What Every Supervisor Should Know

about the author

Lester R. Bittel is currently associate professor at the School of Business at James Madison University in Harrisonburg, Virginia. Before accepting his academic post, he was employed as industrial management editor, editor in chief, and publisher of *American Machinist, Product Engineering, Industrial Distribution,* and *Purchasing Week.* He also held the position of director of information systems for McGraw-Hill Publications Company. Prior to joining McGraw-Hill, he was field engineer for the Leeds & Northrup Company, industrial engineer for Western Electric Company, Inc., and plant manager and director of the Koppers Company. He is a member of the Gantt Medal Board and the Silver Bay Conference on Human Issues in Management and a fellow of the American Society of Mechanical Engineers.

Mr. Bittel is the editor in chief of the *Encyclopedia of Professional Management* and coeditor of the *Training and Development Handbook,* sponsored by the American Society for Training and Development. He is the author of *Business in Action, Improving Supervisory Performance, Management by Exception,* and *The Nine Master Keys of Management.* He also coauthored *Practical Automation.* He is the designer of the *Shenandoah Management Games for Supervisors* and has contributed to the *Industrial Engineering Handbook, Handbook of Business Administration,* and *Maintenance Engineering Handbook.* In addition, he has written more than 200 magazine articles on various phases of industrial management, personnel management, human relations, and business operations.

Sponsoring Editor: Edward E. Byers
Editing Supervisor: Mary Rogina
Production Supervisor: Laurence Charnow
Design Supervisor: Tracy Glasner
Art Supervisor: Howard Brotman

Cover and Text Designer: Jerry Wilke
Technical Studio: Danmark & Michaels
Cartoon Artist: Frank Daniel

Library of Congress Cataloging in Publication Data
    Bittel, Lester R
      What Every Supervisor Should Know.
      Includes index.
      1. Personnel management. 2. Supervision of
employees. I. Title
HF5549.B52   1980   658.3'02   79-16387
ISBN 0-07-005573-4

WHAT EVERY SUPERVISOR SHOULD KNOW
The Basics of Supervisory Management
Fourth Edition

1234567890 DODO 876543210

What Every Supervisor Should Know

FOURTH EDITION

The Basics of Supervisory Management

Lester R. Bittel
Associate Professor, School of Business
James Madison University

McGraw-Hill Book Company

New York
Atlanta
Dallas
St. Louis
San Francisco
Auckland
Bogotá
Hamburg
Johannesburg
London
Madrid
Mexico
Montreal
New Delhi
Panama
Paris
São Paulo
Singapore
Sydney
Tokyo
Toronto

preface

In 1959, when the first edition of this book appeared, its aim was to tell the truth about supervision. There is some evidence that it has succeeded. This book has been consulted by over 300,000 supervisors and potential supervisors. It has been translated into Dutch, Danish, and Spanish and reprinted in paperback by the Tata Press in Bombay, India. It is the basic text for supervisory management in over 100 two-year colleges. It has been adopted for in-house supervisory training programs by hundreds of industrial companies, commercial firms, and nonprofit institutions. And it has stood the toughest test of all—the test for validity and practicality. Thousands of practicing supervisors have bought, read, and kept in ready reach this handbook, which tells them everything they ought to know about their jobs. So, in this fourth edition, let us once again examine the basic premises of *What Every Supervisor Should Know*.

The Truth About Supervision. This phrase defines the focus of the book, which I view as an antidote for too much preaching and too little understanding of the problems that face first-line supervisors. Ever since I plunged into my first supervisory job many years ago, I've had the urge to put into writing what I believe are the realities of supervision. I wanted to examine both the techniques that really work and the ones that are liable to backfire, to show supervisors' proper function in the organization, and to indicate the extent to which supervisors can exercise their judgment and authority.

Integrated Objectives. The overall approach of this book is based on five interrelated objectives:

1. To offer assistance with real-life situations.
2. To take into account changes in today's social environment that might affect the supervisor's job.
3. To provide insights based on experience.
4. To cover all aspects of supervision.
5. To maintain a good-humored perspective.

With objectives like these, *What Every Supervisor Should Know* should prove to be a useful aid to a wide and diverse readership, which includes:

- **Instructors,** who might use it as a basic text for introducing their students to the complex world of supervisory management.
- **Students** of human affairs in commerce, government, and industry, who might turn to it as a centralized source of information about the job of supervision.

- **Supervisors,** who might find it a handy reference manual of methods for handling people and managing their jobs.
- **Their bosses,** who might gain an insight into the problems—human, technical, and personal—that supervisors must face daily.
- **Training directors,** who might use it as a text or guide for supervisory training in interpersonal relations and in technical job skills.

Comprehensive Update.   Since this book was first published, I've talked to and worked with thousands of supervisors. The nature of business, society, and government has undergone marked changes. Nothing, however, has lessened the burden borne by the stalwart men and women who supervise at the first line of their organizations. Increasingly, they perform a vital role in management-employee interface. And they do it under circumstances that are becoming more and more complex.

This revised edition is designed to put supervisors in tune with their changing environment. It includes eight completely new chapters. In Part 1, Chapters 1 and 2 take a fresh look at the supervisor's job and the expectations of people at work today. Part 2 of this book has been restructured to place the supervisor's responsibilities within the framework of the management process. Chapter 7 provides an overview of this process, and Chapter 12 discusses methods of controlling people and processes. In Part 5, Chapter 25 examines the emerging concept of work design, and Chapter 30 helps supervisors understand the role of computers and management information systems in business. Finally, Part 6 offers supervisors valuable pointers on improving their performance: Chapter 32 presents techniques for problem solving and decision making, and Chapter 33 provides insights into how to manage an increasingly regulated business environment.

This revised edition explores dozens of innovative concepts and techniques revolving around supervisory management. Included are sections on OSHA, EEO legislation, affirmative action, ERISA, and CETA; career planning and situational management; power, affiliation, and achievement drives; contingency models of leadership; resolving conflicts; organizing project and task force teams; interviewing applicants; active listening; flexitime, broader aspects of productivity, and the quality of working life; supervising the knowledge worker; and environmental concerns, ethics, and social responsibility.

Of the thirty-one class-tested case studies in this text, sixteen are brand new. They have been chosen to reflect a broad range of organizational settings—in industry, government, and service organizations. There are twenty-eight new tables and figures.

Unique Learning Structure.   As in earlier editions—only to an even greater extent—this text relies heavily on two unique learning methods:

1. A question and answer approach with its immediate feedback develops ideas and shows how to apply these ideas in a manner similar to

that of programmed learning. Additionally, the highlighting of questions enables you to relate concepts to problems you face at your work. It also makes the text itself easy to use as a desk reference, as so many supervisors do.

2. The use of dozens of examples of good and bad handling of interpersonal situations borrows heavily from proven behavioral modeling approaches. These examples show you how to carry out dialogues with employees in a productive manner while also giving examples of the kinds of conversations that are likely to be unsuccessful.

3. Action Summary Checklists, which appear in Part VII, succinctly summarize the key points of each chapter. These will help you review your grasp of basic management concepts. They will also enable you to develop and carry out action plans for improving your on-the-job performance.

Acknowledgments. I accept the responsibility for everything written in this text. I would, however, be doing a great disservice to those connected with supervisory management who assisted and advised me if I did not acknowledge their contributions. In particular, I am indebted to Bernice Johnston, of the Department of Human Resources, Children's Services Division of Salem, Oregon, for her thoughtful counsel on equal treatment of the sexes and to Dr. Joseph Tomkiewicz, professor of management at James Madison University, for his review of the chapters on labor relations and equal employment opportunities.

Many others in the field of supervisory training made valuable contributions, including Joseph T. Allmon of Riegel Textile Corp; Ernest Balkany of Steelcraft Company; Paul Deysher at AMP, Inc.; Frank Diehl of Grove Manufacturing Company; Hubert E. Dobson of FMC Corporation; H. Darwin Haines of the National Board of YMCAs; Robert Johnson of Blaw-Knox Division; Marie Leonard of Morton-Norwich Products, Inc.; Edward Martin, dean of instruction at Hory-Georgetown Technical College; Patricia Moran of Veterans Administration Hospital in Downey, Illinois; George Piccoli of the New York Chamber of Commerce and Industry; Jackson E. Ramsey, coordinator of noncredit programs at James Madison University; Richard Reardon of Virginia Distributive Education Adult In-Service Training; Wallace Richardson, professor of industrial engineering at Lehigh University; Ray Vogt of Pullman Standard Company; Dr. Malcolm W. White; and hundreds of competent people affiliated with the International Management Council.

Finally, I am deeply indebted to Helen Royall, my typist, and to my wife Muriel Albers Bittel, who so ably managed our editing schedules.

Lester R. Bittel

contents

case studies in human relations

supervisory management and human relations

1

Management at any level accomplishes its tasks and goals through the actions of other people. At the supervisory level the interpersonal relations are most frequent and most intense. Accordingly, this part emphasizes six key objectives.

• To grasp the full extent of the supervisory job so as to be able to integrate technical know-how, administrative skills, and sensitivity in employee relations.
• To understand how people view their work so as to be able to create and sustain conditions that provide the most satisfaction and the least dissatisfaction.
• To be aware of the individuality and basic needs of your employees so as to be able to motivate them in a variety of ways.
• To recognize the extent and the power of group influence so as to be able to direct its energy toward productive ends.
• To accept the presence of conflict in organizations but to be able to minimize it and build an atmosphere that encourages cooperation.
• To study the various approaches to leadership so as to develop to the fullest your own innate capabilities.

1

the supervisory management job

Why does first-line supervision get so much attention?

First-line supervisors in industry and commerce represent just about the most important force in the American economy. Over a million strong, they carry out a management tradition that dates back to the building of the pyramids. And yet time has not simplified their work. First the industrial revolution with its division of labor and now mass-production technique with its accelerated mechanization have changed the supervisor's role to one of bewildering and often frustrating complexity.

Today's supervisor (whether a first-line supervisor, a front-line supervisor, or a section or department manager) must be a vigorous leader, a shrewd and effective planner, a source of technical know-how, and a deft mediator between policy-setting management on the one hand and rank-and-file workers (and their union representatives) on the other. Small wonder that the cry goes up again and again: "We need better supervisors."

Recognition—and acceptance—of supervisors by top management has helped them to emerge finally as essential and integrated members of the management group and to assume all the responsibilities of full-fledged managers. The way hasn't been easy. Too often it has been painfully slow. Even today there are companies where the supervisor's status is shaky. But on the whole, no single group of men and women has achieved and deserved such stature and attention in so short a time after so long a wait as have the American supervisors.

Who is a supervisor?

Anyone at the first level of management who has the responsibility for getting the "hands-on-the-work" employees to carry out the plans and policies of higher-level management is a supervisor.

Where did the term come from?

In earlier days the supervisor was the person in charge of a group of towrope pullers or ditch diggers. That person was literally the "fore man," since he was up forward of the gang. His authority consisted mainly of chanting the "one, two, three, up," which set the pace for the rest of the workers. In Germany the supervisor is still called a *vorarbeiter* ("fore worker"); in England the term *charge hand* is used. Both terms suggest the lead-person origin.

The term *supervisor* has its roots in Latin, where it means "looks over." It was originally applied to the master of a group of artisans. Less than one hundred years ago it was not uncommon for the master in a New England shop to have almost complete power over the work force. The master could bid on jobs, hire his own crew, work them as hard as he pleased, and make his living out of the difference between his bid price and the labor costs.

Today the supervisor's job combines some of the talents of the "fore man" (or leader) and of the "master" (skilled administrative artisan).

Legally, what makes a supervisor a supervisor?

The federal laws of the United States provide two definitions of a supervisor.

1. The Taft-Hartley Act of 1947 says that a supervisor is:

. . . any individual having authority, in the interest of the employer, to hire, transfer, suspend, lay off, recall, promote, discharge, assign, reward, or discipline other employees, or responsibility to direct them, or to adjust their grievances, or effectively to recommend such action, if in connection with the foregoing the exercise of such authority is not of a merely routine or clerical nature, but requires the use of independent judgment.

The act specifically prohibits supervisors from joining a union of production and clerical employees, although they may form a union composed exclusively of supervisors.

2. The Fair Labor Standards Act of 1938 (or Minimum Wage Law) specifies that supervisors can spend no more than 20 percent of their time doing the same kind of work as the people they direct. It also stipulates that supervisors be paid a salary (regardless of how many hours they work). This latter provision makes some supervisors unhappy since it makes them exempt from the provision of the law that calls for overtime pay after a certain number of hours worked. Many employers voluntarily compensate supervisors for overtime in one way or another.

The thrust of these two laws is to make supervisors, once and for all, a part of management.

Are supervisors permitted to do the same work as the people they supervise?

There is no law stopping it. But most companies with unions have a contract clause that prohibits the supervisor from performing any work that a union member would ordinarily do (except in clearly defined emergencies, in which the supervisor would do as she or he sees fit).

Here's a point where most managements agree with unions. Few companies want supervisors to do the work their employees are hired to do. Supervisors are most valuable to their employers when they spend 100 percent of their time supervising. It makes little sense for a $300-a-week supervisor, for instance, to do the work of a $120-a-week laborer.

Where do most supervisors come from?

Most supervisors rise from the ranks of the organization in which they serve. Typically they are long-service employees. They have greater experience, have held more different jobs in the organization, and have significantly more education than do the men

and women they supervise. Usually it is apparent that supervisors are chosen from among the best and the most experienced employees in the organization.[1]

What personal characteristics does higher management find most desirable in supervisors?

■■■■■■■ The job of supervision is so demanding that higher management
tends to look for *super*people to fill the role. Most firms establish
criteria against which supervisory candidates are judged. Here
are some of the qualities most commonly sought:[2]

- Energy and good health
- Leadership potential
- Ability to get along with people
- Job know-how and technical competence
- Initiative
- Dedication and dependability
- Positive attitude toward management

Obviously, these are fine attributes in any person. Obviously, too,
persons who measure up are hard to find. Fortunately, however,
many of these attributes can be acquired or improved through
supervisory training and development programs.

How can a newly appointed supervisor make the job of crossing over to the managerial ranks a less turbulent one?

■■■■■■■ A person who is made a supervisor crosses over from one style
of thought to another. As an employee, an individual's concerns
are with self-satisfaction in terms of pay and the work itself. As a
manager, this same person is expected to place the organization's goals above all other job-related concerns. This means that
a supervisor worries first about meeting quotas, quality, and cost
standards; second about the employees who do the work; and
last about himself or herself.

To make the task more difficult, the newly appointed supervisor usually has already made the long climb to the top of the
employee ranks. Now the person must cross over to a new field
of achievement—management, as shown in Figure 1-1. It will
take a while to get a toehold at the supervisory level. For many,
however, it will be the beginning of another long climb—this
time to the top of the management heap.[3]

Such pressure from above and below makes many new supervisors uncomfortable. One Ford Motor Company assembly-line

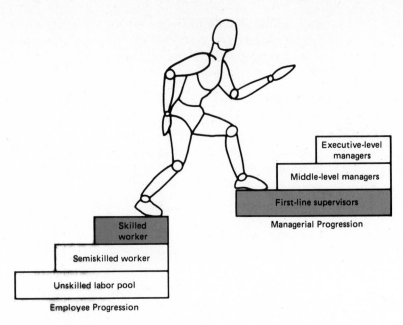

Employee Progression

- Skilled worker
- Semiskilled worker
- Unskilled labor pool

Managerial Progression

- Executive-level managers
- Middle-level managers
- First-line supervisors

FIGURE 1-1. Crossing over from employee ranks to managerial ranks, from "top of the heap" to "bottom of the heap."

supervisor, Ed Hendrix, put it this way: "The foreman is a punching bag. You get your ears beat off from both sides of the fence."[4]

This need not be so, says Professor Keith Davis, one of the most astute observers of organizational relationships. Davis agrees that the supervisor takes pressure from both sides, but he likens the role to a keystone in the organizational arch (Figure 1-2).

Says Davis: "The keystone takes the pressure from both sides and uses this pressure to build a stronger arch. The sides can be held together only by the keystone, which strengthens, not weakens, the arch. The keystone position is the important role of supervisors in organizations."[5]

Experienced supervisors add this advice to the new person:

"Don't throw your weight around. Admit your need for help and seek it from other supervisors and your boss. Make a practice of coming in on time and sticking to your job for the full day; employees despise supervisors who push for productivity but who goof off themselves. Keep yourself physically prepared and mentally alert; the job will be more demanding than you expect. And don't indulge in petty pilfering of supplies or use of shop equip-

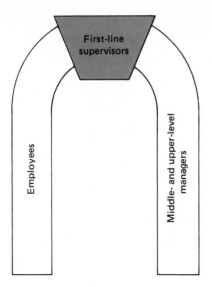

FIGURE 1-2. Supervision as the keystone in the organizational arch.

ment and time to do personal work; employees may try this themselves but they sure don't respect management people who do."[6]

When it comes to job responsibilities, what is expected of supervisors?

Responsibilities encompass four—and occasionally five—broad areas, as illustrated in Figure 1-3.

Responsibility to management. Supervisors must, above all, dedicate themselves to the goals, plans, and policies of the organization. These are typically laid down by higher management. It is the primary task of supervisors to serve as a "linking pin" for management to make sure that these are carried out by the employees they supervise.

Responsibility to employees. Employees expect their supervisors to provide direction and training; to protect them from unfair treatment; and to see that the work place is clean, safe, uncluttered, properly equipped, well-lit, and adequately ventilated.

Responsibility to staff specialists. The relationship between supervision and staff departments is one of mutual support. Staff people are charged with providing supervisors with guidance and help as well as prescribing procedures to be followed and forms to be completed. Supervisors, in turn, aid the work of the

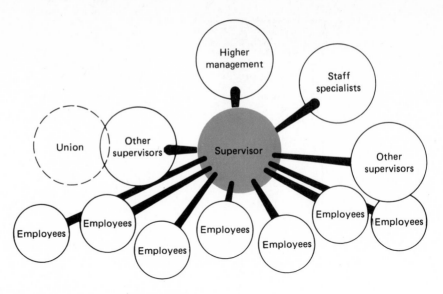

FIGURE 1-3. Supervisor's responsibilities.

staff departments by making good use of their advice and service and by conforming to their requests.

Responsibility to other supervisors.   Teamwork is essential in the supervisory ranks. There is a great deal of departmental interdependence. The goals and activities of one department must harmonize with those of others. This often requires the sacrifice of an immediate target for the greater good of the organization.

Responsibility to the union.   Union and management views are often in conflict, and supervisor and shop steward are often at loggerheads. It is the supervisor's responsibility, however, to keep these relationships objective, neither to "give away the shop" nor to yield responsibility for the welfare of the organization and its employees.

How will supervisory performance be judged by higher management?

It will be judged by two general measures: (1) how well you manage the various resources made available to you to accomplish your assignments and (2) how good the results are that you get from them. (See Figure 1-4.)

Management of resources.   These are all the things that, in effect, set you up in business as a supervisor.[7] They include:

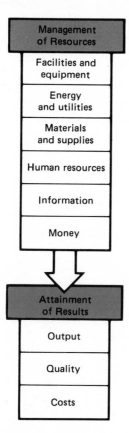

FIGURE 1-4. Measurement of supervisory performance.

- *Facilities and equipment* such as a certain amount of floor space, desks, benches, tools, typewriters, machinery. Your job is to keep these operating productively and to prevent their abuse.
- *Energy, power, and utilities* such as heat, light, air conditioning, electricity, steam, water, and compressed air. Conservation is the principal measure of effectiveness here.
- *Materials and supplies* such as *raw materials,* parts, and assemblies used to make a product and *operating supplies* like lubricants, stationery, typewriter ribbons, and wrapping paper. Getting the most from every scrap of material and holding waste to the minimum are prime measures here.
- *Human resources* such as the work force in general and your employees in particular. Since you do little or nothing with your hands, your biggest job is to see that these people are productively engaged at all times.
- *Information* such as that made available by staff departments

or found in operating manuals, specifications sheets, and blueprints. Your success often depends upon how well you can utilize the data and know-how made available to you through these sources.

• *Money*—all the above can be measured by how much they cost, although the actual cash will rarely flow through your hands. Nevertheless, supervisors are expected to be prudent in decisions that affect expenditures and may have to justify these in terms of savings or other benefits.

Attainment of results. It follows that if you manage each of your resources well, you should get the desired results.[8] Whatever your particular area of responsibility and whatever your organization, you can be sure that you will be judged in the long run by how well you meet these three objectives:

• *Output, or production.* Specifically your department will be expected to turn out a certain amount of work per day, per week, and per month. It will be expected that this be done on time and that you meet delivery schedules and project deadlines.

• *Quality and workmanship.* Output volume alone is not enough. You will also be judged by the quality of the work your employees perform, whether it be measured in terms of the number of product defects, service errors, or customer complaints.

• *Costs and budget control.* Your output and quality efforts will always be restricted by the amount of money you can spend to carry them out. Universally, supervisors attest to the difficulty in living up to cost and budget restraints.

The items in these two lists are spoken of as performance measures.

Of all that is expected of supervisors, which tasks loom largest?

They vary, of course. But one investigator took the time in 1971 to ask this question of 2,054 production supervisors.[9] The tasks found to be the most immediately pressing and most persistently difficult are shown in Table 1-1.

Note how the anxiety over crises, authority sources, and grievances rather quickly dissipates, while the concern for certain basic problems persists.

Another survey, conducted in 1965 of 215 first-line supervisors, found three similar problems to be the most persistent.[10]

1. Meeting tight production schedules. (Take all the fancy talk

TABLE 1-1. Problems facing supervisors.

Problem	Percentage mentioning problem when first appointed	Percentage saying problem persistently recurred
Handling employees with special problems	60	25
Maintaining a neat and orderly workplace	59	43
Dealing with crises or unexpected problems	54	Less than 10
Controlling costs	54	27
Meeting quality requirements	52	33
Learning how much authority a supervisor has	51	Less than 10
Handling labor complaints or grievances	50	Less than 10
Motivating employees	48	23
Meeting work deadlines or production requirements	47	26
Writing reports and handling paperwork	43	24

away, and the supervisor's job is still one of getting out the production.)

2. Keeping production up to standard efficiency. (In simple words, supervisors can't just get the production out at any cost; they have to keep their costs in line.)

3. Maintaining cooperative attitudes with employees. (Automation or not, it's the employees who turn the crank. Getting the employees to turn the crank when they should, how they should, and as fast as they should is the ultimate problem for supervisors.)

What does it really take to succeed as a supervisor?

No one knows for sure, but there are a number of qualities, or dimensions, of the supervisory job that experts look for. For example, General Electric Company, at its Columbia, Maryland, facility, singles out seven important dimensions of the supervisory job: technical know-how, administrative skill, ability to develop a plan to meet department goals, ability to deal with the manager to whom you report, communications skills, ability to deal with people inside and outside the operating unit, and ability to deal

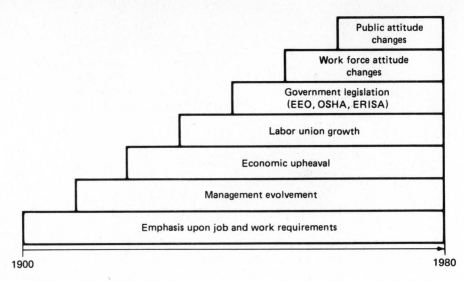

Public attitude changes	
Work force attitude changes	
Government legislation (EEO, OSHA, ERISA)	
Labor union growth	
Economic upheaval	
Management evolvement	
Emphasis upon job and work requirements	

1900   1980

FIGURE 1-5. Evolving sources of pressure on first-line supervisors. Based on a concept in Herbert R. Northrup, Ronald M. Cowin, Lawrence G. Vandon Plas, and William E. Fulmer, *The Objective Selection of Supervisors*, Manpower and Human Resources Studies No. 8, The Wharton School, University of Pennsylvania, 1978, p.6.

effectively with people who report to you.[11] Other researchers also identify such success-related qualities as creativity, stress tolerance, initiative, independence, problem analysis, decisiveness, tenacity, flexibility, risk taking, and use of delegation.[12] Many firms, including American Telephone and Telegraph, attempt to measure these dimensions in supervisory candidates and base their selection on these qualities.

The best part is that many of these talents can be acquired by supervisors who learn from experience and take advantage of developmental opportunities offered by their employers.

How are the pressures on supervisors changing?

What started out as mainly a technical job at the turn of the century has gradually shifted. Pressure is now being put on supervisors to accommodate an increasingly demanding work force,[13] as shown in Figure 1-5. This trend will continue. In the 1980s the general public will ask employers to accept greater responsibility for employment whether or not this employment contributes to profits or effectiveness. This means that supervisors will be expected to make work for their employees in slack times and motivate them to be more productive in active times.

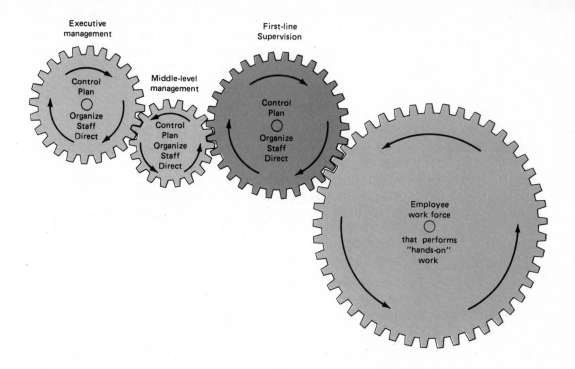

FIGURE 1-6. All managers take part in the managerial process: planning, organizing, staffing, directing, and controlling.

Where do supervisors fit into the management process?

They are an essential part of it. Supervisors perform exactly the same managerial functions as all other managers in their organization—up to and including the chief executive. Each specific task, every responsibility, all the various roles that supervisors are called upon to perform are carried out by the managerial process (Figure 1-6). This process, which is repeated over and over, daily, weekly, and yearly, consists of five broad functions:

• *Planning.* Setting goals and establishing plans and procedures to attain them.
• *Organizing.* Arranging jobs to be done in such a way as to make them more effective.
• *Staffing.* Selecting and placing just the right number of people in the most appropriate jobs.

- *Directing.* Motivating, communicating, and leading.
- *Controlling.* Regulating the process, its costs, and the people who carry it out.

The managerial process is explained in detail in Part 2 of the text.

How do supervisory job roles differ from those of other levels of management?

They differ only in degree. Higher-level managers spend more time planning and less time directing, for example. Two people who studied this matter came up with three useful guidelines.[14] They first divided all the tasks and responsibilities we have listed so far in this text into three kinds of roles. Roles are the parts played by actors on a stage; they are also the real-life parts played by managers and supervisors in an organization. These three roles can be classified as those requiring:

- *Technical skills.* Job know-how, knowledge of the industry and its particular processes, machinery, and problems.
- *Administrative skills.* Knowledge of the entire organization and how it is coordinated, how it records information and its records system, and on ability to plan and control work.
- *Human relations skills.* Knowledge of human behavior, the ability to work effectively with individuals and groups—peers and superiors as well as subordinates.

The observers then concluded that the role of the supervisor emphasizes technical and human relations skills most and administrative skills least. This emphasis tends to reverse itself with higher-level managers, as illustrated in Figure 1-7.

Supervisory balance: What does it mean?

It is a simplification of a very valuable dictum: Pay as much attention to human relations matters as to technical and administrative ones.

In other words, Be as employee-centered as you are job- or task-centered in your interests.

Or said still another way: Spend as much time maintaining group cohesiveness, direction, and morale as you do pushing for productivity or task accomplishment.

This view has been borne out by a number of studies. The basis, however, is research carried on by Rensis Likert. In a survey of clerical, sales, and manufacturing employees, he found that, on the average, employees who worked for supervisors who were

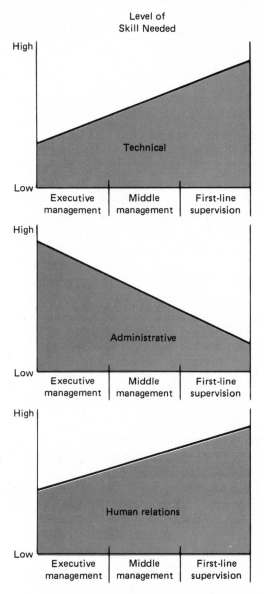

Level of
Skill Needed

FIGURE 1-7. Skills needed according to managerial level.

job- or production-centered produced less than employees who
worked for employee-centered supervisors.[15]

It would be dangerous to draw the conclusion from Likert's
studies that being a nice guy is the answer to employee productivity. It isn't. As in sports, nice guys often finish last. The important conclusion from these studies is that supervisors who focus

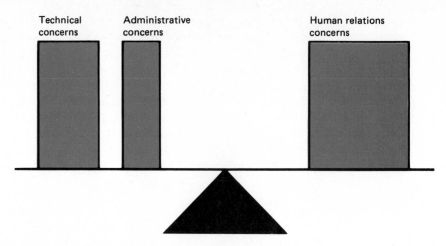

FIGURE 1-8. The balance of supervisory concerns.

on job demands to the exclusion of their interest in the welfare and the development of their people don't get the results they are looking for. Conversely, supervisors who bend over backward to make work easy for their employees don't get good results either. It takes a balance between the two approaches, as shown in Figure 1-8.

For example, David "Red" Goss, a section supervisor in a West Virginia coal mine, speaks of his major headaches. These are directing traffic in the mine's darkness, rearranging power cables, safety, and equipment breakdowns because—as his boss says—"If there's no production, we're down his throat." Yet Red is relaxed and friendly with his workers. His aim, he says, is to treat the miners "like people, like trained men." As a result, Red's crew routinely turns in the mine's highest production. His boss says, "The men respect Red. He knows how to talk to them." Red "gives" a little in accommodating individual wishes among his men, but his men often go out of their way to be helpful. Red points to an instance where the cutting crew used their own initiative to open a new vein without waiting for him to first mark out the next cut, as is traditional.[16]

Being a supervisor can't be all good news.
What are some of the drawbacks?
What can a supervisor do to minimize them?

Generalizations about the negative side of supervision can be misleading because every job is different, companies and industries vary, and each individual is unique. It is usually true, however, that the advancements are limited: The managerial pyramid gets narrower at the top, and college-educated people usually have an inside track. Often the pay isn't much better than that of the people you supervise; efforts to widen the gap often fail. The hours are long, and the human relations part of the job can be torturous. The supervisor is typically torn between loyalties to management and to the work group. In some companies a supervisor's ideas for improving methods may be taken for granted instead of being rewarded via the suggestion box. In most instances a supervisor's security depends not on seniority or union membership but on the individual's ability to produce results. Frequently the supervisor may not have all the resources needed to attain them.

Why do so many supervisors keep on plugging? Because of the reward *not* found in the paycheck.[17] Supervisors keep supervising because of the challenge inherent in the work itself and the sense of accomplishment gained from doing a difficult job better than anyone else can. A few supervisors quit or step down, but most of them hang in. They may grouse and complain, but they keep on swinging—and getting results.[18]

How professional is the work of supervision?

It is getting more professional every day. Two leading management organizations, made up primarily of first-line supervisors, are working hard to make it that way. The International Management Council (IMC), affiliated with the Young Men's Christian Association (YMCA), and the National Management Association (NMA) have pooled their resources to form the Institute of Certified Professional Managers (ICPM). The institute, working with the American College Testing Program (ACT), has devised and is administering professional certification tests. Certification is based on a combination of experience and examinations in three areas: (1) personal skills like communications, government regulation, and time management; (2) administrative skills like planning, decision making, staffing, and controlling; and (3) human relations skills.

Addresses of participating organizations are:

International Management Council
YMCA
291 Broadway
New York, New York 10007 (212-374-2159)

National Management Association
2210 Arbor Boulevard
Dayton, Ohio 45439 (513-294-0421)

Institute of Certified Professional Managers
c/o National Management Association
(at above address)

What's ahead in supervision for women and minorities?

The road ahead is improving, but there is much ground to be covered. In 1960, only 2 of every 100 blue-collar supervisors were black; by 1975, 7 of every 100 were black. The gains by blacks and other minorities among white-collar supervisors seem to be about equal. The picture for women is not as clear, since census data did not anticipate these measures. We do know that of all managers and supervisors in 1965, women made up only about 15 percent of the total. By 1970, the percent of women managers was 17. Of these women, only 4.5 percent were black.[19] The indications are that the employment of women both as managers and as supervisors has grown much faster since 1970. Nevertheless, with women making up more than 40 percent of the work force and blacks and other minorities about 12 percent, there is still considerable room for improvement. Pressures from equal employment opportunity legislation should assure continuing gains both by minorities and by women in the supervisory ranks.

Why do supervisors fail?

When a woman or a man doesn't succeed as a supervisor, only an examination of the particular situation will pinpoint the real reason.[20] And sometimes the individual isn't at fault; the boss may never have provided the right kind of training and encouragement. But if you want to avoid failure, check yourself against the six supervisory pitfalls, pointed out by the National Management Association after a study of 86 companies:

- Poor personal relations with workers or with other management people. (This rated highest on the list.)
- Individual shortcomings such as lack of initiative and emotional instability.
- Lack of understanding of the management point of view.
- Unwillingness to spend the necessary time and effort to improve.
- Lack of skill in planning and organizing work.
- Inability to adjust to new and changing conditions.

So if success is your target, look ahead to the pages of this book that follow. And adapt the advice to your own situation.

---

supervisory word power

Employee. A person who works for a company or an organization for wages or salary and who (for purposes of this text) does not hold supervisory or management status and responsibility. Employees are also called workers, laborers, artisans, technicians, clerks, engineers, and the like. Employees are people who "put their hands on the work."

Supervisor. A person in charge of, and coordinator of, the activities of a group of employees engaged in one type of operation. In the ranks of management the supervisor's position is at, or just above, the entry level. Supervisors determine work procedures, issue written and oral orders and instructions, assign duties to workers, examine work for quality and neatness, maintain harmony among workers, and adjust errors and complaints. Supervisors are also called foremen, group leaders, section chiefs, section heads, and department managers.

Manager. A person who directs supervisory personnel to attain the operational goals of a company or an organization. In the ranks of management a manager's position may range from the entry level to the uppermost echelon, but it usually is in the middle level. Managers plan, initiate, and execute programs; interpret and apply policies; establish goals and standards of operational activities; and motivate, direct, and control supervisors. Managers are also called general supervisors, superintendents, directors, and general managers.

Executive. A person in charge of, and responsible for, the performance of a group of managers. In the ranks of management the executive is in the upper echelons. Executives establish broad plans, objectives, and general policies; they motivate, direct, and control the managers subordinate to them.

Job- or task-centered supervision. Emphasis on the job or task that employees are expected to perform; a major concern for production.

Employee- or group-centered supervision. Emphasis on a genuine concern and respect for employees as human beings and on maintaining harmonious relationships within the work group.

Other Important Terms in This Chapter

dimensions of supervision	results
performance measures	role
resources	

reading comprehension

1. What is the essential point of the legal definitions ot *super-visor*?

2. Why would a company be likely to object if the supervisor of the molding department spent most of his or her time setting up and operating the molding machines?

3. Name at least four groups within the organization for which a supervisor has responsibilities, and briefly describe the nature of the responsibilities to each.

4. Outline the performance measures you might describe to a new supervisor by naming nine measures grouped into two categories.

5. Contrast the likely priorities of a production worker in a glass factory with those of the department's supervisor.

6. Many of the most serious concerns of a new supervisor dwindle in importance as experience grows. What are three or four issues that will remain of prime concern no matter how experienced a supervisor is?

7. How is supervisory management similar to higher-level management? How is it different?

8. When a supervisor is told to achieve supervisory balance, what is it that should be balanced? Why is it important?

9. Describe four drawbacks to a supervisory position.

10. If you had to point to one key area that is most likely to produce failure for a supervisor, what would it be?

supervision in action

A. THE CASE OF THE DIVIDED LOYALTIES. **A case study in human relations involving a supervisor's new job, with questions for you to answer.**

Rick López looked neither to the right nor to the left as he headed back from the shop floor to his desk. Friday had been a long day. In fact, it had been a long week. It seemed like five years, rather than five days, since he had walked into the shop last Monday on his first day as a supervisor in J Shop. Much longer, he thought, than his eight years as an employee in several other departments of the company. Rick had started as a bench hand with only a high school diploma and a three-year hitch in military service under his belt. He had moved ahead quickly through a series of six jobs. The last three years he had been a head assembler in M Shop and then setup person for all the machines in P Shop. Based upon his quickness, his all-around knowledge of shop processes, and his general popularity, Rick had been appointed supervisor of J Shop to replace a veteran supervisor who had retired.

Today, like every other day this week, Rick had encountered situations for which his shop expertise and previous experience had not prepared him. He had expected that, but not what had just happened. Rick was walking the shop—supervising. He stopped for a minute or two to watch each operation and to chat with each employee about his or her work. One particular operation caught his prolonged attention. The point at which a subassembly was joined to a final assembly was going very slowly. The assembler, Jennie Barnes, was a relatively new employee. She was very slow in fitting the two parts together. To pick up her speed she often "forced" the process. In so doing, she damaged an occasional final part. Rick saw that Jennie not only was damaging the final product but also was holding up the rest of the assembly line. "Look, Jennie," he said, "why don't you take a rest for a few minutes. I'll take over here for a while and see that you get caught up with the rest of the lines."

Jennie went off to the lounge while Rick sat in for her. With his quick, deft hands he was able to accomplish two or three times as much as Jennie. When Jennie remained away longer than Rick had anticipated, he began to fix some of the damaged final assemblies. At that moment Rick's new boss, Mr. Tower, came along. "I have been looking all over for you," said Mr. Tower. "We have a rush order I want you to track down for me. But what are you doing here?"

"I'm straightening out a bottleneck in the line," said Rick. "The operator is new at this job and has not learned how to do it right—or fast enough, either."

"Where is the operator?" asked Mr. Tower.

"She went to the lounge a few minutes ago," said Rick.

"I've been looking for you for a half hour," said Mr. Tower. "She must have been gone longer than that."

At that moment Jennie returned to her bench. "It's about time you came back," said Mr. Tower. "It's bad enough that you can't do the job right without your taking half the afternoon off." Jennie looked at Rick, who said nothing. Mr. Tower then called Rick aside. "If Jennie can't do her job, get rid of her. We've got better things for you to do here than covering up for an incompetent employee."

1. What do you think Rick was doing wrong in this situation?
2. Was Mr. Tower fair in his judgment of Jennie? What should Rick have done about this, if anything?
3. What advice would you give to Rick the next time a problem like this comes up?

B. THE CASE OF THE COMPLAINING KEYPUNCH OPERATOR. A case study in human relations involving a supervisor's new job, with questions for you to answer.

Ruth Smyth was the best all-around clerk that Gibraltar Finance Company's data processing section ever had. She was a natural for being promoted to supervisor when the time came. During Ruth's first few weeks as section supervisor, everything went well. She obviously knew the work flow from A to Z. Given this chance, she quickly cleared up long-standing bottlenecks and eliminated a number of duplications. Her experience and good judgment easily won the respect of the people who worked for her. On the other hand, Ruth was a stern and serious taskmaster. She was fair and courteous with her employees, but she showed little interest in them beyond their ability to get the work done.

As Ruth settled into the job, however, she had an uneasy feeling that something wasn't quite right in her section. Her employees came to depend on her decisions in the slightest matters. If a problem arose, they were likely to sit at their machines waiting for orders from Ruth. At first Ruth felt flattered by this dependence. But this caused her work load to gradually build. Increasingly she found herself giving curt instructions and short answers to people in her work group.

One employee in particular, Woodie Beck, a keypunch operator, really irritated her. Regardless of what the assignment was, he found some fault with it. Additionally Woodie regularly complained about his machine, his chair, the lighting, the temperature, or his co-workers. Ruth responded to each of Woodie's complaints and requests with some attempt to accommodate him or to set the problem straight.

To make matters worse, the quality of Woodie's work, which had been unspectacular but acceptable, began to fall off. He made errors. Frequently his tapes had to be checked and re-punched. When this continued, Ruth called Woodie into her office. "I've been very patient with your unending complaints and requests," Ruth said, "but lately your work has been far below what is considered satisfactory. If it continues, I'm going to recommend that you be suspended or discharged."

"I'm sorry about my work," said Woodie. "I've had all kinds of problems at home. My oldest son was expelled from high school for drug dealing a couple of months ago. Neither my wife nor I can seem to keep him out of trouble anymore. It's driving us both crazy."

"Family troubles are a bother, I know," said Ruth, "but you can't let them interfere with your work. What's important right now to you is the fact that the quality of your work is no longer acceptable here. If it continues, you will lose your job. My advice to you is to find some way to keep your concerns about your son from affecting your work. Otherwise, your problems will be even worse. I've been very fair with you, but you owe your first attention now to improving your work. Unless it improves, I'll have to put you on notice."

1. What are Ruth's strengths and weaknesses as a supervisor?

2. How well do you think Ruth handled the problem with Woodie's work? What was good and what was bad about her approach? What do you expect will be the results of Ruth's conference with Woodie?

3. If you were Ruth, how would you have handled Woodie's problems?

4. What suggestions can you make to Ruth in order for her to improve the quality of her supervision?

references cited in this chapter

1. Herbert R. Northrup, Ronald M. Cowin, Lawrence G. Vanden Plas, and William E. Fulmer, *The Objective Selection of Supervisors,* Manpower and Human Resources Studies No. 8, The Wharton School, University of Pennsylvania, 1978, pp. 58–69.

2. Ibid., p. 77.

3. Carl A. Benson, "New Supervisors: From the Top of the Heap to the Bottom of the Heap," *Personnel Journal,* April 1978, p. 176.

4. Laurence O'Donnell, "On the Line: As a Ford Foreman, Ed Hendrix Finds He Is Man in the Middle," *The Wall Street Journal,* July 25, 1973, p. 1.

5. Keith Davis, "The Supervisory Role," in M. Gene Newport (ed.),

Supervisory Management: Tools and Techniques, West Publishing Company, St. Paul, Minn., 1976, p. 5.

6. *Foreman in Indiana Industries,* Manpower Report 70-2, Office of Manpower Studies, Purdue University, Lafayette, Ind., November 10, 1970, pp. 8–10.

7. William H. Cover, "Stepping Back to Basics: Defining Performance Expectations for Operations Supervisors," *Training and Development Journal,* November 1975, pp. 3–6.

8. Saul W. Gellerman, "Supervision: Substance and Style," *Harvard Business Review,* March–April 1976, pp. 89–99.

9. Robert H. Schappe, "The Production Foreman Today: His Needs and his difficulties," *Personnel Journal,* July 1972, pp. 156–172.

10. Bradford B. Boyd and Burt K. Scanlan, "Developing Tomorrow's Supervisors," *Training Director's Journal,* May 1965, pp. 35–40.

11. *What's Ahead in Personnel,* No. 181, Chicago, March 1978, p. 3.

12. William C. Byham, "Assessment Centers," in Lester R. Bittel (ed.), *Encyclopedia of Professional Management,* McGraw-Hill Book Company, New York, 1979, pp. 55–58.

13. Northrup et al., op. cit., p. 7.

14. Basil S. Georgopolous and Floyd C. Mann, *The Community General Hospital,* The Macmillan Company, New York, 1962, "Supervisory and Administrative Behavior," p. 431.

15. Rensis Likert, *New Patterns of Management,* McGraw-Hill Book Company, New York, 1960.

16. Bob Arnold, "The Coal Boss: Foreman's Job Grows Harder as the Miners, Technology Change," *The Wall Street Journal,* November 6, 1975, p. 1.

17. Michael J. Abboud and Homer L. Richardson, "What Do Supervisors Want From Their Jobs?" *Personnel Journal,* June 1978, pp. 308–312.

18. Archie B. Carroll and Ted F. Anthony, "An Overview of the Supervisor's Job," *Personnel Journal,* March 1976, pp. 228–231, 249–250.

19. *Statistical Abstract of the United States,* 1977, U.S. Government Printing Office, Table 601, "Employed Persons—Percent Distribution by Occupation and Race: 1960 to 1975," p. 373; Table 602, "Experienced Civilian Labor Force, by Sex and Occupation, 1960 and 1970, and by Selected Characteristics, 1970," pp. 373–376.

20. William E. Fulmer, "The Making of a Supervisor," *Personnel Journal,* March 1977, pp. 140–143, 151.

2

people at work

What is meant by work?

Webster helps here. The dictionary is on target with five related definitions:

• Activity in which one exerts strength or faculties to do or perform.

• Sustained physical or mental effort valued as it overcomes obstacles and achieves an objective or result.

• Labor, task, or duty that affords one the accustomed means of livelihood.

• Strenuous activity marked by the presence of difficulty and exertion and absence of pleasure.

• Specific task, duty, function, or assignment often being a part or phase of some larger activity.

Note the key words: *physical, mental, effort, exertion, obstacles, difficulty, result,* and *means of livelihood.* Note, too, the implication of work as a part of a larger activity and its age-old association with the absence of pleasure. Modern-day supervisors try to combine work with pleasure as measured by the degree of personal satisfaction derived from it.

Why do most people work?

For two reasons: first, for the money it brings and for what necessities and pleasures that money will buy; second, for the satisfaction work can bring—either from being with other people or from a sense of personal accomplishment.

Which reward is more important to most workers, money or job satisfaction?

That depends. Most of us want both, of course. But until each of us has a paycheck that is big enough for our own highly personal situation, job satisfaction may take a backseat.

In what ways is work different from many other things people do?

Four factors make work unique.

1. Rules, regulations, and procedures are necessarily designed to demand a degree of conformity in each employee's action and thus to limit free choice. Many people find it hard to channel their efforts into paths that are set by others. Modern supervision tries to keep rules to a minimum and to stress the opportunity for self-control.

2. A chain of authority makes each person more or less beholden to the boss, and the boss in turn to another boss, and so on. In practice this means that most companies are run by relatively few top-level managers. Lower-level managers and employees at the bottom of the organizational pyramid often feel that they have little say in what happens. Employees typically think the only right they have is to complain, not to make constructive suggestions about how to run the business. Supervisors who invite help from employees tend to make the work more appealing to them.

3. Those who hold managerial responsibility are expected to place their own personal interests behind those of the organization. It is no secret that a great many managers do not do so. Instead, they take care of themselves first and the company's resources, especially employees, later. Employees who work for

this kind of manager may find their job satisfactions very small. And they may expend their efforts in complaints.

4. Much of what happens or is expected to happen is put into written records. Outside of work, most of our activities are loosely defined and rarely put into writing. Written documents—those that record the past and those that set goals for the future—are threatening to many people. There is the fear that no mistake will be forgotten and that every promise will be remembered. Because of so much formal communication, employees often feel more comfortable with supervisors who pass on the word in easy, give-and-take conversation.

These four factors were first identified in the 1890s by a German sociologist named Max Weber, who prescribed them for an "organized system of work directed by hired managers." He called this system *bureaucracy.*

How many people are truly happy at work?

According to a comprehensive review, published in 1974, of many authoritative studies (*Job Satisfaction: Is There a Trend?*), nearly 90 percent of all employees are satisfied, if not happy. (See Figure 2-1.) Even during the period of affluence and presumed indifference to work in the 1960s and early 1970s, there did not appear to be any substance to the claim that factory workers suffered from the blue-collar blues. The studies showed, however, that factory workers tended to be less satisfied than white-collar workers. One of the clearest conclusions was that job satisfaction tends to increase with age. Young people are by far the most dissatisfied with their work.

What is it that people expect from their jobs in the way of satisfaction?

Different people expect different things. For supervisors this is probably the most significant result of the surveys. It is dangerous to generalize about individuals.

Factory workers place a high priority on wages. Some workers emphasize social and comfort factors such as pleasant and hygienic surroundings, convenient working hours, and good transportation. The more education a person has, the greater the wish for challenging and interesting jobs. This last tendency appears to be true of white-collar employees, too.

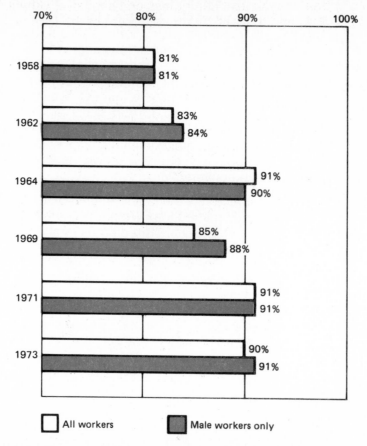

FIGURE 2-1. Percent of "satisfied" workers, 1958 to 1973, based on six national surveys. Adapted from *Job Satisfaction: Is There a Trend?*, Research Monograph No. 30, Manpower Administration, U.S. Department of Labor, 1974, p. 4.

Isn't much of the routine work that people must do simply boring?

Yes, there can be no denying the boredom in many repetitive, routine jobs. Not all or even most jobs, however, are truly boring. Boredom in so-called routine jobs is more likely to result from a point of view or from a shortsighted approach to them than from what the job really contains. I have seen many floor sweepers who attacked the job with the broom as a challenge to their craft. Or assembly-line workers who could add zest by varying their technique. Or file clerks who tried to come up with a productive idea at least once a month. Make no mistake, however: If the boss sees a job as menial and its incumbent as easily replaced, the employee will fall in line with this thinking. The employee will treat the job as meaningless and seek every chance to loaf, to stall, and to head for the rest room or the time clock.

What's the cure for boring work?

Barbara Garson, author of *All the Livelong Day: The Meaning and Demeaning of Routine Work* (Doubleday & Co., Inc., New York, 1975), observed: "People need passionately to do real and serious work: to set a problem for themselves, devise a means whereby the problem can be solved, and then see their realized efforts in a completed task...the need to use judgment, individual skill, or work-educated insight." Garson, a harsh critic of business, points to the solution. Hard and challenging work is real and serious. "Mickey Mouse" jobs are soft and nondemanding. A supervisor can help employees to see the job as a problem to be solved, since that's what a job really is. Supervisors can also show employees what the final results are, even on a short-cycle job like mounting a relay to an electronic breadboard for a TV set. Employees ought to know that supervisors do want the use of their judgment, not indifference or carelessness; personal skill, not automatic machine-dependency; and know-how based on work experience.

What can be done to improve the quality of working life?

There are two views. The first is that improved productivity—greater output from the inputs of labor, materials, money, and machines—continues to be the foundation for a better work life. Higher productivity buys the tools that make work easier and the time for each employee to find the best way of adapting to the task. The second is the conviction on the part of many qualified observers that a greater involvement in decision making at the job level is essential. "The absolutely essential component," says Edward M. Glazer in *Productivity Gains Through Worklife Improvement* (Harcourt Brace Jovanovich, Inc., New York, 1976), "is a real and ever present opportunity for individuals and task groups at any level to influence their working environment, to have some say over what goes on in connection with their work. This requires organization climate and structure that really encourages, facilitates, and rewards questions, challenges, or suggestions relating to improving the existing *modus operandi* in any way... and expeditious, respectful, and appropriate response to such inputs." This is a tall order for any supervisor. But it is a proposition that has made sense to the "work simplification" people, notably Alan Mogensen, for more than 40 years —and they have the productivity records to show its value.

What are the chances of developing a 100 percent gung ho work force?

Very slim. If the statistics presented in Figure 2-1 can be taken as representative, one out of ten employees is likely to be truly dissatisfied. To be on the safe side, you can judge your supervisory performance as "good" if you have only two out of ten employees who regularly sing the work-force blues.

Is there any sure way for a supervisor to make work more enjoyable?

Given the differences in expectations, the answer must be no. Some basic approaches, however, will make for greater satisfaction among employees in general.

Offer employees an opportunity for "bottom-upward" feedback.   This is one good way to find out what each person expects from work, even if it cannot always be provided.

View many supervisory functions as facilitating rather than directing.   Few people want to be told how and when to do every little thing. Not every worker who is given an inch will take a mile. So try to provide the kinds of information and tools an employee needs to get the job done—the right blueprint or specification, a key bit of know-how. A physical or mental assist, when needed or asked for, encourages employees to enforce their own discipline.

Stay flexible when and where you can.   The supervisor whose department rules can't be bent to accommodate a worker's individuality on occasion makes employees feel hopelessly locked in. Keep to a minimum all directives that begin with the words *always* or *never.* Think in terms of *most of the time,* or *on the average,* when you will not permit this or insist on that.

Try to be a part of the total organization.   Know your boss as well as you can. Find out the company's basic objectives about costs, production, and quality. Understand the real intent of company policy toward employees. If you have this information, you will be in a better position to intercede for your employees. The boss who goes to bat for the gang is often the boss an employee can face on a rainy Monday morning when there is a temptation to remain in bed.

supervisory word power

Work.   That task, job, or employment in which a person applies mental or physical skills in order to earn a livelihood.

Bureaucracy.   An organized system of work directed by professional managers.

Facilitating.   An approach to management in which a supervisor assists and guides to employees in their efforts to perform their jobs rather than emphasizing orders and instructions.

Boredom.   The mental fatigue brought on by work that is monotonous, dull, uninteresting, apparently meaningless, or relentlessly tedious and repetitious.

Quality of work life.   The idea that work must—in addition to being productive in a material way—be rewarding in a psychological or spiritual way to the person who performs it.

Other Important Terms in This Chapter

authority
productivity

reading comprehension

1. Contrast the work or job you have done for pay with a task that you may have done on a voluntary basis. Into which did you put more physical or mental effort?

2. List five tasks that you would perform only for money and five that you would perform for personal satisfaction alone. How might you combine a "money" job with a "pleasure" job?

3. Provide an example of an acquaintance who values money as the most important satisfaction from a job. What do you know about the person that would contribute to that viewpoint?

4. Think of persons you know who are happy in their work. Describe one such person, the work performed, and the kind of supervision provided.

5. Describe a job that you consider boring. Can you think of some other person who doesn't feel that way about it?

6. Ron is a file clerk in an insurance company. His task is to take hundreds of documents each day—policies, completed forms, and correspondence—and file them alphabetically in the appropriate folders in file cabinets. What might he do to make his work less boring? Make at least five suggestions.

7. Think of your most recent job. Of the five or ten people you

worked with regularly, how many would you judge to be satisfied with their work and how many dissatisfied with it? What did they say or do that led you to these judgments?

8. Describe the conditions that would make a job ideal for you. Try to be serious and realistic about this.

9. Have you ever had a job that was easy but dull? What could you have done to make it more interesting?

10. Joanne is a stitching machine operator in a shoe manufacturing plant. Her job is to sew the leather soles to the uppers. She uses a device (fixture) to hold the upper in shape while she manipulates the needle of the stitching head around the sole. Joanne stitches 320 shoes per day. The materials she uses include nylon thread and a special adhesive. What might a supervisor do to "facilitate" Joanne's job?

supervision in action

THE CASE OF MILDRED AND THE "MICKEY MOUSE" JOB. A case study in human relations involving a bored employee, with questions for you to answer.

Two employees of the Zebra Hosiery Mills were waiting outside the plant for transportation home on a cold, wet afternoon. Mildred lit a cigarette and said, "One more day like this and it's bye-bye Zebra for me."

"What's the problem?" asked Leon, her co-worker.

"This job is boring me to death," said Mildred. "It's a Mickey Mouse all day long. I work my fingers raw racking up those yarn spools. Two hours straight before the break. Then lunch. Then the afternoon break. That's the same routine four times a day. I handle over 800 spools. Toward the end of each period I can hardly wait until I count the two hundredth spool."

"Wow," said Leon. "I never thought of it that way. It just strikes me that it's an easy way to make $30 a day."

"Easy, nothing," said Mildred. "I could show them how to make it easier. All we'd need is some gizmo to let me rack up two spools at a time. But that pumpkin head I work for hasn't listened to a new idea in 30 years."

"That could be," said Leon. "But I'm satisfied just so long as the supervisor stays off my back. I just don't like to be hassled."

"If she were to hassle you, you'd know you were something besides a machine," said Mildred. "If there were some place closer to home, I'd walk out on Zebra tomorrow."

"I could get a job nearer to my home," said Leon, "but I'd only make $25 a day. The extra $5 is worth 15 minutes longer on the bus."

"Not for me," said Mildred. "I've got kids to feed when I get home. I don't want them out on the streets longer than they have to be. I'd take a cut if my job was next door to where I lived."

At this point Leon's bus arrived. "See you tomorrow—if you don't decide to quit," he said, as he climbed aboard.

"Fat chance," said Mildred to herself. "What other choice do I really have?"

1. Contrast the difference in satisfaction Mildred and Leon get from their work. Which person seems more satisfied? Why?

2. If Mildred doesn't like her job, why wouldn't she simply get a more satisfying job elsewhere?

3. How far should Zebra Mills go to make its jobs satisfying to all employees? Why?

4. If you were Mildred's supervisor, what might you do to make the work less boring for her?

enriching your viewpoint

To gain a broader view of the meaning of work to human beings, the following readings are recommended:

Agassi, Judith, "Women and Work," *Proceedings of the International Conference on the Quality of Working Life,* Arden House, Harriman, N.Y., September 24–29, 1973.

Bluestone, Irving, "Creating a New World of Work," *International Labor Review,* Vol. 115, No. 1, January–February 1977.

Hoppock, Robert, *Job Satisfaction,* Harper & Row Publishers, Inc., New York, 1935.

Job Satisfaction: Is There a Trend? Research Monograph No. 30, Manpower Administration, U.S. Department of Labor, 1974.

Quinn, Robert, and William Cobb Jr., *What Workers Want: Factor Analysis of Importance Ratings of Job Facets,* Survey Research Center, Ann Arbor, Mich., 1971.

Sutermeister, Robert A., *People and Productivity,* 3d ed., McGraw-Hill Book Company, New York, 1976, Chap. 8, "Employees' Search for Job Satisfaction," p. 33; Chap. 7, "Employees' Search for Life Satisfaction," p. 30.

Webber, Ross A., *Management,* Richard D. Irwin, Inc., Homewood, Ill., 1975, Chap. 6, "Work and Extrinsic Rewards," p. 96; Chap. 7, "Work and Intrinsic Satisfactions," p. 116.

Weber, Max, *The Theory of Social and Economic Organization,* A.M. Henderson and Talcott Parsons (trans.), Free Press of Glencoe, Inc., New York, 1947.

3
individual motivation

Why isn't good human relations just plain horse sense?

Because this is a dangerous oversimplification. Life and business experiences are full of paradoxes and inconsistencies showing that good intentions and straight-line reasoning are not enough.

Take this example. Joe Smith supervises two men who work side by side on an assembly line in an auto plant. Their job is to attach the garnish (or trim) to the painted body. For some time Ed and Al, the men involved, had been complaining of knicks and cuts received from handling the sharp pieces of metal. Finally Joe decides the best way to cure the problem is to insist that both men wear gloves on the job. On Monday he approaches Ed and Al together. "Boys," says Joe, "the safety department has approved the issuance of work gloves for this job. This should prevent the rash of cuts you've been getting. Here's a pair of gloves for each of you. From now on I'll expect to see you wearing them all the time."

Next day Joe had to ask Ed on three separate occasions to put his gloves on. But Al wore his all the time. At the week's end Al was sold on the value of the gloves. But Ed just stuck his in his pants pocket. "They slow me down so I can't keep up with the line," he told Joe. But to Al he said, "This work-glove idea is just an excuse to justify speeding up the line. If you give in on this issue, they'll sock it to you even harder the next time."

Why do two men, handled the same way in the same situation, have such differing reactions? After all, weren't Joe's intentions good? Didn't he try to settle Ed's and Al's complaints about the cuts? Wasn't his solution a logical one?

Isn't human relations just applied psychology?

No. Human relations in industry is not psychology, sociology, or anthropology. Most of all, it is not psychiatry. While these four sciences aid in our understanding of what happens to people when they come to work, labels such as these are more misleading than enlightening.

When a job applicant fills out an interview form, the science of psychology is being applied. When a manager asks a supervisor what the employees think about the new rates, the manager is acknowledging the presence of sociological forces. When a plant in Michigan shuts down on the first day of the hunting season because it knows from past experience that most of the workers will take off anyway, anthropologists may identify this action as a concession to group cultures. And when an office manager listens to a near-hysterical clerk without interrupting, the manager may be borrowing a technique from the psychiatrist.

All the above actions involve the behavior of people at work. It has become common—and convenient—practice to call this behavior *human relations*. The operative words are *people, behavior,* and *work.*

Where do you find the important action in human relations?

Human relations is something that takes place between people. It takes place between an employee and the boss, between one worker and another, between a staff specialist and a line supervisor, between a manager and a superior. It takes place between individuals and between an individual and a group. The human interactions may be between executives and their departments, between managers and their associates, or, inversely, between workers and management in general. It takes place between two or more groups also. It may occur between the sales department and the accounting office, between the production department and the maintenance department, or between two factions in the same group. A.V. Graicunas, a noted authority, concludes that the number of potential interactions for a person supervising 14 employees is 114,872.[1]

Why do people act the way they do?

If you mean, "Why don't employees act the way you wish they would?" the answer will take a long time. But if you are really asking, "Why do people act in such unpredictable ways?" the answer is simple: People do as they must. Their actions, which may look irrational to someone who doesn't understand them, are in reality very logical. If you could peer into their backgrounds and into their emotional makeup, you'd be able to predict with startling accuracy how this person will react to criticism or how that person will act when told to change over to the second shift.

The dog who's been scratched by a cat steers clear of all cats. Workers who have learned from one boss that the only time they are treated like human beings is when the work load is going to be increased will go on the defensive when a new boss tries to be friendly. To the new boss such employee actions look absurd. But to the workers it's the only logical thing to do.

So it goes—each person is the product of parents, home, education, social life, and work experience. Consequently, by the time supervisors deal with employees, they are dealing with persons who have brought all their previous experiences to the job.

Then are all people different?

Each person *is* a distinct individual. In detail his or her reactions will be different from anyone else's. But to understand human relations, you must know first *why* people do things before you can predict *what* they will do. If you know that Bill dislikes his job because it requires concentration, you can make a good guess that Bill will make it hard for you to change the job by increasing its complexity. If Mary works at your company because of the conversation she has with her associates, you can predict that Mary will be hard to get along with if she's assigned to a spot in an isolated area.

The important tool in dealing with people is the recognition that although what they do is likely to differ, the underlying reasons for their doing anything are very similar. These reasons, incidentally, are called motives, or needs.

What determines an individual's personality?

███████████████ Just about everything. An individual's personality cannot be neatly pigeonholed (as we so often try to do) as pleasant or outgoing or friendly or ill-tempered or unpleasant or suspicious or defensive. An individual's personality is the sum total of what the person is today: the clothing worn, the food preferred, the conversation enjoyed or avoided, the manners and gestures used, the methods of thought practiced, the way situations are handled. Each person's personality is uniquely different from anyone else's. It is the result of heredity, upbringing, schooling or lack of it, neighborhoods, work and play experiences, parents' influence, religion—all of the social forces around us. From all these influences people learn to shape their individuality in a way that enables them to cope with life's encounters, with work, with living together, with age, with success and failure. As a result, personality is the total expression of the unique way in which each individual deals with life.

What do employees want from life—and their work?

███████████████ Employees, like most of us, seek satisfaction from life for what a very famous psychologist, A. H. Maslow, called the "five basic needs."[2] (See Figure 3–1.) And we seek a good part of these satisfactions at our work. Dr. Maslow outlined the basic needs this way and conceived of them as a sort of hierarchy with the most compelling ones coming first and the more sophisticated ones last.

We want to be alive and to stay alive.   We need to breathe, eat, sleep, reproduce, see, hear, and feel. But in the United States these needs rarely dominate us. Real hunger, for example, is rare. True, according to Masters and Johnson, most men and women don't get all the sex they need. But all in all, our first-level needs are satisfied. Only an occasional experience—a couple of days without sleep, a day on a diet without food, a frantic 30 seconds under water—reminds us that these basic needs are still with us.

We want to feel safe.   We like to feel that we are safe from accident or pain, from competitors or criminals, from an uncertain future or a changing today. Not one of us ever feels completely safe. Yet most of us feel reasonably safe. After all, we have laws, police, insurance, social security, union contracts, and the like to protect us.

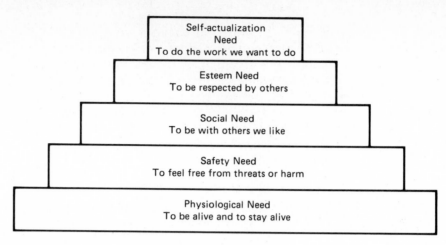

FIGURE 3-1. Maslow's hierarchy of needs.

We want to be social. From the beginning of time we have lived together in tribes and family groups. Today these group ties are stronger than ever. We marry, join lodges, and even do our praying in groups. Social need varies widely from person to person—just as other needs do. Few of us want to be hermits. Not too many people are capable of frank and deep relationships—even with their wives or husbands and close friends. But, to a greater or lesser degree, this social need operates in all of us.

We need to feel worthy and respected. When we talk about our self-respect or our dignity, this is the need we are expressing. When a person isn't completely adjusted to life, this need may show itself as undue pride in achievements, self-importance, boastfulness—a swelled head.

But so many of our other needs are so easily satisfied in the modern world that this need often becomes one of the most demanding. Look what we go through to maintain the need to think well of ourselves—and have others do likewise. When a wife insists her husband wear a jacket to a party, she's expressing this need. When we buy a new car even though the old one is in good shape, we're giving way to our desire to show ourselves off.

We even modify our personalities to get the esteem of others. No doubt you've put on your company manners when out visiting. It's natural, we say, to act more refined in public than at home—or to cover up our less acceptable traits.

We need to do the work we like. This is why many people who don't like their jobs turn to hobbies for expression, and why so many other people can get wrapped up in their work. We all know men and women who enjoy the hard burden of laboring work—or machinists who hurry home from work to run their own lathes. This need rarely is the be-all and end-all of our lives. But there are very few of us who aren't influenced by it.

In the 1960s and early 1970s many young people dropped out of society or set out to "do their own thing." This was largely an expression of the desire to fulfill oneself—what Maslow called "self-actualization."

Which of these needs is the most powerful?

▬▬▬▬▬▬▬ The one or ones that have not yet been satisfied. Maslow's greatest insight was that once a need is satisfied, it will no longer motivate a person to greater effort. If a person has what is required in the way of job security, for example, offering more of it—such as guaranteeing employment for the next five years—will normally not cause the person to work any harder. The supervisor who wishes to see greater effort generated will have to move to an unsatisfied need, such as the desire to be with other people on the job, if this employee is to be expected to work harder.

In what way can a job satisfy a person's needs?

▬▬▬▬▬▬▬ It's a fact: Many people are happier at work than at home! Why? Because a satisfying job with a good supervisor goes such a long way toward making life worth living. While all of us may complain about our job (or our boss) from time to time, most of us respond favorably to the stability of the work situation. At home Jane may have a nagging husband, sick children, and a stack of bills to greet her at the end of the month. At work Jane can have an appreciative supervisor, a neat job with a quota she can meet each day, and assurance of a paycheck (and other benefits) at the week's end. No wonder Jane enjoys herself more at work than at home.

Or look at it this way. A rewarding job with a decent company and a straight-shooting boss easily provides the first two basic needs: (1) a livelihood that keeps the wolf away from the door and (2) a sense of safety from the fears of layoff, old age, or accidents. Satisfaction from the other three basic needs—to be social, to be respected, and to do the work we like—is often more a function of a person's supervisor than of the job itself.

A good supervisor can see that a person's job satisfies the *social need* by demonstrating to the rest of the work group the desirability of taking in a new worker. For instance, "Fellows, this is Pete Brown, our new punch press operator. We're glad to have him with the company. And I've told him what a great bunch of guys you all are. How about taking him along to the cafeteria at lunchtime and showing him how to get a cup of java?"

To satisfy the *esteem need,* a good supervisor will make sure workers know that their work is appreciated. For example, "Pete, here's your locker. I think you'll agree that this is a pretty clean washroom. We feel that if we hire a good man, we've got to give him good conditions to work in so that he can do the best possible work."

To satisfy the *desire to do worthwhile work,* a good supervisor gives a lot of thought to putting workers on the job for which they have the most aptitude and training. Like saying, "Since you've worked this type of machine before, Pete, suppose you start on this one. When you've gotten the hang of things around here, we'll see about giving you a chance to learn some of the better-paying jobs."

If people all have the same fundamental needs, how far can a supervisor go in "push-button" human relations?

Not very far at all. There is a great danger in oversimplifying the analysis of human needs, especially at work.

One explanation of human behavior, for example, is that it depends upon each employee's expectancy (or estimate) of what his or her actions may or may not bring. In effect, the employee makes three estimates: (1) Can I do what management is asking me to do? (2) If I can do it, will management be satisfied and reward me? (3) Will the reward given me be worth the effort? As you can see, a person's effort will be greatly influenced by the answers to these questions. According to Maslow, the supervisor may go through the right motions and still find that the employee doesn't turn out as anticipated.

Satisfaction and dissatisfaction are rather vague terms, aren't they?

Yes. One noted behavioral observer, however, has found a way to be specific about them when they apply to work. Frederick Herzberg (*Work and the Nature of Man*, The World Publishing Company, Cleveland, 1966) set down these interpretations:

Satisfaction for an employee comes only from truly motivating factors such as interesting and challenging work, utilization of one's capabilities, opportunity to do something meaningful, recognition of achievement, and responsibility for one's own work.

Dissatisfaction occurs when the following factors are not present on the job: good pay, adequate holidays, long-enough vacations, paid insurance and pensions, good working conditions, and congenial people to work with.

Herzberg bases these definitions on his two-factor theory. He says that every human being has two motivational tracks: (1) a lower-level one, animal in nature and bent only on surviving and (2) a higher-level one, uniquely human and directed toward adjusting to oneself. Herzberg labels the first set of motivations "hygiene," or "maintenance," factors. We need to satisfy them, he reasons, to keep alive. People try to avoid pain and unpleasantness in life: they do the same on the job. Satisfaction of these needs provides only hygiene for the person. They physically maintain, but they do not motivate. If they are not present in the workplace, an employee will be dissatisfied and may look for a job elsewhere that provides these factors. But the employee will not work harder just because these factors are given to them. Said another way, a general pay increase may keep employees from quitting, but it will rarely motivate an employee to work harder.

On the other hand, Herzberg says, certain other factors provide genuine and positive motivation and should be called satisfiers. Without splitting hairs, we can see that generally the company must provide the factors that prevent dissatisfaction. The supervisor tends to provide the factors that satisfy. Few supervisors can establish the basic pay rates for the organization. Almost all supervisors can motivate. For example, the supervisor can provide an employee with a specific, challenging goal: "Not many people can stack more than 200 cartons an hour. If you can stack 220 today, you'll be a great asset to this department."

Similarly, a supervisor can let an employee know that the work is appreciated: "The boss asked me today who it was that typed these especially neat reports. I was pleased to be able to say it was you."

The supervisor can also help to make work more interesting by suggesting: "Why don't we take 15 minutes today to see whether together we can find a way to break the monotony in your job?"

And the supervisor can always extend responsibility by saying to an employee: "Beginning today, will you make the decision as to whether off-grade products should be reworked or thrown away? If you make an occasional mistake, don't worry about it. Your judgment is as good as mine, and I've learned that we can't be 100 percent perfect in these decisions."

How important is achievement to today's employee?

It is probably more important to supervisors than to employees. One noted observer, David McClelland, believes that the need for achievement is especially strong among most people who enter the management ranks. Nevertheless, a great many people feel its strong pull.

You can recognize the achiever, according to McClelland, if the person:

1. Likes to be able to control the situations in which he or she is involved;

2. Takes moderate risks but not long chances;

3. Likes to get immediate feedback as to how well he or she has done; and

4. Has a tendency to be preoccupied with the job to be done.

This last quality is one that supervisors must guard against lest it distract them from the need to relate well to their subordinates.

McClelland believes that most people learn their motivation patterns from life's experiences rather than by feeling them instinctively, as Maslow suggests. In fact, McClelland believes that in addition to achievement, the needs for power and affiliation are the most common motivators.

Individuals who are *power*-motivated may see every situation in your department as one in which they must seize control or otherwise submit to your domination. The power seekers tend to be abrasive, insisting on doing the job their own way rather than going along with your instructions.

Employees who are motivated by *affiliation* are usually friendly and like to socialize. The affiliation seekers are often hard to motivate toward production for production's sake but may respond to the appeal for cooperation.

Achievement seekers will rise to challenges and seek freedom of choice in deciding how to do the job. But they may be inclined to take off in an independent direction and balk at working with other employees.

Is the object of good human relations to have one big happy family?

Have you ever known a family in which there wasn't some discontent? Where one child didn't feel that another one was favored by a parent? Or where there wasn't an occasional spat between husband and wife? Or where there wasn't a disreputable relative hidden somewhere? I can't believe you haven't. It's the same way in business. As a responsible supervisor you strive for harmonious relationships with your employees and with the others with whom you associate. But it would be foolish to expect that everything is going to be as smooth as cream all the time—or even most of the time. It's only natural for people to have differences of opinion and arguments.

What you should aim for in your area is to have the arguments settled in a peaceful and reasonable manner. Keep emotions and epithets out of it. Sure, you can expect occasional name calling—and loud voices and red necks. But the *general* level of human relations in your area should be friendly. An attitude of: "Okay, let's pull this issue apart. Tell me exactly what's eating you about this assignment. When I've seen your point, I won't promise I'll agree with you. But I'll be a lot better able to give you a straight answer then." And after your decision: "Don't apologize for making an issue about it, Bill. That's your prerogative. And I'm glad you exercised it to get this matter cleared up. But how about in the future coming to me first before you get so hot and bothered about it?"

How far should supervisors go in calling people by their first names?

Almost as far as they like and the nature of the situation permits. Some people take to it right away—feel you're stuffy if you don't use their given names. Other people are standoffish about it and think that first names indicate an intimacy that takes more than an introduction to develop. The important thing is not to make the mistake of assuming that all there is to good human relations is to call people by their first names and to permit them to do the same to you. First names can pave the way to easier relationships. But they are only the first steps.

Of course, when talking with your superiors, you should look at the matter in reverse. Follow the custom of your company—whatever it happens to be. But don't be misled into believing that the familiarity of first-name usage by your boss means complete acceptance and confidence in you as an individual. You'll have to work to develop these.

What happens when workers don't get satisfaction from their jobs?

Morale will be down, attitudes not "right." But most important to you, unsatisfied workers don't produce as much or as well as those who find work rewarding.

Isn't job satisfaction primarily the company's responsibility—not the supervisor's?

The company's stake in good human relations is just as big as the supervisor's. And when a company helps the supervisor to establish the right climate for good human relations, the supervisor's job with people is much easier. But your relationship with your employees is a very personal one. And no amount of policies and procedures, fancy cafeterias, generous fringe benefits, or sparkling toilets can take the place of supervisors who are interested in their people and treat them wisely and well. From your point of view, responsibility for employees' job satisfaction is one you share jointly with the company.

Does good human relations really pay off?

Early in your career as a supervisor you'll find this recurrent criticism of the practice of human relations in industry: It makes good talk, but it doesn't pay the bills; whenever the squeeze is on to cut costs, all the frills will go out the window. That's the trouble with human relations. It's been hard for many companies to prove that its practice saves money. And whenever you come across supervisors who don't believe in good human relations (or who mistake softness for the real thing), they will be able to quote you examples of the well-meaning supervisors who got trampled on by employees they'd tried to do right by.

On the other hand, the casebooks show that supervisors who are intelligent in their dealings with people are able to show more production, lower costs, and greater quality. Good human relations doesn't mean being soft or weak or negligent. But neither does it mean treating people as if they weren't people—which was the mistake of most supervisors for the 20 or 30 years preceding the Great Depression. Good human relations is an art and a science; it's firm, yet flexible; and it's the most difficult ambition in the world to achieve. But be assured that the results are rewarding—in dollars and cents as well as in personal satisfaction for you and the people you supervise.

supervisory word power

Achievement need. A desire for accomplishment, which motivates many people at work. Employees who are motivated by this need usually like to control their own work, like to know immediately whether their work is satisfactory, take moderate risks, and concentrate closely on tasks and goals.

Affiliation need.   A desire to interact with other people and to enjoy social contact. Meeting this need is an important source of job satisfaction for some people.

Behavior.   The actions people take, or the things they say, while coping with other people, with problems, with opportunities, and with situations. Because behavior depends upon so many influences, it may or may not accurately reflect a person's true feelings.

Dissatisfaction.   The state that occurs when "maintenance," or "hygiene," factors such as good pay, fringe benefits, and desirable working conditions are lacking. Merely avoiding dissatisfaction is not adequate to motivate workers.

Individuality.   The character that heredity, environment, education, and experience combine to develop in each person—a unique hierarchy of motives and a unique way of behaving.

Motivation.   The process that impels a person to behave in a certain manner in order to satisfy highly individual needs for survival, security, respect, achievement, power, and sense of personal worth.

Personality.   The individual's unique way of behaving and of seeing and interpreting the actions of other people and things. Personality is shaped by heredity, parents' beliefs, upbringing, work experiences, and many other factors.

Power need.   A desire to control the actions of others and to manipulate events. The control and manipulation may often be seen as ends in themselves rather than as ways to accomplish other important things.

Satisfaction.   The state that occurs when truly motivating factors such as interesting and challenging work, full use of one's capabilities, and recognition for achievement are provided.

Other Important Terms in This Chapter

human relations
job satisfaction
self-actualization

reading comprehension

1. Provide an example from your own experience that shows how two or three people reacted differently to almost the same

set of circumstances. Give an explanation of the reasons for these differences.

2. Find the dictionary definitions for *psychology* and *sociology*. Give an illustration of each science taken from everyday life.

3. Think of a possible confrontation between an employee and a supervisor. Show how their viewpoints and objectives might vary.

4. Do you think that a person's order of priorities for Maslow's five basic needs changes as he or she matures? Why?

5. Comment upon the relationship between an individual's need for esteem and need to do meaningful work.

6. What is your own reaction to people who use your first name before they know you well? Do you like it, or do you think it is an unwarranted familiarity?

7. When worker motivation in a department is still low despite good pay, fringe benefits, and desirable working conditions, what can a supervisor do to increase motivation?

8. Give some examples of behavior that might be expected from three individuals: one who has a strong need for power, another with a strong need for affiliation, and a third with a strong need for achievement.

9. How would you draw the line between *(a)* a supervisor who is well liked and whose department is productive and *(b)* a supervisor who is well liked but whose department is not particularly effective?

10. Contrast a supervisor who tries to manipulate employees and one who tries to motivate them.

supervision in action

THE CASE OF THE THREE EMPLOYEES WHO LOOKED ALIKE. A case study in human relations involving people who appear to be alike, with questions for you to answer.

Lennie, Larry, and Louis began work at the American Specialties plant on the same day. By an odd coincidence the three men not only were about the same age and came from the same neighborhood, but they also looked alike. Their co-workers used to say that the only way to tell them apart was to look at their clock numbers. Lennie was 8291, Larry 8292, and Louis 8293.

The first jobs assigned to Lennie, Larry, and Louis were in the labor pool. Under a rather rough-and-ready gang supervisor, the three fellows would be sent out on different jobs almost every day. One day they'd be in department A shoveling sand, the next day they'd be in the shipping department loading box cars, and the next day helping the packers on the assembly line to seal up cases. But at the end of each day the three men would report back to the labor pool to check out with the gang supervisor. They liked him and he thought well of them. "These kids are okay," he said. "They'll fit in anywhere in the plant."

As the three musketeers (that's what they came to be called in the plant) acquired seniority, one by one they were assigned permanent jobs in the plant. Lennie worked as a lift-truck operator in the shipping department, Larry became a pumpman in the processing department, and Louis went into the maintenance shop as a helper.

A year after Lennie, Larry, and Louis had started their permanent jobs, the personnel manager pulled their record cards from his files. What he saw rather surprised him. Lennie, Larry, and Louis had excellent records while they worked in the labor gang. Except for an occasional excused absence, their attendance and deportment had been almost perfect. But today their records told a different story.

Lennie's personnel record showed that he had been late nine times during the year. He had been absent for one reason or another a total of 27 days. He'd had one lost-time accident and had made over 15 other visits to the dispensary for various reasons. His boss had issued him two written reprimands for infractions of company rules.

Larry's attendance and safety record was about average for the plant. But while he didn't have a production-type job, his supervisor had reported that Larry was a poor producer. In addition there was a notation that Larry had come to the personnel office several times during the year to complain about minor troubles in the shop—once about a mistake in his pay and twice about the kind of work he had been assigned.

Louis's attendance and safety record was also average. But Louis's supervisor had made a special point of noting that Louis was fast and cooperative. In addition he had recommended Louis for promotion to class B mechanic when the next opening arose.

The personnel manager was frankly puzzled by the difference in the men's records—in view of the fact that they all had shown such promise originally.

1. What sorts of experiences at work could have caused Lennie, Larry, and Louis to change?

2. What factors at home or in their lives outside work could have caused these changes?

3. If you were the personnel manager, what conclusions might you draw about each man's supervisor? Why?

enriching your viewpoint

To gain a broader and more comprehensive view of individuality in human relations, the following readings are suggested:

Dowling, William F., and Leonard B. Sayles, *How Managers Motivate,* 2d ed., McGraw-Hill Book Company, New York, 1978.

Gellerman, S.W., *Motivation and Productivity,* American Management Association, New York, 1963.

Luthans, Fred, *Introduction to Management: A Contingency Approach,* McGraw-Hill Book Company, New York, 1976, "Expectancy Models of Motivation," pp. 260–265.

McClelland, David C., *The Achieving Society,* D. Van Nostrand Company, Inc., Princeton, N.J., 1961.

Rosow, Jerome M. (ed.), *The Worker and the Job: Coping with Change,* American Assembly Book, Prentice-Hall, Inc., Englewood Cliffs, N.J., 1974, Chap. 3, "Workers: Attitudes and Adjustments."

Skinner, B.F., *Beyond Freedom and Dignity,* Alfred A. Knopf, Inc., New York, 1964.

Vroom, Victor, *Work and Motivation,* John Wiley & Sons, Inc., New York, 1964.

Winter, D.G., *The Power Motive,* The Free Press, New York, 1973.

references cited in this chapter

1. Henry L. Sisk, *Management and Organizations,* 2d ed., South-Western Publishing Company, Inc., Cincinnati, 1973, pp. 299–300.

2. A. H. Maslow, "A Theory of Human Motivations: The Basic Needs," in H. Leavitt and L. Pondy (eds.), *Readings in Managerial Psychology,* University of Chicago Press, Chicago, 1964.

4

CHAPTER ## work group behavior

What is meant by group dynamics?

This term is applied to the forces brought to bear by individuals, singly or collectively, in a group activity. The choice of the word *dynamics* is especially important. It implies change. For example, you set out to explain to Paul why he should operate a slightly more complex machine without receiving an increase in his pay rate. He enters the situation with the conviction that you are trying to take advantage of him. You begin with the view that he's got to accept your word, willy-nilly. After five minutes of talking, you see that Paul isn't going to take this decision lying down; furthermore, you feel he has a legitimate argument you hadn't anticipated. Paul, on the other hand, feels that you aren't going to go to bat in his behalf, and although he's still apparently listening, he's made up his mind to see his shop steward as soon as he can. Since the conversation began, your attitude has changed and so has Paul's. That's dynamic.

Any two people can make up a group. Their interaction is group dynamics. As more and more people get into the group, the situation gets more dynamic. As time elapses, the situation gets more dynamic. And as new factors enter the situation (a change in workplace lighting, an announcement of a pay increase at the plant next door, etc.), the situation gets even more dynamic.

More than one person—plus change—adds up to group dynamics.

Why are group relations more important today than they were in years past?

Business, industrial, service, and government enterprises are larger and more complex. As a result they depend more upon the effectiveness of group effort. At the turn of the nineteenth into the twentieth century, employees worked more by themselves, and their productivity often depended upon their efforts alone. Then, too, many of the jobs were unskilled. People were hired to do routine work or to perform a specific task that a machine performs today. Automation, computers, and industrial engineering made those jobs scarce. Instead, modern jobs involve great interdependence between individuals and between departments and demand close cooperation among all parties.

What does this have to do with the supervisor?

Just about everything. You must first recognize that all situations are dynamic. Then you've got to develop a way of following the direction of, and coping with, the evolving situation. All too often in group dynamics the supervisor is a couple of laps behind the field. He or she is trying to solve the situation as it was five minutes ago—or five days ago—not as it is right now.

Which groups take priority: the formal or the informal ones?

Formal groups do, such as your own department or assigned work teams within your department. They have been set up routinely to carry out the work in the best fashion. But informal groups require your attention—and consideration, too. A supervisor must be realistic about formation of informal groups within the department:

1. Informal groups are inevitable. They'll form at the water fountain and in the locker room. They will be made up of car

poolers and those with common interests in sports or politics. You will find them everywhere. There is no way to blot them out.

2. Informal groups can be very powerful. They influence your employees strongly. They command their loyalty and often demand conformity. Most important, groups like this can work on your behalf or they can work against you.

To whom does the individual employee owe loyalty: the group or the supervisor?

There is no reason why an employee cannot be loyal to both. An employee warms up to various informal groups for friendship and companionship. A rank-and-file worker is more likely to identify with a buddy than with the boss. And in a time of layoffs or other threats, an employee may reasonably look to the group for protection.

On the other hand, an employee looks to the good supervisor for knowledge about the job, personal training and development, direction and instruction, encouragement, respect, and understanding. The wise supervisor doesn't force an employee to choose between the group and the boss.

Which goals come first: the individual's, the group's, or the organization's?

If anything is to be accomplished, groups as well as individuals must place their goals second to those of the organization. The trick to good supervision, however, is to find a way to keep the goals of all three in harmony. Mary, for example, wants to get the job done as soon as she can so that she can take a break. The group wants to stretch it out so that there will be overtime. The supervisor, who must represent the organization, wants to get the job done on schedule so that a shipment can be made on time and at specified labor cost. Mary and the supervisor are pulling in the same direction. The group is not. The supervisor has to find a way to persuade or insist that the group go along with the company goals, such as "We'll all lose this order if we don't get it out by 4 p.m." Or "Our deadline is 4 p. m. We've been able to make it dozens of times in the past. And regardless, there will be no overtime approved for this shipment."

What are work groups likely to do best?

Solve work problems. Groups, formal or informal, seem to have an uncanny knack for unsnarling complex work situations. In a few minutes they can straighten out crossover procedures between employees. They often know causes of difficulty hidden from the supervisor. Typically, they are acutely aware of personality conflicts between their members. Thus, a group's ability to put together jointly held know-how in a constructive manner is one that experienced supervisors like to tap. The technique of securing group aid this way in solving departmental problems is called *participation.*

In what ways are groups
most likely to cause problems?

██████████████ By ganging up to present mass resistance (spoken or silent) and by pressuring individual members to conform to the group's standards. Strong work groups stick together. They will protect one of their loyal members, and they will force a nonconformist to go along with the majority. The pressure can be so strong that even an eager beaver or a loner can be made to fall in line—or to quit. Groups are powerful. Their support is to be cherished. Their enmity can be awesome. For these reasons prudent supervisors seek the group's help in establishing attainable work goals.

How can a supervisor set goals with the
work group without sacrificing authority?

██████████████ Unless the group of people you supervise believes that what you want them to do is to their advantage as well as to yours, you'll have little success as a supervisor. The solution lies in permitting the group to set their goals along with you and in showing them that these goals are attained through group action—teamwork.

It may be only natural for you to feel that to permit the group to get into the decision-making act will be hazardous to your authority. It needn't be. First of all, make it clear that you'll always retain a veto power over a group decision (but don't exercise it unless absolutely necessary). Second, establish ground rules for their participation beforehand—and make these limitations clear. Finally, provide enough information for the group so that they can see situations as you do. It's when people don't have enough facts that they rebel against authority.

In dealing with work groups, try to make your role that of a coach. Help employees to see why cost cutting, for instance, is desirable and necessary to prevent layoffs. Encourage them to discuss ways to cut costs. Welcome their suggestions. Try to find ways of putting even relatively insignificant ideas to work. And report the team's achievements frequently. Emphasize that good records are the result of the team's united effort, not your own bright ideas.

Of course, it goes without saying that certain decisions—as those concerning work standards or quality specifications —may be beyond the group's control or even yours. Consequently, you should make it clear at the start what work conditions are off limits as far as group participation is concerned.

Why is group participation so effective?

You'll hear a lot about the wonders of participation. And most of what you'll hear is true. In today's employer-employee relations, few techniques have been as successful in developing harmony and the attainment of common goals as has the development of participation by supervision.

Participation is an amazingly simple way to inspire people. And its simplicity lies in the definition of the word: "to share in common with others."

Sharing, then, is the secret. You must share knowledge and information with others in order to gain their cooperation. You must share your own experience so that employees will benefit from it. You must share the decision-making process itself so that employees can do some things the way they'd like to. And you must share credit for achievement.

Once you've learned how to share, participation is self-perpetuating. Supervision becomes easier when employees begin to share responsibility with you. No longer do you alone have to watch for every possibility. An employee will report an overheated motor, raw material with flaws, or an impending bottleneck. Employees won't wait for you to tell them what to do in an emergency. You'll find them using their own initiative to keep the lines producing. So sharing pays off as employees share your burdens and their production records with you.

How often can group participation be expected to work in your behalf?

Only as often as the group's perception of a situation leads them logically or emotionally, or both ways, to the conclusion that what you wish is good for them. Keep in mind that merely permitting participation will not manipulate the group to your point of view. And the larger the group, the more forces are at work in it with which your ideas must cope.

If the majority can be expected to agree with your inclinations when given the same view of the facts you have, then the majority may sway group attitudes in your direction. But even this won't always be the case. If, for example, Mary is cantankerous, but because of seniority or outspokenness has the respect or fear of the rest of the people in the steno pool, the group may never buy an idea of yours that discredits her. Conversely, the group may (for reasons that are hard to determine) rebel against Mary and accept your new idea.

There are two rules of thumb to guide you: (1) Without group support your chance of achievement is slim, and (2) your best chance for winning group support is to let the forces within the group itself struggle toward a decision with minimum interference from you. This isn't to say you must stand helplessly by while the group strikes off in the wrong direction. You can supply sound direction by providing facts that might be overlooked and by asking the group to weigh pros and cons of various alternatives.

How can you tell how a group feels about you?

Surprisingly, one way is to let the group know how you feel about them. In other words, if you're puzzled or angered by a group's behavior, tell them so in clear terms. Then give them a chance to present their excuses or to strike back at you. If you can take a stiff rebuttal or candid criticism, then you're likely to discover how the group really feels about your managerial techniques.

Here's an example. Supervisor Jane is being pressed for better quality control in her department. But month-end reports show that her department is losing ground. Now it does her no good to hold private ideas about who's sabotaging her—or to complain about the matter to the other supervisors. It would be far better for Jane to lay her thoughts on the line. She can call her work group together and say, "I won't make a secret of how I feel. I've asked for your help in licking this quality problem. And all I get is the feeling that you're trying to make a monkey out of me. I don't like it. In fact, I'm downright angry about it. And as far as I can see, the fault is yours, not mine. Now, can you tell me where I'm wrong?" This brings her feeling out into the open. In reply she may—if she can bite her tongue for five minutes—get a response from someone in the group that will show where the trouble lies. Or she may get no verbal response at all. Instead, she may find a subtle shift in the ways in which the group performs and even an improvement in work quality.

Why worry about how people feel about you? Supervising isn't a popularity contest. In the long run, you call the signals, don't you?

A supervisor's first responsibility is to be effective. This doesn't necessarily mean that supervisors have to be popular to be effective. But there are many ingrained habits we acquire that stand in the way of achievement. Many supervisors are naggers without realizing it. Many supervisors have the best of intentions when they offer advice, but don't realize that their subordinates think this is a demonstration of lack of confidence in them. Other supervisors dominate conversations with their employees without recognizing that this breeds a resentment that deafens the employees' ears to instructions. If we could find out how others, especially groups, react to our manner, we might be able to eliminate or minimize those affronts and irritations we don't intend.

How changeable are group attitudes?

They can be very changeable. Take a group's attitude, for example, on a proposed change in its work procedure. Initially all members may resist it. Then one or two try it out and find that it is not so bad as they thought. They persuade a few of their friends to try it out. Soon, like passengers who rush from one side of a boat to another, they can dramatically change the weight of the group's position. Even the reluctant members are swept along with the crowd. Obviously, this effect can be helpful or troublesome. It is a force to be dealt with.

How does a group of employees differ from any single employee in the group?

Take a group of ten employees who work in a small can-filling line in a food-packing plant. This group is respected and feared by its supervisor as one of the most productive, most-likely-to-strike groups in the plant. Yet in the group are three people who, polled separately, are strongly against a walkout. And another three who, when working with other groups, are low producers. This is typical. Each person in a group may be a fairly strong individualist when working alone. But when people work in a group, the personality of the group becomes stronger than that of any single individual in the group. The group's personality will reflect the outlook and work habits of the various individuals, but it will bring out the best (or worst) in some and will submerge many individual tendencies the group does not approve of.

Why are some groups influential, others weak?

One union will pull a strike only to see it fizzle out in a week or two. Another union, with a much less clear-cut issue at stake, may go out on strike and stay on strike for months. The first group of strikers is a weak group, the latter a strong one.

Strong groups, contrary to what you might suspect, are ones in which there are lots of conflict and frequent arguments. But where arguments are welcomed, agreements are stronger, too. And the pressure to conform is great.

Weak groups are those in which the objectives are not very important to most members or in which a few strong leaders make all the decisions.

In the work groups you supervise, try to find out what the workers want as a group. Then help them to set these goals themselves. Try to show that your interest is in seeing that group goals are achieved, that you aren't the roadblock to job security, better pay, more rewarding work. That way the work groups you supervise will be strong groups. And properly inspired, their goals will be very similar to yours.

It's when supervisors set themselves against work groups that the group becomes either strongly against the supervisor and the company or weak and easily seized by a strong leader who may be against the supervisor or the objectives which best satisfy both company and worker.

Why are some groups made up of troublemakers rather than good workers?

At least one significant study has been made to show that the nature of some work itself somehow attracts, or develops, troublemakers. But it's hard to conclude that that's the case most of the time. It's better if you can take the broad view that the group you supervise is also one of the groups of which you, too, are a member. While your company and your boss may have given you a certain amount of authority, that doesn't guarantee that you'll be the leader, or the only leader, in that group. However, if you're in tune with the group, there's a good chance you can find a way to make your kind of leadership and authority harmonize with the group's outlook. If so, even the existing troublemakers in the group won't be able to develop or to encourage the group to challenge you, your objectives, or your way of doing things. It's when the other leadership in the group supersedes yours that the good worker becomes a troublemaker in your eyes.

Which comes first, the individual or the group?

It's almost impossible to say. We do know that the group is not just the sum of the individuals in it. Individually each of your employees may be loyal and honest. But as a group each person may be more loyal to the group's interest than to you. As a result, the individual may cheat a little on output or quality, if that's the standard the group respects.

It seems unavoidable that you must place your bets on the group's being collectively stronger than any of its individuals. Hardly any single person can stand up to group pressures for long. The person who does so may keep on working in your area but is no longer a member of that group. Such persons become odd-balls, difficult for you to deal with fairly and intelligently because you're never sure what standards of performance to impose on them—theirs or the department's. For that reason don't press individuals to support you in favor of the work group. Accept the fact that they will be loyal to you when this loyalty doesn't put them at odds with their peers.

By and large the supervisor's charge is to treat each person as individually as possible without challenging the prerogatives of the group the individual works in. The work group is an organization for which you are expected to provide direction and inspiration, not moral judgments.

supervisory word power

Group dynamics. The interaction between members of a work group and concurrent changes in their attitudes, behavior, and relationships; similarly, the interaction—and changing attitudes, behavior, and relationships—between a work group and others outside the group, in particular, the supervisor.

Formal work groups. Those groups or teams of employees who are assigned by management to similar activities or locations with the intent that they work together toward goals established by management.

Informal work groups. Those groups that form spontaneously among employees who work near one another, or who have common personal interests, or who work toward common job goals, whether or not these goals are the ones set down by management.

Participation.   The sharing, by a supervisor or manager with work groups, of work-related information and of responsibilities, decisions, or both—such as the way a job should be performed, how a group should divide up the work, and what the work goals might be.

Loyalty.   Faithfulness, devotion, or allegiance given by an employee to a person, a supervisor, a group, a company, or an ideal—or to the goals of any of these.

Other Important Terms in This Chapter

group goals
group participation
identify

reading comprehension

1. Why are the forces that operate within groups called group dynamics?

2. Describe a situation you have been in, in which you were part of both a formal group and an informal group within the same organization.

3. Should a supervisor force an employee to choose between loyalty to the group and loyalty to the supervisor? Why or why not?

4. Why would an experienced supervisor encourage group participation in solving a work problem?

5. Which kind of supervision would you prefer if you had your choice—one in which the supervisor carefully and fairly laid out the work but was very firm about your following his or her instructions, or one in which the supervisor carefully and fairly spelled out what results were expected but left it up to you to figure out how to accomplish them? Why?

6. What kind of problems can work groups cause that a supervisor should be especially conscious of?

7. Think of a supervisor or a teacher you have had who never revealed personal feelings and reactions to the work group. Was this a good idea? Why or why not?

8. Think of a group that has changed some of its attitudes or beliefs over a period of time. What caused the change? Was it rapid or gradual? How did it take place?

9. What are some forces likely to create a strong group? A weak group?

10. As a supervisor, what would be your overall goals in establishing relations with your work group?

supervision in action

███████████ **THE CASE OF THE UNSUCCESSFUL PROCEDURES CHANGE.**
A case study in human relations involving group dynamics,
with questions for you to answer.

When Barbara was promoted to supervisor and moved to the claims department of an insurance company, she was viewed with suspicion by the men and women in the new department. Because Barbara was soundly grounded in the clerical procedures used there, she believed there were many improvements that could be made. Not wanting to give the impression of being too eager, however, Barbara spent the first week or two just getting to know the people in her department. On the whole, the staff was pretty standoffish. This was especially true of Jack, one of the older claims analysts. On the bright side, Barbara was able to make friends with Tony, one of the sharp, young new clerks.

One of the costly practices Barbara noticed was that the claims form was initially posted to a logbook by a clerk, then given a preliminary classification by an analyst before being returned to the clerk for detailed verification of the data on the form. After this, the form went back to an analyst for completion. Barbara reasoned that the clerk who entered the form in the logbook could be trained to make the preliminary classification. This same clerk could also verify the detailed data on the form. This way, unnecessary doubling back of the form would be eliminated, and the analysts could spend more of their time on the complex aspects of claims processing.

Barbara waited until Friday and then proposed to the clerks and analysts that on Monday, the new procedure should be followed. She demonstrated to all the clerks how the classifications could be made with the same master list used by the analysts. Since there were no objections and only a few questions, Barbara presumed that the work group understood the new procedure.

On Monday Barbara made a point of working along with Tony because he was the newest clerk in the office. He easily caught on to the new way. Tony seemed sold on the improvement, and by noon he had finished as much work as he normally would have before the additional step was added to his job. That afternoon, however, Tony reported to Barbara that he had run into all sorts of difficulty in following the new procedure. The next morning Barbara discovered that Tony was doing the job in the old way. Barbara checked the rest of the staff and found that no one other than Tony had even given the new method a try. In fact, when she queried Jack about it, Jack said this was an old idea that had been tried before and found to be full of problems. Barbara then went back to Tony and suggested he try a variation in which his problems with the new method might be worked out. Tony shook his head and said, "This is not as good an idea as it looked at first. If it were, other people in the department besides me would be trying it. Anyway, I would rather follow the old procedure. It's much simpler."

1. Why do you suppose Tony gave up on the new procedure so soon?

2. How might Jack's reaction have influenced the other employees?

3. Should Barbara persist in trying to install the new procedure? Why?

4. How might Barbara have gotten her improvement accepted in the first place?

enriching your viewpoint

To gain a broader understanding of work group behavior, the following readings are suggested:

Bartlett, Alton C., and Thomas A. Kayser (eds.), *Changing Organizational Behavior,* Prentice-Hall, Inc., Englewood Cliffs, N.J., 1973.

Eckles, Robert W., Ronald L. Carmichael, and Bernard R. Sarchet, *Essentials of Management for First-Line Supervision,* John Wiley & Sons, Inc., New York, 1974, Chap. 13, "Informal Organizations and Groups."

Katz, Fred, "Explaining Informal Work Groups in Complex Organizations," *Administrative Science Quarterly,* Vol. 10, No. 2, 1965.

Kiesler, Charles A., and Sara B. Kiesler, *Conformity,* Addison-Wesley Publishing Company, Inc., Reading, Mass., 1969.

Porter, Lyman W., Edward E. Lawler III, and J. Richard Hackman, *Behavior in Organizations,* McGraw-Hill Book Company, New York, 1975.

Sayles, Leonard, *The Behavior of Industrial Work Groups,* McGraw-Hill Book Company, New York, 1963.

Schein, Edgar, *Organizational Psychology,* Prentice-Hall, Inc., Englewood Cliffs, N.J., 1970.

Walker, Charles R., Robert H. Guest, and Arthur N. Turner, *The Foreman on the Assembly Line,* Harvard University Press, Cambridge, Mass., 1956.

Zenger, John H., and Dale E. Miller, "Building Effective Teams," *Personnel,* March–April 1974.

LET'S
TALK
ABOUT
IT!

5

conflict and cooperation

Is the presence of bickering and disputes a sign of poor supervision?

Not necessarily. It is human to quarrel and complain. When many people must work together, conflict is inevitable. Accordingly, a small amount of conflict can be a good thing. It is when there is no end of quarreling and confrontation that supervisors should begin to worry about how good a job they are doing.

What are the main sources of conflict in an organization?

They are many. People with different ideas about what should be done and how to do it are a common source. Departments that are sometimes at cross-purposes—like production and maintenance, production control and sales, sales and credit, accounting and retailing, purchasing and engineering—cause intergroup difficulties. But most of the causes of conflict in a supervisor's department are closely related to the work itself: how it is laid out and the way in which the supervisor manages the employees. In particular, a supervisor should be on guard against:

1. A one-way pattern of communications, with the supervisor's making most of the decisions and handing down orders and instructions all the time.

2. Unpredictability, with the supervisor's insisting that something be done this way today and that way tomorrow.

3. The presence of change—in methods, materials, or specifications; in organizational relationships; in company policy. Employees work best when there is a certain degree of stability in the shop.

What's a good way to handle conflict in your department?

First, be alert to its presence. Next, seek out its causes. Then meet it head-on. A basic approach involves four steps:

1. Decide what it is that you wish to be accomplished.   Do you want peace and quiet at any price? Or do you want better quality? Greater productivity? A project finished on time? Fewer mistakes in transcribing? An end to delays caused by quarrels between the maintenance person and your production operator? Nothing will be resolved unless you first make up your mind what the desired outcome should be.

2. Call together the people who can best settle the issue. If the conflict is strictly between you and an individual, limit the confrontation to the two of you. If others are involved, invite them into the discussion. If a disinterested party, such as the quality-control department, can shed light on the subject, ask for its participation. If a referee or someone who can speak authoritatively about the company's viewpoint is needed, then get your boss into the act.

3. Be ready to bargain, not hand out edicts.   Conflicts are truly settled by negotiation. A short answer tends only to put off the problem, and it will keep recurring. If you keep your eye on the objective you have set, there are usually many ways to attain it. Remember that each individual has an objective, too. If the maintenance department, for example, can provide the necessary repairs while still keeping their costs in line—and dependable repairs are your objective—then let them do it their way.

4. Don't be distracted by the red herring of personalities.
While many people do rub one another the wrong way, most
conflicts have a much more tangible basis. That's the value
of keeping the eyes of all concerned on the main objective. It
tends to push personality conflicts into the background. Finally,
try not to get emotionally involved yourself. Above all, don't
choose sides.

How can you avoid prolonging a touchy situation?

As we said earlier, the best thing is to face up to conflict as soon
as you are sure it has substance. In other words, don't heat up a
minor dispute by jumping the gun. But do try to resolve it clearly
once you've seen more than smoke. Because conflict is unpleasant to most of us and because it is not easy to settle, you should
guard against certain practices that tend to prolong it. For example, you should check to see that you are not making any of
the following mistakes:

- Avoiding conversations or contact with those who are involved. You're angry at Sue, for example, and you're not going to
speak to her. Or you purposely cut out the bowling night with the
purchasing supervisor who is undercutting you.
- Emphasizing orders and instructions while shutting off an employee's opportunities to talk up to you. Or relying upon a flurry
of written memos and bulletin board notices. This encourages
employees to carp among themselves, to inflate the issues so
that they become harder to resolve.
- Switching from compliments to complaints. You feel you were
nice to Sam, for example, and he didn't cooperate. Okay, now
you'll show him what it's like by throwing a few zingers to him.
- Allowing the injured parties to gang up. One unhappy person
can "infect" several others. If it is your department against the
sales-order department, for example, continued silent combat
will build up their solidarity. And when you finally do try to settle
the issue, it will be stickier than ever.

People speak of the value of gaining sensitivity. Why?

In dealing with other people, especially people who are
members of your work force, many authorities believe that you
can establish better long-term relations with them if you are sen-

sitive to the way they feel—both about you and about your behavior toward them. The rationale goes something like this: If you're in tune with employees' feelings, your timing of instructions, changes, requests, and criticisms—and your way of going about all this—will be more effective.

The sensitivity point of view assumes that few of us really know how we affect other people. It also assumes that if we had a chance to see ourselves as others see us, we'd change our ways and adopt a more acceptable manner. Unfortunately, these sensitivity authorities generally assume that under normal conditions others disguise their true feelings so well that the chances of our finding out about ourselves are very slim. Accordingly, the prescribed way to acquire this learning is to take part in a sensitivity-training laboratory, often called laboratory, or controlled, training.

In a sensitivity laboratory a number of managers are guided into situations where participants inevitably become candid about one another's behavior. Typically, one group member will comment, "Joe, when you suggest that we ought to cooperate, you sound as phony as a $3 bill. What you really mean is 'play it my way or I won't play ball'!" Joe may be hearing this observation about himself for the first time in his life. And if the comment is valid (the laboratory is so set up that such opinions get plenty of chance to be tested), Joe may be able to use this insight into himself to develop a more sincere approach in dealing with associates and employees back on his job. On the other hand, occasionally Joe can't take this kind of criticism. He may rebel and even walk out of the group. Or he may actually break down altogether. But most people who have undergone sensitivity training believe that the experience has been invaluable in enabling them to improve their effectiveness with other people at work.

What's the significance of a hidden agenda?

One point of view of the sensitivity-training people is that so many ordinary business meetings (where, for instance, supervisors sit down to resolve production or cost problems) get nowhere because each member nurses a "hidden agenda." This hidden agenda prevents the group from making real progress in solving their mutual problems. For example, Teresa, the production-control supervisor, may feel the meeting has been called to make her the scapegoat of a delayed shipment. Consequently, she comes to the meeting with the intention of placing the blame on the purchasing agent for not having stocked the right quantity of subassemblies. This is Teresa's hidden agenda. Until the group gets Teresa to put this agenda on the table, the group meeting will accomplish very little. Proponents of sensitivity argue that it would be far better for the purposes of the meeting if Teresa were to say what is on her mind—that she thinks she's going to be made the goat, that others are to blame. That way, other participants would know how Teresa feels and could clear the air of recriminations before settling down to solutions that usually require teamwork.

Must you be superhuman to get along with everybody?

You would be if you did. That's why psychologists stress the value of accepting yourself pretty much as you are—not smugly, of course, but recognizing that you have many faults, faults that keep you from doing a perfect job and sometimes make you difficult to live with.

If you expect perfection from yourself, for example, chances are that you will become almost impossible for others to get along with because you tend to expect perfection from them, too. Worse still, you expect perfection from them in a lot of matters they couldn't care less about. On the other hand, it's just as dangerous to shield yourself from your own personality deficiencies and to make excuses for them. Admitting your weaknesses is far better. Try to make concessions where they cause others trouble. But don't blame others for your shortcomings.

Whether you strive for perfection or cover up your weaknesses, it often adds up to misery for others. Sensitivity experts believe that (1) just knowing more about yourself may make you more acceptable to others and (2) permitting others to comment to you about your shortcomings can work magic for you. People will then accept you for what you are and will make allowances for you. And they will also more readily accept—and act upon—your criticism of them.

Does sensitivity imply that a responsive manager doesn't demote, discipline, or fire anybody?

Not at all. If the demands of a particular job are such that a subordinate cannot perform it properly, the supervisor must take action. Sensitivity does not interfere with this action. Its purpose is to help people who are working to do a better, more effective job. Sensitivity flourishes in an atmosphere of success (not failure), and vice versa.

How can you invite candid, open discussion with others without recriminations?

First, get the candid talk. That takes guts on your part. Later, the recriminations won't be so bad, if they don't disappear altogether. The trick in getting others to level with you is to try to separate feelings from facts.

Take an employee who has an irritating way of making remarks to other employees while you're explaining the lineup for the day's work. Get this employee aside and say something like this: "I have no idea what it is you're saying when I'm talking. But it irritates me beyond reason. It makes me want to give you the heaviest kind of work I can find. It's crazy for two grown people to get a hang-up like this. Maybe my impression of your attitude is all wrong. Is it?" Given this chance, the person may say, "You bug me, too, the way you lecture us each morning as if we were kids. What's more, you always seem to find a way to make me look like a fool." At that point the employee is beginning to bring a hidden agenda into view—because you've been willing to expose yours. Surprisingly, once feelings have been discussed—not necessarily resolved—the chances are infinitely better that the two of you will be able to agree better on factual matters.

What is an attitude?

An attitude is a person's point of view. It's a way of looking at something. But even more important, an attitude is a person's readiness to react—and to react in a predetermined way.

Baseball batters ready to swing at a pitch, for instance, set their feet, cock their bats, keep their eyes on the pitcher. They've learned from experience that this attitude gives the best chance of getting a hit. In the same way, you—and your employees—learn from your experience to assume a readiness to react when faced with a situation. Employee attitudes toward lateness determine how conscientiously they try to get to work on time. Your attitude toward lateness will determine how much emphasis you place on tardiness as a measure of employee performance.

When are attitudes positive?

Attitudes that reflect optimism and enthusiasm—what professional athletes call desire—are positive. People who are positive in their thinking look for the good things in other people and in their own work. They seek to change and improve those conditions that they don't like rather than merely to complain about them. People who have negative attitudes tend to see only the bad side. They dwell upon their own misfortunes and those of others. Unfortunately, negative attitudes, like positive ones, are contagious. An employee who begins a working career cheerfully may have that positive outlook eroded by the constant carping of sour-dispositioned associates.

What causes poor attitudes?

When an employee faces a situation the way you'd like—such as accepting your corrections in good grace—you're likely to say that the worker has a good attitude. But if the same worker irks you by habitually failing to keep the area neat, you may find yourself saying that the employee's attitude is poor. How do you explain this contradiction? How can the same person's attitude be good one time, bad the next?

It could be that the employee's attitudes (from the employee's point of view) are fine. In the first instance you seem considerate and helpful when it comes to explaining how to do a job. Your favorable action has developed in the worker a good attitude toward criticism. In the second instance this same worker may have learned that you are pretty soft about discipline for sloppy housekeeping. The worker's observation is that you complain a lot about poor housekeeping, but your bark is worse than your bite. So this worker's attitude toward housekeeping is the one you've taught, even though it's bad.

Is the supervisor always
responsible for a worker's attitudes?

No. An employee, just like yourself, has many teachers. Parents, childhood pals, schoolteachers, the woman at the next desk, union representatives have all been teaching him how to react to things for a long time. These other people may have shown him hundreds of times that he could get away with anything just by giving lip service to what the boss says. So he keeps on doing what he pleases. If that's the case, as it often is, you'll have to try hard to build up new, different experiences with this worker. You'll have to show him that his old attitude won't be a good one in his relationships with you.

You can recognize when others have done a better job of teaching attitudes than you have if you find yourself saying, "I've told her and told her. But she just keeps on doing it the way she wants to." Do you really blame an employee if she continues to find out that she can get away with a bad attitude? For her the attitude is a good one to assume with you.

What can you do to understand more about employee attitudes?

Supervisors who are most successful at winning cooperation from their employees are those who have made the most progress in learning why employees feel and act the way they do. It would be a mistake to think such understanding comes easily. It doesn't. But if you sincerely want to understand, you can.

To understand a worker's attitude better, you must take an interest in that person, not just as a productive cog in the business machine but as a person who has dreams and ambitions and troubles just as everyone else has. Your interest mustn't be superficial, or it will be recognized as such and the person will be harder than ever to get to. In fact, you've got to work hard on your own attitudes toward others to get yourself in the mood to want to see each person as a whole.

To begin taking this interest in employees, first form a habit of inquiring into nonwork activities. Begin with less personal things like scores in bowling, do-it-yourself projects, or any hobby they are likely to speak freely about. If you continue to show you're interested in their pastimes and their success or failure in them, you'll build their confidence in you. If they have other personal matters they'd like to tell you about—family affairs, financial troubles, etc.—let them bring them up. That way you won't be guilty of prying.

Little by little, just listening and showing this sincere interest will reveal the reasons for employee attitudes. You needn't attempt to advise them or be overly sympathetic with them in their affairs. It isn't necessary. In fact, it can be downright dangerous. For most people your willing ear is enough.

With most people it's a mistake to use the direct approach—to ask why their attitude is the way it is. More often than not, even they don't know. So it's better to take the roundabout road to discover what employees' attitudes are underneath—and why they have them.

What can you do to change attitudes?

Quite a lot. Understanding attitudes often points the way to changing them. Employees *learn* the attitudes they have. You can teach them new ones. Don't try this by preaching. Do it by setting favorable examples, by providing employees with favorable experiences.

Suppose Mark is a troublemaker in your department. He complains about his own assignment, continually charges discrimination, stirs up the other employees to make grievances. In your eyes his actions show his attitude to be bad.

Now you want Mark to change his attitude. But why is Mark a troublemaker? That's hard to say. And it takes experience and understanding to find out. But think for a moment about what Mark's experience shows him about his troublemaking attitude: It provides him with plenty of attention, it makes him a hero, it wins grudging admiration from his associates.

Now suppose that you could find a way of providing Mark with experiences where his troublemaking didn't get him attention or admiration. And you found other more favorable ways of providing experiences that give him the attention and admiration he desires.

For instance, you might find good reason to compliment Mark openly and frequently about his work. You might ask his opinion about new methods that are under consideration. You might enlist his aid in telling other employees about job changes. All these actions on your part are healthy. And they provide Mark with the type of job satisfaction he looks for. And suppose, for instance, that each time Mark made trouble, you handled his actions discreetly and impersonally. And you avoided any show of emotion or upset. Chances are that the combined effect would be to change his attitude for the better.

You should be cautioned, of course, that attitudes and behaviors aren't often easy to pin down to actual cause and effect. But if you approach each human relations problem without a preconceived notion and with real humility and warmth, attitudes can be changed. The point in Mark's case is that you want to help him, not outsmart him.

Can you always change someone's attitude?

Theoretically the answer is yes, but in practice, no. Some people are just too fixed in their ways to yield very much. Sometimes you, as a supervisor, can do little to change the organizational situations that create unfavorable attitudes. And some combinations of circumstances may be too complex to do much about without professional help from the personnel office, or from a psychologist or a psychiatrist.

You should also be warned that a fairly large number of workers are emotionally unstable. The cause of their poor attitudes is a mental illness that is far beyond the lay person's power to improve. And it's very difficult for a lay person like yourself to identify. If you suspect such a condition in one of your employees, don't play parlor psychiatrist. Speak to the company medical staff or to the personnel office. And then follow their advice.

What's the supervisor's responsibility for the general condition of employee attitudes?

A supervisor is logically in the best position to influence attitudes among rank-and-file employees. Since your contact as supervisor is personal and frequent, you can do much toward understanding attitude changes and taking action to improve attitudes or to keep them from getting worse.

It would be misleading, however, not to recognize that middle management and top management have a significant effect on attitudes. Supervisors are human beings; they're also employees. It's only natural that supervisors should reflect in their attitudes the consideration they get, or do not get, from higher management. And the supervisor's attitude—good or bad—is often reflected among first-line employees. But, by and large, the supervisor holds the key to employee attitudes.

What is an attitude survey?

An attitude survey is a systematic way of finding out how employees feel about their company, their pay, their supervisors, their working conditions, their jobs, and so forth.

The most common attitude survey is based on a multiple-choice questionnaire. This way, a company can take a kind of vote among its employees to find out their attitudes. Questions are phrased something like this:

Check the one answer that most nearly describes how you feel: There's too much pressure on my job. Do you agree, are you undecided, or do you disagree?

Another typical question:

My boss really tries to get my ideas about things. Do you agree, are you undecided, do you disagree?

As many as 100 questions may be asked, with room left for written comments. To make the survey more meaningful, it is kept confidential: No employee signs his or her name, and the tabulation is done by a university or a consulting firm so that company officials never see even the handwriting of the employees surveyed.

Questionnaire answers are tabulated and analyzed. Most companies report survey findings either generally or in specific terms to their employees. It's especially important that once management finds out what employee attitudes are it take immediate action to improve conditions where these attitudes are unfavorable. For instance, a survey may show that most employees don't feel free to discuss job matters with their supervisors. Most people who have studied the relationship of attitudes to effort feel that such a condition is unhealthy and prevents a supervisor from getting the type of cooperation needed. Consequently, the company—and the supervisor—should take steps to improve the condition. For you, it may mean changing your own attitude and conduct to show that you will set aside time to listen to employee questions, complaints, or suggestions. And that you will do this listening with interest and welcome the ideas that are presented.

How good is good morale?

You'll never be able to please all your employees all the time. It would be a mistake to try. The supervisor's job requires that you enforce rules, mete out discipline, and encourage people to do many things they may not be eager to do. The supervisor who strives too hard for popularity may sacrifice some of these important requirements of leadership.

It's fair to ask, though, just how good you can expect morale to get. Studies by the University of Chicago Industrial Research Center of over a half million workers show that two to four out of every ten employees find fault with one thing or another in their work situation. (Table 5-1). And this dissatisfaction will be greater with some things, like pay, than with others, like working conditions. But the University of Chicago study does provide you with a helpful yardstick to measure different attitudes of individual workers toward you and your company.

How's your own morale?

Want to measure your own attitudes against those of the average supervisor? Then ask yourself these questions: Are you management-oriented? Do you feel rather secure in your work? Do you feel that the company gives you enough recognition and opportunity? To be normal, you should answer *yes* to all of these.

But do you think there's lots more that can be done to improve efficiency? That the company's come a long way, but that it has lots more to do before it operates as efficiently as you'd like it to? If you feel this way, chances are you're a pretty good supervisor.

It's normal, too, for you to be a little sensitive on pay mat-

TABLE 5-1 Attitude yardstick to measure morale in your plant.

Category	Questions Asked	Favorable Answers, Percent
Job demands	Work pressure, fatigue, boredom, work load, hours of work	72
Working conditions	Annoyances, management's concern for conditions, equipment adequacy, safety measures, effect of these on efficiency	70
Pay	Adequacy, comparison with pay of others in the company and in other local companies, administration of pay system	44
Employee benefits	All benefits, comparison with benefits in other companies, knowledge of program, administration of benefits	74
Friendliness, cooperation of employees	Bossiness, friction	77
Supervisory-employee relations	Friendliness, fairness, treatment of suggestions, credit for good work, concern for welfare, follow-through on promises	71
Confidence in management	Belief in management's integrity and its concern for employee welfare, adequacy of personnel policies, friendliness	67
Technical competence of supervision	Administrative skill, knowledge of supervision of job, ability to train employees, decision making, work organization	73
Effectiveness of administration	Competence of higher levels of management, efficiency of company operations, cooperation among departments	65
Adequacy of communication	Freedom to express opinion and suggest improvements, complaint handling, information about operations and plans	64
Status and recognition	Standing with the company, fair appraisal of work done, respect for judgment	71
Security of job and work relations	Security from arbitrary discharge and layoff, recognition of length of service, handling of job changes	59
Identification with the company	Pride in the company, interest in its future, sense of belonging and participation with the company	80
Chances for growth and advancement	Opportunities to use one's skills, to grow and develop on the job, to get ahead in the organization	65

ters—to feel that the men and women you supervise get almost too much in relation to your own salary. But if you feel that staff departments are out to get you, or that other supervisors don't cooperate, you're off target. Your attitude is unhealthy and is probably standing in the way of your success.

Why don't some people cooperate?

For a very natural reason: They see no personal advantage in doing so. A terrible attitude? Not at all.

Not one of us does anything for nothing. We do some things for money, others for lots of other reasons. Joe works well because he likes the feeling of being with a gang of people. Sam works hard because he gets a sense of accomplishment from what he is doing. Mary puts in top effort because her job makes her feel important.

Hardly anyone works for money alone. We all expect different satisfactions in different proportions from our work. So don't be annoyed when a worker's attitude seems to say, "What's in it for me?" That's your signal to get busy and to find some way of providing satisfaction for that person on the job.

Why isn't high pay the key to cooperation?

Good pay rates are important, but many companies that have sought the high-wage route to workers' affections have been sadly disappointed. Pay means much to most employees; yet, experience shows that it isn't enough.

One big trouble with pay as an incentive is that employees don't enjoy it while they work. It is after work that the pay brings tangible rewards and good feelings. Consider vacations and pensions. Employees can take advantage of neither while actually on the job. As Herzberg pointed out, your solution to winning employee cooperation is to appeal to employees' needs for respect, for challenge, for interesting work. We agree that each employee has a different set of these needs. Still, the supervisor's skill lies in trying to adjust the employee's work and working relationships to satisfy these "motivating" needs as much as is reasonable. The belief is that employees will cooperate to get this kind of treatment.

What's the best formula for winning cooperation?

The best formula is not to seek one. Despite the simplicity of the basic reasons people work, there is no easy road to securing cooperation. Don't be misled into believing there are gimmicks or pat things to say. There are no standard ways to react that, once memorized, will have employees eating out of your hand. If you attempt to outsmart employees, they will spot your lack of sincerity. And resistance will go up in proportion.

The best way to achieve cooperation is to change your own way of looking at people until you see in them some of the good and bad qualities you see in yourself. Make a point of being sensitive to people. Pause again and again to imagine how employees think about what you tell them or what you ask them to do. Stop talking, too, and listen to what they say about themselves, about the other workers, and about you. For not until you begin to *know* people will you be able to put into practice some of the simple ideas expressed here for getting along with people.

How can you remove resistance?

There are many methods. Don't use the same one in every situation. Learn them all so that you have a choice when resistance shows up.

Try a success example.   Casey doesn't want to work nights? Tell Casey about Jonesy, who thought he wouldn't like working nights, but who, after trying it for a month, won't work any other shift.

Try making a guarantee.   Anne is sure the new method won't work? Tell Anne that if she tries it for a week and doesn't find it better than the old way, you'll promise she can switch back again.

Try a demonstration.   The operator thinks the rate on the new job is too tough? Say, "Here, let me show you how easy the machine is to operate. It looks a lot harder than it actually is."

Try asking questions.   Marie says she can't make bonus? Ask her what she finds hardest about the job, whether she feels it has been properly explained.

Try just plain listening.   Sandy won't work overtime today or any other day? Let him rave. Hear all his arguments in a friendly manner. When he's had his complete say, then try persuasion and reasoning.

How do you go about getting cooperation from your associates?

The secret of getting along well with other supervisors is much the same as winning cooperation from your employees: Find out what they want most from their work, then satisfy these desires. Except that with your associates, it's not so much a problem of providing satisfaction as it is of not blocking their goals and ambitions.

Face up to the fact that, to a degree, you and your associates are competing—for raises, promotions, praise, popularity, and a host of other things. If you compete too hard, or compete unfairly, you won't win much cooperation from the other supervisors. And your chances of getting ahead often depend upon your ability to run your department in smooth harmony with those departments that interlock with yours.

Winning friends among other supervisors means intelligent sacrifice. Occasionally you'll have to put aside your wish to make your department look good just so that you don't put the supervisor of the next department behind the eight ball. Willingness to lend a hand when another supervisor falls behind and avoiding hairsplitting when allocating interdepartmental charges and responsibilities will help.

Above all, let other supervisors run their own shows. Don't try to give orders in their departments or encourage disputes between your workers and theirs.

Just as when an individual employee doesn't play ball with the others, if you don't conform to a reasonable degree, you'll have the supervisory group down on you—and cooperation will be long coming. To turn this group solidarity to your advantage, aim at giving the supervisory organization the advantage of your own positive leadership. Help other supervisors set worthwhile goals, and the chances of your all working together will be improved.

How can you get along best with staff people?

Generally speaking, staff people in your organization are almost entirely dependent upon you and other supervisers for cooperation. And in this case cooperation will breed cooperation. If you cooperate with staff people, their jobs are made infinitely easier. Their superiors judge them by their success in getting your assistance and upon the degree to which you accept and act upon their advice. So if you cooperate with staff people, you're actually helping them to get more satisfaction from their work. And you can be pretty sure that they'll go a long way toward helping you make a good showing on *your* job.

Wouldn't you like to have a data processing specialist report to your boss, "It's a pleasure to work with a supervisor like Jill. She never seems to hide things or get her back up when I offer suggestions. She is quick to see how what we're doing will improve operations in the long run. Not that Jill buys everything I say. She doesn't. She has her ideas, too. But together, I think Jill and I are really accomplishing things out there."

How can "I'm okay, you're okay" help to resolve personality conflicts?

███████████ This kind of analysis, often called transactional analysis (TA), helps to provide insights because it simplifies some of the apparently complex interactions that take place between people. This analysis maintains that there are four possible relationships held by the employee, the supervisor, or both:

1. I'm not okay. You're not okay. This is a negative view that implies an employee's dissatisfaction with her or his own behavior, but also, in effect, says that the supervisor's actions are just as bad. It is somewhat like a rebellious child quarreling with a parent. At work it might arise when an employee accused of pilfering materials says that the boss does the same thing.

2. I'm not okay. You're okay. This is often the mark of the person who has lost self-respect, or of a person who places all the responsibility on the boss's shoulders. This person often feels unable to do the job without continual assistance from the supervisor. Supervisors should strive to get out from under this kind of dependence.

3. I'm okay. You're not okay. This is the parental kind of role supervisors often assume. Essentially it treats the employee like a child. Such an attitude invites rebellion or loss of any hope the individual may have that the job can be done to your satisfaction.

4. I'm okay. You're okay. This is the mature, or adult, way to handle conflicts. It assumes that each individual respects the other. Starting from a point of mutual respect, each person tries to understand—not necessarily agree with—the other's point of view. The supervisor says to the employee, "I understand why you may think I'm taking advantage of your good nature, but listen to me long enough so that you understand my point of view. Once we're sure we understand one another, maybe we can come to some sort of agreement that gives you some satisfaction while making sure that the job gets done."

When transactional analysis is used, any of the first three approaches tends to keep the conflict going, even to heat it up. The fourth approach, sometimes called *stroking*, can be very effective if carried on honestly. It helps to provide a solid basis for cooperation and compromise.

Individual or group of individuals— what's the best way to avoid misunderstanding and to gain willing cooperation?

The starting place is respect for others' points of view, no matter how much they vary from your own. For the manager this implies an appreciation of subordinates for what they really are. It's wishful thinking—and downright harmful—to measure someone against a mythical ideal such as the perfect person for the job.

Try to remind yourself that by definition you, as a supervisor, deal in other people's lives. An order to take any action in the company is interpreted all down the line in terms of personal effects on people. And the effectiveness of the implementation of any order is a matter of approval or disapproval on the part of your subordinates and your associates.

Many managers never learn that their subordinates are constantly evaluating the manager's actions and varying their efforts accordingly. It's certainly the rare subordinate who will risk telling the boss when he or she is making mistakes, particularly if the boss isn't one who takes criticism willingly. Thus many supervisors never get any critical feedback about themselves. Fortunately, if you can make the first step, you'll find yourself a new and better kind of supervisor. You'll gain a new awareness that there are more consequences to any action involving people than those on the surface. And the consequences often interfere with productivity because people who are working on their own frustrations have less energy to devote to the job.

Of course, it isn't always possible to solve the human problems that can result from a necessary and unpleasant management action. But sensitive supervisors enjoy two distinct advantages over their less sensitive counterparts:

1. An awareness of others' needs aids in avoiding unnecessary human problems that ordinarily seem to be cropping up each day.

2. A pattern of awareness of others' needs in itself tends to blunt the edge of problems and conflicts that cannot be avoided, because subordinates and associates know that the supervisor has tried.

Is it smart to show you appreciate employee cooperation, or should you act as if it's something coming to you?

You can overdo your show of appreciation. But neither should employees think you take their efforts for granted. It would be ridiculous, for example, to stand by the time clock congratulating each employee for coming in on time. But it makes sense to look over the attendance record every six months and take a minute to say to each person with a perfect record, "I just reviewed the department's attendance records for the last six months, and I see that you went through those six months without missing a day or being late once. We appreciate that around here. It helps make the department an easier place to work in. Hope you can keep it up."

Yes, it's better to err on the generous side than to get the reputation as a supervisor who takes a pound of flesh each day but never so much as says thank-you.

supervisory word power

Sensitivity. The development of an acute awareness of other people's feelings, attitudes, and motivations, especially as they have an influence upon, or are influenced by, your own behavior and work situations.

Conflict. From a managerial point of view, a disruptive clash of interests, objectives, or personalities between individuals, between individuals and groups, or between groups.

Cooperation. Individuals or groups of people working together in reasonable harmony toward mutual objectives.

Attitude. The way in which an individual or group looks at, and consequently reacts to, a work situation. These are the views and responses toward associates and superiors, the various conditions of employment, and the job itself.

Morale. A measure of the extent (or level, as either high or low) of voluntary cooperation demonstrated by an individual or a work group and of the intensity of the desire to attain common goals.

Other Important Terms in This Chapter

attitude survey
hidden agenda
laboratory training
resistance
transactional analysis

reading comprehension

1. Why do conflicts arise in an organization?

2. Give an example from your own experience of a conflict that was prolonged, rather than resolved, because it was mishandled.

3. How could sensitivity training be any better than on-the-job experience in improving interpersonal skills?

4. Give an example of a hidden agenda in some sort of group meeting or discussion.

5. Would it be wise for a supervisor to insist that an employee's attitude be changed? Why or why not?

6. In what ways might an employee give evidence of a poor attitude toward work?

7. Describe some steps that a supervisor might take to change employee attitudes.

8. Contrast the attitude of employees toward their pay with their attitude toward status and recognition.

9. What kind of action should management take as a result of information gathered during an attitude survey?

10. Can transactional analysis (TA) be of any practical value in handling conflicts?

supervision in action

THE CASE OF THE SHAKY FOUNDATION. A case study in human relations involving conflict and cooperation, with questions for you to answer.

Crews at a construction site for a new supermarket were preparing the foundation. The excavation had been completed. Now the forms crew was busy installing the wood and metal framework into which the cement crew would pour the fresh concrete from the mixer. Duncan, the pouring supervisor, was watching the placement of the forms. "Be sure that inside form is properly secured," he told one of the crew. "That outside form isn't level yet," he advised Wendy Brown, another member of the forms crew. "Last time, your sloppy forms made us look bad." The crew and Wendy just kept on about their work without paying too much attention to the instructions handed down by Duncan. After a while, Duncan left the site to round up his own crew for pouring, which would begin that afternoon.

Nick Motta, the forms supervisor, who had been at the site office verifying the blueprints, returned to his crew shortly after

Duncan had left. He jumped into the foundation pit to show the crew how to make the final alignment of the forms. Wendy Brown, however, told him that the forms had already been leveled and locked up. "They aren't in the right position," said Motta. "Why didn't you wait until I got back before bolting them into place?"

"Duncan was here and showed us what to do," replied Brown.

"Well, he was wrong. And it is none of his business, anyway," said Motta. "I take charge of the forms. All he and his crew do is to dump the concrete into them after we've done the precision work."

At that point the concrete truck rolled up to the excavation. "Get out of the pit!" shouted Duncan, who was now on the site with his crew. "We're ready to pour."

"You'll have to wait," said Motta. "Your meddling has held up the job. We are going to have to realign the forms according to these prints."

"That was what I was trying to tell your crew," said Duncan. "If they had listened to what I told them, we could go ahead."

"Talk to me the next time," said Motta. "But meanwhile, take you and your crew of apes and get out of here."

"You get out," said Duncan. "Or you'll all get a cement over-coat." With that, he opened the chute door on the mixer just enough to let a couple of buckets of wet cement splash into the pit and on Brown and Motta.

Brown jumped out of the pit and pushed Duncan against the mixing truck. Duncan shoved back and in a minute there was a free-for-all as the two crews—forms and pouring—pushed and shoved and swung fists.

Finally someone called the site boss to the scene. The fighting stopped. "What's this all about?" he asked.

"Duncan and his pouring crew put their noses into our job once too often," said Motta. "And he dumped a load of cement on us."

"That's a laugh," said Duncan. "If I wasn't here to check up on what they were doing, we would have one more shaky foundation. And we'd get the blame. I was just making sure that the forms were right before we poured."

1. If you were the site boss, what approach would you use to resolve this dispute? Which supervisor would you sympathize with?

2. What did Duncan do to bring on this conflict?

3. What might Motta have done to avoid the conflict?

4. How might the site boss make sure that similar disputes do not arise in the future?

enriching your viewpoint

To gain a broader understanding of conflict and cooperation, the following readings are suggested:

Albano, Charles, "Transactional Analysis on the Job, Part 4: Motivation and Counselling," *Supervisory Management,* April 1974.

Berne, Eric, *Games People Play,* Grove Press, Inc., New York, 1964.

Chapman, Elwood N., *Your Attitude Is Showing,* Science Research Associates, Inc., Chicago, 1964.

Dalton, Melville, "Conflicts Between Staff and Line Managerial Officers," *American Sociological Review,* Vol. 15, June 1950.

Flippo, Edwin P., *Principles of Personnel Management,* 3d ed., McGraw-Hill Book Company, New York, 1971, Chap. 21, "The Nature and Development of Organization Morale," pp. 416–436.

Horwitz, Murray, "Training in Conflict Resolution," in Leland P. Bradford, Jack R. Gibb, and Kenneth D. Benne (eds.), *The T. Group,* John Wiley & Sons, Inc., New York, 1962.

Likert, Rensis, and Jane Gibson Likert, *New Ways of Managing Conflict,* McGraw-Hill Book Company, New York, 1976.

Moore, David G., and Robert K. Burns, "How Good Is Good Morale?" *Factory Management and Maintenance,* February 1956, pp. 130–131.

Vance, Charles C., *Manager Today, Executive Tomorrow,* McGraw-Hill Book Company, New York, 1974, Chap. 5, "Removing the No. 1 Stumbling Block—Human Conflict."

Webber, Ross A., "Innovation and Conflict in Industrial Engineering," *The Journal of Industrial Engineering,* May 1967.

Weiss, Alan, "Conflict: It's What You Make It," *Supervisory Management,* June 1974.

ONWARD!

6

the arts of leadership

What is leadership?

Everyone will give you a different answer to this one. My definition is this: *Leadership is the knack of getting other people to follow you and to do willingly the things you want them to do.* Regardless of all the fancy talk you'll hear about leadership, this definition pinpoints the real reason for the high premium on this scarce skill.

Is leadership the same as management?

Not exactly. Leadership is only one of many functions a manager must perform for the work force. In addition a manager must plan, organize, communicate, coordinate, evaluate, and exercise control. Nevertheless, leadership is a basic requirement of all managers, especially at the supervisory level.

Are leaders always popular with the people they supervise?

The best leaders seem to combine the knack of leading and the knack of winning friends. But most leaders must be satisfied with respect and followers. Why? Because many of the decisions you must make as a leader will not always favor everybody. Sometimes they will please nobody. Chances are you won't win any popularity contests among employees.

Why should you want to become a leader?

The job of a leader is an unbelievably tough one. But the rewards are high. You'll find them in increased prestige and status among the people with whom you work, among your friends, and in your community. And to many leaders the heady exhilaration of making decisions that prove to be correct is reward enough. To others it's mainly a sense of mission. To still others it's the satisfaction that power brings. In industry you can have all these in varying degrees. You may even have more money—since leadership is a quality that business traditionally pays a high price for.

Are good leaders born or made?

Marshal Foch, famous World War I leader, said of leadership: "These are natural gifts in a man of genius, in a born general; in the average man, such advantages may be secured by work and reflection." Foch's statement pretty much reflects the consensus: Some people are born leaders, but most leaders are good leaders because they have worked hard and thought hard to become so.

What are the ingredients for good leadership?

Men and women who prove to be successful leaders are characterized by such qualities as the following:

Sense of mission. This is a belief in your own ability to lead, a love for the work of leadership itself, and a devotion to the people and the organization you serve.

Self-denial. This essential of leadership is too often played down. It means a willingness to forgo self-indulgences (like blowing your stack) and the ability to bear the headaches the job entails.

High character. Few persons become successful leaders who aren't honest with themselves and with others, who can't face hard facts and unpleasant situations with courage, who fear criticism or their own mistakes, who are insincere or undependable.

Job competence. There's been too much talk about the insignificance of technical job skill to the supervisor. A person who knows the job that is being supervised has one of the best foundations for building good leadership.

Good judgment. Common sense, the ability to separate the important from the unimportant, tact, the wisdom to look into the future and plan for it are ingredients that make the best leaders.

Energy. Leadership at any level means rising early and working late. It leaves little time for relaxation or escape from problems. Good health, good nerves, and boundless energy make this tough job easier.

Here is a word of caution, however. The "trait" approach to leadership can be misleading. Some natural leaders display few of these desirable characteristics. You have only to consider Hitler, Mussolini, and General George Patton to find some of these traits missing.

Is there only one way to lead people?

Here's where a lot of us have been fooled. Take this situation. Jane Smith supervises three material handlers. Each has become an absentee problem. Listen to how Jane deals with each person:

To Al: "It's time you get on the ball. I want to see you in here five days a week every week from now on. Otherwise, I'll put you up for discharge."

To Sid: "Your absences are getting to be a headache for me and the rest of us here. You'll have to see that your attendance improves. Let's you and I work out a way to overcome this problem."

To Terry: "Take a look at your absence record. Not good, is it? I'll leave it up to you to figure out some way to straighten it out."

Which method do you suppose works best? The answer is that all get good results. Al, Sid, and Terry are no longer attendance problems. The reason? There are three basic kinds of leadership because there are three basic kinds of people. To be a successful leader, you need to be able to master all three techniques.

What are the three traditional kinds of leadership called?

Autocratic leadership (the kind used with Al in the last question).   Many people think this technique is old-fashioned, but it often works. The leader makes the decisions and demands obedience from the people supervised. The trouble is that the supervisor better be right.

Democratic leadership (used with Sid).   This is very popular today. The leader discusses, consults, draws ideas from the people supervised, lets them help set policy. It makes for participation and strong teamwork. Some critics call this compromise leadership.

Free-rein leadership (used with Terry).   This kind is the most difficult to use. The leader acts as an information center and exercises minimum control, depending on the employees' sense of responsibility and good judgment to get things done. Advocates of this approach also call it participative or integrative leadership.

Are the traditional approaches the only way to lead?

Not at all. Two somewhat related approaches have become popular in recent years.

Results-centered leadership is akin to the "work itself" approach to motivation or to what you will read about Management by Objectives in Chapter 8 and Chapter 12. Using this technique, the supervisor tries to focus on the job to be done and to minimize the personalities involved. In effect, the supervisor says to the employee, "This is the goal the organization expects you to reach each day. Now let's work together to see how your job can be set up so that you can make your quota."

Contingency, or situational, leadership maintains that leaders will be successful in a particular situation only if three factors are in balance. This approach, advanced by Professor Fred Fiedler and documented in many studies, asks the leader to examine (1) the extent of rapport or good feelings between the supervisor and those supervised; (2) the nature of the job to be done, in terms of how carefully procedures and specifications must be followed; and (3) the amount of real power invested in the supervisor by his or her superiors.

Surprisingly, the authoritative approach, which uses heavy

directing and controlling, is most effective in either very favorable or very unfavorable circumstances. That is, it works best when relationships are either very good or very poor, job methods are precisely defined, and the leader's true authority is either very strong or very weak. In the fuzzier, or middle, situations, the participative approach is likely to be more successful.

For example, an *authoritative approach* works out best (1) in situations where the supervisor has lots of real power, the process requires strong control, and rapport with employees is good; and (2) in situations where just the opposite conditions prevail.

The *participative approach* is best where the supervisor's authority hasn't been clearly spelled out by top management or acknowledged by the employees, where the process and procedures are somewhat flexible, and where the rapport between supervisor and employees is only middling good.

The contingency approach tends to explain why dictatorial supervisors can be effective in some situations and not in others. Similarly it helps to show where participative leadership may work best and to suggest where it might fail. An authoritative approach looks good for assembly-line workers or for labor crews cleaning up the area. A participative approach seems favorable on jobs for which exact procedures are hard to set or for jobs that require creativity or initiative. These conclusions are contingent upon the authoritative leader's having either high or low position power and high or low rapport, and the participative leader's having moderate rapport and only so-so authority.

Which kind of leadership is best?

Most successful managers will tell you that democratic leadership is the best method to use. The fact is that while the democratic way may involve the least risk, you'll hamper your leadership role if you stick only to that one. You can play a round of golf with a driver, but you'll get a much better score if you use a niblick in a sand trap and a putter on the greens.

Suppose you have a problem of cutting down on scrap in your department. You may find it better to consult in a group meeting with all your workers to let them decide how they'll approach the problem (democratic leadership). Then the inspector, when informed of your plan, can adjust inspection techniques accordingly (free-rein). Merely tell the scrap collector how you want the waste sorted (autocratic). You see, you'd be using all three kinds of leadership to deal with the same problem.

Figure 6-1 illustrates what one noted authority calls the continuum of leadership styles. At one extreme the supervisor relies

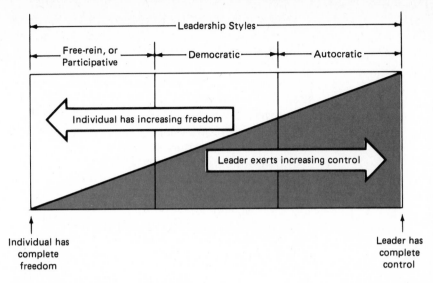

FIGURE 6-1. Continuum of leadership styles. Adapted from Robert Tannenbaum and Warren H. Schmidt, "How to Choose a Leadership Pattern," *Harvard Business Review*, March–April, 1958, pp. 95–101.

upon absolute authority; at the other, subordinates are allowed a great deal of freedom.

How much does personality have to do with leadership?

A good personality helps. Employees may react more easily to a supervisor who has a ready smile and who is warm and outgoing. But personality must be more than skin-deep to be effective. Much more important is your real desire to understand and sympathize with the people who work for you. Fair play, interest in others, good decisions, and character will help make you a stronger leader than if you rely solely on personality.

Likewise, one kind of leadership may fit your personality better than the other two do. And you may rely more on this kind of leadership than on the others. But work hard to keep from depending on just one approach.

What do employee personalities have to do with the kind of leadership you exercise?

Noted author Auren Uris advises that you'll find the following connections between leadership methods and types of personality:

- Aggressive, hostile persons do better under autocratic leaders. Their latent hostility must be firmly channeled to confine their work to constructive ends.
- Aggressive, cooperative persons work better under democratic or free-rein leadership. Their self-assertiveness takes constructive paths, and they will head in the right direction when on their own.
- Insecure persons, who tend to depend on their superiors, do better under the firmer hand of the autocratic leader.
- Individualists, or solo players, are usually most productive under free-rein leadership—if they know the job well.

Uris calls this point of view "followership." It is based on a well-established fact that certain kinds of persons naturally follow certain kinds of leaders better than others. The trick is to match them when you can.

What kind of leadership works best in an emergency?

Autocratic leadership is fast. When an emergency arises—say a live-steam hose breaks loose and whips about endangering lives—you wouldn't want to pussyfoot around consulting employees as to what to do. You'd probably shout, "Hey, Smitty, cut the steam valve! Carl, watch the safety!"

What kind of supervision gets the best results?

At first it may seem hard to believe that supervisors who place less emphasis on production goals actually get higher production from the employees they supervise. This is only one aspect of the picture of the successful supervisor drawn as a result of a landmark study made in 1948 at the University of Michigan. Supervisors in high-production groups were characterized in the following ways:

- Their own bosses gave them a freer hand than was given to supervisors in low-production groups.
- They were more employee-centered and spent more time in supervising and less time on mechanical and paperwork details.
- They encouraged employees to contribute their ideas on how best to get things done.

Note how close these findings come to describing free-rein, or participative, leadership. Rensis Likert, who had much to do with pursuing the Michigan studies, has come to believe that participative leadership, which he calls "System 4," is the only form of leadership truly in tune with twentieth-century life. You may not be able to use it in every situation, but where you can, it brings the best results.

Must you always get participation?

██████████ No. If you plan your big targets by first asking for and considering the opinions of your employees, they'll understand that there isn't time to handle every decision that way. Participation is a long-range affair. If you show that you want and respect employees' opinions—and that your decisions are affected by these opinions—you'll have achieved the goal of making employees feel they are part of a team. An occasional oversight or an infrequent decision made without their counsel won't destroy the feeling that generates cooperation.

By sowing the seeds of participation generously, you'll also find that you won't have to take over many of the minor decisions that occupy your attention otherwise. Employees who know from experience that their opinions are desired know in advance how the team (their team and yours) would act if it had a chance to go into a huddle. They'll act accordingly.

How do leaders win loyalty from their followers?

██████████ You win loyalty by being loyal to your employees—by supporting their best interests and defending their actions to others who would discredit them. "We may not have made a good showing this month," a supervisor who is loyal to the group will say, "but no one can say the staff wasn't in there trying."

Loyalty is also inspired when you show employees your own loyalty to your superiors. For instance, if you have to pass along an order from your superior, you will breed only contempt among your subordinates if you say, "Here's the new operating instruction from the central office. I don't think any more of it than you do. But it was sent down from the top, so we'll have to try to make sense out of it, even if they don't know what they're doing."

Tom Lasorda, who was voted National League manager of the year while manager of the Los Angeles Dodgers baseball team in 1977, was judged to be extremely effective with his players "because he showed them respect, so they respected him in return," according to the Associated Press.

Is good leadership simply good human relations?

You could say that, because to be a good leader, you must be a student of human nature. This is not because you love everybody. Probably you don't. But you must develop shrewd judgment in estimating people's intentions, knowledge, and interests. Even the roughest, toughest industrialists have been keen estimators of human capabilities and have been expert in getting the most from people who work for them.

How much book knowledge of behavioral sciences do you need to handle people well?

There is much that can be done by serious supervisors who wish to improve their relationships with people. While the availability of scientific facts may be slight, the fault lies more with the individual than with the research effort. Individuals who take the time, or make the effort, can learn a lot about human behavior—their own as well as that of others. It will give them a feeling of humility, of course. But this humility need not destroy their confidence.

Leadership depends upon many things. Demonstrated technical ability to plan and coordinate plans wins many followers. Drive, courage, and persistence build a good foundation for leadership, too. People will respond to the supervisor who expresses confidence in them. People will lean toward the supervisor whose behavior is consistent. The supervisor who searches hard for the people-oriented facts when making decisions, who thus creates the impression of trying to be fair, gets approval, if not accolades, from subordinates. These are actions any supervisor can take without being a psychologist, a sociologist, anthropologist, or a parlor psychiatrist.

Theory X, Theory Y. What's this all about?

To get along with people effectively, you must make a couple of fundamental decisions. First you must recognize your responsibility for managing human affairs at work. But you must always weigh this concern of yours against the practical urgencies of technical and administrative matters.

Douglas McGregor, late professor of industrial management at the Massachusetts Institute of Technology, had much to offer supervisors in his thoughtful work *The Human Side of Enterprise.* Most of today's management thinking was forged to meet the needs of a feudal society, reasoned McGregor. The world has changed, and new thinking is needed for top efficiency today. That's the core of this unique philosophy of pitting Theory X against Theory Y.

Theory X, the traditional framework for management thinking, is based on the following set of assumptions about human nature and human behavior:

1. The average human being has an inherent dislike of work and will avoid it if possible.

2. Because of this human characteristic of dislike of work, most people must be coerced, controlled, directed, or threatened with punishment to get them to put forth adequate effort toward the achievement of organizational objectives.

3. The average human being prefers to be directed, wishes to avoid responsibility, has relatively little ambition, and wants security above all.

Do these assumptions make up a straw person for purposes of scientific demolition? Unfortunately, they do not. While they are rarely stated so directly, the principles that constitute the bulk of current management action could have been derived only from assumptions such as those of Theory X.

Theory Y finds its roots in recently accumulated knowledge about human behavior. It is based on the following set of assumptions:

1. The expenditure of physical and mental effort in work is as natural as play or rest.

2. External control and the threat of punishment are not the only means for bringing about effort toward organizational objectives. Individuals will exercise self-control in the service of objectives to which they are committed.

3. Commitment to objectives depends on the rewards associated with their achievement. The most important rewards are those that satisfy needs for self-respect and personal improvement.

4. The average human being learns, under proper conditions, not only to accept but also to seek responsibility.

5. The capacity to exercise a relatively high degree of imagination, ingenuity, and creativity in the solution of organizational problems is widely, not narrowly, distributed in the population among both men and women.

6. Under the conditions of modern industrial life, the intellectual potentialities of the average human being are only partially realized.

What makes Theory Y so applicable today?

██████████████ Under the assumptions of Theory Y, the work of the supervisor is to integrate the needs of employees with the needs of the department. Hard-nosed control rarely works out today. Here are McGregor's words:

> *The industrial manager is dealing with adults who are only partially dependent. They can—and will—exercise remarkable ingenuity in defeating the purpose of external controls which they resent. However, they can—and do—learn to exercise self-direction and self-control under appropriate conditions. His task is to help them discover objectives consistent both with organizational requirements and with their own personal goals. And to do so in ways that will encourage genuine commitment to these objectives. Beyond this, his task is to help them achieve these objectives: to act as teacher, consultant, colleague, and only rarely as authoritative boss.*

Where does the Managerial Grid fit in?

██████████████ The Managerial Grid helps supervisors to assess their leadership approach. The grid, devised by industrial psychologists Robert R. Blake and Jane S. Mouton, makes two measurements of a leader's approach: concern for production and concern for people. As shown in Figure 6-2, these two factors are typically plotted on a grid chart. The least concern for each factor is rated 1, the highest 9. To judge your own approach, first rate yourself according to your concern for people; say you think it is fairly high—a 6 score. Next rate your emphasis on production or job results; say you rate that medium—a score of 5. You then find your place on the Managerial Grid by putting a mark on the chart 6 squares up and 5 squares across.

Blake, Mouton, and others have given nicknames to various places on the grid. The lower left-hand corner (1,1) could be called the cream puff, a supervisor who doesn't push for anything. The upper left-hand corner (1 for production, 9 for people) can be called the do-gooder, a person who watches out for people at the cost of overlooking production needs entirely. The lower right-hand corner (9 for production, 1 for people) is the hard-nose, a supervisor for whom production is all that counts. The supervisor near the middle of the chart (5 for both production and people) is the middle-of-the-roader, a person who makes a reasonable push for both concerns. In the eyes of many, all supervisors should strive to make their leadership performance score 9,9 (highest for both production and people) so that they might be called professionals.

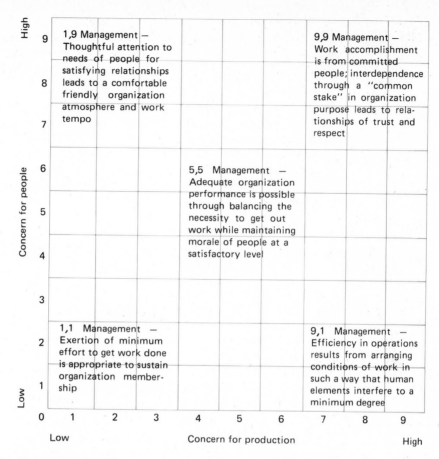

High

9 | 1,9 Management — Thoughtful attention to needs of people for satisfying relationships leads to a comfortable friendly organization atmosphere and work tempo

8 |

7 |

6 | 5,5 Management — Adequate organization performance is possible through balancing the necessity to get out work while maintaining morale of people at a satisfactory level

5 |

4 |

3 |

2 | 1,1 Management — Exertion of minimum effort to get work done is appropriate to sustain organization member-ship

1 |

Low

0 | 1 | 2 | 3 | 4 | 5 | 6 | 7 | 8 | 9

9,9 Management — Work accomplishment is from committed people; interdependence through a "common stake" in organization purpose leads to relationships of trust and respect

9,1 Management — Efficiency in operations results from arranging conditions of work in such a way that human elements interfere to a minimum degree

Concern for people

Low   Concern for production   High

FIGURE 6-2. Managerial grid. From Robert R. Blake and Jane S. Mouton, "Managerial Facades," *Advanced Management Journal*, July 1966, p. 31. Reprinted with permission.

Blake and Mouton believe that a 9,9 rating can be obtained only by a team approach. But as we have seen, the team—or participative—approach doesn't work in every situation. Yet it is a good one to choose if the conditions favor it.

Why is it that some leaders are more poised than others?

Probably because they regard themselves as professional managers and leaders. Even when everything seems to be going wrong, the seasoned leader appears cool and collected. For an immature manager every day can become a series of crash programs. So begin being a professional by keeping calm at crisis time. Don't waste time losing your composure. Accept the fact that crises are always bursting in on business. Use your time for study and analysis.

Try to act like the seasoned leader even if you don't actually feel that way at first. Smile when things get tough, think when problems get mountainous, accept an occasional defeat as part of the game you are paid for playing. Don't get your exercise by jumping to conclusions.

Ask seasoned leaders how they have been able to survive 25 years of heavy production schedules, nagging labor problems, and supervision. They'll answer, "If you can't stand the heat, get out of the kitchen."

Are there any other tips for leaders?

Advice for leaders is free and plentiful. And most of it makes sense for the person who can put it into practice.

Be predictable.   People want to know where they stand with the boss—tomorrow as well as today. You might borrow a page from the books on child psychology. The experts have studied the maladjustments and the frustrations of kids. They suggest one good rule for handling them: be consistent. If a child is praised for an act today and bawled out for the same act tomorrow—bingo, tears. If the child tries to help with the dishes, breaks one, and gets a scolding—watch out for tantrums. If you embarrass the child in front of others, look out—the cat may be painted green just to make it look ridiculous, too. It's the same thing for adults.

Put yourself in the employee's place.   Maybe you recall the last time you were at a ball game. Did you find yourself leaning with every pitch—trying to put body English on foul balls? Do the same thing with people. This mental shift can become a regular and desirable habit. It will help you understand, predict, and direct the responses of people.

Show your enthusiasm.   If you sincerely like an idea, the way an employee did a job, your next assignment, show this feeling to others in words and manner. It is a mistake for a supervisor to "play it cool" in relationships with employees. The personal atmosphere you create determines whether people will have the welcome mat out for you or turn you away.

Be interested in employees' welfare.   People want a supervisor or manager "whom they can trust in time of need, to whom they can go when they need advice about personal affairs," said

Brehon Somervell, late president of the Koppers Company, Inc. "It is a good outfit, indeed," when employees can "ask the boss."

Treat employees equally.   Men and women insist on a leader's having a sense of fair play. They want to believe they are being given assignments entirely upon their merits and that the boss won't play favorites. Not only is favoritism a sign of weak character, but it can also wreck an organization.

supervisory word power

Power.   The capability of a leader to act, the faculty for getting something done because of the ability to influence others over whom the leader holds managerial authority.

Confidence.   A leader's self-reliance in choosing the best course of action for subordinates, coupled with the state of trust that exists between leader and subordinates.

Poise.   A quality of leadership in which an individual's varied powers are equally distributed, resulting in stability and balance from which heavy attacks can be launched.

Theory X.   An essentially negative approach to human relations in which a supervisor presumes that most people don't like to work and, accordingly, must be pushed, threatened, and disciplined; that they wish to avoid responsibility and prefer job security above all. Employees must therefore be pushed constantly and threatened with loss of security and other punishments when they don't produce.

Theory Y.   An essentially positive approach to human relations in which a supervisor presumes that, given meaningful work, most people will try hard to achieve, especially when there is an opportunity to improve their regard for themselves. Given these opportunities, most people will provide their own initiative and challenging objectives and exert self-control in seeking to attain them.

Other Important Terms in This Chapter

autocratic leadership
contingency model of leadership
continuum of leadership styles
democratic leadership
followership

free-rein leadership
managerial grid
participative leadership
situational leadership
system 4

reading comprehension

1. Describe some of the qualities that some people believe are characteristic of successful leaders.
2. Why is leadership essential to effective supervision?
3. Compare *autocratic* leadership with *democratic* leadership.
4. Which kind of leadership is best in an emergency? Why?
5. If an employee tends to be aggressive, but cooperative, which style of leadership might be most suitable? Why?
6. Provide examples of the use of a leadership style at three different points along the continuum of leadership styles.
7. Put together a brief list of supervisory responsibilities that don't particularly require leadership qualities.
8. If you had to choose between a supervisor who was predictable and consistent and one whose enthusiasm was contagious, which one would you rather work for? Why?
9. What might a supervisor do to move his or her placement on the Managerial Grid from 3,7 to 7,7? In what way is the Managerial Grid related to Theory X and Theory Y?
10. According to Fiedler's contingency model of leadership, what is likely to be the best approach in a situation where the supervisor has been newly appointed, relationships with the new group are standoffish, and the task to be performed requires great accuracy? Why?

supervision in action

THE CASE OF THE NEW SALES SUPERVISOR.   A case study in human relations involving leadership, with questions for you to answer.

Ada Force had just been appointed supervisor in a suburban department store. Before her promotion to the management level, she had been a salesperson for five years. Her work on that job had consistently been of superior caliber.

Except for a little good-natured roasting, Ada's co-workers had wished her well on her new job. And for the first week or two most of them had been cooperative—even helpful—while Ada was adjusting to her supervisory role.

Late Friday afternoon of Ada's second week as a supervisor, a disturbing incident took place. Having just made the rounds of her department, Ada stopped in the washroom. There she saw two of her old associates, Mae and Fran, washing up.

"Say, guys. You shouldn't be cleaning up this soon. It's at least

another 15 minutes until quitting time," said Ada.
the floor, and I'll forget I saw you in here."

"Come off it, Ada," said Mae. "You used to slip
yourself on Fridays. Just because you've got a lit
don't think you can come down on us." To this A
"Things are different now. Both of you get back o
make trouble." Mae and Fran said nothing more
returned to the floor.

From that time on Ada began to have problems as a supervisor. Mae and Fran gave her the silent treatment. The rest of the
sales force seemed to forget how to do the simplest things. Sales
checks were prepared improperly. Customer complaints increased. Merchandise was spoiled. By the end of the month
Ada's department was showing the poorest record for performance.

1. How do you think Ada should have handled the washroom
incident? Why?

2. What do you suggest Ada could do about the silent treatment she got from Mae and Fran?

3. If you were Ada, what would you do to get your department's
performance back on track?

enriching your viewpoint

To gain a broader understanding of leadership, the following readings
are recommended:

Blake, Robert R., and Jane S. Mouton, *The Managerial Grid,* Gulf
Publishing Company, Houston, 1974.
Cribbin, James J., *Effective Managerial Leadership,* American Man-
agement Associations, New York, 1972.
Fiedler, Fred E., *A Theory of Leadership Effectiveness,* McGraw-Hill
Book Company, New York, 1967.
Heller, Frank A., "Leadership, Decision Making, and Contingency
Theory," *Industrial Relations,* May 1973, pp. 183–199.
Human Behavior and Leadership, Naval Training Command, NAV-TRA
10058-A, Superintendent of Documents, Washington, D.C., 1973.
Likert, Rensis, *The Human Organization: Its Management and Value,*
McGraw-Hill Book Company, New York, 1967.
McGregor, Douglas, *The Human Side of Enterprise,* McGraw-Hill
Book Company, New York, 1960.
Mosley, Donald C., and Paul H. Pietri Jr., *Management: The Art of
Working With and Through People,* Dickenson Publishing Com-
pany, Inc., Encino, Calif., 1974, Chap. 5, "Supervision: Six Styles of
Leadership."

Steinmetz, Lawrence L., and Charles D. Grennidge, "Realities That Shape Managerial Style: Participative Philosophy Won't Always Work," *Business Horizons,* Vol. 13, No. 5, October 1970.

Stogdill, R. M., *Handbook of Leadership: A Survey of Theory and Research,* The Free Press, New York, 1974.

Tannenbaum, Robert, and W. W. Schmidt, *Leadership and Organization,* McGraw-Hill Book Company, New York, 1961.

principles of supervisory management

Over the past century, trial, error, observation, and research have laid the foundation for the practice of management. Managers and supervisors in all kinds of organizations perform several universal functions. Accordingly, this section stresses the need for the reader to master six related objectives:

- To observe the management process as a whole in which supervisors perform key managerial functions and follow time-tested principles.
- To understand the vital importance of planning so as to set departmental goals and establish effective procedures.
- To see the need for organizational structures and be able to design those that suit a department's goals and resources.
- To relate your knowledge of human needs and behavior to provide the most effective staff for your organization.
- To acquire basic communication skills and use them in concert so that your employees become a unified work force.
- To link the concepts of planning with control so as to be able to keep your processes and employees within prescribed standards of performance.

supervision and the management process

What is the so-called management process?

It is the name given to functions or activities ordinarily performed by managers and not performed by rank-and-file blue-collar workers or clerical employees. These functions are pursued in an orderly sequence. They are carried out, to a greater or lesser degree, by supervisors at every level, by middle managers, and by top executives. Regardless of where these functions are performed by managers—in factories, on construction sites, in banks and retail shops, in hospitals, or at government agencies—they include the following:

Planning. This is the function of setting goals or objectives. Often this specifically means production schedules, quality specifications, cost budgets, deadlines, and timetables. The results of planning include policies or guidelines, operating plans and procedures, regulations and rules. Chapter 8 tells you more about this most important of all managerial functions.

Organizing.   In performing this function a supervisor lines up all available resources. These resources include departmental tools and equipment, materials, and methods, but especially the work force. It is at this stage that the work is divided up in a department and jobs are assigned to the various employees who will staff them. Chapter 9 describes this activity in detail.

Staffing.   This is the function in which the supervisor figuratively puts flesh on the organizational structure. The supervisor first figures out exactly how many employees the department will need to carry out its work and then interviews and selects those people who appear to be most suitable to fill the open jobs. Chapter 10 provides the basic groundwork for effective staffing.

Activating.   It is at this point that the supervisor directs all the department's resources into action by issuing orders and instructions (communicating) and by providing motivation and leadership. Chapter 11 offers suggestions for carrying out this pivotal function.

Controlling.   Once departmental plans are in motion, supervisors must periodically keep score on how well they are working out. Supervisors must measure results, compare them with what was expected, make a judgment of how important any difference may be, and then take whatever action is needed to bring the results into line. In formal language, such activities are called evaluating and controlling. Chapter 12 outlines the essentials of the control function.

In theory, supervisors perfrom the five basic functions of the managerial process in the order listed above. In practice, supervisors may find themselves shortcutting the sequence or turning back on it, depending upon what is observed or what happens in the course of time.

Why is it called a process?

Because it moves from one stage to another progressively in a fairly consistent order. In a production shop, for example, a supervisor first plans the daily schedule, then organizes the resources by assigning people to their work stations, next activates the process by giving orders and instructions, and, finally, controls, or checks up on, results. In a typical office a similar management process takes place as supervisors plan the workday, organize the work and the clerical force, activate by communicating and motivating, and control by seeing that paperwork procedures are followed properly.

This process is carried on over and over again, repeated day by day, month by month, and year by year. For this reason many people refer to it as the *management cycle.*

This process must have an objective, mustn't it?

Yes, of course. The purpose of the management process is to convert the resources available to a supervisor's department into a useful end result. This end result is either a product or a service.

A *product* might be a pair of shoes, a loaf of bread, a bicycle, or steel strings for a guitar. Your product may be partially complete so that it becomes the material resource for the next department in your factory. Or it may become the raw material for use in another manufacturing plant. Or it may be ready, like a pair of shoes, to be sold directly to a consumer without further work performed on it.

A *service* may be in the form of accounting information provided for a production department, inspecting a product as it is being made, or drawing up a schedule for others to follow. A service may be provided directly for a consumer, such as an insurance policy or handling of cash and checks for a bank customer. It may be maintaining machinery in a plant or washing windows in a shopping center.

Whether the end point is a product or a service, the management process is expected to make sure that the result is at least as valuable as the combined cost of the initial resources and the expense of operating the process. In a business enterprise a *profit* is made when the end result can be sold at a price that is higher than the cost of providing it. If the reverse is true, the business assumes a *loss.*

What are the resources managed by the management process?

There are six important resources (or inputs) in the manager's mix:

1. Men and women, the people who make up the labor force. For a supervisor these are the employees, skilled and unskilled, assigned to the department.

2. Machinery, buildings, and tools and equipment needed to make the goods or render the services provided. In a manufacturing company these facilities range from blast furnaces to baking ovens; in construction, from bulldozers to wheelbarrows. In a department store the facilities range from display counters to cash registers. In a bank the equipment includes tellers' cages and coin-counting machines. In an insurance company the equipment may focus on file cabinets, typewriters, calculators, and computers. In a hospital the facilities include beds, bedpans, X-ray machines, and thermometers.

3. **Materials that go into the final product or service or are consumed while making them.** Raw materials in manufacturing and construction run the gamut from iron ore for steel, flour for bakeries, and tires for automobiles to transistor chips for TV sets. Other materials are operating supplies such as grease for machinery and protective clothing for employees. Materials consumed in service industries such as banking or insurance include tons of paper, gallons of ink, and millions of paper clips. In retail trades the "raw" materials are the merchandise manufactured by others and placed on display for sale.

4. **Money, the capital needed to purchase the machinery and the materials and to meet work force payrolls.** Supervisors may see little cash pass through their hands, but every action they take depends upon the availability of funds to pay for these actions and the results of them.

5. **Information, methods, and technology that make up the know-how of a particular company and its industry.** Sometimes this information is written in manuals and procedures. Often it exists only in the minds of talented employees and staff specialists. Regardless of its source, it is invaluable to the efficiency of the conversion process.

6. **Markets, the consumers who buy and use the products and services that result from the management process.** Except for those in sales, supervisors rarely have direct contact with the market served by their company. Nevertheless, it is the market that makes the process meaningful because consumers buy the end results (products or services) and thus provide the money needed to pay for the input resources. In this sense the market is an input, or resource, of the management process.

What do all phases of the management process have in common?

Each requires that a supervisor solve problems and make decisions. Some people believe that these two related activities are what management is all about. If operations ran smoothly, a company could depend upon a computer rather than a supervisor to make decisions. But the organizational workday is crowded with unexpected events. Each represents a problem to be solved, a decision to be made. For supervisors most of these problems require an immediate solution. Otherwise, employees would be standing around waiting for instruction. Machines would be idle. Materials would be damaged. Shipments would be delayed. Chapter 32 gives you dozens of tips on how to improve your problem solving and decision making.

How much of the management process can be handled routinely?

Once your planning has been completed, much of your work can be done routinely—within certain limits. That is, you can apply the same solution you used to handle a problem in absenteeism last month to a similar one this month. Or you may find that your decision about a particular shipping problem will apply to many others like it. On the other hand, there are any number of other problems that are entirely different. These will need fresh inputs. You may have to create a new way to make assignments on the assembly line. Or you may have to initiate a new method of scheduling your keypunch operators. These new situations require that a supervisor be an innovator.

What makes the management process work?

Management and managers: executives, managers, supervisors. Each helps to turn the wheel. Supervisors are out on the cutting edge; higher-level managers are closer to the hub (Figure 1-6).

To what extent can supervisors follow their own inclinations in carrying out the management process?

There is a great deal of leeway. In fact, there are three distinct approaches for management to draw from. Or you can use a combination of all three. The three approaches are sometimes called schools or theories.

1. Systematic management approach. This is known by other names, too, such as scientific, classical, traditional, process, functional, or rational. All names imply a systematic approach that relies upon measurement and analysis of the various tasks and activities that take place at work.

2. Human relations approach. This is also known as the behavioral school because it is based on the thought that a manager who understands human behavior well enough is able to get employees to willingly cooperate with, and produce toward, company goals.

3. **Quantitative approach.** This approach emphasizes the use of numbers and relies upon the sciences of mathematics and statistics. It is also known as the management sciences or systems theory of management.

Many latter-day students of management are skeptical about the value of any of these three approaches. They insist that supervisors and other managers should start again from scratch. These authorities, sometimes called *revisionists,* suggest that each management situation be studied carefully and approached as a uniquely different problem. Sometimes, they say, the scientific approach will be best. Other times the human relations approach will get the best results. Still other times the quantitative approach should be chosen. Because of this iffy kind of advice, this approach has been labeled situational, or contingent, in that what a manager should do depends (is contingent) upon the particular situation at hand.

When does the systematic management approach work best?

A systematic approach is almost always a good way to attack any problem.

It requires that you gather facts first. What has really happened to the agitator tank? When did it happen? Who was operating it? Were reasonable production rates set for its operation? How close has actual output been to what was expected?

It emphasizes the value of accurate measurements. How much? How big? How long? How many?

It presumes that most activities are best performed according to a set path. Are the procedures carefully spelled out? Were they followed?

The problem with the systematic approach is that it too often expects perfection from organizations or that people will function like machines. Its founder, Frederick W. Taylor, was an engineer who hoped that human beings could be motivated by wage incentives to imitate machines. Later advocates of scientific management were also engineers—Henry L. Gantt, who conceived the production control chart, and Frank B. Gilbreth, who perfected the art of motion study of workers. Other proponents were mainly business people. Harrington Emerson, one notable contributor, believed that efficiency would result from better organizational arrangements and elimination of waste—human as well as material. Henri Fayol, a French factory owner, laid down a number of guiding principles that are still useful today. You will read about these in the pages that follow.

At what times should the human relations school of management be used?

████████████ There is rarely a time when it shouldn't be considered. The stickiest problems in business or elsewhere involve human beings. Supervisors need to know all they can about why people act the way they do. Exaggerated human conflict can be very wasteful. Use of what we know about the psychology and the sociology of human behavior can minimize this conflict. A large platoon of authorities, beginning with Elton Mayo and extending to Burleigh Gardner, has demonstrated the controlling influence that human relations can have in any organization. Mayo, in his famous experiment at the Hawthorne Works of the Western Electric Company in the 1930s, indisputably demonstrated that the performance of workers is more nearly related to psychological and social factors than to the physical makeup of the workplace. In 1945 Gardner wrote a basic text summarizing many research studies. Optimism for this approach was highest in the 1950s, when it was thought that a cookbook of methods could be given to supervisors. The idea was that if you follow our directions and prescriptions, people will act the way you want them to. Alas, the real world never came up to this promise.

Recent investigations by the revisionists (people like Herbert Simon and Chris Argyris) strongly suggest that supervisors should use great caution in applying human relations theory. Their watchwords would appear to be: Go slowly. Clear up technical problems first. Let people try to solve their own problems. Don't oversimplify management tasks. They are all complex because so many factors—materials, machinery, instructions, time pressures, conflicting objectives, hidden relationships—can influence the outcome of a supervisor's actions.

Where will the quantitative approach be most reliable?

████████████ Where people problems are fewest and process factors are greatest. The quantitative method is a numbers approach. It helps in setting up production and maintenance schedules, in balancing assembly lines, in controlling quality, in mapping out shipping routes, in setting work loads for bank tellers and airline ticket clerks. Quantitative methods (Part 5, "Managing Work," shows supervisors how to apply a number of statistical and quantitative techniques, as does Chapter 32, "Problem Solving and Decision Making") can be and have been applied successfully to just about any management problem where an employee's interests and motivation aren't controlling factors. Without any doubt the management sciences approach should be in every supervisor's tool kit. More often than not, of course, supervisors will need the help of industrial engineers, statisticians, or systems people to put the technique to work. But these specialists will, in turn, need the supervisor to spot potential applications.

Exactly what are the principles of management?

Just about any good rule of thumb qualifies as a principle. And you will find dozens presented to you in this book. But the basic, or original, principles of management were set down by the French businessman Henri Fayol in 1916. They still make a lot of sense today, as you may agree after examining this list of his more important principles.

1. Work should be divided so that each person will perform a specialized portion. In manning a sailboat, for instance, one person will lay up the hull, another caulk, and another make sails. In running an office, one person will enter orders, another type letters, and another file correspondence. Fayol called these ideas division of work and specialization.

2. Managers must have the right (authority) to give orders and instructions, but they must also accept responsibility for whether or not the work is done right. A supervisor needs the right to ask a work crew to load a freight car, for example, but if the car is loaded improperly, the supervisor must accept the blame.

3. Managers are responsible for extracting discipline and building morale among members of their work force, but they must also be true to their word in return. Said another way, if you want loyalty and cooperation from employees, you must be loyal and cooperative in return.

4. An individual should have only one boss. Fayol called this unity of command. Experience bears this out: If an employee reports to more than one superior, confusion and conflict result.

5. Every organization should have only one master plan, one set of overriding goals. Such unity of direction is lost if the purchasing department, for example, slows down the production department's output by buying materials from a less costly but undependable supplier when the company's overall commitment is to ship orders on time.

6. Similar to the principle he expressed in unity of direction, Fayol insisted that all individuals, especially managers, must place their interests second to those of the total organization. If persons in authority went their own way, Fayol reasoned, all others in the organization would suffer as a result.

7. Pay and rewards (remuneration) should reflect each person's efforts and, more important, that person's contribution to the organization's goal. It was a novel idea then that each employee should be paid according to individual worth rather than at the whim of a manager who might be inclined to play favorites.

8. Orders and instructions should flow down a chain of command from the higher manager to the lower one. Fayol also said that formal communications and complaints should move upward in the same channel. In practice, however, it has proved to be a good idea to permit and encourage the exchange of work information sideways between departments (or commands) as well. The real trouble seems to occur when a manager bypasses a supervisor with instructions to an employee or when an employee goes over a supervisor's head to register a complaint.

9. Materials should be in their proper place. Fayol extolled the virtue of all kinds of order; he believed that routine procedures minimized effort and waste.

10. Employees should be treated equally and fairly. Fayol called this equity. It invites dissatisfaction and conflict among employees, for example, when a supervisor gives one employee a break while picking on another.

11. Managers should encourage initiative among employees. Fayol advised: "It is essential to encourage this capacity to the full. . . . The manager must be able to sacrifice some personal vanity in order to grant this sort of satisfaction to subordinates. Other things being equal, a manager able to permit the exercise of initiative on the part of subordinates is infinitely superior to one who cannot do so."

A contingency approach was mentioned earlier. What is its true significance for supervision?

It adds realism—and safety—to the supervisor's job. The contingency approach (sometimes called the situational or operational approach) implies that a supervisor must be ready to employ one, or all three, of the management approaches. What is used depends upon—is contingent upon—the particulars in the operation or situation. If you are starting a new project or revising an old one, the scientific, or systematic, approach makes sense. If you are enmeshed in a situation (such as a radical change in procedures) where people's reactions are unusually sensitive, a concern for human relations should prevail. If your employees are looking for a solution to a difficult or recurring operational or process problem, the quantitative approach should get first call. Rarely, however, can you rely entirely upon a single approach. Just as there is a continuum of leadership styles, there should be a balance in the application of management approaches. In general choose first the approach that fits your personality and talents best, but do not rely upon it exclusively. Always, or almost always, double-check your results to see if you should apply a second or a third approach to the problem. Above all, try to keep Fayol's management principles in mind.

supervisory word power

Management process. The major managerial functions of planning, organizing, staffing, activating, and controlling carried on by managers in a repetitive sequence or cycle.

Resources (of the management process). The work force, materials and supplies, tools and equipment, money or capital, information and methods, and markets.

Outputs (of the management process). The products or services produced by converting resources into results.

Contingent management. The selection and use of the managerial approach (or combination of approaches) that is most appropriate for a particular problem or situation.

Management principles. The basic, time-tested guidelines that tend to apply universally to managerial functions and the problems these functions are intended to solve.

Other Important Terms in This Chapter

activating	planning
chain of command	problem solving
controlling	product
decision making	profit
division of work	quantitative management
equity	revisionist
human relations approach	service
innovation	systematic approach
management cycle	unity of command
organizing	unity of direction

reading comprehension

1. Give a specific example of an activity that would be included in each of the five functions of the management process.

2. What makes the management process a "process?"

3. How can managers tell whether the process of converting resources to end products is successful?

4. Name six resources on which the management process operates.

5. If supervisors and other managers have plans, why do they have to make decisions and solve problems on a day-to-day basis?

6. Why can't a supervisor rely all the time on the systematic management approach?

7. Name some applications for which the quantitative management approach has been found successful. What do the applications have in common?

8. Why did Henri Fayol say that an organization should have unity of command?

9. In light of modern experience, should communication be rigidly confined to an up-and-down direction in the chain of command?

10. What is the basic message of the contingency view of management?

supervision in action

THE CASE OF WHO'S IN CHARGE HERE?   A case study in human relations involving the management process, with questions for you to answer.

While working as a machinist for a large corporation, Joe Schreck saved his money so that he could start his own business. In 1975 he opened a small custom machine shop with a lathe, a grinder, a milling machine, and an all-purpose tool. At first Joe operated all the machines himself with the aid of a helper. Business grew, and within a few years Joe had six mechanics and four helpers working along with him. It wasn't long thereafter that Joe hired Ruby Burns to take care of his recordkeeping and to handle purchases.

More and more, Joe found himself letting Ruby make decisions about purchases and accounts. He still spent most of his time in the shop working at one or another of the machines. If a difficult job came up, Joe would move the regular operator aside and do the special work himself.

Whenever Joe was busy working on one of the machines, Ruby found herself arranging the job assignments for the employees. If there was a question from a customer, she would handle it directly. In addition Ruby found there were fewer tie-ups if she laid out the work schedules each week.

One day Ruby approached Joe with a suggestion that a new scheduling ticket be used to keep track of jobs as they progressed through the shop. Joe listened to the idea and commented, "That's a good idea, but you should spend your time purchasing and keeping our books. I'm the manager here, and keeping track of jobs is really my job."

Ruby replied, "I don't care what you call yourself, Joe, but I'm doing more to make sure that this shop turns a profit than you are. You act more like one of the hired hands. A skillful one, but really a machinist, not a manager."

"You must be joking," said Joe. "I own this shop, and I am its manager. It is you who are just one of the workers."

"I'm sorry you feel that way," said Ruby. "I've been taking on more and more of the managerial responsibility here, and I've been hoping that you'd give me the title of general manager."

"If anyone should carry that title," said Joe, "I should. The workers in the shop accept your schedules and the way you lay out their work, but if I weren't there, nothing would happen. They get the job done because they know I am boss and that I am the real leader on the floor."

"Let's not argue about it, Joe," said Ruby. "If you want me to be just another worker in the shop, I'll stop managing and stick to calling in purchases and doing the books. But if I do that, you will have to stop most of that 'hands-on' work you get into. And you'll have to spend most of your time really managing."

1. What managerial functions was Ruby performing? Which was Joe performing?

2. What was Joe doing that was not managerial work? Why did he do it? Who would do it if Joe didn't do it?

3. What work did Ruby do that was nonmanagerial?

4. Do you think Ruby should be appointed general manager, or would it be better for Joe to assume that responsibility? Why?

5. Would the fact that Joe is the owner necessarily make him the manager? Why?

enriching your viewpoint

To gain a broader understanding of the management process, approaches, and principles, the following readings are recommended:

Fayol, Henri, *General Principles of Management,* Sir Isaac Pitman & Sons, Ltd., London, 1949. Also in Harwood F. Merrill (ed.), *Classics in Management,* American Management Associations, New York, 1960, pp. 217–241.

Filley, Alan C., Robert J. House, and Steven Kerr, *Managerial Process and Organizational Behavior,* Scott, Foresman and Company, Glenview, Ill., 1976, Chap. 1, "The Evolution of Management Theory."

Follett, Mary Parker, "Management As a Profession," in Henry C. Metcalf (ed.), *Business Management As a Profession,* A. W. Shaw Company, Chicago, 1927. Also in Merrill, pp. 309–322 (see Fayol reference).

Gantt, Henry L., *Organizing for Work,* Harcourt, Brace and Howe, New York, 1919.

Gilbreth, Frank Bunker, "Science in Management for the One Best Way to Do Work," in Harwood F. Merrill (ed.), *Classics in Management,* American Management Associations, New York, 1960, pp. 245–291.

Gilman, Glenn, "The Manager and the Systems Concept," *Business Horizons,* Vol. 12, No. 4, August 1969, pp. 19–28.

Koontz, Harold, "Making Sense of Management Theory: The Management Process School of Thought," in Harold Koontz (ed.), *Toward a Unified Theory of Management,* McGraw-Hill Book Company, New York, 1964, pp. 3–5.

Luthans, Fred, *Introduction to Management: A Contingency Approach,* McGraw-Hill Book Company, New York, 1976, Chap. 1, "The Evolving Field of Management," and Chap. 2, "A Contingency Approach to Management."

Mayo, Elton, *The Social Problems of an Industrial Civilization,* Harvard Graduate School of Business Administration, Boston, 1945, Chap. 3.

Taylor, Frederick W., "What Is Scientific Management?" Testimony before the Special Committee of the House of Representatives to Investigate the Taylor and Other Systems of Shop Management, January 25, 1912; also reproduced in Harwood F. Merrill (ed.), *Classics in Management,* American Management Associations, New York, 1960, pp. 77–81.

Trefethen, Florence N., "A History of Operations Research," in Joseph F. McCloskey and Florence N. Trefethen (eds.), *Operations Research for Management,* The Johns Hopkins Press, Baltimore, 1954.

CHAPTER **8**

making plans and carrying out policy

Why is so much emphasis placed upon planning?

Because the resources that management applies must deal with the future, and the future is rarely the same as today. Planning is a tested way of coping with this change. It helps to make certain that you have enough employees on hand to do the job, the right amount and kind of materials, and tuned-up machinery when you need it. Most important, planning prepares a road map, which enables a supervisor to move resources effectively.

Plans, planning, policies, goals: What is the difference?

If ever there is an area of management where the terms are mixed up, this is it. *Plans* are what come out of the *planning*

113

process. Plans or programs are what you intend to do in the future. Before you can develop plans, however, you must set targets. These targets are called *goals, standards,* or *objectives.* After you have set these goals (that is the simplest term to use), you establish general guidelines for reaching them. These guidelines are called *policies.* Only after policies have been set should plans be formulated. As a final step, you may choose to lay down some *rules* and *regulations.* These will establish the limits (controls) within which employees are free to do the job their own way.

Take this example. You are thinking ahead—planning—about what your department will do during the annual spring cleaning. You make a list of things that you want to accomplish: filing cabinets cleared of all obsolete material, shelving cleaned and re-arranged, tools repaired and in tip-top shape. These are your goals. Next you establish some sort of policy. For example, cleaning will be done during normal working hours without overtime; discarding obsolete papers will conform to legal requirements; repairing tools may be done by your own maintenance department or by an outside machine shop. Then you lay out a master plan of how the housekeeping will be done, when, and by whom. If this plan is detailed as to its exact sequence, it would be called a *procedure.* Finally you set down some firm rules or regulations for your work crew: Only file clerks will make judgments about what paperwork will be discarded; before tools are sent outside for repair, employees must check with you; employees who clean shelving must wear protective gloves. Figure 8-1 illustrates common relationships between these terms.

What is the best way to approach the planning process?

████████████ Systematically. There are a number of factors that contribute to good planning. You will get the best results if you follow them step by step.

1. Consider the goals of the entire organization, not just of your department. Think about the needs and wishes of customers, those the company serves as well as those "customers" your department serves internally.

2. Estimate the strengths and weaknesses of your department. Ask how they will help or hinder you in trying to meet company goals and in trying to serve external and internal customers.

3. Don't jump to conclusions at this early stage. Instead, keep your mind alert to new opportunities—such as ways to improve

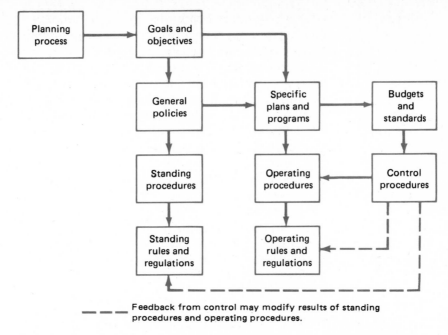

Feedback from control may modify results of standing procedures and operating procedures.

FIGURE 8-1. Relationship Between the Various Outputs of the Planning Process.

quality or lower costs. Don't restrict your thinking to what your goals were last year or how you met them. A forecast of what may happen helps to keep you looking ahead.

4. Pick a reasonable set of goals. These should meet two standards: They (*a*) contribute to the organization's goals and (*b*) can be met by your department, given its strengths and its weaknesses.

5. Arrange your department's goals in a hierarchy of objectives. That is, place the most important ones at the top of your list and the least important at the bottom.

6. Watch out for limitations. Think about restrictions that may be imposed on you by your company or by the need to coordinate with or serve other departments. Your department cannot operate in a vacuum. It must base its plans upon such realistic planning premises.

7. Develop your master plan. This should focus on your main objective. If, for example, the company's goal is for higher-quality products or services, the master plan for your department should give this top priority.

8. Draw up supporting plans. This requires that you think about how each activity in your department can contribute to your master plan. Machinists may need more explicit blueprints. Assemblers may need brighter workplace lighting. Clerks may need a different order-entry procedure.

9. Put numbers and dates on everything you can. Plans work best when employees know how much or how many is required of them. Since plans are for the future—tomorrow, next week, or next month—times and dates are essential.

10. Pin down assignments. Plans are for people. Responsibility for carrying out each part of a plan or procedure should be assigned to a particular individual.

11. Explain the plan to all concerned. Plans should be shared. Their rationales should be explained and their goals justified. Employees who know *why* are more likely to cooperate.

12. Review your plans regularly. Circumstances and restrictions change. Your plans should be examined periodically to see whether they should be changed, too.

How strictly must the planning process be followed?

Experts say that nothing should be attempted without prior planning. There should be few exceptions to this rule of primacy. There is flexibility, however, as to how a supervisor goes about planning. Nevertheless, thought should be given to each of the steps outlined above.

In what way are plans or programs usually classified?

They are usually classified according to their duration and purpose.

Long-range plans are typically set by higher management and are expected to be in operation from two to five years.

Short-range plans are those that supervisors are most concerned with. These are usually based on operations of one year or less. At the department level, short-range plans may be in effect for a day, a week, a month, or a quarter.

Standing plans include just about any activity that goes on without much change from year to year. Standing plans cover general employment practices, health and safety matters, purchasing procedures, routine discipline, and the like.

Single-use plans are used only once before they must be revised. Departmental budgets and operating schedules are examples. They will be good only for a week or a month until new ones are issued.

Generally speaking, then, supervisors will follow short-range, single-use plans for day-to-day operations. But supervisors will also be guided by many standing plans that implement routine, relatively unchanging goals and policies.

When should supervisors plan and how often?

Before starting anything new or different. Planning should take place before a new day, a new week, a new product or service, or introduction of different materials or machinery. As a matter of routine, a supervisor should make up new plans each night for the next day, each Friday for the next week, and the last week in the month for the next month.

Which areas should be targets for a supervisor's planning process?

Just about anything qualifies. Any kind of change should trigger new plans. Every area within the supervisor's responsibility is a candidate for planning. For starters, here is a list of a dozen prime candidates:

• Use of facilities and equipment: departmental layout and working conditions, equipment utilization and maintenance.
• Use and care of materials and supplies: purchases, inventory levels, storage.
• Conservation of energy and power: electricity, steam, water, and compressed air usage; waste disposal; fire protection.
• Cash and credit management: petty cash, billing, collections.
• Work force management: forecasting requirements, safety and health care, sanitation, communications, absences and turnover, employee training and development.
• Information collection and processing: tallies and logbooks, recordkeeping, order processing.
• Time conservation: start-ups, shutdowns, personal time.
• Schedules: routing, delivery performance, shortages.
• Quality management: inspection and control techniques, re-work methods, scraps reduction, employee training and motivation.
• Cost reduction and control: cost estimating, correction of variances, work simplification and methods improvement.
• Productivity: work simplification and methods improvement.
• Self-improvement: planning, organizing, communicating, public speaking, writing for business, leading conferences.

How do controls relate to plans?

Controls are like limit switches that keep plans in line. When a plan is moving directly toward its goal, the track is kept clear. The supervisor need apply no control. But when a plan strays from its target, the supervisor must take corrective action to bring it back in line. When planning a department's goals, a supervisor must also plan its control limits.

What is a good way to double-check your plans and projects?

Try using the five-point planning chart illustrated in Figure 8-2:

- *What* spells out objectives in terms of specifications for output, quality, and costs.
- *Where* sets the location for the assignment (its workplace) and the place where the product or service must be delivered: the adjoining department, the shipping dock, the home office.
- *When* records your time estimates for the work to be performed and, most important, pins down starting and finishing times and dates.
- *How* verifies short- and long-range methods, procedures, and job sequences.
- *Who* designates the individual responsible for the assignment and specifies that person's authority and extent of control over the resources needed: tools, machinery, additional labor, materials.

FIGURE 8-2.

Five-Point Planning Check Chart		
What	Objectives	Specifications
		Cost/price limits
Where	Locale	Delivery point
When	Time elapsed	Starting date
		Completion date
How	Tactics	Methods Procedure
	Strategy	Sequence
Who	Responsibility	Authority Control Assignment

What is meant by company policy?

Company policies are broad rules or guides for action. At their best these rules are a statement of the company's objectives and its basic principles for doing business. They are intended as a guide for supervisors and managers in getting their jobs done. Many policies give supervisors the opportunity to use their own best judgment in carrying them out. Others are supported by firm rules, which supervisors must observe if they are to run their departments in harmony with the rest of the organization.

Does policy apply only at high levels?

Policy is generally set by managers high up in the company organization. But policy can be no more than a collection of high-sounding words unless the supervisor translates them into action on the firing line.

Take an example of a disciplinary policy. Here's how it might sound as it works its way down from the front office to first-line action by the supervisor:

Company president: "Our policy is to exercise fair and reasonable controls to regulate the conduct of our employees."

Manufacturing vice president: "The policy on attendance in this plant is that habitual absenteeism will be penalized."

Plant superintendent: "Here are the rules governing absences. It's up to you supervisors to keep an eye on unexcused absences and to discharge any employee absent or late more than three times in three months."

Supervisor; "Sorry, I'm going to have to lay you off for three days. You know the rules. You put me in a bad spot when you take time off on your own without warning or getting approval."

Note that no real action takes place until the supervisor puts the words of the policy into effect.

What sort of matters does policy cover?

A company may have a policy to cover almost every important phase of its business—from regulating its method of purchasing materials to stipulating how employees may submit suggestions. As a supervisor you will probably be most concerned with policies that affect (1) employees and (2) the practices of your department.

Employee policies most commonly formalized are those affecting wages and salaries, holidays and vacations, leaves of absence, termination of employment, safety, medical and health insurance and hospitalization, service awards, and retirement and pensions.

Department practices most often reduced to policy are requisitioning of supplies, preparation of records, timekeeping, safeguarding classified materials, cost-control measures, quality standards, maintenance and repair, and acquisition of new machinery and equipment.

These listings are not all-inclusive. Some companies have more, others fewer policies.

Is policy always in writing?

Far from it. Many rigid policies have never been put down in black and white. And many firm policies have never been heard from an executive's lips. But employees and supervisors alike recognize that matters affected by such policies must be handled in a certain manner and usually do so.

The existence of so much unwritten policy has led many authorities to the conclusion that all policy is better put into writing so that it may be explained, discussed, and understood. Nevertheless, there are many companies that don't subscribe to this way of thinking, and their policies remain implied rather than spelled out.

How does policy apply to rules and regulations?

One of the great misunderstandings about policy is the belief that it's always something negative like "Don't do that" or "Do it this way or you'll get in trouble."

Policy can also be positive, encouraging, and uplifting. Just examine the written policy of a nationally respected company as expressed in a booklet published by its board of directors:

Importance of the individual. We believe the actions of business should recognize human feelings and the importance of the individual and should ensure each person's treatment as an individual.
Common interest. We believe that employees, their unions, and management are bound together by a common interest—the ability of their unit to operate successfully—and that opportunity and security for the individual depend upon this success.
Open communications. We believe that the sharing of ideas, information, and feeling is essential as a means of expression and as the route to better understanding and sounder decisions.
Local decisions. We believe that people closest to the problems affecting themselves develop the most satisfactory solutions

*when given the authority to solve such matters at the point where
they arise.*
High moral standards. *We believe that the soundest basis for
judging the "rightness" of an action involving people is the test of
its morality and its effect on basic human rights.*

Words? Yes. Policy? Definitely. And as an official guide to action committed to print by the top officers of the organization, these statements are an excellent example of the positive side of policy.

Should a supervisor change policy?

▄▄▄▄▄▄▄▄ No. That's a very dangerous thing to do. Policies are set to guide action. It's a supervisor's responsibility to act within policy limits.

Supervisors can influence a policy change, however, by making their thoughts and observations known to the boss, the personnel department, and the top management. After all, supervisors are in the best position to feel employees' reactions to policy—favorable or otherwise. You do your boss and your company a service when you accurately report employees' reactions. And that's the time to offer your suggestions for improving or modifying the policy.

Do supervisors ever set policy?

▄▄▄▄▄▄▄▄ In a way, supervisors always set policy at the department level. Supervisory application of policy is their interpretation of how the broader company policy should be carried out for employees. It's important for you to recognize that company policy usually allows you discretion at your level—even though this discretion may be limited.

Suppose your company has a policy that forbids bookmaking in the area. Anyone caught will be fired. You can carry out that policy many ways. You can bait a trap, hide behind a post, and fire the first person you catch. Or you can quietly size up and warn the most likely violator that if caught, there won't be a second chance. You can put a notice on the bulletin board calling employees' attention, generally, to the policy. Or you can hold a group meeting and announce how you will deal with bookmakers. You can choose to regard only taking of horseracing bets as bookmaking, or include professionally run baseball, basketball, and football pools. Or you can rule out any kind of gambling. Whatever you decide, so long as you carry out the intentions (and the letter where it's spelled out) of the company policy, you are setting your own policy.

How responsible will
employees hold you for company policy?

██████████ If you have done a good job of convincing employees that you fully represent the management of their company, your actions and company policy will be one and the same thing in their eyes. Naturally, you will sometimes have to carry out policy that you don't fully agree with—policy that may be unpopular with you or with your employees. Resist the temptation to apologize for your actions or to criticize the policy to employees. When you do, you weaken your position.

If you have to reprimand an employee, don't say, "I'd like to give you a break, but that's company policy." Or when sparking a cleanup campaign, don't say, "The manager wants you to get your area in order." Handle such matters positively. Give the policy your own personal touch, but don't sell the company down the river or you're likely to be caught in the current yourself.

How can you prevent your
policy interpretations from backfiring?

██████████ Try to protect your actions in policy matters by asking yourself questions before making decisions:

- Is policy involved here? What is the procedure? What is the rule?
- Am I sure of the facts? Do I know all the circumstances?
- How did I handle a similar matter in the past?
- Who can give me advice on this problem? Should I ask for it?
- Would my boss want to talk this over with me first?
- Does this problem involve the union? If so, should I see the union steward or should I check with our labor relations people first?

Must you consider more
than one policy at the same time?

██████████ Yes. Frequently you will be called on to handle a situation that involves several policy matters simultaneously. For instance, suppose you were informed that the company was dropping a product from its line. It will mean reducing labor costs in your department 25 percent, since the work volume will fall off the same amount. One of your employees, hearing of the cutback, asks whether instead of laying off people, the work can be shared— that you retain all the employees but have them all work fewer hours per week. You check with your boss, who says, "The company's policy (and it's written into our agreement with the union) is that we will not 'share work.' The employees we retain must work a full week. But anything else you can do to reassign work is all right with me—as long as it's in line with company policy."

What can you do? Company policy knocks out a work-sharing plan. How about keeping the most skilled workers and laying off the less skilled? No. Can't do that. Company policy is that in "permanent" layoffs, employees with least seniority will go first. How about reducing the number of material handlers? That's okay. Nothing to prevent you from doing that. How about having the setup person double as an inspector? Oops, policy says, "Quality will be considered before every other operating policy except safety."

"Well," you say to yourself, "what I propose to do needn't sacrifice quality, so I'll make the double-up move.

"Now what can I do with my direct labor? I can drop ten from the gang if I can work four operators to an assembly instead of our usual six. Let's see, the union contract specifies that the number of operators needed to staff an assembly job operation cannot be changed except when changes in work load warrant a reduction. That seems like pretty clear policy to me. But I better check with the shop steward to see if there's some angle I've overlooked."

Before you have made your final plans, you've had to check them—and adjust them—against five company policies. Yet you make your own decisions and run the department as you see fit—except that you are guided by the rules set down for integrating your action with that of all the other departments of the company.

What is a supervisor's policy manual?

Many companies have actually taken their general company policies and written down interpretations as a specific guide to supervisory action. Those written guides for supervisors are usually placed in a loose-leaf folder and called a Supervisor's Manual. Supervisors use these manuals as references whenever a policy question comes up that they aren't certain about handling. If your company has such a manual, and it's up to date, it's an invaluable aid in handling your job.

What do employees want to know about policy?

Employees are rarely concerned with nice phrases. General statements of policy will mean little to them. But they do have a keen—and critical—interest in the specific and concrete aspects of policy whenever it hits home.

If your company's policy is to "treat employees equitably in disciplinary affairs," this will probably be unclear to them. You can help a lot if you rephrase the broad statements of policy (which may necessarily be generalized) into language that every employee understands. In this case, "We intend to give everyone a fair and square deal if a rule is broken."

But even such a clear summary of a regulation still doesn't answer for an employee: "What does this mean to me?" You'll have to be still more specific: "If more than three out of every hundred pieces you turn out don't measure up to standards, I'll give you a warning the first time. The second time, you'll be given time off without pay. If it continues, you may be discharged." You wouldn't get far with policy, for instance, if you say to the employee, "If the quality of your production is substandard, we may have to take disciplinary action." The employee may very well ask, "What's quality? What's my production? What's substandard? What's disciplinary action?"

TABLE 8-1. Typical Performance Goals for a First-Line Supervisor

Area of Measurement	Last Year's Record	Next Year's Goals
1. Ratio of jobs completed on schedule to total jobs worked	85% average, 92% highest, 65% lowest in June	90% average, minimum acceptable 75%
2. Percentage of job costs held within 3% of standard costs	91% average, 95% highest, 75% lowest in June	90% average, bring up low figure to 87% or better
3. Rejects and rework	Less than 1% rejects. Rework averages 7%	Keep rejects to less than 1%, but cut rework to 3%
4. Labor stability	Two quits, one discharge	No quits of employees with over three years service
5. Absences, latenesses	5% absences, 7% latenesses	5% absences, 2% latenesses
6. Overtime	Only on jobs okayed by sales department	Only on jobs okayed by sales department
7. Accidents	No lost-time accidents; 37 calls to dispensary for minor ailments	No lost-time accidents; reduce number of dispensary visits

What kinds of goals are typically set for supervisors?

Objectives or goals—especially at the supervisory level—are usually targets that you or your department must aim for in order to (1) put policy into practice and (2) specifically assist the firm in making a reasonable profit or in living up to its service commitments. Typically, the goals for your department are short-range. These goals pin down your cost, quality, and performance targets for next week, next month, or next year. Frequently these goals are quantitative (with numbers on them) rather than merely qualitative (described by words such as improve, maintain, good, better). Typical performance goals for a first-line supervisor are shown in Table 8-1. In many companies the manner in which you and your department attain your goals becomes the determining factor in what kind of a raise you'll get or how good a job you can be groomed for.

supervisory word power

Objectives. Goals, targets, and purposes—both short-term and long-range—toward which an organization strives; the long-range objectives in particular must be supported by guidelines for management action and decisions.

Policies. Broad guidelines, philosophy, or principles which management establishes in support of its organizational goals and which it must follow in seeking them.

Procedures. Methods prescribed by management as the proper and consistent forms and channels to be followed by individuals and units of an organization.

Regulations. Specific rules, orders, and controls set forth by management restricting the conduct of individuals and units within an organization.

Standards. Specifications, criteria, and prescribed measurements that define the limits within which, or the level at which, organizational performance is presumed to have met its goals.

Other Important Terms in This Chapter

long-range plans
planning premises
short-range plans
single-use plans
standing plans

reading comprehension

1. Give an example from your work or personal life of a time when prior planning would have made things work out better than they did.

2. How can you judge whether particular objectives are reasonable for your department or work group?

3. Name some specific areas in organizations to which planning should be applied.

4. How are plans and controls related?

5. Contrast the way in which policy affects top management decisions and the supervisor's actions.

6. What are some of the things typically covered by company policies?

7. When would it be wise for a supervisor to check with the boss before carrying out a particular policy?

8. Give an example of how a supervisor's decision in a particular instance might be influenced by more than one policy.

9. One company's policy manual stated: "It is our intention to listen with an open mind to employees' complaints." What supplementary information might a supervisor add to that statement when explaining it to employees?

10. Which do you think is more important to a company in the long run: the policies it sets or the actions its supervisors take? Why?

supervision in action

THE CASE OF THE EXCUSED ABSENCE.   A case study in human relations involving company policy, with questions for you to answer.

"The company's policy regarding time off from work is a reasonable one, Dick," said the plant superintendent to Dick Deeds, the new supervisor in the stamping room. "If an employee has a personal emergency to take care of during working hours, we're only too glad to let him punch out and take care of it. However, we frown on the practice of granting time off to fish or hunt or to take care of any other personal matters that can be done after working time."

Three weeks later Tad Wade, a machine operator, asked Dick if he could report in late the next morning. He needed to do so, he said, because he had just bought a new car and wanted to register it at the motor vehicle agency. There was always a long line of applicants at the lunch hour or in the afternoon. "Sure you can," said Dick. "But come to work as soon as you have tended to your business."

The following morning, while Dick was lining up the day's schedule, Ray Featherstone, supervisor of the mixing department, stopped by Dick's desk. "You certainly put me in a tough spot with a couple of my people today. The boys got wind of the fact that you let Tad off today to register his new car. I've never accepted an excuse like that. I tell my people that so long as it's urgent, I'll let them go. But nix on rearranging work schedules just to suit one man's convenience."

1. Do you think Dick was right in letting Tad have the time off? Why?

2. What do you think of Ray's interpretation of company policy? Of Dick's?

3. Would it be better if Dick's boss had been more explicit in explaining the policy to Dick? Why?

4. What can Dick do to avoid having this situation arise again?

enriching your viewpoint

To gain a broader understanding of planning and policy, the following readings are recommended:

Albanese, Robert, *Managing: Toward Accountability for Performance,* Richard D. Irwin, Inc., Homewood, Ill., 1978, Chap. 3, "Managerial Planning," pp. 97–120.

Bittel, Lester R., *The Nine Master Keys of Management,* McGraw-Hill Book Company, New York, 1972, Chap. 5, "Act From a Plan," pp. 121–149.

Bower, Marvin, *The Will to Manage,* McGraw-Hill Book Company, New York, 1966, Chap. 4, "Policies, Standards, Guide Lines, and Procedures," pp. 98–118.

Dale, Ernest, *Management Theory & Practice,* 4th ed., McGraw-Hill Book Company, New York, 1978, Chap. 12, "Forecasting and Planning," pp. 227–255.

Glueck, William F., *Management,* The Dryden Press, Inc., Hinsdale, Ill., 1977, Chap. 12, "Techniques for Effective Planning," pp. 348–378.

Koontz, Harold, and Cyril O'Donnell, *Essentials of Management,* 2d ed., McGraw-Hill Book Company, New York, 1978, Chap. 7, "Strategies and Policies," pp. 131–144.

Wilson, Charles F., *How to Develop and Apply Work Plans: A Federal Supervisor's Guide,* Superintendent of Documents, U.S. Government Printing Office, 1974.

CHAPTER 9
organizing an effective department

Must supervisors always hold the "in-between" spot in the management organization?

Too often, supervisors (and occasionally their superiors) see themselves only as people in the middle, put in an awkward position to serve as a buffer between the company and the workers. The upper group wants them to put the pressure on; the lower group wants them to be good guys.

Good supervisors in a good organization are much more than just intermediaries. They are really the key people. Situated where they are, first-line supervisors can clear the way for intelligent top-management actions directed toward the rank and file and also serve to let top management know how workers feel. Acting as key managers, they knit the whole organization of management and workers together.

A particularly bad situation is where the supervisor with no real status is a figurehead who is bypassed by both managers and workers. This can be sheer torture.

Not being just a buffer or a figurehead depends upon two things—your company's attitude toward supervisors and your own attitude toward yourself. Most companies truly want supervisors to be full-time managers who think and feel and act at the department or section level the way other executives do at middle- and top-management levels. Surprisingly, more supervisors than companies have shirked this responsibility. These are the supervisors who continually complain of being sold down the river or of being whipping boys. The record will show that most supervisors determine for themselves whether they will be key managers or merely in the middle.

What is an organization?

An organization is a grouping together of people so that they can work effectively toward a goal members of the group want to achieve.

The goal of a business organization is primarily profits for stockholders and salaries and wages for managers, supervisors, and employees. There are other important goals, too, like supplying goods and services to the general population or producing military materials for our defense in time of war. And members of the organization all aim for other satisfactions, too, such as fellowship, accomplishment, and prestige.

Why organize?

We'd have nothing but havoc without it. We take organization for granted because we have lived so long with it at home, in places of worship, and at school. Little we do together would be effective if we didn't agree among ourselves as to who should do what. And since business organizations are under tremendous pressures to be effective, their organization tends to be more formal and rigid.

After the Dallas Cowboys won the professional football Super Bowl in 1978, one sportswriter made the comment that the victory wasn't the real accomplishment. "The thing that sets the Cowboys apart from other strong National Football League teams," said Phil Elderkin of the *Christian Science Monitor,* "is their ability as an organization. From the front office to the playing field, everything is done with calculated precision."

Are all organizations formal?

No. In a good many of our activities, even in complex manufacturing plants, some people just naturally take over responsibilities and exercise authority without anyone's ever spelling it out. Chances are that in a group of 15 employees who you might imagine are all at the same level, you'll discover some sort of informal organization. It may be that the person who sweeps the floors actually swings weight in that group. Acting as staff assistant may be the lift-truck driver, who is the informant. The rest of the group may either work hard or stage a slowdown at a nod from a third member of the group, who has authority as surely as if the company president had given it.

So be alert to informal organization—among the employees you supervise, in the supervisory group itself, and in the entire management structure.

Which comes first, the organization or the work to be done?

If there were no job to do, there would be no reason for having an organization. So don't make the mistake of being organization-happy and trying to set up an elaborate organization just for the sake of having one. The best organization is a simple one that puts people together so that the job at hand gets done better, more quickly, more cheaply than any other way.

In business the job at hand in an industrial plant, for example, is very big and complex. The number of people involved is large, and their different skills are many. Some authorities say that organizations must manage four key resources:

- Work force. The people who manage others, as well as those who do the work.
- Machines. The machinery, buildings, and equipment that enable the work force to produce the goods and services.
- Material. The raw materials and other goods that go into the product or are used to refine it.
- Money. The dollars and cents that provide the machines and materials for people to manage and work with.

Your job, too, is one that involves management of these four resources. Your place in the company's organization should be designed to help you do that management job better. But recognize that the big organization can't be tailor-made to the last inch to suit all your preferences. Within the framework of your own department, however, it's up to you to see that your organization is tailor-made to the job as well as it possibly can be.

What is the purpose of organization charts?

To help you understand organizational relationships. Such charts are really pictures of how one job or department fits in with others. Each box, or rectangle, encloses an activity or department. Those boxes on the same horizontal level on the chart tend to have the same degree of authority or power and to have their work closely related. Departments in boxes on the next higher level have greater authority; those at lower levels have less authority. Clusters of boxes that enclose departments performing closely related functions (such as shaping, fabricating, assembly and finishing in a manufacturing plant) are typically connected in a vertical chain to the head manager of that particular function (such as the production manager).

Boxes containing line departments tend to descend from the top of the chart to the bottom (where supervisors' departments typically are) in vertical chains. Boxes that enclose staff departments tend to branch out to either side of the main flow of authority from top to bottom.

Organization charts can be drawn any way that shows relationships best, even in circles; but for practical purposes most charting is done in the manner just described and illustrated in Figure 9-1. One caution: Organization structures and staffing change constantly. Accordingly, organization charts go out of date very quickly.

What's the difference between line and staff?

An organization works best when it gets many related jobs done effectively with the minimum of friction. This requires coordination and determination of what to do and how to do it. Those managers and supervisors whose main job it is to see that things get done are usually considered members of the *line* organization. Other management people who help them to decide what to do and how to do it, assist in coordinating the efforts of all, or provide service are usually called *staff* people. (See Figure 9-1.)

In manufacturing plants, production departments, sales departments, and occasionally purchasing departments are the most common line activities. The production supervisor or first-line supervisor is likely to be a member of the line organization.

Departments that help the line departments control quality and maintain adequate records are typically staff activities. Industrial engineering, maintenance, research, accounting, industrial and

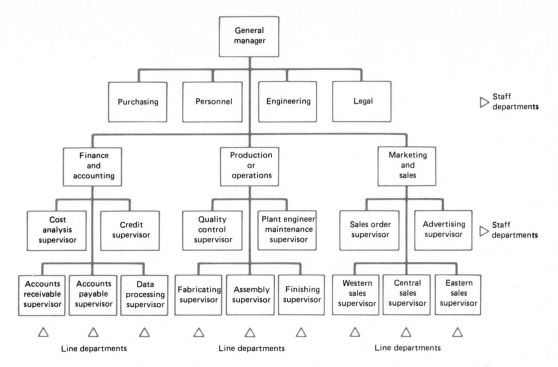

FIGURE 9-1. Line-and-Staff Organization in a Manufacturing Company.

personnel relations are some other examples of typical staff activities.

In service organizations such as banks and insurance firms, the line organization may represent the primary "action" operations (like deposits and withdrawals and recordkeeping, or premium collections and claim settlements) and the staff organization such support activities as computer departments and actuarial.

In hotels and motels the line may be everything connected with the operation of a geographic unit, and the staff such activities as advertising, accounting, and legal.

In transport companies the line department may be fleet operations; the staff, equipment repair and maintenance.

In a hospital, medical and nursing may represent the line groups, with laboratory, culinary, and housekeeping the staff.

It may help you to think of line people as the doers, staff people as the advisers. Each function—line or staff—is important in its own way, even though there has often been rivalry between line and staff for credit and recognition.

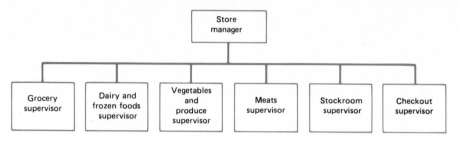

FIGURE 9-2. Example of Functional Organization Design for a Supermarket.

Is the line-and-staff structure the only way to organize?

No, although it is the most common and is found in most organizations. There are other commonly used ways to put together an organization:

Functional. Each group of related activities is collected under one functional head, as shown in Figure 9-2. Most line-and-staff organizations tend to be somewhat functional in concept, however, and it may often be hard to make the distinction.

Divisional or product. All functions needed to make a particular product, for example, are gathered under one highly placed manager. If a firm manufactures tractors for farmers, road graders for construction contractors, and lawn mowers for home use, it might "divisionalize" in order to make and sell each major product in its product line, as shown in Figure 9-3. Note that under each division head this organization is essentially a functional

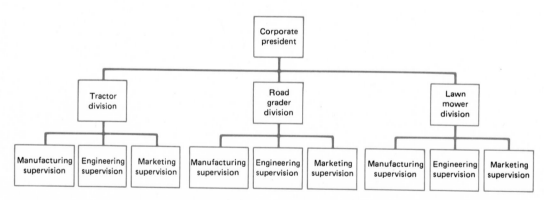

FIGURE 9-3. Example of Product or Divisional Organization Design for a Manufacturing Company.

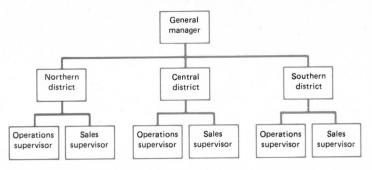

FIGURE 9-4. Example of Geographic Organization Design for an Insurance Company.

one; as a consequence, labels such as functional or divisional can be misleading.

Geographic.   A firm may divide some of its activities, such as sales, or all of its activities, according to the geographic region where these take place (Figure 9-4).

Customer.   A company may also choose to organize some or all of its activities according to the customers it serves, such as farmers, contractors, or home owners. This kind of organization (Figure 9-5) is closely related to the product organization.

Project or task force.   This form is commonly used in research and development organizations and engineering firms for one-of-a-kind projects or contracts. It allows a project manager to call upon the time and skills of personnel—for a limited period of time—from various functional specialties. When the project is completed, the specialized personnel return to their home units

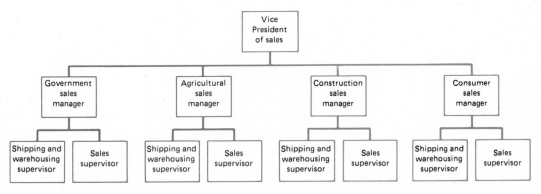

FIGURE 9-5. Example of Customer- or Market-Oriented Organization Design.

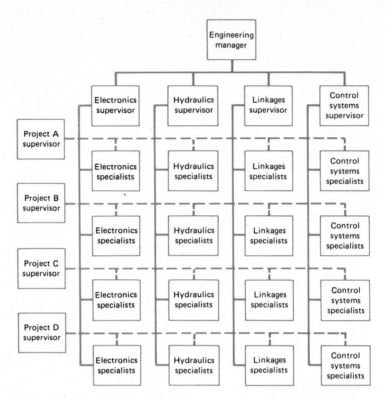

FIGURE 9-6. Example of Project or Task Force (Matrix) Organization Design.

to await assignment to another project. Because project managers can exercise their authority horizontally across the basic organization while the specialists receive permanent authority from their functional bosses above them vertically on the chart (Figure 9-6), this form is called a matrix organization.

Regardless of organization type, always remember that the purpose of the organizational structure is to make your department's work more nearly fit together with the work of other departments.

What is the distinction between a centralized and a decentralized organization?

A *centralized* organization tends to have many levels of management, to concentrate its facilities in one location, to perform certain functions such as engineering, labor negotiations, computer operations, and purchasing from a single source, and to gather together its power and authority at headquarters. A *decentralized* organization tends to have the opposite characteristics, especially when a company is divided into distinctly separate units with varying degrees of independence. These units may be set up along product lines, by geography, or by methods of marketing and distribution.

What is the Table of Organization (TO)?

This expression (derived from military staffing practices) implies that for each department or unit (1) staffing is limited to certain specified positions and (2) for each position a specified number of people are prescribed. When a department is not up to its TO, it means that either vacancies exist as positions with no incumbents or the number of incumbents in one or more position classes is less than that prescribed, or some combination of both. The TO principle can beneficially be applied to business if the specific TO capacity (or productivity) is carefully related to the organization's responsibilities and goals.

How wide can a manager's span of control be?

Authorities disagree on this point, but it is a good rule of thumb that no manager or supervisor should have the responsibility for more than six separate activites. The more specialized and complex the activities, the shorter the span of control. The more uniform and less complicated the activities (as with many supervisory responsibilities), the greater the span can be. Sometimes the span of control (or of management) is defined by the number of people, rather than by the number of activities. If such is the case, it is not unusual for a supervisor to have a span of 30 or more employees, provided they are engaged in only a few simple, related activities. On the other hand, a middle-level manager might be responsible for the activities managed by the supervisors of six different departments.

Are authority and responsibility the same thing?

No. Authority should go hand in hand with responsibility, but the two are no more alike than are the two sides of a coin. Your *responsibilities* are those things you are held accountable for—like costs, on-time deliveries, and good housekeeping. Responsibilities are also spoken of as your duties—like checking time cards, investigating accidents, scheduling employees, or keeping production records. *Authority* is the power you need to carry out your responsibilities. A supervisor's authority includes the right to make decisions, to take action to control costs and quality, and to exercise necessary discipline over the employees assigned to help carry out these responsibilities.

It's an axiom that you shouldn't be given a responsibility without enough authority to carry it out. If a supervisor is given responsibility for seeing that quality is up to specifications, that supervisor must also be given authority to stop the production line when the quality falls off or to take any steps necessary to correct the condition.

Where does your organizational authority come from?

Authority, like responsibility, is usually handed down to supervisors from their immediate bosses. The bosses in turn receive their authority and responsibilities from their immediate superiors. And so it goes, on up to the company president, who receives assignments from the board of directors.

The biggest chunk of authority and responsibility rests with the company president, who may split this chunk in as few as 3 pieces (to the vice presidents of production, sales, and financing) or as many as 20 (to vice presidents in charge of 20 different products). As the responsibilities and authorities come down the line to you, the pieces get smaller and smaller. But they also get much more specific.

Your plant superintendent may have the responsibility for producing goods in sufficient quantities to meet sales requirements, while your responsibility may be to see that ten milling machines are operated at optimum capacity so that 200,000 product units are produced each month. Similarly, the plant superintendent's authority may permit the exercise of broad disciplinary measures, while yours may be limited to recommending disciplinary action for employees who break rules or whose output is not up to production and quality standards.

Most companies try to make the responsibilities and authorities at each level of management fairly consistent. For instance, a supervisor in Department A should have the same general responsibilities as a supervisor in Department Z. And their authorities would be generally the same even though the specific duties of each might differ widely.

Figure 9-7 is a checklist that might help you and your boss to decide duties, policies, and actions for which you are held responsible.

Even in the best of firms, however, communications are never so clear between a supervisor and a boss that both agree completely on authority limits. At least that's the conclusion that

Bradford B. Boyd and J. Michael Jensen drew from a survey of 1,000 manufacturing firms. Respondents to this survey (sponsored in 1971 by the Supervisory Institutes of the University of Wisconsin's Department of Business and Management) found that such disagreement occurred more than half the time. Key areas of conflict were over such matters as registering protests to the engineering department over unrealistic standards, moving up a maintenance schedule on critical equipment, granting time off to employees, revising production schedules to accommodate good customers, spending money for a safety guard, and turning down a job applicant the personnel department said was qualified.

What other sources can you draw upon for your authority?

In addition to your organizational "right" to get things done, you may often need to draw from other, more personal sources. Your employer tries to establish your organizational rights by granting you a title or a rank, by depicting your position on an organization chart, and by some visible demonstration of status such as a desk or an office or some special privilege. Ordinarily you must reinforce this authority—or power—with one of the following:

- Your job knowledge or craftsmanship
- Your personal influence in the organization (whom you know and can get to help you or your team)
- Your personal charm (if you have it)
- Your ability to see that things get done (performance)
- Your persuasive ability (a communication skill)
- Occasionally your muscle or physical strength

All these sources are important because employees tend to restrict their acknowledgment of organizational rights over them. They expect their supervisors to show a little more real power than that. When employees come to accept your authority as deserved or earned (acceptance theory of authority rather than institutional), you will find that your people relationships will improve.

Should a distinction be drawn between authority, responsibility, and accountability?

Yes, although it may appear to you to be only a technical one. As your boss, for example, I might be held accountable to higher management for the way in which operating supplies are con-

FIGURE 9-7.

Supervisory Responsibility Survey

Do you feel it is your responsibility to . . .		Yes	No	Don't Know
	1. Request that additional employees be hired as needed?	___	___	___
	2. Approve new employees assigned to you?	___	___	___
. . . select and train your employees?	3. Explain benefit plans such as group insurance and hospitalization to employees?	___	___	___
	4. Tell employees about upgrading and pay ranges?	___	___	___
	5. Make sure employees know rules of conduct and safety regulations?	___	___	___
	6. Train an understudy?	___	___	___
	7. Hold regular safety meetings?	___	___	___
	8. Prepare employee work schedules?	___	___	___
	9. Assign specific duties to workers?	___	___	___
	10. Assign responsibilities to assistants or group leaders?	___	___	___
. . . make work assignments and maintain discipline?	11. Delegate authority?	___	___	___
	12. Discipline employees?	___	___	___
	13. Discharge employees?	___	___	___
	14. Specify the kind and number of employees to do a job?	___	___	___
	15. Determine amount of work to be done by each employee in your group?	___	___	___
	16. Authorize overtime?	___	___	___
	17. Enforce safety rules?	___	___	___
	18. Transfer employees within your department?	___	___	___
	19. Interpret the union contract?	___	___	___
. . . handle employee problems with the union?	20. Process grievances with shop stewards?	___	___	___
	21. Prepare vacation schedules?	___	___	___
	22. Recommend changes in the contract?	___	___	___
	23. Lay off employees for lack of work?	___	___	___
	24. Grant leaves of absence?	___	___	___
	25. Explain to employees how their pay is calculated?	___	___	___
. . . know how pay and incentive systems work?	26. Determine allowances for faulty material or interruptions?	___	___	___
	27. Approve piece rates or standards before they become effective?	___	___	___
	28. Answer employees' questions regarding time studies or allowances?	___	___	___

Figure 9-7 (continued).

Supervisory Responsibility Survey

Do you feel it is your responsibility to . . .		Yes	No	Don't Know
. . . make these operating decisions?	29. Start jobs in process?	——	——	——
	30. Stop jobs in process?	——	——	——
	31. Authorize setup changes?	——	——	——
	32. Approve material substitutions?	——	——	——
	33. Requisition supplies to keep your department running?	——	——	——
	34. Determine whether material should be scrapped or reworked?	——	——	——
	35. Replan schedules due to breakdowns?	——	——	——
	36. Take unsafe tools out of service?	——	——	——
	37. Correct unsafe working conditions?	——	——	——
. . . tie in with other departments?	38. Know how an order flows through the company from start to finish?	——	——	——
	39. Understand what the staff departments do? Your relationship to them?	——	——	——
	40. Authorize maintenance and repair jobs?	——	——	——
	41. Requisition tools?	——	——	——
	42. Investigate accidents?	——	——	——
. . . be concerned with the way the job gets done?	43. Make suggestions for improvements in operating procedures in your department?	——	——	——
	44. Recommend changes in department layout?			
	45. Suggest materials handling methods to be used in your department?	——	——	——
	46. Discuss with staff the operating problems caused by proposed design changes?	——	——	——
. . . think about how much things cost?	47. Cut down on waste of materials and supplies?	——	——	——
	48. Keep adequate production records for checking output per machine and per worker-hour?	——	——	——
	49. Participate in setting up your department budget?			
	50. Investigate charges against your budget?			

served in my department. But I have the prerogative to delegate this responsibility to you—if I also grant you the authority to take any steps needed to protect these supplies. If you were to misuse these supplies or to lose track of them, I might discipline you for failing to discharge your responsibility in this matter. But I'd still be held accountable to my boss (and would be subject to discipline) for what happened—no matter which one of us was at fault. Similarly, when you delegate a minor responsibility to one of your employees (together with the necessary authority to carry it out), you will still be held accountable to your boss for the way in which this responsibility is carried out by your subordinate. In other words, you can delegate responsibility, but you cannot delegate accountability.

How much leeway do supervisors have in taking authoritative action?

██████████████ You can't draw a hard-and-fast rule to follow. Generally speaking, a company may establish three rough classifications of authority within which supervisors can make decisions:

- Class 1. Complete authority. Supervisors can take action without consulting their superiors.
- Class 2. Limited authority. Supervisors can take action they deem fit so long as the superior is told about it afterward.
- Class 3. No authority. Supervisors can take no action until they check with the superior.

If many decisions fall into class 3, supervisors will become little more than messengers. To improve this situation, first learn more about your company's policy and then spend time finding out how your bosses would act. If you can convince them that you would handle matters as they might, your bosses are more likely to transfer class 3 decisions into class 2, and as you prove yourself, from class 2 to class 1.

Note that the existing company policy would still prevail. The big change would be in permitting supervisory discretion. And this would be because you have demonstrated that you are qualified to translate front-office policy into front-line action.

Who can delegate authority and responsibility?

██████████████ Any member of management, including the supervisor, can usually delegate some responsibility—and authority. Remember, the two must go together.

A supervisor, for instance, who has responsibility for seeing that proper records are kept in the department may delegate that responsibility to a records clerk. But the clerk must also be given the authority to collect time sheets from the operators and to interview them if the data seems inaccurate. The supervisor wouldn't, however, delegate to the records clerk the authority to discipline an employee. Likewise, a supervisor can't delegate all the responsibility for seeing that accurate records are kept.

What is the chain of command?

▆▆▆▆▆▆▆▆▆▆▆ The term *chain of command* is a military phrase used to imply that orders and information in an organization should originate at the top, then proceed toward the bottom from one higher management level to the next lower without skipping any levels or crossing over to another chain of command. The same procedure would be followed by information and requests going up the line.

Is it a bad practice to go out of channels?

▆▆▆▆▆▆▆▆▆▆▆ It's best to conform to the practice in your company. Channel is just a word to indicate the normal path that information, orders, or requests should travel when following the chain of command. The channel for customer orders to travel from the sales manager to the production supervisor might be from the sales manager to the production manager, from the production manager to the department superintendent, and from the department superintendent to the supervisor. It would be going out of channels if the sales manager gave the order directly to the supervisor.

The channel used by a supervisor to ask for a raise might be from the supervisor to the department head, from the department head to the production manager, and from the production manager to the manufacturing vice president. The supervisor would be going out of channels if the vice president were asked for a raise before each one of the other managers had been seen in progression.

Since authority and responsibility are delegated through the channels of a chain of command, for the most part it's better to handle your affairs (especially decisions) through them, too. It avoids your making changes without letting your boss know what's going on. And it prevents others from feeling another manager is going over the boss's head.

On the other hand, there are occasions when chain-of-command channels should be circumvented. In emergencies, or when time is essential, it makes sense to get a decision or advice from a higher authority other than your boss if your boss is not readily available.

For purposes of keeping people informed and for exchanging information, channels sometimes get in the way. There's really nothing wrong with your discussing matters with people in other departments or on other levels of the company—so long as you don't betray confidences. If you do cross channels, it's a good practice to tell your boss you are doing so, and why. That way, you won't seem to be doing something behind your boss's back. And that is something you should never do.

How do staff people exert influence?

█████████████ Staff departments exert influence, rather than real authority, because their responsibility is to advise and guide, not to take action themselves.

Before the days of staff departments (and when companies were smaller), an office manager or a shop superintendent tried to be informed on all kinds of subjects related to their fields. These subjects might include personnel management, merchandising, cost control, quality control. As companies grew larger and processes became more complex, many managers found it was wiser to employ assistants who could devote their full time and attention to becoming authorities in each of these phases of operations. These assistants have become known as staff assistants, and the departments they manage, staff departments.

It's a mistake to assume (in most cases) that a staff department tells you how to do something. More often than not the staff department suggests that you do something differently, or advises that your department is off target (on quality, for instance), or provides information for your guidance. This isn't evasion. It's an honest recognition that the line people must retain the authority to run the department, but that to stand up to today's competition, you need the counsel of a specialist in some side areas.

If supervisors are smart, they will make every use they can of the staff department's knowledge. If you were building a house yourself for the first time and someone offered to furnish you free the advice of a first-rate carpenter, a top-notch mason, a heating specialist, and a journeyman painter, you'd jump at the chance. The same holds true in accepting the advice and guidance available from the staff departments and other specialists when you are tackling a management problem.

When should you delegate some of your work?

█████████████ Delegate when you find you can't personally keep up with everything you feel you should do. Just giving minor time-consuming tasks to others will save your time for bigger things. Let one employee double-check the production report, for example, and send another employee down the line to see who wants to work overtime.

Arrange to have certain jobs taken over when you're absent from your department in an emergency or during vacation. Keep it to routine matters, if you will, and to those requiring a minimum of authority. But do try to get rid of the task of filling out routine requisitions and reports, making calculations and entries, checking supplies, and running errands.

How can you do a better job of delegating?

Start by seeing yourself as a manager. Recognize that no matter how good a person you might be, you'll always have more responsibilities than you can carry out yourself.

The trick of delegating is to concentrate on the most important matters yourself. Keep a close eye, for instance, on the trend of production costs: That's a big item. But let someone else check the temperature of the quenching oil in the heat treater. That's less important.

Trouble begins when you can't distinguish between the big and the little matters. You may feel you can put off checking the production record: It can wait until the day of reckoning at the end of the month. You may think that unless the quenching oil temperature is just right, the heat treater will spoil a $500 die today. But in the long run you'll lose your sanity if you don't see that the small jobs must get done by someone else.

Be ready, too, to give up certain work that you enjoy. A supervisor must learn to let go of those tasks that rightfully belong to a subordinate. Otherwise, larger and more demanding assignments may not get done. And don't worry too much about getting blamed by your boss for delegating to an employee work the boss has given to you. Generally speaking, supervisors should be interested only in seeing that the job is done the right way, not in who carries it out. See Figure 9-8 for an idea on how to decide what jobs to target for delegation.

Should you delegate everything?

Don't go too far. Some things are yours only. When a duty involves technical knowledge that only you possess, it would be wrong to let someone less able take over. And it's wrong to trust confidential information to others.

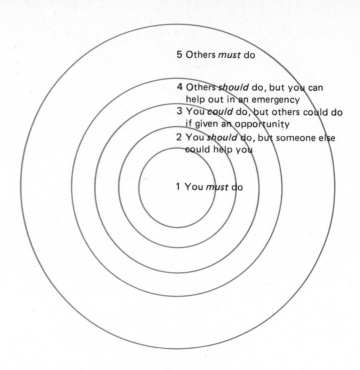

5 Others *must* do

4 Others *should* do, but you can help out in an emergency

3 You *could* do, but others could do if given an opportunity

2 You *should* do, but someone else could help you

1 You *must* do

FIGURE 9-8. Supervisor's Task and Delegation Chart.

What should you tell employees about jobs delegated to them?

Give them a clear statement of what they are to do, how far they can go, and how much checking you intend to do. Let employees know the relative importance of the job so that they can judge how much attention it should receive. There's no point in letting an employee think that making a tally will lead to a promotion if you consider it just a routine task.

Tell employees why you delegated the job. If it shows you have confidence in them, they will try that much harder. But if they think you're pushing off all the dirty jobs on them, they may deliberately make mistakes.

Don't mislead employees about authority. You don't want them trying to crack your whip. But do define the scope of the task and see that others in your department know that this new task isn't something an employee assumed without authorization. Let it be known that you gave the assignment and that you'll expect cooperation from the other workers.

Why should employees accept a delegated job?

Employees who accept a delegated job outside of their own job responsibilities are really taking the job on speculation. They have a right to know what's in it for them:

• Employees who take on an extra duty get a chance to learn. If they have never seen how the individual records in the department are tabulated, here's a chance for them to get a better perception of what's going on.
• Delegated jobs provide more job satisfaction. Employees thrive on varied assignments. This is a chance to build interest by letting employees do something out of the ordinary.
• Delegation is sometimes a reward for other work well done. If you can truthfully say that you wouldn't trust anyone else with a certain delegated task, this will help build employee pride and feeling of status.

Are there any organizational don'ts?

Yes, but not very many. Once an organization is set up, pragmatism and practicality ought to prevail. In fact, some odd—and informal—arrangements occasionally work out very well. For example, a highly successful Canton, Ohio, firm operated for years without a visual organization chart. Its president thought the staff would develop the most effective relationships without one, and apparently it did. Nevertheless, in the design stages, at least, there are a few hazards of organization that ought to be guarded against.

1. Don't let the chain of command get too long. Keep the number of responsibility levels at a minimum; otherwise, some information never trickles all the way to the bottom.
2. Don't ask one person to report to two bosses. Anyone caught in this nutcracker knows the dilemma: Which boss's work comes first?
3. Don't make fuzzy job assignments. When there is a gray area between two positions, overlap, conflict, and duplication of effort are invited.
4. Don't put responsibilities with different objectives into the same group. For example, to make the production department responsible for monitoring the quality of its own output, with the power of acceptance or rejection, can lead to harmful collusion.
5. Don't be too rigid. Try to retain flexibility for contingent situations—those problems that inevitably crop up and need nonstandard assignments. It is said that Napoleon would not have lost at Waterloo if he had applied contingency management.

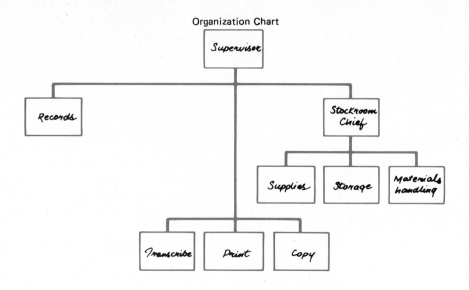

Organization Chart

FIGURE 9-9. Organization Planning for a Reproduction Department.

How can supervisors
best organize the work in their departments?

Use the same approach that top management does. This can be done in four steps, as illustrated in Figure 9-9.

1. Analyze the work that must be done to accomplish the objectives of the department. In this example of an office records reproduction department, the supervisor knows that the work

Step 1 Work to be done	Step 2 Main operations	Support services	Step 3 Consolidate work	Step 4 Add managerial controls
Transcribe	Transcribe	Store supplies	} Central stores	Stockroom Chief
Print	Print	Store copies		
Copy	Copy	Move materials		
Stock supplies		Keep records		
Store finished copies				
Move materials				
Keep records				

primarily involves transcribing, printing, and copying. But the supervisor also realizes that this requires operation of a stockroom for supplies, a storage area for finished copies, and some way of moving materials within the department. This supervisor knows, too, that some sort of records of supplies, inventories, costs, orders, etc., will have to be maintained personally.

2. Determine the best pattern of grouping activities for long-term operation. In this case the supervisor divides the work to be done into main operations and support (or staff) services—a line-staff structure.

3. Consolidate operations or services in such a way as to provide for lowest costs with greatest effectiveness. This supervisor combined supplies, storage, and material handling in one group, leaving recordkeeping as a separate unit.

4. Set up management, or management-oriented, positions to furnish optimum planning, coordination, supervision, and control. In this illustration the supervisor appointed a stockroom chief to head the consolidated stock-supplies handling service. All other employees would report directly to the supervisor.

supervisory word power

Organization. The structure derived from systematic grouping of the tasks to be performed and establishing formal relationships that strengthen the ability of people to work more effectively together in pursuing common objectives.

Responsibility and authority. An obligation on the part of a manager or supervisor to see that certain organizational tasks are performed, coupled inseparably with the power necessary to carry out these tasks.

Accountability. A supervisor or manager's liability for the way in which organizational obligations are discharged, either personally or by those managers and supervisors to whom he or she has delegated responsibility and authority to perform them.

Delegation. The assignment, or entrustment, to subordinates of organizational responsibilities and obligations along with appropriate organizational authority, power, and rights.

Line and staff. The most common kind of organizational structure, in which line managers hold accountability for results that most directly affect profits, or other corporate goals, while staff managers hold accountability for results that most directly affect the processes by which line managers accomplish their goals.

Other Important Terms in This Chapter

acceptance theory of authority
chain of command
functional organization
geographic organization
institutional authority
matrix organization
organizational channels
power
product organization
project or task force organization
span of control
Table of Organization

reading comprehension

1. What can a supervisor do to avoid being only an intermediary or a messenger?

2. What is the purpose of an organization chart? Is it possible to do without one?

3. Compare the formal organization with the informal organization.

4. In a manufacturing organization, which departments are likely to be line and which ones staff?

5. In a service organization such as a bank, which departments are likely to be considered line and which staff?

6. Managers and supervisors choose the kind of organization structure that will best fulfill its basic purpose in their work group or department. What is this purpose?

7. Based on what you know of human relations, should managers who have the choice stress authority derived from the institution or stemming from employee acceptance? Why?

8. Why must authority and responsibility be passed together to subordinates?

9. Give examples of companies, departments, or other groups that might likely be structured by using matrix organization. What do these groups have in common?

10. Would it be a good thing to have an especially versatile employee report to the maintenance supervisor as well as to the production supervisor? Why?

supervision in action

THE CASE OF THE FAST-FOOD CLEANUP. **A case study in human relations involving organizational practices, with questions for you to answer.**

"Which is it going to be?" asked Charlie J., a porter at the Bronze Burger, a fast-food franchise restaurant in Cincinnati. "Am I going to sweep the parking lot, or am I going to mop up the kitchen?"

Charlie's question was directed at Karen W., manager of the Bronze Burger.

"It should be obvious to you that the kitchen takes precedence over the parking lot," said Karen. "Food is our business. We must keep the kitchen clean at all times. And if the cook tells you to clean the kitchen, you better hop to it."

"That's what you tell me now," said Charlie. "But you should have heard the blistering I got from the out-front service chief a couple of minutes ago. He said that if I didn't get the parking lot swept before noon, I could look for a new job."

"The out-front chief is right," said Karen. "You've got to keep after the outside of the shop or we will be losing business from customers who drive in and see containers and slopped food all over the lot. But, for the moment, the kitchen job comes first. Grab your mop and get going."

"You better tell that to the out-front chief. He'll have my hide otherwise," said Charlie.

"Don't worry about him," said Karen. "Just get the kitchen mopped now. When you finish that, get your broom and go outside to the parking lot."

Charlie J. returned to the kitchen, got his mop, and within a few minutes was swabbing its quarry-tile floor. When he was half through, Jerry, the out-front chief, rushed into the kitchen. "What's going on here?" Jerry demanded. "I told you to get the parking lot swept before noon. It's a mess out there."

"I'm only doing what I've been told," said Charlie.

"No, you're not. I told you to sweep the parking lot."

"Tell that to the cook," said Charlie. "And tell it to Karen, too. She's the boss, and she said to do what the cook told me to."

With that, Jerry stomped out front to where Karen was watching the work of the serving clerks.

Jerry grabbed her by the arm. "Karen," he said, "you'll have to do something about Charlie. And about the cook, too. Charlie is paying no attention to me. And the cook keeps insisting that Charlie do the kitchen work first."

"In this instance," said Karen, "Charlie and the cook are right.

The kitchen needs mopping before any more food comes out of it today."

"The parking lot needs sweeping," said Jerry, "if you are going to have any customers. The place is a mess. You told me that the outside areas must be kept spotless. You also told me that Charlie was assigned to me for that duty."

"He is," said Karen, "but sometimes the kitchen work will have to come first."

Jerry threw down his apron and walked away.

Two days later Jerry told Charlie that the restaurant tables needed cleaning and that he should get to them when he could. Charlie shrugged and said, "I'll get to them when I've finished in the kitchen."

Karen, coming on shift, took one look at the state of the uncleaned tables in the restaurant, found Jerry, and said, "What's happening out front? The tables are in terrible condition. Your responsibility is to see that they are kept spotless. We'll lose customers if this keeps up."

Jerry replied, "I am doing all I can. I spoke to Charlie about getting them cleaned up. As you told me the other day, his first responsibility is to the cook. After he finishes in the kitchen, he will get to the tables."

"That won't do," said Karen. "You and the cook will have to work out a better way of sharing Charlie's time."

1. What do you suggest Jerry do now?
2. What do you think of Karen's organizational setup?
3. If you were Charlie, what would your reaction be?
4. If you were Karen, how would you organize Charlie's work and his reporting relationships?

enriching your viewpoint

To gain a broader and deeper knowledge of organization practices, the following readings are recommended:

Black, James M., *The Basics of Supervisory Management,* McGraw-Hill Book Company, New York, 1975, Chap. 5, "How to Get Results Through Improved Delegation."

Carzo, Rocco Jr., and John Yanouzas, "Effects of Flat and Tall Organizational Structures," *Administrative Science Quarterly,* Vol. 14, 1969, pp. 178–191.

Dale, E., and L.F. Urwick, *Staff in Organization,* McGraw-Hill Book Company, New York, 1960.

Drucker, Peter, "New Templates for Today's Organizations," *Harvard Business Review,* January–February 1974, pp. 45–52.

Galbraith, J.R., "Matrix Organization Designs," *Business Horizons,*
Vol. 14, No. 1, 1971, pp. 29–40.

Glueck, William F., *Management,* The Dryden Press, Inc., Hinsdale, Ill.,
1977, Chap. 15, "Organizing and Coordinating Work Units."

Haimann, Theo, and Raymond L. Hilgert, *Supervision: Concepts and
Practices of Management,* 2d ed., South-Western Publishing Company, Inc., Cincinnati, 1977, Chap. 10, "Creating an Effective Organization."

Petit, Thomas A., *Fundamentals of Management Coordination:
Supervisors, Middle Managers and Executives,* John Wiley &
Sons, Inc., New York, 1975, Chap. 22, "Design of the Organization."

Viola, Richard, "The Span of Management in the Life Insurance Industry," *Economic and Business Bulletin,* No. 1, 1975, pp. 18–25.

Woodward, Joan, *Industrial Organization: Theory and Practice,* Ox-
ford University Press, New York, 1965.

MAKE ROOM FOR ME!

10

CHAPTER staffing with
human resources

What are the symptoms
of poor human resources staffing?

Costs so high that they don't allow your department to operate at
a profit are the most obvious symptom. And your first corrective
step should be to see that you have only the right number of employees on the job.

Signs of inefficient work force management also include a high
turnover rate, excessive absences and lateness, lots of grievances, poor quality of work, and lowered output. Each one tells
you that there's a big chance you don't have the right person
working for you, or if you do, that person isn't working on the right
job at the right time.

What does it cost to
put a new employee on the payroll?

It is not unusual for a manufacturing company to find that it costs over $3,000 for one net addition to its labor force at the assembly-worker level. This is not unusual when you consider costs of running want ads, operating an employment office, handling paperwork, and breaking in the new person. For a technician or engineer the figure could be $6,000 or more.

How much does it cost to keep
an employee on the payroll for a year?

A conservative estimate of the cost of keeping a semiskilled factory or office worker on the payroll for one year is $12,000. Figure it this way. Salary for a good employee runs more than $7,500 a year. It costs an average of $1,200 to train and bring a new employee up to normal production. Another $400 is included to offset the cost of the one in three employees who doesn't work out. Add $1,700 in fringe benefits that don't show up in salary. And cap this off with another $1,200—cost of the depreciation on the capital investment that makes the job possible.

Consequently, each employee who works for you must return about $12,000 in productive efforts before the company can break even. If you supervise ten employees, you can figure you're managing a payroll of more than $100,000 per year. That's why human resources management is so important.

What phases of work
force staffing concern supervisors most?

The supervisor's chief responsibilities for a plant's work force management could be summed up by saying the supervisor should have the right worker on the right job at the right time. How can this be done? By making accurate forecasts of the number of workers needed to staff the department, by taking an active interest in the kind of employees the company hires, and by maintaining working conditions that can attract and hold the best employees.

How do you forecast work force requirements?

It's really a matter of looking ahead—and applying simple arithmetic. Time studies and labor standards all make a forecast more accurate, but you can do very well without them.

Step 1. Find out what your department is scheduled to produce for the next week, month, quarter, or as far ahead as you can determine. If you don't know that, the chances are slight that you'll make efficient use of the people who work for you.

Step 2. Calculate how much the work schedule means in terms of total worker-hours. You can do this by getting an estimate from the time-study, industrial engineering, or planning and scheduling department—if one exists in your company. Their schedules are certainly based upon machine time and work force estimates.

If man-hour requirements aren't available elsewhere, you'll have to make your own estimate. Do this either by checking times for previous or similar jobs or by making careful estimates of the time required for each job. Keep your figures in terms of man-hours or man-days. But be specific and allow time for setups and teardowns. Try to recall delays associated with each job and allow time for these.

Where jobs are machine-controlled (that is, the job can't be done any faster than the speed at which the machine runs), base your estimates on (1) how long the machine will take to do each job—allowing for breakdowns and idle time—and (2) how many operator-hours are needed to run the machine.

Step 3. Convert your totals to man-hours and divide by 8 to see how many man-days it will take you to complete your schedule for the period you've selected.

Step 4. Divide the total man-days by the number of working days during the period to find the number of employees you'll need. But don't stop here.

Step 5. Check how many indirect persons—sweepers, material handlers, setup persons—you'll need to service the required number of employees during this period (unless you included these in step 2).

Step 6. Add the number of employees (direct labor) to the number of indirect persons to get the total needed.

Step 7. Make allowances for absences. How many days absent per month do employees in your department average? How many man-days a month do all your employees combined lose? Suppose, for example, it's 5 man-days a month. That's just the same as saying that you can expect to be short-handed 5 days a month, which may interfere with meeting your schedule. If you add an extra employee, you can expect to be overstaffed 15 days a month—which is costly.

What is an example of
forecasting work force requirements?

1. Suppose your schedule shows that during July your department must produce 1,000 widgets, 250 gadgets, and 60 umphlets.

2. Widgets and gadgets are hand-assembly jobs. Umphlets are produced on a machine. Previous production records, or time studies, or standards show the following:

Widgets: Average 50 per day with 10 employees

$$\frac{1,000}{50} = 20 \text{ days}$$

20 days × 10 employees × 8 hours = 1,600 man-hours

Gadgets: Average 10 per day with 2 employees

$$\frac{250}{10} = 25 \text{ days}$$

25 days × 2 employees × 8 hours =   400 man-hours

Umphlets: Average 3 per day, allowing for down time, require 1 operator

$$\frac{60}{3} = 20 \text{ days}$$

20 days × 1 operator × 8 hours =   160 man-hours

Total man-hours for all three units:
1,600 man-hours (widgets) + 400 man-hours (gadgets) + 160 man-hours (umphlets) = 2,160 man-hours

3. Convert to man-days:

$$\frac{2,160 \text{ man-hours}}{8 \text{ hours per day}} = 270 \text{ man-days per month}$$

4. Average number of employees needed for month:

$$\frac{270 \text{ man-days}}{20 \text{ days/month}} = 13\frac{1}{2} \text{ employees for the month}$$

5. Add number of indirect employees. Three materials handlers take care of the gadget and umphlet operation. A combination setup person and packer handles the widget line. That's four employees each day all month.

6. Average number of employees needed in July:

$$13\tfrac{1}{2} \text{ direct}$$
$$\underline{4 \text{ indirect}}$$
$$17\tfrac{1}{2} \text{ employees}$$

7. Allowance for absences. Record for department shows your employees lose on the average of a half-day per month:
$17\tfrac{1}{2}$ employees $\times$ 4 hours per month absent $=$ 70 hours absent per month
70 hours is about one-half of one employee for a month. So

$$17\tfrac{1}{2} \text{ employees needed}$$
$$\underline{\tfrac{1}{2} \text{ employee for absences}}$$
$$18 \quad \text{employees needed for the month of July}$$

You should be cautioned that this is a simplified example. In some cases the numbers of employees needed cannot be averaged by estimating gross man-hours. Transfers of employees between operations can become impractical or can even be prohibited. The supervisor in the example, for instance, might not be able to use the umphlet operator on the widget line, or the widget operator on the umphlet line. In addition, you cannot presume that in practice you will have unlimited machines for assignment. Accordingly, you will encounter scheduling bottenecks because of machine or space limitations and may have to plan second or third shifts.

Should you overstaff or understaff?

That depends. If you plan for too many employees, department costs will go up unless your schedule and machine availability will permit you to assign them to productive jobs. It's bad, too, to have idle people in the shop or to use them on make-work jobs. Overstaffing, however, does allow you to set up production in emergencies and assures your meeting delivery dates.

Understaffing can be just as bad. It can get you behind in schedule and in trouble on deliveries. It can also give employees the feeling of being overworked. And it doesn't give you much flexibility.

Your company can minimize either overstaffing or understaffing by pooling the work force estimates of each supervisor and maintaining an optimum-size labor pool as a cushion against unpredictables—such as unusual absences or a sharp upward adjustment in schedules.

How far ahead should you plan?

██████████████ As far as you can—even a year ahead if possible. Demands by employees for a guaranteed weekly or annual wage have mainly been for a guarantee of a more stable job.

Job stability is just as desirable to management as it is to labor. Layoffs and rehiring are costly. One very good way to minimize both is to make your forecast of work force requirements accurate and to make them as far ahead as possible. That way you can smooth the hills and valleys of your labor requirements. There's little point in laying off five workers this week if you're going to need ten more workers a week from now. It's much better if you can level out the scheduling in your department so that you keep, say, seven or eight of these employees working continuously all the time.

It's recognized that such optimum forecasting cannot always be done—that interruptions in supply, restrictions to storage capacity, and unpredictable demands by customers interfere with the best plans.

What is meant by balancing the work force?

██████████████ Making sure that the number of employees on hand just matches the work load. Most departments have peaks and valleys that last an hour or a day. Mismatches that extend over a week, however, are costly and should be avoided. One way to balance your employee work load more consistently is to prepare a look-ahead work force trial balance, using a work sheet like the one illustrated in Figure 10-1. This example looks 12 months ahead. If your work load is changeable, you could make such a sheet month by month.

How do you measure turnover?

██████████████ Turnover is the name given to the measure of how many people come to work for you and don't stay for one reason or another. Turnover includes employees who are hired or rehired and employees who are laid off, who quit, or who are discharged. It also includes those who either retire or die.

For consistency's sake the U.S. Department of Labor suggests that the rate of turnover compare only the total number of separations (quits, fires, deaths, etc.) with the average number of employees on your payroll during a particular period. The *rate of turnover* is calculated as follows:

$$\frac{\text{Number of separations} \times 100}{\text{Average size of work force}} = \text{Turnover percentage}$$

Figure 10-1.

Work Force Trial Balance Planning Sheet*

Dept: _____   **Period: from** _____ **to** _____.

1. Number of workers needed to meet present work load:
   Direct   _____
   Indirect   _____
   Subtotal
                                                                        _____
2. Number of additional workers to allow for:
   A. Scheduled workday losses
      Holidays   _____
      Vacations   _____
      Subtotal
                                                                        _____
   B. Unscheduled workday losses
      Sickness and other excused absences   _____
      Unexcused absences   _____
      Subtotal
                                                                        _____
3. Total number of workers needed to staff department at beginning
   of period: (line 1 + subtotal 2A + subtotal 2B)
                                                                        _____
4. Number of workers to be added during the period to:
   A. Replace anticipated work force losses
      Retirements   _____
      Promotions and transfers   _____
      Discharges   _____
      Leaves of absence   _____
      Subtotal
                                                                        _____
   B. Replace unanticipated work force losses†
      Resignations and quits   _____
      Disabilities   _____
      Deaths   _____
      Subtotal
                                                                        _____
5. Total number of employees needed to replace losses during the
   period
      Subtotal 4A + Subtotal 4B
                                                                        _____
6. Number of employees needed to meet anticipated change in
   department work load during the period
   A. Additions to meet increase in work load   _____
   B. Less removals to allow for decrease in work load   (−)_____
7. Total number of workers needed at end of period:
      Number on line 3   _____
      Number on line 5   _____
      Number on line 6A or B (+ or −)   _____
      Total   _____

*All entries are in number of workers.
†If no past records are available, use 5% of the total on line 1.

For instance, if you had an average of 50 employees during the month, but you laid off 3, the turnover would be 3. Your turnover rate would be $\frac{3 \times 100}{50} = 6$ percent per month. If that rate persisted, your turnover rate for the year would be 72 percent (6×12).

Turnover rates vary from department to department, from company to company, and from industry to industry. The national average for all business in the United States is about 7 percent per month, or 82 percent per year!

Decisions as to what kind of separations and hires to include in turnover computations vary from organization to organization. Obviously, if certain kinds of separations or hires are excluded, the turnover rates will be lower. So it's good to know exactly what the specifications are when comparing turnover rates.

What causes turnover?

Turnover is generally considered to be the single best measure of morale. Poor morale can result from many things. Two of the most important of these are poor supervision and having the wrong person on the wrong job. The wrong person on the wrong job can mean poor hiring procedures—or poor placement procedures after a good person is put on the payroll. This chapter will discuss the latter causes.

What's so bad about absenteeism?

Absences (like turnover) are costly—to the company as well as to the employee. If it costs about $12,000 per year to keep a person on the payroll, then each day that person is absent could cost your department something like $60. Even the direct cost doesn't tell the whole story. Absences frequently cause overtime, through delays in getting an operation started or a machine running. And every supervisor can testify to the aggravation absence and lateness cause. It's the biggest obstacle you have in your work force planning—from day to day or from month to month.

There are two popular ways to compute absenteeism rates:

$$\text{Absenteeism rate} = \frac{\text{Total days absent}}{\text{Average size of work force}} \qquad (1)$$

$$= \text{Average days absent per employee}$$

$$\text{Absenteeism rate} = \frac{\text{Total days absent} \times 100}{\text{man-days worked and man-days lost}} \quad (2)$$

$$= \text{Percentage of scheduled man-days lost}$$

For example, suppose at the end of 6 months a supervisor found that the schedule showed a crew of 25 employees working for 120 days. Examining the record, the supervisor found that 10 employees had worked every day (10 × 120) for 1,200 man-days; 10 employees worked 116 days (10 × 116) for 1,160 man-days; 3 employees worked only 110 days (3 × 110) for 330 man-days; and 2 employees worked only 100 days (2 × 100) for 200 man-days. The total man-days worked is 2,890. If all 25 employees had worked every day for 120 days, the total man-days would have amounted to 3,000. Therefore, 110 man-days were lost (3,000 − 2,890). The department's absenteeism rate would be:

$$\frac{110 \text{ days absent}}{25 \text{ employees}} = 4.4 \text{ days lost per employee} \quad (1)$$
$$\text{in 6 months or 8.8 days per year}$$

The percent of man-days lost each year would be calculated as follows:

$$\frac{110 \text{ days absent} \times 100}{2,890 + 110} = \frac{110 \times 100}{3,000} = 3.7 \text{ percent of} \quad (2)$$
$$\text{scheduled}$$
$$\text{man-days lost}$$

National averages for days lost per employee range from 9 days per year to as high as 3 days per month (36 days per year). Absence and lateness, like turnover, can be controlled by good supervision. But it's better to avoid this demand upon your supervisory time and skill if you can. And you can, by screening out applicants who have displayed these undesirable characteristics in the past or are likely to develop them on the job in your company—simply because they are unsuited for the work they were hired to do.

How can better hiring reduce turnover and absences?

Selecting the proper person to fit first the company and then the available job opening hits at the turnover and absenteeism problem at its source. There are hundreds of thousands of people looking for work who would be misfits almost anywhere. But there are millions who would probably be out of place in your company. Joe doesn't like close work. Pete can't stand heavy work. Sue wants a job with lots of room for initiative. Alma wants a job where she doesn't have to think. And so on. Turnover and absences show that Joe, Pete, Sue, and Alma didn't find work to suit them in your company.

To complicate the matter further, Sue may want a job that allows for initiative, but maybe she doesn't have the native ability to produce without close supervision. Alma wants a job where she doesn't have to think, but maybe all those jobs call for someone who can work rapidly and Alma is slow as can be.

A third complication, and perhaps the most serious, is that the ability to handle the human side of the job varies widely with different people. And, of course, the human relations requirements of jobs vary, too. If you put employees who like to be one of the gang back in the corner working alone, they won't be happy no matter how much they like the work or how skillfully they can perform it. Similarly, a person who has never been able to get along well with superiors won't be much of a help on a job where there has to be a lot of close supervision.

In what ways can you improve your hiring results?

Just formalizing the employment procedure and making it systematic help rule out the big mistakes that often occur during haphazard hiring. For instance, every applicant should fill out some sort of form before being given consideration. On such a form the applicant should furnish critical information about work experience and education. A glance at the form will rule out people who don't meet educational or job-experience requirements.

The application form can tell you something more. A work record will show up the job hopper who has held a dozen jobs in three or four years. This kind of person is always a big employment risk. Periods of prolonged employment are good indicators of stability, even if the indicator doesn't always prove reliable.

Chances are that your responsibility in your company will be limited to cooperating with the employment or personnel department. If you understand what they are trying to do for you, they'll be able to do a better job for you. A prominent personnel executive put it this way: "The personnel department gives the candidate the first interview, checks references, and may conduct mechanical or clerical aptitude tests. The medical department makes certain the applicant is physically fit. But there is no substitute for the supervisory interview. The supervisor has to live and work with the employee. The supervisor should be satisfied the new person fills the bill."

Will tests help to select better employees?

Over 50,000 firms think so. Properly selected, administered, and evaluated, so-called psychological tests can be a big help in picking better workers. Tests may be simple and direct, such as those that show whether an applicant can read and write or perform the simple arithmetic that recordkeeping on the job may demand. Other, highly specific tests may enable an applicant to demonstrate the ability to perform the skills your job demands. For instance, any person looking for a job can assure you of competence in operating a multiple-spindle automatic or a calculator. A ten-minute tryout will prove whether the claim is valid. These "can do?" tests, called *performance tests*, are widely used.

Which tests are most sensitive to restrictions of the Civil Rights Act of 1964?

Psychological tests that attempt to find out whether a person has the capability to learn a particular kind of job (aptitude tests) can also be fairly reliable, but under present United States laws these are often open to challenge by the applicant. For that reason your company may or may not choose to use them.

Personality, intelligence, and job or career *interest* tests are widely used for applicants seeking higher-level management positions. But these, too, must be fully validated and their reliability proved before they can pass the civil rights hurdle. *Validity* simply means that the test really measures what it is supposed to measure. *Reliability* means that if an applicant were to take a test several times, the score would always be the same.

Underlying the challenges of validity and reliability is the requirement that any test given to applicants (1) should be directly related to the job's content and (2) should not discriminate unfairly against the person taking them. In other words, it would not be right to require that an applicant for a typist's job pass a test designed for an administrative secretary. Nor should the test be worded in such a way that it favors a person with a particular background over another who does not have it—unless it can be shown that the job requires that background.

Who gives the psychological tests to job applicants?

Most companies employ either a psychologist or someone else professionally trained to administer tests to job applicants. But it's important that the supervisor know what the tests are trying to prove and how reliable the tests are in selecting employees who will be successful on the job.

What good are physical examinations?

As a supervisor, you'll want to know whether a person assigned to your department has any physical limitations. There's no way of actually finding out about poor eyesight, a hernia, or a heart condition, for instance, without a complete physical examination. A physical defect doesn't necessarily rule out an applicant, but knowledge of it does assure that person's being put on a job where the best work can be done and where the disability is not aggravated.

What can a supervisor do to improve the selection process?

Whenever a supervisor is given a chance to interview a prospective job candidate, that's a golden opportunity to help make sure the department gets a first-rate employee. Interviewing points that apply most directly to selecting employees are reviewed here.

Know what kind of employee you want. Don't describe the person vaguely as a good worker who will stay on the job. That doesn't tell you a thing about the qualities you are looking for to suit the job that is open. Try making a checklist of necessary or desirable qualifications:

* Experience. The applicant should have worked a couple of years on multiple-spindle drill presses, for example, even though they weren't exactly like ours.
* Blueprint reading. The person has to be able to work directly from prints.
* Speed. This job doesn't require a quick worker as much as it requires a steady, consistent worker.
* Initiative. Does the applicant's previous experience show work without close supervision?
* Attendance. Has the applicant a good record of attendance (because this job needs someone who's going to be here every day)?

See enough candidates. Your personnel department will probably screen out the obvious misfits before an applicant is sent to you for approval. But if you do the hiring directly, make a point of interviewing at least three candidates before making up your mind. That way you get a chance to make comparisons and to get the feel of the prevailing labor market. For some hard-to-fill jobs, you may have to see as many as 20 or 30 persons.

What should you talk about to job candidates?

Preview the job for the applicant. It's a great time-saver to tell the applicant what the fixed requirements of the job are. Mention such things as job title and relationships to other jobs, and the main activities involved in the job like walking, standing, sitting, performing heavy work. Tell the applicant what kind of materials and machines are used and describe the working conditions.

It's especially wise to forewarn an applicant about any undesirable conditions like fumes, dampness, night work. Don't scare the applicant, but be sure the facts are known ahead of time. Better that the applicant turn down the job than walk off it after three days.

You can describe the good parts about the job—what kind of advancement there is, the company's benefit programs, and so forth. This is the time to do some sound, factual selling.

What kind of questions should you ask the applicant?

Don't turn the interview into a third degree by asking too many point-blank questions—especially those that can be answered by a simple yes or no. The job seeker is likely to be on guard during the interview, anyway. The answer will ordinarily be "yes" to a question like, "Did you get along well with your boss in the last place you worked?"

Ask questions that begin with what, where, why, when, who. This gives the applicant a chance to talk and while talking, to show you the kind of person he or she really is. If the applicant does most of the talking and you do most of the listening, you'll have lots of time to form an opinion. And that's the purpose of the interview.

Ask questions like these:

• What about your education? How do you feel that it would help you do the kind of work we do here?
• Where did you get your most valuable experience? Suppose you tell me about your working experience, starting with your first job.
• Whom did you report to in your last job? Can you describe that supervisor?
• When did you first decide you liked to do this sort of work? What have you found most difficult about it? Most pleasant?

- How would you describe your health? What kind of an attendance record have you maintained during the last year?
- Why did you leave the job at the XYZ Company?

In addition, ask questions about the applicant's occupation. You can find out pretty quickly whether the person is exaggerating. And if you discover that some of the applicant's facts don't jibe, ask for clarification of the discrepancy. Say something like, "Let me see now, who was it you said you worked for in 1973?" Or, "What did you do just before you took that job at GM?"

What kind of questions are you forbidden to ask a job applicant?

Be careful. Listen to whatever your personnel department advises. Otherwise, you as well as your company may get into trouble over some unintended equal employment opportunity infringement. The following is just a partial list of prohibitions:

- *Race or color.* Don't ask. Don't comment.
- *Religion.* Don't ask. Don't say, "This is a (Catholic, Protestant, Jewish, or other) organization."
- *National origin.* Don't ask. Don't comment.
- *Sex.* Don't ask. Don't comment. Don't indicate prejudgment about physical capabilities.
- *Age.* Don't ask, "How old are you?" Don't ask for a birth date. You *may* ask if the applicant is between the ages of 18 and 65.
- *Marital status.* Don't ask for this, or for ages of children, or where a spouse works.
- *Disability.* You may ask if the person has a present disability that will interfere with the job to be performed, but not about past disabilities or illnesses.
- *Address.* You may ask for this and how long the person has lived there. You may ask if the applicant is an American citizen and, if not, whether the person has the legal right to remain permanently in the United States. It is generally unlawful to press for answers beyond this point.
- *Criminal record.* You may ask if the person has ever been convicted of a crime and when and where it took place. You may *not* ask if a person has ever been arrested, nor can you deny employment on this basis unless it can be proved it would damage the employer's business.
- *Physical capabilities.* Don't ask how tall or how strong an applicant is. This may indicate a sexist prejudice. You may explain physical aspects of the job such as lifting, pulling, and so forth, and show how it must be performed. And you may

require a physical examination. The hope is that if the applicant has a clear chance to estimate the job's physical requirements, the application will be withdrawn if the job appears too demanding or beyond the person's capabilities. Legally, however, you may not make that decision during an interview.

Questions about *education* and *experience* are pretty much unrestricted. The main point to check against in any interviewing area is that the question's relevance to the job for which the individual is applying can undeniably be shown. This legal requirement is called a bona fide occupational qualification, or BFOQ.

What do you look for while interviewing an applicant?

Besides the factual things you obviously need to know about an applicant's skills and know-how, you'll want to be alert to what the interview tells you about:

Background. Do the applicant's education and experience, and even residence and off-the-job associates, indicate the person will be happy working with the people in your company? If education isn't a strong point and hobbies are bowling and baseball, the applicant won't find many friends among employees who take their education seriously and spend their spare time discussing opera and stamp collecting.

Characteristics. Are the applicant's achievements outstanding? Did the person work five years at the XYZ Company without missing a day?

How about personal interests? If the jobs liked best in the past have been outdoor ones, like truck driving, why is the applicant looking now for a confining job on an assembly line?

Try to spot attitude. Does the person act mature, or sound as if given to childish boasting? Does the person listen to what you say? An example of an attitude you'll want to steer clear of is one where an individual goes out of the way to criticize the last company worked for, the people worked with, or the quality of the product. You'll probably be making no mistake to conclude this individual is the kind of person who'd find everything wrong at your company, too.

You can tell a lot about physical condition, too, from the interview. The person applying for a job who appears slow-moving and lethargic may have no oomph on the job, either. Remember, most people looking for work are trying to put their best foot forward. If an interviewee can't show you a very good side during the interview, there's a chance that you won't see anything better on the job.

What should you avoid in conducting a job interview?

James Menzies Black, a leading authority on this subject, cautions:

1. Don't be overly formal. The more you do to help the applicant relax, the more effective the interview will be.

2. Don't take notes. A busy pencil writes off a productive interview. Train your memory so you can make your notes after the interview is completed.

3. Don't high-pressure applicants. If you paint a glowing picture to job seekers that quickly fades after they are on the payroll, you have disappointed employees on your hands. Worst of all, you have employees who don't trust your word.

4. Don't hire a chief when you really need a worker. If an applicant is too intelligent or experienced to be happy in the job and there is little opportunity for quick promotion, say so. You want employee and job to match. That's why you conduct an interview.

5. Don't tell applicants you are rejecting them for personality reasons. If you think the experience or the knowledge to hold a job is lacking, be frank and say so. If you are refusing to hire for intangible reasons like a poor personality, and uncertainty about reliability, or a dislike of general attitude, keep your reasons to yourself. Frankness may offend applicants and will certainly discourage them for no good reason.

6. Don't make moral judgments or give advice. The applicant's personal life is no concern of yours.

7. Don't ask trick questions that may embarrass. If you see that there is conflict in the applicant's statements, you should certainly explore the matter, but do so discreetly. Your job is not to "catch" the prospect. It is to find out what you can about the individual.

8. Don't let your facial expression, tone of voice, or gestures reveal your feelings. You give applicants confidence by showing interest and sympathy. If they think you disapprove of what they are telling you, they will become silent or try to shift ideas around to where they will please you.

9. Don't be impatient. Try not to let the applicant know you're in a hurry, even if you are. A look at a watch has killed many an interview.

10. Don't be misled by your prejudices. Keep an open mind. Good interviewers never allow their biases to cloud their judgment.

Whom should you hire?

Deciding which applicant to hire isn't easy. But you can make a better decision if you separate facts from hunches—not that you should ignore your intuition or inferences. It's a good idea to take five minutes after you've interviewed an applicant to jot down what you think are the significant facts, and list your hunches, too.

Facts may show that the job seeker has had ten years of experience on a milling machine, has good health, and can read blueprints. But your conversation may have brought out the feeling that the individual is stubborn and boastful and might be hard to supervise. Only you can tell which items you'll give most weight to. Some supervisors don't mind having a prima donna on their staff so long as that individual can produce. Others fear that a prima donna is likely to upset teamwork. And, of course, your hunches can be wrong.

You can be sure, however, that your choice will be better than flipping a coin if you've gone about your interview in a systematic way; and if you've kept personal prejudices as to race, religion, age, sex, or nationality out of your figuring.

How do you pick the best from the list of qualified applicants?

First, be sure that you have dropped no one from the list of possibilities because of discrimination or prejudice; in other words, be sure that all things are equal according to the law. Then, pick the applicant who fits your sense of what kind of person will do the job best. This is where your experience and intuition can help. For example, Bobby Knight, the highly successful Indiana University basketball coach, lists three things he looks for when recruiting basketball players: "(1) *Strength.* Wiry strength to hold onto the ball, to maintain a position on the boards or a defensive stance. (2) *Quickness.* The slow, plodding team will have trouble over the long season. (3) *Concentration.* There isn't a right way to play the game, but there are a lot of poor ways. You have to play in a way that utilizes the abilities of your team. Concentrate, and you will be successful."

Your department won't be playing basketball. But you can look for such things as (1) *perseverance,* as demonstrated by a work record that shows the applicant can stay with a difficult situation; (2) *alertness,* as indicated by the applicant's ability to follow your description of the work to be done—since many jobs require a person who can sense when a deviation from rigid procedures is desirable; (3) *cooperation,* as illustrated by the applicant's willingness to go through the red tape of employment interviewing and processing without quibbling about it. Other jobs, of course, may need another set of personal qualities. Initiative in a salesclerk, for example, may be more important than cooperation. Single-mindedness may be more valuable than alertness in a chemical processing plant that requires rigid conformance to prescribed sequence.

Should you check employee references?

Absolutely yes! It's foolhardy to hire anyone without checking with the last employer to find out about the actual job the applicant held, attendance, and honesty. Most employers cooperate if the information is kept confidential. (It's a good practice to tell the applicant that you are going to verify references.) Checking can be done either by telephone or by letter.

Personal references are usually not of much value. No one is going to supply the name of a person who will say something bad. And school references are of value primarily to verify whether the employee actually has the education claimed.

supervisory word power

Application blank. A form used by a company to gather and record information and data systematically about a job applicant's qualifications, education, and work experience.

Psychological tests. Written examinations, conducted by trained professionals, of a person's qualifications, interests, and aptitudes in order to judge objectively the individual's suitability for a particular job or kind of work.

Employment interview. A face-to-face exchange of information between a job applicant and an employer's representative in order to develop qualitative information about the applicant's suitability for employment.

Work load. The amount of work an individual, or a group of individuals, can be expected to perform during a given period of time under normal conditions.

Attrition.   The gradual reduction of a work force by means of natural events and causes, such as retirements, deaths, and resignations, as opposed to reductions planned by management, such as discharges, layoffs, and early retirements.

Other Important Terms in This Chapter

absenteeism
aptitude tests
bona fide occupational qualification (BFOQ)
direct labor
indirect labor
performance test
reliability
turnover
validity
work force balancing

reading comprehension

1. What is meant by balancing the work force? Why should a supervisor try to do it?

2. What are some of the hidden costs of adding an employee to, and separating an employee from, the payroll?

3. State a basic rule supervisors can follow to make their selection and hiring practices comply with the Civil Rights Act of 1964.

4. What is the fundamental purpose of tests, application forms, and interviews that are used in hiring new employees?

5. What are some of the factors that contribute to turnover?

6. Would it be wise to hire a college graduate for a job that requires only a high school education, so long as the applicant were willing to take it at prevailing wage rates? Why?

7. Would a supervisor be likely to use more than one method of calculating absence rates? Why?

8. What's the difference between an aptitude test and a performance test?

9. What are some of the things you might want to know about an applicant, which can be elicited in a job interview?

10. In conducting an employment or a placement interview, what are some of the techniques a supervisor can use to make it more effective?

■■■■■■■■ **THE CASE OF TOO MUCH OVERTIME.   A case study in human relations involving work force management, with questions for you to answer.**

"This overtime has got to stop," stormed the plant superintendent to Jake Barnes, supervisor of the finishing department in a toy factory. "You've had to schedule overtime three times already, and the month has only just begun. What's the trouble out there?"

"Well, boss, it's this way," said Jake. "When the pressure was on to pare costs to the bone, I laid off three of our finishers. According to the schedule we got from sales, we would have been able to produce all they required without putting on any overtime. But the sales manager has been out here every day moving up orders. And increasing some, too. We'll still be in good shape by the end of the month. But right now I don't have as much help as I need to get the stuff out as fast as sales is calling for it."

"Jake, I've told you time and again not to accept delivery changes from sales without first making sure you can handle them. It's easy for sales to make promises. But the way you're running up overtime, we're the ones who will have to pay for those promises."

"To tell the truth," said Jake, "I thought we'd be able to move up those orders—and we would have, except that we had four employees out this week. Seems as if the flu is knocking out more people every day. I can't predict things like this. You tell me to keep my labor force down to the minimum. I don't want to recall anyone for just a few days. I think that if the company wants delivery, we'll have to schedule the overtime."

"Jake, I still don't think you've handled this problem well at all. There's going to be the devil to pay if you don't bring your labor costs into line."

Two days later, the finishing department was still in trouble. At 3 p.m. the phone rang. It was the sales manager. "Jake, the shipping department tells me you're holding up the McWorth order. It's got to go out tomorrow for sure. Can I call McWorth and promise the order will be shipped?"

1. What do you think of the instructions Jake got from his boss?

2. What do you think of the sales manager's request?

3. What do you think Jake should have said to his boss when the overtime problem arose?

4. If you were Jake now, how would you handle this situation?
5. What would you do to avoid the problem in the future?

enriching your viewpoint

To gain a fuller understanding of recruiting, interviewing, and staffing your work force, the following readings are suggested:

Anastasi, A., *Psychological Testing,* 4th ed., The Macmillan Company, New York, 1976.

Bauer, Ernie, "A Matter of Balance," *Think,* March/April 1975, pp. 4-7-11.

Black, James Menzies, *How to Get Results from Interviewing,* McGraw-Hill Book Company, New York, 1970, Chap. 4, "The Job Interview."

Eckles, Robert W., Ronald L. Carmichael, and Bernard R. Sarchet, *Essentials of Management for First-Line Supervisors,* John Wiley & Sons, Inc., New York, 1974, Chap. 17, "The Selection Process and the Supervisor."

"The Effective Manager," sample issue, Warren, Gorham, & Lamont, Boston, 1977, pp. 4–5.

Fear, Richard A., *The Evaluation Interview,* 2d ed., McGraw-Hill Book Company, New York, 1973.

Kirkpatrick, J. J., R. B. Ewen, R. S. Barrett, and R. A. Katzell, *Testing and Fair Employment,* New York University Press, New York, 1968.

Minter, Robert L., "The Hiring Interview," *Supervisory Management,* December 1974, p. 210.

"Selection and Utilization of Personnel," Supervisory Development Program, Civilian Personnel Pamphlet 41-B-2, Department of the Army, Washington 25, August 28, 1962.

Stanard, Steven J., "Psychological Testing," in Lester R. Bittel (ed.), *The Encyclopedia of Professional Management,* McGraw-Hill Book Company, New York, 1978.

11

CHAPTER **activating the work force by communications**

**What is the significance
of the term communications
when used in connection with supervision?**

The term *communications* is defined as the process in human relations of passing information and understanding from one person to another. As a supervisory responsibility, it is frequently called employee communications, although the communicating process is equally important between supervisor and supervisor and between supervisor and boss.

The term was, of course, originally applied to mechanical means for transmitting and receiving information, such as newspapers, bulletin board announcements, radio, telephone, and television. Employee communications have many of the qualities—and limitations—of mechanical means, but they are infinitely more subtle and complex. So try to treat communications carefully.

How does communications activate the organization?

By providing the linking pin between plans and action. You may have put together the best set of plans ever and staffed your department with the best people available. But until something begins to happen, you will have accomplished nothing. Communications with your employees is what puts the whole plan into motion.

When do human communications get off the track?

In trying to get our ideas across to others, human communication (like radio or television transmission) systems suffer from poor reception, interference, or being tuned in on the wrong channel. Poor reception often occurs when a supervisor gives an order that an employee hasn't been conditioned to expect. Interference takes place when a supervisor gives conflicting instructions. An employee may be tuned in on the wrong channel if a supervisor talks about improving work quality when the employee wants to find out about taking a day off. Only through skillful communications can these human transmission failures be avoided. Some experts on communications refer to these kinds of distractions as noise.

How much must supervisors know about communications?

Good supervisors can't know too much about employee communications. Their leadership is affected by what information they can pass on to others through communications. Unless employees know how you feel and what you want, the best management ideas in the world go astray. This is especially true where group effort is essential.

Group attitudes will depend on how well you can interpret your company's interests and intentions to workers. And you'll need all the communicating skill you can muster to secure the cooperation so necessary from your work team.

Is any one method
of communications better than another?

Each situation has its own best method or combination of methods. To show some employees how much you appreciate their cooperation, all you may need to do is give them an occasional pat on the shoulder. But others may need frequent vocal assurance. Still others will believe only what you put down on paper. So it goes to show that the most successful communicating is done by supervisors who know many ways of getting their ideas, instructions, and attitudes across.

Where does the management information
system fit into the communications process?

A company's management information system (MIS) is the formal process it uses to collect data about production, quality, sales, and costs. In many companies this system is no more than its routine clerical and accounting processes. In others the system is highly complex and utilizes a computer to process and analyze the data or information. When such a process is truly a management information system, its real purpose is to provide just the right kind of information for each of the company's decision makers, from first-line supervisor to top-level executive. Each of you may get different information and different documents to look at, but the purpose will be the same. The MIS goal is to give you just enough of the right kind of information so that you can make good decisions.

At the supervisory level the data you collect on employee time cards, production tally sheets, quality-control records, stockroom inventories, cash register receipts, and sales tickets become raw data for the MIS. In return you may get budget or variance reports and attendance and turnover reports from the MIS. These tell you what you need to know about how well your department is doing in maintaining discipline, in meeting its production targets, and in controlling costs.

In general the MIS focuses on the operating needs of management rather than on the information needs of employees, although there may be a great deal of overlap. In the main, information that employees need to do their jobs and to conform to company policies flows down from the top in the form of written memos and bulletins or by word of mouth, primarily from their supervisors. Thus, the choice of the communication system you will use to run your department is a vital one. When information comes down from the top, your system must pick up where the company's MIS leaves off. When communicating upward, your system must connect with the company's MIS if you and your employees are to be heard clearly upstairs.

What are the two basic ways to approach employee communications in your department?

███████████ By using either a wheel (or satellite) or a web (or system network). In a wheel system, communications tend to be restricted. The supervisor stands at the center, or hub, as shown in Figure 11-1. Information is passed out to, and received from, employees via the spokes. Employees are not encouraged to exchange ideas between one another. In web networks, communications tend to be more open. The supervisor still stands at the center of the system, but employees are encouraged to exchange information freely in any channel they can find open.

In the wheel network the supervisor controls the flow of information. This helps to avoid inconsistencies in interpreting what was said. The wheel approach seems best with simple, repetitive tasks. It protects privacy and allows the supervisor to be very personal in talks with employees. But it tends to be slow and ponderous when new or complex problems are being dealt with.

In the web network the supervisor acts more as facilitator and verifier than as communicator. The system distributes ideas quickly and helps to get agreement for them and application of them on a broad front. The system does have drawbacks. Rumors often get out of control. Progress toward goals and changes in methods may not be fed back to the supervisor until too late. But the advantages tend to outweigh the disadvantages. Furthermore, an attitude toward open communications invites employee participation in solving problems. And it helps to build a strong team spirit.

Experts advise, however, that if you have established a communication system that works, don't change it. Employees who have found the way through company channels don't particularly like to have the channels upset.

How does communications help to unify an organization?

███████████ By letting each person see a continuing relationship to the action of others as, collectively, they work to attain a common goal. Laurence Leamer, writing in *Harper's Magazine* (December 1971, p. 105), illustrates this principle when he tells of a simple communications device that ties together a whole shift of coal miners despite the fact that they work alone or in very small teams in remote areas of the mine:

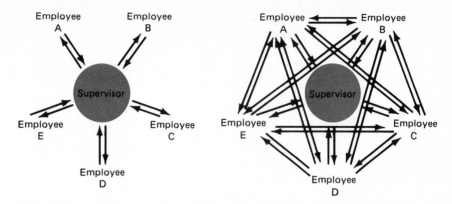

FIGURE 11-1. Examples of Restricted and Open Communication Systems.

"Wheel" or "Satellite" System: Supervisor maintains control. There are no exchanges between employees. System is relatively restricted.

"Web" System: Supervisor serves as stimulator and validator. There are few or no controls. There is free and open exchange among employees and between employees and supervisor.

While they work they can tell where Harry (the shift superintendent) is by listening to the voices on the amplified single-circuit telephone system that runs through the mine.
"Harry, Harry Flatts. Calling Harry Flatts."
"What the (hell) is it now, Willis?"
"We got a motor off the track."
"Well, get it out of there first thing. I'll be right down."
"Six right boom boy. Six right boom boy."
"Yeah. What you want now, Beard?"
"Why's the belt off now, Charlie? We gotta run some coal, buddy."
"We're outa coal cars. They're bringin' 'em up now."
"Harry, Harry, I'm having a hell of a time with this here belt at B Panel boom."

The miners listen to the phone and know what is happening all over the mine. It makes of each shift a single organism, with tentacles stretched thousands of feet up the various tunnels, each one pulling down coal and sending it back to the elevator at the base of the Eccles tipple.

Should a supervisor use the company grapevine as a means of communication?

Listen to it. It's one way of getting an inkling of what's going on. But don't depend upon it for receiving accurate information. And never use it to disseminate information.

The grapevine gets its most active usage in the absence of good communications. If you don't tell employees about changes that will affect them, they'll make their own speculations—via the grapevine. As a result, the grapevine carries rumors and outright lies more often than it does the truth. Surveys show that while employees may receive a lot of their information from the rumor mill, they'd much rather get it straight from a responsible party—the boss. In fact, you build goodwill by spiking rumors that come to your attention. So show employees you welcome the chance to tell them the truth about company matters that concern them.

Some authorities, however, believe that if you talk to enough employees and prove yourself to be a reliable source of company information, the grapevine will work for you. This is probably true. But leaking information to the work group deliberately through the grapevine isn't the same thing—and will tend to isolate you from them in the long run.

Some people talk about three-dimensional communications. What are they referring to?

Communication should not be a one-way street. For a complex, modern organization to function smoothly, communications must move three ways. Not only must you furnish information downward to employees, but employees must communicate their ideas and feeling upward to you. And since staff and interdepartmental cooperation is so important, there must be horizontal, or sideways, flow of information, too. This up, down, and across process is called three-dimensional communications.

Supervisors can't have the answer to everything that is happening in the company, can they?

No. But it is your responsibility to keep informed on matters of importance. If you don't know what's going on, you can't tell others. This applies to many areas that are of concern to employees—like social security, pension plans, the way an incentive is applied, or a leave of absence policy. When an employee asks you something you don't know about, you'll lose face if every time you have to say that you'll find out from someone else. Soon employees will figure you're not knowledgeable and will go to someone else—like their shop steward—for information.

When you are caught unprepared, however, don't bluff. And don't say something like, "How should I know? Nobody tells me anything." Instead, strive to be in a position of confidence with higher management so that you can say, "I don't know the answer to that one. But I'll certainly try to find out and let you know as soon as I can."

Do employees believe what you tell them?

Not all the time, any more than you believe everything you hear. But if you shoot as straight as you can in all your conversations with them, they'll look to you as a reliable source of information. It is just as important that employees have confidence in the purpose of your communications. They should never wonder, "Why did the supervisor say that?"

If the reason you complimented an employee yesterday was so that you could stick that person with a hard job today, there will be suspicion the next time you offer praise. If you would build confidence, avoid trickery and don't blind yourself to the inferences an employee may draw from what you say. Better to be brutally frank about your purpose: "I'm having this heart-to-heart talk with you now because we're going to crack down on low producers," than to pussyfoot about your intentions: "I want to get your ideas as to what you can do to improve your output."

Is there danger in saying too much to employees?

Yes, although this isn't the most common hazard. Supervisors who run off at the mouth continually, who are indiscreet, or who violate confidences do overcommunicate or communicate wrongly. It's much better to speak only about what you are certain than to get a reputation for being a blabbermouth.

Some supervisors, too, in their eagerness to keep employees fully informed, try too hard. They find themselves spending too much time communicating information that employees don't need or have no interest in.

How can you decide what to talk to employees about?

Talk about those things employees want to know—those things that directly affect them or their work. Talk about work methods, company rules, pay practices, the values in employee benefits, opportunities for advancement, your appraisal of how well the employee is doing the job.

Talk also about department and company matters that are news—while they are news. Your influence as a communicator will be watered down if what workers hear from you is only a stale confirmation of something they have learned from another worker or from their union representative. Your employees should depend on you for dependable information.

Are there things you shouldn't talk about?

Yes. Politics and religion are dangerous subjects, as are other intensely personal matters like men versus women. Steer clear of these issues—even if an employee brings up the subject.

On the subject of business economics—which should be discussed with employees if they are to get a good perspective of their work environment—be careful to let employees form their own judgments and express their own opinions.

How much communication should you have upward with your boss?

Just as your success as a leader depends upon how freely employees will talk to you and tell you what's bothering them, your superior, too, needs similar information from you. Make a point of keeping your boss informed on:

Matters for which the boss is held accountable by his or her superior. This would include performance standards such as deliveries, output, quality. If you see that you're not going to be able to meet a schedule commitment, don't yield to the temptation of trying to conceal it. Instead, build confidence with your boss by saying, "I want to warn you that Job No. 1257 won't be finished on time. We ran into off-grade material and had to rework some of the units. I can guarantee that delivery will be made by next Tuesday, however."

Matters that may cause controversy. If you've had to take action that may be criticized by another department, your boss should know about it to be able to talk intelligently about it if interdepartment disagreements are brought up. Suppose the quality-control section has advised you to shut down a line because production is off-standard, but you've thought that you must keep it running in order to make a delivery date. Better get to your superior fast—with the facts.

Attitudes and morale. Middle and top managers are continually frustrated because of their isolation from the work group. They need your advice and consultation as to how people in the company feel, generally or about a specific issue. Make a point of speaking to your boss on this subject regularly. Tell your boss about good reactions as well as bad. But never play the role of a stool pigeon or go to your superior with information gained in confidence.

Which kinds of communications are likely to speak louder than words?

▬▬▬▬▬ Talking and writing are the communications media most frequently used, of course. But regardless of what you say, employees will be most affected by what you communicate to them by your actions. What you do—how you treat them—is the proof of your real intentions. When you go to bat for an employee who is in trouble, that's concrete communication of how well you value that person's contributions to your production team.

Even on simple matters, such as training an employee to do a new job, the act of showing how to do it (demonstration) is eloquent even when no words are spoken.

The best kinds of communications are generally those that combine the spoken or written words with action. "Show and tell" is a good formula for you to remember.

Body language. What's that?

▬▬▬▬▬ The way your body or facial expressions tip off to others what is really on your mind. These nonverbal signals are revealed by a frown, a nervous touching of the nose, the way you shrug your shoulders, or a gesture with your hands. Don't concern yourself with changing or controlling your body language, but do recognize that many employees will read it to tell how sincere you are.

How can you avoid having an employee take offense at what you say?

▬▬▬▬▬ Each of us has a great big ego—and some of us are more sensitive than others. The tone of your voice, your choice of words, your tactlessness may make an employee feel menaced or hurt. Whenever you put something in such a way that an individual may infer a threat to pay or status, personal feelings will get in the way of rational thinking.

Take this example of a statement to an employee: "You remember I told you they wouldn't approve that transfer you asked for. Well, they won't."

Compare the tone of that statement with this way of saying the same thing: "I'm sorry, but the super won't approve that transfer right now. You recall, we thought it might have to be held up as long as we're short-handed here and they're full in the keypunch department. But you speak to me about it again in the spring, and we'll try it when we're slack in this department."

Watch out, too, when you start a conversation. Sometimes you can be more aggressive than you intend to be, especially when speaking to a superior. Or when you're afraid you won't get your point across. That's because it sometimes takes courage. You have to push yourself, and some of that push gets into your voice.

Don't start an appeal this way, for example: "Now listen, I know you won't agree with me. But you've got to listen." This makes the tone of your message aggressive. It puts you on the defensive and may defeat your purpose.

How can you be sure that people understand what you mean?

A very simple device is to ask an employee to repeat back to you what you have said. If the person can't do this, it's the signal for you to tell your story over again.

Another way is to get the employee to ask questions. What is asked will tip you off to areas of weak understanding. And once a conversation is established on a give-and-take basis, communications are always improved.

One reason for poor understanding is that words mean one thing in one relationship and something very different in other situations. Everyone had ideas, for instance, of what is meant by faster, slower, harder, up a little, bear down. To make the meaning clearer, be more specific. Say, "Go a little slower—down to 2,100 rpm." Or, "I want you to bear down a little harder on quality this month. Last month we had complaints about poor finishes on six of the cabinets you turned out. Will you be especially careful about the application of the 00 emery cloth in the future?" Said with this explanation, "bear down" now has explicit meaning.

Should you keep personalities out of the picture?

Don't be impersonal or cold-blooded in your approach to people. In fact, you should tailor your presentation to best fit the person you're talking to. Some employees like rough language. Others feel it is a sign of disrespect. Some employees respond well to an informal request like, "When you've got time, will you sweep up the loading dock?" Others want you to be more formal, like, "Please get a broom and sweep the shipping platform. Start now and be sure it's done by three o'clock."

On the other hand, it's a good policy to deemphasize personalities in your communications. Think of communications as a process essential to the firm's organization. Try to avoid interference from personal factors that don't belong in the picture. Watch your tone so that it is objective and keeps emotional opinions out. There are helpful ways of rising above personalities. For instance:

"Now let's look at this from the point of view of company policy."

"This isn't between me and you. This is a question of whether office discipline will be maintained or not."

"Let's get back to the facts of the case."

"This is really a question of interpretation of the union contract. Let's see what they say in personnel."

It should go without saying, of course, that bias and prejudice should be held in check. You will arouse anger and resistance if you let your prejudices about sex, color, religion, handicaps, age, or national origin creep into your communications.

What will encourage
employees to communicate with you?

Good faith, mutual confidence, welcome for their ideas, and a friendly attitude are the foundations on which employees will learn to talk to you. But a more specific way is for you to develop the fine art of listening.

Real communication is two-way. In the long run people won't listen to you if you won't listen to them. But listening must be more than just a mechanical process. Many employees (in fact, most people) are poor communicators. This means that you have to be an extraordinary receiver to find out what workers may be trying to say.

Here are a few suggestions that may improve your listening power:

Don't assume anything.   Don't anticipate. Don't let an employee think that you know what is going to be said.

Don't interrupt.   Let the individual have a full say. The employee who is stopped may feel there will never be an opportunity to unload the problem. If you don't have the time to hear an employee through just then, ask that the discussion stay within a time limit. Better still, make an appointment (for the same day, if at all possible) for a time when you can get the whole story.

Try to understand the need.   Look for the real reason the employee wants your attention. Often this may be quite different from what appears to be the immediate purpose. For instance, the real reason for a request for a half-day off may be to test the employee's standing with you against another worker who has recently gotten a half-day off.

Don't react too quickly.   We all tend to jump to conclusions. The employee may use a word that makes you see red, or may express the situation badly. Be patient in trying to make sure that you are both talking about the same thing. Above all, try to understand—not necessarily agree with—the other's viewpoint.

Can listening be overdone?

Listening should make up at least a third of your communications. But it shouldn't take the place of definite actions and answers on your part.

When an employee begins to ramble too far afield in discussions, return to the point with astute questioning.

If an employee is wrong on a point of fact, make that clear, even if it means contradicting the individual. But watch your tone!

When conferences or group discussions tend to turn into purposeless rap sessions, it's time for you to set talk aside and take action.

Finally, when an employee comes to you with a problem and its solution is clear to you, give a straightforward reply. It does help, if you have the time, to permit the individual to develop the solution. But when the employee has come to you by virtue of your knowledge and experience, chances are a direct answer is wanted, not a session of hand holding.

Which kind of communications technique is the best?

For a supervisor, nothing can beat face-to-face communications. This way the common situation is shared with whomever you're talking to. And right at the time, you get a chance to see where your timing, tone, or choice of words has misfired. The biggest drawback to face-to-face communication is that it can be very time-consuming. You may feel at the end of some days that you've done nothing but talk. This can interfere with other work.

Because person-to-person communication, talking to one person at a time, is so time-consuming, you will want to consider some of the other effective ways for communicating to employees. There are many forms of communications and an almost infinite combination of them. Combinations are usually more effective than any particular technique used by itself. To aid in your choice of technique, think of employee communications in two ways—either person-to-person or with groups of employees.

How can person-to-person communications be conducted effectively?

The maximum of "custom tailoring" for the individual is not only feasible but definitely in order. It becomes increasingly so as the relationship accumulates a common background. That's because an individual who is addressed singly (but like anyone else) is usually resentful in proportion to the degree of previously assumed familiarity.

Spoken. In spoken communication the immediate situation is shared, and the person addressed is aware of the conditions under which the message takes place. Therefore, haste, tone, mood, gestures, or facial expression may seriously affect the way the individual reacts.

1. **Informal talks.** Still the most fundamental form of communication. They are suitable for day-to-day liaison, direction, exchange of information, conference, review, discipline, checking up, maintenance of effective personal relations. Even if brief, be sure they provide the opportunity for a two-way exchange.

Face-to-face communication should always be used (in preference to the telephone) when the subject is of personal importance to either party.

2. **Planned appointments.** Appropriate for regular review or liaison, recurring joint work sessions, and so forth. The parties should be adequately prepared to make such meetings complete and effective by being up to date, by providing adequate data and information, and by limiting interruptions to the fewest possible.

Many supervisors have regular planned appointments with each major subordinate—daily (brief), weekly (longer), and monthly (extensive). It's valuable to note the gist of the discussion, for future reference.

3. **Telephone calls.** For quick checkup, or for imparting or receiving information, instruction, or data. They play a part in the personal relationship of the individuals concerned, which is sometimes overlooked. Your telephone personality sometimes contradicts your real self. An occasional personal note can alleviate the sometimes resented impersonality of routine calls, which may sound indifferent.

Written. All messages intended to be formal, official, or long-term or that affect several persons in a related way should be written. Be sure that you use only a written communication to amend any previous written communication. Oral changes will be forgotten or recalled indifferently.

4. Interoffice memos. For recording informal inquiries or replies. They can be of value, too, if several people are to receive a message that is extensive, or when data are numerous or complex. Use of memos should not be overdone, or they will be ignored.

5. Letters. More individualized in effect than a memo and usually more formal. They are useful for official notices, formally recorded statements, or lengthy communications, even when the addressee is physically accessible. Letters are often valuable for communicating involved thoughts and ideas for future discussion and development, or as part of a continuing consideration of problems.

6. Reports. More impersonal than a letter and usually more formal. Reports are used to convey information associated with evaluation, analysis, or recommendations to supervisors or colleagues. They are most effective when based on conferences, visits, inspections, surveys, research, or study. Reports should carefully distinguish objectively determined facts from estimates, guesses, opinions, impressions, and generalizations.

How can you communicate most effectively with groups of employees?

Plant or office groups that are uniform in status, age, sex, compensation level, occupation, and length of service provide a valid basis for highly pointed messages. This approach helps avoid the gradually numbing stream of form letters, memos, and announcements that really have meaning for only a few of the recipients. Establishment of such groups on a continuing basis helps to build a sense of unity and group coherence that fosters favorable group reaction and group response, especially where there is routine personal contact among the members.

Spoken. Effective spoken communication with groups calls for special skills. Those that are effective in a committee of equals may be inadequate in a mass meeting. Ability to conduct a conference of your own staff doesn't mean you will have equal ability to participate effectively as a staff member in a conference called by your superior. Conflicts of interest need more tactful handling than does a discussion of factual topics.

1. Informal staff meeting. This provides an opportunity for development of strong group cohesiveness and response. Properly supplemented with individual face-to-face contacts, it is an outstanding means of coordinating activities and building mutual understanding. Hold brief, informal staff meetings daily (if your schedule permits)—early in the morning, at the end of the day, or at lunch.

2. Planned conferences. A relatively formal affair. The commonest error is for the person calling the conference to set up the agenda without previous consultation with those who will attend. It is usually desirable to check with most of the prospective participants in advance; provide time for the preparation and the assembling of needed data, information, reports, and recommendations; allow opportunity for suggestions as to agenda and conduct of the meeting.

Properly conducted, a planned conference can be extremely useful. If improperly managed, participation will be limited or misdirected. As a result it can be not only wasteful of time but even harmful in effect.

3. Mass meetings. Of large numbers of employees or management. They can be a valuable means of celebrating occasions, building morale, changing attitudes, meeting emergencies, introducing new policies or key personnel, or making special announcements. Mass meetings can also be used to clarify confused situations, resolve misunderstandings, or identify dissident elements. But such procedures require of the presiding individual great skill and a forceful personality. And there is always the danger of interference or interruption.

Written. The effect of a single, isolated written communication to a group of employees is generally unpredictable. But a carefully planned program of written communications can develop a desirable cumulative effect.

4. Bulletin board notices. For lengthy or formal announcements. These notices can be used for a series of illustrated messages and are most effective when readership is constantly attracted by changes and by careful control of content, including prompt removal of out-of-date material. Most bulletin board announcements should be supplemented by other forms.

5. Posters. Small or large, at suitable locations, used in series, changed frequently, they can do much to supplement your other communications media. The usual and most effective subjects are safety, quality, and good housekeeping.

6. Exhibits and displays. Can serve a useful purpose when appropriate space is available, and when they can be properly prepared. Such preparation is often expensive. The commonest subjects are company products, advertising, promoting quality production, increasing safety, cutting waste and costs, and stimulating suggestions.

7. Visual aids.   Films, filmstrips, easel presentations, audio cassettes, and other special visual materials have great potential value but are only as good as the way they are used. Few are self-administering. A good film will be far more effective, for instance, if presented with a soundly planned introduction and follow-up. Much material that could be of considerable value will be relatively worthless if not presented appropriately. Careful, competent preparation and planning should be applied to the use of all visual materials.

supervisory word power

Communications process.   The giving and receiving of information as a result of thinking, doing, observing, talking, listening, writing, and reading. In supervision, the exchange (especially of accurate meaning) between supervisor and employee.

Information.   The knowledge (such as basic background data about a particular job), skills (such as a specific work procedure), and feelings (such as a display of confidence in an employee's ability to respond favorably) that are exchanged in the communications process through the various media.

Communications media.   The method, manner, form, or technique by which information is communicated, such as attitude, performance, appearance, speech, decision, demonstration, or deed; conversation, discussion, dialogue, interview, conference, or lecture; writing, memorandum, letter, report, or book; telephone, recording, radio, public address system, or television.

Rumors.   Inaccurate, ambiguous, or incomplete information circulated informally within an organization by means of an unorganized, often unreliable, but extremely pervasive and quick communications channel (the underground or the grapevine). Rumors flourish in inverse proportion to the effectiveness of the formal communications channels.

Listening.   The conscious, active process of securing information of all kinds (including feelings and emotions) by paying acute attention to what people say and how they say it—for the purpose of improving the communications process and consequently the quality of the performance and understanding that depend on it.

Other Important Terms in This Chapter

body language
face-to-face communication
grapevine
group communication
management information system (MIS)
noise
overcommunication
person-to-person communication
three-dimensional communications
visual aids
web (open) communications system
wheel (restricted) communications system

reading comprehension

1. Why is communication needed in an organization in the first place?

2. What kinds of information are usually handled by a management information system (MIS)? Can an organization do without an MIS?

3. Of the wheel and the web communication networks, which is more restricted and which more open? What are some advantages and disadvantages of each?

4. Discuss the shortcomings of the grapevine.

5. How can the credibility gap between a supervisor and the employees be narrowed?

6. If a supervisor finds that the department cannot deliver an important order on schedule, should the boss be told about it immediately, or should the supervisor wait until the order is finally shipped? Why?

7. Is it ever possible for a supervisor to overcommunicate? If so, is it harmful? How?

8. If a supervisor is quick to get the gist of an employee's complaint, why shouldn't the conversation be cut off right away, thus permitting an immediate reaction or decision by the supervisor?

9. If an employee in your department seems to make far too many mistakes, how might you effectively let that employee know of your growing concern?

10. Discuss the pros and cons of a supervisor's holding a mass meeting with everybody in the department.

supervision in action

■■■■■■■■ **THE CASE OF THE TANGLED GRAPEVINE.** **A case study in human relations involving communications, with questions for you to answer.**

Mary Lou was appointed head teller of the Arlington branch of SNB bank six months ago. The branch, which employs eight tellers, is located in a rapidly growing suburban community. Unlike the bank's main office and other branches that work some nights and weekends, the Arlington branch works only from 9 a.m. to 5 p.m. Monday through Friday. The SNB bank, however, is an old one. It places great emphasis upon proper relationships and formal channels of communication. Whenever changes in procedures are made, the main bank first issues a bulletin to all supervisors. Only after the supervisors have had a chance to get this information are general announcements made to rank-and-file employees.

Last week one of the drive-up tellers was asked by a depositor when the branch would be open Saturday mornings, as the main bank was. The teller said that it wasn't likely, since most of the tellers had taken their jobs with the assumption that there would be no Saturday work. "That's interesting," said the depositor. "My sister, who works at your head office, implied that a change in banking hours was imminent." On a coffee break the drive-up teller mentioned this to two of the employees who were in the lounge at the time. Bill B., one of the more talkative clerks in the bank, ventured the opinion that "where there's smoke, there's likely to be fire. I'll bet that plans are already under way to open this branch on Saturdays. And, as usual, we'll be the last ones to know."

Two days later Jill J., a savings teller, asked Mary Lou whether there was any truth to the rumor that the branch would soon be open Saturdays.

"I can't believe that this could happen in the near future," said Mary Lou. "Other branches like ours did not begin to open Saturday mornings until after their weekly deposits exceeded $500,000. We are nowhere near that level now. Anyway, nobody has said anything to me about it. As you know, if any changes are planned, we supervisors are informed before anyone else."

"If the Arlington branch wants me to work on Saturdays," observed Jill, "I'll have to quit. I want to spend time with my family on the weekends. I can always find another five-day, 9-to-5 job elsewhere."

"Don't worry about it," said Mary Lou. "It's just a rumor. I don't know how stories like this get started. It's probably someone like Bill B. He sees ghosts around every corner. Anyway, I'll let you know right away if anything develops along that line."

At the end of the week Jill again asked Mary Lou about the rumored change in the bank's operating times. She was especially concerned now because she had a chance to take another job whose hours would suit her better. She had to make up her mind right away. Mary Lou again assured her that there was nothing in the works for additional openings. On the strength of this, Jill turned down the job opportunity.

Two weeks after this incident, the SNB *Bulletin to Supervisors* had the following announcement:

> *Beginning the first Friday of next month, all branches, regardless of size or deposits, will be open for business from 9 a.m. to 9 p.m It is expected that all full-time employees will share this extended schedule equally.*

Mary Lou immediately gathered her tellers together at quitting time and relayed the announcement to them. The news was not received enthusiastically.

"There goes my weekend," said one employee.

"Next move will be for Saturdays," said Bill B.

"It won't be all that bad," said Mary Lou. "By rotating schedules, each of you will only have to work every fourth Friday."

"That's not good enough for me," said Jill J. "I'm not about to work on Friday nights. That's league night for my bowling team."

"I'm sorry about that," said Mary Lou.

"You should be," said Jill, "especially after telling me to pass up a job where it was guaranteed that I wouldn't work anything but straight 9 to 5, five days a week."

"I didn't guarantee anything," said Mary Lou.

"Well, you sure weren't clewed into what the bank was going to do," said Jill. "You really didn't have any more information about this change in hours than we did. You said it was all a rumor, and it turned out to be true. Next time I'll listen to the grapevine."

1. Did it make any difference that the details of the rumor were inaccurate?

2. Could Mary Lou have avoided this situation? How?

3. What should Mary Lou do, if anything, to make the next shift less difficult for Jill J.?

4. What should Mary Lou say about Bill's comment that Saturday work will be next?

enriching your viewpoint

For a broader and more comprehensive view of the concepts and specific information presented in this chapter, the following readings are suggested:

Aranguren, José Luis, *Human Communication,* McGraw-Hill Book Company, New York, 1967.

Becvar, Raphael J., *Skills for Effective Communications,* John Wiley & Sons, Inc., New York, 1975.

Coffin, Royce A., and Ric Estrada, *The Communicator,* Amacom, New York, 1975.

Hershey, R., "The Grapevine . . . Here to Stay but Not Beyond Control," *Personnel,* Vol. 43, No. 1, 1966. pp. 62–66.

Hicks, Hebert G., and C. Ray Gullett, *The Management of Organizations,* 3d ed., McGraw-Hill Book Company, New York, 1976, Chap. 26, "Organizational Communications."

Lesikar, Raymond V., *Business Communication: Theory and Application,* 3d ed., Richard D. Irwin, Inc., Homewood, Ill., 1976.

Miner, John B., *The Management Process: Theory, Research, and Practice,* 2d ed., The Macmillan Company, New York, 1978, Chap. 9, "Management Information Systems."

Morris, John O., *Make Yourself Clear!* McGraw-Hill Book Company, New York, 1972.

Steinmetz, Lawrence L., and H. Ralph Todd Jr., *First-Line Management,* Business Publications, Inc., Dallas, 1975, Chap. 11, "Communications: A Management Tool."

Wofford, Jerry, Edwin A. Gerloff, and Robert C. Cummins, *Organizational Communications,* McGraw-Hill Book Company, New York, 1977.

CHAPTER 12

exercising control of people and processes

What is the basic purpose of a supervisor's control function?

To keep things in line and to make sure your plans hit their targets. In the restrictive sense, you use controls to make sure that employees are at work on time, that materials aren't wasted or stolen, that some persons don't exceed their authority. These controls tend to be the don'ts of an organization, the rules and regulations that set limits of acceptable behavior. In the more constructive sense, controls help to guide you and your department to production goals and quality standards.

What can controls be used for?

For just about anything that needs regulation and guidance. Controls, for example, can be used to regulate:

- *Employee performance* of all kinds, such as attendance, rest periods, productivity, and workmanship.
- *Machine operation and maintenance,* such as its expected daily output, power consumption, and extent of time for out-of-service repairs.
- *Materials usages,* such as the percentage of expected yield and anticipated waste during handling and processing.
- *Product or service quality,* such as the number of rejects that will be accepted or the number of complaints about service that will be tolerated.
- *Personal authority,* such as the extent of independent action employees can take while carrying out the duties outlined in their job descriptions.

Exactly what is a control standard?

A control standard, usually called simply a *standard,* is a specific performance goal that a product, a service, a machine, an individual, or an organization is expected to meet. It is usually expressed numerically: a weight (14.00 ounces), a rate (200 units per hour), or a flat target (4 rejects). The numbers may be expressed in any unit, such as inches, gallons, dollars, or percentages.

Many companies also allow a little leeway from standard, called a *tolerance.* This implies that the performance will be considered to be in control if it falls within specified boundaries. A product, for instance, may be said to meet its 14.00-ounce standard weight if it weighs no less than 13.75 ounces or no more than 14.25 ounces. The control standard would be stated as 14 ounces, ± 0.25 ounces. The tolerance is the ± 0.25 ounces.

In what way are plans and controls linked?

Controls are directly related to the goals that have been set during the planning process. In fact, controls are often identical with these goals. Suppose, for example, that as supervisor of a commercial office of a telephone company, you have planned that your department will handle 100 service calls per day during the next month. The 100 calls per day is your goal. It also becomes your control standard. If your department handles 100 calls per day, you have met your target and need exert no corrective controls. If, however, your department handles fewer than 100 calls and begins to fall behind, it is below its control standard. You must take some sort of action to correct this performance.

Take another example. Suppose that you are the supervisor of a machining department in a brass foundry. Your superintendent has advised you that the company has set a goal of only 3 percent rejects of products scheduled to leave your area. In this case you may have to study each separate operation in your department to determine what you can consider its acceptable quality (or workmanship). You must keep in mind that the net effect must be only 3 rejects out of every 100 castings machined.

The lathe operators may be told that they cannot damage any castings at all, since their work is easiest to control. The boring machine operators may be given a standard that allows them to bore center holes no more than 0.1 inch off center. And the grinding machine operators may not be given a standard in terms of rejects at all. They may be told that the surface finish of casting they work on must meet the specified dimensions, between ±0.005 inches. In your estimate, if everything went as wrong as it could for each operator, while still meeting the standards you set, the department will still meet its targeted goal of 3 rejects per 100, regardless of which operation used up all its tolerances.

If the department found that it was rejecting 5 of 100 castings, your job as supervisor would be to find which machine operator had exceeded the limits of control that you had set. And then you would have to decide what caused this to happen. It may be that the machine needs maintenance because it wobbles too much to bore a perfect center. Or the fixture that holds the casting in place while it is being machined may have slipped. Or the tools may need sharpening. Or the employee may need training in how to operate the machine more accurately. Or, there is always the possibility that the operator is careless or has willfully damaged a casting. Each of these causes would require a different kind of control action on your part.

Where do the control standards come from? Who sets them?

A great many standards are set by the organization itself. They may be set by the accounting department for costs or by the industrial engineering department for wage incentive (or time) standards. They may be issued by the production-control department for schedule quantities or by the quality-control people for inspection specifications. It is typical for control standards in large organizations to be set by staff specialists. In smaller companies supervisors may set standards themselves. But even in large companies the supervisor may have to take an overall, or department, standard and translate it into standards for each employee or operation.

Upon what information are control standards based?

Standards are based upon one, or all three, of these sources.

Past performance.   Historical records often provide the basis for controls. If your department has been able to process 150 orders with three clerks in the past, this may be accepted as the standard. The weakness of this historical method is that it presumes that 150 orders represents good performance. Perhaps 200 would be a better target. This might be true if improvements have recently been made in the processing machinery and layouts.

High hopes.   In the absence of any other basis, some supervisors ask for the moon. They set unreasonably high standards for their employees to shoot at. While it is a sound practice to set challenging goals, standards should always be attainable by employees who put forth a reasonable effort. Otherwise, workers will become discouraged, or rebel, and won't try to meet them.

Systematic analysis.   The best standards are set by systematically analyzing what a job entails. This way the standard is based upon careful observation and measurement, as with time studies. At the very least, standards should be based upon a consideration of all the factors that affect attainment of the standard—such as tooling, equipment, training of the operator, absence of distractions, clear-cut instructions and specifications.

How accurate are standards and control measurements likely to be?

They won't be perfect. It is the supervisor's responsibility, however, to check regularly to see that measurements are being made as honestly and as accurately as possible.

Unintentional errors creep in from carelessness when original figures are recorded, from mistakes when data is transferred from one record to another in keypunching, or from the halo effect when an observer is impressed by unusually high or low performance.

Deliberate falsification can take place when an operator or a salesperson—whose wages depend upon performance—distorts the figures, when an employee covers up for a friend, when someone wants to give the impression of progress by holding up Friday's production count so that it appears in next week's record, or when someone works to lull the supervisor into thinking that everything is going all right.

Inaccuracies aside, it is also very important to check regularly to see that (1) the standards have not changed because of an improvement in machines or methods and (2) the measurements really do help you to make control decisions.

How is the control process carried out?
The control process follows four distinct steps:

1. **Set performance standards.** Standards of quantity, quality, and time spell out (*a*) what is expected and (*b*) how much of a deviation can be tolerated if the person or process fails to come up to the mark. For example, the standard for an airlines ticket counter might be that no customer should have to wait in line more than five minutes. The standard could then be modified to say that if only one out of ten customers had to wait more than five minutes, no corrective action need be taken. The standard would be stated as "waiting time of less than five minutes per customer with a tolerance of one out of ten who might have to wait longer." The guideline is that the more specific the standard, the better, especially when it can be stated with numbers as opposed to vague terms like good performance or minimum waiting time.

2. **Collect data to measure performance.** Accumulation of control data is so routine in most organizations that it is taken for granted. Every time a supervisor or an employee fills out a time card, prepares a production tally, or files a receiving or inspection report, control data is being collected. Whenever a sales ticket is filled out, a sale rung up on a cash register, or a shipping ticket prepared, control data is being recorded. Of course, all information is not collected in written form. Much of what a good supervisor uses for control purposes is gathered by observation—simply watching how well employees are carrying out their work.

3. **Compare results with standards.** From top manager to first-line supervisor, the control system flashes a warning if there is a gap between what was expected (the standard) and what is taking place or has taken place (the result). If the results are within the tolerance limits, the supervisor's attention can be turned elsewhere. But if the process exceeds the tolerance limits—the gap is too big—then action is called for.

4. **Take corrective action.** You must first find the cause of the gap (variance or deviation from standard). Then you must take action to remove or minimize this cause. If travelers are waiting too long in the airline's ticket line, for example, the supervisor may see that there is an unusually high degree of travel because of a holiday. The corrective action is to add another

ticket clerk. If, however, the supervisor observes that the clerks are taking extra long coffee breaks, this practice will have to be stopped as soon as possible.

To what extent can a supervisor depend on automatic controls?

More and more, operating processes rely on mechanical or automatic control. They try to minimize the human element. We all expect the thermostat to tell the furnace to keep the room warm. In many automobiles we expect a buzzer to tell us whether the seat belt is fastened or whether we are exceeding a preselected speed limit. In some cars we even let a mechanism take over the accelerator so that the speed of the auto is automatically maintained for us. Many processes in business and industry are controlled by the same principles. A worker feeds a sheet of metal into a press, and the machine takes over. A clerk slips a piece of paper into a copying machine, and the machine automatically reproduces the number of copies the clerk has dialed onto the control mechanism. The trend toward such automatic controls is very strong.

Human activities, however, still require supervisory control. Supervisors continually have to find ways to make sure that employees meet their job standards. Especially important are those of (1) attendance, (2) speed and care in feeding or servicing automatically controlled machines, and (3) even greater care needed by employees in joining their efforts with those of people in their own organizations and others they interface in their company or client organizations.

What specific kinds of controls are most likely to aid or restrict supervisory actions?

These will depend largely on the nature of the organization in which the supervisor works. The following controls, however, are most common:

Quantity controls. These relate to the demand of almost every organization for some standard of output or production. The quantity of production required is often the basis for all other aspects of control. In other words, a supervisor must first make sure that output quantities measure up. Then the supervisor's attention can turn to controls that specify a certain quality or time, for example.

Quality controls. If, in meeting the production standard, a department skimps on the quality of its work, there can be trouble. Quantity and quality go hand in hand. The inspection function is intended to make sure the final product or service lives up to its quality standards (specifications). As a supplement to routine inspections, many companies practice statistical quality control, a way of predicting quality deviations in advance so that a supervisor can take corrective action before a product is spoiled. (See Chapter 28 for details.)

Time controls.   Almost every organization must also meet certain deadlines or live within time restraints. A product must be shipped on a certain date. A service must be performed on an agreed-on day. A project must be completed as scheduled. Such time standards point up the fact that it is not enough just to get the job done if it isn't finished on time.

Material controls.   This is related to both quality and quantity standards. A company may wish to limit the amount of raw or finished materials it keeps on hand; thus it exercises inventory controls. Or an apparel firm, for instance, may wish to make sure that the maximum number of skirts be cut out of a bolt of cloth so that a minimum amount of cloth is wasted—a material yield standard.

Cost controls.   The final crunch in exercising controls involves costs. A supervisor may meet the quantity and quality standards, but if, in so doing, the department has been overstaffed or works overtime, it probably won't meet its cost standard.

How do budgets fit into this picture?

Budgetary controls are very similar to cost standards. Typically, the accounting or financial department provides a supervisor with a list of allowable expenses for the month. These will be based on the expectation of a certain output, say, 4,000 units of production. These allowable expenses become its cost standards to be met for the month. At the end of the month the accounting department may issue the supervisor a cost variance report (Figure 12-1). This tells whether the department has met its standards, exceeded them, or fallen below them. Note that in Figure 12-1 the deparment has exceeded its overall budget by $800. It has, however, met a number of its standards while spending more for material handling, overtime, operating supplies, and maintenance. The supervisor will be expected to do something to bring these cost overruns back into line next month. On the other hand, the department used less than was budgeted

FIGURE 12-1

Cost Variance Report

Department <u>Assembly</u>   Dept. no. <u>707</u>   Month <u>July</u>
No. of units scheduled for production <u>4,000</u>
No. of units actually produced <u>4,020</u>
Production variance <u>+20 units</u>

Account Title	Actual	Budget	Variance (+over −under)
Direct labor	$ 8,000	$ 8,000	0
Indirect labor			
Material handling	900	600	+300
Shop clerical	500	500	0
Supervision	1,200	1,200	0
Overtime	100	0	+100
Shift premium	0	0	0
Operating supplies	500	400	+100
Maintenance and repairs	1,900	1,400	+500
Gas, water, steam, air	1,600	1,800	−200
Electrical power	800	800	0
Total controllable budget	$15,500	$14,700	+$800

for gas, water, and steam. If this keeps up, the accounting department may develop a new standard for those expenses and allow the supervisor less money for them in the future.

Some authorities speak of systems control. What is meant by that?

In simplest terms, systems control means that you can't control one activity or performance factor without affecting the control of another. All activities carried on in a department or a process are interrelated. Quantity, quality, time, materials, and costs cannot really be separated if you look at the big picture. They are part of a system.

Take an example. If the sales department wants the shop supervisor to push an order in a hurry, the supervisor may have to sacrifice quality (by working too quickly) or costs (by working overtime). Something in the system has to give. In practice, someone must always decide whether the cost of getting out an order ahead of schedule can be justified by the benefits involved. One customer may be pleased (a benefit), while several others may be displeased because their orders were bumped back (a cost). Even the customer who is pleased to get an order sooner than expected may be displeased if the quality of the shipment doesn't measure up to expectations.

Supervisors are often at the receiving end of systems-control decisions. Just as frequently they may have to make systems-control decisions in their own departments.

Must supervisors spend all their time controlling?

It would appear that way. But by using a simple principle called management by exception, time taken for control activities can be held to a minimum. *Management by exception* is a form of delegation in which the supervisor lets things run as they are so long as they fall within prescribed (control) limits of performance. When they get out of line (as on the cost variance report in Figure 12-1), the supervisor steps in and takes corrective action.

Figure 12-2 show how a supervisor can use the management-by-exception principle as a guideline for delegating much of the control work to subordinates.

Take, for example, a broiler chef in a fast-food restaurant. The boss says that the chef should expect to broil between 180 and 200 hamburgers per hour. This is control zone 1. So long as results fall within the prescribed limits, the chef is completely in charge.

If the requests for hamburgers, however, fall below 180 but above 150, the chef keeps the grill hot but puts fewer hamburgers into the ready position; or, if requests build up to 225, the chef moves more hamburgers to the completed stage. This is zone 2. The chef takes this action without first checking with the boss but tells the boss what has been done.

If business falls from 150 to more than 100 hamburgers an hour, the chef may ask the boss whether the grill can be turned off for a while; or, if the requests build up to 250 per hour the chef may ask if one of the counter clerks can help. This is zone 3.

If conditions now move to either extreme—hamburger requests drop below 100 or exceed 250, the chef calls this to the supervisor's attention. This is zone 4. The supervisor may in the first instance (below 100) decide to shut down the grill; in the second instance (above 250) decide to start up an auxiliary grill.

What about the people problem in controls?

Many people do not like to be "controlled." They don't like to be told what to do, and they feel boxed in when faced with specific standards. Few persons like to be criticized or corrected. Yet criticism or correction is what control often comes down to. When correction means discipline or termination, controls can seem

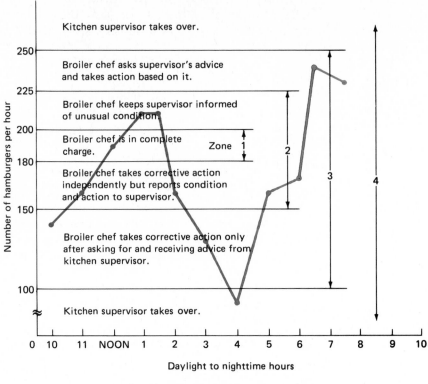

Zone 1: Expected or planned conditions
Zone 2: Unusual but acceptable conditions
Zone 3: Undesirable or highly unusual conditions
Zone 4: Unacceptable conditions

FIGURE 12-2. Use of Management-by-Exception Chart for Controlling Operation of Hamburger Grill.

very harsh indeed. For this reason a supervisor should be realistic about controls. Thus controls can have a very negative effect on employees, to say nothing of what they may do to the supervisor.

The negative aspects of controls, however, can be minimized. Supervisors should consider any of the following more positive approaches:

Emphasize the value of controls to employees. Standards provide employees with feedback that tells them whether they are doing well or not. Standards minimize the need for the supervisor to interfere and often allow the employee to choose a way of doing the job so long as standards are met. "You do the job, and I will stay out of your hair."

Avoid arbitrary or punitive standards.   Employees respond better to standards that can be justified by past records that support the standards. "Our records show that 150 per day is a standard that other operators have consistently met." Standards based upon analysis, especially time studies, are even more acceptable. "Let's time this job for an hour or two so that we can be sure the standard is reasonable." Compare this with: "We'll just have to step up our production rate to 175 units each day."

Be specific; use numbers if possible.   Avoid expressions like "improve quality," "show us better attendance." Instead, use numbers that set specific targets such as "fewer than two days' absence in the next six months," or "decrease your scrap percentage from 7 out of 100 to 3 out of 100."

Aim for improvement rather than punishment.   Capitalize on instances of missed standards to try to help employees learn how to improve their work. "Your output was below standard again last month. Perhaps you and I ought to start all over again to see what it is that is preventing you from meeting them. There may be some place or something that I haven't shown you about this particular operation.

Resort to punishment as the last step.   A supervisor must balance rewards with punishment. Most employees respond to positive motivation. Many do not. All employees, however, good and poor alike, want to know what the "or else" is about their jobs. The guiding rule is to hold off punishment if you can, but to make it clear to everyone that standards must be met. Specify in advance what the penalty will be for those who don't meet them.

Avoid threats that you can't or won't back up.   If an employee is to be disciplined for failing to meet a quota or a standard of workmanship, be specific about the nature and timing of the discipline. "If you don't get your production up to 150 per day by the first of April, I will recommend that you be laid off for good." Don't say, "If you don't shape up soon, your head will be in a noose." If you do make the specific threat, it is good to make certain in advance that the company will help you to make it stick. (See Chapter 22.)

Be consistent in the application of controls.   If you have set standards that apply to the work of several employees, it should go without saying that you will be expected to make everyone measure up to them. If you do feel that exceptions can be made, be prepared to defend that position. In the main, however, standards should be the same for everyone doing the same work.

Similarly, rewards and punishment should be the same for all those who meet, and fail to meet, these standards.

What about encouraging self-control?

Self-control is beautiful for those who can exert it. Douglas McGregor insisted that many people needed only to be given the targets for their work—the standards. After that, he said, they wished to be left alone and to be judged on the basis of their results in meeting or not meeting these targets. Employees will, McGregor said, provide their own control and do not need a supervisor to threaten them or cajole them into meeting standards.

My advice is to give an employee the benefit of the doubt. Give a free hand to those who take charge of themselves. Keep the rein on those who soon show that they need, or expect, the control to come from the supervisor.

When do management goals become control standards?

Very often, as shown when the linkage between planning and controlling was explained. More specifically, however, many companies convert their organizational goals into control programs by using a system of Management by Objectives. *Management by Objectives* (MBO) is a planning and control process that provides managers at each organizational control point with a set of goals, or standards, to be attained. The process is usually repeated every 12 months. These MBO goals are similar to the supervisory performance goals listed in Table 8-1 in Chapter 8. It is presumed that if all supervisors reach their goals, the organization will also reach its goals. In companies where MBO is practiced to its full extent, the supervisors' goals literally become the standards of performance that must be met. The assumption is that the supervisors are capable of, and will exert, their own controls in striving to meet these objectives. The MBO system also presumes that the supervisors have been given enough freedom of action so that they can meet these goals within the resources provided by staff and budget. In essence, MBO is simply a formalization at managerial levels of the principle of self-control.

supervisory word power

Standard.   The measure, criterion, or basis for judging performance of a product or service, machine, individual, or organization.

Specification.   A collection of standardized dimensions and characteristics pertaining to a product, process, or service.

Variance.   The gap or deviation between *actual* performance or results and the *standard* or expected performance or results.

Tolerance.   The permissible deviation from standard.

Feedback.   Relaying of the measurement of actual performance back to the individual or unit causing the performance so that action can be taken to correct, or narrow, the variance.

Budget.   A financial or cost standard that establishes the amount of allowable expenses for operating a supervisor's department over a limited period of time.

Management by exception.   A principle of control that enables a supervisor to delegate corrective action to a subordinate so long as the variances in performance are within specified ranges.

Other Important Terms in This Chapter

automatic control	quality control
budgetary control	quantity control
cost-benefit analysis	self-control
cost variance report	systems control
management by objectives (MBO)	time control
material control	yield

reading comprehension

1. How are control standards related to the goals established in plans?

2. If standards are set by higher management in a company, does the supervisor ever have any responsibility for establishing controls? If so, how?

3. Of the three chief ways of setting standards, which is the best? Why? What's wrong with the other two?

4. What kind of errors should supervisors look for in control information or in the measurements on which standards are based?

5. What is the ultimate purpose of the control process?

6. Give some examples of automatic controls in everyday life.

7. Briefly describe five specific controls a supervisor is likely to be concerned with.

8. How are management by exception and control standard tolerances related?

9. Is there anything positive in controls for the *people* who work in an organization? If so, what?

10. How should a supervisor approach the issue of self-control among employees?

supervision in action

███████████ **THE CASE OF THE MISSED BOGEY.** **A case study in human relations involving budgetary controls, with questions for you to answer.**

Ross J., supervisor of the assembly department of the Traverse City Transmissions Plant, had just received his budget for the month of May. Among other things the production control department had increased his monthly output standard, or bogey, from 2,000 units to 2,500. The budgeting department had taken this into account when setting the various allowable expenses for the month. The department's total allowable costs were usually $100,000. For May this figure had been raised to $125,000. This is a one-quarter increase to balance the one-quarter increase in the output bogey. The budgeting department called this approach "flexible budgeting," since it increases or decreases Ross's allowable expenses in proportion to the monthly output bogey. If the bogey had been lowered to 1,500 units, for example, the allowable expense total would have been lowered also, probably to $75,000.

Ross studied his bogey and expense budget carefully. He saw that he would have to add another person to the assembly line. He also decided that the department would have to work overtime for an hour or two each day to meet the bogey. When Ross called this to the attention of his superior, his boss said, "I can't approve your adding another person into your department, but I will approve overtime—so long as you don't exceed the total allowable expense for the month."

"That won't be too easy," said Ross. "You are asking for an increase in output of 25 percent. I may have to work the department as much as 25 percent overtime to meet that bogey."

"The expense budget won't handle it," said Ross's boss. "It allows for only a 15 percent increase in overtime. You'll have to make up the difference by getting increased productivity from your regular workers."

Ross wasn't too happy about that decision. He did go back to his desk, however, to see what improvements he could think of.

Then he went out to the shop floor to study the operations there. After considerable observation, Ross did discover a couple of places on the line where improvements could be made. At one point, where the gears were placed in the housing, there was a bottleneck. This slowed the line while employees downstream waited for housings to finish. Based upon this observation, Ross decided to transfer one worker from the finishing operation to the gear-insertion stage. That way, the line would be better balanced. Production ought to rise the needed 10 percent.

Ross made the necessary changes in assignments the second day of May. There was some resistance to this. The employees in the finishing stage complained about being overloaded now. Work at the gear-insertion station was somewhat crowded, as the additional employee tended to get in the way. Nevertheless, Ross stuck with his plan and by the end of the second week in May, the line was running pretty smoothly. Ross checked his output and found to his chagrin that the department had completed only 1,000 assemblies. The month was half over, and even with the increased production rate the department would probably fall short of its 2,500-unit bogey by 250 units. Accordingly, Ross took it upon himself to work his crew overtime every day for the last two weeks of the month. At the end of May, however, Ross was pleased that his department had, in fact, met the bogey of 2,500 units.

A few days after the end of the month Ross received a call from his boss. "What happened to your budget last month? the boss asked. "You went over it by $5,000."

"It must have been the overtime we worked during the last couple of weeks," said Ross.

"I thought I told you that you had to keep your overtime in line," his boss replied.

"I did, during the first two weeks," said Ross. "But when I saw that we wouldn't meet our bogey, I added overtime every day."

"You shouldn't have done that," said his boss. "Ordinarily it costs your department $50 to put together each unit. At the rate you were going, it cost more than that. In fact, it cost $130,000 to put together the 2,500 units, or $52 per unit. That's an increase of 4 percent. We hardly make that kind of percentage of profit on the transmissions in the first place."

"I am sorry about that," said Ross. "But I thought that the main thing you wanted from me was the 2,500 units. Besides, the changes I've made in setting up the assembly line will enable me to keep costs in line next month."

"It's too late now," said Ross's boss. "The scheduling department is cutting us back to 1,500 transmissions next month. You'll have to be thinking about cutting at least one person from your line. Meanwhile, I want you to write out a complete explanation as to why you failed to come inside your expense bogey during May. I have to meet with the general manager this afternoon, and he will want a full explanation."

1. How reasonable was Ross's boss in this situation? What might he have done to make the situation clearer to Ross?

2. What do you think of Ross's plan? What was good about it and what was bad about it? How does it reflect the need for a cost-benefit decision?

3. In what way might Ross have avoided this situation? How can he avoid a recurrence in June?

enriching your viewpoint

To gain a broader understanding of supervisory controls, the following readings are suggested:

Bittel, Lester R., *Improving Supervisory Performance,* McGraw-Hill Book Company, New York, 1976, Chap. 1, "Performance Criteria for Supervisors."

————, *Management by Exception,* McGraw-Hill Book Company, New York, 1964.

Daugherty, William, and Donald Harvey, "Some Behavioral Implications of Budgeting Systems," *Arizona Business,* April 1973, pp. 3–7.

Jasinski, F. J., "Use and Misuse of Efficiency Controls," *Harvard Business Review,* July–August 1956, pp. 105–112.

Jones, Reginald, and H. George Trentin, *Budgeting: Key to Planning and Control,* Amacom, New York, 1971.

Koontz, Harold, and Cyril O'Donnell, *Essentials of Management,* 2d ed., McGraw-Hill Book Company, New York, 1978, Chap. 23, "Control Techniques."

Newman, W.H., *Constructive Control: Design and Use of Control Systems,* Prentice-Hall, Inc., Englewood Cliffs, N.J., 1975.

Reddin, W.J., *Effective Management by Objectives,* McGraw-Hill Book Company, New York, 1971.

Reeser, Clayton, *Management Functions and Modern Concepts,* Scott, Foresman and Company, Glenview, Ill., 1973 Chap. 58, "Budgetary Financial Control."

Sartain, Aaron Q., and Alton W. Baker, *The Supervisor and the Job,* 3d ed., McGraw-Hill Book Company, New York, 1978, Chap. 4, "Controlling."

supervising people at work

3
PART

Because of their everyday and intimate contact with employees, supervisors must acquire certain specialized interpersonal skills. These cover a gamut of administrative and personnel relationships, which underscore the objectives of Part 3:

- To develop more fully oral communications skills so as to be able to direct and instruct employees more effectively.
- To further pursue understanding of organization design so as to facilitate job analysis, evaluation, and compensation processes.
- To relate job specifications to the performance requirements of those who perform these jobs and to conduct appraisals that provide proper correction and motivation for the incumbents.
- To apply knowledge of job requirements and human resources to the training and development of employees.
- To acquire the knowledge and skills needed to educate the work force in accident-free practices and enforce standards of safe conduct.
- To comprehend the basic labor management laws so as to safeguard management prerogatives and maintain harmonious union relationships.

13

CHAPTER **giving orders and instructions**

How can you get better results from the instructions and orders you issue?

By being sure your order is the right one for the particular situation at hand and by being specific about what the employee is to do and what kind of results you expect.

Your orders are even more effective when you use care in selecting the person most likely to carry them out well. And you add power to your orders by being confident (not cocky) and calm as you deliver them. Finally, your orders will stand the best chance of accomplishing what you intend if you make a practice of checking to be sure they are carried out at the time and in the manner you prescribe.

Should you repeat an order?

Yes, by all means. Repeat your instructions to be certain the employee understands them clearly. All of us are expert at misunderstanding. So give a worker an opportunity to ask questions if there seems to be doubt about what you want. In fact, it's a good practice to ask the employee to repeat your instructions back to you. That way you can readily find out where the stumbling blocks might be.

When should you request an employee to do something?

As often as possible. It used to be thought that order giving was a one-way street, that all a supervisor had to say was, "I tell you. You do it." Such an attitude gets you nowhere. Today's workers want and deserve more consideration. And many of them have unions to back this desire. In addition we now know lots more about employees' attitudes. For instance, psychologists who study employee behavior tell us that most workers will rate a boss high and will cooperate more willingly as a result if the boss gives orders pleasantly. We know, too, that employees like to feel they are offered some say in decisions that affect them and will work harder when they have had a chance to participate.

So there's nothing wrong and there's much good in saying, "Will you try to get that machine cleaned up before quitting time?" Or, "Won't you please make an effort to get to work on time Monday?"

Generally speaking, a request carries the same weight as a direct order. But it does impart a feeling that workers have some freedom of action, that they can question any part that bothers them. And it's especially useful with thin-skinned employees who tend to see every boss as a dictator.

When should you command an employee to do something?

Commands are dangerous. But they may be necessary in emergencies. In case of accident or fire, for instance, your instructions should be direct, clear, and unequivocal to avoid conflicting actions.

Orders should be specific and firm, too, in operating situations that demand active leadership. It's desirable to be especially decisive, for instance, in directing a crew that requires rapid coordination on an unfamiliar job—like supervising a crew that is lowering a 100-ton machine onto its foundations, or starting up a new and complex machine.

But, in general, commands cause resentment. It's best to avoid them until you need them. If you use commands only occasionally, your employees will know that you're not being bossy just for the sake of showing your authority. They will recognize that your change in approach is necessary and will snap to accordingly.

Is it your fault if an employee misses an order?

Not necessarily. In fact, the employee may be the one who goofed. This points up the wisdom of seeing order giving as a two-way street.

Look at it this way: An order is given only to get something done. You see a situation. You see what the situation calls for. Your job as an order giver is to make sure the person who is to do the job sees the situation the same way you do.

For example, say you're supervisor of the packaging department in a soap flake plant. You come by the discharge end of a packaging machine that fills and seals boxes of soap flakes. You test-weigh a box and find that it is overweight. From your experience you know that an adjustment of the filling mechanism will correct the situation. The only reason you will give an order is to help the package machine operator see the situation and the action it calls for, as you do.

How would you give your order? "Wake up, Joe! Shut down your machine and get it fixed." That's not too bad, but it doesn't tell Joe what's wrong or recognize that Joe might know what to do without your telling him. This is better: "Joe, your machine's running overweight. Better shut down until I send the repairman up." Even better, if you have confidence in Joe, just hold up a box to get his attention. Then say, "Overweight!" Let Joe take over from there.

So try to look at your orders as solutions to action-demanding situations that both you and your employees must see in the same light if orders are to be carried out willingly and well.

What should you do when an employee willfully refuses to do what you ask?

The first piece of advice and the toughest to follow is: Don't fly off the handle. Count to 100 if insubordination makes you want to blow your top. Then ask yourself whether the order was a fair one, whether you've chosen the proper person to follow it. Have you made yourself understood?

If you think you've done your part, next try to find out what the employee objects to. Ask for specifics: "What is it that you object to? Why do you think it's unreasonable?" Chances are an employee who is willfully disobedient is looking for an excuse to blow off steam. It may be that if you listen for a couple of minutes, the resentment will pass. For that reason it's smart not to talk about your authority or threaten with discipline. Not then, anyway.

But if an employee is stubborn and can't or won't be cooled off or have a change of mind about doing what you say, you're faced with a disciplinary problem. You still have alternative choices of what to do, so don't be quick about firing, penalizing, or suspending. You may find it wise not to insist—at that moment—that the order be carried out. Or you may want to modify the order so that it will be accepted. If you choose to do either of the latter, don't let the matter drop there.

Find an early opportunity to talk calmly, constructively, and in private. Don't permit the employee to think that you were soft. Let it be known that you will take disciplinary steps if the employee doesn't straighten up and fly right.

Your other choice is to take whatever disciplinary action your plant permits—that same day, while the incident is fresh in everyone's mind. But this is a choice supervisors should avoid if possible. Punishment is a last resort only. That's why it's unwise to force a showdown situation—especially if there are other employees watching or listening and especially if you'd like to change your mind later on.

Is there anything you can do about a worker who carries out your instructions in a slipshod manner?

There are two effective actions you can take in such a case. First, be sure you have told the worker exactly what you expect the finished work to be. And then follow up to see that it measures up. If it doesn't, insist that it be done over until it's acceptable.

A second approach, and one that will win you cooperation and respect, is to offer to demonstrate some little knack of your own that will help the person work in a more professional manner.

Take Rod Peters, who is sealing up corrugated cases of perfume in a toiletries factory. He's having a hard time keeping up with the employees who pack the boxes. So he gets sloppy with the glue brush, smears the cases, and puts on either too much or too little glue. Ann True, his supervisor, doesn't chew Rod out. Instead Ann says to him, "Having trouble keeping up with the packers? I know, they're pretty fast. Let me show you a trick I learned from somebody who used to hold this job. See, line up three cases before you swing the glue brush. This way you do three cases at a time.

"Here, you try it. And try to be as neat as you can. Our customers hate to display sloppy-looking cases. And if they're not glued properly, they break open in shipment. So let's see how you make out sealing them this way. I'll be back later in the morning to find out how you're doing."

When should you put an order in writing?

Whenever you change an order that was previously in writing, put the new order in writing, too. Or if you give an order that must be carried over into another shift, it's wise to jot it down in writing—on the bulletin board, in the department logbook, or as a note to be passed on to the employees concerned. This is much more reliable than word of mouth.

When instructions are complex and contain variations from normal in amounts and sequence, it's wise to write them down, too. On the other hand, don't depend too much on written orders. Not everyone follows written instructions easily. In fact, if you do write instructions down, look for an opportunity to review them orally with employees to see if they understand them. That way the written orders serve the employees as a reference.

Is it wise to let employees use their own judgment in following your instructions?

Sometimes it's a good idea just to suggest what you want. Then let the employees use their own discretion in carrying it out. This leaves it up to them whether or not anything will be done and how it will be done. For instance, "I wonder if there's anything you can do to get this job finished by quitting time." Or, "It looks as if our scrap record will be off this month. Is there something you can do to get it back on the beam?"

Such an implied order stimulates initiative and cooperation—among more responsible workers. It's a form of delegation, and it helps develop your employees' judgment.

The suggestion approach is risky to try with inexperienced or unreliable people. And you shouldn't use it when you have decided in advance exactly what you want done and how. After all, you can't expect your workers to be mind readers.

Should you let anyone else give instructions to your employees?

Unless you have expressly asked someone else to pass along orders to people who work directly under you (and this should be done only infrequently), it's best to see that you're the only one who gives orders to your employees. Otherwise, your employees will find themselves working for two bosses. And your status and effectiveness will be weakened.

You were hired to direct your employees. That's your responsibility. If someone else tries to take over this part of your job, it's up to you to politely, but firmly, hold on to your rights. If your boss makes a habit of bypassing you in issuing instructions to your employees, you should speak to your boss at once about it. Be tactful, of course, but be convincing that this works against department morale and efficiency; otherwise, you're in for trouble.

Employees are paid to work, aren't they? Why, then, should you handle them with kid gloves?

Because in the long run it's easier on the supervisor. Actually, giving orders pleasantly and thoughtfully really isn't babying employees. It's just common sense to make it as easy as possible for them to say "Yes" to what you ask them to do. It's an old adage that a willing worker does better work.

One reason old-fashioned supervisors had trouble with order giving (and consequently cost their companies lots of money by having to fire disobedient workers) was that they overlooked one and sometimes two of the three important ingredients of order giving. It may be obvious that you should tell workers what to do. But it's easy to forget that they may not know how to do it—that you must take time out to show them or tell them how to go about it. But the biggest error of all is not to tell them why.

Telling employees why something must be done gives them a reason for wanting to do it. There's a world of difference, for instance, between "Starting tomorrow I want you to show me personally each piece of off-quality raw material you charge for credit" and "The purchasing department wants a report on how well our new supplier is meeting specifications with our raw material. For a couple of weeks, I'll have to furnish them with a detailed report. So will you set aside for me each piece of off-quality stock so that I may inspect it? I have to tell the purchasing department exactly what's wrong with it."

Should you give an order when you're angry?

If you can avoid it, don't give orders when you're uptight. There's always the possibility that you'll make a threat that you can't, or won't want to, carry out.

You probably know of a case similar to this one: Ralph, machine-shop supervisor, has just been chewed out by his boss for the number of damaged hand tools charged to his department. So as soon as the boss leaves, Ralph blows his stack to his employees. "Next one who turns in a damaged tool, no matter what the reason, you'll pay for it out of your own pocket." So what happens? That afternoon Sylvia, who has been with the company 15 years and who is as conscientious as can be, accidentally ruins a micrometer. Whom does that put on the spot? Nobody but Ralph!

How is your tone of voice important?

Remember the story of the cowboy who said, "When you call me that, smile." Employees are the same way. They'll read your voice like a book to hear whether you're trying to throw your weight around, whether you mean what you say or are just talking through your hat. So when you give an order that's going to be hard to carry out, smile to show that you know what you ask isn't easy. But let the tone of your voice show that you expect it to be done regardless.

Should you ask an employee to do anything you wouldn't do?

You don't have to do everything you ask others to do. But, in principle, you should show that you'd be willing to do it if you had to.

Giving orders is a test of your leadership courage. General Patton used to say that an army was like a piece of cooked spaghetti. You can't push it, you can only pull it. You might not have to lead an army, but you should always imply your willingness to stand up where the shots are being received.

If there's a dirty or unpleasant job, be sure you expose yourself to the same conditions your workers do. If they must work in the rain or cold, get out there with them. If they have to get in the muck under a machine, show that you're not above getting your hands dirty, either.

But shouldn't each person be handled differently?

Yes, if you can find time. Some people like their bosses to be specific about what they want done. Others want only an opportunity to raise a question or make a suggestion. Still other people work best when given a free hand. To assign orders accordingly, you'll want to improve your ability to size up people. Then you will improve your leadership by tailoring each order to fit the individual.

Do you issue group orders differently?

Many people believe that orders given to groups of people are ineffective unless the group is permitted to discuss them and decide how the group can best carry them out. This isn't always practical or desirable, of course. But when you issue orders to groups, keep in mind that getting across to groups is many times harder than reaching one person. It's always better if you can find a suitable time and place to discuss the reasons behind the order and to get suggestions from the group as to how it might best be carried out.

One rule to follow in group instructions is to pin down who is to do what. If you dont, you're likely to find each person waiting for someone else to carry the ball.

How can active listening help gain acceptance for your orders?

When supervisors actively listen to an employee's negative reaction to an order, for example, they may hear the reason for that resistance. Most of the time, however, we tend to put our minds into neutral when others resist us. We engage in passive listening, hardly hearing what the other person says, and we're ready to attack again. Compare these two examples:

Passive listening

Employee: What does the scheduling office think I am, Rose— a miracle worker? There is no way this job can be finished today!

Supervisor: That's the order, whether you like it or not. Just make sure you've finished it by 5 p.m.

Employee: I'm already behind schedule because of the press breakdown this week. Doesn't anybody understand what kind of pressure that puts on me?

Supervisor: Look, I don't make up the schedules here. It's my job to see that they get carried out. We're all under pressure this week. So, like it or not, you've got to get hopping right away so that we meet the deadline.

Employee: I'll do it, but this is the last time you're going to treat me like dirt.

Active listening

Employee: What does the scheduling office think I am, Rose— a miracle worker? There is no way this job can be finished today!

Supervisor: Sounds like you're really angry about it, Joe.

Employee: You're darned right I am. I've been working all week to catch up after that press broke down. Now that I'm about on schedule, this lousy order comes in.

Supervisor: As if you didn't have enough to do already. Seems as if you're shoveling sand against the tide.

Employee: Yeah. It's all uphill around here. I can hardly catch a breath.

Supervisor: You feel like it's unfair to unload a rush job on you when you've been trying so hard to get back on schedule.

Employee: That's right. I'm willing to pull my share of the load, Rose, but it's discouraging to feel that you're being dumped on all the time.

Supervisor: You feel that we have been asking more than you can handle?

Employee: Not more than I can handle. I can get this lousy job out today. But it sure puts me near my breaking point.

Supervisor: I understand how you feel. Actually, Joe, we haven't been picking on you. The whole shop is in a bind this week. But I appreciate your taking on what seems like an unjustified overload.

The difference between the two examples is that the supervisor is actively listening in the second one. Joe is, in effect, saying that he is being misused. Rose is listening and responding to make it clear to Joe that she appreciates the feeling he is expressing. Active listening won't solve all order-giving problems, but it does provide a good base for acceptance. It helps to show that the supervisor is not just mechanically passing on instructions and that the supervisor views the employee as a human being with very personal feelings and problems.

What can supervisors do to detect hidden resistance?

By trying to put themselves in the employees' shoes. When you are giving an order, it is only natural for you to see the need only from the top down. If you turn yourself around mentally, you may begin to see what the need is from the bottom up. One good way to get this turned-about feeling is to answer an employee's challenge with a response that reflects what the employee has said. For example:

Employee's challenge: Just who is responsible for those filing cabinets, anyway?

Supervisor's response: Do you feel that someone is trying to take over your authority for them?

Employee's challenge: Isn't it about time that younger, more able people get a shot at a promotion before the older guys do?

Supervisor's response: It seems to you that younger people should get a chance now.

Employee's challenge: How does the company think I'm going to turn out clean letters on this broken-down typewriter?

Supervisor's response: You really are fed up with this machine, aren't you?

Employee's challenge: Don't you think my work has gotten better over the last few months?

Supervisor's response: Sounds as if you feel that your work has picked up since we last talked about it.

Responses like this are not sweet talk. Their purpose is to keep open the flow of communication from the employee. Kept talking to a sympathetic ear, the employee may expose the real source of irritation. If so, the supervisor may be better able to shape the order or instruction to the employee's preference. Or at the very least, the supervisor may be able to take the sting out of the assignment.

Technically speaking, this approach provides empathy (understanding of, not necessarily sympathy for, another's feelings). This, in turn, helps to establish rapport (harmony, closeness, and confidence) between supervisor and employee.

What can be done to avoid ambiguity in instructions?

Many words and phrases have a double, or at least an unclear, meaning. Here is a list of troublemakers. Avoid words or terms like these when handing out assignments. Instead, try to add clarifying details to make them more specific.

* *Quality factors*, words like good, smooth, well-done, or clean. Try instead: *fewer than 3 rejects per day, so smooth that a dust cloth won't catch on the surface, a steak without a trace of red in it, completely free of the grease that protected it when shipped.*
* *Quantity factors*, words like *large, small, heavy,* or *tight.* Try instead: *over ten inches, smaller than a ten-cent piece, over two ounces, as tight as a 20-psi wrench can make it.*
* *Time factors*, terms like *quickly, as soon as possible, in a few days.* Try instead: *25 per minute, within 24 hours, by Thursday at 2 p.m.*

Which guidelines in particular may keep a supervisor out of trouble when directing, ordering, assigning, or instructing?

There are no assurances that employees won't get hung up about a particular assignment, but here are 11 guidelines that should minimize trouble:

1. Don't make it a struggle for power. If you approach too many order-giving situations in an I'll show-you-who's-boss frame of mind, you'll soon be fighting the whole department. Try to focus your attention—and the worker's—on the goal that must be met. The idea to project is that it is the situation that demands the order, not a whim of the supervisor.

2. Avoid an offhand manner. If you want employees to take instructions seriously, then deliver them that way. It's all right to have fun, but be firm about those matters that are important.

3. Watch out for your words. As you have seen, words can be unreliable messengers of your thoughts. Watch the tone of your voice, too. Few people like to feel that they are being taken for granted or pushed around. Most employees accept the fact that it is the supervisor's job to hand out orders and instructions. Their quarrel is more likely to be with the way these are made.

4. Don't assume that the worker understands. Give the employee a chance to ask questions and to raise objections. Have the employee confirm an understanding by repeating what you've said.

5. Be sure to get feedback right away. Give the employee who wishes to complain about the assignment a chance to do so at the time. It's better to iron out resistance and misunderstanding before the job begins than afterward.

6. Don't give too many orders. This is an area where a communications overload will be self-defeating. Be selective in issuing instructions. Keep them brief and to the point. Wait until an employee has finished one job before asking that another be started.

7. Provide just enough detail. Some jobs require more information than less complex ones do. Some workers need more detailed instruction than others do. Think about the information needs of the person you're speaking to. For an old hand there's nothing more tiresome than having to listen to familiar details.

8. Watch out for conflicting instructions. Check to make sure that you're not telling your employees one thing while supervisors in adjoining departments are telling their people another.

9. Don't choose only the willing worker. Some people are naturally cooperative. Others make it difficult for you to ask them to do anything. Be sure that you don't overwork the willing person. Make sure the hard-to-handle people get their share of the rough jobs, too.

10. Try not to pick on anyone.   It is a temptation to punish a person by handing out an unpleasant assignment. Resist this temptation if you can. Employees have the right to expect the work to be distributed fairly. So if you have a grudge against an employee, don't use a dirty job assignment to get even.

11. Above all, don't play the big shot.   New supervisors are sometimes guilty of flaunting their authority. Older supervisors feel more confident. They know that you don't have to crack the whip to gain employees' cooperation and respect.

supervisory word power

Command.   To exercise authority forcefully with the expectation of obedience.

Order.   To communicate authority to employees so as to arrange a more systematic and productive sequence of activities.

Instruct.   To furnish knowledge or information in a disciplined, systematic way with the expectation of compliance.

Direct.   To guide or regulate in order to achieve a smooth and efficient operation.

Request.   To ask courteously, to make known your wishes without the implied assurance that they will be fulfilled.

Other Important Terms in This Chapter

active listening   passive listening
empathy   rapport

reading comprehension

1. When should a supervisor be expected to repeat an order?

2. Under what circumstances might a supervisor command an employee to carry out an order?

3. Contrast a request that something be done and a suggestion that it might be done.

4. When you give orders, why is it important to try to get the employee to understand the situation in the same way you do?

5. Suggest at least two ways a supervisor can call an employee's attention to a misread order.

6. In an instance of an employee's apparent willful disobedience, what recourses are open to the supervisor?

7. What are some disadvantages of passing orders through other people?

8. Under what circumstances should a supervisor try to refrain from issuing orders?

9. Why should supervisors try to develop the ability to listen actively when giving orders?

10. Give some examples of how objective units can be used in orders to improve their clarity.

supervision in action

████████████ THE CASE OF THE SNARLED PARKING LOT. **A case study in human relations involving the knack of giving orders and instructions, with questions for you to answer.**

Dr. McClinans, the director of administrative affairs for a Midwestern technical training institute, had been concerned for some time about the way in which staff personnel regularly ignored or disobeyed the school's parking regulations. His policy had been to assign parking spaces in order of seniority, with the most convenient spaces going to the senior staff members. Employees with the least seniority were placed in remote parking lots. On rainy days, however, these junior employees regularly cruised the senior parking lots looking for spaces that might be open. This was a distinct possibility, since staff hours varied according to the day of the week or whether employees were on daytime or evening schedules. It was a great source of irritation to older staff people to arrive at the institute for work only to find that their assigned space was occupied. Often, by the time the license plate of the interloper was identified, the car had been moved.

To counter this problem, Dr. McClinans regularly had the parking lots patrolled by security officers who were instructed to ticket the cars of parking violators. This practice was aided to some extent by the way in which parking lots were color-coded. Each staff person who applied for parking privileges was issued a color-coded decal that designated the particular lot in which that person's car could park—red, yellow, green, and so forth. When a security officer saw a "red" car in a "yellow" parking lot, it was simple to place a ticket on it and to report the decal number to the administrator's office. Violators who were caught were made to pay a stiff fine: $2 for the first offense, $5 for the second, and $25 for the third. Nevertheless, the parking lot interlopers were an ingenious group. They often knew the security patrol schedule and would be in and out of the prohibited lot before they were identified. Some drove unregistered cars to work so there could be no identification by the color-coded decal system.

Dr. McClinans finally reviewed the whole system and decided to revise the policy. His decision was to assign parking lots to a group of individuals rather than individuals to specific parking spaces. This would provide greater flexibility, he thought. Furthermore, he decided that he could overassign parking spaces by 10 percent, since there were always about that many no-shows on any given day or at any given time.

To carry out this new policy, Dr. McClinans had his administrative assistant revise assignments so that, for example, 55 of the most senior staff were assigned to the red parking lot, which had 50 available spaces; 88 of the next most senior to the yellow parking lot, which had 80 spaces; 110 to the green lot, with 100 spaces, and so on. Next, Dr. McClinans issued a general announcement to describe the new procedure. Tech Institute General Order No. 276, dated December 10, read:

> *Beginning January 1, no one will be issued a specific parking space at the institute. All assignments will be on the basis of a particular lot only. Each employee will, before January 1, be issued a new color-coded decal designating his or her lot. All employees will be expected to respect the new assignments. However, should you arrive at your parking lot and find that there is no space for you, you may seek an open space in the next most senior lot. As in the past, employees who willfully ignore this new assignment policy will be fined.*
>
> *W. X. McClinans, Director of Administration*

January 1 was a holiday, but when the institute opened on January 2, chaos broke out. One senior staff member, finding his old parking space occupied by someone else's car, parked his car in the turning lane so as to block access and egress. A yellow car driver purposely rammed the fender of a red car driver who was trying to take the last open spot in the yellow lot. The red driver insisted that the new policy gave her first claim.

Many less senior employees headed directly for the best parking lots and cruised around till they found a space. Those that couldn't find spaces added to the traffic congestion in already closed lots. Three people assigned to the green lot reported to the director that more than seven spaces were occupied by drivers from red and yellow lots. When the security patrol tried to prevent drivers from entering unfilled, more convenient lots, they were reported by the drivers to the director as not cooperating in the new assignment plan. Drivers of those cars that were ticketed by the security patrol refused to pay fines on the grounds that they had tried to respect the new assignments as best they could or that they had not willfully ignored the regulations.

On January 3, Dr. McClinans and his assistant locked the door to the administration office and turned off the phones. "What shall we do now?" asked Dr. McClinans.

1. If you were Dr. McClinans, what would you do now? Would you try to make the new system work, or would you rescind General Order No. 276 and try a fresh approach? Why?

2. What are three main failings in the way in which instructions for the new systems were given to the staff?

3. What could Dr. McClinans have done to make the instructions regarding the new system clearer?

enriching your viewpoint

For a broader and more comprehensive view of the concepts and specific information presented in this chapter, the following readings are suggested:

Argyris, Chris, *Interpersonal Competence and Organizational Effectiveness,* The Dorsey Press and Richard D. Irwin, Inc., Homewood, Ill., 1962.

Blake, Robert R., and Jane Srygley Moutoin, *The Grid for Supervisory Effectiveness,* Scientific Methods, Inc., Austin, Tex., 1975.

Carnegie, Dale, and Associates, *Managing Through People,* Simon and Schuster, New York, 1975, Chap. 18, "The Human Aspects of Control."

Crosby, Philip B., *The Art of Getting Your Own Sweet Way,* McGraw-Hill Book Company, New York, 1972.

Dowling, William F., and Leonard B. Sayles, *How Managers Motivate,* McGraw-Hill Book Company, New York, 1971.

Flippo, Edwin B., *Principles of Personnel Management,* 4th ed., McGraw-Hill Book Company, New York, 1976, Chap. 21, "Communication and Counselling."

Glueck, William F., *Management,* The Dryden Press, Hinsdale, Ill., 1977, Chap. 9, "Effective Communication."

Mosley, Donald C., and Paul H. Pietri Jr., *Management: The Art of Working With and Through People,* Dickenson Publishing Company, Inc., Encino, Calif., 1975, Chap. 8, "Management Communications: Six Ways to Improve It."

Reeves, Elton T., *So You Want to Be a Supervisor!* Amacom, New York, 1971, Chap. 2, "Skills and Abilities You Will Need."

Tannenbaum, Robert, Irving Weschler, and Fred Massarik, *Leadership and Organization,* McGraw-Hill Book Company, New York, 1961, "Sensitivity for the Management Team," pp. 167–187.

14

CHAPTER job analysis, evaluation, and compensation

What's the underlying purpose of job evaluation?

The purpose of job analysis and job evaluation is to determine systematically the relative worth of jobs within plants and offices.

Have you ever wondered how the job of a washroom porter can be compared in terms of wages with that of a machine operator? Or the duties of a file clerk with those of an executive secretary? Do the unpleasant tasks of the porter's job make it worth as much as that of the machinist, who has better working conditions but who needs more skill? What's the worth of the continuous attention demanded by the filing job compared with the versatility and responsibility of the secretary's?

How would you compare the dollar value to a company of a supervisor who supervises an assembly crew of 75 people with that of a quality-control engineer who supervises only 10 people

227

but who needs much more technical education than the supervisor? Would you pay a steeplejack more than a toolmaker in order to reward the steeplejack for the risks taken? Job evaluation is designed to form a systematic basis for answering such difficult questions, and it leads to fairer pay systems.

How foolproof is job evaluation?

▮▮▮▮▮▮▮▮ It is pretty reliable, although it is not altogether without injustices. Job evaluation is a systematic art, but it is not a science yet. In job evaluation you still have to exercise judgment to appraise the worth of jobs. But job evaluation is the most reliable and the fairest way we know to compare the value of one job with that of another. Its checks and balances help rule out personal prejudices and see that each job is measured by the same set of yardsticks.

What are some of the values that come from job evaluation?

▮▮▮▮▮▮▮▮ When jobs are rated fairly and employees are paid accordingly, there are usually fewer grievances about wages and pay rates. It's said that employees are not so much interested in "how much I get" as in "how much the fellow next to me gets." Job evaluation assures that people doing the same work under the same conditions get the same pay.

In addition, job evaluation provides a structure so that an employee may progress within defined lines to a higher wage grade. The same structure can be used to rate a new job quickly when it is added. And it can be used to compare the pay for jobs within the company with those in nearby or similar plants.

What is the relationship between how much is paid for a certain job and how it is rated under a job-evaluation plan?

▮▮▮▮▮▮▮▮ Under a job-evaluation plan, the job's rating should be the major factor in determining its pay, but there are other influences. The total wage can be affected by the prosperity of the company, the industry involved, or its geographic location. For instance, in 1980 a machinist in an auto plant in Detroit might receive anywhere from 35 to 90 cents more per hour than a machinist with the same classification in a textile plant in Columbia, South Carolina.

Another factor that influences wages is the power of the individual or of the group to bargain for higher wages. And where wage-incentive plans exist, two workers with identically rated jobs may draw the same base rate but have different earnings because of differences in their effort and output.

Which is rated, the individual or the job?

The first principle of job evaluation is that only the job is rated—not the individual who performs it. Here's why: Suppose two employees have identical jobs and turn out about the same quality and quantity of work. But one has a better education than the other. So far as the jobs are concerned, both should still be rated the same. In job evaluation, what is important is only what the job demands, not what extra personal qualities the employee may or may not bring to it. After all, if the job requires only an elementary school education or its equivalent, what purpose would be served in paying an employee extra for a college education when this extra education can't be applied to that job?

How do you find out what the job entails?

The basic tool of job evaluation is a job analysis. It is a method for finding out in an orderly way the duties, requirements, and skills of a job.

Job titles, in and of themselves, mean very little. In one plant a machinist is a lathe operator, in another a grinding machine operator. Even in the same plant, a grinding machine operator in Department B will work to 0.002 inch on routine work. In Department C, the operator will work to 0.001 inch on custom jobs. In Department G, a horizontal grinder may be operated; in Department H, a centerless grinder.

Only by studying it in detail can you find out what the job really entails.

How is a job analysis made?

Information is gathered for a job analysis by any of three methods:

• Sending a questionnaire to supervisors and employees, who fill the survey form out in detail. Accuracy and comprehensiveness of this method depend almost entirely on the supervisor and the employee.
• Interviewing supervisors and employees and recording significant facts on a survey form. This method is more accurate than

the first one, but it depends on good cooperation from the people interviewed.

• Actually observing the job as it is performed. This is the most dependable way, although there can be a loophole if the operator performs a variety of jobs and the observer doesn't see a representative sample of all of them.

Who can make a job analysis?

Anyone, properly instructed, can make a job analysis. But most companies either employ a professional specialist to do this job or train someone to do it on a full-time basis.

What's included in a job description?

The job description or job analysis is not a step-by-step account of the way a job is done. Instead, it summarizes in more general terms what the job entails.

A typical job description for a light assembly job might read something like this:

> **Work performed.** *Assembles small electronic components like capacitors, resistances, tubes, rheostats, shunts, etc., to radio chassis. Works with hand tools like socket wrenches, screwdrivers, and pliers and with overhead power-driven wrench. Refers to instruction sheets and diagrams. Keeps tally sheet of the units worked on. Keeps workplace clean and performs miscellaneous related duties. Is under close supervision of supervisor.*

How clearly are job requirements spelled out in a job description?

Through interviews with the employee and the supervisor and through comparisons with other jobs, the analyst determines specifically what the performance requirements are. For instance, in the light assembly job described in the last question, the analyst might enter on the job description:

> **Responsibilities.** *Is responsible for assembling parts according to specifications. Is responsible for care of tools and housekeeping.*
> **Job knowledge.** *Must know how to read from job instructions and diagrams. Must know how custom changes are handled.*
> **Mental application.** *Requires moderate concentration. Must recognize poor fit or parts that are faulty mechanically.*
> **Dexterity and accuracy.** *Requires high degree of dexterity.*
> **Machines or tools used.** *Hand tools and power-driven screwdriver.*

The analyst will also specify other requirements such as:

Experience required. None.
Training data. One week of vestibule training.
Education requirement. Equivalent of two years of high school.
Relation to other jobs. Transfer from other assembly work.
Transfer to other assembly work like soldering and wiring. Promotion to lead assembler.
Supervision. Under supervision of department supervisor.

The analyst will then run through a checklist of over 100 items that describe *physical activities* (like walking, stooping, carrying, hearing, color vision); *working conditions* (like hot, cold, dusty, noisy, or toxic conditions, electrical hazards); and *occupational characteristics* (like strength of hands, ability to work rapidly for short periods, memory for written instructions, arithmetic computation, tact in dealing with people).

It is of utmost importance that the job requirements be truly justified and not in any way represent prejudices or habitual preferences toward white males, for example. All job-evaluation plans are subject to review by the Equal Employment Opportunity Commission (EEOC) for this reason.

How does a job analysis become a job evaluation?

Data collected during the analysis becomes the raw material for job evaluation. But without the analysis, job evaluation on a large scale is practically impossible. The more accurate the data, the better the evaluation.

Four principal methods are used to convert the job analysis data into a job-evaluation system. The first three are described just briefly here because only about one-fifth of all companies having job-evaluation plans use any of them.

Ranking is the simplest and earliest form of job evaluation. Simple title and descriptions of each job are written on separate cards. Then a committee sorts the cards, ranking them from highest to lowest worth. The trouble here is that it's almost impossible for everyone on the committee to know each job or to agree on the importance of the various factors—working conditions, supervision required, and so forth.

Classification is a refinement of the ranking methods. The committee begins by classifying all possible work at the location into grades of work: for example, A—messenger work, B—simple clerical work requiring no training, C—work requiring recognized clerical ability or considerable experience on certain machines. Next the committee slots the existing jobs into the

FIGURE 14-1.

Job rating—substantiating data		
Job Name LATHE OPERATOR–ENGINE (Up to 30")		**Class** A
Factors	**Deg**	**Basis of Rating**
Education	3 (42)	Use shop mathematics, charts, tables, handbook formulas. Work from complicated drawings. Use micrometers, depth gauges, indicator gauges, protractors. Knowledge of machining methods, tools, cutting qualities of different kinds of metals. Equivalent to 4 years high school plus 2 to 3 years trade training.
Experience	4 (88)	3 to 5 years on wide variety of engine lathe work, including diversified setups.
Initiative and ingenuity	4 (56)	Wide variety of castings and forgings of complicated form Close tolerances. Difficult setups of irregular-shaped parts. Considerable judgment and ingenuity to plan and lay out unusual lathe operations, select proper feeds and speeds, devise tooling, for varying materials and conditions.
Physical demand	2 (20)	Light physical effort. Setups may require handling of heavy material mounting on faceplate. Machine time greatest part of cycle. Most of time spent watching work, checking, making adjustments.
Mental or visual demand	4 (20)	Must concentrate mental and visual attention closely, planning and laying out work, checking, making adjustments. Close tolerances may require unusual attention.

various grades. Here again, the committee must guard against thinking of the individual rather than the job. Nevertheless, this system is simple and is used effectively in most government jobs.

Factor comparison is a reliable, but complicated, method of evaluating very different types of jobs—like comparing manual jobs with jobs requiring creative thinking. Essentially, the method consists of ranking about twenty key jobs according to several different factors common to all jobs. A proportionate amount of the present wage for a key job will represent each of the factors. The sum of the amounts paid for each of the factors is the money

FIGURE 14-1 (*continued*)

Job rating—substantiating data		
Job Name LATHE OPERATOR–ENGINE (Up to 30")		**Class** A

Factors	Deg	Basis of Rating
Responsibility for equipment or process	3 (15)	Careless setup or operation, jamming of tools, dropping work on ways, jamming carriage, may cause damage seldom over $500.
Responsibility for material or product	3 (15)	Careless setup or operation may result in spoilage and possible scrapping of expensive castings, forgings, shafts, etc., e.g., machining below size inaccurate boring of diameter and depth. Probable losses seldom over $500.
Responsibility for safety of others	3 (15)	Flying chips may cause burns, cuts, or eye injuries. Improperly fastened work may fly from faceplate or chuck. May injure another employee when setting work in machine.
Responsibility for work of others	1 (5)	None
Working conditions	2 (20)	Good working conditions. May be slightly dirty, especially in setups. Some dust from castings. Usual machine shop noise.
Unavoidable hazards	3 (15)	May crush fingers or toes handling material or from dropped tools or clamps. Possible burns, cuts, or eye injury from flying chips and particles. Finger or hand injury from rotating work.
Total	311	Grade 4

rate for the job. This is the only job-evaluation method that brings money into the calculations before the job classifications are determined.

What is the most popular method for evaluating jobs?

The point method. Point plans have been installed in several thousand companies—small and large.

Under the point method, jobs are defined in terms of factors that are common to all—like responsibility, skill, education, effort required. The amount of each factor will vary according to the job. So the first step is to take the job analysis or job description and transfer the data to a point-system job-rating sheet (see Figure 14-1).

For each of the "compensable" factors (11 are in the illustration), there is a range of points (see Table 14-1). According to the demands of the particular job on each of the factors, the job will get a certain amount of points. To determine just how many points, it is common to rate each factor for each job according to the degree of demand for that factor (see Table 14-2).

For example, in the case of the engine lathe operator's job, look at the description of Responsibility for Material or Product. The basis for rating (obtained from the original job analysis) says that the probable losses are seldom over $500. On Table 14-2 this is considered a third-degree demand for that factor. Table 14-1 allocates 15 points for third-degree demand for this factor.

Points on the job-rating sheet are totaled, and the total for the job plus each of the point scores for each factor is posted to a master summary sheet. The analyst, together with the supervisor, can then compare the factor rating of each job with others that are similar, and next, the total points for each job with the total points for other jobs.

TABLE 14-1. **Points Assigned to Factors**

	First Degree	Second Degree	Third Degree	Fourth Degree	Fifth Degree
Skill:					
1. Education	14	28	42	56	70
2. Experience	22	44	66	88	110
3. Initiative and ingenuity	14	28	42	56	70
Effort:					
4. Physical demand	10	20	30	40	50
5. Mental or visual demand	5	10	15	20	25
Responsibility:					
6. Equipment or process	5	10	15	20	25
7. Material or product	5	10	15	20	25
8. Safety of others	5	10	15	20	25
9. Work of others	5	..	15	..	25
Job Conditions:					
10. Working conditions	10	20	30	40	50
11. Unavoidable hazards	5	10	15	20	25

TABLE 14-2. **Responsibility for Factor 7 (Material or Product)**

Degree	Requirements
First:	Value of material that may be wasted, damaged, or lost is small (maximum $50), or possibility of loss or damage is slight.
Second:	Probable loss due to damage or waste of materials or product is low (maximum $200).
Third:	Probable loss due to damage or waste of material or product is limited (maximum $500), or if amount of possible loss is high, probability of occurrence is exceedingly low.
Fourth:	Probable loss due to waste or damage of material or product is high (maximum $1,000).
Fifth:	Value of material that may be wasted, damaged, or lost by the employee is very high, up to several thousand dollars.

How are job points converted into job grades?

A typical point system sets up a range or cutoff scores. Minimum and maximum scores are established for each labor rating or grade. For example: 100 to 150 points is a grade 10 job (lowest on the scale); 151 to 180 is a grade 9; 181 to 205 is a grade 8; and so on up to the maximum number of points, which would rate as the number 1 job in the system.

It is not uncommon to find two very different kinds of jobs, such as a specialty machine operator and a roving inspector, with similar point totals and thus in the same labor grade. One job may build up points for experience and physical demand, the other for initiative, visual demand, and responsibility for product. It is the total of all factors, not just a high score on one, that counts.

Are all point systems the same?

No. There are many "standard" plans, such as the old National Metal Trades Association (NMTA), the National Electrical Manufacturers' Association (NEMA), and the Life Office Management Association (LOMA) plans. But even if your company uses such a plan, there's a good chance that it has been adjusted slightly to better fit the jobs that are peculiar to your organization.

Are job-evaluation plans different for white-collar jobs?

Most of the time a different scale of points is used for white-collar jobs from that used for factory workers. Office plans may give special weight to "contacts with other departments." Service-type jobs may emphasize "client" or "customer" contacts.

Special plans are used for (1) highly creative work, such as research and development or editing, and for (2) management positions where credits for number of people supervised, extent of initiative required, and responsibility for profits are heavily weighted.

Where do supervisors fit into this picture?

Supervisors can be of great help to the job-evaluation specialist. First, they can aid the job analyst in getting the true picture of the job. After all, supervisors probably know better than anyone else how a job might vary from time to time. And since they look at many jobs, their opinions as to the degree of the various demands are likely to be more objective than those of employees.

Supervisors are especially helpful in determining the degree to be assigned the various factors for each job. For instance, a supervisor may have felt originally that the experience factor for a heat treater was fourth degree. But when comparing this factor with other jobs, the supervisor sees that a layout person's job is rated fourth degree also. The supervisor might now say, "No, the heat treater's experience isn't quite so necessary as that of the layout person, so let's drop the heat treater's rating back to third degree."

When are the money values assigned to the various jobs classifications?

Only after the labor grades have been assigned. That way, the ratings are apt to be fairer because the raters up until now have been talking only in terms of the job itself—not the individual currently performing it or the wages that person should receive.

How are actual wages determined?

Job-evaluation ratings are usually converted to wage rates in three steps:

1. Plot a chart of money paid employees *now* against the evaluation job grade. This shows up the current inequities in job payment. It's not uncommon to find two persons working in the same job classification—one getting $3.75 per hour, another $4.50. This is the situation that job evaluation corrects.

2. Make a survey of wages paid by comparable companies in

the community. In making this survey, the job-evaluation specialist is careful to compare job descriptions—not just job titles,
since titles are misleading.

3. Combine the study of actual wages paid with wages other
companies in the area pay to develop a pattern for paying wages
in the particular organization.

What are rate ranges?

Rate range is the term typically applied to the spread between
the minimum and the maximum wage rate for each job grade.
Many companies, however, pay only a single rate to wage-roll
employees in each grade and prescribe rate ranges for salaried,
white-collar, and supervisory jobs only.

What happens to employees' pay when they move from one job to another job in the same grade?

A transfer from one job to another in the same job grade is not
considered a promotion, even though an employee may feel it is
and consider one job more desirable. The employee will continue to get the same rate as on the old job. The only way for the
employee to get more money (if there are no rate ranges) is to
be promoted to a higher job grade.

Does the wage pattern always remain the same?

Under job evaluation the difference in pay rate between a higher-
grade job and a lower one provides an incentive for employees
to take jobs that demand more from them. So the steps between
rates are very important. This becomes a problem, and a management decision has to be made when general increases or
across-the-board increases are negotiated with the union or
otherwise put into effect. If the company decides to pay everyone
10 cents an hour more than he or she now receives, this has the
effect of lowering the percentage difference between steps.

Take an example. In a foundry in 1975 the lowest-paying job
two was $2 divided by $4, or 50 percent. During the ensuing
years all the raises were made across the board and accumulated to a total of $1. Now the percentage difference be-
tween the bottom rate of $5 and the top rate of $7 has been
reduced to $2 divided by $5, or 40 percent. And the percentage
difference between each two consecutive job grades has been
narrowed accordingly.

To avoid the narrowing of pay differentials, many companies try to apply general wage increases as a percentage of the present rate. Instead of giving 20 cents an hour across the board, the raise might be 10 percent of each grade's wage rate. So a 10 percent increase in 1975 in the example above would mean a raise of 40 cents for the lowest-paying job and 60 cents for the highest. This would maintain the percentage differentials between grades and also continue to provide an incentive for employees to move up in grades.

Has a cost-of-living raise anything to do with job evaluation?

Not directly, although cost-of-living raises can affect differentials between grades, as shown in the last question. Cost-of-living, or escalator, raises usually are introduced to gear wages to rises and falls in the consumer price index of the U.S. Bureau of Labor Statistics, commonly referred to as the cost-of-living index. In some companies, if the index rises one full point, all wages go up 1 percent—or some agreed-upon fraction of a percent.

Another factor that sometimes affects a company's pay system is when it adopts a raise in the federal minimum wage. If pay for higher-grade jobs is not raised proportionately, the lowest-grade job squeezes the pay scale from the bottom. The law's intention is not to require an across-the-board raise, but employees in the higher labor grades often feel that it is an inequity if their wage rates remain where they were.

How much should employees know about job evaluation?

Job evaluation takes the mystery out of why some jobs pay more than others. Nothing can destroy morale more than the thought that someone else is getting more for doing the same job that you are doing. So, within the limits of your company's policy, job-evaluation methods should be an open book to employees. Supervisors ought to make it their business to know more about how their company's plan works than any other employees know. That way supervisors remain the employees' main source of information. And supervisors can do much to explain what may appear to be discrepancies and thus keep grievances from growing.

In discussing job evaluation with employees, emphasize these points:

- Job evaluation rates the job, not the person performing it.

- Many factors are compared and evaluated—not just the one that seems most important to the particular individual.
- The same set of yardsticks is used to measure every job.
- Job evaluation is based on the gathering of factual evidence, not just a casual description of the job.
- Job titles are misleading and can mean different things in different parts of the company. Descriptions are what count.
- While judgment still plays a role in determining a job's worth, it has been held to a minimum because the method is systematic and involves enough people so that discrimination and favoritism are practically ruled out.

When it comes to pay, how many companies rely upon a job-evaluation plan for a foundation?

Relatively few small companies, but three-quarters of larger companies and almost all state and federal agencies use some form of job evaluation. For example, the classification system is prescribed by the Classification Act of 1949 for all jobs regulated by the United States Civil Service Commission.

Regardless of job evaluation, what are the basic ways in which employees get paid for their work?

There are essentially three different forms of direct compensation or pay.

1. Hourly wages. Pay is based solely on how many hours the individual works. If the job of a welder calls for $4.55 per hour and the welder works only 28 hours during a particular week, the pay will be $4.55 × 28, or $127.40. Hourly wage systems prevail for blue-collar workers.

2. Straight salary. Pay is based on a flat weekly or monthly sum and is often paid in full regardless of the hours worked, provided the hours not worked are excused. For example, the salary of a receiving clerk may be $155 per week. If the clerk has to miss six hours' work during the week for a legitimate reason, the full $155 is still received. The straight salary system prevails for office and clerical workers, white-collar employees generally, and managerial personnel.

3. Incentive systems. There are dozens of variations in incentive-pay systems, but the principle is that pay is based in full or in part on the results attained by the individual. In an apparel factory, for example, sewing machine operators may be guaranteed a base wage rate of, say, $3.50 per hour. They will be given an additional percentage of that wage rate, however, in proportion to how much more they produce above a certain standard of output. Suppose the standard is 20 shirts stitched per hour, and the operator puts together 24 in an hour. The incentive (sometimes called a bonus) will be 20 percent (4/20) multiplied by the hourly rate ($3.50), or 70 cents. The total pay for that hour then would be $4.20. Many salespeople also work on similar incentive arrangements, based on how much they sell.

An organization may use any one or all three of these methods. The combination of payment methods and the resulting pay pattern within an organization is called its compensation plan.

Where does the guaranteed annual wage fit in?

A few companies that employ blue-collar workers attempt to put them on straight salary just like white-collar workers. Where business is very stable and does not suffer ups and downs of employment (as so much factory work does), this system has been successful. In essence it tries to assure employees of a certain number of hours of work per year. This assurance is sometimes in the form of a contractual guarantee. But it almost always depends on whether business remains good enough for the company to fulfill the promise.

What about profit sharing?

Like wage incentives, there are almost as many profit-sharing plans as there are companies that offer them to employees. Most plans are based on a system that shares the company's year-end profit with employees. Some plans attempt to relate the employees' share to the overall productivity of the company, based on some agreed-upon standard of performance. There are arguments pro and con regarding profit sharing. Many workers would rather have their pay completely unrelated to how well their employers fare in business. Many others feel that a share in the profit is their due. Companies that offer profit sharing do so because they believe it improves internal cooperation and workmanship, and often productivity.

Are fringe benefits the same as pay?

Technically, no. But to the companies that provide employee benefits—and all companies do to a greater or lesser degree—it might as well be pay. Surveys regularly conducted by the United States Chamber of Commerce peg the cost of employee benefits at over 30 percent of base wages or salaries. Many of the fringe benefits most employees take for granted are included in this figure. These include vacations, holidays, sick leave, health care and insurance, life insurance, education assistance, and pensions. A person has only to be self-employed to find out quickly the staggering cost of social security payments, medical, hospitalization, and life insurance and to find out how costly it is to be sick or to take a vacation without an employer to share these payments.

supervisory word power

Job analysis. The process of gathering information about, and determining the component elements of, a particular job by means of observation, interview, and study, for purposes of wage and salary administration.

Job description. A combination of simply written, short statements that describe both the work to be performed and the essential requirements of a particular job or position.

Job requirements. A listing of the specific knowledge and skills, education, and experience needed by an employee to perform the work described.

Job evaluation. The process by which the overall value of a particular job, as specified in its description and requirements, is measured.

Compensation plan. The total pay system set up by an organization to provide the direct financial return to employees in the form of wages, salaries, incentives, and other cash payments for the work they perform.

Other Important Terms in This Chapter

classification plan	labor grade
cost-of-living raise	point method
factor comparison plan	profit sharing
fringe (employee) benefits	ranking plan
guaranteed annual wage	rate range
hourly wage	straight salary
incentive plan	wage survey

reading comprehension

1. Compare the benefits derived by management from a job-evaluation program with those enjoyed by its employees.

2. Explain why it is so important to rate the job rather than the person who holds it.

3. List at least five typical requirements that might be itemized in a job description.

4. Name the four principal methods used for job evaluation.

5. Give an example of the kind of inequity in pay that might irritate an employee.

6. What is the difference between wages and a straight salary? For what kinds of jobs are the two pay methods traditionally used? Give examples of jobs for which each might be used.

7. Explain how a series of across-the-board wage increases can lower the relative pay differentials between classifications.

8. What are some of the things a supervisor should tell employees about the company's job-evaluation plan?

9. What is the basic principle by which pay is determined in an incentive system? Give an example of such a system.

10. In the point plan illustrated in the text, 11 factors are provided. Some factors are more heavily weighted than others. Which are they? Why do you suppose they are assigned the most points?

supervision in action

THE CASE OF THE DISGRUNTLED LIFT-TRUCK OPERATOR. A case study in human relations involving job evaluation, with questions for you to answer.

"Say, Smitty," said Bill Todd to his supervisor one day, "I thought we had a job-evaluation system here that guaranteed that everybody with the same job got the same pay. How come I don't get the same money as Abe Tower over in Department 303? He and I got to talking at the bowling matches the other night, and I found out that he and I do the same work. Except he gets 25 cents an hour more than I do. Don't I know the right people?

"First I thought Abe was off the beam—or giving me the needle. But we're both lift-truck operators. We both work for the same company. And he showed me his pay envelope. He gets $160 base pay for 40 hours while I get only $150.

"Furthermore, Abe's got it lots easier than I. His boss leaves him pretty much on his own. And he can go in and out of the warehouse without getting an okay. But you know how I have to work—I've got every operator in the department on my back all day.

"What I want to know is, who do I have to see to get a square deal around here?"

1. Do you think Bill is right in his request for more money? Why?

2. What kind of information will Smitty need to know in order to judge this request?

3. What sort of answer do you think Smitty should give Bill?

4. Could this situation have been avoided? How?

enriching your viewpoint

A number of sound books and readings are devoted in great measure to job evaluation and wage and salary administration. These seven in particular can provide you with a more comprehensive understanding of the subject:

Dunn, J. D., and Frank M. Rachel, *Wage and Salary Administration,* McGraw-Hill Book Company, New York, 1971.

Flippo, Edwin B., *Principles of Personnel Management,* 4th ed., McGraw-Hill Book Company, New York 1976, Chap. 14, "Base Compensation—Job," and Chap. 15, "Incentive Compensation—Person."

Janes, Harold D., "Issues in Job Evaluation: The Union View," *Personnel Journal,* Vol. 51, No. 9, September 1972, pp. 675–679.

Miner, Mary G., "Pay Policies: Secret or Open? And Why?" *Personnel Journal,* Vol. 53, No. 2, February 1974, pp. 110–115.

Sibson, Robert E., *Wages and Salaries: A Handbook for Line Managers,* rev. ed., American Management Association, New York, 1967.

Smyth, Richard C., "Financial Incentives for Salesmen," *Harvard Business Review,* Vol. 46, No. 1, January–February 1968, p. 111.

Teague, Frederick A., "Job Analysis" and "Job Evaluation," in Lester R. Bittel (ed.), *The Encyclopedia of Professional Management,* McGraw-Hill Book Company, New York, 1979, pp. 581–586.

15

appraisal of
employee performance

What is the difference between job evaluation and an employee performance appraisal?

In job evaluation, only the job is considered. In an employee performance appraisal (sometimes called a merit rating), you measure how well an employee is doing on that job. Essentially, one technique evaluates a job; the other evaluates an individual.

At its root, what is the true purpose of an appraisal?

There are three basic reasons for making an appraisal of employee performance:

244

1. To encourage good behavior or to correct and discourage below-standard performance. Good performers expect a reward, even if it is only praise. Poor performers should recognize that continued substandard behavior will at the very least stand in the way of advancement. At the most drastic, it may lead to termination.

2. To satisfy our curiosity about how well we are doing. It is a fundamental drive in human nature for each of us to want to know how well we fit into the organization for which we work. An employee may dislike being judged, but the urge to know is very strong.

3. To provide a firm foundation for later judgments that concern an employee's career—pay raises, promotions, transfers, or separation. It is a cardinal mistake, however, to stress the relationship of pay raises during the appraisal period. It is only human for persons who have been told their work is good to expect an increase in pay to follow. If your company's compensation plan doesn't work that way, you may suffer a very red face when an employee tells you later on that "you told me my good work would bring a raise or a promotion."

How formal will the performance rating procedure be?

It varies. Some companies prescribe and carefully follow through on their appraisal programs. Others leave it pretty much up to the individual supervisor. Many formal programs use a "forced choice" form (Figure 15-1) to record the supervisor's rating. Its purpose is to force the supervisor to make a decision on each of the rating factors considered. These ratings can often be converted to achievement scores, which are provided in the illustrated form.

Is it proper to ask an employee to help you make an appraisal of another employee's performance?

Evaluation of an individual's performance and ability is a definite management responsibility. You cannot properly share it or delegate it to someone else outside the managerial ranks. It's perfectly all right, however, and often helpful, to discuss your opinions with your boss or occasionally with your associates (like an assistant supervisor). But management alone can determine the relative value of individual employees and their place in the organization.

Employee Performance Rating Form

Dept. _____ Clock No. _____

Rating For _____

Factor	Range	
QUALITY 1 Performance in meeting quality standards	Careless **4**	Just gets by **8**
JOB KNOWLEDGE 2 Understanding in all phases of the work	Expert in own job and several others **25**	Expert but limited to own job **20**
QUANTITY 3 Output of satisfactory work	Turns out required amount but seldom more **8**	Frequently turns out more than required amount **12**
DEPENDABILITY 4 Works conscientiously according to instructions	Dependable, no checking necessary **20**	Very little checking **16**
INITIATIVE 5 Thinks constructively and originates action	Good decisions and actions but requires some supervision **9**	Minimum of supervision **12**
ADAPTABILITY 6 Ability to learn and meet changed conditions	Prefers old methods, does not remember instructions **3**	Learns slowly, reluctant to change **6**
ATTITUDE 7 Willingness to cooperate and carry out demands	Good team worker **10**	Cooperative **8**
ATTENDANCE 8 Amount of excessive absenteeism	2 to 3 days normal or 2 days own accord **6**	1 to 2 days normal or 1 day own accord **8**
SAFETY AND HOUSEKEEPING 9 Compliance with safety and housekeeping rules	Safe and orderly worker; equipment well cared for **10**	Workplace clean and safe **8**
POTENTIAL 10 Potential ability to lead and teach others	Has no more growth **2**	Future growth doubtful **4**
PERSONALITY 11 Ability to get along with associates	Disagreeable **2**	Difficult to get along with **4**
SUPERVISORY ABILITY 12 Additional rating for supervisors only	Poor organization and planning **7**	Inadequate supervision **14**

Date rated _____ Signed _____

FIGURE 15-1. **Typical Employee Performance Rating Sheet to Be Completed by the Supervisor.** Note that to minimize halo effect, rating scales for some factors are reversed, such

INSTRUCTIONS

1. Disregard your personal feelings. Judge this employee on the qualities listed below
2. Study the definitions of each factor, and the various phases of each before rating
3. Call to mind instances that are typical of employee's work and actions
4. Using your own careful judgment—check the phrase in each factor that is typical
5. If employee performs no supervision—do not rate additional factor for supervisory ability
6. Explain on reverse side any unusual characteristic not covered in regular factors

Range			Rating
Does a good job **12**	Rejects and errors rare **16**	Exceptionally high quality **20**	
Knows job fairly well **15**	Improvement necessary—just gets by **10**	Inadequate knowledge **5**	
Slow—output is seldom required amount **4**	Exceptionally fast. output high **20**	Usually does more than expected **16**	
Follows instructions **12**	Frequent checking **8**	Continuous checking and follow-up **4**	
Thinks and acts constructively; no supervision required **15**	Requires constant supervision **3**	Fair decisions— routine worker **6**	
Normal ability; routine worker **9**	Short period for mental adjustment. willing to change **12**	Learns rapidly— adjusts and grasps changes quickly **15**	
Limited cooperation **6**	Passive resistance **4**	Poor cooperation. argumentative **2**	
No days lost **10**	3 to 4 days normal or 3 days own accord **4**	More than 4 days absence **2**	
Occasional warning about safety and orderliness **6**	Warned repeatedly about safety and cleanliness **4**	Area dirty. safety rules ignored **2**	
Slow development ahead **6**	Bright future growth **8**	Exceptional possibilities **10**	
Average or reasonable **6**	Well liked and respected **8**	Winning personality **10**	
Nothing outstanding **21**	Good planning and effective organization **28**	Outstanding leadership **35**	

TOTAL _____

as for job knowledge, dependability, attitude, and safety and housekeeping. Other scales are mixed in order, such as for quantity, initiative, and attendance.

It should be added that a few organizations use peer ratings successfully. But unless this is an established part of the appraisal program in your company, it should be avoided. Without proper preparation, it will cause far more problems than it will solve.

Doesn't an employee's rating represent only the supervisor's opinion?

A good performance rating includes more than just a supervisor's opinion. It should be based on facts, too. In the consideration of quality, what is the employee's scrap record? As to quantity, what do the production records show? Dependability—what's the absence and lateness record? Can you cite actual incidents where you may have had to discipline the employee or speak about the quality or quantity of output? Answering these questions makes your rating less opinionated, consequently more valid and worthwhile.

Such documented incidents become critical examples (often called critical incidents) of an employee's performance. These incidents should undeniably represent the quality—good or bad—of an employee's work. It is a good practice to make notes of such occurrences and place them in the employee's file. At appraisal time they serve to illustrate what you consider good or subpar performance and to support the ratings you make.

What factors should you consider when appraising an employee?

These can vary from plan to plan. What you are trying to answer about an employee's performance, however, are these three questions:

- What has the individual done since last appraised? How well has it been done? How much better could it be?
- In what ways have strengths and weaknesses in the individual's job approach affected this performance? Are these factors ones that could be improved?
- What is the individual's potential? How well could the employee do if really given a chance?

Factors that are judged in appraisal also tend to fall into two categories: objective judgments and subjective judgments. *Objective factors* focus on hard facts and measurable results— quantities, quality, attendance. *Subjective factors* tend to represent opinions, such as those about attitude, personality, and adaptability. Distinguish between the two. Be firmer about appraisal of objective factors than about those involving opinion only. But even subjective factors can be rated with confidence if they are supported by documented incidents. The sample performance rating form shown in Figure 15-1 includes both objective and subjective factors, together with verbal definitions of the various kinds of performance.

How often should you rate an employee?

Twice a year is a happy medium. If you rate too often, you're likely to be too much impressed by day-to-day occurrences. If you wait too long, you're likely to forget many of the incidents that ought to influence your appraisal. Even if your company has a plan that calls for rating only once a year, it's good practice on your part to make an informal appraisal more often.

How can you make sure your ratings are consistent from employee to employee?

One good way to make sure you rate each employee fairly is to make out a checklist with the name of each of your employees down one side of a sheet of paper and the factor to be rated across the top. Look at only one factor at a time. Take quality, for instance. If you have previously rated Tom only "fair" and Pete and Vera "good," decide whether Pete and Vera should still be rated "good" when compared with Tom's rating. Perhaps you'll want to drop Pete's rating to "fair" because Pete and Tom produce about the same quality of work, while Vera's quality is consistently better than either of the other two.

Another way to check your ratings for consistency is to see whether there is a variation of appraisals, or whether you have rated all your employees the same. In any group there should be a variety of performances. Roughly speaking, three-quarters of your employees should be in the middle ratings—"fair" to "good." About one-eighth will stand out at the top with "very good" to "exceptional." And another eighth will be at the bottom, rated from "fair" to "unsatisfactory."

How do you convert employee performance ratings to money?

This is strictly a matter of your company's policy. About the only generality that can be drawn is that employees whose ratings are less than satisfactory should not be recommended for increases.

Where a company has a rate range (maximum and minimum wage rates) for each job, many people believe that only workers who are rated "very good" or "exceptional" should advance to the maximum rate for the job.

If you can't give an employee a raise, why rate the employee at all?

Performance rating is so often associated with money that supervisors and employees alike lose sight of the other important benefits. Periodic performance reviews help a supervisor to:

- Point out strengths and weaknesses to employees so that they can cultivate the former and correct the latter.
- Provide a fair and unbiased method for determining qualifications for promotions, transfers, and rate increases.
- Recognize those employees who have exceptional ability and deserve training for higher positions and responsibilities.
- Weed out those who aren't qualified for the work they are now doing and help assign them to more suitable work. Or, if they are wholly unqualified, to separate them from the company's payroll.

Why should you bother to tell employees where they stand?

People like to know how they shape up, as long as your evaluation is fair and constructive. Informal discussions of ratings with an employee will:

- Give the employee a clear understanding of how well the boss thinks the job is being done.
- Provide the employee with a chance to ask questions about your opinion and give views on his or her own efforts.
- Clear up any misunderstandings about what you expect from the employee on the job.
- Set a course for the employee to improve attitudes and job skills.
- Build a strong relationship based on mutual confidence between supervisor and employee.

Don't employees resent being told?

The biggest fear in most supervisors' minds is that an employee will dislike being criticized. Surprisingly, this fear is unfounded—if the appraisal is based on facts rather than opinion only and you display a willingness to change ratings if an employee can show you you're wrong. People want to know where they stand—even if it isn't good. But don't interpret this to mean that appraisal interviews are easy, or that employees will make it easy for you. Chances are they won't.

Furthermore, do not let your discussion with the employee being rated take on the nature of an end-of-term school report. Mature adults resist this. Subordinates can easily regard the performance appraisal as just another way for the company to increase its control over them if this attitude prevails.

How do you handle charges of discrimination or favoritism?

Unfavorable criticism stings an occasional employee so hard that it's not unusual for the person to react by charging you with favoritism. Don't try to argue the employee out of it. Your direct denial probably won't be accepted anyway. Instead, try acknowledging that possibly you have erred in making your rating.

For instance, say, "Tony, why do you think I might be favoring Sam? If I've given you that impression, perhaps you can help me see where I've been wrong." So Tony says, "Well, you give Sam all the easy jobs, and I get all the junk that no one else wants."

Your reply ought to be along these lines: "I don't agree that I give Sam the easy jobs, but I do find that I ask him to do lots of jobs that need first-rate attention. He seems easier to get along with when I need something done in a hurry. On the other hand, I've been hesitating to ask you to do anything out of the ordinary. That's because you act as if I'm taking unfair advantage of you. Don't you agree that it's just human nature on my part to lean on people who show they want to cooperate? Maybe it's been my fault that you feel I've favored Sam. I'll watch that in the future. But how about your pitching in and taking your share of the load? Will you try it that way with me, Tony?"

How can you tell employees their work is way below par?

Don't be too harsh on poor performers. Be especially sure that your treatment has encouraged the best kind of performance. Otherwise they may feel that their poor showing is more your fault than their own.

Your guides should be these: Be firm. Nothing is to be gained by being soft. If work has been bad, say so.

Be specific, such as, "We've been over this before. During the last six months I've made a point of showing you exactly where you have fallen down on the job. Remember the rejects we had on the X-56 job? And the complaints on the motor shafts? Only last week you put the whole shop in a bad light by the way you mishandled the shaft job again. It looks to me as if you just aren't cut out for machine shop work. So I'm recommending that you be transferred out of this department. If there's no other suitable work available, I guess you'll have to look for work elsewhere."

Don't rub it in, though. Leave the employee's self-respect. End the discussion by summarizing what you have found satisfactory as well as the things that are unsatisfactory.

Isn't it true that no matter how well some employees do their job, there's little chance of their getting a better job?

Yes. It's especially hard on a good worker who is bucking a seniority sequence and who knows that until the person ahead gets promoted or drops dead, there is little chance to move up. Suppose a number 2 operator on an oil still said to you, "Each time I get reviewed, you tell me I'm doing a good job. But this hasn't done me any good. I'm getting top dollar for the job I'm on, and until the number 1 operator changes jobs, I'm stuck. All the performance review does to me is to rub salt in the wound!"

A good way for you to handle this gripe is to admit the situation exists, but don't oversympathize. Try saying something like this: "Sure, I agree that it's hard waiting for your chance. But some workers make the mistake of depending entirely upon seniority for their advancement. I don't want you to fall into that trap. When the next better job opens, I hope both of us can say that you're fully qualified. That's one of the good things about performance ratings. You can find out where your weak spots may be and correct them. For a person who has your ability and does as well on the job as you do, there's no reason why you have to limit your ambitions to the number 1 operator's job either. Maybe you'll be able to jump from a number 2 job to a supervisor's spot."

Should you discuss one employee's rating with another employee?

Not if you can possibly help it. Avoid comparisons when you can. And be sure that each employee knows that you treat each rating as confidential. Try to establish the entire procedure on the basis of confidentiality.

What is the best way
to handle the appraisal interview itself?

While there are any number of approaches you might use, there are seven steps that are a pretty good path toward understanding and acceptance of the appraisal.

Step 1.   Prepare the employee, as well as yourself, to come to the meeting expecting to compare notes. That way, you have your facts at hand and the employee has the same opportunity to recollect about performance during the previous period.

Step 2.   Compare accomplishments with specific targets. Don't be vague or resort to generalizations. Be specific about what was expected and how close the employee has come to meeting these expectations.

Step 3.   Be sure to give adequate credit for what *has* been accomplished. It is a temptation to take for granted those things that have been done well and to concentrate on the deficiencies.

Step 4.   Review those things that have *not* been accomplished. Emphasize where improvement is needed. And explore together with the employee how this can be done and why it is necessary for the employee to improve.

Step 5.   Avoid the impression of your sitting in judgment. If there is blame to be shared, acknowledge it. Don't talk in terms of mistakes, faults, or weaknesses. Never compare the employee with a third person. Stick to a mutual examination of the facts and what they imply to both of you.

Step 6.   Agree on targets to be met during the period ahead. Be specific about them. Relate them to what has not been accomplished during the current period. This sets the stage for a more objective appraisal discussion next time around.

Step 7.   Review what *you* can do to be of greater help. Improvement is almost always a mutually dependent activity. An employee who knows that you share responsibility for it will approach the task with greater confidence and enthusiasm.

Where should you carry on
performance rating or appraisal interviews?

Do it privately, in your own office or in a private room. You'll want to be able to give the interview your undivided attention. And you won't want to be in earshot of other employees, either. Allow yourself enough time—at least a half hour. Otherwise the whole procedure will be too abrupt.

What's the "sandwich" technique for telling employees about unfavorable aspects of their work?

The sandwich technique means simply to sandwich unfavorable comments between favorable comments: "I've been pleased with the way you've stepped up your output. You've made real improvement there. I am a little disappointed, however, by the quality of what you produce. The records show that you're always near the bottom of the group on errors. So I hope you'll work as well to improve quality as you did quantity. I feel sure you will, since your attitude toward your work has been just fine."

The same technique is a helpful guide to the entire appraisal/ review discussion. Use it by starting the talk off with a compliment. Then discuss the work that must be improved. Finish by finding something else good to say about the employee's work.

Should you leave room for employees to save face?

Call it what you want, but give employees every chance to tell you what obstacles stand in the way of their making good. Don't interrupt or say, "That's just an excuse." Instead, take your time. Let the person talk. Often the first reason given isn't the real one. Only if you listen carefully will you discover underlying causes for poor attitude or effort.

Confidence in you as a supervisor and in the performance rating system is important. So don't be too anxious to prove that the employee is wrong. Above all, don't show anger, regardless of what kind of remark the employee makes. That advice goes even if the employee becomes angry.

Isn't it dangerous to tell employees you've given a high rating? Won't they expect to get an immediate raise or a promotion out of it?

Knowledge of where an individual stands with the boss is every bit as important to a top-notch performer as it is to a mediocre employee—maybe even more so. If you fail to show your recognition of a good job, an employee is likely to feel, "What's the use of doing a good job? No one appreciates it."

Good workers are hard to come by. They should know how you feel, even when you can't show them an immediate reward. Remember, people work for lots more than what they get in the pay envelope.

What's the halo effect? How can you avoid it?

Nearly all of us have a tendency to let one favorable or unfavorable trait influence our judgment of an individual as a whole. This is called the *halo effect*. You may feel that Carl is a hard person to socialize with, that his attitude is wrong. This becomes a halo effect if you let this one trait color your whole judgment of Carl so that you forget that Carl's workmanship is outstanding or his attendance is good. In the other direction, you may be so impressed with a worker's loyalty that you may tend to overlook shortcomings. Either kind of halo effect is bad.

To avoid the halo effect, it's helpful to rate all employees on one of the rating factors before going on to the next factor.

What are some common errors a supervisor may make when appraising employee performance?

Plain old bias or prejudice is something that will ruin an otherwise good appraisal unless you make a definite effort to keep it out. Ask yourself, "Am I measuring this person's performance only against the job? Or am I dragging in dress, accent, color or nationality, physical appearance?"

Overemphasizing a single incident will also distort your rating. Guard yourself against saying, "Mary is one of the best people we have. I remember three years ago when she saved our skin by turning out the Thompson job in six hours." Or, "Mack will never be any good. He proved that to me last year when he botched the Smith job."

What sort of follow-up should a supervisor make after the performance rating interview?

Appraisal isn't something that's done today and finished. To be of lasting value to you and your employees, you should follow up the appraisal interview this way:

Stick to your side of the bargain. If you have promised to examine an employee's work more carefully to see if you've given a fair rating, do so. Check the past record and show the employee any of the data that's been questioned. If you must change your rating, do it promptly and let the employee know that his or her point of view has been supported.

Provide ways for the employee's development. An employee will need your help to improve—especially skills. Give the worker the kind of instruction your review indicated will help. If the employee needs more versatility, broaden the assignments by giving different and challenging jobs to do. If workmanship is inferior, study what the worker is doing wrong and show how it can be done right.

Continue to show interest in the individual's work. Drop by the workplace occasionally with a view toward letting employees know they have improved—or gone downhill—since the interview. If they're making progress, give them credit. If they are slipping, point out where you're dissatisfied.

Will the management by objectives approach work with your employees?

Yes, if you don't carry it too far. At step 6 of the appraisal interview, described above, you can be very specific about performance goals for the next period. If you and the employee mutually agree upon them, they become objectives of the employee, who can provide self-control (or self-management) in order to attain them. The MBO approach (see page 206) appeals to well-motivated, self-starting, responsible individuals. It is less attractive to, and less effective for, those employees who rely heavily on the supervisor for planning and control of their work.

Some employees try very hard, but their performance remains below par. What is the reason for this? What can be done about it?

If there is a weakness in performance appraisal programs, it is that management assumes employees have only to try harder in order to measure up to standards. This is often not the case. Many factors can contribute to employee performance.

1. Individuals may be assigned to work that does not match their capabilities. It may be too easy or too difficult. One solution is a transfer to a more suitable job. Or the job might be redesigned to give the employee a better fit. An employee may not be able to handle the paperwork required. Perhaps it can be done by someone else. Or the job may require too little judgment for a highly intelligent person. Perhaps it can be rearranged to provide options that use this person's analytic ability.

2. Employees may not have received proper training. In any case of continued poor performance, the supervisor should first

reexamine the training program and find a way to review the job procedure with the employee from start to finish. A key operating point may have been missed.

3. Individuals may be victims of pressures from the work group. An employee may be trying to conform to your job standards, but co-workers give the person a hard time. To correct this situation, you may need to approach it from the group's point of view to change or modify their position.

4. Workers may not be up to the job requirements, physically or emotionally. A checkup by the company nurse or doctor may be in order. If there are persistent family problems—divorce, death, severe illness—you may try gentle counseling. Your objective should be to show that you are sympathetic, but that there is a limit as to how long the related poor performance can be accepted.

5. Your own supervision may be at fault. It takes two to tango, and poor performance may be related to a supervisor's failure to provide clear-cut standards, to train employees effectively, or to help with problems and changes as they arise.

6. There is always the possibility, too, that there is some hitch in the operating process or a conflict in prescribed paperwork procedures. You may want to review these problems with your own boss or with the appropriate staff departments.

supervisory word power

Performance appraisal.   A yardstick used to measure how well an individual fits the job and fills the appropriate role in the organization.

Appraisal interview.   A meeting held between an employee and the supervisor to review the performance rating and, using that rating as a basis, to discuss the overall quality of the employee's work.

Objective factors.   Those signs in an employee's job record that can actually be measured: quantities, qualities, attendance, accident record, and housekeeping. They are observable facts and, as such, tend to be free of bias.

Subjective factors.   Those characteristics in an employee's approach to the job that cannot easily be converted to quantitative measures, but which must also be accounted for in the performance rating of an employee. They include factors like dependability, initiative, adaptability, attitude, and personality.

Halo effect. A generalization when one aspect of performance, or a single quality of the individual's nature, is allowed to overshadow everything else about that person.

Other Important Terms in This Chapter

critical incident   peer rating
forced choice   sandwich technique
merit rating

reading comprehension

1. Distinguish between employee performance appraisal and job evaluation.

2. How important is it, when rating an employee's performance, that you use the same yardstick you use with other employees?

3. Distinguish between rating for performance and rating for pay increases.

4. Under what circumstances will an employee accept criticism in an appraisal interview?

5. Should performance ratings be treated confidentially, or is it all right to show one person's rating to another? Why?

6. What can a supervisor do during normal operations to help make subjective judgments more reliable when the time comes for performance appraisals?

7. Contrast the sandwich technique with the halo effect.

8. Would it be better to go easy during an interview rather than risk hurting feelings so that the employee can't save face? Why?

9. What are some possible causes of poor employee performance, other than carelessness or lack of effort?

10. When the semiannual appraisal interview is over, why can't the supervisor forget about it for six months?

supervision in action

THE CASE OF THE SPOILED LETTUCE. **A case study in human relations involving appraisal of employee performance, with questions for you to answer.**

At the close of the shift on Thursday, Andy Baker, a handler in the central division warehouse of the Waterman Wholesaling Company, made the biggest mistake of his career. He loaded 250 cases of perishable lettuce on a truck heading for St. Louis. It should have gone on the truck standing in the next bay, scheduled to make its run that night to Cleveland. The St. Louis truck was well on its way before the error was caught. Rico Lopez, Andy's supervisor on the loading dock, tried to catch the St. Louis driver at truck stops along the way, but after a couple of hours of frantic telephoning, he gave up. "There's $1,000 of the company's money you threw down the drain!" he shouted at Andy. "By the time that lettuce gets back here from St. Louis, it will be garbage."

"I checked the bill of lading," said Andy, "and I checked my case count carefully. But I didn't understand that the shipping code we use for perishables is different from what we use for canned goods. Besides, the driver should have caught it."

"The driver thought the cartons contained celery, not lettuce. He'll be in trouble, too. But you are the guy who made the trouble for Waterman Wholesaling."

The following day Rico received a note from the personnel department through interoffice mail, advising him that his semi-annual performance rating for Andy Baker was due next week. Rico seized this opportunity to straighten Andy out. On Monday afternoon he called Andy into the shipping office. "Sit down, Andy. The time has come for you and me to have a serious talk."

"About what?" asked Andy.

"About your performance rating. It is six months since we had our little talk, and your work has gotten worse rather than better."

"I thought my work had been getting better," said Andy.

"Better? After last week's foul-up! You are just lucky you weren't fired for sending those 250 cartons of lettuce off to St. Louis."

"But that was just a bad day for me." said Andy. "Most of the time my work has been good. You said so yourself a couple of weeks ago."

"I said that your attendance was finally on target, not that your work on the whole had improved," said Rico.

"What else have I done wrong?" asked Andy.

"Well, your attitude hasn't been all that it should be. Last month when the weather was so cold, every time I looked for you, you were inside standing under the space heater."

"What was I supposed to do? Stand out in the snow waiting for the next shipment?"

"You should have been showing some initiative. There is always a lot of stock that needs shifting around. If you have nothing to do, just come ask me and I'll keep you plenty busy," said Rico.

"I work as hard as the next guy on the dock," said Andy. "You never said anything about my shifting stock on my own before."

"If you took an interest in this job," said Rico, "you wouldn't make the kind of boo-boo you made last Thursday. That tops them all."

"Tops them all!" said Andy. "That's the first mistake I've made so far this year. You keep a logbook on the dock. You show me where I goofed up any other time."

Rico got out the logbook. After scanning it for a minute or two, he pointed out an entry to Andy. "See, you messed up a shipment of melons like this a couple of months ago."

"I forgot that," said Andy, "but I told you at the time that the coding system at Waterman is confusing. If you look at the other entries, you can see that I'm not the only person making that mistake."

"That's not the point," said Rico. "Your work has simply got to improve. I'm filling out this performance form on you today, and it won't be good."

"That's not fair," said Andy. "I'm doing my best. I'm sure that I do as well as the other handlers."

"I'm rating you now, not the other handlers," said Rico. "They will get theirs when the time comes."

1. How objective is Rico's appraisal of Andy's performance?
2. How valid was the critical incident of the mistaken shipment to St. Louis in judging Andy's overall performance?
3. What did you think of the way in which Rico conducted the appraisal interview?
4. Do you think that Andy's performance will improve? Why or why not?
5. If you were in Rico's place, how would you have handled the appraisal and the interview so as to get better results from Andy?

enriching your viewpoint

For a broader understanding of the concepts underlying performance appraisals, the following readings are suggested:

Anderson, Harry B., "The Rating Game: Formal Job Appraisals Grow More Prevalent but Get More Criticism," *The Wall Street Journal,* May 23, 1978, p. 1.

Flippo, Edwin B., *Principles of Personnel Management,* 4th ed., McGraw-Hill Book Company, New York, 1976, Chap. 13, "Performance Appraisal and Management by Objectives."

Kellogg, Marion S., *What to Do About Performance Appraisals,* rev. ed., Amacom, New York, 1976.

Latham, Gary, "How to Evaluate Work Performance," *Work Performance,* Vol. 2, No. 1, November 1975.

McGregor, Douglas, "An Uneasy Look at Performance Appraisal," *Harvard Business Review,* May–June 1957, p. 89.

Miner, John B., *The Management Process: Theory, Research, and Practice,* 2d ed., The Macmillan Company, New York, 1978, Chap. 26, "Control Models and Performance Control."

Odiorne, George S., *Management by Objectives,* Pitman Publishing Corporation, New York, 1965.

16 CHAPTER training and development of employees

Will employees learn without being trained?

Yes. That's the danger. Whether you train employees or not, they learn anyway. Even if you do the training and don't do it the right way, someone else is likely to do it the wrong way for you. It's a sad story that employees who learn by trial and error or from co-workers are rarely trained to do the job efficiently.

Why should a supervisor have to do the training? Isn't this job better done by a training specialist?

Make up your mind that training is your concern and one of the most important ones. It needs to be done day in and day out, for training is the only surefire way to build a work force that returns full value for every dollar invested in labor cost. As a supervisor, you no longer work with your hands. You are judged by your ability to get the people who work for you to produce accurately and well and to turn out more goods at lower costs. Employee training is your biggest tool in accomplishing that end.

When can you tell that training is needed?
████████████ Training needs are often the underlying cause of other problems. Be on the alert whenever you observe any of these conditions: too much scrap or rework, subpar production rates, operating costs that are out of line, a high accident rate, excessive overtime, and even a general state of poor morale. Any of these symptoms may respond better to a training program than to a crackdown on discipline, for example.

What are the special rewards for a supervisor who does a good job of training workers?
████████████ In addition to making a better showing for your department in terms of better quality and quantity of output, training puts you in a favorable light in other ways. Effective employee instruction:

- Helps you handle intradepartment transfers better.
- Allows you more time for planning and scheduling your work.
- Provides a reserve of trained personnel in your department for emergencies.
- Wins the confidence and the cooperation of your workers.

Perhaps most important of all for a supervisor who wants to get ahead, training your employees makes you "available" for advancement.

When does good training begin?
████████████ When a new employee is hired. New workers who get off on the right foot are like a baseball team that gets off to a ten-run lead in the first inning. There's a good chance of eventual success.
Training recently hired workers, called *induction training* or *orientation training,* is a little like introducing friends at a club meeting where they are strangers. You'd want to introduce them around and try to make them feel at home. You'd show them where to hang their hats and coats, where the rest rooms are. If you wanted to have them think well of your club, you might tell them something about its history and the good people who

belong to it. If you had to leave them for a time to attend to some duty or other, you would come back occasionally to see how they were getting along. It's the same way with new employees who report to you. Treat them as persons you'd like to think well of you and to feel at home in your department.

What should you tell brand-new employees about their jobs?

An induction talk should cover the following subjects, where they apply:

- Pay rates, pay periods, how employees are paid—by cash or by check—the day first pay is received, and the pay deductions
- Hours of work, reporting and quitting time, lunch periods, washup time
- Overtime and overtime pay
- Shift premium pay
- Time cards, where they are located, how to punch in and out
- How to report out sick
- What to do when late
- Location of lockers and washrooms
- Location of first-aid facilities and how to report accidents
- Basic safety rules, employee's as well as company's responsibilities under the Occupational Safety and Health Administration (OSHA)
- Explanation of employee's options under company's benefits plans such as group life and health insurance

Induction activities should include:

- Tour of department or company
- Introduction to co-workers
- Assignment to work station

Just this basic information is a lot for new employees to swallow at once. So don't be afraid to repeat what you tell them several times. Better still, give them some of the more detailed information in small doses. Some today, a little more tomorrow, and as much as they can take a week from now.

Note that in many companies a new employee receives an induction talk from a central service, like the personnel or training department. As valuable as this talk may be, it won't help the new employee half as much as an informal, straight-from-the-shoulder chat with you.

How do you get down to the real business of training employees to do a job the way you want them to?

Training can be either the simplest—or the most difficult—job in the world. If you can grasp just four fundamentals, you can be a superior trainer. If you don't buy this approach, you'll spend the rest of your life complaining that employees are stupid, willful, or not like workers used to be in the good old days.

The foundation of systematic, structured job training has four cornerstones:

Step 1. Get the workers ready to learn. People who want to learn are the easiest to teach. So let trainees know why their job is important, why it must be done right. Find out something about the employees as individuals. Not only does this make them have more confidence in you, but it reveals to you how much they know already about the job, the amount and quality of their experience, and what their attitude toward learning is. This familiarization period helps the trainees to get the feel of the job you want them to do.

Step 2. Demonstrate how the job should be done. Don't just tell the trainees how to go about it or say, "Watch how I do it." Do both—tell *and* show them the correct procedure. Do this a little at a time, step by step. There's no point in going on to something new until the trainee has grasped the preceding step.

Step 3. Try the workers out by letting them do the job. Let the employees try the job—under your guidance. Stay with the trainees now to encourage them when they are doing right and to correct them when wrong. The mistakes they make while you're watching are invaluable, since they show you where they have not learned.

Step 4. Put the trainees on their own <u>gradually</u>. Persons doing a new job have to fly alone sooner or later. So after they have shown you that they can do the work reasonably well while you're standing by, turn them loose for a while. Don't abandon them completely, though. Make a point of checking on their progress and workmanship regularly. Perhaps three or four times the first day they are on their own, then once or twice a day for a week or two. But never think they are completely trained. There's always something the employee can learn to do, or learn to do better.

Training the four-step way is costly, isn't it?

All training, structured or catch-as-catch-can, is costly. It is the results that count. You may obtain inexpensive training by simply having a new employee work along with an experienced one. That way the costs won't show up immediately on the books. Or you can spend a little out-of-pocket money on a systematic plan like the four-step method.

At one Johns-Manville Corporation plant in 1975, supervisors tried it both ways while breaking in new operators of extruding machines that convert raw materials into plastic pipe. The unstructured way put new employees on their own at about $60 per trainee. The structured plan cost almost $440 per person for the first trainee. When the total cost of the program was spread out over ten new employees, however, the cost per trainee averaged closer to $80. But what about the results? There was a big difference. The actual time for a new employee to reach a job-competence standard was 16.3 hours for the unstructured way, compared with 4.6 hours for the systematic way. And that was not the only savings. The structured employees operated their equipment almost two-thirds faster during training and turned out only 5.3 pounds of scrap per individual compared with 22 pounds for the unstructured.

How much should you teach at one time?

This depends on (1) the speed with which a trainee can learn and (2) how difficult the job is. Each learner is different. Some catch on fast. Others are slow. It's better, therefore, to gauge your speed to the slow person. Try to find out why the person has trouble learning. With new employees it may simply be that they are nervous and trying so hard that they don't concentrate. So be patient. Give them a chance to relax. And when they complete even a small part of the task successfully, be sure to praise them.

Going ahead slowly is especially important at the start, since learning is like getting a three-speed car into motion. You first warm up the engine, then start slowly in low gear. You shift into second only as the car picks up speed, and finally into high when it's rolling along under its own momentum.

What can you do to make the job easier to learn and to teach?

Jobs that seem simple to you because you're familiar with them may appear very hard to a person who has never performed them before. Experience has shown that the trick to making jobs easier to learn is to break them down into simple steps. That way, an employee needs to learn only one step at a time and then add steps, rather than try to grasp the whole job in a single piece.

Breaking a job down for training purposes involves two elements:

First, you must observe the job as it is done and break it into its logical steps. For instance, if the job were to in-feed grind on a centerless grinder, the first step would be to place the piece on the plate against the regulating wheel. The second step is to lower the lever-feed and grind. The third step is to raise the lever-release. And so on until the job is finished.

Second, for each step in a job breakdown, you must now consider the second element—called the *key point*. A key point is anything at a particular step that might make or break a job or injure the worker. Essentially, it's the knack or know-how of experienced workers that makes the job go easier for them. The key point for the first step in the centerless grinding job in the previous paragraph would be to know the knack of not catching the workpiece on the wheel. For the second step it would be the knowledge of how to avoid tapering or oval surfaces.

Figure 16-1 shows how this centerless grinder job might be broken down into seven steps with their appropriate key points for training purposes. Table 16-1 lists a number of factors that typically become key points for training purposes.

In what sequence must a job be taught?

The best way to teach a job is to start with the easiest part and proceed to the most difficult. This isn't always possible, of course. But if you can arrange your employee training in this sequence, learning will go more smoothly and teaching will be easier. Figure 16-2 shows how you can arrange your training sequence so that the learner works up to the difficult parts gradually.

How soon should you expect an employee to acquire job skill?

This, too, depends on the employee and on the job being learned. But, regardless, it's smart to set a timetable for learning. This can be a very simple one like Figure 16-3, or it can be as detailed as you like. The important thing is to use it to (1) record how much each worker knows already; (2) indicate what each worker doesn't need to know; (3) plan ahead for what each

Job Breakdown Sheet for Training

Part: Shaft

Operation: In-feed grind on centerless grinder

IMPORTANT STEPS IN THE OPERATION Step: A logical segment of the operation when something happens to advance the work	KEY POINTS Key point: Anything in a step that might: Make or break the job Injure the worker Make the work easier to do i.e., knack, trick, special timing, bit of special information
1. Place piece on plate against regulating wheel	Knack—don't catch on wheel
2. Lower lever-feed	Hold at end of stroke (count 1-2-3-4) Slow feed—where might taper Watch—no oval grinding
3. Raise lever-release	
4. Gauge pieces periodically	More often as approach tolerance
5. Readjust regulating wheel as required	Watch—no backlash
6. Repeat above until finished	
7. Check	

FIGURE 16-1.

Sample Job Instruction Breakdown. This illustrates steps in an operation that advance the work, together with the appropriate key points.

worker has to learn; and (4) set definite dates for completing training in each required phase of the job.

An analysis like that illustrated in Figure 16-3 is sometimes called a skills inventory because it tells you what skills each worker has already acquired as well as the total skills capability of your department.

Must supervisors do all the training themselves?

No. Instruction is a job that can be delegated—provided the employee who is to conduct the training is a qualified trainer and provided a job breakdown sheet with key points has been prepared. Just as you must know the ins and outs of teaching a

TABLE 16-1. Key-point Checklist

Key points are those things that should happen, or could happen, at each step of a job, which make it either go right or go wrong. Key points include any of the following:

1. *Feel.* Is there a special smoothness or roughness? Absence of vibration?
2. *Alignment.* Should the part be up or down? Which face forward? Label in which position?
3. *Fit.* Should it be loose or tight? How loose? How tight? Can you show the trainee? When can you tell that a part is jammed?
4. *Safety.* What can happen to injure a worker? How are the safety guards operated? What special glasses, gloves, switches, shoes are needed?
5. *Speed.* How fast must the operation proceed? Is speed critical? How can you tell if it's going too fast or too slow?
6. *Timing.* What must be synchronized with something else? How long must an operation remain idle—as with waiting for an adhesive to set?
7. *Smell.* Is there a right or wrong smell about anything—the material, the cooking or curing during the process, the overheating of a machine?
8. *Temperature.* Is temperature critical? How can you tell whether it is too hot or too cold? What can you do to change the temperature, if necessary?
9. *Sequence.* Is the specified order critical? Must one operation be performed before another, or doesn't it make any difference? How can the worker tell if he or she has gotten something out of order?
10. *Appearance.* Should surfaces be glossy or dull? Should the part be straight or bent? How can you correct an unsatisfactory condition?
11. *Heft.* Is weight important? Can you demonstrate how heavy or light a part or package should be?
12. *Noise.* Are certain noises expected (purring of a motor)? Unacceptable (grinding of gears)?
13. *Materials.* What is critical about their condition? How can the worker recognize that? When should the material be rejected? What should be done with rejected material?
14. *Tools.* What is critical about their condition? Sharpness? Absence of nicks or burrs? Positioning? Handling?
15. *Machinery.* What is critical about its operation? How is it shut down in emergencies? What will damage it? How can this be avoided?
16. *Trouble.* What should be done in the case of injury to persons, damage to materials, parts, products, tools, or machinery? How can damage be recognized?

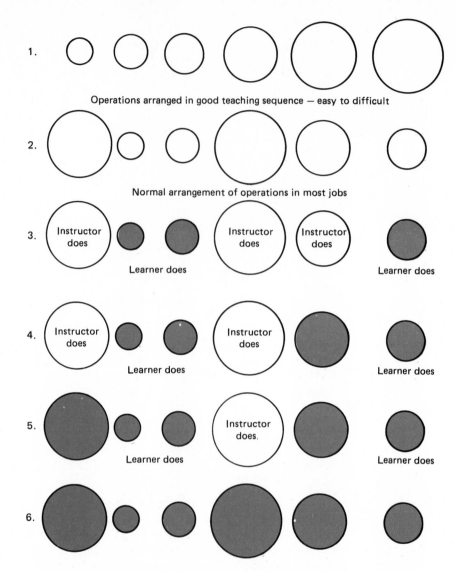

1. Operations arranged in good teaching sequence — easy to difficult

2. Normal arrangement of operations in most jobs

3. Instructor does | Learner does | Instructor does | Instructor does | Learner does

4. Instructor does | Learner does | Instructor does | Learner does

5. Learner does | Instructor does. | Learner does

6.

FIGURE 16-2. How to Teach the Difficult Operations. If a job can be taught by proceeding from the easy steps to the difficult, teaching becomes easier. Few jobs, however, have their working sequence arranged in an order of increasing difficulty, as shown at the top of the chart. Instead, the difficult parts of the job are usually mixed in with the easy ones, like the second line on the chart. These steps have to be done on the job in the correct order, and, therefore, they should be learned in that order. What can supervisor-instructors do? They can keep the job in proper sequence and still teach the easier parts first by setting up their teaching plans as shown by the dark spots in each row of the chart. The instructor does the difficult, or white, spots, while the learner does the easy, or shaded, spots, thus maintaining a learning sequence even in a difficult or long operation.

	Answer telephone calls	File correspondence	File reports	Make logbook entries	File sales order forms	Prepare day-end report	Etc.	Etc.	Etc.
White	√	√	√	√	√	√			
Nolan	√	√	√	11–10	–	–			
Smith	11–1	11–20	–	√	√	12–1			
Jones	–	–	√	11–15	12–1	12–8			
Etc.									

√ means the worker can already do the job.

– means the worker doesn't need to know the job.

11–1, 11–15, etc., indicate the dates the supervisor has set to have the workers *trained* to do the jobs required.

FIGURE 16-3. **Sample Job Instruction Timetable or Skills Inventory.** This illustrates (a) jobs in which the employee has already been trained, (b) jobs in which the skill or knowledge is not necessary, and (c) dates for training of various individuals in specific jobs or skills.

job, any employees you appoint as instructors must also know how to train others. This means that they should have completed a course in Job Instruction Training (JIT) or have been thoroughly indoctrinated by you or by the company's training director in how to train. Nothing is worse than bringing a new employee over to an older employee and just turning that person loose. If the older worker doesn't know how to train, chances are 1,000 to 1 that the new employee will never learn the job correctly. And the training process itself will be slow and costly. So never depend on an older employee to show a new one the ropes.

Caution: Even if you have a qualified job instructor in your department, you can never completely delegate your training responsibility. It's up to you to show a personal interest in every trainee's progress and to supervise the training just as you supervise any other of your responsibilities.

Can you depend on an employee to learn a job by reading an equipment manufacturer's instruction manual?

Absolutely not. It's a very exceptional person who can learn how to operate equipment solely on the basis of an instruction manual. Instruction manuals are valuable training aids, however, and they will help you draw up job breakdown sheets. But they are no substitute for personal instruction.

How much training can be accomplished through outside reading and by correspondence instruction?

If employees are ambitious to learn and to improve themselves—and if they are the rare persons who can absorb knowledge and skills through reading and self-help—they can learn much through reading or through correspondence courses. But make no mistake about it, this is the hard way! Few employees are up to it. And despite the claims of many advocates of correspondence courses, the percentage of workers who have learned their jobs this way is very small.

This is not to say, however, that outside reading combined with personalized instruction by the supervisor is not effective. It is, but the two must go hand in hand.

How good is group training?

Personalized training seems to be best for job skills, but it is expensive and time-consuming. Training employees in groups is obviously less expensive. And for many purposes it is just as effective as individualized training. Sometimes, like explaining the theory behind an operation, it's even better. If you are working with disadvantaged employees under the Comprehensive Employment and Training Act (CETA) of 1973, the U.S. Department of Labor offers this advice:

> *Group instruction generally doesn't work; use the individualized approach. Find out exactly what the individual doesn't know and concentrate on teaching that rather than a rounded course of instruction. Use a frequent method of testing to provide feedback on learning progress. Instruction must be set for each individual at his or her own pace without peer group pressures or public disclosure of ignorance.*

What is programmed instruction?

In 1912 Edward L. Thorndike, an educator, wrote: "If, by a miracle of mechanical ingenuity, a book could be so arranged that only to him who had done what was directed on page one would page two become visible and so on, much that now requires personal instruction could be managed by print."

Programmed instruction has achieved that miracle of mechanical ingenuity. In brief, it presents information in very small bits and then gives questions that must be answered correctly before the trainees go on to the next lesson. Answers are given immediately after the questions.

There are two techniques of programmed learning: linear and branching.

In *linear* programming the information is presented in a series of frames. Frame 1 presents a small bit of information, frame 2 reinforces frame 1 and adds another small bit, frame 3 reinforces frame 2 and adds another small bit, and so on.

In the *branching* technique the questions asked in each frame are multiple-choice questions. Then, if trainees give one of the wrong answers, they are directed to information that clears up the specific misunderstanding. For example, they will be told that if they checked wrong answer *a,* they should see a certain page that explains why this was wrong. If they checked wrong answer *b,* they are directed to turn to a different set of instructions. If they checked the right answer, they go on to the next frame. Programmed instruction may be provided by a textbook, a series of pages, or a teaching machine.

What are teaching machines?

Recognize first that teaching machines cannot be used without programmed instruction. Typically, a teaching machine may require written answers, and as soon as trainees have written answers, they press a button or move a paper to see the correct answer. Or they may press a button to record the answer to a multiple-choice question. Usually the machine is designed so that trainees cannot move the machine to the right answer until they have given their own answers.

Why is programmed instruction considered so valuable?

Since information is presented in such small bits, the learners find little difficulty in absorbing it. And since they are almost al-

TABLE 16-2. Programmed Versus Conventional Instruction.

	Programmed Instruction	Conventional Teaching
Average time spent by trainees	12.8 h	17 h
Average scores on examination	91%	81%

ways able to give the right answers, they are encouraged by their progress and so keep at it. Also, they can learn at their own pace and without an instructor.

Many experiments have shown that trainees learn faster and retain more when they learn through programmed instruction than when they are taught in conventional classes. For example, the Du Pont company divided employees being taught how to read engineering drawings into two groups. One group was taught by an instructor in a classroom, the other by programmed learning and a teaching machine. The results are shown in Table 16-2.

How quickly do people forget what they have learned?

According to the Research Institute of America, the startling figures in Table 16-3 indicate how fast our learning disappears unless we keep at it.

So for employees to become expert at the job you're teaching, they must practice constantly. And you must keep repeating the important things that these figures show they are likely to forget. This is one reason why follow-up (step 4) in training is so vital.

What's the purpose of visual aids?

The classic Chinese proverb still tells the story best: One picture is worth 1,000 words. Any device that helps trainees visualize what you're telling them speeds up the learning process. After all, most of us use our eyes to pick up 80 percent of what we know. So it's only natural for training that utilizes the visual sense to be more effective.

Visual aids may include a variety of devices such as transparencies, slides and filmstrips, motion pictures, and opaque projectors; charts and chart boards, posters, flannel and magnetic board presentations; simulated equipment and mock-ups, cut-

TABLE 16-3. Learning Retention Rates.

Time Interval Since Learning	Percentage Forgotten	Percentage Retained
$\frac{1}{3}$ h	42	58
1 h	56	44
$8\frac{3}{4}$ h	64	36
1 day	66	34
2 days	72	28
6 days	75	25

away models of machines, and actual displays of products, materials, and so forth.

Visual aids may also be simple and obvious, such as writing on a blackboard or demonstrating a point on a machine. Practically nothing beats making the demonstration right on the equipment a worker will use.

Increasingly in the last few years, audiovisual instruction has invaded the training field. Tape cassettes linked to programmed texts, audio-TV cassettes with capsulated instructions, and closed-circuit television demonstrations and lectures—live or on tape—have demonstrated their capability to ensure consistent instruction. In the main, however, such methods are prohibitively expensive and are used only selectively where their cost can be justified.

How good is apprentice training?

Traditionally, the top-notch, all-around skilled artisans have been schooled through apprenticeship. This is a long, thorough, and costly practice. It may take anywhere from 12 months to 4 years. A man or woman who has learned a trade through an approved apprenticeship program will be able to handle with skill almost any kind of job that occurs within that skill class. But as jobs have tended to become more and more standardized, much of what the person who has completed apprenticeship knows never gets used. For this reason the percentage of employees trained through apprentice programs becomes lower and lower. Most employees today are trained for only one specific job at a time. As a result the training is more to the point, is done faster, and costs less. But if you were to examine apprentice training, you'd find that it incorporates the four points of job training outlined previously. The main difference lies in the length of the training period and the variety of skills learned.

What's vestibule training?

When employees are trained by the company on the kind of work they are hired to perform before they begin to work on in-production materials, the training is called vestibule training. It gets its name from the fact that such training is often done outside the area—as if it were performed in the vestibule of the company before actual entry into the working part.

Can you teach old dogs new tricks?

Yes. Older workers can and do learn new methods and new jobs. And while they may learn at a slower rate than younger workers, this is mainly because older workers frequently have to unlearn what was taught them in the past. Older workers often don't have the same incentive to learn that younger ones do. They tend to feel more secure in their jobs and have less interest in advancement. For these reasons, step 1—getting the worker ready to learn—is of prime importance when teaching older workers.

How do you get employees to want to learn?

Employees must see how training will pay off for them before they pitch into training with a will. So show the younger employees how training helped others to get ahead, how it built job security for them and increased their incomes. For older workers, stress the prestige that skill gives them with other workers. Show them how learning new jobs or better methods makes the work more interesting.

Telling workers why a job is done a certain way is often the key to securing their interest. To see the necessity for training, an employee needs to know not only *what* to do and *how* to do it, but *why* it needs to be done. This process may be compared with a technical problem in transmitting color television. As you may know, the picture is broken down into three separate channels, one of which carries the red, another the green, and the third the blue part of the picture. Unless all three are transmitted in harmony, the picture is blurred and distorted. So, too, unless all three requisites of training are transmitted to the employees, it makes little sense to them.

Do labor unions object to training programs?

Few unions are opposed to the principle of training. How you set up your training activities and how you carry them out is where suspicion might arise. It's a good idea for you to lay your training cards on the table so that the shop stewards know exactly what you propose to do. Aim for their cooperation, since mutual confidence and trust between you and union representatives help make your training efforts successful. Explain to them how training will benefit employees in security, pay, and pride.

How smoothly should the training process proceed?

The learning process doesn't go smoothly for most people. We all have our ups and downs. Expect trainees to learn quickly for a while, then taper off on a plateau temporarily. They may even backslide a little. That's the time to reassure them that their halt in progress is normal. Don't let them become discouraged. If necessary, go through the demonstration again so that they can get a fresh start. And pile on the encouragement.

If supervisors are responsible for training, what's the purpose of a company's training department?

The function of a company training department will vary from organization to organization. But almost all training directors are agreed that unless supervisors are sold on training as their responsibility, the efforts of the training department won't be very effective.

Generally, the training department people are experts in teaching methods. They won't lay claim to technical skill about the job (except in cases where technical specialists are employed for certain types of instruction, such as blueprint reading). The training department serves best as an aid and a guide to supervisors in improving the skills of their workers.

For example, training directors can be of real help in determining specific training needs. They can help you recognize and interpret the training symptoms mentioned previously. You'll want their help, too, in learning how to be a good instructor and in training some of your key employees to be trainers. And the training department is invaluable in getting you started in making job breakdowns and training timetables.

Certain employee training is best done by a central training group. Such general subjects as company history and products, economics, and human relations are naturals for them. Other classroom-type instruction (like arithmetic and work simplification) lends itself to centralized training, too. But when the training department does these jobs for you, you must still assume the responsibility for requesting this training for your employees and for making sure they apply what they learn to their work.

Induction (orientation) training. The education and orientation of recently hired employees. It focuses on basic information about hours of work, pay, time cards, location of lockers and washrooms, safety rules, and so forth, and includes an introduction to co-workers and assignment to a work station.

Job Instruction Training. A systematic four-step approach to training employees in a basic job skill: (1) prepare the workers to learn; (2) demonstrate how the job is done; (3) try them out by letting them do the job; and (4) gradually put them on their own.

Job breakdown analysis. Segmentation of a particular job into those important elements, or steps, during which the employee must perform, induce, or supervise an action that advances the work toward its completion.

Key point. The unique insight, knack, trick, timing, or special information that enables a worker to advance the work or task through a particular step in skillful and accident-free fashion. Literally, the make or break of the job.

Programmed instruction. A self-administered teaching technique (using a specially prepared text or electromechanical device), which presents information in very small, readily absorbed bits. These bits are followed immediately by related questions that test the trainee's comprehension and that must be answered correctly before the trainee proceeds with the lesson.

Other Important Terms in This Chapter

apprenticeship training
retention rate
skills inventory
structured training
training timetable
vestibule training
visual aids

reading comprehension

1. In what ways can a training specialist supplement the efforts made by supervisors to train their employees?
2. How does apprentice training differ from Job Instruction Training?

3. Contrast vestibule training with induction training.

4. Explain why a high accident rate in a machine shop might be related to the absence of, or an inadequate program for, employee training.

5. Would it be wise for a supervisor to let an employee try a new job before the supervisor got around to showing how it is done?

6. Compare the preparing-to-learn phase of training with the identification of a key point.

7. Why is individual rather than group training usually preferred for disadvantaged people (like those trained under CETA) and for specific job skills training generally?

8. Would it be a good idea to let an employee learn all about the operation of a new machine by reading the manufacturer's instruction manual?

9. What are some of the advantages of programmed instruction for certain kinds of job training?

10. In what way should the training of an older worker differ from that of a younger one?

supervision in action

███████████ THE CASE OF JOHN W.'s INDOCTRINATION.   A case study in human relations involving employee training, with questions for you to answer.

When the Grimes Refrigerator Co. plant switched over from batch spray-painting to a continuous automatic-spray line, the number of painters was reduced from 23 to 5. All the displaced painters were placed in other jobs throughout the plant. One of the 18 displaced painters, John W., was assigned to the cabinet department to learn the job of a class B spot-welder.

When John reported to the cabinet department, Bill Mollier, his new supervisor, said to him, "I don't know whether you'll stay here for keeps. We're a little slow now, and we really don't need an extra welder. But in the meantime, I'll see that you get a place to hang your hat and a bench to sit at." So for the first few days, all John did was stand around and watch the other welders. Finally, at the end of the week, Bill told John, "I've got news for you: Work is picking up in our department and we'll be able to put you to work for real on Monday."

On Monday Bill assigned John to a welding machine. It was a very simple rig. All the operator needed to know was how to slide a metal refrigerator panel into a jig, clamp on the holding mechanism, and punch an electric switch. The welding was done automatically. When the weld had been made, an air blast automatically ejected the panel onto a moving belt.

"Here," said Bill to John, "watch me do this operation. It's as easy as ABC. A moron could do this job if he'd just learn these three steps. In fact, I sometimes think a moron would be better at it than a normal person." Bill demonstrated the three steps very slowly to John. As he did each step, he explained what was happening. After he'd repeated the operation a half dozen times, he got up from the machine and said to John, "Now you try it." John did it right the first time he tried. With Bill standing by, he welded 20 panels without mishap. "There," said Bill, "I told you there was nothing to it. You'll be able to do this job in your sleep." That was the last time John saw Bill to speak to until Friday.

Between Monday morning and Friday, these things happened to John: The air ejection mechanism jammed twice, and he had to get a co-worker to show him how to free it. Several panel sheets came to him that looked slightly shorter than the others, but he welded them just the same and sent them ahead to the next operation. On Friday, as he was sliding a sheet into the machine, a sharp edge caught the fleshy part of his thumb and ripped a one-inch gash in it. That was when Bill found time to talk to John again.

1. How do you think John feels about his new job? His new boss?

2. In what way were the incidents that happened to John between Monday morning and Friday afternoon related to his training?

3. What was wrong with the way Bill trained John to operate the welding machine?

4. If you were Bill, what would you have done that he did not do?

enriching your viewpoint

For a deeper understanding of some of the specific areas covered in this chapter, the following readings are especially helpful:

"Basic Education and Manpower Programs: The Research and Demonstration Experience," *Manpower Research Monograph No. 38,* U.S. Department of Labor, Superintendent of Documents, Government Printing Office, Washington, D.C., 1976.

Bittel, Lester R., *Nine Master Keys of Management,* McGraw-Hill Book Company, New York, 1972, Chap. 8, "Employ the Power of Training."

Christian, Roger W., "Programmed Learning," *Factory,* March 1962, p. 74.

Cullen, James G., Steven Sawzin, Gary R. Sisson, and Richard A. Swanson, "Training, What's It Worth?" *Training and Development Journal,* August 1976, p. 1220.

Johnson, Robert M., "Maintenance-Trades Training," in Lindley R. Higgins (ed.), *Maintenance Engineering Handbook,* 3d ed., McGraw-Hill Book Company, 1977, Chap. 2-1.

McCord, Bird, "Job Instruction," in Robert L. Craig, (ed.), *Training and Development Handbook,* 2d ed. McGraw-Hill Book Company, New York, 1976, Chap. 32.

On-the-Job Training: An Answer to Training Needs of Business, Chamber of Commerce of the United States, Washington, June 1963.

On-the-Job Training: Guide for Planning and Conducting, Air Force Manual, U.S. Department of the Air Force, Washington, D.C., August 1966.

O'Sullivan, Kevin, "Audiovisuals and the Training Process," in Robert L. Craig (ed.), *Training and Development Handbook,* 2d ed., McGraw-Hill Book Company, New York, 1976, Chap. 43.

Wikstrom, Walter S., "On-the-Job Training," *Supervisory Training,* The Conference Board, Inc., Report 612, New York, 1973, pp. 20–35.

CHAPTER 17 employee safety and health and OSHA

What causes accidents?

People do. And for a variety of reasons. Sometimes employees are careless. Sometimes the boss hasn't given proper instructions. Sometimes employee attitudes are to blame. Sometimes the supervisor hasn't helped employees to understand the dangers involved in their work. Sometimes equipment fails. Sometimes machines are not properly guarded. But it's *always* a person who could have prevented the accident by proper protective or control action.

What role does the federal government play in the prevention of accidents?

Since 1971, a major one. Until that time the safety of an employee at work was largely the result of efforts on behalf of state gov-

282

ernments, insurance companies, independent safety organizations like the National Safety Council, and the employer. Passage of the Williams-Steiger Occupational Safety and Health Act of 1970 (effective April 28, 1971) and the creation of the Occupational Safety and Health Administration (OSHA) have put the federal government and the Department of Health, Education, and Welfare (HEW) squarely into the safety act in every significant plant and office in the United States. The purpose of OSHA is to establish safety and health standards with which every employer and every employee must comply. And to make sure that there is compliance, OSHA makes more than 100,000 inspections annually.

How much leeway for variances does OSHA permit?

Very little. The act minces no words. For example, the General Duty Clause states that each employer:

1. Shall furnish to each employee employment and a place of employment that are free from recognized hazards causing or likely to cause death or serious harm to employees.

2. Shall comply with occupational safety and health standards promulgated by the act.

The poster that OSHA requires each employer to display in the area adds this:

The act further requires that employers comply with specific safety and health standards issued by the Department of Labor.

The standards (called National Consensus Standards) are derived from the American National Standards Institute (ANSI) and the National Fire Protection Association (NFPA) and are supplemented by the Established Federal Standards, which were derived from previous acts. Set down in a tightly packed, 250-page volume called "Occupational Safety and Health Standards; National Consensus Standards and Established Federal Standards," published by the *Federal Register* (Vol. 36, No. 105, Part II), May 29, 1971, the standards specify just about everything imaginable. They include specifications for guarding walks and walking surfaces, means of egress, powered platforms, environmental controls, noise, radiation, hazardous materials, sanitation, first-aid services, fire protection, compressed gases, material handling, machine guards, portable tools, welding, electrical installations, and particular attention to paper, textiles, laundry, sawmill, and bakery operations.

What happens to a company
when it doesn't meet the OSHA standards?

It is given a citation. More specifically, the citation is issued to the manager in charge of the facility. It may even be issued, for example, to a supervisor who refused to make certain that a prescribed machine guard was in place. A company and an individual may seek a temporary variance from the standard, but in most instances the only recourse is to take corrective action as soon as possible. In many cases, heavy fines and even jail sentences have been imposed on companies and managers who failed to comply promptly with the citation.

Some accident hazards are more
serious than others, aren't they?

Yes, and OSHA tries to separate them out. For example, it recognizes five categories of violations or potential hazards:

- *Imminent danger.* Any conditions or practices that could be expected to cause death or serious physical harm immediately before the danger could be eliminated. In this case, a company can be shut down fast by a court order.
- *Serious.* Conditions where there is a substantial probability that death or serious physical harm could result from the alleged violation, whether the employer knew of or, with reasonable diligence, should have known of the hazard. Guidelines have been set up in the OSHA Compliance Operations Manual to help evaluate such terms as "substantial probability."
- *Willful and repeated.* Violations are willful when the employer either intentionally or knowingly violates the act or, although not consciously violating it, is aware of hazardous conditions without making an effort to eliminate them. Repeated violations are those for which a second citation has been issued.
- *Nonserious.* Violations that are not serious but have a direct or immediate relationship to occupational safety and health.
- *De minimus.* A violation that has no immediate or direct relationship to the safety and health of the employees. No citation is issued.

How far beyond safety does OSHA extend?

The Occupational Safety and Health Administration looks deep into the areas of employee health that may be affected by substances in, or conditions of, the process or working environment and to *general sanitation* on the premises. These sanitation

standards are spelled out under the section General Environmental Controls. An important area is housekeeping. For example, containers for waste disposal must be available and
should be the kinds that don't leak and can be sanitized. Exter-
mination programs must be in effect for vermin control. Food and
beverage consumption on the premises is regulated.

Washrooms, toilet facilities, and water supplies are considered. Provision must be made for clearly labeling potable and
nonpotable water. Toilet facilities are specified according to the
number and sex of employees. Showers, change rooms, and
clothes-drying facilities must be provided under certain circumstances.

To what extent does OSHA specify accident recordkeeping?

It insists that every company or separate establishment maintain
a log of illnesses and accidents as they occur. Beyond that, the
forms already used by your organization to monitor these matters
and to investigate accidents are probably satisfactory.

The OSHA log (Form 200) is used to record each occupational
injury or illness and identify whether it has caused a fatality, a
lost workday, a permanent transfer to another job, or a termination of employment. In the area of *illness identification* OSHA has
expanded typical coverage; OSHA requires a report on occupational skin diseases or disorders, dust diseases of the lungs
(pneumoconioses), respiratory conditions due to toxic agents,
poisoning from systematic effects of toxic materials, disorders
due to other physical agents, and traumas (emotional shocks).

Also, OSHA standards require that additional specialized
records be maintained on such items as scaffolding, platforms,
man lifts, fire extinguishers, cranes, derricks, and power presses.
These records should include maintenance and inspection
dates. Still other records are required for radiation exposure,
flammable and combustible liquids inventories, and monitoring
logs of toxic and hazardous substances.

While your company will probably specify what records must
be kept and who will maintain them, the supervisor—as in so
many other areas—is a pivotal person in collecting the data.

How has OSHA affected safety training?

It has made it mandatory. Supervisors are expected to make certain that safe procedures are taught not only to new employees
but also as an ongoing program.

General safety training applies to the proper observance of safety regulations, routing for emergency egress in case of fire or other common danger, accident and injury treatment and reporting, and fire and explosion emergency activities.

Specific employee training required by OSHA applies to occupational health and environmental controls, hazardous materials, personal protective equipment, medical and first aid, fire protection, materials handling and storage, machine guarding, and—for welding—cutting and brazing.

Where do employees fit into the OSHA picture?

The law insists that they, too, act safely within established standards—provided that employers live up to their responsibilities. In other words, an employee who refused to wear the safety glasses provided by the employer in prescribed areas could be cited. Specifically, OSHA states:

> *The Williams-Steiger Act also requires that each employee comply with safety and health standards, rules, and orders issued under the Act and applicable to his conduct.*

Employees have several important rights under OSHA, however. For example, they may:

1. Request an inspection if they believe an imminent danger exists or that a violation of a standard exists that threatens physical harm.

2. Have a representative (such as a union steward) accompany an OSHA compliance officer during the inspection of a workplace.

3. Advise an OSHA compliance officer of any violation of the act that they believe exists in the workplace, and question, and be questioned privately by, the compliance officer.

4. Have regulations posted to inform them of protection afforded by the act.

5. Have locations monitored in order to measure exposure to toxic or radiation materials, have access to the records of such monitoring or measuring, and have a record of their own personal exposure.

6. Have medical examinations or other tests to determine whether their health is being affected by an exposure and have the results of such tests furnished to their physicians.

7. Have posted on the premises any citations made to the employer by OSHA.

Where do most accidents happen?

Accidents can happen anywhere. But the most common places for industrial accidents to happen are:

- Around hand lift trucks, wheelbarrows, warehouses, cranes, and shipping departments. More industrial accidents (nearly one-third) are caused by handling and lifting materials than by any other activity.
- Near metal- and woodworking machines, saws, latches, and transmission machinery like gears, pulleys, couplings, belts, and flywheels.
- On stairs, ladders, walkways, and scaffolds. That's because falls are the third most common source of industrial injury.
- Anywhere hand tools are worked with. Chisels, screwdrivers, hammers, and the like account for 7 percent of industrial disability.
- Everywhere electricity is used, especially near extension cords, portable hand tools, electric droplights, wiring, switchboards, and welding apparatus.

How do you prevent accidents from happening?

For years the National Safety Council has said that accident prevention depended on the three Es—engineering, education, and enforcement:

- To *engineer* a job for safety is to design the equipment, lay out the work, plan the job, and protect the individual—all with accident prevention as a first ingredient. Safety guards on machines are one example of engineering. Arranging the job so that employees work in another room instead of one where toxic fumes are generated by the process is another example. Still another is the wearing of protective eye shields, gloves, or safety shoes.
- To *educate* for safety is to show employees where, why, and how accidents can happen and to develop in them safe work habits and the desire to avoid injury. Helping workers to analyze the danger spots in their jobs and training them to build a defense against each is an example of education for safety.
- To *enforce* safety is to make an actuality of the slogan Safety first. Employees work most safely when they want to be safe, but they need guidance in the form of regulations and discipline to protect safe workers from those who would cause accidents by unsafe acts.

Isn't accident prevention
the safety specialist's job?

Safety engineers do an excellent job of carrying out the three Es of safety. But they would be the first to admit that without the supervisor's help, safety programs would flop. The supervisor is the key safety person, especially in education and enforcement.

Doesn't insurance or workers'
compensation take care of accident costs?

Not by a long shot. A company's liability insurance usually pays only the cost of a worker's compensation for an injury received at work. The cost of liability insurance to a company depends on how good a safety record the company has. The difference between a good and a bad record isn't peanuts. It means real money in insurance rates. Workers' compensation is a term applied to the procedure of most state governments for determining how much money an employee should get to compensate for the injury—assuming that it leaves the employee temporarily or permanently disabled to some degree.

It's been estimated that for an accident that comes to $600 for compensation, a company pays another $3,000 for related expenses. Examples of related expenses are cost of time lost by employees who stop to watch or assist; time lost by supervisors' helping and investigating the accident, making changes in production schedules, assigning and breaking in new workers; cost of medical care; loss of material, damage to equipment, productive time lost on machines, and—not to be overlooked—cost of the insurance that pays for the compensation.

With whom does accident prevention begin?

Good supervision is the starting place for an effective accident-prevention program. No amount of machine guards or safety rules will stop accidents from happening if supervisors aren't absolutely sold that it can be done—and that it's their responsibility.

Take the slogan "Safety first". What does it mean to you? Does it mean "Safety measures come ahead of everything else in my department," or is it just another slogan? Keep asking yourself that question every time you urge a worker toward higher production or better quality. Be sure that you don't ever give quantity or quality priority over safety. If you do, you'll find that your accident record suffers—and someone may get hurt.

One of the best examples I know of in setting the highest possible priority for safety takes place at a Du Pont plant in Germany. Each morning at Du Pont (Deutschland) GmbH polyester and nylon plant, the director and assistants meet at 8:45 to review the past 24 hours. The first matter they discuss is not production, but safety. Only after they have examined reports of accidents and near misses and satisfied themselves that corrective action has been taken, do they move on to look at output, quality, and cost matters.

Doesn't the individual employee have a responsibility for safety?

People cause accidents. Supervisors can't be everywhere at once. They shouldn't want to be. So in the long run it will be your employees who cause—or prevent—accidents in your company. But they won't prevent accidents unless you've gone all the way down the line to show them how.

First of all you've got to instill in employees the belief that *they* are the most influential source of accident prevention. Do this, with the aid of your safety engineer if you have one, by discussing the accidents that have happened in your organization. Seize every opportunity to let employees see cause and effect for themselves.

Preaching is not much help. Instead, when an accident happens, talk it over with one—or many—of your employees. Get their ideas of how it could have been prevented. Ask them if similar situations could arise in their jobs. Continually bring the conversation around to the human element.

Second, help your employees to develop safe working habits. People have to be trained to work safely just as they must be trained to work accurately. Few persons are just naturally cautious—or know instinctively where danger lies. The first day on the job in a foundry, a worker may be worried most about burns from the hot metal and hardly realize that eye injury, dermatitis, or crushed toes are just as likely to happen. The supervisor can start the worker out right, however, by explaining all these things, by showing how such accidents can happen, and by showing how to do the job so that they don't happen.

The third step in helping employees to be safe lies in the supervisor's ability to enforce job instructions for safety. Too many employees think of safety as "Don't do this or that"—as just so many rules and regulations. To get acceptance of job methods—as well as rules—you've got to show why they are necessary. And let employees know of the danger to themselves and your dissatisfaction when they don't follow the guides you've established for them. If you catch yourself saying, "Workers in my department just won't wear their safety goggles," it's no one else's fault but your own. It's up to you to see that they do. Reason and encourage first. But penalize if you don't get conformity.

What is an accident-prone employee?

Examination of safety records often shows that only a few employees account for the bulk of the accidents—that the great majority of employees rarely have accidents. Those people who get injured frequently are spoken of as *accident-prone.* This means that for one reason or another the person has an innate tendency to have accidents and hence is prone to injury. Psychologists have shown, however, that only a small percentage of so-called accident-prone employees are truly accident-prone. Most of these habitual sufferers can actually be made accident-free by proper job placement, training, and encouragement. So if one of your workers appears accident-prone, don't give up. Encourage the development of work habits that will protect the worker as well as the co-workers (see Chapter 20 on problem employees).

How effective are safety posters?

This is a debatable subject. Most authorities feel that "scare" posters on highways have done little to reduce accidents. Posters in the company can be more effective when they are keyed to your area's condition and your own safety program. For instance, if your emphasis is on safety goggles this month, posters that reinforce or repeat this emphasis will help. The mistake is to expect a series of posters to do your safety job for you. They'll help a little. But the big job is up to you.

Posters, like other forms of communication, need frequent changes in order to attract fresh attention. It's better to have none than to have a dust-covered one that's been on a bulletin board for two or three months.

Should a supervisor give
an injured employee first aid?

That depends on the practice in your company and on your own qualifications. There should be no question, however, about your responsibility to see that an injured employee gets first aid— quickly and properly. Permit only trained people (like graduates of the Red Cross first-aid course) to attend the patient. Know who these people are ahead of time and how to summon them without delay.

If your plant has a nurse or a physician who has been called, stay until you are sure that the injured employee is under medical care.

What can you do about employees who you think are malingering?

Check with the company medical department, if you have one. Avoid charging employees with faking illness unless your medical department can support you. Otherwise, you may have a hard time supporting your viewpoint. If workers feign sickness, ask yourself what there is about the job or about the employees that makes them want to get away from work so badly that they'll put on an act. In the long run, the answer to malingering lies in better understanding and in improving the employee's attitude.

How do you prevent lifting and material-handling accidents?

Heavy loads are only one reason for lifting accidents. Most lifting accidents happen because an employee doesn't have the knack of lifting with the legs, rather than the back. If you try to pick something up by bending over it and pulling backward and upward with your arms, it tends to strain the muscles and ligaments in the back. Instead, get as close to the object as possible. Crouch down beside it; if it's a case or carton, get the inside of your thighs as close to it as possible. Get a firm grip with your hands and arms. Keep your back straight as you pull the object toward you. Then simply stand up.

Try this knee-lift method yourself until you get the feel of it. Whenever a new employee enters your department, show how it's done. Let the person practice the lift a few times while you watch.

Of course, it goes without saying that when loads get too heavy—over, say, 50 to 100 pounds—you should instruct employees to get help. This may be another pair of hands, or a lift truck, jack, crowbar, block and tackle, crane, or any handling device that suits the purpose.

Accidents often happen when a worker trips when carrying materials. That's one reason clean floors and aisles are so important.

Accidents that happen while using mechanical lifting devices are frequently the result of overloading or improper usage. Make it a point to check load ratings on slings, cables, and cranes. Don't permit an inexperienced employee to operate any mechanical equipment without first checking the person out to show the right way.

How do you prevent accidents on machinery, machine tools, and power-transmission equipment?

Not only is machinery the number 2 cause of accidents in manufacturing, it also causes the most severe injuries. Since the turn of the century, both employers and machine builders have done much to protect machine operators through the judicious use of safety guards and devices. But don't take this action for granted. Whenever a new machine is installed in your department, inspect it before it goes into action. Try to be certain in your own mind that a worker would be adequately protected.

Many machine tools cannot be fully protected. So it's a good practice to caution employees about wearing loose clothing, long-sleeved shirts, string neckties, and so forth, around moving machinery. Stay with new and old employees alike until you're sure that each is aware of the danger a machine holds and how to steer clear of trouble. Of particular importance is knowledge of how to shut machinery down in a hurry. You should drill machine operators until they know enough about "off" and "on" control locations so that they can turn their machines off blindfolded.

How do you prevent falls?

In theory, falls can be prevented 100 percent. In practice, it's not quite that easy. One big obstacle to perfection is that employees tend to take falls for granted. It's the mark of a timid person, workers often say, to worry much about them.

To minimize falling injuries in your department, keep an eye out for these causes:

Unsafe floors and work surfaces. See that employees keep floors and work places swept clean. Don't permit spillages to remain unguarded or uncleaned a minute. Your keen interest in this matter helps dramatize its importance.

Unsafe ladders, stairways, and scaffolds. Ladders should never be used if there is any doubt about their condition or suitable length. Stairways should have railings and be well lit. Scaffolding should be checked by a qualified mechanic or an engineer.

Improper footwear.   There's a lot of stress on safety shoes to protect the feet. But sensible, low-heeled shoes, with soles in good shape and uppers laced to support the foot, are an excellent guard against falls, too.

Unsafe practice.   Employees may think you're nagging if you insist they hold on to a railing when going up or down stairs. But if you insist on safe practices when walking and climbing, or especially when working overhead, they will respect you for your interest in their welfare. That's the point to stress—how safe practices protect them and not just the shop's accident record.

How do you prevent hand-tool accidents?

Squashed thumbs and scraped knuckles by the hundreds of thousands bear painful tribute to the misuse of hand tools. Tools in bad shape, like a chisel whose head looks like a mushroom, should be taken out of service and repaired or thrown away. Proper tools for the job should be available, and employees should be instructed as to the danger in using the wrong tool for a job—like using a knife as a screwdriver or a file as a driftpin to remove a drill from a chuck.

Some employees, especially those who have not come up through the apprentice ranks, won't know how to handle tools properly unless you show them how. In securing employee cooperation in this, appeal to their sense of professional skill. No one likes to look like an amateur. So see that a file is used with a handle, never hit with a hammer (it might shatter), thumbs are out of the way of handsaws, open jaws of monkey wrenches are facing you when you pull on the handle.

Portable hand tools all have their own peculiarities, too. Check with the manufacturer's instruction manual to be certain you know, and your employees follow, the maker's guide for safe use.

How do you prevent low-voltage electric shocks?

The term *low voltage* covers anything under 600 volts. Since deaths due to contact with 110 volts (ordinary house-lighting circuits) are common, it's absolutely foolhardy to take any chances with electrical hazards. Injuries from electrical sources happen from touching live parts, short circuits, accidental grounds, overloads on the system, and broken connections.

Advise your employees to report to you any evidence of hot wires, tingling shocks from machines or equipment, abnormal sparking, frayed insulations, loose connections, or any other electrical fault. Don't investigate the cause yourself. Get the plant electrician—and quickly.

Portable electric power tools should always be grounded before being connected to an electric outlet. This is done by connecting a separate wire between the frame of the tool and a good ground—like a pipeline or I beam. Today many companies have grounded, three-prong outlets to accept three-prong plugs, but the existence of a three-prong plug doesn't guarantee the circuit is grounded. Check with the plant electrician on this.

Electricity's safety valves are fuses, fused switches, and circuit breakers. These protect equipment and circuits from overloads. Disconnect switches are dangerous. Do not permit production operators to touch them. That's the job for an electrician.

If one of your employees is knocked out by an electric shock, see that he or she is removed from the electrical source first (be careful, or others may also be shocked) and then given artificial respiration.

Frequency and severity—what's the difference?

Both are measures of how good your plant or department's safety record is. *Frequency* tells how often accidents have occurred. *Severity* tells for how long injured persons are disabled. The key to each measure is the *lost-time accident.* If an employee is injured and loses no time from work, the accident is not computed in the records. If the employee does lose time, it is.

Take this example: Foreman Joe has 50 employees averaging 40 hours work a week each. In 12 months one worker is injured. Total time lost is 37 days.

Injury frequency rate =

$$\frac{1 \text{ injury} \times 1,000,000}{50 \text{ workers} \times 40 \text{ per week} \times 50 \text{ weeks per year}}$$
$$= 10 \text{ lost-time accidents}$$
$$\text{per million hours worked}$$

Injury severity rate =

$$\frac{37 \text{ days lost} \times 1,000,000}{50 \text{ workers} \times 40 \text{ hours per week} \times 50 \text{ weeks per year}}$$
$$= 370 \text{ days lost}$$
$$\text{per million hours worked}$$

Note that OSHA uses its own special formula based upon the assumption that 100 employees will work fifty 40-hour weeks for a total of 200,000 hours annually. Thus, the OSHA formulas are:

Frequency = number of incidents $\times$ 200,000 $\div$ total hours worked

TABLE 17-1. Key-point Safety Planning

Job Planning	Hazard	Safe Practice
Get material on job	Acid stored in tank	Wear full eye protection and acid-resistant gloves
Dig out sewer	Hand tools	Keep tool handles dry
Repair sewer	Acid splash	Shut off tank outlet valve; proper use of chisels
Backfill	Hand tools	Keep tool handles dry
Clean up	Acid on surface	Use water freely on hands or any place acid splashes; spread lime on ground to neutralize acid

Severity = number of lost days $\times$ 200,000 $\div$ total hours worked

Rates compiled this way appear each year in the *Statistical Abstract of the United States.*

National Safety Council figures (compiled the standard way) show that frequency rates range from a low of 1.2 accidents per 1 million hours worked in the communications industry, to an average of 6.5 for all industry, to 28.4 for construction, and to a high of 36.7 in underground coal mining. Severity rates are lowest in wholesale and retail trades (71 days lost per 1 million hours worked); they average 695 days for industry in general, amount to 2,642 for construction, and reach a high of 7,542 in coal mining.

What's key-point safety?

Key-point safety is a form of job analysis in which the supervisor lists the safety hazards on the job and the preventive measure an employee should take for each.

Suppose you were a maintenance supervisor in a chemical plant. You're about to assign a work crew to repair an acid sewer. You'd first fill out a key-point safety-planning card. It might look like Table 17-1.

The next step is to discuss the key points with the operator who has to follow them. Have the operator repeat the instructions—and follow up to see that safety is being practiced on the job.

If you supervise a job that is done about the same way each

day, and consequently has the same hazards most of the time, you'll want to make up a permanent key-point safety card for each job. Post it at the machine or the workplace. Quiz workers regularly about it. (See the section on key points in Chapter 16.)

How do you investigate an accident?

If an accident should happen in your department or to an employee under your supervision, one of the best ways to prevent its happening again is to investigate the accident to find out exactly why it happened. Once you have determined this, you can establish safeguards to protect individuals from any unnecessary dangers. This is an important point to understand, since there is a little risk in everything we do—even staying at home in bed. But many of the chances employees take are unnecessary. Accident investigation will uncover these and enable you to do something about minimizing them. When checking on accidents, your object is to find causes, not to fix the blame. Look for:

- What object or substance caused the accident—such as a hand chisel.
- What part of the object did the damage—such as a cutting edge.
- What kind of accident it was—such as being struck by the chisel.
- What the unsafe mechanical or physical condition was—such as a dull edge.
- What the unsafe act was—such as not grasping the chisel firmly.
- What the unsafe personal factor was—such as lack of skill.

The easier it is for you to answer any of these questions, the more obvious it is that unnecessary chances have been taken and that you can help an employee avoid taking those chances in the future.

Many companies provide an accident investigation form for the supervisor to fill out. A typical one is shown in Figure 17-1.

How much good is safety clothing if employees won't wear it?

It's generally been proved that employees will wear safety goggles and other protective clothing *if* they have been trained to do their work with it, *if* employees understand how it protects them, and *if* everybody—co-workers as well as the supervisor—expects them to wear it.

Supervisor's Accident Review

Date reported _____

Name of injured worker _____ Clock No. _____

Date of accident _____

Brief description of accident _____

_____

_____

Indicate below by an "X" whether in your opinion the accident was caused by:

Physical causes

_____ Improper guarding?

_____ Defective substances or equipment?

_____ Hazardous arrangement?

_____ Improper illumination?

_____ Improper ventilation?

_____ Improper dress or apparel?

_____ No mechanical cause?

_____ Not listed? (Describe briefly) _____

Sometimes the injured person is not directly associated with the causes of an accident. Using an "X" to represent the injured worker and an "O" to represent any other person involved, indicate whether, in your opinion, the accident was caused by:

Unsafe acts

_____ Operating without authority?

_____ Failure to secure or warn?

_____ Working at unsafe speed?

_____ Made safety device inoperative?

_____ Used unsafe equipment or hands instead of equipment?

_____ No unsafe act?

_____ Not listed? (Describe briefly) _____

_____ Unsafe loading, placement, mixing, etc?

_____ Worked on moving equipment?

_____ Took unsafe position?

_____ Teased, abused, distracted, etc.?

_____ Did not use safe clothes or personal protective equipment?

Personal causes

_____ Physical or mental defect?

_____ Lack of knowledge or skill?

_____ Wrong attitude?

_____ Not listed? (Describe briefly) _____

Actions that I have taken to prevent a similar future accident.

_____

_____

Supervisor's signature _____

FIGURE 17-1. Typical Accident Investigation Form Used by Supervisors to Report Their Investigations. (Rollin H. Simonds and John V. Grimaldi, Safety Management: Accident Cost and Control, Richard D. Irwin, Inc., Homewood, Ill., 1956).

To make safety clothing more acceptable to employees, there are many things you can do:

1. Let employees help decide which kind of protection suits the situation best. Discuss the hazardous situation with them first. If working near a degreaser requires wearing a respirator, talk over with them the various kinds of respirators available. Give them a chance to make suggestions as to what they think is best.

2. Offer a selection. If employees say that such and such a safety goggle makes them uncomfortable, it helps if you can offer a choice of three or four different kinds. "Surely," you can say, "you ought to be able to find one that you like."

3. Set an example yourself. If the job calls for hard hats, wear the heaviest, brightest one yourself. Then you can say, "I know that the hard hat looks uncomfortable. But I hardly even know I'm wearing it anymore."

4. Get help from the informal leaders in the work group. If you can get an older, respected employee to set the style in safety gear, other workers are likely to follow suit.

5. Show you mean business. If employees can't be cajoled, encouraged, or led to wear their safety clothing, then take disciplinary action. If you're consistent and if the protective equipment is suitable, OSHA and even most unions will back you up strongly on this point.

Should a supervisor get involved with locker room sanitation?

Yes, if only to demonstrate a concern for employee well-being. Locker rooms speak eloquently to employees about a company's attitude toward them as individuals. When locker and service rooms are clean, workers know that they have the boss's respect. When these rooms are messy or unsanitary, employees are likely to feel that the company is unconcerned about its workers.

Regardless of whether the responsibility for washrooms and locker rooms is assigned to a single supervisor (say, in the maintenance department), be sure you take a personal interest in service-room conditions. Encourage the employees who work for you to keep sinks clean, to throw paper towels in the trash can. Check to see that they don't keep dirty clothing or soiled towels in their lockers very long. If general conditions of lighting, care of showers, and soap supply are below standard, speak to your higher management about it. You needn't be a troublemaker in this regard. But recommendations from the supervisor are much more in order than waiting for employees or their union representatives to complain first.

Just how much of a threat is fire to industrial and commercial buildings?

More than many people suspect. Loss of life is shocking to contemplate. And purely from a business viewpoint, a plant or office destroyed by fire often means hundreds of jobs permanently destroyed. That's right. According to *Occupational Hazards* magazine, 71 percent of all business establishments that are severely damaged by fire fail within three years, 43 percent never open again, and 28 percent have to give up within 36 months! So when you hear an employee say, "What do I care if this old company burns down? It's time they built a new one," give an ungarbled account of what fire can do to employees' jobs.

Where are industrial fires most frequent?

Industrial fires, like most fires anywhere, tend to start where there are few people or where the fires are difficult to spot until they've made headway. Few houses are burned down by sparks from a roaring fire in the living-room fireplace while the room is full of people to watch it. If the fire is caused by a fireplace, chances are that it begins from sparks thrown out of the chimney or onto the living-room rug after everybody's gone to bed. It's the same way in the company. Sparks from a welder's torch can be dangerous (as in the case of the famous General Motors fire at Livonia, Michigan), but fires that begin where you least expect them are much more dangerous.

So look for fire hazards in out-of-the-way places as well as in the obvious spots. Spend some time usefully by probing into corners of warehouses to prevent accumulation of papers and other debris that might make perfect nesting places for a lighted cigarette butt. Look under benches for oily rags stuffed in tight corners, just loaded with the right ingredients for spontaneous combustion. Climb up near the roof to see whether dust is heavy on rafters and pipes—just the stuff to help spread a flash fire that originates somewhere else.

What sort of fire prevention measures should you enforce?

Good housekeeping is one of the best. Where floors, benches, desks, corners, and machines are kept clean and neat, fire has a hard time getting a foothold. Watch out for material piled too close to overhead sprinklers, fire extinguishers, and hoses. Material too close to the sprinklers cuts down on their effectiveness.

Blocked fire extinguishers may mean the difference between a fire that is put out in a few seconds and one that gets a toehold in a minute. And never permit a fire extinguisher or a fire bucket to be used for any purpose other than to fight fires. Also check regularly to see that they're full.

Check with your safety engineer, personnel manager, or superior to determine the best practices for handling flammable liquids, like solvents of any kind. Some of the precautions will seem overdone, but in the long run no safety measure with flammable materials can be too extreme.

Don't be lenient with employees who smoke in unauthorized areas. It may seem like a little thing. But it's the carelessly flipped butt where people don't expect it that can cause the big trouble.

Set this rule for yourself and your employees: Regard every open light, every flame, every match and cigarette, every bit of oily waste or thimbleful of flammable liquid as potentially dangerous. Discipline taken to enforce safety measures is the least difficult to gain support for from labor unions. So sell each employee on the personal stake held in fire prevention in the plant or office.

How does the National Fire Protection Association (NFPA) differentiate between the kinds of fires?

The NFPA and the Underwriters' Laboratories, Inc., recognize four kinds of fires:

Class A.   Ordinary combustible materials like wood, which are put out by a quenching agent like water.

Class B.   Flammable liquids or greases such as gasoline, which require a blanketing or smothering agent like foam.

Class C.   Involving energized electrical equipment, which requires a nonconductive extinguisher like a dry chemical or CO_2.

Class D.   Fires of combustible metals where the quenching agent must cling to surfaces, conduct heat away, and smother burning.

What's the significance of the four classifications?

Each kind of fire is fought with a different kind of agent. Most wood and paper fires (A type) are fought with the typical soda-acid extinguisher or a hose—both of which use water as a quenching agent to cool off and wet down the fire.

Oil, grease, and solvent fires (B type) are fought with foam-type, dry chemical, or carbon-dioxide gas extinguishers. These all act to blanket the fire by keeping the air away from it. Water on a fire like this would simply spread the fire around. Lighter oils would float on top of it.

An electrical fire (C type) *could* be put out with almost any kind of extinguisher, but the person holding the hose or extinguisher (if it's soda-acid) would get a severe, possibly killing, shock. That's why a bromotrifluoromethane, dry chemical, or CO_2 extinguisher must be used; none conducts electricity.

A burning metal (like magnesium, uranium, sodium, or potassium, and now known as a D-type fire) has been controlled for years by G-1, a graphite granule and phosphorus powder, applied by scoop or shovel. But a new dry powder in fire extinguishers flows freely and provides a heat cake to cool metal. It has a sodium-chloride base and additives to assist flow and water repellence. Its ability to cling to vertical surfaces makes it quite suitable for magnesium casting fires since it is not necessary to bury the casting.

The point is that you need the right kind of extinguisher for each fire. Usually you can depend on your safety engineer or insurance company to be certain that the most suitable extinguisher is handy to the kind of fire that might start. But you should make a habit of knowing what kind of fire-fighting equipment is in your department, how to use it, and on what kind of fire. Then see that your employees know, too.

Figure 17-2 shows NFPA's recommended markings to indicate which kind of extinguisher is good for what kind of fire.

In case of fire, what should you do?

Experts disagree as to which one of these things you should do first. But they all agree that these three things should be done immediately:

1. Report the fire by telephone, or see that the message is carried to the company or local fire department. Many building-wrecking fires have gotten away from persons who were sure they could put them out themselves.

2. See that employees are evacuated. Safety to persons comes before property. See that all employees in the department know about the fire and are evacuated from the building or out of the area—except those officially designated to fight the fire.

3. Fight the fire with hand extinguisher or hose. Speed is abso-

ORDINARY | FLAMMABLE | ELECTRICAL | COMBUSTIBLE

COMBUSTIBLES | LIQUIDS | EQUIPMENT | METALS

FIGURE 17-2.   **NFPA Recommended Markings for Fire Extinguisher Use.** Markings placed on extinguisher indicate suitable use for each class of fire.. Extinguishers suitable for more than one class of fire may carry as many markings as appropriate. When symbols are colored, A is green, B is red, C is blue, and D is yellow.

lutely essential—thus the need for keeping fire extinguishers unblocked and knowing how to use them.

What can be done to make safety committees more useful?

If you or your company has organized departmental safety committees, see that the committee has a real job to do. Don't let meetings turn into coffee klatches. And don't use them solely as a sounding board for your inspirational appeals for safety. Treat the safety committee as a business organization:

Assign specific problems.   If your medical department or first-aid room tells you there's been a rash of small cuts on hands and arms, get the committee to investigate this condition to find out what the facts are, where they occur, to whom. Then ask for a specific recommendation on how to correct the situation.

Expect results.   Make it clear that being on a safety committee entails more than sitting in on a meeting. Assign area safety responsibilities to the members. Let them assist with inspections. Ask for a report of minor accidents in each area. Have the members tell what improvements have been made, what more can be done.

Have members participate on investigations.   Talking about safety isn't as effective as getting out on the floor to see what's being done about it. Use this opportunity to demonstrate the company's efforts and expenditures for safe working conditions. Emphasize that unsafe practices are just as important to watch out for.

Delegate duties.   If the committee plans a safety competition, let them handle the publicity, the method of making awards, and the establishment of rules. They know their co-workers better than anyone else does—and can guess what will work best.

What conditions should a supervisor look for when making safety and housekeeping inspections?

Conditions and OSHA requirements vary, but you'll find a good starting set in Table 17-2. For each item listed, it is a good idea to check with your superior to see what the specific OSHA standard is so that you can know exactly what to look for.

What's the best way to sell safety to your employees?

There are three keys here:

Believe in your product. "If you'll study your job with me so that you always do it the safe way, I'll guarantee you'll never get a cut or a bruise, let alone lose an eye—as someone might who doesn't work safely."

Know your product. "Safety first is more than a slogan here. There's a safe way and an unsafe way of doing every part of your work. Before you start up your machine, see that your safety goggles are on. Check the tool, is it firmly in the chuck? Now stand clear as you push the button to start the motor."

Show benefits to employees. "Safety practices are designed with one person in mind—and that's you. These practices not only make your job safer, they often make it easier. And we can show you the records to prove that the safety device won't cut down on your earnings. Safety here at work pays off for your family at home, too. They can relax knowing that you are working the safe way, that they needn't fear that someday you'll come home in an ambulance."

supervisory word power

Hazard. A potentially dangerous object, condition, or practice that is present in the workplace, to which employees must be alert and from which they must be protected.

TABLE 17-2. Safety and Housekeeping Checklist

	Condition Okay	Needs Correction
Unsafe Practices:		
Employees operating without authority	————	————
Employees working at unsafe speeds	————	————
Employees making safety devices inoperative	————	————
Employees using unsafe equipment	————	————
Employees lifting improperly	————	————
Employees assuming unsafe positions	————	————
Bulletin Boards and Safety Signs:		
Clean	————	————
Readable	————	————
Material changed frequently	————	————
Material removed when obsolete	————	————
Protective Equipment and Clothing:		
Equipment and clothing in good condition	————	————
Equipment and clothing used when needed	————	————
Additional equipment or clothing needed	————	————
Sufficient storage space for equipment	————	————
Floors:		
Loose material	————	————
Slippery, wet, or oily	————	————
Badly worn or rutted	————	————
Garbage, dirt, or debris	————	————
Stairways and Aisles:		
Passageways, aisles, stairs unblocked	————	————
Stairways well lighted	————	————
Aisles marked and markings visible	————	————
Lighting:		
Lamp reflectors clean	————	————
Bulbs missing	————	————
Any dark areas	————	————
Material Storage:		
Neatly and safely piled	————	————
Passageways and work areas not blocked	————	————
Fire extinguishers and sprinklers clear	————	————
Machinery:		
Machines and equipment clean	————	————
Sufficient containers for waste materials	————	————
Guards on and operating	————	————
No drips or oil leaks	————	————
Cutoff switches accessible	————	————
Buildings:		
Windows clean and not broken	————	————
Painting and upkeep satisfactory	————	————
Door jambs clean	————	————
Fire doors unblocked	————	————

TABLE 17-2. **Safety and Housekeeping Checklist (*continued*)**

	Condition Okay	Needs Correction
Employee Facilities:		
Drinking fountains clean	———	———
Locker rooms and toilets clean	———	———
Soap and towel supply satisfactory	———	———
Tools:		
Right tools for the job	———	———
Tools used correctly	———	———
Tools stored properly	———	———
Tools in safe condition	———	———
Electrical hand tools grounded, used properly	———	———
Ladders in good condition, used properly	———	———
Electrical:		
Motors clean	———	———
No exposed wiring	———	———
Temporary wiring removed	———	———
Switch boxes closed	———	———
Proper fusing	———	———
Pressure:		
Gauges working properly	———	———
Cylinders secured from falling	———	———
Pressure vessels inspected regularly	———	———
Steam:		
Steam or water leaks	———	———
Insulation condition	———	———
Gases, Vapors, Dust, and Fumes:		
Ventilation all right	———	———
Masks and breathing apparatus available where needed	———	———
Dust-collection system satisfactory	———	———
Material-handling Equipment:		
(Check for cleanliness, safe condition, and operation)		
Cranes, platforms, cabs, walkways	———	———
Chains, cables, ropes, block and tackle	———	———
Industrial trucks	———	———
Railroad equipment—rolling stock, tracks, signals, roadbed	———	———
Conveyors—drives, belt condition, guards	———	———
Elevators, hoists	———	———
Hand trucks and wheelbarrows	———	———
Fire Protection:		
Hoses and extinguishers well marked	———	———
Hoses and extinguishers not blocked	———	———
Extinguishers inspected regularly	———	———

Accident. An unplanned or uncontrolled event in which the action or reaction of an object, material, or person results in personal injury.

Lost-time accident. An accidental injury at work that causes an employee to lost time from the job and thus becomes recorded in official statistics.

Worker's compensation. Financial reparations or awards granted by an employer (often in accord with rate tables prescribed by a state's legislature) to an employee who has suffered an injury at work that is judged to have permanently restricted the employee's earning capacity.

Spontaneous combustion. Ignition of a substance (such as oily cotton waste) from the heat generated by the rapid oxidation of its own constituents when exposed to air and with no other heat source applied.

Other Important Terms in This Chapter

accident frequency	fire classes A, B, C, and D
accident-prone	imminent-danger hazard
accident severity	key-point safety
citation, OSHA	malingerer
compliance officer, OSHA	National Consensus Standards
de minimus hazard	sanitation

reading comprehension

1. Differentiate between the three Es of safety.

2. What is the purpose of OSHA? What are employees' rights under the act?

3. Why do so many serious fires start in out-of-the-way places?

4. What can a supervisor do to instill safety consciousness in employees?

5. What limits the effectiveness of safety posters, campaigns, and other appeals for safety?

6. What is the danger in trying to put out a fire yourself, without first calling the fire department?

7. Distinguish between injury frequency and injury severity rates.

8. When investigating an accident, what role should key-point safety play?

9. Would it be a good idea to make the wearing of safety clothing optional? Why?

10. If a company's safety committee turns up nothing but

slogans, what might you suggest to make their suggestions more useful?

supervision in action

◼◼◼◼◼◼ **THE CASE OF THE SIX-HIGH STACK.   A case study in human relations involving safety, with questions for you to answer.**

Mike studied the OSHA poster on the wall of the Dairy/Drug chain store where he was employed as a stock clerk. Mike's job consisted of unloading cases from trucks, opening cartons in the stockroom, wheeling their contents out into the store proper, stamping prices on each item, and placing these items in their assigned shelf space. If Mike understood the OSHA poster correctly, it meant that he did not have to do anything that he thought was unsafe. And here he was piling these heavy cartons as they came off incoming trucks six high in the stockroom. Why, that was outright dangerous! They might topple down on someone's foot if the person weren't careful. To say nothing of the fact that he was going to strain his back for sure, lifting the fifth and sixth cases above chest level to stack them. Mike decided that he was going to do something about this right away. He went looking for Edna, the assistant store manager.

"Hey, Edna," Mike said, "from now on, I'm not stacking those incoming cases like you want. Not until you provide some sort of racks so that they are only stacked three or four high. The way it is, those cases are a safety hazard. Somebody's going to have a bad accident if they fall. And it may be me. We ought to have a powered lift truck out in that stockroom anyway. Or at least someone to help me stack cases when a truck comes in."

"Who do you think you are fooling?" asked Edna. "You're just looking for an excuse to get out of the heavy work here. We have been stacking cases six high for years, and I never saw one fall. And neither did you."

"We've been lucky," said Mike. "OSHA wants us to step in now and make sure no accident can happen because of an unsafe practice. And stacking cases six high is unsafe."

"We'll see what's unsafe around here," said Edna. "In the meantime, get that truck unloaded. And keep on stacking the cases six high. Otherwise, there won't be room in the stockroom to walk around or to sort out the case contents. *That's* what might really cause an accident."

"No way," said Mike. "I know my rights. Stacking six high is a threat to my safety. Dairy/Drug has got to remove any hazards that are likely to cause me or anyone else serious bodily harm."

"As a matter of fact," said Edna, "I'd like to see one of those cases fall on your head where it would do some good. But the heaviest case can't weigh more than ten pounds. And besides, those cases aren't going to fall. That's a safe way to stack them. You are just looking for trouble. Or for someone else to help you do your work."

"Since you put it that way," said Mike, "I am not going to stack those cases at all until the OSHA inspector comes in here and tells me whether it is safe or not. I'll keep on moving stock out into the store, but I won't unload trucks."

1. What do you think of Mike's argument?
2. How do you think Edna has handled this situation?
3. If you were Edna, would you insist that Mike unload trucks? Stack cases? How high?

enriching your viewpoint

To gain a broader understanding of safety and of accident and fire protection, the following readings are recommended:

Accident Prevention Manual for Industrial Operations 7th ed., National Safety Council, Chicago, 1974.

Binford, Charles, Cecil Fleming, and Z.A. Prust, *Loss Control in the OSHA Era,* McGraw-Hill Book Company, New York, 1975, Chap. 6, "Standard Procedures Instructions."

Coccola, Richard, "What To Expect From the OSHA Man, *Factory,* August 1972, pp. 25–49.

Fundamentals of Industrial Hygiene, 1970, National Safety Council, 425 North Michigan Avenue, Chicago, Ill.

"How Two Companies Are Promoting Safety," *Supervisory Management,* March 1975, pp. 35–39.

OSHA Safety & Health Standards Digest for General Industry, OSHA 2201, revised March 1975, U.S. Department of Labor Occupational Safety and Health Administration, Government Printing Office.

Sampson, Arthur F., *Fire Safety: A Management Concern,* U. S. General Service Administration, 1973, Government Printing Office.

Supervisors Safety Manual, 4th ed., 1973, National Safety Council, 425 North Michigan Avenue, Chicago, Ill.

Waisanen, Christine, *What to Do About OSHA,* National Chamber of Commerce of the United States, Washington, 1977.

the supervisor's role in labor relations

What part does the first-line supervisor play in labor matters?

In the eyes of the law, supervisors are the responsible agents of their company. Your employers are held responsible for any action you take in dealing with employees or with unions, just as if they had taken the action themselves. For this reason, if for no other, it's essential that a supervisor be familiar with the labor contract the company has signed with its union and with the other policies, practices, and procedures that make for good labor relations.

How does a supervisor's authority in labor relations vary according to the company?

Your primary responsibility to your company in labor matters is to protect the interests and the rights of management. How far supervisors can exercise authority in carrying out this responsibility will depend on the extent to which the front office feels they can act without first checking to see if their decisions are in line with company policy.

In most companies supervisors may have no authority to adjust wage rates directly; they may be limited merely to reporting a wage-rate request and analyzing the job conditions. On the other hand, in most companies supervisors will be expected to take direct and immediate action in the case of willful damage to equipment, unsafe actions, or refusal to follow a work assignment.

But regardless of administrative differences from company to company, the first-line supervisor is usually the first contact between employees and management and between union representatives and management. Since what you do and say in labor matters has such vital consequences to your company's overall relationship with employees and their representatives, you must be alert to your company's labor practices. Your actions are not confined only to yourself and a single employee. They could very well have companywide impact. Under certain circumstances, your actions could cause your employer to be charged by the union with breaking the contract, or even with breaking the law.

What does collective bargaining include?

When authorized representatives of the employer and authorized representatives of the employees bargain together to establish wages, hours, and working conditions, this process is called *collective bargaining.* Various labor laws have determined what are fit matters for collective bargaining and what are not. Generally speaking, however, the term *working conditions* is so broad that almost anything that affects employees at work or the manner in which they carry it out can be included.

The mere fact that a matter, such as the establishment of piece rates, is a fit subject for collective bargaining doesn't assure that the union can necessarily control the way it is handled. The union can bargain for its position, and management has to bargain in good faith over the issue. But the company does not have to accept the union's position. Several considerations will determine its final disposition: the reasonableness of the union demand; the desirability of the demand to employees, management, and stockholders; the ability of the company to pay for its cost; the judgment of management as to its worth; and, finally, the bargaining strength or weakness of the union or the company.

Does collective bargaining apply only to contract negotiations?

Collective bargaining usually starts with the negotiation of the union agreement and the signing of the labor contract. But it doesn't end there. Supervisors, managers, employees, and union stewards must live with the agreement for the next 365 days or longer. Applying the contract and interpreting its meanings from day to day are what make collective bargaining effective. The contract, like any other contract, is rarely changed during its life. But there are dozens, sometimes hundreds, of occurrences between supervisor and employee that need astute judgment as to how the situation should be handled in order to carry out the meaning of the contract. It is such interpretation and differences of opinion between management and unions that make labor relations a key supervisory headache and responsibility.

Wasn't everything much simpler before the Wagner Act?

There's no denying that supervisors had a much freer hand in dealing with employee matters before the Wagner Act. But there is also considerable evidence that, unions or not, supervision has actually become more intelligent and more effective since the right of employees to organize has been protected by law.

The Wagner Act (correctly called the National Labor Relations Act) describes the conditions under which workers can bargain collectively through their authorized representatives. The act did not create any new rights. It was intended to safeguard and enforce existing rights.

The Wagner Act does not set up any specific working conditions (as so many people erroneously believe) that employers must give to their employees. It does not concern itself with the terms of the union agreement. All it does is guarantee that employees may act in a group together—rather than as individuals —if they so desire, in bargaining for their wages, hours, and working conditions.

The supervisory job has been made tougher, where unions exist, simply because whenever a supervisor deals with an individual employee's problem, he or she must always take into account the whole employee group's position as set forth in the labor contract.

Supervisors in the past have been charged with unfair labor practices of interference and discrimination. What's this all about?

Supervisors are most directly affected by the section of the Wagner Act that prohibits unfair labor practices. Actually, there are five unfair labor practices, but two most frequently involve supervisors.

Interference. This would most likely take place during a union's organizing drive or a National Labor Relations Board (NLRB) representation election. Supervisors should be especially careful at that time to avoid (1) any actions that affect an employee's job or pay, (2) arguments that lead to a fight over a union question, (3) threatening a union member through a third party, or (4) dealing without advice from top management with any of the organizing union's officers.

Discrimination. This term applies to any action (such as discharge of an employee, layoff, demotion, or assignment to more difficult or disagreeable work) taken by any member of management on account of the employee's union membership or activity. To be on safe ground, it's wise not to discuss union matters as such with employees, or to express an opinion for or against a union or unionism. This is good practice off duty as well as on.

The simplest way to avoid charges of discrimination is to disregard completely an employee's union membership when you make decisions regarding job assignments, discipline, and promotions. Before you act, make sure in your own mind that you have separated ability, performance, and attitude toward the job from the employee's stand on unionism or zeal in supporting it.

Why don't supervisors sit in with the management bargaining team at a union contract negotiation?

Bargaining is a delicate matter of strategy and power. It's a little like playing poker. If there are too many kibitzers, a good hand can be spoiled by unwanted expressions and remarks.

If your company does not invite you to sit in on negotiations, don't feel slighted. Not many companies have other than a hand-picked bargaining team of the top plant management group.

How does the supervisor's day-to-day administration of the contract influence contract negotiations?

In many ways. If day by day a supervisor neglects or ignores grievances, assigns jobs unfairly, or neglects safety and other working conditions, collective bargaining will be made more difficult. Each time during the year you throw your weight around indiscriminately or take advantage of letter-of-the-law loopholes in the contract, you add to the store of incidents that the union representatives will bring to bear in order to win their demands at contract time.

Take seniority as an example. Suppose you stand on your management right (and the absence of a specific contract clause to the contrary) to assign overtime only to the workers you favor, regardless of their seniority. Once or twice you defend your position by saying that the overtime required the special skills of the two class A operators you held over. But the union observes that several times you've held over class A operators just as convenience: The bulk of the work could have been done by laborers. When contract time rolls around, you can bet that the union negotiators will be in there pitching for a definite clause to spell out exactly how overtime will be distributed.

It's far better to handle your decisions reasonably and equitably during the year so that at contract time the union will accept more general provisions. This leaves the details to be worked out during the year on a mutual basis as the occasion arises. Experience seems to show that the more general type of contract is easier for all members of management to administer.

Union shop, closed shop, what's this all about?

The closed shop was outlawed by the Taft-Hartley Act. Under a closed shop, a man or woman had to belong to the bargaining union before he or she could be hired. The union shop is somewhat similar. The difference lies in the fact that a person need not be a union member at the time of hiring. But an employee must (usually after a 30- or 60-day trial period) become a member of the union in order to stay on the payroll.

Under the Taft-Hartley Act, the only reason a union may force a company to fire a worker is that he or she does not pay union dues. This protects the individual from being discriminated against by the union. In the union shop agreement, it's common for a company also to sign a checkoff agreement with the union. This means that the company will collect employees' union initiation fees and dues and turn them over to the union. The employee must first sign an authorization card that gives the company permission to do so.

How did the Taft-Hartley Act change the Wagner Act?

The labor law of the land is the National Labor Relations Act (the Wagner Act) as amended by the Taft-Hartley Act (Labor-Management Relations Act) in 1947. The Taft-Hartley Act clarified and added to the list of unfair practices that could be charged against management. But more significantly, the act imposed upon unions certain controls over their organizing activities, their internal union organization, and their collective bargaining methods.

Under the law, unions or their agents are forbidden to:

• Attempt to force an employer to discharge or discriminate against former members of the union who have been expelled for reasons other than nonpayment of regular union dues or initiation fees.
• Attempt to force an employer to pay or deliver any money or other things of value for services that are not performed. This outlaws featherbedding or other make-work practices.
• Restrain or coerce other employees into joining or not joining a union.
• Require excessive or discriminatory fees of employees who wish to become union members.

In addition, individual employees are protected in their desire to bargain or not to bargain collectively:

• They may take up a grievance directly with management—provided that the settlement is in line with the union contract, and a union representative is given an opportunity to be present.
• If they are professional employees, they have a right to vote with a company's other professional employees whether they want a collective bargaining unit of their own.

Other significant changes enacted by the Taft-Hartley Act are:

The 60-day notice of contract termination. Either company or union must give the other party 60 days' notice that it wants to end the contract—even though the contract has a definite termination date. During the 60-day period no employee can strike or slow down; management cannot alter, contrary to the contract requirements, the employment status or working conditions of any employee.

The 80-day injunction.   Should a labor dispute, in the opinion of the President of the United States, imperil the health and safety of the nation, procedures are set up so that after proper investigation the President may petition the federal district court for an injunction to stop the strike or lockout. During this 80-day cooling-off period, certain other procedures must be followed. Toward the end of the cooling-off period, if the dispute remains unsettled, the NLRB must take a secret ballot of employees to ascertain whether they wish to accept the terms of the employer's last offer. If still unsettled after 80 days, the strike or lockout may resume.

Right to sue for damages.   Both companies and unions may sue in federal court for damages caused by breach of contract. Employers may also sue for damages arising out of illegal strikes and boycotts.

Plant guards' units.   Plant guards are permitted to form their own bargaining group but may not bargain collectively through a union associated with other employees.

Freedom of speech.   Employers and unions are given equal rights to speak their minds freely about each other—except when they actually utter a "threat of reprisal, or force, or promise of benefit." (Note that "promise of benefit" is not considered to restrict a union from describing the potential benefits to be derived from union membership.)

Are there any other labor laws that a supervisor should know about?

Two important laws are the Walsh-Healey Public Contracts Act and the Fair Labor Standards Act. Generally, your company will watch for compliance, but since the laws influence decisions that affect you, here's a fast rundown:

Walsh-Healey sets the rules for any company that works on a government contract in excess of $10,000. The act forbids hiring boys under 16 and girls under 18. It limits the basic hours of work to 8 per day and 40 per week. The employer must pay time and one-half for overtime that results. It sets up strict standards for safety, health, and working conditions and also may establish a minimum wage for a particular industry.

Fair Labor Standards (Wages and Hours Law) regulates methods of wage payment and hours of work for any industry engaged in commerce between two or more states. The law restricts the employment of children over 14 and under 16 to nonmanufacturing and nonmining positions and will not permit the employment of children between 16 and 18 in hazardous jobs, including driving or helping a driver of a motor vehicle. The law sets the minimum wage ($3 an hour in 1979) and prescribes that time and one-half must be paid for all hours worked over 40 in a week. It also establishes what is "work" and what is not—such as waiting in line to receive paychecks, changing clothes, washing up or bathing, checking in or out. (All this may be considered work in a union agreement if the parties so agree.)

The Fair Labor Standards Act also sets up guides for determining which supervisors must be paid overtime and which need not. In order to be classed as an exempt executive, a supervisor must:

• Have as a primary duty the management of a recognized department or subdivision.
• Customarily and regularly direct the work of two or more other employees, exercise discretionary powers, and have the power to hire or fire or make suggestions and recommendations which will be given particular weight as to the hiring, firing, advancement, and promotion of subordinates.
• Not perform nonexempt (clerical, nonadministrative) work more than 20 percent of the time (40 percent in retail trade).
• Receive a salary of at least $125 per week.

If an employee's salary is over $200, there are fewer restrictions on what he or she can do and still be exempt from overtime. Nonexempt employees include almost all wage-roll and clerical people; overtime provisions of the law apply to them. Professional employees who require advanced knowledge, customarily acquired through prolonged instruction and study of a specialized field, are usually considered exempt. However, apprenticeship, a college degree, or routine training will not necessarily qualify an employee as a professional.

What is the purpose of the Disclosure Act of 1959?

Officially designated as the Labor Management Reporting and Disclosure Act of 1959, Public Law 86-257 (also known as the Landrum-Griffith Act) compels employers to report:

• Payments to labor union officials, agents, or shop stewards (for purposes other than pay for work).
• Payments to employees (other than regular wage payments) or to groups or committees of employees for purposes of persuading other employees regarding choice of a union or other union matters.

- Payments to a consultant on labor union matters.

Payments that must be reported also include reimbursed expenses. More important, the law also compels a labor union to make a more complete disclosure regarding the sources and disbursement of its funds.

Primarily, the law is aimed at (1) preventing unethical collusion between a company and a union or other interference with the due process of collective bargaining, (2) preventing the misuse of a union's funds by its leaders, and (3) otherwise minimizing the possibility of labor "racketeering."

Do the new laws make it illegal for your company to refuse to hire members of a minority group?

Yes, if you do not hire them because of the color of their skin or because of their religion. The equal opportunity law (Title VII of the Civil Rights Act of 1964) actually goes further than that. It prohibits employers in interstate commerce from discriminating against job applicants because of race, color, sex, religion, or national origin, except where religion, sex, or national origin is a bona fide occupational qualification (BFOQ) reasonably necessary to the normal operation of the business. For example, religion may be a bona fide occupational qualification for an educational institution supported by a religious denomination. Or there may be a legitimate pay differential because of sex if the job content for a man and a woman is truly different in physical requirements.

Other restrictions prohibit separate lines of progression for men and women or separate seniority lists. Advertisements must indicate that the jobs are open to both men and women. Furthermore, the need to provide separate facilities is not considered an excuse for not employing women unless it would be unreasonably expensive. And the law considers that discrimination against married women is no longer acceptable.

In trying to comply with the law, you cannot shift the responsibility to the preferences of your customers or others who come in contact with your employees. For example, you can't say, "Our customers prefer to deal with men" or "Our customers don't like blacks."

The equal opportunity law is a federal law. It supersedes conflicting laws of some states and supplements or reinforces existing laws (such as those preventing discrimination on the basis of age) in other states. The law was initially legislated to apply to larger firms, but by 1968 it applied to all employers with more than 25 employees.

What about affirmative action?

██████████ In enforcing the provisions of equal employment opportunity laws (Chapter 10 and Chapter 19), the Equal Employment Opportunity Commission (EEOC) has encouraged firms to engage in *affirmative action programs*. When these firms are handling federal contracts, the EEOC insists that they do so. Affirmative action programs consist of positive action taken to ensure nondiscriminatory treatment of all groups protected by legislation that forbids discrimination in employment because of race, religion, sex, age, or national origin. These programs emphasize that results count, not good intentions. If company statistics on pay or promotion, for example, show that the current status of minority groups is inferior to that of most other employees in that company or geographic area, the company may be directed to set up an affirmative action program. Companies with federal contracts over $50,000 and more than 50 employees have no choice. They must have a written program in good operation.

Obviously, equal employment opportunity legislation was designed to protect minority groups from discrimination and specifically to encourage more rapid utilization of blacks and women in the work force. Note that the law is not a labor-management law: It is directed at employers, and they must comply without obstruction by a labor union, if one is present.

ERISA? Is that a labor relations law?

██████████ The Employee Retirement Income Security Act of 1974 (ERISA) made sweeping changes in the way employee benefits are handled, with or without a union. While ERISA is not a labor relations law as such, because it is essentially a directive to management, it affects workers everywhere. Of special importance to supervisors is the ERISA requirement that details of benefit plans be "fully disclosed" to employees. Supervisors and other management representatives are expected to explain clearly benefits such as pensions and profit sharing, hospital insurance, reimbursement for medical and surgical expense, and compensation for accident, disability, death, or unemployment.

How about OSHA?

██████████ The Occupational Safety and Health Administration (see Chapter 17) is directed at management *and* labor, but it does not stipulate or regulate their relationships; OSHA, of course, greatly regulates working conditions, which in the past have been a prime bargaining issue between management and labor.

What is the outlook
for growth in labor union membership?

Only one in four American workers belongs to a labor union. Changing values among workers and management's enlightenment would seem to forecast a decline in membership in the future. Many states have enacted right-to-work laws, which preserve the right of an individual to refuse to join a union even after the union has been certified as the legal bargaining agent. Many companies seek to start up new plants on a nonunion basis, too, not because of lower wages (many pay higher wages) but because they believe there is a potential for higher productivity in nonunion operations.

How far does a union shop steward's authority go?

A steward is to the union what you are to the company. It's a union steward's job to protect the rights of union members just as it's yours to protect the rights of management. But in protecting these rights, union shop stewards have no authority to run your department or to tell you or any employee what to do.

You may get the impression that a steward is telling you what to do. A new steward may even feel that it is his or her job to do so. All the steward has authority to do, however, is to advise you or an employee of how the steward understands the contract to limit your actions and decisions. It goes without saying that you are the department executive, and you are not obligated to share your responsibility with anyone.

It is good practice, however, to keep stewards informed of what you are doing—so that they can make their position known. It also shows that you are not trying to take unfair advantage of the stewards.

How friendly should
a supervisor be with a shop steward?

Be as cordial as you can without giving up your right to run your department. You may personally resent a steward who is a continual thorn in your side. But remember, the steward is an elected representative of the group. Stewards speak not only as individuals but also for the employees they represent.

You can gain confidence, if not cooperation, from shop stewards if you let them know what's going on. They have status to protect, just as you do. If you try to keep them in the dark or treat them as if they are insignificant, they may react by showing you just how important they are. So don't keep a steward at arm's length. Get to know him or her as you would any other employee. You will have many mutual problems. There's nothing wrong with enlisting a steward's help in solving some of them.

Suppose you are planning to start up a second shift on one of the machines in your department. You intend to post a bidding sheet for a new operator. You lose nothing by telling the steward of the new job opportunity in advance. And it gives you a chance to enlist the steward's help when you say "We're going to be needing a good operator to run the number 6 machine on the second shift. We agree with the union that the job should go to the worker with the most seniority who is really qualified to do a good job. But let's see that we get some good people bidding."

Some stewards just won't cooperate. How do you handle them?

You can help aggressive stewards blow off steam if you maintain a constructive approach and show them you understand their problems. After all, their jobs can be thankless ones. Check yourself, too, to be sure that it's not your own aggressive actions that make a steward hard to get along with. Try to approach each problem, not as a battle between the two of you, but as one that you both are trying to solve in accordance with the labor agreement. Don't say only, "Let's see what the contract says." Show that you, too, are interested in justice for your employees: "Let's see how we can do the most we can for this employee without making a decision that is out of line with the contract."

Always keep in mind, however, that it is cooperation you are seeking, not comanagement.

What should be your attitude toward the union?

Don't be anti-union. Adopt the attitude that most unions are here to stay and that once your company has made an agreement with one, your best bet is to work as hard as you can to get along with the union. Don't waste your energy trying to undermine the union. Instead, put your efforts into making your department a better place to work.

It would also be a big mistake, however, to turn over to the union your interests in, and your responsibilities to, your employees. It's more important than ever, when your company has a union, to show employees that you still consider them your department's greatest asset. If you abandon their interests, you're likely to find employees looking to their union representatives rather than to you for leadership.

Should you feel hurt when your employees join a union or display strong loyalties to union stewards and officers?

▬▬▬▬▬▬▬ No. An extensive study of employees' loyalties showed rather conclusively that it's natural for workers to have dual loyalty—to their supervisors and to their union leaders. Employees look to their boss for sound business judgments and for the satisfactions that come from doing a purposeful job under good working conditions. Employees look to their union for the social prestige of belonging to an influential group and as a protector of their economic interests and job security. An employee who works for a good company and a considerate boss and who also is represented by an honest, active union enjoys this relationship. Asking an employee to choose between the boss and the union would be a little like asking a child to choose between mother and father.

Why is there a grievance procedure? Wouldn't it be better to settle gripes informally without all the red tape?

▬▬▬▬▬▬▬ Most union contracts establish a step-by-step grievance procedure. Experience has shown both management and labor that it's best to have a systematic method of handling complaints. Without a formalized procedure, management (in dealing with unionized employees) would find it difficult to coordinate labor and personnel practices from department to department.

The formal procedure provides an easy and open channel of communications for employees to bring complaints to the attention of supervision. And it guarantees that these complaints won't be sidetracked or allowed to ferment without corrective action being taken. Good supervisors and wise managements know that an unsettled grievance, real or imaginary, expressed or hidden, is always a potential source of trouble. The grievance machinery helps uncover the causes and get the grievance out into the open. (See Chapter 21.)

Is there a standard grievance procedure set down by law?

No. The actual grievance procedure will vary from company to company. It will depend on what the company and the union have agreed upon and have written into the labor contract.

A typical grievance procedure has from three to five steps:

• Step 1. Supervisor discusses complaint with employee and union steward.
• Step 2. Superintendent and industrial relations manager discuss with union grievance committee.
• Step 3. Plant manager and industrial relations manager discuss with union grievance committee.
• Step 4. General company management discusses with national union representative and union grievance committee.
• Step 5. Dispute is referred to impartial umpire or arbitrator for decision.

It should be emphasized that a serious and a prolonged effort should be made by both parties to settle the grievance at each of the steps—including the first.

Why do supervisors sometimes get overruled?

If supervisors have made every effort beforehand to be sure their decisions and actions are in line with the company's interpretation of the contract, there can be only three reasons why they should be overruled. The supervisor may have acted on insufficient or incorrect facts. This is probably the most common reason. The supervisor may occasionally be made the sacrificial lamb when the company realizes at the third or fourth step of the procedure that its interpretation of the contract won't stand up to the union's position. Or both the supervisor and the company may be overruled by the arbitrator at the last step.

Why don't grievances go right to the arbitrator in the first place?

Unions and managements seem to agree on this point: They'd both rather settle their household quarrels between themselves than invite a stranger in to settle disputes. Both parties reason, and rightly, that they know more than anyone else about their affairs. In the long run, union and management must learn how to settle their differences themselves without continually depending on a third party. It's been said by both union and management that nobody wins an arbitration. But when it's needed, peaceful arbitration is far better than strikes or lockouts.

What's the purpose of the NLRB?

The National Labor Relations Board (NLRB) is made up of five members appointed by the President of the United States. Its duty is to:

- Administer the National Labor Relations Act and, in so doing, determine proper collective-bargaining units.
- Direct and supervise representation elections.
- Prevent employers, employees, and unions from violating the act by committing unfair labor practices defined in the statutes.

The NLRB is not a federal court with power to settle disputes. But it makes the major decisions about how the NLRA should be interpreted. Since it is not a court, you may occasionally read of a company or a union petitioning a federal district court or the United States Supreme Court to set aside a ruling made by the NLRB. The federal court or the Supreme Court, in such a case, would have the final say—not the NLRB.

supervisory word power

Collective bargaining.   The process of give and take between the management of a company and authorized representatives of its collective employees (a labor union) to reach a formal, written agreement about wages, hours, and working conditions.

Unfair labor practices.   Those practices engaged in by either management or labor unions that are judged by the federal labor law (National Labor Relations Act) to be improper, especially in that they (1) interfere with the rights of employees to organize or (2) discriminate against them for labor union activities.

Labor contract.   The written agreement that binds a company's management and its employees' organization (labor union) for a stipulated period of time to certain conditions of pay, hours, and work, and any other matter the parties deem appropriate.

Grievance procedure.   A formalized, systematic channel for employees to follow in bringing their complaints to the attention of management. Typically, it prescribes a progression of appeals from lowest to highest authority within the company and the employees' organization.

Arbitration.   Settlement of a labor dispute or employee grievance by an impartial umpire selected by mutual agreement of the company and the union.

Other Important Terms in This Chapter

affirmative action
bona fide occupational qualification (BFOQ)
checkoff
closed shop
discrimination
exempt and nonexempt employees
interference
right-to-work laws
union shop
working conditions

reading comprehension

1. What three principal matters are always fit subjects for collective bargaining discussions?

2. Contrast the negotiations for a collective bargaining agreement and the day-to-day administration of that contract.

3. What is the difference between unfair labor practices involving interference and those involving discrimination?

4. Compare the objectives of the Wagner Act with those of the Taft-Hartley Act.

5. How does an exempt employee differ from a nonexempt employee?

6. Which particular labor law is designed to protect employees from discrimination because of race, color, sex, religion, or national origin? When does this law not apply?

7. Contrast a shop steward's responsibility under a labor contract with that of a supervisor.

8. Describe a typical grievance procedure. At what point does a supervisor usually bow out?

9. Contrast the role of an arbitrator and that of the NLRB in settling labor disputes.

10. Under what circumstances would a company be likely to be required to set up and adhere to an affirmative action program?

supervision in action

███████████ **THE CASE OF THE SUSPENDED DYE MIXER.** **A case study in human relations involving labor relations, with questions for you to answer.**

"Eddie, this is the third time this year you've pumped the wrong mixture into a dipping tank," said Frank, the supervisor of a chemical plant, to a dye mixer. "I can't understand how you can make such a mistake. You mustn't be paying enough attention to what you're doing. So I'll give you something to help you remember. Punch out now, and don't come back to work until next Monday. And if the same thing happens again, you'll be fired."

Eddie punched out, but before doing so, he checked with his shop steward, Tom Tyler. "We'll see what we can do for you," he was told by the union representative.

That afternoon Tom Tyler spoke to the supervisor. "Don't you think that a suspension is a little steep for Eddie? You've never done this to anyone else."

"No," said the supervisor. "And nobody else has pumped the wrong tank three times in a year. Our contract says we can take necessary disciplinary action to correct poor performance. Eddie has had enough chances. Now he needs to know we mean business. Besides, Eddie's attendance has been lousy lately. He's been late a couple of times this month and was absent at least once when he wasn't excused. And you should have heard the hassle he gave me last week, too. Eddie's head is getting too big for his hat, and he needs something to put him straight. The suspension will have to stick."

The shop steward's only reply was, "We'll see about that."

The union filed a written grievance. When the case came before the plant superintendent, here's what the steward said then: "Sure, it looks as if Eddie made a mistake. But when I checked up, it wasn't at all clear to me. Eddie says that Frank's directions were confusing, that he misunderstood. In fact, Eddie says that on one occasion recently he asked Frank to explain his orders over again and all he got from him was 'You understand what I mean.'

"Besides, when I spoke to Frank about this case, Frank was more interested in telling me all the other things that were wrong with Eddie than about the pumping mistake. In fact, he went so far as to say that Eddie's head was getting too big for his hat and he was going to straighten him out. It's my opinion that Frank had it in for Eddie and gave him the business the first phony excuse he could find."

The plant superintendent turned to Frank. "Is this true, Frank? Let's hear your side of the story again."

1. If you were Frank, how would you explain your position?
2. What do you think of the shop steward's defense to protect Eddie?
3. What sort of mistakes do you think Frank made in handling this case? Why?
4. What do you think of Frank's relationship with Eddie? With Tom?

enriching your viewpoint

Labor relations is an ever-changing field, subject every day to new interpretations in the laws and their application. Consequently it is helpful to have a comprehensive understanding of the principles that underlie them. For further study the following readings are suggested:

Affirmative Action and Equal Employment: A Guidebook for Employers, U.S. Equal Employment Opportunity Commission, Vol. 1, January 1974.

Dowling, William F., and Leonard R. Sayles, *How Managers Motivate: The Imperatives of Supervision,* 2d ed., McGraw-Hill Book Company, New York, 1978, Chap. 13, "The Supervisor and the Union."

Glueck, William F., "Labor Relations and the Supervisor," in M. Gene Newport (ed.), *Supervisory Management Tools and Techniques,* West Publishing Company, St. Paul, Minn., 1976, Chap. 12.

How to Eliminate Discriminatory Practices: A Guide to EEO Compliance, Staff of Humanic Designs Division, Information Science Incorporated, Amacom, New York, 1975.

Marshall, H. D., and N. J. Marshall, *Collective Bargaining,* Random House, Inc., New York, 1971.

Prascow, Paul, and Edward Peters, *Arbitration and Collective Bargaining,* McGraw-Hill Book Company, New York, 1970.

Selby, Rose T., and Maurice L. Cunningham, "Grievance Procedures in Major Contracts," *Monthly Labor Review,* October 1964, pp. 1125–1130.

Stagner, Ross, and Hjalmar Rosen, *Psychology Of Union-Management Relations,* Wadsworth Publishing Company, Inc., Belmont, Calif., 1965.

Stone, Morris, *Labor-Management Contracts At Work,* Harper & Row, Publishers, Inc., New York, 1961.

The Supervisor's Guide to Labor Relations in the Federal Government, 5th ed., U.S. Civil Service Commission, Bureau of Training, Labor Relations Training Center, August 1972 (CST 26-9494) RN 59.

supervising special people at work

Many employees present unique supervisory problems and require special considerations. These employees cover a wide spectrum of individuals and groups. Accordingly, the objectives of this part are:

• To grasp the intentions and the ramifications of legislation that guarantees equal employment opportunities so as to be able to implement these laws properly.
• To become aware of, and counsel effectively with, employees whose performance is weakened by personal problems such as mental illness, drugs, and alcohol.
• To develop a sensitivity to employees' complaints and grievances and handle them fairly and positively.
• To be able to administer firmly both positive and negative discipline as the occasions arise.
• To identify the aspects of clerical work that make it unique so as to be able to manage office employees more effectively.
• To understand the idiosyncrasies of those "knowledge workers" whose jobs require advanced knowledge and training so as to create the most supportive work environment.

19

equal employment opportunities for all

In the eyes of the law, who is a minority employee?

Just about anyone who is not a middle-aged white male of European heritage and the benefactor of a fairly adequate primary education. Minorities include blacks, Mexican Americans, Spanish-speaking Americans, American Indians, women (white as well as black), disadvantaged young, handicapped workers, and persons over 40 years of age. The basic equal employment opportunity laws say that an employer cannot discriminate against a person because of race, religion, sex, national origin, or age. In trying to make these laws work, various agencies of the United States government have interpreted them to apply to all victims of prejudice and discrimination, especially those who are undereducated and have grown up in extreme poverty such as occurs in many ghettos and rural areas.

What has caused this concern for minorities today? Hasn't America always been a land of struggle as well as opportunity for the latest wave of immigrants?

Great social forces at work in the past 30 years have altered the values of many people. Family life-styles and marriage patterns have radically changed. Most people enjoy relatively affluent living. This makes for harsh comparisons with those who do not have jobs or are relegated to second-class work and often second-class pay. The power of television and instant communications intensifies the awareness of these differences. People—especially those who believe that their second-class status is the result of discrimination—are impatient for improvement. The newer laws are a direct expression of the public's general dissatisfaction with these conditions and its wish to provide equal employment opportunities.

What is the legal basis for equal employment opportunity programs?

There's no reason for you to be bogged down with the details, but for reference purposes here are the major laws with a brief description of their main points.

The *Equal Pay Act* (June 1963) amended the long-standing Fair Labor Standards Act of 1938 to require the same pay for men and women doing the same work.

Title VII of the Civil Rights Act (1964) is the biggie. It prohibits employers, unions, and employment agencies from discrimination (race, sex, or national origin) in hiring; in wages, terms, conditions, and privileges of employment; in classifying, assigning or promoting, and extending or assigning use of facilities; and in training, retraining, and apprenticeship.

Executive Orders 11246 and 11375 prohibit discrimination in employment for organizations having contracts of $10,000 or more with the federal government. They require that these organizations institute affirmative action programs. Specifically, these contractors—and there are hundreds of thousands of them, including almost all large organizations—cannot:

Make any distinctions based on race, sex, or national origin in any conditions of employment, including fringe benefits and pension plans.

Distinguish between married and single people of one sex and not the other.

- Deny employment to women with young children unless the same policies apply to men with young children.
- Penalize women because they require time away from work for childbearing.
- Maintain seniority lists based solely on sex or race.
- Deny a woman the right to a job for which she is qualified even though the state may have "feminine protective legislation."

In 1971 the United States Supreme Court ruled in the *Griggs* vs. *Duke Power* case that if any employment practices or tests had an adverse (or differential) effect on minorities, the employers were guilty until they proved themselves innocent. In other words, if a test or a requirement (no matter how well intended it is, such as the requirement of a high school diploma) actually screened out minorities, it had to be shown indisputably that it was related to successful performance on the job. A company that requires a high school diploma for a floor sweeper's job, for example, would probably be in trouble. Based on this decree, the government said that exceptions could be made only if the company could prove that discriminatory selection practices were truly related to the job, that is, bona fide occupational qualifications (BFOQ). These are discussed in Chapter 10 and Chapter 18.

Revised Order IV (1971) strengthened equal employment opportunity guidelines to require that contractors (1) analyze their work force to determine if women are underemployed and (2) set numerical goals and timetables by job classification and organizational unit to correct any deficiencies. This order was tested by the landmark AT&T consent decree of 1973, in which the nation's largest employer agreed to make fundamental changes in personnel policies and to promote women as well as men into jobs from which they were traditionally excluded.

Age Discrimination in Employment Act (1967) forbids discrimination against workers 40 to 64 years old in hiring, firing, promoting, classifying, paying, assigning, advertising, or eligibility for union membership.

Rehabilitation Act (1973), especially section 503, requires employers with a federal contract of $2,500 or more to take affirmative action to hire and promote handicapped persons.

Vietnam Era Veteran's Readjustment Assistance Act (1974) requires certain affirmative action in the employment of veterans.

What is meant by reverse discrimination?

This is what many persons believe happens to men and also to members of the white race when preference in employment is shown to women, minorities, or both. In the *Bakke* case of 1978, the Supreme Court said in effect that it was wrong to use quotas designed to accommodate women and blacks in such a manner as to withhold employment from eligible men and whites. At the same time, however, the Supreme Court upheld the principle of affirmative action programs.

How are the hard-core unemployed different from others?

They are especially disadvantaged. For example, in reports prepared by the National Industrial Conference Board and Industrial Relations Counselors, Inc., of Princeton, New Jersey, the hard-core unemployed typically had these characteristics.

- They are school dropouts, usually with only a sixth- or seventh-grade education. Many do not speak or write English. As many as 30 percent have less than fifth-grade reading and arithmetic skills.
- They are unemployed heads of households, men and women with large family responsibilities that tend to overwhelm them with problems.
- They have poor work histories. Few have worked at anything but day labor or in casual service as dishwashers or porters, for example. They have not been prepared for work by their families, their communities, or their schools.
- They are plagued by personal problems. They have little experience in managing a regular income and may need help in handling credit, balancing a diet, or even learning how to cash a paycheck.

Table 19-1 lists skills in which the hard-core unemployed do not have training.

Is it true that many disadvantaged people get "tested" out of jobs?

It was true to a great extent until 1971, when the United States Supreme Court (*Griggs* vs. *Duke Power*) handed down a decision barring "discriminatory" job testing. Few tests, however, are intentionally discriminatory; it is just that most tests have been built around cultural models of white, middle-class people. As you can see by definition, privileged people are not typical of the hard-core unemployed, and tests—when used indiscriminately—screened out the latter. Nevertheless, as a result of the Supreme Court decision, testing for selection, placement, or

TABLE 19-1. Environmental and Interpersonal Skills Often Needed by Hard-Core Unemployed

1. Handling money.
2. The meaning of and use of bank accounts, savings, and reserves for the future.
3. Credit and installment buying.
4. Simple consumer economics.
5. Routine business practices.
6. Community health and welfare services.
7. How to get and keep a job.
8. The structure and functions of society's organizations and institutions.
9. Relating satisfactorily to one's co-workers.
10. Relating satisfactorily to one's supervisors.
11. Responding satisfactorily to rules, regulations, production requirements, and social expectations in the organization.

Copyright, National Industrial Conference Board, New York, 1969; reprinted with permission of the publisher.

training in industry has been modified to identify aptitudes and skill of disadvantaged persons rather than unwittingly to separate out from the labor force people with untapped potential.

Federal guidelines for employment testing require that tests be validated (if adverse impact is present) so that the test really measures what it says it measures and does not exclude minorities or women in a discriminatory fashion. Tests must be validated on two counts:

Content validity. This means that the test content is truly related to the job requirements. It would be unfair to give a complex typing test requiring 100 words per minute when the job requires only the simplest sort of typing at 60 words per minute.

Construct validity. This means that the test is put together in such a way that it does not screen out applicants who could pass the content part if only they could understand the test questions themselves. For example, applicants might be able to demonstrate mechanical aptitude if they could read the questions. Perhaps the test should be administered orally rather than in writing.

What does it take to motivate hard-core employees?

Candidly, it takes plenty. Their disbelief in the "system" is so ingrained that only extraordinary measures can overcome it. As the National Industrial Conference Board (NICB) *Report on Education, Training, and Employment of the Disadvantaged* says, "The trainee must be brought to believe that there is something in this for him; that, at the end of the road, there is a real job." At Lockheed-Georgia Company, for example, trainers of hard-core employees introduce two motivational aspects designed to strengthen belief on the part of hard-core employees: (1) a status of trust and (2) a showing of concern. For many it is the first time that they have been truly trusted by an establishment person, and for just as many it is likely to be the first time that a "straight" person has shown a real concern for their self-improvement.

At the 3M Factory Training Center in St. Paul, Minnesota, trainers concluded that the disadvantaged who try to succeed in society by adopting its codes of behavior become frustrated. Accordingly, their trainers say that the disadvantaged see the system as closed and want only to satisfy physical needs—to obtain minimal food, clothing and housing. They are not interested in luxuries, because these never were seen to be accessible. The middleclass worker who sticks to a poor job because he can buy treats outside of work has few counterparts among hard-core workers. The disadvantaged on blue-collar jobs have only 'meat and potatoes' goals.

Another key insight into the motivation of disadvantaged persons is that they seem far more concerned with peer recognition than with supervisory approval. If the group with whom a hard-core employee is working has trouble with the job, the participant will be more strongly inclined to fail along with the group than to succeed to please the boss. Consequently, the favorable influence of co-workers from the community is to be encouraged. The employee who admires the accomplishments of another will try hard to succeed.

Another challenge to the supervisor is the tendency of hard-core people to resist involvement. They see the job scene as what many West Coast disadvantaged persons call the "poverty hustle": it's an activity with no real substance. One of the first questions a hard-core employee is asked by the community neighbors is, "What do you do?" Consequently, it is a good assumption that workers who know what a finished product will look like will outperform others who don't. Specifically, if they work on a part for a toaster, they ought to see just how that part fits into the toaster—and have a picture of the toaster to show the family. Similarly, if they are filing policy records in an insurance company, they ought to see what a policy actually looks like and have a brochure about the company's services that can be taken home.

What works and what doesn't work in training hard-core employees?

Training fundamentals do not vary from situation to situation or from person to person. It is more a matter of intensifying the fundamental techniques. Companies like Chrysler, Western Electric, Lockheed, and the Equitable Life Assurance Society have found that the following guidelines need special emphasis:

1. **Make the training specific.**   Avoid generalizations and abstractions. Talk about concrete things like pounds, inches, steel, or paper. Show how each new subject relates to a job or to a product.

2. **Rely on demonstrations.**   Actions and illustrations, plus live demonstrations, communicate far more effectively than do words alone with an audience for whom speaking, reading, and other verbal skills are underdeveloped. Repeat and repeat the demonstration until you are sure the trainee has understood what you are doing.

3. **Overtrain rather than undertrain.**   Err on the side of providing more information and more skills than are needed for the work to be done. That way, trainees will be less likely to underperform on the job, and they'll have more confidence in their ability to do it well.

4. **Offer personal aid.**   It may not seem germane to a training effort for a supervisor to help a trainee get a ride to work, have a garnishment reduced, or even provide jail bail, but it helps to keep the trainee's mind on what is being learned and, of course, it builds confidence in the boss.

5. **Provide lots of follow-up.**   In some cases, the most meaningful training takes place when a supervisor shows a trainee again on the job what may have already been shown in training. That's because it is on the job that learning becomes most relevant and least academic.

6. **Reassure and recognize frequently.**   It may seem like pampering to assure a person repeatedly that progress is good, or to tell that person (and others) constantly how well the work is going; but with people who have been on the receiving end of put-downs most of their lives, it takes an overabundance of encouragement to reinforce their confidence in themselves.

7. **Use the buddy system.**   Appoint a co-worker, preferably a disadvantaged person, from whom the trainee can get private counseling. The first days on a new job are often full of hazing and mistakes. At one St. Louis plant, for instance, a trainee inadvertently was doused with oil on his first day in the shop. He would not have returned to the job after lunch, he said, if his

buddy hadn't shown him that it was an accident and that it wouldn't happen again.

What role does CETA play in the employment of the disadvantaged?

The Comprehensive Employment and Training Act (CETA) of 1973 provides federal monies to state and local agencies to train and seek employment (primarily in the public sector) for those in the community who are hard to employ, especially persons who are undereducated, unskilled, or inexperienced; (2) are considered by many employers to be too young or too old; (3) are unable to work full-time; (4) are subject to discrimination or restrictive labor market practices, despite equal employment opportunity laws; and (5) lack the basic work disciplines and abilities necessary to get and hold a steady job.

The Youth Employment Act of 1977, similarly administered, focuses on training and employment of teenagers and other young people.

Should a woman's place be in the home?

There was a time not so long ago when many people thought so. But if you are a man, and that's your attitude toward women who work in your company, you're likely to be in for trouble. Far more important than the charge of the various feminist organizations to gain equal rights for women has been the impetus provided by the federal government and sustained by the rising levels of education that find men as well as women inclined to support the basic issues of the women's movement.

Women play a major role in the work force of the United States. That role continues to grow. By the mid-1970s women in the total work force exceeded 39 million, approximately 40 percent of the total number of people working. As the labor force grows, more than half the increase is made up of women.

Why do so many women work outside the home?

Many women simply have no choice. Others work outside the home as so many men do, for the sheer exhilaration and satisfaction they get from their jobs.

While many women may work to earn extra money, nearly half of those in the labor force have to work because they are single, widowed, divorced, or separated (and thus self-supporting), or they are married to husbands who have low incomes. All these women must earn in order to subsist.

It is instructive to look at the turnaround in the nature of women earning money since the beginning of this century. United States Department of Labor figures reported that in 1900 only one out of twenty married women was at work while two out of every three women in the labor force were single. By 1971, four out of every ten married women were at work, and only one out of every four women in the work force was single. In 1971, 55 percent of the women in the work force were married (the rest were single, widowed, or divorced).

In what ways might a woman's basic reason for seeking employment affect her job performance?

A glib reply would be to say that her performance will be affected in exactly the same way as a man's. It can be presumed, for example, that a single man may not be so highly motivated by wage rates and job security as a man with a family. Similarly, it can be presumed that a 19-year-old woman engaged to be married may not be so career-oriented as a 35-year-old unmarried woman. If these presumptions are correct, it would imply that a young man might respond less favorably to boring work than a married man would. And a young woman might be less interested in long-term advancement opportunities than a middle-aged one would be. Following this line of reasoning (and based on my own experience and that of dozens of other managers with whom I've discussed this problem), I think it is reasonable to anticipate a woman worker's attitude and resultant response to motivations on the basis of her reasons for working and the extent to which she expects her job to contribute to her life goals. For example:

A relatively young woman, newly entered in the work force, may have only short-term work goals. Good pay, an attractive workplace, a chance to socialize, holidays and vacations, and a friendly boss probably rank highest on her list of requirements. Another young woman, especially one with advanced education and a liberal view of the woman's role in society as well as in marriage, might rate most attractive only those jobs that offer intellectual challenge and a chance to prove her true worth as an individual. Either young woman may be difficult to manage: the former, because her mind is not on the bigger picture; the latter, because she wishes to approach her work not as a subordinate who routinely follows orders, but as an intellectual equal whose opinion and judgment are sought and accepted. Obviously, there will be a little of each view in each woman because these examples represent the extremes of a spectrum; most young women are somewhere in between.

A working wife (or mother) may be so dominated by family responsibilities that her job can mean little else to her than a source of needed income. If so, pay may be her biggest motivator, with the hope that the workday will not drain her energies, emotional as well as physical, to the detriment of her home life. At the other end of this spectrum is the wife or mother for whom work is her most rewarding effort. Such a person is far more likely to expect mental stimulation at work and to exert pressure for equitable treatment. In between, of course, are the women who find both family and work rewarding and for whom work may or may not be necessary. These women will be neither docile nor excessively aggressive. They are more likely to fit the concept of an average, well-balanced employee and will respond most predictably to normal, unself-conscious, good supervisory techniques.

An older woman, married or widowed, who returns to the work force at middle age represents another challenge to sensitive supervision. If she has worked at a specialty before "retiring" to raise children or to manage her home, her skills are likely to be rusty, and her adjustment to the sustained pressures (and often impersonal nature) of the workplace may require adjustment on her part. But she is typically steadier, more patient, and less demanding than many people in the work force, men as well as women. Since this group of potential employees seems to keep growing in the United States economy, the returned-to-work woman represents a particularly attractive employee to seek out and encourage.

Somewhere in this mix is a large group of women who view work in exactly the same manner as men traditionally do. These career women look to work not only for income and occupation, but as the principal avenue for fulfilling their life-career goals. Typically, they are competent, dedicated individuals. Treat them that way, regardless of whether they work for you or with you as associates or serve you in a staff capacity, or whether you work for one of them. These women seek no unusual quarter. All they ask is to be provided with the opportunity to perform at the level of their competence without favor or prejudice because of their sex. This is all that men with similar ambitions should ask for, too.

**For most women, what appears
to be the main ingredient missing
in the labor market in general
and in their jobs in particular?**

An opportunity equal to that of men for securing intellectually challenging employment and a chance for advancement in proportion to their performance and capabilities. Too often in the past, the traditional or stereotypical attitude of management and supervision was essentially protective. The question asked was, "Is the work fitting for a woman?" not, "What is she capable of?" Accordingly, women generally found themselves restricted to secretarial and clerical routines in the office and to bench work or nonthink jobs in the plant. Even today, one-third of all women working are found in only seven occupations: secretaries, sales workers, private household service workers, elementary school teachers, bookkeepers, waitresses, and professional nurses.

According to the U.S. Department of Labor, in 1974, of all managerial and administrative jobs, women held only 18.5 percent. Of clerical jobs, however, women held 77.6 percent of the total. Of professional and technical jobs, women held 40.5 percent, but this was because women dominated almost completely the nursing and elementary school teacher areas. Women hold only 4.5 percent of the relatively skilled craft positions in the United States and 31 percent of factory work, mainly at the less-skilled levels. It is little wonder that women complain they have been channeled into the less attractive and often lower-paying jobs and industries.

In the eyes of many, worse still has been the tendency for a supervisor to grow dependent on the know-how and can-do of a particular woman worker while at the same time concealing the true extent of her capabilities from others in management; thus her advancement and development are stymied, to say nothing of limitations that are put on her income. And of course there are endless instances where the capability of an individual is freely acknowledged in an organization, so long as it is confined to activities considered suitable for women. The figures cited in the previous paragraph are a direct reflection of this pervasive attitude.

The time has come—in fact, is long overdue—for supervisors and managers to open, rather than to block, the way outward (in terms of job scope) and upward (in terms of training, status, and financial opportunity) for the women who work for them. The returns to the supervisor who is progressive and liberated in the management of women will find *all* the employees more highly motivated and with a greater loyalty and devotion to the company objectives.

How differently from men should you treat women at work?

There should be no basic difference in how you supervise women. The principles of sound, equitable, and considerate management should apply fully as well to the supervision of women as to the supervision of men. It probably can't be repeated often enough that a person is a person is a person. Regardless of sex—and color and national origin and religious preference—the starting point in good human relations is recognition of each person's unique individuality and the conviction that he or she will respond most favorably when treated with respect and thoughtfulness.

But women are different from men, aren't they?

There are some distinct and indisputable biological and physiological differences between the sexes, but they are not nearly so many nor so pronounced as we once thought they were. And there is the question, often unanswered by the researchers, of how these differences affect behavior—if, in fact, they do affect it at all.

Practitioners of human engineering, for example, in designing gear for the work-station environment, take into account such factors as a woman's (on an average) thinner skin and less hirsute body (and her consequently greater sensitivity to colder temperatures). A woman's more acute color perception enables her to handle color-related assignments (again, on the average) better than her male counterpart does. Her shorter stature and smaller fingers make her a better bet for jobs that might physically cramp the average man's bulk. A woman's elbows are slightly curved inward and more supple at the joints than are the more muscular male's, giving her an edge in jobs where flexibility of arm rotation is desirable. Most men are stronger than most women, too. This has led, in many states, to legislation limiting the weight of the load a woman might carry on her job; in many occupations and industries it has also provided an excuse for reserving some jobs exclusively for men.

Observations like these about men and women have led to the widespread practice (now greatly restricted by federal legislation) of classifying jobs as either men's or women's. The Equal

Employment Opportunity Commission, on January 24, 1969, set down guidelines making it unlawful to place help-wanted ads segregated in this manner unless a bona fide occupational qualification (BFOQ) dependent on some of the delimiting factors listed above truly exists.

It should be obvious that, in principle if not always in practical fact (because of the limits of the available labor market), for any job there is a woman or a man who can perform it satisfactorily. To prejudge suitability or capability on the basis of sex alone (except as noted above) is patently unfair and illegal.

But what about absences and turnover?

The most serious disagreement, when a person is being judged for job suitability, revolves around a woman's menstrual cycle and her child-bearing capability—and the effect these have, if any, on her attendance and her job stability. It is a foregone conclusion of many employers that a woman worker will be absent one or more days a month during her menstrual period. The statistical facts do not bear this out. Study after study over the years purports to prove one view or the other, but a recently available study made in 1970 by the U.S. Department of Labor showed that women lose only 5.2 days a year because of illness or injury; men lose slightly fewer, 5.1. The surprise in this study was that single women were absent from their jobs 3.9 days a year compared with 4.3 for single men. In any event, for working wives and mothers, there is always a time conflict when a child or a husband becomes sick; often the woman will remain home to provide the necessary care.

What about the charge of excessive job turnover that so many managers imply is related to women who drop out from the labor market to marry and have children? The evidence seems to show that, give or take a little (and excepting the 25 to 55 years for turnover), absenteeism and turnover are not hurtfully different in women from what they are in men. Much more seems to depend on the individual, the family situation, the company worked for, the nature of the job itself, and the supervisor.

Are women better at some jobs than at others?

You'll get lots of arguments based on individual experiences, which vary. Aptitude tests have shown repeatedly that women can perform just about any job as well as men can. Women are now represented in virtually every one of the 479 occupations listed in the 1970 census. Consequently, an assertion that there are men-only jobs, or even women-only jobs, is for the most part inaccurate.

A valuable and unexpected by-product of one notable experience was the discovery that women who registered high tardiness and absenteeism rates at desk work scored near-perfect punctuality and attendance when transferred to less monotonous physical factory work. Not so unexpected (contrary to feminist views) was a vast improvement in safety and housekeeping when the women took over.

Can a woman do every job a man can do?

For every job a man now does, there is a woman, somewhere, who can do it as well. But, in general, there is no good reason to make such a demand. In a great number of jobs requiring heavy physical effort, women—compared with men—have limited capabilities.

In spite of all these limiting factors, to say nothing of stereotyped thinking in making job assignments, the 1970 United States Census reported one or more women in every one of the 479 occupational classifications. In fact, there were thousands working as welders, draftswomen, and painters and at maintenance crafts. Certainly, the employment of so many women in nontraditional jobs is an object lesson on the speciousness of withholding from any woman the opportunity to perform the kind of work for which she may be qualified.

Must women receive the same pay as men?

Absolutely! Ever since the passage of antisex discrimination legislation, the law is unrelenting in its insistence that women receive pay equal to that of men for equal work, and rightfully so. Separate seniority lists, positions so constructed as to artificially support a pay differential between men and women, and other wage biases based on sex are severely penalized.

Do working women have fewer accidents than working men do?

Women seem to have fewer accidents at work than men do, although this hasn't been proved conclusively. What is certain is that the accidents men have are more severe. Some people attribute this record to the practice of assigning women to lighter and less hazardous work.

Is it true that women don't like working for other women?

■■■■■■■■ Some studies support this claim, but their validity has been challenged. According to Dr. Harry Levinson, in an observation made when he was head of the Menninger Foundation industrial division, women employees do tend to create more difficulties for women supervisors. Here's his reasoning:

> In the course of growing up, girls are usually more closely controlled by their mothers than boys are by their fathers and often are rivals with their mothers for the attention of their fathers. Women supervisors tend to act as they think men would act in the same situation. They are often more rigid than men would be, therefore. Women can become better supervisors of women if they can be helped to understand that the best kind of supervision is not just firm, but considerate as well. And some women supervisors will need to become aware of the fact that if they have half-hidden feelings of hostility to women who have husbands and families, both they and those who are under their supervision will have a rough time of it.
>
> The woman who becomes a supervisor of men will have even more problems than the woman who supervises women. For men, ideally, bosses are models. The boss should be someone a man can learn from and identify with. (It is more acceptable for him to depend on another man than a woman.) Work groups inevitably test a new superior. They will test a woman even more. She will have to expect to earn the respect, trust, and confidence of her subordinates.

What characterizes the younger work force?

■■■■■■■■ It is composed of two kinds of workers, who have many things in common. The typical younger worker under 25 enters the labor force with a jaundiced eye toward business—toward what is called the establishment. The disadvantaged younger worker enters the labor market keenly distrustful of the establishment's intent.

Typical younger workers may come from backgrounds that are rich or poor. Their education may be complete or they may be dropouts from the school—or straight—scene. They may have ambition in the traditional sense—to achieve—or they may wish only to collect enough paychecks to underwrite their next adventures. They may be white Caucasians or black, Puerto Rican, or Chicano. Their politics may be radically left; they may be head-knocking, hard-hat right; or they may have no social concerns at all. Their distinguishing characteristics are (1) a deep preoccupation with themselves as individuals with unique prerogatives, and (2) an almost universal rejection of everything traditional.

The disadvantaged younger workers begin the battle for survival, let alone work, with several handicaps—most of which are neither of their own choosing nor of their own making. They suffer from all the usual wounds of the poor—poor background at home, poor education, poor diet, poor health, poor legal protection. They may be white, but the chances are that their skin is brown, yellow, or black. The probability is that they have never worked at a decent job with fair pay or in an enlightened environment. They may never have enjoyed any of the social comforts that the vast majority experience. Their politics may be militant, but they are more likely to be nonexistent. Their distinguishing characteristics are (1) an outlook that recognizes no values beyond those of today, (2) a disbelief in the possibility that business will ever provide an honest opportunity to succeed, and (3) a hopeless feeling that the cards are stacked against them.

Deep down, the typical younger worker asks, "What's in it for me now?"

Deep down, the disadvantaged younger worker asks, "What's the use of trying?"

Why bother to accommodate the young, if they are that troublesome?

Because young workers offer business a rich labor resource. Especially in industrial areas, nearly half the population is under 25. Younger job candidates, affluent or disadvantaged, represent a largely underutilized labor pool. Their potential, for those supervisors who find ways to release it, is unlimited.

How serious is the generation gap in business?

It is at its most critical in the realm of what any older person will accept without complaint and what a younger person will refuse to do, regardless of pay. Whereas an old-timer will brag about the scars from welding sparks, a 22-year-old packs up and quits. A veteran grimly clenches his nostrils as he seals up a coke-oven door in a steel mill; the recent high school graduate balks at that and asks his union steward to get him off that job. A woman who has worked for years as a blotter clerk in a stock broker's cage swallows her boredom; a young woman says that life is too short for that.

What is the root of this difference? The answers vary. Some say it is the permissiveness and the relative affluence in which most young people have grown up. Others say it is simply the difference between a compelling reason to earn a full-scale livelihood (as most older, married persons must) and the wish only to make enough cash for walking around. Regardless, younger persons are not docile. Either the job must be made more tolerable for them—or they will walk away from it.

What are the main complaints you hear from younger workers?

Complaints differ in number and intensity according to the industry and the geography, but these three seem to shout the loudest for attention:

1. "I want the same rights as my boss." Despite demurrals by many about the value of an education, better-educated young people, especially, equate their advantage with authority. They want to be able to challenge their bosses on just about anything that has to do with the job. For example, in one large auto assembly plant, the company typically retains the right to maintain order and efficiency, to hire and lay off, to assign and to transfer, to determine starting and quitting times. Said a grizzled union officer at that plant, "To the young person, this means the company has all the rights. When the employee, who seems to be just part of the machinery, challenges a supervisor, there may be discipline, and this raises another cry of injustice."

2. "I won't work where my health or safety may be endangered." Young people do not want to prove their ruggedness. They think that to do so is foolish. Just as the appeal to go off to war to prove oneself has been seen by many as an old person's trick on the young, so thousands of young people find it difficult to accept the fact that all work cannot be made clean, cool, and accident-free. Sometimes, of course, this complaint is exaggerated to include any job that might not be particularly pleasant.

3. "I expect improvements to be made fast." Young workers simply do not want to wait. They certainly will not accept promises, even when made in good faith. Change, for them, must come as soon as a condition warrants it. Nor do they want to be burdened with a responsibility for making this change or with a comprehension of its difficulties. With a specific complaint, for example, they protest that the grievance machinery is too slow. Says one worker, "If a situation is unfair, I don't want to wait a year while it goes through channels. I want the benefits of the change right now." Underneath this impatience, of course, is a mistrust of management's intention—a belief that time is being used as a way to delay action and possibly to avoid it altogether.

What can a supervisor do to better motivate and manage young workers?

███████████████ Supervisors should take their cues from younger workers' complaints. Specifically, a supervisor must:

1. **Exert authority only from reason.** Dependence on power invites rebellion. A supervisor's authority ought to make sense in terms of its conservation of effort and resources, its recognition of the humanness of employees, its understanding of the value in change as well as in conformance.

2. **Seek to improve working conditions.** Along with higher management, a supervisor needs to acknowledge that work need not be hard or hot or dirty to be worthwhile; in fact, the supervisor should devote thought to ways of making it less demanding physically, safer, and more conducive to creative effort.

3. **Learn to move faster in making changes.** This century moves ever faster in its development of knowledge and technology. Tradition has lost much of its value and meaning. It should be tested constantly against current needs. Letting go of the old must be achieved with dispatch. Neither progress nor capable young workers will wait very long for you to embrace the new.

4. **Convey the meaning of each assignment.** There is nothing unique about the younger worker's cry for relevance. Men and women have wished to gain this from their work since time began. In order to apply oneself, one needs to know why a job must be done a certain way, why it must be done at all, and how it relates to what is going on around one.

5. **Make sure the younger workers know what results are expected of them.** Vague admonitions rather than specific goals and targets will weaken a younger person's resolve. Make certain, too, that the wage system is clearly understood—exactly how pay will be related to accomplishment.

6. **Provide support and assistance, especially in job training.** A supervisor's desire to help employees become proficient is welcomed as an expression of respect and confidence.

7. **Praise freely when it is deserved.** Younger people are less confident of their performance and need constant feedback as to its quality. Conversely, when you criticize, it is important to be tactful. Similarly, discipline must appear to be reasonable rather than arbitrary.

8. **Enrich the nature of the work.** Monotony stems from rep-

etition that allows no room for improvisation and ingenuity. By stretching the limits of each job and by incorporating into it elements of depth, employees will have the freedom, should they choose it, to provide their own variety while they are still committed to a specific, demanding goal.

Who is an older worker?

The Age Discrimination in Employment Act categorizes people between 40 and 65 as older. Most authorities, however, observe that by age 45, employees have become older. They are mature, settled, experienced, and usually well trained. But they already have family responsibilities, often heavy ones; and signs of both physical aging and emotional wear are becoming evident.

What is important to keep in mind is that age affects each person differently. Its effect depends on a large number of factors: heredity, durability, physical condition, exposure to weather, extreme living or working conditions, climate, indulgence in food or drink, drug abuse, and emotional and psychological strains. Nevertheless, it is a good rule of thumb for a supervisor to look for signs of change due to age in any employee over 50 years old. Changes may be physical or mental, slight or marked. Changes may affect the older worker's performance for better or for worse. But change there is.

Why is the older worker so important to industry if experience seems to have less value today than in the past?

Sheer numbers of older people in the labor force cannot be ignored. From 1960 to 1970, half the growth in the labor force came from the 45-and-over age group. This situation is changing slightly now as the relative population of male workers over 54 begins to decrease; although the growth of the female segment in that age bracket continues to increase, so that the percentage of the United States labor force who are over 54 will continue to be about 17 percent through the 1970s (see Figure 19-1). Interestingly, the percentage represented by the middle working ages from 25 to 54 historically remains constant at about 60 percent. What this means, of course, is that there are over 20 million older men and women upon whom the economy is still very dependent. To keep your operations running smoothly, you'll need to continue to make better use of your aging workers.

It is true, however, that in selected areas where technology or social values have changed radically, experience has lost much

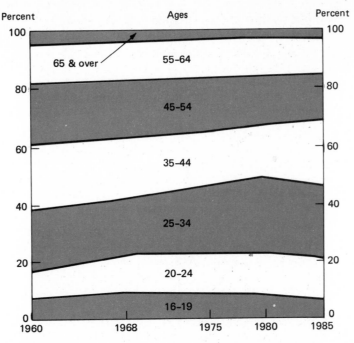

FIGURE 19-1. **Percentage Distribution of the Labor Force by Age.** *Based on projections made by the U.S. Bureau of Labor Statistics.*

of the intrinsic value it once had. This presents a real challenge to maturing employees and their management. Experience is only as good as it remains relevant or is updated to cope with present-day problems and situations.

How do older workers compare with younger workers as to their desire and ability to hold their jobs?

On the all-important matters of job turnover, older workers stand head and shoulders over younger workers. In an important study made by the U.S. Department of Labor, workers over 45 were found to be twice as stable as those under 25. Compared with workers under 45, workers over 45 were considerably superior in their ability to stick to a job. And these findings were generally the same for older women as for older men, if not better.

What are the chief assets of older workers?

They have many. According to Dr. William A. Sawyer, formerly medical director of the Eastman Kodak Company and later medical consultant to the International Association of Machinists, AFL, these are the assets older workers take to work:

Safety. They have far fewer accidents.

Attendance. They have a better absence record. They are sick less often, although illnesses tend to last longer than those of younger people.

Judgment. The variety of their work and social experiences tend to improve older workers' judgment and to familiarize them with a variety of work situations.

Loyalty. Broad experience has helped older workers to recognize good supervision when they get it—and to reward that supervision with the loyalty it deserves.

Skill. Once acquired, job skills rarely start to fade before a person reaches 60, often not until much later.

What are the chief drawbacks of older workers?

Older workers have many liabilities. But their experience and skills often permit them to compensate for the liabilities. On the whole, older workers tend to be:

Slower. Age slows athletes and workers. But while older people work more slowly, they may make fewer mistakes.

Weaker. Their strength fades, too, although by now they may have learned to work more intelligently, not harder.

Less resilient. Older workers haven't the endurance they once had. Fatigue—mental and physical—sets in faster. And illnesses and accidents keep them off the job longer than they would a younger person. But remember, they are less likely to have either happen.

Suffering from poor eyesight. Near vision may suffer —they may need bifocals to correct it. But if vision also includes the ability to understand what we see, then older workers aren't much worse off than their sharp-eyed children.

Does an older worker age all of a sudden?

It may appear that an older employee comes apart all at once. But actually, the aging process is one of gradual decline. As we grow older, we foolishly try to conceal the fact from others and even from ourselves. Then, what has been happening to us over several years is brought to light only when we have a serious illness. If we were to have a physical examination each year, the examining doctor could trace our physical decline as it happens and would be in a better position to advise us how to adjust our living habits to compensate for our aging. This is why physical examinations for older workers are so important—for the worker as well as for the company.

Is it true that older workers learn less easily than younger ones?

This is a tricky question because the learning process is so complicated. It's best answered by saying that older persons with their greater experience, could learn just as quickly as younger persons—if the older persons were as well motivated. Younger people learn faster because they want to learn, because they see learning as a key to their futures. Older persons may see no benefit from learning. They have done their bit, they may think. So why try to learn something new?

Under what conditions do older workers learn best?

Knowledge of how well they are doing is especially important to older persons. This is a form of motivation that experience has taught them to recognize. The value the older workers place on their pride is so high that in a learning situation, an error is less acceptable to them than to younger persons.

Take this example. Pete is 56 years old and has been on the same welding machine for ten years. Now his plant buys a gas arc welder and assigns Pete to learn how to run it. Pete's boss, Jane Smith, first shows Pete the many ways in which the gas arc technique is similar to what he's been doing. Then she points out where the welding method differs from the old—and demonstrates what happens if Pete should make a mistake. After Pete has tried out the new machine under Jane's supervision for an hour or so Jane lets Pete handle it by himself for the rest of the day. First thing in the morning, however, Jane gets together with Pete and inspects the work he's turned out. They agree as to what's acceptable and what's below par. While Jane stands by, Pete reruns the off-quality material until he gets the hang of how to do the job right. Once Pete has the quality problem licked, Jane gives him a pretty specific idea of how fast he's supposed to work. That way Pete can judge for himself if he's running out enough work.

Day by day Jane lets Pete know how well he's doing as to quality and quantity of work until both Jane and Pete are sure that Pete can handle the job by himself. In other words, Jane hasn't made a nuisance of herself by explaining to Pete the things Pete already knows about his new job. But Jane does emphasize the job's newfangled aspects and is very definite in letting Pete know how well he's doing.

Under what conditions do older workers have the most difficulty in learning a new job?

Older adults have the most trouble learning a new skill when that skill conflicts with one they have already learned. Experience grows strong roots. When learning a new skill means cutting off those roots, psychologically the older workers may not be ready to learn something new.

To make a difficult learning task easier, it's wise to demonstrate to older workers the similarities between what they have been doing and what you're asking them to do now. For instance, in the case of the older heat treater, the supervisor could show that the processes for hardening carbon steel and high-speed steel are basically the same, that the differences are mainly a matter of degree. It's always easier for anybody to learn if the move is gradual from the familiar to the unfamiliar.

Here's another point. Rarely is it really necessary for an older worker to learn an entirely new job. It's poor management on your part if you require such a radical change. Why? Because it's just plain smart to keep someone on a job where previous experience isn't wasted.

At what sort of work will older persons find it hardest to become skilled?

At machine-paced work. Most older workers do much better at jobs they can pace themselves. An older person's loss of speed is often combined with a loss of responsiveness to what a situation demands. For instance, a very old person who is crossing a street may cautiously look up and down the road to see if there are any oncoming cars. But by the time the person evaluates the situation and decides it's safe to cross, he or she may step into the path of an oncoming vehicle. The person simply can't see and analyze a situation fast enough for decisions to be reliable. The same is true to a lesser degree for almost any older worker.

Similarly, many persons over 50 have proved to make poor retail sales workers simply because they found it difficult, if not impossible, to pace themselves to the fast-changing sales situation.

For this reason, as a worker's age increases, it's best to assign jobs requiring caution and accuracy rather than those requiring the worker to react quickly or to keep pace with a machine or a group of faster workers.

How can you motivate older workers?

By understanding them and helping them to understand themselves. As all of us grow older, the gap widens between what we are and what we'd like to be. It's only natural for us to adopt an I-am-what-I-am attitude—especially when someone asks us to improve or to change our ways. In fact, the very stability that makes older workers an asset also makes it harder for them to learn, since this stability is based on their having found contentment with their present lot. So the problem of getting them to want to change, or to do better, resolves itself in your ability to get them to try.

To get older persons to try, you must help them to be less critical and less self-conscious. Show them what other older workers are doing—in your company, if possible. Urge them to talk to others who have changed.

Demonstrate to older workers, if you can, that even at their worst they will make fewer errors than younger persons do. Let them compare their work records with those of younger persons. If possible, let them try new things in a place where they aren't too conspicuous. It would be a mistake, for example, to announce: "Old Pete is going to try to learn to operate this new-fangled machine." Instead, quietly team up with Pete and make it a problem of both his and your learning something new. Let him see you make mistakes, so he won't feel foolish when he does. Only when he's gained a little confidence should you let his efforts be spotlighted.

A final word of caution: Keep performance standards high—for both output and quality—for older workers. There should be no rewards for age in terms of relaxed requirements. It is precisely these qualities that make older workers valuable to the organization.

supervisory word power

Aging. The chronological process in which persons grow older and during which they suffer to one degree or another from obsolescence, physical or mental wear and tear, and a general wasting away of knowledge or skill because of insufficient use or challenge.

Discrimination. A distinction that is made in favor of, or against, a person (typically, but not necessarily, a member of a minority group) in employment, placement, training, advancement, pay, or working conditions.

Minority worker. An employee or candidate for employment who, because of color, national or geographic origin, religion, education, sex, or age represents a relatively small segment of workers in a particular employment situation.

Disadvantaged worker. An employee or candidate for employment who, because of shortcomings in education and environment, enters the established and more stable world of business and opportunity with penalizing handicaps.

Young worker. Generally any employee or candidate for employment between the ages of 18 and 25, although increasingly anyone, regardless of age, who embraces the views of youth toward work—that it should be meaningful and its decisions participative.

Other Important Terms in This Chapter

protective legislation
quota system
reverse discrimination
tokenism
validity of tests (content and construct)

reading comprehension

1. If a minority-group employee doesn't measure up to the job, should the employee be the only one to blame? Why?

2. What is meant by the quota system in hiring blacks?

3. Which technique do you think would motivate the company's hard-core van driver most—an offer of membership in the company's recreational club or allowing the driver to take the keys to the van home at night? Why?

4. Why do you suppose so many married women participate in the work force now compared with the number doing so at the turn of the century?

5. Compare a possible difference in attitude toward her work on the part of a young single woman and of a married woman of 30.

6. Discuss the charge that women are more prone to be absent and to change jobs than men are.

7. What's wrong with classifying a job as either a man's or a woman's?

8. When a younger employee is dissatisfied and blames his or her unrest on the meaninglessness of the work, what is the possibility of this charge being justified? What should the supervisor do about it?

9. Why do you suppose older workers have fewer accidents than younger ones do?

10. Would it be a good idea for a supervisor to assign newly hired older persons to a fast-paced team of employees in the hope that they would learn the ropes more quickly in that kind of atmosphere? Why?

supervision in action

THE CASE OF THE UNEXPECTED RESIGNATION. **A case study in human relations involving supervision of the new labor force, with questions for you to answer.**

Paul Garcia had been hired by Inter Ridge Company as part of its contribution to an urban coalition employment program. Paul was typically underdeveloped in reading and arithmetic skills, but he was bright, quick, and personable. He responded well to the remedial programs and to the specific job training that Inter Ridge Company offered. As a starting position, however, the only job the company could place Paul on was that of a mail boy. Paul appeared to like the job, nevertheless. In particular, he enjoyed going about from office to office. It gave him a chance to chat with people and to make new friends. Unfortunately, it also gave him a chance to carry on a little business on the side—that of running the balota numbers in the building. In the course of the day, Paul would pick up about 25 numbers slips along with about $15 in cash. His deal with the numbers man was that Paul kept $3 of this daily take, and if someone hit the numbers, Paul would get 10 percent of the winning sum.

Paul began his mail job in May, and the first Tuesday in July a clerk in the shipping department hit the numbers for $1,500. Paul was elated. The next day, however, Paul saw his supervisor, Mr. Kent, and told him that his aunt, who had helped to send Paul to the city, was very sick and he'd need a week off to go home to visit her. Mr. Kent told Paul that this would be impossible. Paul should postpone his trip to the weekend and try to see his aunt then. Paul said nothing, but the next day Paul's sister called the office and told them that Paul had an upset stomach and couldn't report for work that day. Mr. Kent heard nothing from Paul for the rest of the week or during the next week either. On the Monday following the second week of absence, Paul's sister came to the Inter Ridge Company personnel office and asked for Paul's paycheck. He had decided to resign and had a job elsewhere, she said.

1. Do you think that Paul's resignation could have been avoided? Why?

2. How do you explain Paul's running the numbers when he had a steady job?

3. Was it a good idea for Mr. Kent not to have given Paul the time off when he wanted it?

4. What do you think could be done at this point to reinstate Paul in his job with Inter Ridge Company?

enriching your viewpoint

Interpretation and application of equal opportunity laws continually change. For a sound background and a more comprehensive understanding of these developments, the following references are suggested:

"The American Woman: On the Move—but Where?" *U.S. News and World Report,* December 8, 1975, p. 54.

Jobs for the Hard-to-Employ, Committee for Economic Development, Research and Policy Committee, New York, January 1978.

Purcell, Theodore V., "The Case of the Borderline Black," *Harvard Business Review,* November–December 1971.

——— and Gerald F. Cavanagh, *Blacks in the Industrial World: Issues for Management,* The Free Press, New York, 1973.

Rhine, Shirley H., "The Senior Worker—Employed and Unemployed," *The Conference Board Record,* Vol. 13, No. 3, May 1976, p. 7.

Scanlan, Burt K., "Motivating Young Adults in Retailing," *Journal of Small Business Management,* Vol. 4, No. 2, April 1976, pp. 46–54.

Schwartz, Eleanor Brantley, "Women in Industry," in Lester R. Bittel (ed.), *The Encyclopedia of Professional Management,* McGraw-Hill Book Company, New York, 1979, pp. 1195–1201.

Shaeffer, Ruth G., "Non-Discrimination in Employment, 1973–1975,"
The Conference Board Record, Inc., New York, 1975.
Stroh, Thomas F., *Managing the New Generation in Business,*
McGraw-Hill Book Company, New York, 1971.
The Supervisor's EEO Handbook: A Guide to Federal Antidiscrim-
ination Laws and Regulations, rev. ed., Executive Enterprises
Publications Co., Inc., New York, 1977.
U.S. Department of Labor, 1975, *Handbook of Women Workers,*
Employment Standards Administration, Bulletin 297. Washington, DC
Wallace, Phyllis A., *Equal Employment Opportunity and the AT&T*
Case, The M.I.T. Press, Cambridge, Mass., 1976.
"Women at Work," *Newsweek,* December 6, 1976, pp. 68–82.

20

CHAPTER
counseling problem employees

Who are the problem employees?

The chronic absentee, the rule breaker, the boss hater, the psychosomatic, the malingerer, the person who's lost self-confidence, the heavy drinker, the alcoholic, the pill popper, the troublemaker, and, yes, even the work obsessed.

Why worry so much about them?

Simply because there are so many of them. Authoritative estimates place the number of potential mentally disturbed employees at one out of every four or five American workers.

There are many sociological and humanitarian reasons for being concerned about problem workers. One big reason is that a problem employee is also probably a problem husband, son, daughter, or wife. But industry's concern, admittedly, is primarily one of economics. Problem employees are expensive to have on the payroll. They are characterized by excessive tardiness and absences. They are difficult to supervise. And they have a tendency to upset the morale of the work group. Consequently, a supervisor should worry about (1) hiring problem employees in the first place, (2) handling them on the job so that they reach maximum productivity with the least disruption of the company's overall performance, and (3) determining whether problem employees have become so seriously maladjusted that they need professional attention.

How successful have companies been in handling problem employees?

Probably the most notable success with problem employees has been that of the Western Electric Company. Back in 1927 the company sponsored a series of research studies aimed at finding the relationship to production of employee working conditions, such as rest pauses and length of workday.

To determine how effective the changes were, the researchers started interviewing employees. Then a perplexing change began to take place. Regardless of the mechanical or physical changes made in the working arrangements, productivity seemed to increase. Finally, the researchers realized that as workers were asked for their opinions and were able to register their complaints, these workers became more favorably disposed toward management in general—and actually produced more.

The worthwhileness of letting employees get things off their chest finally proved to be so valuable that Western Electric set up an interviewing (or counseling) program for just that purpose. This talking out their problems changed the nature of the original program to one of employee-adjustment counseling. It began formally in 1936 and supplanted the original program of interviewing for the needs of management.

This discovery of the value of interviewing employees for the purpose of helping them understand their problems, known as the *Hawthorne experiment,* took place at the Hawthorne Works of Western Electric in Cicero, Illinois. It has provided the basis for much of what we know about getting along with all employees and with problem employees in particular.

How can you recognize an employee with an emotional problem?

There are problem employees, and then there are employees who are really problems. The most serious problem employees are those who are emotionally disturbed, and it is very difficult to tell when an employee has crossed over the line into the more serious category. Generally speaking, the symptoms of employees with emotional problems are similar. These people tend to run away from reality. They do this by going on sick leave, by too frequent visits to the dispensary; they believe that their supervisors are against them, blame their failures on other people and other things rather than accepting any blame themselves.

Many problem employees fall into these categories: They are perpetually dissatisfied, are given to baseless worries, tire easily, are suspicious, are sure that superiors withhold promotions, believe their associates gossip maliciously about them. Some are characterized by drinking sprees, are given to drug abuse, are insubordinate, or have ungovernable tempers.

Among themselves problem employees differ widely, just as more normal people do. But within the framework of their symptoms, they are surprisingly alike in their reactions.

Are emotionally disturbed employees insane?

Most emotionally disturbed employees definitely are not "crazy." In fact, a psychological consultant for Eastman Kodak Company, Ralph Collins, says, "One out of four workers is subject to emotional upsets that visibly disturb his or her work." Such employees' behavior under certain kinds of stress is not normal. When goaded by fear (such as the threat of a bill collector) or by anger (because of being refused a day off), they may act in a way that you would describe as "crazy." But they are not (except for a very few) insane or even abnormal.

What about psychotic and neurotic employees?

Both terms sound pretty ominous. But only the employee with a psychosis is seriously ill. The most common type of psychosis is schizophrenia, or split personality. Schizophrenics live partly in a world of imagination. Especially when the world seems threatening to them, they withdraw. They may be able to adjust to life, even have a successful career. But when they lose their grip, their problem is way beyond the scope of a lay person.

On the other hand, most people are neurotic to a degree. People who have exaggerated fears, who feel the need to prove themselves, or who are irritable, hostile, opinionated, timid, or aggressive (which somewhere along the line describes most of us) have the seeds of neurosis in them. It's when this condition becomes exaggerated that a neurotic employee becomes a problem to associates and to the supervisor.

Here are a couple of examples of neurotic employees: the lift-truck operator who boasts about drinking and sexual prowess; the supervisor who gets pleasure from reprimanding an employee in front of others; the mechanic who visits the nurse every other day with some minor ailment; the punch press operator who meticulously arranges the workplace in the same manner every day, who can't begin the job unless everything is exactly right.

What makes problem people problems?

The key lies in the word *adjustment.* Most problems of neurotic employees are trivial. And they can adjust to them readily. But they may for months, years, keep their disturbed feelings hidden—even from themselves—then be stricken by a fear that is so great they can't control it. And then they do something that even to themselves they can't explain. They have lost, perhaps temporarily, the ability to adjust.

What sort of management action can put pressure on employees with emotional problems?

All human problems are the result of cause and effect. A supervisor does something and an employee can't adjust—the result, a human explosion. Typical of some managers who unthinkingly put pressure on workers are:

• The supervisor who thinks it's smart psychology to set production and quality goals just a little higher than an employee can reach. What could be more frustrating?
• The supervisor who thinks it's poor psychology to praise an employee for doing a good job. Is there anything so damaging to a person's morale than to do something well and have it taken for granted?
• The supervisor and management who think that employee relations are better whenever the threat of a layoff hangs over employees' heads.

What are the signs of a worried worker— the employee who is about to become a problem?

Until now we've been discussing the general symptoms of problem employees. But you'll be more interested in pinning down the specific kinds of behavior that make employees a problem in your company. That way, you'll be better able to know what to do to aid them. Some specific signs of a worried worker are:

Sudden change of behavior.   Pete used to whistle on the job. He hasn't lately. Wonder what's wrong?

Preoccupation.   Judy doesn't hear you when you speak to her. She seems off in a fog. When you do get her attention, she says she must have been daydreaming. Is something serious bothering her?

Irritability.   Albert is as cross as a bear these days. Even his old buddies are steering clear of him. He didn't used to be that way.

Increased accidents.   Bob knocked his knuckles on the job again today. This is unusual. Up until a couple of months ago, he hadn't had even a scratch in five years.

More absences.   Sara is getting to be a headache. She wasn't in this morning again. She never was extra dependable, but now we'll have to do something to get her back on the ball.

Increased fatigue.   Mary seems to live a clean life and keep good hours. But she complains about being tired all the time. Is it something physical or is she worried about something?

Too much drinking.   Ralph was so jittery at his machine this afternoon, I felt sorry for him. And he had a breath that would knock you over. I know he used to like going on the town, but this is different.

What can you do about problem workers?

Let's make this clear. We are not talking here about psychotic persons or the ones with serious neurotic disorders. We'll talk about them later on.

You can help problem employees toward better adjustment only after you have reassured them that you are trying to help them keep their jobs—not looking for an excuse to get rid of them. No approach does more harm with persons who have problems than the better-get-yourself-straightened-out-or-you-will-lose-your-job attitude on a supervisor's part. You have to believe, and make them believe, that your intentions are good, that you want to help. Then, you must give them every opportunity to help themselves. This approach is called *counseling*.

How do you counsel employees?

The researchers who conducted the Hawthorne experiment described previously suggested that a supervisor could best counsel employees if these five rules are followed for each interview:

1. Listen patiently to what the employee has to say before making any comment of your own.

2. Refrain from criticizing or offering hasty advice on the employee's problem.

3. Never argue with an employee while you are counseling.

4. Give your undivided attention to the employee who is talking.

5. Look beyond the mere words of what the employee says—listen to see if the person is trying to tell you something deeper than what appears on the surface.

What results should you expect from counseling?

Recognize what you are counseling an employee for, and don't look for immediate results. Never mix the counseling interview with some other action you may want to take—such as discipline.

Suppose Ruth has been late for the fourth time this month. The company rules say she must be suspended for three days. When talking to Ruth about the penalty, try to keep the conversation impersonal. Your purpose at that point is to show her the connection between what she's done and what is happening to her.

Now in the long run you may wish to rehabilitate Ruth because she's potentially a good worker. This calls for a counseling interview. And it's better to hold the interview with Ruth at a separate time. (Of course, it would have been better to hold the interview before she had to be disciplined.)

A counseling interview is aimed at helping employees to unburden themselves—to get worries off their chest. Whether or not the conversation is related to the problem they create for you at work is not important. The payoff comes as they get confidence in you—and consequently don't vent their resistance and frustrations on the job. Experience seems to show that this will happen if you are patient. It won't work with every problem employee, of course, but it will with most of them.

How do you start a counseling session?

■■■■■■■■■■■■■ Find a reasonably quiet place where you're sure you won't be interrupted and won't be overheard. Try to put the employee at ease. Don't jump into a cross-examination. Saying absolutely nothing is better than that. If Ralph has become a problem because of spotty work, you can lead into the discussion by saying something like this: "Ralph, have you noticed the increase in the orders we're getting on the new model? This is going to mean a lot of work for the company for a long while ahead. I guess it has meant some changes, too. How is it affecting the operation of your machine? What sort of problems has it created?"

In this case, you are trying to give Ralph an opportunity to talk about something specific and mechanical. If you listen to his ideas, he may begin to loosen up and talk about his emotional problems or his worries.

Another approach is simply to talk to Ralph casually about things he'd be interested in that have no connection with his work. Then let him lead the conversation to the subject that is uppermost in his mind: "Ralph, what do you think of the Braves' chances this year? That's the team you've rooted for, for how many years? Did you used to play ball yourself?" This approach, which lets the employee set the course of the interview, is called *nondirective counseling.*

How many counseling interviews
should you have with a problem employee?
How long should a counseling interview last?

■■■■■■■■■■ These are hard question for clear-cut answers. For a less serious case, one interview might clear the air for a long time. With employees whose emotional problems are more serious, it may take five or ten 15- to 30-minute conversations just to gain confidence. And with still others, the counseling will have to become a regular part of your supervisory chores with them.

You can readily see that counseling can be time-consuming. That's why it's so important to spot worried workers early and take corrective action while you can help them with the minimum drag on your time.

As to how long an interview should last—you can't accomplish much in 15 minutes, but if that's all you can spare, it's a lot better than nothing. At the very least, it shows the employee you're interested in the problem. Ideally, an interview should last between three-quarters of an hour and an hour.

How can you best handle these touchy problems objectively?

Make no mistake: Handling an employee who has become a problem isn't easy. Sometimes it can become downright unpleasant, and it's only natural to want to duck this responsibility. But the solace you can extract from it is that the sooner you face up to this key supervisory responsibility, the sooner the problems get solved. To be objective, you must:

• Get conditioned to the fact that this is your job and you can't run away from it.
• Look at your task as a fact-finding one—just as in handling grievances.
• Control your own emotions and opinions while dealing with the employee.
• Be sold on the value of listening rather than preaching.

Finally, as a word of caution: Recognize your own limits in handling these situations.

How can you recognize when an employee needs emotional first aid?

Dr. Harry Levinson, a nationally recognized authority and founder of the Levinson Institute, advises that the basic steps for you to take in administering emotional first aid are to:

• Recognize the emotional disturbance.
• Relieve acute distress by listening (counseling).
• Refer cases beyond your limits to professional help.

To recognize the employee who needs counseling help, says Dr. Levinson, look for three major signs:

Extremes. The ordinarily shy person goes even deeper into a shell. The hail-fellow-well-met steps up social activities to a fever pitch.

Anxiety. If withdrawal or activity brings no relief, the employee may become panicky or jittery, show extreme tension, flush in the face, or perspire heavily.

Breakdown.   If still unable to cope with the anxiety, the problem employee may break down altogether, be unable to control thoughts, feelings, or actions. Thinking becomes irrational. The person doesn't make sense to others. Emotions may become irrational. For instance, the tidy person may become slovenly, the quiet person noisy.

How can you provide relief for
the emotionally troubled employee?

Dr. Levinson suggests you may be helpful simply by letting the emotionally disturbed employee know how much the current distress is affecting the job—and how much of this the company will tolerate. Above all, a person under strain may add to it materially with fears of what the company might do if and when it discovers the condition. If you can offer some rule of thumb ("We appreciate the fact that you have something bothering you. And we're willing to go along with your present performance for a couple of weeks or so. But if it doesn't improve after that, we'll have to find a solution.") even if it's not entirely sympathetic, you at least provide something concrete to guide the employee's actions.

If the employee voluntarily brings the problem to you, you can help most by listening, advises Dr. Levinson. This is more difficult than it appears, he cautions. Listening must mean truly *nonevaluative* listening—no interruptions, advice, prescriptions, solutions, pontifications, or preaching.

When should you call
for professional help?

Dr. Levinson offers this rule of thumb: *If after two listening sessions you seem to be making little headway in establishing confidence, you should report the case (in confidence, of course) to the company nurse or the company physician.*

Dr. Levinson also advises that your approach in referral should be that of opening another door for additional help. Don't ever suggest by action or word that the employee is "crazy," hopeless, or unworthy of attention.

Is an accident-prone employee
likely to be emotionally disturbed?

Dr. Gerald Gordon, of the Du Pont company, which has one of the best safety records of any company in the world, had this to say:

*Our studies have revealed a small group of individuals around whom occupational injuries seem to cluster in disproportionate numbers. Obviously there is something more than hard luck plaguing a man whose career shows a long series of injuries. What's back of his trouble? The answer is that **the accident maker is suffering from a form of mental illness so widespread that it may be found to some degree in most of us**. . . . It is the failure of the employee as a whole person that is the core of his problem. He tends to evade the rules, both of working and of living. . . . In most cases the potential accident victim has a long service record and is well trained for his job. But all too often he's a victim of his own bottled-up emotions, which he turns against himself.*

What can a supervisor do about an accident-prone employee?

Du Pont's Dr. Gordon advises that so-called accident-prone employees can be helped fairly easily if they are discovered early enough and something is done to help them:

*A basic approach involves requiring employees to follow safety rules and develop sound work habits. In my opinion, the fact that a worker violates a safety rule is more important than **why** he violates it. Pampering the emotionally disturbed individual only serves to increase his demands and, at the same time, aggravates the severity of his illness.*
If a supervisor openly and honestly exercises his authority to obtain good performance, he is helping both the employee and the company for which they both work.
On the other hand, a supervisor who evades responsibility for the safety of his men becomes mentally ill himself and spreads this illness to others.

Absentees are a special kind of problem people. How lenient should you be with them?

It depends on the reasons for absence. Professor P. J. Taylor of London University, who was formerly medical director of Shell (UK) Ltd., observes that 60 percent of all absences are due to serious or chronic illness and 20 percent to acute, short-term illnesses like the flu; 10 percent feel unwell because of a minor illness like a cold and they do or don't report to work according to their attitude about their jobs; and the final 10 percent are completely well but feign illness to enjoy a day off.

It is the group of absentees who make up the bottom 20 percent who are suspect. Industrial psychologists call their virus "voluntary absence" or, more ominously, "motivation morbidity." In many, this is deeply rooted. The Puritan ethic of work does not apply to them. There is an inevitable conflict between the desire for more leisure and more work. This tug is especially evident among the younger workers.

Many authorities, however, still contend that employees who are chronically absent from work are mentally ill. They reason that the reality of work must be so unbearable to these emotionally disturbed employees that they literally escape from reality by staying away from work. Regardless of the reason, you can help reduce absenteeism by:

- Firming up your rules about it.
- Being consistent in applying penalties.
- Trying to get at the reasons why an employee is frequently absent.

The last method requires the counseling technique. Widespread absenteeism is cured by getting one person to come to work, then another, and so on. Consequently, it's important that each individual case be followed up promptly. In your discussion of the problem with employees, be sure to permit them to explain their reactions to the job itself, the people they work with, the working conditions, their tools and equipment, the kind of training they receive. You thus avoid their feeling that you are placing all the blame on them. And if they are specific in their reactions, you then have specific complaints, rather than vague dissatisfactions, to deal with.

Don't overlook, however, the power of job satisfaction in luring absence-prone workers back to the job. Surprisingly, however, working conditions seem to have little effect. In company after company, attendance figures show little variation between the dirty, unpleasant areas and those that are clean and well lighted. Even most incentive schemes to reduce absences are relatively ineffective. Closeness of the work team, its homogeneity, and the state of its morale seem to have the greatest effect.

How effective is counseling in reducing absenteeism?

Success depends on the root cause of individual absences. See how the patterns and the motivations differ:

Chronic absentees. The people who have little capacity for pressure, either on the job or off, may be prime candidates for counseling. But first they must be made fully aware of the consequences of poor attendance. Theirs is a habit, usually of long standing, and correction requires pressure to attend, as well as handholding.

Vacationing absentees.   The people who work only so long as they need the cash and who then treat themselves to a day or two off are difficult cases. These employees are often extremely capable on the job, but they feel no deep responsibility for it. Vacationers make a conscious choice to be absent and are rarely helped by counseling.

Directionless absentees.   The younger employees who have as yet found no real purpose in work may simply follow the lead of the vacationer who appears to lead a footloose, exciting life. A Dutch-uncle talk with the directionless absentee may be more effective than counseling.

Aggressive absentees.   The persons who willfully stay away from work in the hope that their absence will cause an inconvenience for you are probably emotionally disturbed. This kind of behavior, however, requires professional counseling to correct it, not the kind the ordinary supervisor can provide.

Moonlighters.   The persons who hold more than one job are often either too tired to come to work or faced with conflicting schedules. Straight talk, rather than counseling, is prescribed. When attendance is affected, the moonlighter must be forced to make a choice between jobs.

Occasional absentees.   The persons who seem to have slightly more absences than the rest of your staff are probably prime candidates for counseling. Their absences are legitimate. Their illnesses are real. Their problems are often temporarily insurmountable. These people deserve a mixture of sympathy, understanding, and sometimes outright advice.

In summary, you can probably help people who are absent for the following reasons: (1) Getting to work is a problem, real or imagined. (2) Off-job pressures are so strong that they weaken the employee's resolve to get to work. (3) The employee is imitative, easily led or misled. (4) The work appears boring, disagreeable, or unattractive. (5) Working relationships are unpleasant. (6) There are in fact off-job problems—child care, serious illness, court appearances—that need immediate attention. (7) Absence or lateness has become a habit.

You will have difficulty helping people who are absent because of these reasons: (1) The work or the pay associated with it holds no strong attraction. (2) Off-job pleasures have a greater appeal than work. (3) The employee is willfully absent in order to disrupt or inconvenience the organization.

What can you do for alcoholic employees?

████████████ Whatever you attempt, proceed slowly and cautiously. Not all heavy drinkers are alcoholics. And the more they drink, the less likely they are to admit to anyone (even themselves) that their ability to handle liquor has got out of their control.

An alcoholic employee is really just another kind of problem employee—only the case is an aggravated one and may need the help of a professional (see later question). Nevertheless, many alcoholic workers have rescued themselves with the aid of Alcoholics Anonymous, an association of ex-alcoholics who, because they don't preach and because they emphasize the individual's need to face weaknesses, have perfected the art of listening without being either sympathetic or critical.

Your best bet, however, is to recognize an alcoholic in the early stages. Then you can apply the same techniques to gain the person's confidence that you would with any other problem employee. Your objective is to provide security at work and to help with talking out problems. If these employees can be helped to recognize that excessive drinking is a problem they aren't handling, then you can refer them to the company doctor or nurse, who in turn may be able to persuade them to look into Alcoholics Anonymous or to visit a psychiatrist or a special clinic for alcoholics.

To guide you in recognizing alcoholic employees, Professor Harrison M. Trice of Cornell University advises that you look first to the employee's absence record. A sharp rise in overall rate of absences almost always accompanies the development of drinking problems, he says. In a study of 200 cases of alcoholism in industry, Professor Trice also noted three differences from the normal conception of absences among problem drinkers:

Absences are spread out through the week. Neither Monday nor Friday absences predominate (probably because the alcoholic is trying to be careful not to draw attention to the condition).

Partial absenteeism is frequent. A worker often reports in the morning but leaves before the day is over.

Tardiness is not a marked feature of alcoholism in industry. The widespread notion that a problem drinker comes late to work was not substantiated by Professor Trice's study.

How should you approach counseling an employee you believe to be an alcoholic?

Alcoholism requires a special form of counseling, say those who have coped most effectively with it. For example, the U.S. Department of Health, Education, and Welfare in its *Supervisors' Guide on Alcohol Abuse* offers these hints to supervisors who are faced with this problem among their employees:

1. Don't apologize for confronting the troubled employee about the situation. Your responsibility is to maintain acceptable performance for all your employees.

2. Do encourage this employee to explain why work performance, behavior, or attendance is deteriorating. This can provide an opportunity to question the use of alcohol.

3. Don't discuss a person's right to drink. It is best not to make a moral issue of it; HEW views alcoholism as a progressive and debilitating illness, which, if untreated, can eventually lead to insanity, custodial care, or death.

4. Don't suggest that the employee use moderation or change their drinking habits. A person who is an alcoholic cannot, at the start, voluntarily control drinking habits.

5. Don't be distracted by the individual's excuses for drinking—a difficult spouse, problem children, financial troubles. The problem as far as you are concerned is the employee's drinking and how it affects work, behavior, and attendance on the job.

6. Don't be put off by the drinker's assertion that a physician or a psychologist is already being seen. The employee may claim that the physician or the psychologist doesn't consider the drinking a problem, or that they think the use of alcohol will subside once the "problems" are worked out. Therapists probably wouldn't say that if they knew the employee's job was in jeopardy because of alcohol abuse; they would attach a new importance to the drinking habits.

7. Do remember that the alcoholic, like any other sick person, should be given the opportunity for treatment and rehabilitation.

8. Do emphasize that your major concern as a supervisor is the employee's poor work performance or behavior. You can firmly state that if there is no improvement, administrative action—such as suspension or discharge—will be taken.

9. Do state that the decision to accept rehabilitative assistance is the employee's responsibility.

10. Ann St. Louis, personnel counselor for Canada's Department of National Revenue, whose program maintains a 90 percent recovery rate among alcoholic government workers, adds this thought:

An employer—far better than wife, mother, minister or social agency—can lead an alcoholic to treatment by "constructive coercion." Give an employee every chance to take treatment, but make it clear that he must cooperate or lose his job. This has proven to be more effective than loss of friends or family.

How widespread is drug addiction among employees?

It is not so pervasive as you might think. Because regular drug use is incompatible with regular attendance, drug users tend not to select most regular or demanding kinds of employment. Attempts on a company's part to screen out hard drug users before employment have not been particularly successful. Dismissal afterward can be difficult because drug users are good at hiding the tools of their habit even if they cannot conceal its symptoms.

Symptoms of drug use are well known. At work they manifest themselves objectively in terms of poor or erratic performance, tardiness, absenteeism, requests to leave early, forgetfulness, indifference to deadlines and safety, and in many instances theft of company property.

Treatment and rehabilitation for drug users are as difficult and complicated as for alcoholics, and the treatments are somewhat similar. Policies of companies against drug addiction, however, tend to be firmer than against drinking and alcoholism. For one thing, the addict is different from the alcoholic because many addicts try to involve other people in drugs. The danger of an alcoholic's inducing another employee to begin alcoholism is slight. Then, too, drug use is illegal; in most instances, use of alcohol is not.

Here again, a supervisor's responsibility should be limited to the detection of drug addiction, prevention of its use or sale on company property, and counseling and referral—if indicated—of drug users to the appropriate company authority.

What makes some people overwork to the point of sickness?

A great many people suffer from work addiction. To mask deep emotional problems, and sometimes very real difficulties in their economic or home lives, they burrow into their work. It is a form of retreat from reality. It helps them forget what seem like insurmountable problems. The difficulty from a supervisor's point of view is that the work of work addicts tends to be nonproductive. Paradoxically, as these work-obsessed individuals intensify their diligence, it impedes their output. Furthermore, they often stir up such waves in the office or plant that they cut down the output of their associates.

It is difficult for a supervisor to do much other than to recognize the work addict. These compulsive individuals are usually highly moral, ambitious, intelligent, honest, and intensely loyal to their employer. At higher levels, they are the persons who stuff the briefcase for what is often needless work in the evening or weekends. They suffer from anxieties and depressions and generally will not respond to advice to take it easy. They need professional therapy that aims at improving self-understanding, flexibility, and creativity.

What do the professionals do for problem employees that the supervisors can't do?

Two kinds of industrial professionals usually work with mentally disturbed employees who are beyond the supervisor's limits to help adjust:

• The psychiatrist is a fully qualified physician who has practiced medicine before qualifying for this specialty. An industrial psychiatrist, because of specialized training and experience, can diagnose more closely what an individual's trouble is and prescribe the proper kind of treatment. No supervisor should try to do either.
• The counselor, or industrial psychologist, works with the great majority of emotionally disturbed employees who do not need full-scale psychiatric treatment. Because of specialized training, the counselor's biggest asset is the ability to listen understandingly to an employee's account of problems. The professional counselor has an advantage over the line supervisor, since the counselor doesn't have the authority to discipline, promote, or fire the employee and therefore has a greater chance of winning the employee's confidence.

supervisory word power

Neurosis.   An emotional disorder, relatively mild in nature, in which employees have feelings of anxiety, fear, or anger that drive them unknowingly or unwillingly to say and do things they would not normally choose to say and do and which often act against their own interests.

Psychosis. A severe mental disorder or disease in which employee feelings of hostility or persecution are gravely magnified and actions are irrational and unmanageable to the extreme.

Hostility. A feeling of enmity or antagonism; an aggressive expression of anger displayed by problem employees as an unconscious, unwitting relief from fears about their security or other feelings of inadequacy.

Withdrawal. A passive way for emotionally disturbed employees to cope with their anxieties, in which they retreat from confrontations, appear unduly preoccupied, discourage social overtures, and keep very much to themselves.

Adjustment. The process whereby healthy as well as disturbed individuals find a way to fit themselves to difficult situations by yielding to a degree and by modifying their feelings and their behavior to accommodate the stresses of life and work.

Other Important Terms in This Chapter

absence-prone
alcoholism
counseling
Hawthorne experiment
industrial psychologist
nondirective counseling
nonevaluative listening
psychiatrist
schizophrenia
work addiction

reading comprehension

1. What was the major finding of the research at the Hawthorne Works of the Western Electric Company?

2. List at least five symptoms of an employee with an emotional problem.

3. Differentiate between a neurotic employee and a psychotic employee.

4. Which kinds of problem employees are supervisors likely to be able to help, and which kinds had they best refer to a more highly qualified counselor?

5. Describe the essentials of a counseling interview.

6. What symptoms characterize an extremely disturbed employee who ought to receive professional help without delay?

7. In what ways are the accident-prone employee, the alcoholic, and the drug-addicted worker similar?

8. Discuss the difference between valid absences due to a bona fide illness and those absences that psychologists describe as voluntary absences. What is the supervisor's role in minimizing the latter?

9. What should a supervisor stress when counseling an employee who has showed signs of being an alcoholic?

10. Why are professionals like psychiatrists and industrial psychologists better able to handle seriously disturbed employees than a supervisor is?

supervision in action

THE CASE OF THE DOCUMENT CLERK'S SICKNESSES. A case study in human relations involving absenteeism, with questions for you to answer.

Aretha Ford, deputy assistant director of the Water Control Unit of a Western state environmental protection agency, pondered her unit's absentee record. There were a couple of real losers on the list. She had tried very hard to get them back into line with little success, and she had just about made up her mind to speak to the director about starting administrative procedures to separate them. But what caught her eye was the record of Beno Axelsone. His absence record had been steadily climbing above the unit's average for the past three years.

Beno was a medium-grade documents clerk with nearly 12 years of service in various state agencies. He had come to the Water Control Unit about four years ago. His overall performance was just about satisfactory. He was relatively quiet and showed little initiative. Nevertheless, he managed to do his work satisfactorily so long as he was there. The problem was that he regularly used up his sick leave with a variety of short absences. Each of these absences, taken one by one, seemed legitimate. Because he was a documents clerk, it was a nuisance when he was not there. It meant that someone had to search his files for critical records if these were needed in a hurry, as they often were when a call came from the state capital or from Washington for information.

Aretha decided to speak to Beno about his increasing number of absences. She asked her secretary to call Beno into her office. Here is what transpired.

"Beno, can we talk a little this morning?" said Aretha.

"Yes, Ms. Ford," answered Beno.

"How have you been feeling?" asked Aretha.

"Fine, fine," said Beno.

"No problems at home?" asked Aretha.

"Everyone's got problems, Ms. Ford," replied Beno.

"What kind of problems do you have?" asked Aretha.

"I got no problems," said Beno.

"I thought maybe you did," said Aretha.

"Why?"

"Because I notice that your sick leave days have been steadily increasing in the last year."

"I'm entitled to them, aren't I? I have 12 years' service with the state now."

"You are entitled to them if you are sick. But you seem to be sick so often."

"I can't help it if I'm sick."

"Well, you cause us a problem when you are out so often."

"I do my work all right, don't I?"

"When you're here you do. But you have missed 24 days so far this year."

"I'm entitled to them. I've earned them."

"You are entitled to them only if you are sick."

"I am sick when I'm absent. I can't help it."

"Are you sure there isn't something at home that causes you to be sick so often?"

"I don't know what you mean, Ms. Ford. I get sick because I'm not as healthy as some other people, I guess."

"The records show that you are among the few in the department who are sick so often they use up their entire sick leave."

"Isn't that what the sick leave is for, Ms. Ford? To let me stay home without losing pay when I'm sick?"

"Yes, but you and a couple of others in the unit are the only ones who are sick so often."

"That's what I mean. Others get sick, too. And when they get sick, they stay home. I don't stay home unless I'm sick. I've worked for the state 12 years and my record is good."

"Well, your absence record isn't that good, and I'd like to see you improve it."

"I can't help it if I'm sick, Ms. Ford. My work record is good with the state. You can't get rid of me because I get sick a little more than others who are lucky to be healthy."

"I didn't say we were going to fire you. I only want your absence record to improve."

"Why are you putting this pressure on me because I get sick? I do my best. I can't help it if I'm not well."

"Beno, I'm not trying to get you fired. All I want is for you to improve your attendance. All right?"

"I'll try, Ms. Ford, but I'm doing my best anyway."

Beno left the office. Ms. Ford looked again at the records and shook her head. Why, she asked herself, is it so hard to get employees to admit that their absences cause a problem?

1. What is your estimate of the rapport Aretha established between herself and Beno? Who is at fault?

2. What is your reaction to Beno's reason for being absent so often?

3. How might Aretha have probed further into Beno's problem?

4. What did Aretha fail to do in discussing this problem with Beno?

enriching your viewpoint

Try digging more deeply into this complex and sensitive subject by reading the following references:

"Alcoholism: The $15 Billion War," *Applied Training,* February 1977, pp. 10–15.

Collins, Robert, "Drinking on the Job," *Imperial Oil Review,* No. 2, 1973, pp. 3–7.

Dickson, William J., and F. J. Roethlisberger, *Counseling in an Organization: A Sequel to the Hawthorne Research,* Graduate School of Business Administration, Division of Research, Harvard University, Cambridge, Mass., 1966.

Frunzi, George L., and Joseph R. Dunn, "Counseling Subordinated: It's Up to You," *Supervisory Management,* August 1974, pp. 3–9.

"How Companies Control Absenteeism." *Personnel Policies Forum,* Survey No. 57, The Bureau of National Affairs, Inc., Washington, 1960.

HSMHA Supervisors' Guide on Alcohol Abuse, Health Services and Mental Health Administration, Employee Health Program on Alcoholism, U.S. Government Printing Office, December 1972.

Maier, Norman R. F., *Psychology in Industry,* 3d ed., Houghton Mifflin Company, Boston, 1965.

Mee, John F., "Understanding the Attitudes of Today's Employees," *Nation's Business,* August 1976, pp. 22–28.

Oates, David, "Luring Back the Absent Workers," *International Management,* December 1971.

21

CHAPTER handling complaints
and avoiding
grievances

How much attention should supervisors pay to employee complaints?

Just as much as is necessary to remove the employee complaints as obstacles to their doing a willing, productive job. That's the main reason supervisors should act as soon as they even sense a complaint, gripe, or grievance. A gripe, imagined or real, spoken or held within, blocks an employee's will to cooperate. Until you've examined the grievance and its underlying causes, an employee isn't likely to put out very much for you. And if the complaint has merit, the only way for you to get the employee back on your team 100 percent is to correct the situation.

Can you settle every grievance to an employee's satisfaction?

No. It's natural for people sometimes to want more than they deserve. When an employee complains about a condition that the facts don't back up, the best you can do is to demonstrate that the settlement is a just one—even if it isn't exactly what the employee would like.

Jake may want the company to provide him with work clothing on a job he considers dirty. Suppose you are able to show Jake that the working conditions are normal for the kind of work being done, that other workers in the company doing the same kind of work provide their own coveralls, and that this practice is common in the industry. Jake should be satisfied with this answer. He's getting equal treatment. But there's nothing to prevent Jake from still feeling dissatisfied with the settlement of his complaint. He may still feel the company should provide work clothing.

Look at it this way, though. You didn't give Jake the brushoff. You listened to his argument attentively. You didn't give him a snap answer. You checked with other supervisors and with the manager to see what the company practice was. You found out that the company practice conforms with that of the industry. All this adds up to something of value in you that Jake can see. He can take his troubles to you and get a straight answer. That's good leadership!

Is there danger in trying to talk an employee out of a complaint?

Talk if you will. But don't try to outsmart an employee—even if that's what the employee may be trying to do to you. Grievances are caused by facts—or what an employee believes to be facts. Clever use of words and sharp debating tactics won't change these facts or dissolve the grievance.

Patience and sincerity are the two biggest keys to settling a grievance. In many cases, just listening patiently to an explanation will result in the employee's forgetting the grievance.

What is meant by an imagined grievance? If it's a figment of a worker's imagination, why give it serious attention?

Marie, an unskilled machine operator, files a grievance saying that you've been picking on her, accusing her of doing substandard work. As far as you're concerned, Marie is off her rocker. In fact, you've hardly paid any attention to what she's been doing. Where'd she ever get a notion like that?

Well, where did she? Let's see. Your department has been pretty rushed lately—that's why you haven't seen much of Marie. You've been spending a good deal of your time with two new apprentices that have just been turned over to you for assignment. *You* knew that their presence had nothing to do with Marie or her job. But did Marie?

Here's how Marie looked at the situation: "I've been here four years busting a gut for Joe. So what does he do when they send up a couple of bright young apprentices? He puts me on the blacklist. He thinks he's going to freeze me out of my job by not speaking to me for two weeks. Then when he does, he tells me that the last batch of fasteners I turned out have to be reworked. And first thing this morning he jumps me for breaking a drill. Next thing I know he'll have one of those apprentices showing me how to do a job I've done for four years. Or taking my job on some phony pretext and bumping me back to the foundry. I'll squawk now before it's too late."

Marie has imagined this grievance, hasn't she? She's got the situation all wrong, too. But if Joe doesn't take time out right now to get to the bottom of this complaint, he'll have a real problem on his hands. Joe will make a good beginning by saying, "Marie, if I've been picking on you, it certainly wasn't personal. In fact, if I thought you had any complaint, it was that I hadn't been giving you enough attention. For the last couple of weeks, I've let you pretty much alone because you're an older hand here. I feel I can trust you to go ahead without my standing over your shoulder. But somewhere maybe I've gotten off the track. Can you tell me what you mean by picking on you? I certainly want to get this matter straightened out."

What's the most important thing you can do when handling grievances?

It can't be said too often: Above all, be fair. Get the employees' point of view clear in your mind. If they have an opportunity to make themselves understood, their grievances may turn out to be something different from what appears on the surface.

To be really fair, you must be prepared to accept the logical conclusion that flows from the facts you uncover. This may mean making concessions. But if the facts warrant it, you often have to change your mind or your way of doing things if you are to gain a reputation for fair dealing.

If you find you've made a mistake, admit it. A supervisor isn't expected to be right all the time. But your employees expect you to be honest in every instance—even if it means your eating crow on occasion.

Should a supervisor bargain on grievances?

No. Be like a good baseball umpire: Call each one as you see it. An umpire who blows a decision is really in for trouble if he tries to make up for it on the next call. It should be the same way with grievances. An employee either has a case or hasn't a case. Consider each case on its merits. And don't let the grievances become political issues.

Should supervisors change their story if they find the facts won't support their original conclusions?

Supervisors have no other choice if upon investigation they find their actions or decisions have been wrong. But they should avoid this embarrassing situation in the first place. Just be sure to get the facts—all the facts. Get them straight to begin with—before you give the employee or a shop steward your decision. It costs you nothing to say, "Give me a couple of hours (or a couple of days) to look into this matter thoroughly. Just as soon as I know all the facts, I'll be able to discuss this grievance so that we come up with the fairest solution."

In trying to round up the facts of a case, explore further than just the obvious places. For example, if the grievance involves a dispute over pay, look beyond just the time-card and payroll data. Ask yourself: Has the worker been upset about the jobs assigned? Has the worker had a fair share of easier jobs? Have we had occasion to turn the worker down on a bid for a better job? Does the worker know how to fill in a time card properly? Does the worker know the procedure for getting credit for machine breakdown time? Have the worker's materials and tools been up to standard?

All these factors could affect a person's pay and should be examined before you commit yourself.

Records are especially useful in assembling the facts and backing you when you present your decision to the employee or the union. If your complaint is that output has been below par, you'll need the worker's records and the records of others to prove it.

Isn't there a danger that if you make a big thing of a grievance, you'll encourage the employee and the union to think it's more legitimate than it really is?

There's that chance. But you've got to risk it. In the long run, treating each grievance with care and consideration pays off. That's different, of course, from giving in on a grievance. That might lead employees to believe you're soft and that you'll make concessions just to avoid arguments.

On the whole it is best to follow this rule for handling grievances: Be businesslike in your discussions. Talk with an employee someplace where you'll be free from distractions and interruptions. You should by all means treat the grievance as a private matter; discuss it away from other employees. Once the employee refers the grievance to the union for handling, don't attempt to settle it except in the presence of the union representative.

When you have made your own investigation and are ready to discuss how the grievance should be settled, advise the union steward. Ask the steward to invite the employee to be present. After all, your reply is to the employee as well as to the union. Even though the employee has gone to the union for representation, you still want to maintain your personal relationship. And the employee can observe that you maintained the initiative, that the steward didn't have to tell you off.

As in any business situation, handle all your discussions in a civil tone. Avoid discussing personalities. Keep the steward's focus, as well as your own, on the grievance situation. Show the steward you, too, wish to settle it fairly. Keep control of your temper, even if the employee or steward doesn't. Resist the temptation to blow your top. It's all too easy to permit a grievance to fall to the level of a personal squabble among you, the employee, and the steward. Avoid this at all cost.

When you give your decision on a grievance, how specific should you be? Should you leave yourself a loophole?

A supervisor is paid to make decisions. When the grievance has been fully investigated and you've talked it over with the parties involved, make your decision as promptly as possible. Be definite in your answer. State your decision so that there's no mistake about what you mean. If it involves a warning rather than a more serious penalty, for breaking a safety rule, for instance, don't give this kind of reply: "I'll withhold the warning this time, but next time it happens it won't be so easy for you."

Instead, use this clear-cut approach: "There appears to be good reason to believe that you misunderstood what I expected of you. So I'll tear up the warning and throw it away. Next time, you'll get a written warning. And if it happens a second time, it will cost you a week off without pay."

It is also a good idea to make sure that the worker understands the reasons for your decisions. For instance, in the safety warning case above, the supervisor might have said: "Ordinarily, ignorance of the rule is no excuse. The rule is in the employee handbook and has been posted conspicuously in the department. Your case seems to be different because you asked me about this rule last week, and you misunderstood what I told you about it. I told you that you were to report any injury, no matter how minor, to me before going to the nurse. You seem to have thought that you didn't have to report the injury so long as you didn't go to the nurse—which you didn't. I've explained it now that I want to know about every injury—and I'll decide whether we treat it here or send you to the dispensary."

Must you give your decision right away?

No. But don't sit on it forever. Nothing breaks down the grievance procedure like procrastination. If you can't make up your mind on the spot, or need to check even further than you did originally, tell the employee and the steward that you'll give a definite answer this afternoon or tomorrow. Stick to this promise. If you run into an unexpected delay, let them know about it. Like: "Sorry I can't let you know this afternoon as I'd hoped, because the paymaster has been tied up all morning. I won't be able to check the time sheets until late this afternoon. But I will let you know first thing in the morning."

Incidentally, where stewards are involved, get your answer back to them directly. It ruins their prestige in the company if your decision leaks out before you've had a chance to speak to them personally.

Suppose your boss or your boss's superior asks you to hand down a grievance decision that you don't agree with. Should you accept responsibility for it?

This is that old supervisor-in-the-middle situation. It's bound to come up from time to time. Sometimes you'll find that company practice is easier on the employee than you think it should be. Sometimes just the reverse—it's tougher than what you'd do if you had no one but yourself to answer to. In either case, don't pass the buck. If you as a supervisor say that you agree with the employee but that the company manager can't see it your way, you destroy the whole management teamwork. If you don't agree with company policy, try to adjust your own thinking. In any event, and hard as it may be to swallow, you should pass the decision along as your own.

Should a supervisor help employees save face if they have had a grievance go against them?

It seems as if it's asking too much for a supervisor to be noble about winning a grievance—especially when the employee or union has been nasty or aggressive in pursuing it. But here again, it's a bad practice in the long run to make the employee eat humble pie. If you help employees save face, they may be considerate to you when the tables are turned. If you rub in the decision, you may irk them so much that they'll be on the lookout for a gripe they can't lose.

This shouldn't be interpreted to mean that you must be so downright nice as to appear as if you were sorry you were right. Try saying something like this: "I've checked your complaint from every angle, but it still looks like no to me. You made two comparisons when you stated that I was playing favorites. In each case the facts show that both employees you referred to outranked you in both output and quality of production. On my scorecard they deserve the better assignments. I'm far from glad that I had to say no to you. But I am glad that you brought your position out into the open. Perhaps now that I know how you feel, I can give you some help to improve your performance so you can do some of the jobs requiring greater skill."

What's the best way to wind up a grievance settlement?

Carry out your part of the bargain and see that the employee does, too. Once an agreement has been made, follow through on corrective action promptly. You may lose all the good will you've built in settling the grievance if you delay in taking action.

How important is the grievance procedure as such? Wouldn't it be simpler if employee grievances were all handled informally?

Where a union is involved, the grievance procedure becomes a very important matter. The procedure may vary from company to company (see Chapter 18), but in any case your guide should be: Know the authorized grievance procedure in your plant and stick to it. It's up to you, too, to see that the steward also observes the provisions of the grievance clause.

Take special notice of what may appear to be tiny technicalities, and be sure you observe them. For instance, some contracts call for the supervisor to give an answer within 24 hours after the complaint has been presented in writing. Be sure you do, so that you can't be accused of stalling, or even lose the grievance entirely on such a technicality.

Of course, it would be desirable if grievances could all be settled in a casual, informal manner. But where a union is concerned, experience shows that it's best to be businesslike and stick to the letter of the contract procedure. On the other hand, don't get so engrossed with the process itself that you overlook the original purpose of the grievance procedure—to settle grievances fairly and promptly.

What happens to grievances that go unsettled?

They continue to fester. Frequently a supervisor may feel that he or she has taken care of a complaint just by soft-soaping the aggrieved employee. This is a mistake. The grievance will continue to simmer in the employee's mind, even if nothing more is said about it to the supervisor. And dissatisfaction is contagious.

An unsettled grievance is like one rotten apple in a basket. It spoils the good ones—the good ones don't make a good apple of the rotten one. An offended or angry employee tends to make other employees lose confidence in the supervisor. The co-workers may encourage the dissatisfied employee to pursue the matter if it appears that you have been evasive.

When does a grievance go to arbitration?

Most union-management contract agreements call for a grievance to go to arbitration if the grievance cannot be settled at any of the steps of the authorized procedure. Once the complaint has been turned over to an impartial arbitrator, the arbitrator acts somewhat like a judge, listens to the facts as presented by both parties, then makes a decision. The arbitrator does not mediate, that is, try to reopen the discussions between the company and the union. Both parties agree to abide by the decision.

Where are grievances most likely to occur?

It's hard to pinpoint just what situations are most likely to breed grievances. But there are some indicators for you to follow:

TABLE 21-1. Common Grievances and Their Causes

Grievances (listed in order of their frequency)	Typical Causes (as an employee sees it)
Wages and Salary	
1. Demand for individual wage adjustment	I'm not getting what I'm worth. I get less than other people doing work that requires no more skill.
2. Complaints about job classifications	My job is worth more than it pays and it should be reclassified.
3. Complaints about incentive systems	The method used to figure my pay is so complicated that I don't really know what the rate is. My piece rate is too low. You cut my rate when my production went up.
4. Miscellaneous wage complaints	You made a mistake in figuring my pay. The wages here are too low for what you ask me to do.
Supervision	
1. Complaints about discipline	My supervisor doesn't like me and has it in for me. Any mistakes that I made were because my boss didn't instruct me properly. My supervisor plays favorites.
2. Objections to general methods of supervision	There are too many rules and regulations. The rules are not posted clearly.
Seniority and Related Matters	
1. Loss of seniority	I was unfairly deprived of seniority when the department was reorganized.
2. Calculation of seniority	I didn't get all the seniority due me.

- First of all, don't lose sight of the fact that grievances are symptoms of something wrong with employees, or with working conditions, or with immediate supervision.
- Second, employees are most likely to be worried about situations that threaten their security: such things as promotions, transfers, work assignments, layoffs, the supervisor's evaluation of their performance, mechanization or elimination of their jobs.

For an indication of situations that stir up grievances, together with some ideas of how employees are likely to feel about them,

TABLE 21-1. Common Grievances and Their Causes (*continued*)

Grievances (listed in order of their frequency)	Typical Causes (as an employee sees it)
3. Interpretation of seniority	You didn't apply my seniority the way it should have been when assigning overtime.
4. Layoffs	I was laid off out of sequence. You didn't recall me in sequence.
5. Promotions	There is no chance to get ahead in this job. You promoted the other person ahead of my seniority.
6. Disciplinary discharge	The company has been unfair. What I did didn't warrant this severe a penalty. You were just looking for an excuse to get rid of me.
7. Transfers	I've had more than my share of dirty work. I don't want to work in the mixing department. Will you get me off the midnight shift?
General Working Conditions	
1. Safety and health	The lockers are too crowded. This place is unsafe because it is too damp, too noisy, and there are dangerous fumes.
2. Miscellaneous	I lose time waiting for materials. Overtime is unnecessary. The company should pay for my work clothing. You can't do the job right without better tools than you provide.

take a look at Table 21-1. It is based on (and updated from) studies made by the U.S. Bureau of Labor Statistics.

It's easy to see that it would be better to prevent grievances in the first place. What can you do to keep from having to wait until one occurs?

The trick lies in detecting situations that breed grievances and then correcting these situations. Don't make the mistake of planting seeds of trouble where trouble doesn't exist, though. A perfectly happy worker may be able to find something to complain about if you ask directly, "What is there about your job that you don't like?" Better leave that type of open-ended prospecting to company-directed attitude surveys.

As a rule of thumb, however, you can reduce the number of grievances by applying common sense to your relationships with your staff. For example:

1. Give employees prompt and regular feedback about how well they are doing their jobs. Uncertainty in this area is a major source of employee dissatisfaction.

2. Remove, or try to ease, minor irritations as they arise. The presence of unnecessary aggravations tends to magnify the more serious complaints when they occur.

3. Listen to and encourage constructive suggestions. Take action whenever it is reasonable and nondisruptive.

4. Make certain of your authority before making a commitment to an employee. Then be sure to keep your promises.

5. When making changes, take special care to explain the reasons—and as far in advance as possible.

6. Assign work impartially. Try to balance the distribution of attractive and disagreeable work so that employees share it equally.

7. Be consistent in your standards of performance and the way in which you reward or punish those workers who comply or fail to measure up.

8. Render your decisions as soon as possible when responding to employee requests. A prompt no is often more welcome than a long-delayed yes.

9. If you must criticize or take disciplinary action, do not make a public display of it. Keep it a private matter between you and the employee.

supervisory word power

Grievance. A job-oriented complaint stemming from an injury or injustice, real or imaginary, suffered by an employee, for which redress or relief from management is sought.

Settlement. Adjustment of an employee grievance, based on careful investigation and analysis of the facts influencing the situation; the decision arrived at either unilaterally by management or after discussion, negotiation, or both with the employee or a representative of the employee.

Security. The presence in an employment situation of conditions and safeguards that protect an employee, especially from casual, frivolous, or unjust transfers, demotions, or discharge.

Seniority. The rights and privileges, safeguards, and security afforded an employee by reason of length of service, either with the company or in a particular unit of the company, or in some combination of both.

Promotion. A significant enlargement in job responsibility, but also any increase in pay, prestige, rank, or status; an upgrading within a certain job classification; any increase in responsibility that provides additional privileges, comforts, or prestige.

reading comprehension

1. Contrast a real grievance with an imagined one.
2. Why should every complaint be treated as if it were important?
3. For supervisors to be fair in settling a grievance, they must expect that occasionally they will lose one. Why should they resist the temptation to give in on one grievance so that they can win on another?
4. In searching for facts that contribute to a grievance, what are some of the places where a supervisor should look?
5. How specific and conclusive should a supervisor's settlement of a grievance be?
6. Is it wise for a supervisor to refer an employee's complaint to a staff department rather than try to deal with it first? Why?
7. To what extent are grievances handled differently when there is a formal grievance procedure prescribed by the labor contract?
8. Name several administrative procedures and situations from which grievances are likely to arise.
9. Is it a good idea to ignore or belittle minor irritations and complaints? Why or why not?
10. What are some ways that effective communication will help to minimize the number and severity of employee complaints?

supervision in action

THE CASE OF THE DELAYED REPLY. **A case study in human relations involving grievances, with questions for you to answer.**

When Lew first brought his complaint to the attention of his shop supervisor, Belle Baker, he felt fairly satisfied. "Belle listened to what I had to say about why I should have gotten the overtime rather than the man from the second shift," Lew told his bench-mate. "I can't see how Belle can handle it any other way than to give me what's coming to me." This conversation took place the day after Lew had spoken to his supervisor.

Three days later when Lew saw that his paycheck didn't reflect any additional money, he spoke to Belle again. "What happened to that overtime pay I spoke to you about? I figured that so long as I didn't hear from you, the company had approved my request. How long do I have to wait for my money?"

"Well, now," said Belle. "I didn't promise you that you'd get the money. All I said was that I'd look into it. But I've been so busy lately that it clean slipped my mind. Tell you what. I'll go up to payroll this afternoon for sure and find out what can be done."

That afternoon Belle checked the matter with the personnel manager and with her boss. They both listened to the facts. Then they showed Belle that a similar case had been settled at a third-step grievance with the union—with no overtime pay for the em-ployee concerned.

Belle didn't look forward to telling Lew that he wouldn't get the overtime, so for a couple of days she avoided going into Lew's part of the shop. The following payday, however, Lew went up to Belle's desk: "I still didn't get the overtime pay. Are you going to do something about it or aren't you?"

Belle then told Lew that he wasn't entitled to the overtime pay. Lew replied, "We'll see about that. My shop steward told me to file a written grievance and said that's the only way to get any action around here. And I can already see that the steward is right!"

1. Do you think the written grievance could have been avoided? How?

2. If Lew really had no case, will it make any difference in the long run whether he files a grievance or not? Why?

3. How could Belle have improved her handling of this com-plaint?

4. If you were Lew, what would you think of Belle as a super-visor?

enriching your viewpoint

■■■■■■■■■ To gain a fuller understanding of this sensitive and significant subject, the following readings are suggested:

Black, James Menzies, *The Basics of Supervisory Management,* McGraw-Hill Book Company, New York, 1975, Chap. 7, "How to Ad-minister a Grievance Program Properly."

Chapman, J. Brad, "Constructive Grievance Handling," in M. Gene Newport (ed.), *Supervisory Management Tools and Techniques,* West Publishing Company, St. Paul, Minn., 1976, Chap. 14, pp. 253–274.

Flippo, Edwin B., *Principles of Personnel Management,* 4th ed., McGraw-Hill Book Company, New York, 1976, "The Processing of Grievances," pp. 429–437.

Gellerman, Saul W., *Managers and Subordinates,* The Dryden Press, Inc., Hinsdale, Ill., 1976, Chap. 8, "Grievances."

Kepner, Charles H., and Benjamin B. Tregoe, *The Rational Manager,* McGraw-Hill Book Company, New York, 1975, Chap. 7, "Finding the Cause."

The Supervisor's Guide to Labor Relations in the Federal Government, 5th ed., U.S. Civil Service Commission, Bureau of Training, Labor Relations Center, CST 26-9404, August 1972, Chap. 4, "Handling Grievances and Arbitration."

White, James R. H., *Successful Supervision,* McGraw-Hill Book Company, Maidenhead, England, 1975, Chap. 6, "Understanding Complaints and Grievances."

22

CHAPTER **how and
when to discipline**

What is the real purpose of discipline?

The real purpose of discipline is quite simple. It is to encourage employees to meet established standards of job performance and to behave sensibly and safely at work. Supervisors should think of discipline as a form of training. Those employees who observe the rules and standards are rewarded by praise, by security, and often by advancement. Those who cannot stay in line or measure up to performance standards are penalized in such a way that they can clearly learn what acceptable performance and behavior are. Most employees recognize this system as a legitimate way to preserve order and safety and to keep everyone working toward the same organizational goals and standards. For most employees, self-discipline is the best discipline. As often as not, the need to impose penalties is a fault of management as well as the individual worker. For that reason alone a supervisor should resort to disciplinary action only after all else fails. Discipline should never be used as a show of authority or power on the supervisor's part.

Why do employees resent discipline?

Employees don't object to the idea of rules and regulations, but they frequently object to the way a supervisor metes out discipline. In civil life, if a person breaks the law, the police officer only makes the arrest. The person is tried before a jury of peers who are guided by the rulings of an impartial judge, who in turn determines the punishment.

Now compare the civil procedure for handling lawbreakers with what happens in the company. As supervisor, you're often called on not only to put the finger on the wrongdoer, but also to hear the case and decide the penalty. To many employees this seems unfair because you've acted as police officer, judge, and jury.

So don't take your job as disciplinarian lightly. It's a great responsibility and requires impartiality, good judgment, and courage on your part.

Incidentally, when rules are thought by the work group to be reasonable, the group itself will impose a discipline to keep its members in line.

Why do employees break rules?

As in most personnel problems, only a small percentage of workers cause disciplinary problems. People who break rules do so for a number of reasons—most of them because they are not well adjusted. Contributing personal characteristics include carelessness, lack of cooperation, laziness, dishonesty, lack of initiative, lateness, and lack of effort. The supervisor's job, as a result, is to help employees to be better adjusted.

People break rules less often when the supervisor is a good leader, when a sincere interest is shown in employees, when employees get more enjoyment from their work. After all, if an employee finds the work uninteresting and the boss unpleasant, is it surprising that the employee will find reasons for being late or for staying away from work altogether?

If the supervisor gives the employees little or no chance to show initiative on the job or to discuss ways the work should be done, there should be no surprise if the employees talk back, shirk their responsibilities, or create a lot of scrap. That's what some people do who can't express themselves any other way.

Sometimes the real reason an employee breaks rules or seems lazy on the job has nothing at all to do with working conditions. The employee may be having worries at home—money problems or a nagging spouse—or may be physically sick. You might ask, "What concern is that of the supervisor?" It isn't—unless the supervisor wants that employee to be more cooperative and productive at work. If you're smart enough to see the connection, then you can do much to improve this worker's performance. Don't snoop in personal affairs, but do offer a willing and uncritical ear. Let the employee get to know that you're an understanding person, that the boss is someone to talk to without getting a short answer or a lot of phony advice.

So when an employee breaks a rule, make discipline your last resort. Instead, search hard for the reason the employee acts that way. Then try to see what you can do to remove the reason.

What kind of handling do employees expect from a supervisor in the way of discipline?

Justice and equal treatment. Being soft, overlooking nonstandard performance, giving chance after chance to wrongdoers does not win popularity among most employees. In fact, it works the other way to destroy morale. That's because the majority of people who work hard and stay in line are frustrated and disappointed when they see others get away with things. Of course, no one likes to be punished. But everyone likes to be assured that the punishment received is in line with the error. ("Let the punishment fit the crime" is the advice given in Gilbert and Sullivan's *Mikado*). No one likes to be treated better or worse than anyone else for the same fault.

Some people talk about negative punishment and say positive discipline is better. What does this mean?

When you have to penalize someone, that's negative. If you can get an employee to do what you wish through constructive criticism or discussion, that's positive.

Supervisors, more so than employees, understand that disciplining is an unpleasant task. All a supervisor wants is to run the department in peace and harmony, to see that things get done right, and that no one gets hurt. The supervisor who can establish discipline through good leadership won't have to exercise negative discipline through scoldings, suspensions, or discharges.

What is meant by progressive discipline?

██████████████ The penalties for substandard performance or broken rules get increasingly harsh as the condition continues or the infraction is repeated. Typically, a first offense may be excused, or the worker is given an oral warning. A second offense receives a written warning. A third infraction may bring a temporary layoff or a suspension. The final step occurs when an employee is discharged for the fourth (or very serious) infraction.

What is the "hot-stove" rule of discipline?

██████████████ It is used to illustrate four essentials of a good disciplinary policy. If the stove is red-hot, you ought to be able to see it and to know that if you touch it, you will be burned; that is the principle of *advance warning.* If you touch the hot stove, you get burned (penalized) right away; that is the principle of *immediacy.* Every time you touch a hot stove, you will get burned; that is the principle of *consistency.* Everyone who touches a hot stove will get burned because it plays no favorites; that is the principle of *impartiality.*

How far can a supervisor go in handling discipline?

██████████████ That depends on your company's management policy—and on the labor agreement, if your company has a union.

Legally, a supervisor can hire and fire. But firing is a costly action. To break in a new employee can cost from $250 to several thousand dollars for a skilled mechanic. So most companies have tried to approach discipline from a positive direction. And since discipline puts a supervisor in such a responsible position, many companies have carefully spelled out just how far a supervisor can go before having to check with the boss.

Labor unions, in their desire to provide the maximum protection from injustice or unfair treatment, maintain that discipline shouldn't be handled by management alone. Unions contend that they, too, should help decide on an employee's punishment. How much say a particular union will have depends on how successful the union has been in writing this privilege into the contract or in establishing precedents for its participation.

So tread carefully in discipline matters. Find out from your company's policy-level management (your immediate superior or the personnel manager) just how far the company wants you to go—and how much participation you must permit the union.

Aren't supervisors likely to be no more than figureheads if they can't take discipline into their own hands?

No. Not if supervisors act only in accordance with their authority. Trouble comes when you try to throw more weight around than you actually possess. That's when you look foolish!

Hardly anyone anywhere can take action that affects others without at the same time being responsible to still other people. This applies to your boss, who must answer to higher executives and to the company president, who in turn may have to answer to a board of directors.

Being a supervisor isn't an easy job. Handling discipline when you know that if you make a mistake, you may be reversed or overruled makes the job even more difficult. To make it easier, you must become a legal eagle on the points of how far you can go before it's wise to check with your boss. Some companies actually formalize this process by having the supervisor's superior and the supervisor work out a checklist so that supervisors know exactly where they stand on each point. When it's done this way, you'd be surprised how much real authority you have, how many decisions you can make yourself—even though in some cases your authority is necessarily limited. You'll find an example of such a checklist in Figure 22-1.

Should you act when you're angry?

It's a very unusual person who can think and act sensibly when angry. For that reason it's a good idea for a supervisor not to take any disciplinary action while boiling over. How can this be accomplished? Try one of these:

Count to 100.   An oldie, but it works.

Take a walk.   Ask the employee to walk over to the window or to your office—anything that takes time. This is especially good, since it gets the person away from other employees and from familiar surroundings where you may be resisted.

See the employee later.   Simply tell the employee you'll speak about the matter in a couple of hours. This gives you a chance to cool off, to think the matter through, to check with your boss, if necessary.

How do you decide what to do?

No one can make a decision without all the facts. If a situation arises that looks as if you've got to take disciplinary action, look

FIGURE 22-1.

Responsibility and Limit of Authority for Handling Employee Relations and Disciplinary Problems

Authority Limits:

Class 1. Complete authority. Supervisor can take action without consulting superior.

Class 2. Authority is limited to the extent that supervisor must inform superior of any action taken.

Class 3. Limited authority. Supervisor must consult superior before taking any action.

	Authority Limit Classification
New Employees:	
Hire additional employees	_____
Accept new employees	_____
Report on probationary employees	_____
Job Assignments:	
Schedule employees	_____
Make changes in schedules	_____
Transfer employees within department	_____
Transfer employees within company	_____
Discipline:	
Suggest appropriate discipline	_____
Issue written reprimand	_____
Suspend	_____
Discharge for cause	_____
Grievances:	
Adjust grievances with employees	_____
Accept written grievances from union	_____
Give written reply to union	_____
Termination and Leaves:	
Grant leaves of absence	_____
Prepare vacation schedules	_____
Lay employees off for lack of work	_____
Information:	
Maintain bulletin boards	_____
Explain company policy to employees	_____
First Aid and Accidents:	
Send employees to first-aid station	_____
Send employees to doctor or hospital	_____
Notify family of injured employee	_____
Prepare report of accident	_____
Safety and Good Housekeeping:	
Take unsafe tools out of service	_____
Correct unsafe conditions	_____
Stop work where conditions are unsafe	_____
Establish housekeeping standards	_____

hard before you leap. Take time to investigate. Let the employee tell the full story—without interruptions. Check with witnesses for their observations. Look in the company records to see what other supervisors have done in the past. Speak to your boss or the personnel manager to get their advice.

For instance, someone tips you off that Will Jones is going to take home a baby Stillson wrench in his lunch box tonight. You stop Will at the time clock. Sure enough. There's the wrench tucked underneath a wad of sandwich wrappers. Your first reaction is to fire Will on the spot for stealing. But should you?

Suppose, on checking, you found any of these circumstances:

• Will had asked the toolroom supervisor for the wrench and received permission to borrow it overnight for a home-repair job.
• Two of Will's co-workers tell you Will had said he was just borrowing the wrench overnight and planned to return it in the morning.
• Will could prove that the wrench was one he actually had bought himself to use on his job.
• When checking with the personnel department, you found that the company had agreed with the union not to fire any ten-year employee for petty thefts, that the most Will's penalty could be for a first offense would be one day off without pay.

Wouldn't any of these facts change your decision?

When should you consult the union on disciplinary problems?

Practices will vary from company to company. Some supervisors, however, have found it helps to inform the union immediately of any planned disciplinary action. The supervisor who sees that a disciplinary problem has arisen holds an informal hearing with the employee with the shop steward standing by. This way, the shop steward is a witness to the situation from the beginning. The steward can observe that the supervisor's handling of the case is fair. It also makes it harder for the employee to change the story later on; it avoids the case where the shop steward says to you, "That's not what I was told."

Unless your company has a practice to the contrary, you should avoid asking the union or the shop steward what you should do or what penalty is appropriate. You should make it clear that the union representative has been invited only for the purpose of keeping him or her informed. Keeping order in the shop is your job, not the union's, although you may welcome its cooperation.

Do warnings do any good?

Yes, warnings do a lot of good—if you make them more than idle threats. Your warnings put employees on notice that their performance isn't up to standard. It gives you a chance to explain a rule that they may have taken only lightly before—and to make the penalty clear to them. When you warn employees that's the perfect time for you to be constructive, to offer help, to practice positive discipline.

To make a warning a valuable piece of evidence in a union grievance, you should always make a written record of it. You'd be surprised how much weight arbitrators and union officials give to notations that you have written in your pocket notebook or the department logbook, or have inserted in the employee's personnel file.

Some companies make this written notation a formal practice by requiring supervisors to fill out a form to be filed by the personnel department. These notations are called written reprimands, and copies of the reprimand are sent to the employee and the union.

When should you fire an employee?

As mentioned previously, the supervisor's authority is limited by the company's policy and by its agreements with the labor union, if one exists.

Speaking generally, however, some employee offenses are worse than others. Drinking or sleeping on the job, smoking in restricted areas, willfully destroying property, and falsifying time cards are often charges that result in discharge. It is easier to generalize about offenses like fighting on company property and gross insubordination. But all these wrongdoings have one thing in common—they are single incidents rather than an accumulation of minor offenses, and many of these single acts require immediate action by the supervisor.

To handle any of these serious offenses and still leave yourself free from reversal later on, there's an effective action you can take. It's short of discharge, but it certainly gets the culprit out of the company quickly and legally. This action is called suspension. It follows the advice arbitrators give employees: "Obey first—argue later."

To suspend an employee, you merely say something like this: "You've come to work with a load on. I think you're under the influence of liquor right now and are unfit to do your job. You could be subject for dismissal for being in this shape. I haven't made up my mind yet whether that's what I'll do. But in the meantime, you're suspended. Punch out your time card and don't come back to work until I call you. I'll try to let you know definitely tomorrow."

By suspending, you have demonstrated your willingness to enforce your authority when needed. And yet you have protected both yourself and the company from looking weak, foolish, or indecisive. If tomorrow, in the opinion of your boss, the personnel manager, or the company's lawyer, you can't make the discharge stick, you and the company are still in an effective position. It's when you cast the die—fire a employee and then have to take him or her back—that you have to eat crow.

When can't you make disciplinary action stick?

Here are some famous last words: What's difficult about discharging a third-rate employee? Get rid of the person whose work is poor, who talks back or breaks a rule.

Many supervisors with that attitude have ended up behind the eight ball. And the company has been involved in an arbitration case, had to fork over back pay to a discharged worker, and even faced a charge of an unfair labor practice. Why? Because the situation that requires the most delicate handling is the provision for discipline and discharge. Dead beyond recall are the days when a supervisor could act and talk tough, when an employee had no recourse but to curse.

As difficult as the discipline problem is, many discharges or other penalties could be made to stick if the following mistakes weren't made:

No clear-cut breach of rule.   In one company a supervisor fired an employee for sleeping, only to see the decision reversed by the arbitrator. The union brought out the fact that the supervisor had made the observation from 60 feet away. The arbitrator ruled that at this distance the supervisor was "likely to see what he wanted to see."

Inadequate warning.   Arbitrators frequently feel that workers are entitled to sufficient warning that their conduct won't be tolerated—even though the rules and penalties are in an employee manual. Typical is the case where an employee has had a record of poor attendance for months without having been disciplined. Suddenly the supervisor cracks down without warning and fires the employee.

Absence of positive evidence.   Take this case of loafing—always a difficult charge to make stick: The company went along with the supervisor and fired a worker caught loafing. The arbitrator reversed the company because (1) the supervisor had not been in the department continually but had popped in and out during one afternoon and (2) the person's job entailed occasional waits for material. Furthermore, the company could produce no time sheets that showed reduced output in black and white. The arbitrator ruled that the supervisor might have come into the department at the times the employee had been legitimately waiting for materials.

Acting on prejudices.   Real or imagined discrimination or favoritism weakens a disciplinary ruling. If a supervisor has showed that she has it in for a worker and just waited for an opportunity to enforce a penalty, an arbitration case may bring this out. If the supervisor has let others get away unpunished with the same offense for which she punishes another, she'll have a hard time justifying such unequal treatment.

Inadequate records.   The value of written records of warnings and reprimands can't be overemphasized. It's especially valuable for documenting action taken to correct an accumulation of minor offenses. You may not want to discharge a person who's been late the first time—or even the fifth. But when it gets to be a frequent and costly habit, you'll want to take action. Unless you've build up a record of warnings and kept a file of them that can be shown to the union and an arbitrator if necessary, your case will be hard to prove.

Too severe punishment.   Many arbitrators recommend "progressive punishment" and look unfavorably on too severe discipline—especially for first offenses. For instance, a supervisor in a can company noticed a worker away from his work station ten minutes before the end of the shift. A look at the employee's time card showed that he had punched out a half minute early. The man was fired because not long before that he had received a written reprimand for doing the same thing. He had been warned that the next time he'd be fired. An arbitrator ruled that a penalty was called for—but not such a tough one. Do it progressively, the arbitrator said—just a little tougher each time. A lighter penalty would keep an old (seven years' service) and valuable employee on the payroll.

What consideration should be given to an employee's good work record?

There's danger in carrying the rule book too far. Treating each offender equally does not mean that you should not weigh personal factors, too. For instance, what was the worker's attitude when the rule was broken? Was it done deliberately or accidentally? Was the worker emotionally upset by a circumstance beyond control (like worrying about a sick child at home)? How long has the person worked for the company? What kind of work record has there been? Remember, it costs money to fire a good employee. Even civil courts put on probation a guilty person who has been considered a good citizen in the past.

In many instances, it is also good to wipe an employee's slate clean now and then. For example, if an employee who had a poor absence record two years ago has been near perfect since then, the employee should not have the past record brought up if at a later date there is another absence problem.

How much should employees know about your discipline policy?

The more the better. Technically you can make your rules and penalties stick as long as they are posted on bulletin boards, written in union contracts, or expressed in employee manuals. But employees should be reminded of rules from time to time.

It's especially good if you tell them the purpose of the rules. Take a no-smoking rule. How much more effective it would be if in addition to posting a sign, you told employees:

"You can smoke most places in the company, but not in Department 29. We use a lot of solvents there. If you dropped a lighted match or butt in that department, we'd all blast off! And it would knock the department and maybe the company out of operation and jobs for a long time. So don't light up in Department 29—or even carry a cigarette in there accidentally. We'd hate to do it, but you might be fired on the spot."

Here's another thought: When you've had to discharge an employee, be sure that the other employees know what the circumstances were and why that person was fired. Don't use the person you fired as an example, but do convince other employees that you were impartial. Use this opportunity to emphasize that you don't want to discipline—that you want only to see that the department is run smoothly for the benefit of all concerned.

supervisory word power

Discipline. The imposition of a penalty by management on an employee for the infraction of a company rule or regulation in such a manner as to encourage more constructive behavior and to discourage a similar infraction in the future.

Penalty.   A punishment or forfeiture imposed by management on an employee in order to impose discipline. Typically, such penalties include suspensions, loss of time and/or pay, demotion, or loss of job—that is, discharge.

Suspension.   The temporary removal by management of a privilege (particularly the right to report to work and receive pay for it) from an employee until the proper penalty for a rule infraction has been determined and imposed.

Reprimand.   A severe expression of disapproval or censure by management of an employee, usually written as well as oral, and retained in an employee's personal file.

Warning.   A reprimand so worded as to give formal notice to an employee that repetition of a particular form of unacceptable behavior, such as infraction of a rule, will draw a penalty.

Other Important Terms in This Chapter

consistency
hot-stove rule
immediacy
impartiality
negative discipline
positive discipline
progressive discipline

reading comprehension

1. Discuss the similarities between rules and regulations at work and laws in civil life.

2. In what way does the enforcement of discipline in business differ from that in civil life?

3. What kind of people are most likely to break work rules regularly?

4. Distinguish between negative and positive discipline.

5. What kind of restraints are placed on a supervisor's authority to handle discipline independently?

6. When Carlos saw Jane sneaking out early again, he fired her on the spot, even though he hadn't given her any prior warning. What should he have done to make discipline progressive?

7. The "hot-stove" rule is meant to help supervisors remember four important points about discipline. Briefly describe the four.

8. To what extent should a supervisor consult the union representative before meting out discipline?

9. Explain the importance of making written notations of discussions held with employees regarding disciplinary matters.

10. Describe at least three reasons why a supervisor's decision to discharge an employee might not be upheld.

supervision in action

████████████ **THE CASE OF THE MISSED STITCHES.** **A case study in human relations involving employee discipline, with questions for you to answer.**

Business was booming at Ottobine Overall Outfitters, a manufacturer of heavy-duty work clothing. In the shirt department Phil Ford, section supervisor, had 35 sewing machine operators turning out nearly 2,000 denim work shirts a day. The quality-control inspector, however, had cautioned Phil several times about the stitching of seams. "Your operators frequently miss stitches and are often off the mark by a sixteenth to an eighth of an inch. And they are failing to catch and close the thread at the ends of the seams. We are going to get in big trouble with the buyers if you don't tighten up on your operation."

"Sorry," said Phil. "We are doing the best we can. The sales manager has made promises all over the lot. We are just about hitting our shipping dates as it is. And I've had to scrape the barrel to find 35 sewing machine operators."

"Don't blame me, then," said the inspector, "if you get hit with a truckload of returns from one of the big department stores. The little guys will take anything. But the big stores have an inspection routine that makes ours look like child's play."

As a matter of fact, no shirts were returned to Ottobine during this peak period. But when the sales staff made their next seasonal round of calls on customers, they received criticism for the poor quality of seam stitching on the work shirts. The word got back to Phil from higher management to correct this situation before the next season began.

Immediately, Phil carefully examined the work of his operators. There were only 20 regulars employed now, and it was easier to keep track of what was going on. Phil found that even among his regulars, however, the quality of seam work was not up to Ottobine's reputation for first-class workmanship. Beginning on the next Monday, Phil advised the quality-control inspector to tighten her inspections. She was not to pass anything that was below specifications. At the end of the day, the report came to Phil's desk: Of the 1,000 shirts made, 95 had been rejected. These were returned to the operators, who had to rip out the seams and redo the sewing. Even then, many of the shirts had to be marked "seconds." Since the operators were on piecework (a wage-incentive system that enabled them to make about 20 to 30 percent over their basic hourly wage), the time spent on rework cut into their earnings. As a result, there was a constant battle between the operators and the inspector as to what work was acceptable and what was not.

"You'll have to straighten your operators out," the inspector advised Phil. "I am not going to spend all my time arguing with them. When their work isn't up to standard, I am going to reject it. You have been letting them run away with the shop. We will all be in trouble if you don't crack down."

The next morning, after having studied the reject tally for the previous day, Phil identified the operator with the poorest record—Annie Clark. He went out to her machine and picked up the shirt she was working on. "These seams won't do, Annie," said Phil. "If you don't get them 100 percent right by Friday, I'm going to have to let you go."

"What's wrong with that seam?" asked Annie. "It looks okay."

Phil got out the marker, a pattern that showed exactly where the seams should be. He demonstrated to Annie that her seam was a sixteenth of an inch off the mark.

"Look at this, Annie. Your seams are way out of line."

"They look pretty close to me," said Annie. "Besides, since when is a sixteenth of an inch off standard? Last month we were shipping stuff that was as much as an eighth of an inch off."

"We had a lot of temporary help then who didn't know any better. And we were under pressure from the sales department to ship. You are one of our regular operators. You've got to do better. There's no reason for your seams not to be on the mark."

Phil left Annie's machine and stopped to warn three other operators that their work was off standard, too.

On Friday morning Phil examined the inspector's quality-control record again. He found to his annoyance that Annie's rejects had dropped off a little, but she was far from perfect. The other three operators he had talked to had not improved as much as he had asked for, but their work was better than Annie's.

Phil called Annie into his office. "I'm sorry, Annie, but your seam work is still below what we can accept. I'm going to speak to the personnel department. You will be laid off. Don't come in Monday. We may call you when the plant gets busy. But for now, you are suspended because your performance is unsatisfactory."

"Why me?" asked Annie. "I'm not the only person around here who is having rejects. Anyway, the markers are too tight for the kinds of shirts we do for the department stores."

"Your work is not satisfactory," replied Phil. "I warned you at the beginning of the week that it had to improve. It's practically as bad today as it was then."

"It's not fair," said Annie. "You were happy enough to get my work when you were busy. And my quality was lots better than your temporary help then. Now all of a sudden, my work isn't good enough. If you're going to lay someone off, it ought to be all of us who are having rejects, not just me."

"Yours is the worst," said Phil. "And I am going to make sure that you are suspended until you can show me that you can measure up to Ottobine's standards."

1. What circumstances have contributed to this problem?

2. What do you think is wrong (or right) about Phil's approach to this problem? Why?

3. If you were the personnel manager for Ottobine, what would you do now? What would you suggest Phil do to make his discipline more effective?

enriching your viewpoint

To gain a more comprehensive understanding of the complex matter of employee discipline, a reading of the following references is suggested:

Dowling, William F., and Leonard R. Sayles, *How Managers Motivate: The Imperatives of Supervision,* 2d ed., McGraw-Hill Book Company, New York, 1978, Chap. 6, "Administering Positive Discipline."

Duncan, W. Jack, *Organizational Behavior,* Houghton Mifflin Company, Boston, 1978, Chap. 12, "Power Relations in Organizations."

Hellriegel, Don, and John W. Slocum Jr., *Management: Contingency Approaches,* 2d ed., Addison-Wesley Publishing Company, Inc., Reading, Mass., 1978, Chap. 9, "Control Process."

Reeser, Clayton, and Marvin Loper, *Management: The Key to Organizational Effectiveness,* Scott, Foresman and Company, Glenview, Ill., 1978, "Organizational Justice," pp. 268–273.

Steinmetz, Lawrence L., and H. Ralph Todd Jr., *First-Line Mangement: Approaching Supervision Effectively,* Business Publications, Inc., Dallas, 1975, Chap. 13, "Disciplinary Matters and Unions."

Strauss, George, and Leonard R. Sayles, *Personnel: The Human Problems of Management,* 2d ed., Prentice-Hall, Inc., Englewood Cliffs, N.J., 1967, Chap. 14, "Discipline."

Walters, Kenneth D., "Your Employees' Right to Blow the Whistle," *Harvard Business Review,* Vol. 53, No. 4, July–August 1975, p. 26.

23
CHAPTER

supervising office employees and clerical work

Must office administration always be considered just so much overhead?

Not necessarily, if office operations are viewed as an opportunity to generate what the Administrative Management Society calls the "third profit." Traditionally, business people have recognized the "first profit," which is the profit from the manufacturing operation. It also acknowledges the "second profit," which results from the sales effort. Only lately has it seen the potential in the third profit—the profit to be gained from efficient operation of the administrative activities of an enterprise. For example, if a company realizes a 5 percent profit on gross sales ($1,000 on sales of $20,000), it figures that a like reduction in administrative office

405

costs of $1,000 will have the same effect on corporate profits as an increase in sales of $20,000.

To what extent are office jobs in one company similar to those in other companies?

To a very great extent—in general. In their detailed particulars, however, office jobs may vary radically from company to company. In trying to identify secretarial jobs, for example, the Bureau of Labor Statistics lists junior and senior stenographers, secretaries A, secretaries B, and executive secretaries. With regard to details and amount of work performed, these carefully defined jobs frequently differ from one office to another.

Office work, of course, covers a broad range of occupations, mainly clerical, which support specialized activities in sales order, purchasing, scheduling, accounting, inventory control, and data processing departments. In today's world data processing is often the term used to cover any kind of work involving data and information recording, manipulation, retrieval, and transmission.

Are office and clerical workers different from hourly workers?

From a supervisor's viewpoint, they are. Office workers may have the same number and variety of motives that blue-collar workers have, but they have them to a varying degree. For instance, job status is of great importance to most white-collar workers, while it is usually of secondary importance to blue-collar workers. The same is often true of working conditions. On the other hand, wages are of serious importance to both.

To supervise office, clerical, and other white-collar workers successfully, you'll have to study their idiosyncrasies and deal with them accordingly.

How good is the white-collar worker's morale?

Generally speaking, white-collar workers are pretty reserved, according to studies conducted by the University of Chicago, which are still valid today. (See Figure 23-1.) This means that they tend to be neither strongly for nor strongly against their job situation. The net result, however, is that office employees' morale on the whole is better than that of production workers. Much of this is attributed to the better working conditions and the correspondingly higher status usually associated with offices.

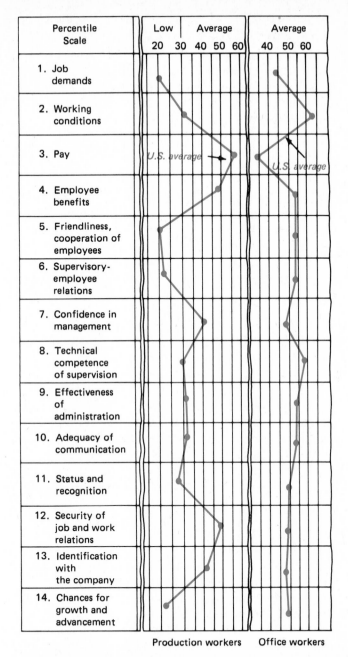

FIGURE 23-1. **How Attitudes of Office Employees Differ from Those of Production Workers. Heavy zigzag lines show how morale of office employees and production workers is either higher or lower than average for all workers.** *David G. Moore and Robert K. Burns, "How Good Is Good Morale?" Factory Management and Maintenance,* McGraw-Hill Publications, *New York, February 1956.*

How important is
pay to white-collar workers?

▆▆▆▆▆▆▆▆ Very important. For years it was a mistaken impression that office workers enjoyed their working conditions and status so much that their wages were of little importance. This isn't true, as the survey figures show. White-collar workers tend to feel underpaid and overworked.

Do office employees take
fringe benefits for granted?

▆▆▆▆▆▆▆▆ Yes. On the whole, clerical workers don't turn handsprings just because you give them a 15-minute coffee break, for instance. If anything at all, they view fringe benefits negatively. In other words, they're more likely to complain about what you don't give them (and the ABC Company next door does) than to be much impressed—and grateful—for what you do for them.

How prevalent today is office unionization?

▆▆▆▆▆▆▆▆ Only about 7.5 percent of all office employees who work in nationally known companies are members of unions. Probably less than 4 percent of all office people are union members. Despite the efforts of labor unions to organize white-collar workers, unionism has not had a particularly strong appeal to office employees. Office work tends to attract people who like the status associated with clean work and who have a strong sense of individuality. If you can respond to those desires—and provide intelligent leadership—you can probably keep the appeal of unionism from taking hold in your office.

Of what part of their jobs are office
employees likely to be most critical?

▆▆▆▆▆▆▆▆ Your attention to the human side of an office employee's job is likely to be the critical factor of your success or failure in supervising. Studies show that office employees place high importance on the social and human aspects of the organization.

One feature of office work that makes it particularly attractive is the opportunity for employees to talk together while they work. Although this can sometimes be disruptive, it is a powerful force in knitting a work group together, and it offers a form of real job satisfaction quite apart from pay and status.

There is a negative aspect, however, to the office employees' concern for the social side of the work. Office employees (compared with blue-collar workers) are often critical of others who have better or worse education, dress differently, or live in inferior or superior parts of town. The office work group strives for homogeneity. The pressure is strong for conformance. Any newcomer has a hard time breaking down the "typewriter curtain." Offbeat newcomers will find it almost impossible to gain acceptance unless you introduce them gradually—and stand by to give them assurance when needed.

So strive hard to put together people who have similar interests. Don't put too much emphasis on technical skills. A good disposition in a typist will go a long way toward offsetting slow fingers.

Must white-collar workers be handled with velvet gloves?

It helps—so long as there is a firm hand inside them. Remember that white-collar workers choose that kind of work because it implies social distinction. Consequently, they expect their supervisor to act and speak courteously. They won't complain because you're a little stiff and unbending as long as you treat them with genuine respect.

Office jobs are routine, often boring. What can you do to relieve the monotony?

Be careful with this one. What may appear to be monotonous work to you may be just what the doctor ordered for your office workers. Unless you see real signs of boredom, don't upset the office applecart by well-meant, but resented, attempts to liven up the job.

When a worker indicates that the job is boring, one sensible move to make is to find ways of varying the daily routine. Can tasks usually done in the morning be shifted to the afternoon? Can the worker develop a different and more stimulating order of work without disturbing the routine of others?

Better still, look for ways to rotate work assignments. If sorting mail is a tiresome job, break it up into smaller pieces so that each of five people share it for only one day each week. Likewise, if the reception desk is a pleasant assignment in your office, don't give this choice plum to only one person. Make it an assignment that several employees can look forward to each week.

In the office, as in the shop, jobs often become boring simply because employees can't see the point in what they're doing.

They think they're just another cog in a machine. To counteract this form of the blues, sharpen your listening technique. Ask employees for their opinions about office procedures. See if you can't adapt some of their ideas. Let them establish their own way of doing minor tasks. It's said over and over again: To get employees interested in their work, you've got to get interested in them.

How effective are participative and job enlargement techniques in motivating office workers?

Apparently there is an endless horizon for goal sharing and laissez-faire management in the office. In a notable job enrichment program at American Telephone and Telegraph Company, supervisors in the treasury department changed the jobs of 120 women employees so that these jobs would include appeals to learning, achievement, recognition, responsibility, and advancement. The supervisors in this "work itself" program decided that these employees should research, compose, and type their own letters without being checked. Results were dramatic. Turnover of employees dropped 27 percent, and 24 clerks did the work that 46 had previously done. In all, savings totaled $558,000 in 18 months. After that experiment, which took place in 1965, the program expanded. Keypunch operators were given full units of work, such as the payroll for an entire department, and were asked to schedule their own days as well as to maintain their own quantity and quality records. Telephone operators were encouraged to use their own words, rather than prescribed phrases, when speaking to customers. By 1980 over 30,000 AT&T employees had taken part in this program. Many other companies have had comparable success with such programs. The Prudential Insurance Company, for example, has a "job design" program in 100 of its divisions, and over 2,000 employees have benefited from the changes.

How do you handle the career-oriented office worker?

Most office employees are women. Many of them (in the beginning) do not view their work as a lifetime career. Handling these employees takes the greater part of your time and your skill. But there is a significant and increasing group of office employees who desire more from their work than just a place to occupy their time between high school and motherhood. These are career-oriented employees.

The career woman (or man) needs stimulating assignments, a chance to learn—even if there's small chance to get ahead. Be careful not to have this attitude: "What's the point of letting Amy learn how to strike trial balances? She won't stay here long enough to become a chief accountant." It's true that in the past there was little or no chance in many offices for promotion for women. But legislation and social awareness (see Chapter 19) have opened the door for advancement. Regardless of the sex of the individual, nothing dashes cold water into the face of an ambitious person so much as having the boss block chances for improvement at every turn.

Many people to whom work is a complete outlet will willingly accept broad assignments and won't confine themselves to narrow job descriptions. These willing workers get satisfaction from the importance derived from doing more and doing better. So give them a chance to flex their muscles.

Should you treat your secretary differently from other office employees?

The relationship between a boss and his or her secretary is a delicate one. Technically, supervising a secretary is just like supervising any other clerical employee. But anyone who's ever had a secretary will tell you that in practice it doesn't work out that way.

First of all, your secretary is doing work for you personally—in contrast with other kinds of workers who are more likely to see their work as being done for the company. A secretary often has access to confidential matters—both about business and about your own affairs. This makes it difficult to be reserved and impartial in your relationships. On the other hand, you should avoid being too chummy. A dignified distance between boss and secretary will wear better in the long run. Be friendly, but keep your friendliness on the formal side. In the office it looks better to the rest of the employees—and to outsiders—to be businesslike.

What kind of turnover is normal for office personnel?

It varies with the state of the local economy, of course. It was 14 percent per year in 1975, according to a survey conducted by the Administrative Management Society. At that time it was lowest in the eastern United States (12 percent) and highest in the west-central regions (16 percent). Large companies had better records than small ones did. Separations for nonexempt employees occurred for the following reasons:

Reason	Percentage of all separations
Another job	28
Dismissal	16
Leave city	12
Reduction in staff	10
Stay home	8
Return to school	8
Pregnancy	6
Retirement	5
Health	3
Marriage	2
Military service	1
Death	1

The Administrative Management Society noted that turnover in 1975 was far lower than in 1973, when it was 21 percent, and even 1971, when it was 19 percent. These figures compare very favorably with turnover among manufacturing employees, which in 1975 averaged 4.2 percent per month, or nearly 50 percent per year, according to the U.S. Bureau of Labor Statistics.

What's the best way to hold on to your good clerical workers?

Surprisingly to some people, it is not long vacations or exotic fringe benefits. A study by Deutsch, Shea & Evans, recruitment specialists, cited the two biggest reasons for job jumping: (1) lack of interesting work and (2) lack of prospects for additional responsibility. Their study, however, emphasized the need to provide a favorable balance of job conditions in order to attract and hold the best office people. Accordingly, interesting work, attractive salaries, good location, adequate fringe benefits, the company's reputation, and the treatment received from supervision go into the mix.

Deutsch, Shea & Evans also cautioned about the impression many supervisors have in thinking that most younger clerical people do not take their work as a serious occupation. For the most part, the surveyors concluded, secretaries and other clerical candidates tend now to think in career terms rather than "just a job." They want to make a contribution to the company's activities and want this viewpoint recognized by their supervisors. Furthermore, the drive for women's equality on the job puts far greater stress than ever before on upward mobility from the typing pool and the file room.

In human resources planning for an office, how much output can you expect from filing clerks, typists, and stenographers?

Under normal conditions a filing clerk can take good care of 60 file drawers. (Incidentally, you can ordinarily fit 4,000 sheets of paper into a single file drawer.) The Administrative Management Society once recommended (1954) the following standards of performance: typing, about 70 words per minute (although many firms accept 45); shorthand, 120 words per minute (although most firms accept 80); and transcription from notes, 45 words per minute (although here again, the standard for many firms is only 30).

In its *Records Management Handbook* (1973) the U.S. General Services Administration's National Archives and Records Services prescribed these far more conservative rates:

* To type from copy a standard page of 30 to 40 lines: 3 pages per hour
* To transcribe one standard page: 25 minutes
* To address envelopes by typewriter: 140 envelopes per hour
* To type letters from steno notes: 2 letters per hour
* To type form letters: 20 letters per hour
* To type average straight copy: 42 words per minute
* To take shorthand: 24 words per minute
* To transcribe shorthand notes: 15 words per minute
* To transcribe machine dictation: 30 words per minute

You might conclude from these contradictory figures that staffing should be based on careful study of the unique nature and demand of the work performed in your particular office.

How error-free should you expect clerical people to be in performing their work?

According to many authorities, you can be satisfied if your people meet the following standards of performance:

Filing cards. Only 1 misfile out of each 10,000 units.

Filing correspondence. Only 3 misfiles out of 1,000 letters.

Punching cards.   About one-half of 1 percent wrong, excluding errors corrected by the puncher.

Cutting mail stencils.   About one-half of 1 percent of all items incorrect, or about 3 percent of all stencils with an error.

Preparing invoices.   One oil company found that good clerks can still be expected to make errors on six-hundredths of 1 percent of all vouchers.

Preparing bills.   One public utility found that four-tenths of 1 percent contained clerical errors, but that the best employee made errors on only about one-tenth of 1 percent of the work.

Should there be a limit to the number of paperwork forms used in a single office?

Form design and control is a science in itself. But it is usually a wise idea to make one person in your office a forms "commander"—with absolute authority to say yes or no on any new form. Your other people will then take the forms problem seriously. Duplication of information from form to form can be avoided; forms can be consolidated, and the proliferation of forms that demand time and attention can be minimized.

Such a control procedure ought to apply also to the insidious kind of form such as (1) the unprinted kind that's run off casually on the copying machine or (2) the monthly letter that requests tabulated information. This informal type of form frequently sneaks by forms control; yet it is just as time-consuming as a printed form for the recipients to handle.

What can you do to make the filing chore in your office more inspired and to keep the files more orderly?

Just as most files are filled with tons of never-used paper, so have tons of papers been presented on proper procedures. The subject is really too broad to be covered in a single answer. But there are important things that can be said in this book about the people who do the filing. Here are a few insights into their thinking:

"Filing is a task to be done, not a service to be rendered."   You may be concerned with the suitability of what's filed and its placement in the metal archives; the clerk's view is likely to be more prosaic. The clerk will file today what seems important now—with little judgment of how important it will be to the organization a month or a year from now. Probably only you can furnish this perspective.

"It's better to err on the side of saving than of throwing out."   Timeworn, cynical employees know that the boss can cause trouble about the loss of what is considered a precious document at a given moment. Rather than risk the boss's wrath, file clerks reason, "Why not stick everything into the files somewhere. After all, a letter takes up only one-hundredth of an inch in a manila folder." If you'd avoid this rationale, you've got to show your employees that you can accept the fact of an occasional tossed-away or misplaced document. Experience seems to show that valuable documents do get lost anyway—even in the best-designed and best-manned filing systems.

"The system was designed by someone who didn't have the filing clerk in mind."   The filing instructions were set up, clerks imply, by a theorist who wanted to be able to prove that anything that went wrong was an employee's fault. Since it's almost impossible for you to supervise the filing of each paper, clerks naturally tend to evolve their own filing system—the simpler and more effortless for them, the better.

To put your files in harmony with these human viewpoints, it's essential that you spend more time getting across the proper attitude toward the filing job than detailing the filing operation itself. You'll find that employees will show more common sense than you may have anticipated if you can express and maintain a philosophy that (1) retention should be based on long-term usefulness, (2) a minimum of duplication is desirable, and (3) a slim file is a worthwhile objective.

It's easier to say that files should be kept slim than to see that they stay that way. What are some good rules to follow in order to attain that objective?

██████████ One expert suggests you weigh these eight factors before relegating anything to your filing cabinets:

1. How useful is this information for the operation of your department?
2. How often do you need this information?
3. Does it summarize other records (that could be discarded now if you hold on to just this one record)?
4. Can this information be duplicated easily from other sources if you need it (so that it need not be held in your files)?

5. Is the information essential for meeting government or company regulations? (The latter test is sticky because so much can be justified as conforming to company policy.)

6. Is it necessary to retain this document for legal purposes? Might it be needed later as evidence to avoid or to settle suits about unemployment, accidents, specifications, deliveries, contracts, and so forth?

7. How important is this material to persons other than those in your department? Is your file the main source for this information? Do others depend on you to maintain this record?

8. How long should you hold on to this information? Can it be marked with a green tab for removal after six months? A yellow tab for discard after a year? Should it be branded with a red flag if it must be held indefinitely?

In applying work simplification to office methods, where should you begin?

Work simplification is too often left up to the systems and procedures department. Actually, there are many simple improvements you can make or initiate on your own. As a starter, try any of these approaches:

• Look for single steps of a job that are performed by more than one person. These steps can often be combined or eliminated.

• Look for identical data that is recorded on more than one form. A single, well-designed form can often replace two or more forms.

• Look for records that are seldom used. Question their value. These are the ones most susceptible to elimination.

• Look for records that duplicate other records. Those records can usually be consolidated.

• Look for people doing too little work. Chances are that half your people could do more work than they do now if work flow was smoother and assignments were better planned.

• Look for people doing too much work. About one-tenth of your people will take on too big a work load—and often not do it as quickly as it might be done if assignments were better balanced.

• Don't pass up small opportunities. Especially where many employees or transactions are involved, pennies saved can add up to hundreds of dollars. For example, your typist can save a separate operation in making file cards by slipping a card and a carbon inside each envelope while addressing it. Or for some correspondence purposes, the reply can be written on the back or bottom of an incoming letter—or a form designed for this use can be substituted for typed letters.

What is the role of systems and procedures in office management?

████████████ This deals with the study and improvement of information, communications, and paperwork flow within an organization. It is usually conducted by trained specialists with the advice of various department supervisors. Typical areas investigated are forms and records, paperwork preparation and flow, work measurement and standardization, equipment usage, and computer adaptability. In principle, systems and procedures is not unlike work simplification.

How will the trend toward word processing affect office and clerical work?

████████████ Word processing is the production of written communications (letters, forms, reports, and so forth) through a systematic combination of automated equipment and human effort. It requires a major change in office staffing and procedures. In its simplest phase, word processing combines dictation equipment with automatic typewriters. In its most advanced stage, word processing uses (1) machines that store data for forms and letters and have features for correcting, revising, deleting, and aligning copy; (2) machines that set type from the output of the storage unit; (3) computers to link all this together; and (4) telephones or satellites to transmit data in its raw or printed form between departments in one building or between plants and offices thousands of miles apart. Figure 23-2 illustrates a basic word processing system.

Experts say that even the simple word processing systems save between 15 and 40 percent of secretarial and typing costs. Obviously, word processing will change the work of secretaries, typists, file clerks, and those in mail rooms, duplicating services, and telephone operations. It will require the addition of personnel specialized in such skills as grammatical construction, correspondence procedures, and conceptualization and operation of electronic office equipment in systematic arrangement.

How can you minimize work peaks and overloads?

████████████ P. K. Eschbach, a perceptive office manager for the Blue Diamond Corporation in Nevada, has suggested this approach:

1. Prepare your staff for flexibility by rotating jobs and assignments among different employees. Almost every job can thus be handled by more than one person. This is especially valuable

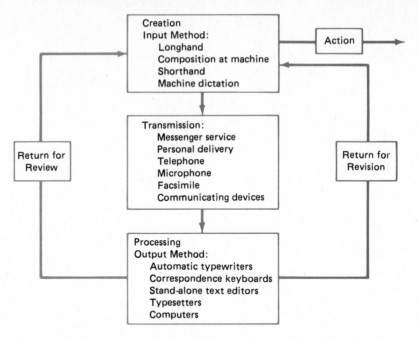

FIGURE 23-2. Basic Word Processing System.

during vacation periods when doubling up or filling in is a necessity.

2. Put your job procedures into writing so that the person who has to fill in will have a reasonable idea of what's to be done and how to do it. Such written procedures need not be overly detailed or comprehensive.

3. Schedule work assignments far in advance. You'll be surprised how many peaks can be melted ahead of time simply by pushing anticipated routine work ahead on the schedule. Furthermore, when you know that Tom will be out on vacation at such and such a time, that Jack is planning to get married in June, and that your keypunch operator is expecting in October, you can plan fill-in assignments beforehand.

4. Build a backlog of substitute pinch hitters. Keep in touch with good employees who have left your employ to set up housekeeping or who are recently retired. Frequently you can call on them to step in at a moment's notice and with a minimum of instruction.

5. Set up an interdepartmental employee loan program to meet emergencies. Of course this can be done only if working relations between departments are good. But there's much to be said for swapping employees back and forth. It makes for a break in

monotony for the employees, too—provided they aren't made to feel like so much chattel.

6. Clean up as much work as possible ahead of known peak periods. Don't go into a month-end closing, for example, with a backlog of unfinished routine work. Carefully plan ahead of time the specific work assignments for the peak period. That way, each employee starts with a clean slate and with full knowledge of what's expected when the pressure is on.

Of course, you can always resort (with your boss's approval) to the employment of professional temporary people or to the extension of work into overtime for regular employees. The latter course of action is a dangerous habit to get into, however. Employees tend to take the overtime for granted and may resist future solutions to peak-period staffing that do away with it.

When requisitioning office machines, how can you be sure these machines will pay off?

A fancy new machine frequently has great eye, or gimmick, appeal. Or if the office down the floor has one, there's a tendency for you to want one for your department, too. For these reasons it's a good idea to look hard before you make a strong plea to your boss for that new machine. First, you might check the answers to these four questions:

1. How much does the machine really cost? Not just what someone said it cost, but the price of the model your office will need. Then, too, what will be the installation charge? The cost of operating supplies? The cost of maintenance?

2. Will your employees use it effectively? Are they capable of using it without further training? Will they like to use it? If you can get only one, will there be a squabble over who has priority for its use?

3. What are the machine's payoff characteristics? Will it save labor? How much? Will it produce more copies? Better copies? Can one person perform a complexity of jobs on it? How soon will it pay for itself in saved labor or supplies.

4. Is this machine what your office needs now? Will it fit into your existing paperwork system? Is its speed something that's nice to have but not absolutely necessary at this time? Will it be outmoded quickly?

What are the most likely accident hazards in offices?

More than half of all serious office accidents are caused by falls. The most common hazards are highly polished floors, a single unsuspected step just inside a door, unanchored rugs, wet or slippery stairs, poor lighting, extension cords, ladders, and wastebaskets.

Office people also have a penchant for cutting or bruising themselves on relatively simple equipment like paper cutters, scissors, razor blades, moving parts of typewriters and comptometers, electric fans, mail carts and dollies, and glass-top desks.

Office fires also take their toll. Watch out for employees who carelessly throw matches or ashes in wastebaskets, who smoke when using flammable typewriter-cleaning fluid or who use the floor for an ashtray.

What are reasonable office safety rules to enforce?

The American Management Association lists these as being especially applicable to office work:

1. Open doors slowly to avoid hitting anyone approaching from the other side.

2. Don't stand in front of closed doors.

3. Use the handrail when you go up or down stairs; don't carry materials so heavy or bulky that you have no hand free with which to grip the railing.

4. Don't tip back in swivel chairs.

5. Don't run or horseplay in the office. Don't play practical jokes.

6. Don't yank at file-cabinet drawers. If they're difficult to open, ask the maintenance department to repair them.

7. Never stand on the open drawer of a desk or file cabinet.

8. Never stand on chairs—especially swivel chairs—to reach something on a high shelf.

9. Don't leave drawers of a desk or file cabinet standing open.

10. To remove staples, use a staple remover only.

11. Keep razor blades and other sharp equipment in a closed container so that employees won't be cut while reaching into a drawer.

12. Keep drawers neat and orderly so that employees won't be accidentally stabbed by a pen or a pair of scissors hiding under a pile of papers.

13. When handling large stacks of papers, use rubber finger guards to eliminate the hazard of paper cuts.

To what extent can you
monitor personal telephone calls?

This may be no problem if your office has only a few telephones from which an unrestricted number of calls can be placed. If so, consider yourself lucky. Policing telephone calls invites snooping on your part, which often leads to embarrassment, if not hard feelings.

In today's society most people have come to take the telephone privilege for granted. They use the telephone indiscriminately in their own homes, so it's hard for them to feel that they're doing something wrong when they make free use of telephones in your office. This doesn't mean that you should make no attempt at all to control telephone use. When a dozen employees bang away daily on commercial telephones, the telephone bill will accelerate wildly. And, of course, such use ties up the telephone for business purposes and can also be a costly employee time waster.

One approach to telephone control is to ask the telephone company for a billing system that breaks out separate, identifiable calls and charges for each phone. In this way, calls can be traced back to the originator and billed. Of course, this practice does not halt incoming personal calls, which can be just as undesirable.

Probably the most effective approach to telephone control is to combine an appeal to fair play with a certain amount of hard-nosed checking. Try to set some acceptable standards for personal calls, such as (1) no charge for calls made within the area, (2) permission granted to call home when weather or business delays normal arrival, and (3) no criticism for incoming or outgoing personal calls that don't exceed five minutes each or for making no more than two calls per day. Admittedly, critics may ask why such calls should be permitted at all. The reason is that limited, reasonable usage seems better than unlimited, surreptitious usage. If you can arrive at a permissible standard, you also imply your prerogative to enforce this standard. You'll also feel freer to question anyone who is frequently on the telephone or who uses it for long periods of time. You can ask such users directly whether the call is personal or not. If the call is not a personal one, there's no reason why you can't press for details about it.

Nevertheless, it's hard to avoid the fact that it is difficult indeed to enforce tight telephone restrictions without appearing like a martinet to your employees.

supervisory word power

Office employee. A white-collar worker who performs work typically of a clerical nature in an office (as opposed to a manufacturing area) of an industrial or a commercial enterprise or an institutional establishment.

Data processing. Transmission and manipulation of data, paperwork, records, and other information essential to the production and distribution of goods and services. It may be accomplished manually, mechanically, or electronically or by some combination of these.

Records retrieval. The methods and techniques used to locate and recover data, documents, and information from filing systems, libraries, and other records storage or retention areas.

Forms control. An administrative control technique for standardizing, coordinating, and minimizing the number of forms needed to carry on properly the functions of the organization.

Word processing. A specialized aspect of data processing that involves a systematic approach to producing written communications (letters, forms, reports, and so forth) by integrating human skills with highly complex, automated equipment.

Other Important Terms in This Chapter

career orientation
systems and procedures
third profit
work itself

reading comprehension

1. How likely is it that a stenographer's duties in an office in Missouri would be similar in fundamentals to those of a stenographer in a plant in Massachusetts.

2. Compare the morale of white-collar workers with that of blue-collar employees.

3. Which is more important to a white-collar employee: status or pay?

4. How might a supervisor minimize the monotonony of some office jobs? When should the supervisor exercise caution in making changes?

5. What are the key ingredients of a job enrichment or "work itself" program?

6. Would you agree that most younger women are not seriously concerned about the value of their work? Why?

7. What is your reaction to the standards recommended for typing and shorthand speeds as opposed to what is generally acceptable to employers?

8. What would make a file clerk tend to save papers and records that are really of little potential use or value?

9. What sort of problems do peak work-load periods cause in an office? How can they be minimized?

10. What kind of accident accounts for most of the serious office injuries?

supervision in action

THE CASE OF THE BULLETIN BOARD NOTICE. A case study in human relations involving supervision of office employees, with questions for you to answer.

When Lora Bland was hired as a supervisor by the claims section of the Granite Surety Corporation, she wanted to make a name for herself. Lora came to the company with broad experience in accounting procedures, and it wasn't long before she had demonstrated her knowledge of the field. In six months Lora streamlined the tabulating procedures and completely eliminated the need for making hand entries on client file cards. Ms. Bland was often heard to say, "Where there's a machine, there's a better way."

Part of Lora Bland's improvement program for the claims office was a general sprucing up of the work areas. She persuaded the general manager to repaint the office, install brighter lights, and purchase more modern furniture. The office certainly looked a lot better than it ever had, but some of the old-shoe comforts were lost in the process. Ms. Bland frowned on anything that implied disorder. As a result, she ordered the stenographers to get rid of any pictures formerly pasted on the inside of their typewriter cubicles. Desks had to be cleared every night before going home. But even this wasn't enough.

One day, employees reported to work and found a notice on the bulletin board. It read, "The company has purchased special wax-impregnated dusting cloths. Each employee will be issued a fresh cloth every month. Beginning this week, each employee will wipe down all furniture and woodwork at his or her workplace on Friday before shutting down for the weekend."

That afternoon at 4:15 p.m., Lora Bland was visited in her office by a committee of three employees. "Ms. Bland," said one of the employees, "we feel we speak for the rest of the office when we say we think your request that we polish furniture is completely unreasonable. After all, we're employed to perform clerical duties—not menial work."

1. Do you think the employees' complaint was reasonable? Why?

2. What do you think of Ms. Bland's program for improvement of office conditions?

3. In what way could Ms. Bland achieve her objectives and still avoid human relations problems with her employees?

enriching your viewpoint

So that you may enlarge your knowledge of office and clerical work management, the following sources are suggested:

Bassett, Ernest D., and David G. Goodman, *Business Filing and Records Control,* South-Western Publishing Company, Incorporated, Cincinnati, 1974.

Correspondence Management, Records Management Handbook FPMR 101-11.2, Federal Stock Number 7610-187-3858, General Services Administration, National Archives and Records Services, Office of Records Management, 1973, U.S. Superintendent of Documents. Washington, D.C.

"Designing the Mailroom as a System," *Administrative Management,* March 1978, pp. 36–47.

Gottheimer, Debra, "What's Wrong With This Office?," *Administrative Management,* June 1977, pp. 30–32.

Graham, Ben S., "Paperwork Simplification," in Lester R. Bittel (ed.), *The Encyclopedia of Professional Management,* McGraw-Hill Book Company, New York, 1979, pp. 863–867.

Grossman, Lee, *Fat Paper: Diets for Trimming Paperwork,* McGraw-Hill Book Company, New York, 1976.

Guide to Records Retention Requirements, rev. January 1, 1975 (GS 4.107/A:R 245/975), General Services Administration, National Archives and Records Services, U.S. Superintendent of Documents, Washington, D.C.

Heyel, Carl (ed.), *Handbook of Modern Office Management,* McGraw-Hill Book Company, New York, 1971.

Kleinschrod, Walter A., *Management's Guide to Word Processing,* The Dartnell Corporation, Chicago, 1975.

Martin, R. Keith, "Don't Overlook Clerical Productivity!" *Industrial Engineering,* February 1977, pp. 28–311.

Maynard, H. B. (ed.), *Handbook of Business Administration,* McGraw-Hill Book Company, New York, 1967, Sec. 14, "Office Administration."

Ripnen, Kenneth H., *Office Space Administration,* McGraw-Hill Book Company, New York, 1974.

Starting a Revolution in Office Efficiency: A Handbook of Word Processing Procedures, Equipment Data, and Conversion Techniques, Geyer-McAllister Publications, Inc., New York, 1973.

supervising engineers and the knowledge worker

Who are the "knowledge workers"?

They are the growing army of people who combine an advanced education with work requiring a high degree of mental effort such as analysis, reasoning, interpretation, and creativity. Their occupations cover a wide scope. Knowledge workers are engineers, scientists, researchers, planners, and technicians. They are librarians, editors, economists, market analysts, statisticians, data processing designers, programmers, and the like. They include, of course, doctors, lawyers, nurses, dentists, architects, and all other occupations generally regarded as professional. The real test of a knowledge job, however, is the degree to which it requires the incumbent to apply a specialized body of knowledge or information, usually acquired by extended study in colleges or universities, and considerable experience in that particular field.

What is the significance of this rise in knowledge workers?

Peter Drucker makes this point:

> Fifteen to twenty years ago manual workers were the central productive factor in this society. Today, in our society, and increasingly in **all** developed societies, the central cost factor—which is not quite the same as the central productive factor—consists of knowledge workers. These people do not work with their hands, do not use brawn or manual skills. They use concepts and theories.

Drucker believes that business profits cannot improve without an intense application of this "knowledge talent." And he insists that it is "information," not "technology," that diffuses through our economy at the faster rate today. Consequently, the engineer and the scientist, together with the vast body of technicians and others who apply specialized knowledge, must be made more productive if our society is to grow and improve.

In what way will the progress toward greater automation and computer applications affect the growth in the number of knowledge workers?

It won't do away entirely with blue-collar or routine clerical work, but it will develop an intense demand for highly skilled artisans and knowledge workers with advanced, specialized training. Figure 24-1 (adopted from one prepared originally by the International Labour Organization in Geneva, Switzerland) illustrates the trend. Automation has already hit hard at repetitive, strong-back, no-think jobs. At the same time it shifted much of the blue-collar factory employment to white-collar or service industries. Computers, the whiz kids of automation, then descended on almost every conceivable office or clerical operation. But, initially at least, the net effect was to create more jobs. The trend today, however, is toward (1) a leveling off of routine clerical work and (2) a growth in specialized, conceptual jobs to support computer activities and to serve in fields opened by technology, automation, and computerization. There is little doubt that Peter Drucker is correct: We are entering the age of the knowledge worker.

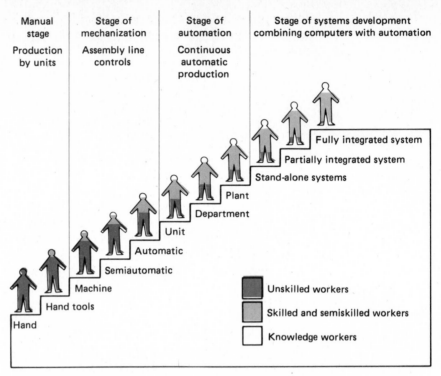

FIGURE 24-1. Gradual Increase in Percent of Knowledge Workers as Industrial Processes Progress From Manual to Automated and Computerized Systems.

To what extent does a higher level of education make a difference in the knowledge worker's expectations?

The higher the level of education beyond high school, the more the employee will put a premium on a job that offers (1) real challenge, (2) the chance to make a contribution to society, (3) the ability for self-expression, and (4) free time for outside interests. Furthermore, most people with college degrees do not believe that hard work will pay off. Even young people with master's degrees in management find themselves at odds with what business offers them. For example:

• Most organizations provide greater job security than these highly educated people want.
• On the other hand, most organizations expect greater conformity in behavior and acceptance of corporate goals and values than graduates are ready to give.

- Furthermore, organizations believe the ability to work with groups is more important than people with advanced degrees think it is.

As a supervisor of college-trained knowledge workers, then, you face the difficult task of trying to bring together organizational and individual goals. Your best bet is to look for some sort of trade-off. For example, you may have to give a little in demands for conformity of dress and behavior in return for exceptional job results. Or, you may have to provide more flexible working hours in exchange for unstinting dedication to the work to be done. As to the need to work with groups, some highly creative people may do their best work alone—and their interests should be accommodated as much as is possible. But for most organization members, the need to sacrifice some of their independence to the work group is so great that noncooperating individualists may be a luxury the organization cannot tolerate.

Between high and low performers among knowledge workers, are the expectations much different?

In some areas they are. According to a study of 730 engineers and engineering managers employed in aerospace and technology-based companies, conducted by Brigham Young University in 1975, poor performers—just as much as high performers—expect salary increases, challenging work, and more job freedom. The big difference lies in expectations of promotion to a managerial position or of assuming positions of great complexity. In actual fact, the high performers get their wishes fulfilled, while the poorer performers are disappointed.

These attitudes imply that supervisors are more likely to run into apathy and performance problems with their less effective employees. The danger would appear to be that supervisors will be called on to spend a disproportionate amount of their time counseling and motivating second-rate and third-rate employees. On the other hand, the high performers among knowledge workers tend to be self-starters and to be able to work effectively with minimum outside direction and stimulation.

How does the age factor affect motivation of knowledge workers?

According to the Brigham Young University study, the appeal of promotion falls off rapidly with advancing years. But the desire for job freedom, challenging work, and salary increases holds up

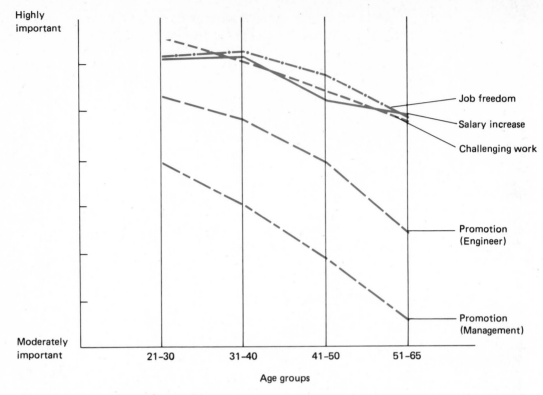

Highly
important

Job freedom

Salary increase

Challenging work

Promotion
(Engineer)

Promotion
(Management)

Moderately
important

21–30   31–40   41–50   51–65

Age groups

FIGURE 24-2. **Relative Importance of Various Kinds of Motivation to Engineers and Other Knowledge Workers as They Grow Older.** *From P. H. Thompson, J. Bowden, and R. L. Price, "What Motivates Engineers?", Mechanical Engineering, March 1975, pp. 40–47.*

almost as well for those in their sixties as for recent college graduates. (See Figure 24-2.)

How different are engineers, scientists, and other knowledge workers from other employees?

They are different from other employees in that they feel they are different. They believe that they are professionals and resent treatment that indicates they are thought of as ordinary workers. In a study performed for Esso Research and Engineering in the early 1960s, the average engineer was found:

• To view the job as interesting and challenging and to be proud of the field. The average employee does not have this viewpoint.
• To rate challenge, advancement, and salary as key factors of

the ideal job. There's not too much difference here, except that technically oriented people are more likely to expect to find these rewards at work—and to leave if they don't.

• To feel that the degree of professionalism of the job is not understood by either the company or the general public.

• To be an avid reader of employment ads and to be readily open to pirating overtures by other companies.

In what ways do scientists differ from engineers?

Engineers apply scientific information. Scientists develop this information. They usually have more advanced education than engineers do. More important, their viewpoint is more academic or theoretical; the engineer's is more practical.

Scientists are even more concerned than engineers about operating in a freewheeling way. For example, one frustrated manager laments: "They like to take coffee breaks whenever they want to."

Other distinctions are more troublesome. Observes one person who must deal with scientific personnel, "Our research and development people simply won't defer to another person's priorities or backlog. Even though the job they want done may seem fairly trivial, they want it right away. For example, a scientist may wait three months for a machine to be delivered. If it comes in at four o'clock Tuesday afternoon, it has to be running by 9 a.m. Wednesday. They make it seem that the whole project will go down the drain otherwise." Still another observer complains, "The main problem in the design of laboratories is pinning the research people down to what they want and getting them to relinquish some of their more exotic ideas." You'd better be prepared to accept the fact that the more highly educated the employees are, and the more intellectual and creative their work, the more likely they are to be touchy to deal with.

But are engineers really professionals?

The weight of opinion is that engineers are not more than partly professional, despite the fact that many states license them as professional engineers. If they were truly professional, goes one opinion, they would have a rounded balance of specialized training and experience, professional legal responsibility, professional personal relationships, and professional ethical relationships (qualities generally attributed to a professional). Another viewpoint says, "It depends on the engineer's attitude about responsibility to society. Some research engineers are outstanding in applying science to meet some objective, but then show only the technician's limited interest in what their endeavors actually do to people." The point, however, is that most engineers—and technicians—do consider their work professional. Regardless of the harsh judgment of others, they think they are a cut above rank-and-file employees. They respect their superiors only if the superior encourages them to display a disciplined—or professional—attitude toward their assignments.

One big problem with engineers stems from their great need to be right. William D. McGuigan, who has managed thousands of engineers, puts it this way:

> *Criticism of an engineer's ideas tends to be translated into personal criticism—of his intelligence, competence, standing in the community, and even his ancestry. Thus, particular care must be taken to minimize criticism, particularly in the initial stages when ideas are still in an intuitive stage. The desire to avoid being wrong may make engineers poor decision makers. One role of the manager of such people is to assume this responsibility, making it his neck that is out rather than theirs. Furthermore, engineers also tend to be critics themselves. Thus the very tendencies which make an engineer—to be meticulous, detailed, analytical—are the factors least needed by a manager of engineers—particularly of creative ones.*

What other kinds of employees might be thought of as professionals?

Webster defines a profession as "a calling requiring specialized knowledge and often long and intensive preparation. The so-called learned professions—theology, law, and medicine—all require intense, advanced, and specialized education; guided experience; and some form of licensing. However, many other occupations have acquired professional status: Teaching is one of the more obvious. Accounting is another. Many people in technical occupations (such as laboratory technicians, draftsmen and draftswomen, and surveyors) are often thought of as professionals—even though not every professional stipulation is met in every case or to a full degree. In addition, many clearly definable occupations—such as traffic manager, purchasing agent, systems analyst, and training director—have tended to develop professional standards of practice. When jobholders adhere to high standards of responsibility—and maintain a high level of self-discipline—in the execution of their jobs, they may think of themselves as professionals and expect to be treated accordingly.

In what ways can hospital personnel be considered professionals?

Registered nurses (RNs) are, without doubt, professionals. Licensed practical nurses (LPNs) consider themselves professionals, too, although technically this may not be so. Laboratory technicians, because of their long training and the precise quality of their work, are usually granted professional status, also. But there's something unique about hospital and related health care work that tends to make all hospital employees feel that their work is professional. First of all, they assist, in one way or another, the most respected professionals of all—medical doctors. Second, the ultimate impact of their efforts, no matter how humble, on the health—even the very life—of human beings demands a sterner self-discipline than is required in most jobs.

What characterizes work as professional?

These four unique characteristics differentiate professional chores from administrative and managerial work:

Professional work is investigative in nature. Professional assignments always involve conducting investigations for the purpose of drawing scientific conclusions or solving technical problems. Obtaining and recording data, making analyses and computations, and similar activities (although they may be performed by a professional) are not peculiar to professional work. Such activities are characteristic of the work of nonprofessional technicians. Therefore, by definition, a person not directly concerned with drawing conclusions or solving problems based on technical investigations is not doing professional work.

Professional work requires individual contributions. A professional worker is primarily concerned with the execution of technical work and not primarily with planning, organizing and directing work carried out by others. Even though he or she may be a leader of a team or group attempting to reach a common objective, the professional will, nonetheless, be making a substantial part of the contribution personally and directly. In such a case, the other team or group members, both professional and nonprofessional, act as extenders or multipliers of the leader. In other words, professional technical persons are employed to carry out technical assignments, and any team or group that they lead or coordinate is brought together primarily to assist. The professional knowledge worker therefore differs from a managerial employee, technical or otherwise, whose position exists for the prime reason of organizing, directing, and controlling the work of others.

Professional work is not routine or repetitive. It does not follow a pattern or cycle, nor does it consist of specified duties and responsibilities as does the work of most managerial or administrative positions. Professional work consists of a series of assignments, each having a definite beginning and an end; and, in most cases, each is quite different from the others with respect to the steps taken in carrying it out and the end results achieved. Therefore, the professional position is neither defined nor limited by reporting relationships, or responsibility for resources—human, physical, or financial. Rather, it is defined and limited by the technical complexity of assignments carried out.

Increases in the importance and difficulty of professional work do not occur in discrete stages. Professional work covers a wide range of complexity. The range can be defined at one end by the type of assignment given a beginning, inexperienced engineer or scientist; and at the other end by the most complex kind of assignment given to a professional employee. Between these extremes, of course, assignments represent a progressive order of complexity in a more or less continuous spectrum.

In what ways can supervisors modify their approach when dealing with individuals who have a high sense of their professionalism?

Try any of these actions to suit the unique needs of professional employees:

1. Realize that professional employees want to be recognized as members of a profession. The professional employees are often career-oriented rather than company-oriented. They are usually individualists who are constantly evaluating themselves. They dislike regimentation and compulsion.

2. Ensure credit and recognition from top management for outstanding work and unusual accomplishments. Generally, professional employees are jealous of their own ideas and accomplishments. They understandably resent the supervisor who takes credit for their work. They want their unusual contributions to reach the attention of top executives.

3. Give proper dignity to the title of each position held by a professional employee. Job titles are important and should be consistent with the stature of the responsibilities involved. The

use of the term *engineer* in jobs that do not require formal technical training and professional status should be avoided. Similarly, such titles as Junior Engineer or Class B Planner have an adverse effect on the professional's morale.

4. Adopt liberal policies with respect to time off for personal reasons. Knowledge workers enjoy a work environment where clock-punching and other rigid controls are absent. They are frequently required to work extra hours to meet emergencies, or voluntarily spend a considerable portion of their own time coping with their employer's problems. This is considered part of the game. Accordingly, when personal matters require their absence, they expect to be allowed reasonable compensating time off.

5. Encourage knowledge workers to take part in the activities of their professional or technical societies. Since stature in the profession is important, professional interests should be promoted at every opportunity.

What is it that knowledge workers are most likely to complain about?

The typical knowledge worker resents being asked to do what he or she considers subprofessional work—routine work of a technician or clerk. The knowledge workers also feel that their salary is determined more by seniority than by merit, and they resent this. Furthermore, they dislike being regimented and believe they should be allowed to manage themselves—at least to a reasonable degree. *Machine Design* magazine has observed that engineers, for example, claim they need more technical and nonprofessional help—ranging from draftsmen and draftswomen and technical writers to clerks and typists; they would like management to better define project and company goals; and many complain that communications are inadequate on scope, planning, and progress of their projects.

What do supervisors find most wanting about knowledge workers?

Typical criticisms are: "They lack experience, common sense, and maturity." "They lack practical knowledge of market needs and company problems." "They are technically strong but naive in the realm of business practicality." Supervisors may also say: "They don't keep abreast of their field" or, worse still, "They don't have the ability to determine when a job is complete." If you are aware of these tendencies, you can avoid being taken by surprise when professional performance doesn't measure up to your expectations.

Scientists and paperwork: any problems?

C. Guy Suits, former vice president and director of research, General Electric, Schenectady, says:

> In a research program, we have found that the requirement of reports on a calendar basis is unrealistic. The results of scientific research investigations do not emerge with chronological regularity. There may be no result for five months, and a jackpot a day later. Any ingenious researcher can produce a 1-inch-thick report each week, if required. But he may have time for little else, and most of his reports will be extremely dull reading. A better plan, we feel, is to require reports only when there is something to report, regardless of the calendar. The reports that are written on this plan are worth reading.

Another authority has this to say on the subject:

> Young scientists tend to be unaccustomed to paperwork because at the university they generally had to do things themselves. Worse still, they may even believe that anything the technical services can do, they can do better. In getting up their reports, for example, they may want help from the drafting department. But they are hard to satisfy because they feel superior to anyone in the drafting department. If they are senior scientists, you may have to tolerate it. But usually they can gently but firmly be persuaded that the drafting department's suggestions may have some merit.

Control of the progress of scientific work is difficult. Apparently, excessive paperwork won't make your job any easier. Day-to-day or week-to-week personnel contact and discussions are probably more productive.

How can you keep researchers and engineers from carrying their projects past the point of no return?

Research in any field, social or technical, is largely unpredictable. Progress, furthermore, is made in small steps. And research personnel, by their very nature, are eternally hopeful and optimistic. Be prepared to listen to the plea for just $1,000 more or just one more week's work or just one more something to clear up the difficulties that seem to be bogging down progress. It will take not only good judgment but courage as well, on your part, to decide to abandon a project after considerable time and money have been spent on it. Therefore, be comforted by the generally accepted fact that between 50 and 90 percent of all research projects come to no useful end. It obviously makes a great deal of difference, however, whether the 50 or 90 percent is dropped after $1,000 has been spent or after $100,000 has been spent.

Engineering and other technical projects, while more definitive, often present the same sort of problem to the manager. The main danger here lies in the tendency of the engineer to broaden the scope of the project. Firm goals and specific budgets that are agreed on at the start seem the best way to avoid undeserved prolongation of engineering projects.

How closely should research people be supervised?

Most experienced managers believe that supervision of research people should not be too close. One missile scientist, for example, defined what the supervisor should do as "just leave me alone." Scientific personnel seem to respond best to colleague authority. That is, they want their work approved by other scientists as well as by the supervisor. Despite this preference, many authorities still believe that closer supervision is necessary to prevent scientists from straying too far afield. This approach, however, is most effective where scientists are engaged in development work rather than in exploration of new fields.

Happily, the true professional is basically self-regulating. A supervisor, therefore, need not necessarily know more than the subordinate scientists do—or bear down continually on them. The supervisor should function as a catalyst, a bridge to higher management, a coach, or even a critic. But if you function as a warden or a turnkey, the professional resents, rather than respects, both the concept of supervision and the person who supervises.

How much control of time and workmanship should you exert over employees who perform engineering or development work?

The hourly cost of engineering and creative work is typically very high. It is best controlled not by excessive personal supervision but by the maintenance of a few simple tabular records. For example, project cost control should compare hourly inputs with those in the original estimates. A continuing record should be kept of nonproductive time that accrues to individuals because of the failure to assign them to specific projects. Work sampling studies, which make random observations of what engineers, designers, and researchers actually do in the course of a week, often reveal that more than 25 percent of the knowledge worker's time is nonproductive for one reason or another. (See Chapter 27 for a discussion of work sampling.)

As to quality of work, it is just as important to establish quality standards for the knowledge worker as for manual, routine, or clerical work. Many engineering organizations maintain detailed checklists of design items that must be inspected and verified to prevent errors and omissions. Standards typically include dimensioning, lettering, preparing title blocks, and procedures for issuing drawing numbers.

What's the best way to keep younger knowledge workers interested in their work?

Impatience characterizes young knowledge workers. They want to make their mark fast. So it's important to get across to them in a challenging manner the idea that big achievements rarely come easily or quickly. Point out that the little successes are essential. Show that they in turn become the foundation on which reputations are built and from which more important tasks can be attacked.

A variety of job assignments, including job or project rotation, also keeps a job from becoming dull. While it's natural for some individuals to want to move ahead immediately to more difficult assignments, under proper guidance they can continue to learn and to gain versatility by working on a number of jobs that are essentially of the same complexity. This way they gain breadth, if not depth.

Probably the greatest offense to guard against when dealing with younger specialists is to reject ideas out of hand. You must listen—and listen objectively—to their suggestions. Avoid being overcritical. You want to nurture an inquiring mind with a fresh approach. You'll discourage it quickly if you revert too often to "We've tried that before and it won't work here."

One sure way to disenchant young college graduates is to flagrantly misuse their talents. Expect them to do some routine work, of course. But don't make their daily work just one long series of errands. This includes such break-in assignments as performing routine calculations, digging up reference material, or operating reproduction equipment. One large manufacturing company recently interviewed a number of promising engineers who had left them. The company found that the overwhelming complaint was that the company not only did not provide work that was challenging but also expected far too little from them in the way of performance.

As a sidelight to this, it is important not to overselect engineers or other technical people for your department. If the nature of your work is such that you can't keep good personnel working near their capabilities, they are almost certain to get jaded. Overstaffing, too, can lead to the same kind of problem. Keeping good knowledge workers waiting around for assignments to materialize frequently results in boring, unproductive idleness. Most technically oriented departments would probably function better with too few employees than with too many.

What is the best communications pattern to encourage among knowledge workers?

It should be free and open and encouraged to take place at the lowest possible level. Knowledge workers should feel free to consult other workers across organizational lines. Informal groups develop from these contacts, and this fosters cross-fertilization of ideas and innovation. Often the best solutions to problems come from these informal communications channels.

Should you handle the nonprofessional hospital employee differently from RNs, for example?

Supervising hospital personnel presents a delicate problem. Some of the personnel are undeniably professionals; others merely think that their work is professional. The true professionals are typically granted certain status and privileges. When you withhold these conditions from the nonprofessional staff, you tend to demoralize them, or at least to lessen their dedication—a dedication that is so badly needed. On the other hand, things can get out of hand if housekeeping employees for example, refuse direction on the basis of their "professionalism."

In the main, it would appear better to lean a little in favor of too much recognition of rank-and-file employees than to reveal an attitude that judges their work to be routine or, worse still, menial. For that reason the word *dedicated* occupies a special place in describing the work of hospital employees. It tends to place their efforts above those of people employed in other industrial or service occupations without, at the same time, leading these employees to demand or expect status and privileges equal to those of the recognized professionals on the staff.

Conversely, experience has shown that registered nurses and technicians sometimes want all the status associated with professionalism without wanting to assume their share of its self-discipline and responsibilities. For example, the practice of tipping nurses and presenting them with gifts has tended to detract from their professionalism. Pervasive as the practice is in hospitals today, it is not consistent with a policy of equal treatment of all patients regardless of income, reputation, or disposition. The rule of thumb for the true professionals might be to treat them with full respect for their status but at the same time to let them know you expect the ultimate from them in dedicated service.

What criteria should be used when appraising the performance of knowledge workers?

One guideline has been provided by the National Society of Professional Engineers (2029 K Street, N.W., Washington, D.C.). It cautions, however, that evaluations are essentially a matter of judgment and not a matter on which there can be hard-and-fast rules about how to rate. Nevertheless, the society suggests the criteria and possible weightings shown in Table 24-1. Most appraisal systems seem to be informal rather than formal. Typically, a manager observes the knowledge worker and discusses the work with him or her, judging output by projects completed successfully, process and product improvements, patents, and published articles. Some companies feel that productivity and performance should be measured over a period of years (perhaps three years) because so many projects take a long time. Shorter-interval rating could be misleading, they say.

Those companies that use appraisal forms most often include the following factors: attitude and cooperation, reliability, productivity, job and technical knowledge, judgment, planning and administrative skills, contribution of workable ideas, accuracy, adaptability, personality, quality of work, capacity for development, leadership ability, relations with others, drive, and ability to communicate.

What can you do to retain good scientific, engineering, and technical people on your staff?

You have to work hard at it because professional and scientific personnel are highly mobile. This means that unemployment among them is usually low, and they can often pick and choose their jobs. Private companies must compete for these profes-

TABLE 24-1. Appraisal Standards for Engineers

Criterion	Point Value
Job and technical knowledge	15
Application and productivity	10
Originality and initiative	20
Quality of work	15
Judgment, planning, and organization	10
Cooperation	3
Effective communication	8
Leadership	6
Attitude	4
Dependability and responsibility	10
Capacity for learning	9
	110 maximum

sionals not only with other companies but also with federal agencies.

The best approach is to offer (1) as much freedom of job direction as possible and (2) truly worthwhile and challenging assignments. Assuming that pay scales are equitable, this kind of employee will stick to an employer under even miserable working conditions if the task is interesting enough and the supervisor is understanding enough. The employee may appear to be discontented; knowledge workers are very able and vocal complainers. But they also can get so wrapped up in their work that you couldn't persuade them to leave even if you wanted to.

Are the management mind and the engineering-scientific mind likely to be at odds?

Yes. Their viewpoints tend to be much different. According to Herbert Wissman, former manager of education and training for American Motors, engineers (and other highly trained, often socially conscious people) tend to see management as measuring results in dollars only, having little depth of knowledge, and oversimplifying problems. Engineers find it hard to grasp that management must often act quickly and on the basis of limited knowledge. Ideally, engineers would like to live in a world where thoroughness is the principal criterion. Management, on the other hand, must always face up to the profitability problem.

Wissman suggests that you might bring your views and those of your engineers closer together by explaining the reason behind your decisions. Intelligent and well educated as they may be, many engineers do not extend their vision beyond their immediate project. Consequently, they remain uninformed and naive about the facts of business life unless you take the initiative.

What about advancing people who are good at their specialty, but have poor management potential, into the managerial ranks?

Some companies handle the problem by rewarding outstanding researchers and other specialized knowledge workers with a two-track promotion plan. One track is for those who want, and have the potential, to advance by the management route; the other is for those who want to stick to research. The idea is that persons who want to devote their talents to research can still achieve the same pay and status as the persons who go into supervision and management. Even if your company does not follow this plan, it is probably better in the long run to keep good researchers researching than to advance them into management echelons if their personalities and inclinations are not suitable.

Task force or project assignments: How do these affect supervisors of knowledge workers?

It puts great demands on the supervisors to coordinate one set of specialized skills or knowledge with several others. In medical research, for example, a parasitologist may have to work effectively with a tissue specialist. On a mechanical design project, a metallurgist may have to work with structural, aeronautical, and chemical engineers. On an urban development project, economists, sociologists, and behavioral scientists may have to work together with land-usage engineers, planning specialists, and architects.

Leadership of such interdisciplinary teams requires a unique balance. On the one hand, the leader will extract the greatest contributions and cooperation from the participatory approach. On the other hand, the leader must also exert firm progress and cost control to keep team members focusing on the project's objectives and scheduled completion date.

The situation is complicated further because members of task forces often are assigned only temporarily to a particular project. They owe their more permanent allegiance to managers of the specialized departments from which they have been detached. Thus, knowledge workers find themselves torn between two bosses and two sets of standards. There is no easy solution here.

The project supervisor must recognize this possibility and maintain a flexible approach to minimize its effect.

Where does the so-called matrix organization fit in?

The matrix organization is closely associated with special projects, task forces, and committee work. It presumes that each group of specialists is organized in a separate, but typical, line organization. You can picture this part of the matrix as a series of vertical organizational chains hanging from a clothesline. The other part of the matrix (the horizontal segment) occurs when one or more project managers are given authority to use the time of a number of different specialists. These projects managers come in horizontally from the left side of the clothesline to pick out from each vertical organization the particular specialists needed. The matrix (or grid) has the net effect of putting each specialist into a square from which he or she looks (1) upward to the manager of the specialized organization and (2) sideways to the manager of the project to which he or she is assigned.

Matrix organizations are becoming increasingly popular since so many modern problems need solutions that stem from many sources rather than a single one. Matrix organizations are most commonly found in engineering, research and development, planning, and investigational work.

The matrix organization, however, is by no means the only way to organize knowledge workers. Whatever the organizational form may be, its purpose should be to bring these informed people together to get jobs done, not to classify jobs and establish barriers between zones of authority and responsibility. The most effective organizational groups for these people are often the informal ones set up by the knowledge workers themselves.

supervisory word power

Knowledge worker. A person who applies specialized knowledge or information, usually acquired by extended study and considerable experience, to an occupation that requires a high degree of mental effort such as analysis, reasoning, interpretation, and creativity.

Professional.　A person whose occupation requires highly specialized training and experience, legal responsibility—such as a license to practice the occupation—and prescribed standards of performance and ethics.

Scientist.　A person whose occupation is concerned with the development of information based on a study of the facts, truths, and laws that define the arrangement of the physical and material world.

Engineer.　A person who applies scientific information to the design, construction, or use of machinery and equipment.

Technician.　A person skilled in the application of a particular art or trade or of one of the engineering or scientific disciplines.

Other Important Terms in This Chapter

interdisciplinary teams
licensed practical nurse (LPN)
matrix organization
professional work
project teams
registered nurse (RN)
task force

reading comprehension

████████████　　1. In what ways do engineers and other knowledge workers think they are different from ordinary workers?

2. If knowledge workers are so jealous of their professional status, does that mean that managers can exert no control over their performance? Explain.

3. What is it that distinguishes professional work from nonprofessional work?

4. If a choice had to be made, would a professional tend to defend the profession or the employer most vigorously? Why?

5. Compare a knowledge worker's attitude toward the length and regularity of the hours of work with that of, say, a clerk in a large office.

6. If a knowledge worker balked at being asked to perform regularly subprofessional work like filing correspondence, would it be a good idea to insist on the assignment? Why?

7. Why should a supervisor want to bring to a conclusion a knowledge worker's research project just when the individual wants to continue it until it is certain the best solution has been reached in the research?

8. Contrast the supervision considered ideal for a knowledge

worker with that considered necessary for an assembly line worker.

9. To what extent does it make sense to consider noncertified occupations professional because of the professional demands of the work? Give some examples.

10. Engineers, scientists, and technicians from a number of disciplines in an electronics research firm organized in a matrix structure are being assigned temporarily as needed to project managers. What are two difficulties the project managers might encounter?

supervision in action

THE CASE OF THE MISSED DEADLINES. **A case study in human relations involving knowledge workers, with questions for you to answer.**

John B, a project leader, supervises a group of three mechanical engineers. Their mission is to redesign a gear track for a motion-picture projector in which Teflon gears are to be substituted for bronze ones. When John was first handed the assignment from the chief engineer, he called his group together. He explained that the new design would have to conform to a new set of parameters. For example, the new gear train had to be totally enclosed and dust-free and operate at speeds of more than twice the speed of the bronze ones, and the gear box would have to be interchangeable with previous models. Furthermore, this called for a crash program—the project was to be completed within three months. After the preliminary discussion, John proceeded to make specific job assignments. He asked Sabra to draw up a table indicating the range of Teflon gears available in stock sizes. He asked Tom to develop a gear-box design that would be readily interchangeable with existing and projected models. He asked the veteran in his group, George, to develop sketches for the new gear-train design.

At the end of the next week, John met with each of the engineers to check their progress. He found that Sabra had gathered all her information within a day or two and then had turned her efforts toward another project. Tom, on the other hand, had no designs to show and had spent only a few hours during the week talking to members of the production department about assembly specifications. The rest of the time he had spent on another urgent project. George had made a few preliminary calculations and then set the project aside in the belief that it would be next to impossible to develop a design to meet the new operating specifications using a synthetic material.

In speaking to each of his engineers at this time, John listened carefully and discussed the progress or lack of progress without criticism. In his own mind, however, he decided that the group would never meet the project deadline if he didn't set more rigorous timetables for each intermediate target. That Friday afternoon he laid out a schedule pinpointing what sort of progress would be expected from Sabra, Tom, and George by the following Friday. His secretary typed the schedule and distributed it to all three. The following Friday, when John met with each of the engineers to discuss progress, he discovered that none of them had made any significant progress during the week.

1. If you were John, what tack would you try now?

2. What could be some of the reasons why John's original approach did not work?

3. Was there anything fundamentally wrong with his follow-up approach? Why?

4. Why didn't each engineer accomplish more during the first week of the project?

5. What could John have done to get the project moving faster in the first place?

enriching your viewpoint

To better understand the field of professionalism and those who participate in it, the following readings are recommended:

Bass, Lawrence W., *Management By Task Force: A Manual on the Operation of Interdisciplinary Teams,* Lomond Books, Mt. Airy, Md., 1975.

Cook, C. F., "Troubled Life of the Young Ph.D. in an Industrial Research. Lab," *Research Management,* Vol. 18, May 1975, pp. 28–31.

Diehl, Peter, and John R. Howell, "Engineering Teams: What Makes Them Go?" *Mechanical Engineering,* May 1974, pp. 25–29.

Drucker, Peter, "The New Knowledge Worker," *Bell Telephone Magazine,* September/October 1971.

McAleer, William K., "Engineering Management," in Lester R. Bittel (ed.), *The Encyclopedia of Professional Management,* McGraw-Hill Book Company, New York, 1979, pp. 348–353.

Rueth, Nancy, "Special Report: The Mechanical Engineer: An In-depth Profile," *Mechanical Engineering,* March 1975, pp. 24–47.

Schulz, Rockwell, and Alton Johnson, *Management of Hospitals,* McGraw-Hill Book Company, New York, 1976.

Seiler, Robert E., *Improving the Effectiveness of Research and Development,* McGraw-Hill Book Company, New York, 1965.

Silverman, Martin, *Project Management,* John Wiley & Sons, Inc., New York, 1976.

managing work

Supervisors are judged by their ability to get employees to perform the organization's work. Accordingly, this part sets for the reader a number of task-oriented objectives:

• To become proficient at work design so as to be able to make job content and environment more attractive and job incumbents more effective.

• To be able to convert overall company plans into specific job assignments and departmental work schedules.

• To observe and measure work processes and job methods in order to simplify work flow and improve job efficiency.

• To gain an understanding of factors that contribute to poor quality and be able to motivate employees to higher standards of workmanship.

• To develop and administer work and cost standards so as to raise the levels of departmental productivity.

• To comprehend the way in which a management information system (MIS) and computer technology operate and use both to strengthen planning, communications, and controls in your department.

THIS IS GOING TOO FAR!

WORK SWEET WORK

25
job design and enrichment

What is a job?

It is the task, duty, or chore assigned to one individual. It is the smallest unit of work performed by one employee in a particular unit, section, or department. Within a unit there may be many similar, almost identical jobs—such as the job of a filing clerk, keypunch operator, welder, pipe fitter second class, journeyman machinist, bench assembly hand, textile spinner, salesperson, bus driver, checkout counter clerk, and bank teller.

A job may be called a position or an occupation. The fourth edition of the *Dictionary of Occupational Titles*, published in 1977 by the Employment and Training Administration of the U.S. Department of Labor, lists 20,000 different occupations. To illustrate how narrowly a job may be defined, this volume uses a nine-digit code for each occupation. Thus, a "boot and shoe side laster" who cements the last is designated 690.685.358; the laster who staples the last is 690.685.632!

Who decides how big or small a job should be?

████████████ This is a management decision, but it usually is carried out as a joint process. One or more specialists help the manager or supervisor make the decision. In a manufacturing plant, for example, an industrial engineer may provide the initial job design. In an office, a systems and procedures specialist may prescribe the job dimensions. Or the professional advice may be furnished by someone from the personnel department like a job analyst. Usually, however, a job just evolves as a company or an organization grows. As a particular job gets too big for one person to handle, it is divided into smaller, more specialized jobs. Later on these jobs may be fine-tuned—slightly reduced, enlarged, or modified in some way to best fit the organization's needs. A supervisor can make the most effective contribution to the design of a job in this fine-tuning stage.

What is meant by job design?

████████████ *Job design* is simply the process of dividing work into units that one person will be asked to carry out. Often called *work design,* it is the process of defining what a job should be. When existing jobs are reshaped in any way, the process may be more accurately called work or job *redesign.*

On what basis are jobs designed?

████████████ Two ways: to fit the process and to fit the people who must perform the jobs. Back in the days of scientific management, the aim was to design jobs that most perfectly supported the movement of the product or service as it was shaped by the manufacturing or administrative process. The ultimate idea was to have a machine do the work. When this couldn't be done, the job and the person were made to function as much like a machine as possible. This method of job design—the process-centered approach—was effective for a number of years. It wasn't particularly good for people, but it was good for efficiency.

Gradually, job design has acquired a greater and greater people-orientation. People aren't machines. They can never do what a machine can do as well as the machine can do it. But people can do an incredible number of things that machines can't do. People can think better. They can make changes more easily and faster. They are more flexible. They don't have to be programmed. People can solve problems more creatively, and they can make decisions based on information that only human beings can sense and consider. When job design takes this into account, it is called the people-centered approach.

Which approach to job design is better: the process-centered approach or the people-centered approach?

Neither—although the people approach was given so little attention for so many years, it still needs a lot of catching up.

Jobs are the means for getting work done, for helping an organization meet its goals. If a brass foundry, for example, has to make 6-inch gears, someone performing a job or jobs must make the pattern, put the pattern in the mold, fill the mold with sand, remove the pattern, lock up the mold, pour the molten brass into the mold, and shake out the mold after the metal has set. The design of each of these jobs must conform to the needs of the process.

On the other hand, thought must also be given to the person or persons who will perform these jobs. Is the job more challenging and more interesting if a single person performs the entire job cycle? Or would it be too fatiguing a job for one person? Or would the skill needed to make patterns be wasted on shaking out molds? The job designers—supervisors and specialists—must seek the best balance between process and people.

What limits the degree of people considerations in job design when the process or technical approach is used?

The extent to which:

1. The job is performed entirely by hand and at whatever pace is comfortable or attainable by the operator. Example: An assembler in a toy factory who puts together prefabricated parts to make a dollhouse.

2. The job is performed with the assistance of a machine, which dictates some of the conditions the employee must accept or maintain. Example: A stenographer who transcribes from a pedal-controlled dictating machine. The stenographer, who de-

pends on the machine for voice inputs and cannot control the speed while the machine is running, can control the process by starting and stopping the machine.

3. The job is largely machine-controlled, machine-paced, or both, and leaves very little room for people considerations. Example: A packer at the output end of an automatic box-making machine who catches the boxes as they come off the line and places them into cartons. The operator must keep up with the machine and can shut it down only in an emergency.

When the process approach is used, what process or technical factors must be satisfied by the job design?

Several process factors must be satisfied by the job, whether or not it is accomplished entirely by hand or by automatic equipment.

Product specifications. The finished product must be a certain size, shape, weight, and appearance. A customer who buys a refill for a ballpoint pen, for example, expects the refill to fit.

Process flow sequence. Whenever anything is produced or serviced, certain steps must be performed before other steps are performed. Roofers at a home construction site, for example, must wait until the frame and the rafters have been erected. An accounting clerk in the sales order department of a shoe company cannot prepare the customer invoice until after the order has been recorded and priced.

Time constraints. The way in which a job is done almost always depends on two factors: (1) how long it takes to do the job (even in an automated bakery it will still take from 30 to 40 minutes to bake a loaf of bread) and (2) how soon the customer or client wants the product or service. If a company has a policy of shipping everything within 48 hours, the job may be designed one way; if the company makes few commitments about delivery dates, the job can be designed another way.

Costs and profits. If cost is no object (for a product that has a high profit margin, for example), the job may be designed for maximum craftsmanship and quality. If the product has a low profit margin (so often the case with highly competitive items), the job may be designed to cut corners, to have a large machine input, and to put pressure on employees to get output at the sacrifice of quality.

What determines how efficiently the job will be designed under the process approach?

Three things: (1) the methods employed; (2) the tools, machinery, and computers used to perform the job; and (3) the arrangement of equipment and people.

The workplace layout (3) is especially critical, whether the job is hand-paced or machine-controlled. For jobs that are largely hand-controlled, the workplace design must go far not only in easing work flow but also in accommodating the physical aspects of human movements. Figure 25-1 illustrates a popular bench arrangement designed with the human body in mind. This approach typifies scientific management and the concept that the human body can be engineered somewhat like a machine. The engineering is soundly based on studies of human movement and body limitations. The studies were made in the early 1900s by Frank B. Gilbreth. In what he called motion study, each motion was broken down into its smallest element, a *therblig*. When this technique is brought completely up to date, it is called human factors engineering or biomechanics. Most contemporary equipment, ranging from automobile instrument panels to machine tools, is designed with this in mind. Chapter 26 offers more ideas about work methods and workplace design and their use in improving jobs by making them simpler, easier, and more efficient.

How does the people-centered approach to job design differ from the process-centered approach?

It strives for maximum employee involvement in the design of each individual's job. It does not ignore process considerations. Instead, it encourages employees to view demands and restrictions as problems they are invited to help solve. The way in which this involvement takes place has led to its having many names: job enlargement, job enrichment, and work design or, sometimes, work redesign. The big difference is that the people-centered approach stresses genuine participation by employees, singly or in groups, in making their work effective and their jobs more attractive.

The boon to supervisors in the people approach is that it focuses everyone's attention on the work itself (another term sometimes used). Supervisors aren't expected to be part-time psychologists or extraordinary leaders in seeking cooperation from their employees. It is the work that is examined, criticized, and restructured rather than human beings. The responsibility for these changes is no longer the sole burden of the supervisor but

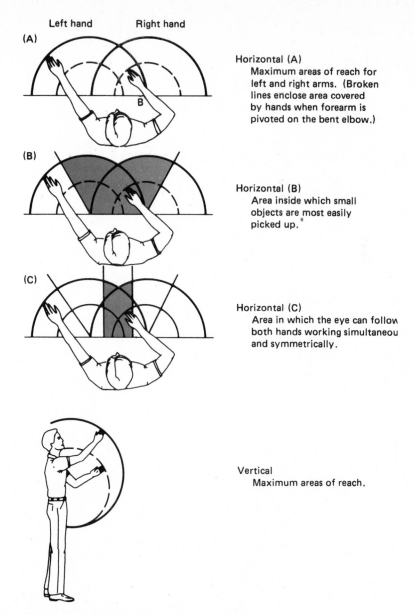

Left hand   **Right hand**

(A)

Horizontal (A)
Maximum areas of reach for left and right arms. (Broken lines enclose area covered by hands when forearm is pivoted on the bent elbow.)

(B)

Horizontal (B)
Area inside which small objects are most easily picked up.

(C)

Horizontal (C)
Area in which the eye can follow both hands working simultaneou and symmetrically.

Vertical
Maximum areas of reach.

FIGURE 25-1. Workplace Design for Easiest Reach. *From H. B. Maynard (ed.), Industrial Engineering Handbook, 2d ed., McGraw-Hill Book Company, New York, 1963, pp. 2–84.*

is shared by all those employees who are able to, and wish to, get involved.

See Table 25-1 for comparisons between the process-centered and the people-centered approaches.

TABLE 25-1. Job—and Work—Design Considerations

Process-centered Approach		People-centered Approach	
Degrees of process control:		Degrees of organizational restrictions:	
Low	Manual work	Low	Involves work of only one employee
Moderate	Machine-assisted work	Moderate	Involves work of group of employees within a department, section, or unit
High	Machine-paced work	High	Involves interfaces between departments or affects work of entire company, organization, or system

Process requirements that must be met:	Organizational requirements that must be met:
Product specifications	Output, quality, and cost goals
Process flow sequence	Job evaluation and wage schedules
Time constraints;	Motivational factors to be satisfied:
Process cycle time	Functional completeness
Promised delivery dates	Relationships with clients
Costs and profits	Skills and task variety
	Autonomy
	Direct feedback from work itself
	Opportunity for self-development

Areas affected by supervisor- and employee-initiated changes in job design structures which influence both approaches:
Work methods
Work tools and equipment
Support facilities
Workplace space and arrangements
Work schedules
Interpersonal relationships

When the people approach is used, what organizational restrictions must be recognized?

As in the process approach, there are basic realities to which the job designers must give thought. For example:

1. The extent to which changes in job content and methods will affect only the individual employee. Example: A stock clerk in a supermarket finds it more efficient to stamp prices on items while they are in the stockroom (rather than at the shelves) before bringing them into the store and placing them on the shelves. This decision affects no other workers and attains the results wanted: price-marked items on the appropriate shelves.

2. The extent to which job changes will be confined to a single department, section, or unit. Example: Employees in the purchasing department agree to rearrange their work so that order and posting clerks share some of the buying responsibilities. This work redesign fulfills the department's goals without interfering with, or affecting adversely, the quality and timing of its services.

3. The extent to which job changes will affect the entire company, organization, or system. Example: Machine shop employees and their supervisors wish to restructure their work in a way that will improve their operations but will require changes in plant scheduling procedures and a major revision in assembly and finishing operations.

Supervisors can usually encourage and assist job design in the first and second instances. It requires someone (or a special committee with plantwide knowledge and authority) to coordinate projects of the third kind.

What factors of job design are most likely to increase the motivational aspects of work?

Two authorities from AT&T (where more than 30,000 employees have been involved in work design), H. Weston Clarke Jr. and Richard O. Peterson, advise that there are six critical factors. When added to the job, these factors—or dimensions—help to meet organizational needs and thus to promote productive performance in support of departmental or organizational goals. These dimensions include:

A whole job from beginning to end. This functional completeness enables an employee to start his or her part of the work from scratch and see a definable product or service when the job is completed. Obviously, a worker in an auto factory cannot build a whole car. But it would be better if a wheel, for example, could be followed from the time it is uncrated until it is mounted on the car's hub.

Regular contact with users or clients.   The provision for an employee to have direct, consistent relationships with the person (department, regional office, or customer) who uses what is made or processed greatly enhances the individual's sense of being a person rather than an unknown cog in the machinery. Example: The person recording a sales order can call the salesperson for clarification if need be.

Use of a variety of tasks and skills.   The need to employ more than one skill and accomplish more than one task in getting the job done helps to relieve the sense of confinement and monotony. Example: An assembly worker uses a soldering iron as well as a wrench to join parts and to adjust critical mechanical tensions.

Freedom for self-direction.   This is the reality as well as the feeling of autonomy—that the employee can run the show as far as the job is concerned. In particular, it provides the opportunity to make choices about how the work will be done. Example: At the General Foods plant in Topeka, Kansas, autonomous work groups of from seven to fourteen members decide for themselves how to divide the work, screen and select new members, and counsel members who do not meet team standards.

Direct feedback from the work itself.   The employee can tell immediately by looking at the finished product or service whether it has been done right or wrong. The worker does not have to wait for the supervisor, an inspector, or an accounting report to get this information. Example: In one AT&T department, keypunch operators decided to schedule their own work, verify their own output, and keep track of their own errors. In work that had previously been judged deadend and boring, turnover was cut 27 percent, and 24 clerks found they could do what 46 had previously done.

A chance for self-development.   Work that requires employees to stretch their minds and sharpen their skills makes these employees more valuable to themselves as well as to the company. It demonstrates that the benefits from work need not be one-sided, that an employee's goals and a company's goals can mutually be satisfied.

Should distinctions be made among
the various kinds of people-centered job design?

Not necessarily, but it helps to add perspective to the ways that job design can be accomplished.

Job enlargement, for example, extends the boundaries of the job. First tried at IBM, the concept is to let manufacturing employees be responsible for the production step just before and just after the one they currently are doing. Thus, punch press operators might fill their own tote boxes and carry the punched parts to the next operation. It provides an opportunity to get away from a fixed place all day, a chance to converse for a minute or two with adjoining operators, and to feel that the job isn't limited to the second or two it takes to load the press and wait for the die to stamp out a part.

Job enrichment is an outgrowth of the job enlargement concept. It allows participating employees to perform job-related activities that are usually done by specialists. For example, the punch press operators might set up their presses with the die required for each new job, inspect their own work with gauges typically used by roving inspectors, and maintain their own output tallies.

Work simplification, as you'll see in the next chapter, stresses employee participation in what is essentially a process-centered approach to work design. Using this technique, employees are trained to think about their jobs much as engineers would think about their jobs.

Goal-oriented management is the approach developed by M. Scott Myers while at Texas Instruments Company in Dallas. It is not unlike "work itself," except that it emphasizes the need for supervisors to shift their thinking from "I am the boss who must think of everything" to "These are the goals we must reach together." Under the Myers system the supervisor leads (by "facilitating") and controls when necessary; employees are responsible for planning tasks and accomplishing them. Conversely, authority-oriented supervisors typically plan, lead, and control the doers, who have little say in planning how their work is to be accomplished. (See Figure 25-2.)

Autonomous work group is a group-centered concept originally developed at the Tavistock Institute of Human Relations in London, England, in work with coal miners. Its basic premise is that the social or human system and the technical or machine system are, in fact, one interlocked system. The goal is to build relatively independent work groups that can exert control over the technology (or process) involved in their work. This is the

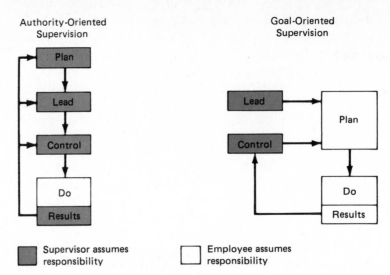

Authority-Oriented
Supervision

Goal-Oriented
Supervision

Plan

Lead

Control

Do

Results

Lead

Control

Plan

Do

Results

Supervisor assumes
responsibility

Employee assumes
responsibility

FIGURE 25-2. Job Design Differences Using Authority-Oriented and Goal-Oriented Supervision. *Adopted from a concept developed by M. Scott Myers,* Every Employee a Manager, *McGraw-Hill Book Company, New York, 1970, p. 99.*

approach used at the General Foods plant in Topeka, Kansas, and at the Volvo auto assembly plant in Sweden.

Work itself was the term initially used by AT&T for the program it now labels *work design.* It typifies the people-centered job design approach featured in this chapter because it looks for a balance among process demands, organizational goals and restrictions, and employee abilities and interests.

Where does the biggest payoff come from in job design?

For the company or organization it comes in greater output per employee; improved quality of product or service; and—often most important—fewer absences, lower turnover rates, and greater cooperation from employees.

For employees there can be little doubt that job design adds a number of attractive ingredients to their work. Experts say that it improves the quality of work itself. It offers greater freedom and flexibility and at the same time makes the work more challenging. Job design utilizes more of an employee's skills and does this more effectively than with traditionally frozen methods.

What steps are typically included in a formalized job design program?

David A. Whitsett, a noted consultant for work design programs, recommends these four steps:

Step 1. Make a feasibility study. This includes data on productivity, quality, absenteeism, turnover, and morale. Find out from employees what their interests might be in participating in such a program and from supervisors the degree to which they will lend their support.

Step 2. Plan the work design changes. This includes training of employees and supervisors in job analysis work simplification and job relationships, after which a large number of ideas must be generated by all the participants. The pool of ideas is then reviewed in a series of committee meetings. The best ideas are selected and the bugs are eliminated. Needed resources are specified: new tools, power, machinery, layouts. Costs are estimated. Implementation schedules are drawn up.

Step 3. Put the job redesigns into action. Some changes, such as those that affect only one employee or a single department, can be put into place in a few weeks. Those that have systemwide implications may take as long as three years.

Step 4. Measure the results. Job design should not be an exercise for the sake of making changes. It should produce tangible results—measurable improvements in output, quality, costs, and attendance and other, less measurable improvements in morale and quality of working life in the organization.

Must job design follow a carefully prescribed and supervised program?

That is the way to get the best results. But there is no reason a supervisor cannot introduce informally many job design improvement factors—both process- and people-oriented. The principles are there to be applied. Organizational support and guidance give a great boost, but supervisory initiative can go a long way toward improving job design at the departmental level.

How can supervisors get started in people-centered job design on their own?

Simply approach directly the employees you think might respond. Try this uncomplicated method.

With an individual employee

1. You ask: If you could remake your present job so that you still got the same amount and quality of work performed, what would you do?

2. The employee suggests: New methods, different tools, restructured workplace layout, rescheduled stop and start time, fewer or additional things to do, changed relationships with other employees, revised paperwork, innovative ways of doing anything related to the job.

3. Together you and the employee check the employee's ideas against

		OK	Not OK
a. Process constraints			
(1) Product specifications	_____	____	____
(2) Process flow sequence	_____	____	____
(3) Time constraints	_____	____	____
(4) Costs	_____	____	____
b. Organization requirements			
(1) Output and other goals	_____	____	____
(2) Relationships with other jobs	_____	____	____

4. Your boss approves, suggests modifications, or disapproves.

5. Together, you and the employee implement the job design plan. Example of job redesign for an individual: A chemical plant pumper now makes simple hookups to valves and piping, then operates on and off switches on pump motors. The operator asks to be allowed to replace leaking pipe fittings and pump packing as required, and to begin the shift an hour earlier on days when the work load is heavy. The company says it is okay to handle pump packing, but replacing pipe fittings would interfere with the job of pipe fitters in maintenance crews. Flexibility in starting time is approved.

With a small group of employees

Follow steps 1 through 5 as above, except that allowances must be made for considerable interactions and adjustments among employees at steps 2 and 5. They will need to find ways to make each person's ideal job structure fit those of other employees. Example of job redesign for a group: Five office employees now have separate jobs. A sorts and delivers mail and serves as receptionist, B files all day, C transcribes dictation from a machine, D types records and form letters, E types letters and reports. Their redesign plan calls for all employees to share the mail job and the reception duties on a daily rotation basis. Otherwise, they suggest a rotation plan in which an employee works a full week each on filing, transcribing, form typing, and letter typing. The rotation cycle for these four segments repeats every four weeks. The company says okay so long as the work is done on time with no increase in errors.

Caution. When a job-evaluation plan exists in your organization, job restructuring may affect wage rates. The possibility of a change in wage and salary structure should be checked out with your boss, the personnel department, or both, at step 4 and before implementing step 5.

Is everything about job design all good?

Far from it. Like almost every other managerial technique, job design has its good points and its drawbacks. They can be summarized this way:

Advantages	*Disadvantages*
Higher output per employee	Time taken in planning meetings
Better product or service quality	Time and production lost in making conversions
Less waste of materials	Cost of new tooling, machinery, and other facilities
Reduction in number of standby personnel required	Higher wage rates (not total payroll)
Less absenteeism	Longer training for new employees
Lower total costs	Greater work space requirements
Staff more flexible in meeting changes	Higher servicing and maintenance costs
Better use of employee talents	Less efficient use of production equipment because of its duplication at some work stations
Greater use of employee initiative	Requirement for high degree of managerial and supervisory commitment
Shorter, more effective communication routes	Potential resistance from labor unions
More attractive workplaces	Risk of program failure
Higher quality of working life	

supervisory word power

Job. The task, duty, chore, position, occupation, or work unit assigned by an organization to one individual to be performed routinely or repetitively on an hourly, weekly, monthly, or annual basis in return for wages.

Job design. Known as job redesign or work design; the process of dividing work to be done by an organization into carefully structured and defined individual jobs so as to foster productivity and appeal to the employees who carry them out.

Work itself. The concept that the nature and the design of the job that employees hold will influence employee performance and satisfaction as much as or more than the interpersonal motivation provided by supervisors and management.

Quality of work. The extent to which the work itself provides motivation and satisfaction because of the existence in the job design of functional completeness, contact with users, varied tasks and skills, autonomy, direct feedback from the work, and chance for personal growth.

Workplace design. The layout and arrangement of tools, equipment, and support facilities of the space assigned to an employee so as to make the job easier and less fatiguing.

Other Important Terms in This Chapter

autonomous work groups
functional completeness
goal-oriented management
human factors engineering (biomechanics)
job enlargement
job enrichment
machine-paced work
people-centered job design
process-centered job design
process flow sequence
product specifications
time constraints

reading comprehension

1. Lester Morton says he's responsible for job design in the plant. What would his main activity be?

2. What is the basic difference between process-oriented and people-oriented job design?

3. At a furniture manufacturer, wood frames must be assembled and the glue allowed to set for four hours before the facing can be fitted. What two constraints on process redesign do these requirements represent?

4. Give two reasons why supervisors are often enthusiastic about the "work itself" approach to job redesign.

5. Although Margaret is a firm believer in people-oriented job redesign, she turned down Janice's suggestion because of "organizational restrictions." What most likely caused her to refuse the suggested change?

6. Name at least five factors that, if built into jobs, usually help to motivate employees.

7. After some changes had been made in the job, an employee complained to the supervisor: "This is job enlargement, all right, but it sure isn't job enrichment." What did the employee mean?

8. Which main functions does the supervisor carry out under authority-oriented supervision? Which under goal-oriented supervision?

9. Why would a company bother with job enrichment or redesign in the first place?

10. The head of production for an insulation manufacturer turned down a job design program because "it had too many disadvantages." What are four that might have been mentioned?

supervision in action

THE CASE OF THE FARM EQUIPMENT REPAIR SHOP.   A case study in human relations involving job design, with questions for you to answer.

For years it had been considered your good fortune if you could get a job at J. O. Shepley & Sons Farm Equipment Sales Company. The work was steady, the pay was adequate, and the management was considerate. As the firm grew larger, however, the work did not seem quite so attractive to many of Shepley's employees. Especially in the service and repair shop, there was a disturbing amount of turnover. Part of this was attributed to the entry into the area of larger factories that were able to offer higher wages to the kind of all-around service mechanics that work at Shepley's developed. But among those who stayed at Shepley's, there was a certain amount of dissatisfaction that was hard to pinpoint.

The service shop was not unlike a very large garage. It was equipped with overhead cranes and hoists large enough to lift an engine out of a tractor for repair. There were several small lathes, welding rigs, and other machines available for making or repairing small parts. During the summer the shop doors were kept open. In the winter they were closed to keep out the cold, for heating was provided only by a few space heaters mounted on the shop walls.

Six mechanics worked in the shop under the supervision of Mrs. Clem, a daughter-in-law in the Shepley family. Mrs. Clem was about 50 years old and had been working in the service shop since she was a teenage stock clerk. Her big advantage was her knowledge of spare parts lists and location of manufacturer's replacement parts, which were kept in the company's rather extensive stockrooms.

Originally, the six mechanics had pitched in and worked together in groups of twos or threes on whatever job or equipment happened to be in the shop. With the growing variety of specialized farm equipment, however, Mrs. Clem thought that this approach was no longer efficient. Beginning a year ago, she had changed over the shop itself so that each corner was devoted to work on one type of equipment. The northeast corner was for tractors, the northwest corner for baling equipment, the southeast corner for mowers, rakes, and plows, and the southwest corner for planting equipment. In the center of the shop, Mrs. Clem placed the shop's machinery.

Additionally, the shop doors were kept closed now and a modern air-conditioning and heating system installed. Customers—farmers—who used to wander in and out of the shop while their equipment was being worked on now were asked to wait in a lounge in the showroom, where coffee was served and they could look at the new equipment for sale.

Under the new setup one mechanic was assigned to each of the four specialty shops, the fifth mechanic was assigned to operate the lathes and similar machines, and the sixth mechanic did all the welding. The specialty shop mechanics would perform all the work in their areas, but when lathe work or welding was required, they would bring the part to the center of the shop or have the welder roll the rig to their area, where the work would be performed.

The lathe operator and the welder seemed to like the new arrangement. The main trouble was with the specialty shop mechanics. "I can't understand it," said Mrs. Clem. "I've put all these people in business for themselves. And air-conditioned the place to boot. They ought to love it this way. Besides, it is the only way to keep up to date on what's been put into all this new-fangled farm equipment. It was too much to expect everyone to know all about every tractor, plow, rake, windrower, and manure spreader we have to work on now. Furthermore the old way was too slow, and our costs were too high."

1. What do you think might be bothering the dissatisfied mechanics?
2. What is good and bad about the new shop layout?
3. How do you react to Mrs. Clem's comment that since all the mechanics are in business for themselves, they ought to love the work?
4. Given the problem of the variety and complexity of the new farm equipment that must be repaired, how would you approach this problem to find a solution?

enriching your viewpoint

To explore this expanding new field, the following references are recommended:

Annual Report to the President and Congress, National Center for Productivity and Quality of Working Life, Superintendent of Documents, Washington, 1977.

Bittel, Lester R., *Improving Supervisory Performance,* McGraw-Hill Book Company, New York, Chap. 13, "Improvement Through Work Simplification," pp. 348–365.

Cemach, Harry P., *Work Study in the Office,* MacLaren & Sons, London, 1969.

Davis, L., and A. Cherns, *The Quality of Working Life,* 2 vols., The Free Press, New York, 1975.

Ford, R. N., *Motivation Through the Work Itself,* American Management Associations, New York, 1969.

Hackman, J. Richard, "Is Job Enrichment Just a Fad?" *Harvard Business Review,* Vol. 53, No. 5, September–October 1975, pp. 129–138.

Katzell, Raymond A., and Daniel Yankelovich, *Work, Productivity, and Job Satisfaction,* The Psychological Corporation, New York, 1975.

Nadler, Gerald, *Work Design,* Richard D. Irwin, Inc., Homewood, Ill., 1970.

Peterson, Richard O., "Human Resources Development Through 'Work Design,'" *Training and Development Journal,* August 1976, pp. 3–6.

Shaw, Anne G., "Motion Study," in H. B. Maynard (ed.), *Industrial Engineering Handbook,* 2d ed., McGraw-Hill Book Company, New York, 1963, Chap. 5, pp. 2-60–2-86.

26

CHAPTER ## job assignments and work schedules

If a person has a job to do, why must supervisors get involved in making assignments?

To be certain that each employee's efforts are placed on the most important or the most pressing work to be done. A job simply defines the scope of an individual's work. In most instances supervisors must also provide specific direction in the form of job assignments. If six employees hold checkout-counter jobs in a supermarket, for example, the supervisor must assign each employee to a particular register, by time of day or by day of week. Making assignments, then, becomes a matching process between jobholders and the work to be done.

Job assignments, or matches, tend to fall into three categories:

1. Repetitive, routine assignments. An employee who has received an assignment reports to the same machine and performs essentially the same work over and over again for weeks or months until the assignment is changed. Repetitive assignments are typical of work in mass production operations or large offices.

2. **Variable routine assignments.**   As the department work load rises and falls or shifts from one order or product to another, the jobholders may also be shifted from one workplace, machine, or assignment to another. The duration of the assignment may range from an hour or two to a day or a week at most. Variable assignments are by far the most common, especially in job shops and smaller offices.

3. **Special projects assignments.**   An employee or a group of employees are given highly specific, usually nonrepetitive assignments that require extended time to complete (from a week to a year or two), with a firm beginning and ending date. Such assignments are most common with knowledge workers or with artisans in developmental operations.

How restrictive will a job definition be in the assignments an employee will accept or can handle?

This will vary. The point of designing, defining, and evaluating an employee's job is to provide some kind of specialized divisions in the work force. Obviously, you want to put the employee with the appropriate job skills on each task to be done. You wouldn't expect a lathe hand, for example, to do the work of a toolmaker. On the other hand, you wouldn't want to waste too much of a secretary's talent on routine filing. People rightfully expect to work within reasonable limits of their job design, although they may accept extraordinary assignments temporarily or in emergencies. If these out-of-job-scope assignments are prolonged, however, you will run into trouble. The overqualified person will protest; the underqualified person may want a wage increase.

Which comes first, job assignments or the department's overall production schedule?

The production schedule comes first. It should guide the supervisor in making assignments. Said another way, each job assignment should be part of the supervisor's plan for meeting the overall schedule. Every assignment that steers an employee in another direction (a special cleanup job, an unanticipated request for a search of the files, or a nice-but-not-necessary embellishment) takes away from the overall schedule. These distractions may cause you to miss the schedule—or to add extra employees or overtime to meet the schedule.

Supervisors' major responsibility is to get out the work. Why should they be burdened with planning and scheduling?

███████████ Regardless of how much planning help supervisors may get from a company's centralized scheduling department, they just won't be able to turn out the work without detailed planning on their own part.

Turning out the work requires skillful planning right at the department level. Planning transforms master plans into day-to-day operations. Otherwise the supervisor will waste (1) time—because of avoidable delays; (2) materials—because of haste, spoilage, or unnecessary inventories; (3) machines—because they are not operated to their best capacity; (4) space—because of overcrowding and poor coordination of incoming supplies and outgoing production; (5) personnel—because employees are not fully occupied.

How far ahead should supervisors plan their work?

███████████ Long-range planning should be handled largely by those in higher levels of management. Your target is necessarily much closer at hand. The American Management Association suggests that supervisors spend 38 percent of their thinking time on problems that come up the same day, 40 percent on those one week ahead, 15 percent on those one month ahead, 5 percent on those three to six months ahead, and 2 percent on those one year from now.

Check your own habits. If you feel you're too busy to worry about anything but today, chances are you spend most of your time fighting fires that can be avoided by planning a week to a month ahead of time.

Typically, a supervisor is responsible for short-range (or tactical) plans; higher executives, for long-range (or strategic) plans. In military language tactical plans are those concerned with a particular engagement or skirmish or battle; strategic plans are those on which the major battle or entire war is based.

In what ways does good scheduling affect morale?

███████████ Employees have confidence in a supervisor who is willing and able to plan their work well for them. One of the worst destroyers of morale is the constant recurrence of emergency situations. Nothing breaks down security like continual crises. Employees don't like change. They fear it and would prefer that the company was run smoothly all the time. Poor planning adds to that fear and often hits them where it really hurts—in the pocketbook.

Good planning makes it possible for employees to go home at night fairly certain of the job they are going to work on tomorrow. It builds their respect for you. Employees want the feeling that they know what they're doing at the company. If you've shown them that you can schedule work smoothly, employees will be more willing to pitch in when the occasional emergency arises.

Isn't it true that scheduling often entails a lot of paperwork? Isn't there danger of your becoming just another pencil mechanic?

Records and reports are an essential part of planning and scheduling. But they shouldn't be overdone. Each record should stand the test of "Is this absolutely necessary?" and "Does it give me the specific information, and only that information, I need to plan this job?"

Keep your own schedules simple, just enough to give you what you need. A large wall calendar is a handy tool. Jot on it the critical items that are coming up in the days or months ahead. It not only acts as a reminder but also helps you keep your sights on the future.

Another useful device is a pocket notebook with a page for each day of the month. Try to make a habit of writing down in it those items that you must check from time to time. Put a flag in the notebook a few days before a shipment of supplies is expected, for instance. Then check beforehand to find out if the shipment will be delivered when expected. If it isn't, you've still got time to adjust your plans without waiting until the last minute.

Planning systems are sometimes based on the exception principle. What is it?

Under the *exception principle* of planning, a supervisor sets up a system of records and reports so that recurring problems are handled simply as a matter of routine. These are handled without the supervisor's getting into the picture at all. What the supervisor looks for are the exceptions to the routine. He or she acts only on those items that are unusual or involve change from day-to-day practice. (See pages 203–204.)

A supervisor of a pattern shop, for instance, who plans to have 50 forms completed each week during the current month would simply make a daily check of how many forms were finished. Each day the supervisor would enter the number on the calendar (or on a sheet of paper). Whenever the production fell, say, 10 percent below 50 forms, this would be noted as an exception that needed attention. The supervisor would then find out what action was needed to get the production back to normal.

Sound too simple? Most record systems are simple in principle. It's when you don't understand them that they get complicated. But even this simple system can warn you of impending trouble. Suppose the pattern-shop supervisor put another figure on the calendar each day—the number above or below the production scheduled for the month. If the company made only 49 forms each day, taken one at a time the situation wouldn't look bad. But at the end of ten working days, the company would be ten forms, or a fifth of a day, behind. This figure is large enough to stand out and would give the supervisor warning in time to step up production to 51 forms a day for the rest of the month.

Should you schedule your department to operate at 100 percent capacity?

No. This is a poor practice because it leaves no cushion for emergencies. It's best to call on your past experience and plan only for short periods at 100 percent. No department can run for very long without some unforeseen emergency arising. These emergencies may be only unexpected absences or special rush orders. But you must leave room for them.

What happens if you underschedule your staff?

Exactly what you would expect: They find a way to stretch the job to fill the time. One way to minimize this is to have a backlog of second-priority jobs on tap for assignment. If regular orders are slow coming in, you can catch up with some of the work that often needs to be done but is not allowed for in the master schedule. These assignments might include cleaning out files in an office, sorting and discarding obsolete inventory in the stockroom, or any kind of general cleanup.

It should go without saying that if this condition persists, some employees must be transferred or laid off.

Can you expect as much from employees when they work overtime, or should you make an allowance for it in the schedule?

██████████ You should probably expect a 5 to 10 percent drop in productivity. Authorities differ on this one, probably because there has been very little definitive research on the subject. For example, studies conducted years ago by the Bureau of Labor Statistics showed that employees in daywork industries could work 10 hours a day, 6 days a week, on daywork (where standards are looser and not so measured) without loss in efficiency over the 8-hour day and 5-day week. However, two industrial engineering authorities offer disclaimers. Gerald Griffin (writing in *Industrial Engineering,* July 1969) flatly states that efficiency among incentive workers drops during overtime because of stress and fatigue. Gene Shue offers a documented study of dayworkers in a printing plant to show that when their $7\frac{1}{2}$-hour day, 5-day week was stretched to 6 days, efficiency dropped by 4.8 percent. My own impression is that this figure is low, and a 10 percent figure is more reliable for scheduling purposes.

Must you make allowances now for the four-day week?

██████████ With the growing emphasis on an individual's efficient use of leisure time, more and more companies will schedule employees on a 4-day week. Techniques will vary, with the target of reaching a 35-hour or 40-hour week in the shorter span. Moonlighting on a second job will be common, because about 10 percent of such employees are more interested in additional income than in extra leisure.

The 4-day week has attractions in many industries where shift scheduling has been complex and tiresome when employees were scheduled around the clock, 7 days a week, and a 5-day workweek was still desired. Figure 26-1 shows a unique but broadly applicable scheduling scheme especially suitable for service employees in hospitals. It has been used successfully at a large health center to schedule the activities in the nursing, food service, housekeeping, and plant operations departments.

What kind of special problems should you anticipate when scheduling shift work?

██████████ Shift work is becoming more, rather than less, common today—both in manufacturing and in office work. White-collar workers

1st week

	M	T	W	T	F	S	S
A	0	1	2	3	4	0	0
B	4	0	0	1	2	3	4
C	2	3	4	0	0	1	2

2nd week

	M	T	W	T	F	S	S
A	1	2	3	4	0	0	1
B	0	0	1	2	3	4	0
C	3	4	0	0	1	2	3

3rd week

	M	T	W	T	F	S	S
A	2	3	4	0	0	1	2
B	0	1	2	3	4	0	0
C	4	0	0	1	2	3	4

4th week

	M	T	W	T	F	S	S
A	3	4	0	0	1	2	3
B	1	2	3	4	0	0	1
C	0	0	1	2	3	4	0

5th week

	M	T	W	T	F	S	S
A	4	0	0	1	2	3	4
B	2	3	4	0	0	1	2
C	0	1	2	3	4	0	0

6th week

	M	T	W	T	F	S	S
A	0	0	1	2	3	4	0
B	3	4	0	0	1	2	3
C	1	2	3	4	0	0	1

FIGURE 26-1. Four-Two Schedule. This schedule for three employees (or groups of employees), A, B, and C, shows how each receives one complete and two partial weekends off duty during a six-week period. Tinted spaces indicate workdays; white areas are days off. Numbers show each block of four consecutive days for each employee group.

who never conceived of anything but a nine-to-five day now find themselves scheduled from 4 p.m. to 12 midnight. It's because their output is needed to keep a highly expensive computer busy.

As you know, more than one shift usually creates a special set of problems for supervisors to contend with. For example:

Employee attitudes. Nightworkers feel left out. They need more attention from both day and night supervisors to make them feel they're really part of the team.

Employee training. More often than not, seniority prevails in staffing for the second shift. This means that the night gang is made up of beginners or relatively inexperienced personnel. So your training effort for nightworkers must be more patient and thorough than that for dayworkers.

Accidents. Fatigue and poor lighting make nightworkers more susceptible to accidents than dayworkers are. Consequently, greater precautions must be taken, and education must be more detailed.

Communications. Projects carried from the day shift to the second shift frequently bog down or get off course because of faulty communications. Supervision ought to overlap—at least a half hour between shifts, preferably more. And logbook instructions should be written out in painful detail. What appears clear

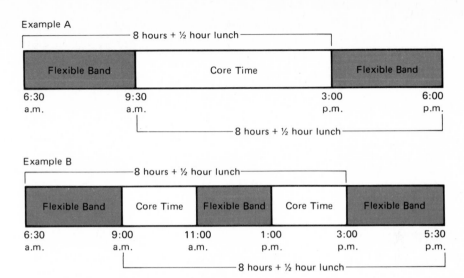

FIGURE 26-2. Two Ways of Designing Flexitime Schedules. From Barbara L. Fiss, *Flexitime—A Guide,* U.S. Civil Service Commission, May 15, 1974.

to the employee who's been working with a process all day may seem cryptic to the person who takes over at 4 p.m.

Cooperation. A little competition between shifts is a good thing. But if this competition grows into antagonism, you've got trouble. Typically, employees from the first shift leave the unattractive jobs—like cleaning up spills—for the second shift. Or second-shift employees "forget" to prepare the equipment for a quick start-up by the day shift. Here's where it will pay off if you can devise ways to bring personnel from both shifts together occasionally—for production conferences and for recreation. If they get to know one another more intimately, mutual sympathy—and respect—are more likely to develop.

What about flexitime?

You will see more of this phenomenon. Especially prevalent in government and in office work in smaller firms, flexitime (flexible working hours) permits employees to choose their own working hours to some extent, provided they work the normal number of hours. Flexitime schedules (see Figure 26-2) generally include several (often six) hours of core time during which all employees must be on the job. An employee may choose to come to work an hour late and make up the hour after normal closing time, or an hour early and leave an hour before normal closing time. This kind of scheduling has advantages where transportation is a problem, and it appeals to many workers. It isn't so good where there is a need for continuous interaction between employees—for example, on an assembly line. It also requires a degree of co-operation between employees. For every person who may wish a variation, there may be a need for another employee to choose the opposite alternate to cover the job of the person who is early or late.

How do companywide plans dictate department-level schedules?

Through the preparation of a *master production schedule* (Figure 26-3-A). This sets the overall schedule for end items (or final products) that the company must make—in terms of number of units and their delivery dates.

Every final product consists of a number of different parts. Thus, to make end item 27-135 in Figure 26-3-A, a list of parts called a *bill of materials* must be prepared (Figure 26-3-B).

If a part, such as 219 (frame) in Figure 26-3-B, is to be made in the plant, a *route sheet* must be prepared (Figure 26-3-C). This shows the operations that must be performed to make the part, their sequence, and the machine on which the work will be performed. The route sheet (sometimes called the order-of-work sheet) may also provide an estimate of the time needed to perform each operation.

It is usually the supervisor's task to assign each of the operations listed on the route sheet to a qualified worker in the supervisor's department.

If your company prepares detailed schedules for you, what will be your main responsibilities?

You'll help most by checking and controlling. And here are some other important things you can do:

• Cooperate with your planning department. It can make your job easier if you'll only let it.
• Follow your schedules carefully. If you know in advance what is expected from your department, you can plan your activities accordingly.
• Find the bottlenecks in your department. Help the planning department understand how they limit your operations. Many supervisors' complaints about an overload come down to the fact

FIGURE 26-3.

Development of Route Sheet from Master Schedule

A. Master Production Schedule

End Item catalog no.	Amount on hand	Amount to be produced weeks of:			
		10/22	10/29	11/5	11/12
27-135	2,000	2,000	2,000	3,000	3.000
28-136	1,000	1,000	1,000	0	0
17-206	500	0	500	0	500
05-721	10	10	10	10	10

B. Bill of Materials
For End Item Catalog No. 27-135

Part no.	Description	Quantity needed	
		To make 1 unit	To make 2,000 units
219	Frame	1	2,000
526	Bracket	5	10,000
735	Fastener	12	24,000

C. Route Sheet
Part No: *219* Description: *Frame* Usage: *End Item*
Cat. No. *27-135*

Opera-tion no.	Operation description	Machine no.	Time Estimates		Employee assigned
			Setup (hr)	Rate (per 1 hr)	
1	Rough-grind edges	521	0.7	100	_____
2	Drill C Holes 0.500 ± 0.001	D17	0.1	260	_____
3	Deburr	D15	0.1	200	_____

that they have not made the planning department fully aware of the department's limitations.

• Watch the number of setups. Too many reduce your output and raise your costs. When a setup is a long one, check with planning to see if you can produce additional material for stock.

• Notify your superior and the planning department whenever you feel that (1) you can't meet the issued schedule or (2) your department is falling behind schedule.

What should supervisors do when
they are pressured for faster deliveries?

Resist the desire to promise what you can't deliver. Hopes and expectations have no place in planning. Your schedules and promises must be based on fact. Only facts—available equipment and its condition, people and their reliability, material supply and its delivery—can be used as a successful base for planning.

A firm, dependable promise will satisfy most superiors. But don't yield to the temptation to be overcautious. Don't allow for more time than you think the situation actually warrants.

Don't say, for instance, "We can't possibly deliver these parts before the sixteenth," and then finish the job on the eleventh. Others in your plant depend on the accuracy of your forecasts. If everyone allowed too much leeway, that would eat up time and money just as overscheduling might.

Give the best sure date you can figure on. Otherwise you'll lose friends and respect among your associates and your superiors.

When a supervisor draws up work schedules,
what personnel time factors should be considered?

Planning a work schedule involves many employee variables—all of which must be accounted for in your final plans. Here are some of the most recurrent:

Holidays	Absences
Vacations	Shift rotation
Rest periods	Meal reliefs
Leaves of absence	Quits and discharges
Training time	Time off to vote (where applicable)

A study made by the department of economics of the University of Michigan in 1977 turned up some valuable information for scheduling purposes. This study found that the average employee spends 27 minutes a day on unscheduled breaks in addition to whatever is allowed in the schedule. This means that when estimating labor hours required, you should figure in another 10 per cent to make up for the facts of working life.

If your company has no planning
department, what can you do to
schedule production smoothly and efficiently?

Don't try to improvise. Work up some sort of schedule and use it as a guide for assigning work and checking completions. As each order reaches you, make a rough estimate (based on experience or time study) of how long it will take—the number of man-hours or machine-hours per operation. Then build up machine loads. At all times, know how many hours of work are ahead of each operator and each machine.

Check regularly with supervisors in the departments before yours and after yours. This way you keep track of when to expect goods to work on and when the next department expects goods from you. If your timing gets off, you're likely to have employees standing around waiting for work or you will hear the same complaint from the department that's waiting for goods from you.

Keep an eye constantly on supplies. On a regular basis, check to see that you have enough operating supplies on hand such as raw materials, packaging materials, and any other items that you add to the product in your department.

Each afternoon start checking to see that there will be enough materials and work in process on hand to keep your employees busy the next morning. If you anticipate delays, try to maintain a backlog of low-priority jobs that can be set up and torn down quickly.

What is a Gantt chart?
How does a supervisor use it?

During World War I Henry Laurence Gantt, an industrial engineer, developed the first production control chart. Its form seems obvious today, since most organizations now use one or another version of it to plan and chart output performance. Its essentials are displayed in Figure 26-4.

To understand the unique value of the Gantt chart, put yourself in the place of a supervisor who has just been handed five production orders, stamped serially from 101 to 105. These orders indicate what machines the work must be processed on, the sequence that must be followed, and the estimated number of hours it will take each machine to complete its work.

These orders contain essentially the same kind of information found on a route sheet. The route sheet, however, often includes operations performed in different departments. Thus, it is not unusual for the supervisor to collect this information from several route sheets, or the production-control department may issue a number of separate orders to each departmental supervisor.

If the supervisor were to load the machines (they could be benches, work stations, desks, and so on) with the assumption that each order must be finished before another one was begun (straight-line or point-to-point scheduling), the schedule would

Log of Orders for Charts A and B

Order no.	101			102			103			104			105		
Operation sequence	1	2	3	1	2	3	1	2	3	1	2	3	1	2	3
Machine no.	A	B	C	C	A	B	B	A	C	A	C	B	B	C	A
Machine time (h)	4	8	2	10	4	6	6	4	8	4	10	12	4	2	6

Chart A

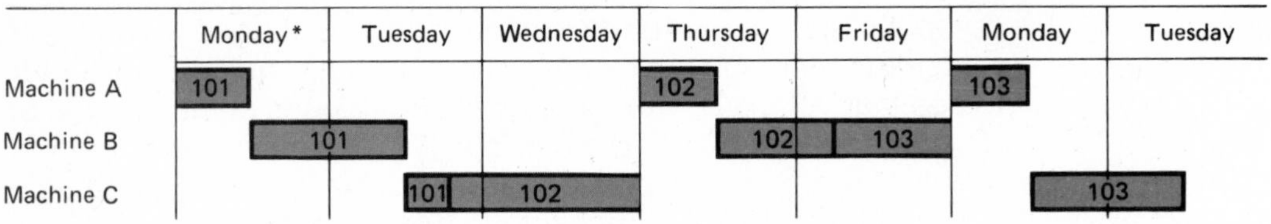

	Monday*	Tuesday	Wednesday	Thursday	Friday	Monday	Tuesday
Machine A	101			102		103	
Machine B		101			102	103	
Machine C			101	102			103

Chart B

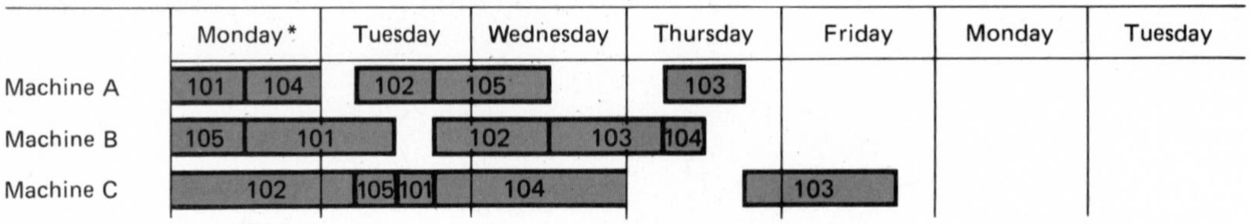

	Monday*	Tuesday	Wednesday	Thursday	Friday	Monday	Tuesday
Machine A	101 104	102 105		103			
Machine B	105 101		102 103 104				
Machine C	102	105 101 104		103			

Note: Each day represents 8 hours.

FIGURE 26-4. Development of a Gantt Chart From a Series of Production Orders. Chart A shows jobs lined up in sequence as they were received. Chart B shows jobs rearranged (overlapped) for maximum machine loading, with prescribed sequence of operations for each job maintained. *Each job represents 8 hours.*

be something like Chart A in Figure 26-4. The flow of work would be orderly, but the equipment would be extremely underutilized. Worse still, many orders would be delayed. To correct these deficiencies, Gantt overlapped orders and disregarded the sequence in which they were accepted, while still rigidly adhering to the operation sequence each order specifies. Chart B in Figure 26-4 shows how the supervisor can juggle orders, starting number 105 on machine B and number 102 on machine C and at the same time beginning number 101 on machine A. By rearranging and overlapping the jobs, all five orders can be finished by Friday afternoon. Furthermore, the supervisor has greatly increased the overall machine utilization. Machine A is now scheduled to be in operation 18 of the first 24 hours of the

FIGURE 26-5.

Progress Control Chart for Maintenance Projects

Job No.	Description	Mechanic assigned	Probable start	Target finish	Man-days estimated
107	Replace and clean lamps	Miller	Jan.	Dec.	200
109	Repaint building interiors	Stover	Apr.	Sept.	200
115	Repair sidewalks/roadways	Stover	Jan.	Feb.	300
117	Repair chimney stack	Ajax Co.*		Jan.	contract
118	Replace warehouse transformer	Corso	Apr.	Sept.	90
119	Rewire machine shop	Corso	Jan.	Mar.	260
121	Install sewer drains plumbing	Urn Plumbing Co.*		May	contract
122	Install fire doors	Texco Co.*		Feb.	contract
125	Power line for computer	Corso	Mar.	June	320
126	Weatherstrip windows	Miller	Nov.	Dec.	120
128	Replace office partitions	Miller	Mar.	May	120
129	Rewire office area	Corso	June	Oct.	230
130	Replace fuel lines	Miller	Sept.	Sept.	20
131	Check out ventilation system	Corso	Oct.	Dec.	80
132	Paint office areas	Stover	Oct.	Dec.	240
135	Rebuild craneways	Miller	Sept.	Dec.	170

*External contracts.

week (through Wednesday). It works 4 hours on 101, 4 hours on 104, is idle for 2 hours, then works 4 hours on 102, 6 hours on 105, and is idle again until the close of the shift on Wednesday. Machine B utilizes 22 hours during the same period: 4 hours on 105, 8 hours on 101, idle for 2 hours, 6 hours on 102, and 4 hours on 103. Machine C utilizes all 24 hours: 10 hours on 102, 2 hours on 105, 2 hours on 101, and 10 hours on 104. This predicts utilization rates of 75 percent, 92 percent, and 100 percent. While the supervisor might not be able to juggle the work so efficiently all week long, it is an indication of what judicial overlapping of jobs can accomplish.

Is the Gantt chart useful only for production scheduling?

Far from it. Just about any kind of project can be scheduled with it. In fact, with only a few minor additions, it can serve as a progress control chart, too. Figure 26-5 shows such usage for planning and controlling a series of maintenance projects over a year's time. Instead of days, as in Figure 26–4, this chart would be divided into months. Each job would be blocked out in an open rectangle spanning its probable start and target finish dates. As each job moved ahead, its rectangle would be filled in to represent its degree of completion. Progress could be checked at any particular date by drawing a vertical line from the top to the bottom of the chart. Open rectangles to the left would show jobs behind schedule, and filled-in rectangles would show those that were on target.

What is PERT?

It stands for program evaluation and review technique. In plainer English, PERT is a technique for planning any project that involves a number of different tasks that must be coordinated. It is a graphic technique that enables the planner to see the progressive relationships between many jobs; PERT is also known as the critical-path method (CPM), arrow diagraming, and dozens of other variations.

The technique dramatizes the value of conceiving of doing two or more things simultaneously. It may take 12 minutes to get a haircut, 5 minutes for a shoeshine, and 10 minutes to browse through the newspaper. You could take 27 minutes to do all three—in sequence, one after the other—or you could do all three in 12 minutes by doing them simultaneously or (as planners say) in parallel.

The PERT method is most useful for scheduling one-of-a-kind projects. It is used to plan and schedule construction projects like roads, bridges, and dams. It is used to plan the building of very large engines, airplanes, and ships; PERT is helpful, too, in scheduling a number of jobs that must be done in a short period of time. For example, a plant closes for two weeks in the summer and tries to get everything cleaned and repaired during that period. It is also useful for starting a new program in a government agency or for introducing a new product to the market.

What makes PERT so different from ordinary scheduling methods?

The program evaluation and review technique helps a scheduler to plan ahead, to look for critical jobs that will tie up a whole program unless they are begun and completed before they become bottlenecks. For example, it may be logical to wait until a machine foundation pit has been dug and the concrete has been poured before constructing the supporting ironwork for the machine. But if steel is in short supply and the ironwork job will take four weeks to fabricate, then perhaps it's wiser to begin this part of the job before digging the pit. And if there are several other jobs that can't be begun until the ironwork is in place, you can see how critical it is to anticipate the ironwork job and assure its completion in time; PERT charting helps you to identify these critical jobs ahead of time.

Why is it so important to identify the critical tasks of a large project?

Usually, only about 10 to 20 percent of the jobs in a major project control the time needed for the whole project. Any delay in these critical jobs will delay the final completion date. By putting the heat on them, however, the entire project can be completed sooner, and at far less cost than would be involved if the project were put on a crash basis straight across the board. There is always at least one continuous chain of these critical jobs running through every project, from start to finish. This chain is called the *critical path.* Proper control and manipulation of the jobs that make up this critical path can give you control over the time and cost involved in an entire project—regardless of its size.

A common error of traditional scheduling is that someone arbitrarily plucks a target completion date out of the air, and everybody digs in to meet it. With critical-path scheduling, you estimate the time needed for each of the critical jobs, add them together, and then reach for the calendar. If you're unhappy with that date, you know just what jobs you can expedite, by how much, at what cost, and with what effect on the rest of the project.

How does PERT work?

When PERT is used, planning and scheduling are usually approached in four steps.

1. Diagram job sequences. List everything that has to be done. Put these jobs in proper sequence. (An obvious example: The wooden forms will have to be finished before you can pour the concrete.)

The next step—arrow diagraming—is the heart of the technique. Each job is indicated by an arrow. The length of the arrows is not important, but their direction indicates the sequence of jobs. The diagram is constructed by taking each job in turn and asking three questions: (a) What immediately precedes this job? (b) What immediately follows this job? (c) What other jobs can be done at the same time?

The seven-job project diagramed in Figure 26-6 is a simple

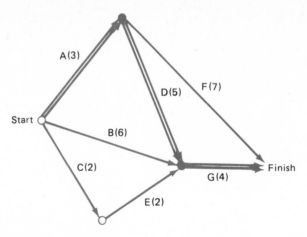

FIGURE 26-6. Simplified PERT Diagram. Double arrows represent the critical path.

example that is easy to follow. See the interrelationships of the project jobs. For instance, it's obvious that job G can't start until jobs B, D, and E are completed. But before that, jobs A, B, and C can all get under way.

2. Add time factors. Now you estimate the duration of each job. Wild guesswork at this stage will destroy any benefits you might receive from the technique, so get the best estimates available. (Possibly the most realistic estimate will be that given by the artisans—or the crew chief—who will perform the work.) At this stage you want figures for straight time and normal delivery schedules, with a typical work force. The normal time estimate in days for each job is written in parentheses beside the arrow that represents that job.

Now add up the duration of all the jobs along each possible path. The longest one is the critical path (A-D-G, or 12 days, in this case). Any delay in the completion of these jobs will delay completion of the whole project. The rest of the jobs are floaters. You have a certain amount of leeway in completing them without affecting the target date of the project.

3. Look for the fastest, cheapest way. Most projects can be done in a number of ways, from minimum cost (maximum time) to minimum time (maximum cost). The beauty of critical-path scheduling is that it permits you to make an educated choice between these extremes at a point that's best for your operation. To gain time, all you must do is compress the schedule along the critical path, which automatically shortens the overall project time. This is more efficient and far less costly than pushing everything on a crash basis across the board.

4. Choose the lowest total cost. This step introduces the cost of lost production, the availability of labor and materials, and the associated outage costs. Here's where you weigh not only the time and the direct cost factors of the project, as shown by the arrow diagram, but also those indirect costs that go with crash jobs or machinery not in operation.

What is the basis for scheduling and assigning office and clerical work?

Office scheduling should be based on the same considerations given to manufacturing scheduling: (1) the number of tasks to be done, (2) the time it will take to do each task, (3) the number and qualifications of employees available to do the work, and (4) the capacity and availability of proper machines and equipment, when machinery plays a part. A good way to put this all together is to use a work distribution chart, which provides a rule-of-thumb guide to indicate how much work the department can handle with its present staff.

Figure 26-7 shows how repetitive, routine work in an office might be balanced among eight employees by means of a work distribution chart. (Machine capacity and availability is not considered to be a factor in this example.) Note that this supervisor has tried to group together activities of roughly the same skills level into the job assignments for each person. For example, Apgar handles all the mail and part of the copying, fairly simple work. Bond and Crisi handle filing and the balance of the copying, slightly more difficult work. Dalt and Eigo have secretarial jobs, while Finch's job is mainly stenography. Grey is a key-punch operator who also handles the check-writing machine, and Hruska is a posting clerk.

What's meant by short-interval scheduling?

This is an industrial engineering technique for improving output by means of issuing many specific work assignments of relatively short duration. Called by various proprietary names by a number of management consulting firms, short-interval scheduling has met with growing popularity in office applications because of its unusual suitability to clerical work and some service work, such as maintenance and repair jobs.

In essence, the short-interval scheduling technique calls on the supervisor to block out only a small portion of work at a time for each employee, rather than lining up a whole day's or week's work at once. For example, you give a filing clerk a sheaf of cor-

FIGURE 26-7.

Work Distribution Chart for Office Planning and Scheduling									
Tasks or activities to be done each week	Total time (in hours) for each task each week	Weekly time distribution in hours per employee							
		Apgar	Bond	Crisi	Dalt	Eigo	Finch	Grey	Hruska
Mail in	15	15							
Mail out	15	15							
Dictation	20				10	10			
Transcription	30				10	10	10		
Typing	80			10	20	20	30		
Copying	30	10	10	10					
Filing in	25		20	5					
Filing out	15		10	5					
Keypunching	30							30	
Check writing	10							10	
Posting	50			10					40
Total hours	320	40	40	40	40	40	40	40	40

respondence and say that it should be filed within the next half hour. Or you hand a dozen invoices to a clerk and ask for their preparation within the hour. When each of these particular blocks of work has been completed, you assign another chunk of work (that again covers only a short interval in the workday) to each employee.

A key advantage of the short-interval approach is that in a very short time you will know whether an employee is keeping up or falling behind in output. This system also forces you to estimate and enforce output standards, and it calls your attention to typical wishful thinking on management's part. For example, in the past you may have assumed that a clerk could handle 70 documents in a day. When you break this assignment up into 10 documents per hour, you might be surprised to discover that unexpected peculiarities in your kind of work make it impossible for the clerk to average more than 7 documents per hour—and consequently only 50 or 60 per day.

Short-interval scheduling functions well because many clerical people are not capable of, or particularly interested in, establishing or following for themselves a work schedule of a duration of much more than an hour. Consequently, they tend to welcome your taking the responsibility for the planning and scheduling part of their job.

Short-interval scheduling may be difficult because it depends on (1) the accuracy with which you can estimate reasonable work loads; (2) the extent to which you can find time to make these estimates and assignments; (3) the degree to which you observe and control performance and make the necessary adjustments in your expectations; (4) the effectiveness with which employees can be motivated to accept a work pace that is higher than that to which they have been accustomed; and (5) the ability and time available to train people to work with greater skills, concentration, and persistence.

Whether your office installs a formal short-interval scheduling system or not, however, the principle is a sound one for you to follow. You'll find that you can apply the general idea informally, even sporadically, and still get unusually good results.

supervisory word power

Stockout. An occurrence wherein a product or a part listed for sale or internal consumption is not immediately available; literally, something that someone needs is out of stock.

Backlog. Orders received and on hand but not yet scheduled for production or processing.

Down time. The condition wherein a machine, a process, or an operation is out of service waiting for repairs and, consequently, is not available for scheduling.

Short shipment. A shipment or delivery of goods in which the order is shipped incomplete; literally, the order is shipped short of one or more of its items.

Expedite. A relatively costly technique (one usually accomplished by intense personal attention) for speeding the progress of an order through the production process to meet or advance a scheduled shipment.

Other Important Terms in This Chapter

bill of materials	master plan
critical path	PERT(or CPM)
exception principle	progress control chart
flexitime	project assignment
four-day week	route sheet
Gantt chart	short-interval scheduling
job assignment	work distribution chart

reading comprehension

1. Describe two simple ways to record plans without becoming overly burdened with paperwork.

2. Why would it not be wise to plan for as much production on the night shift as on the day shift?

3. An electric motor manufacturer is considering flexitime on its assembly line. Is that a good idea? Could flexitime have any advantages if used in the office instead?

4. If a supervisor's company provides a master production schedule, why does the supervisor have to schedule at all? What is the supervisor's role in carrying out the master plan?

5. What are some of the things a supervisor should do to make the work of a central planning and scheduling department more effective?

6. In what ways is a Gantt chart like a calendar? Different from a calendar?

7. In what ways is a PERT chart similar to a Gantt chart? What is its principal difference?

8. What is the critical path? Why is it called "critical?"

9. Peggy was moved from supervising manufacturing workers to a new job supervising office workers. How much of what she learned about scheduling in her old job can she use in her new job? What will be different?

10. Under what circumstances is short-interval scheduling particularly effective?

supervision in action

THE CASE OF MATT HOPPER'S BOTTLENECK.   A case study in human relations involving work schedules, with questions for you to answer.

When Matt Hopper's boss asked him to see if he couldn't straighten out scheduling bottlenecks in his department, Matt got busy right away. He made a thorough analysis of work loads, staffing requirements, and process flow. He designed a form for loading machines and for scheduling work for each operator. And he double-checked his plans with his boss and with the production planning department. Everybody agreed that Matt's work schedules now ought to be dependable. Time proved they weren't.

To determine where the difficulty lay, the industrial engineering department sent a methods engineer in to observe actual practices in Matt's department. Here are some of the observations:

8:00 a.m.: Whistle blows. Of 18 workplaces, 15 are occupied. Only 12 of the 15 are actually operating.

8:12 a.m.: All workplaces occupied, 15 now working.

8:45 a.m.: One workplace not occupied, 15 working, 2 waiting for material.

9:22 a.m.: Observed one worker watching neighbor to learn how to work on special job.

11:12 a.m.: Supervisor in area. All workplaces filled, all working.

11:55 a.m.: Fifteen workplaces occupied, two women putting on makeup. One man eating lunch.

12:30 p.m.: Ten workplaces occupied.

12:35 p.m.: All workplaces occupied.

1:15 p.m.: One worker reports to nurse with headache.

2:05 p.m.: All workplaces occupied. Three employees talking with material handler.

3:57 p.m.: Two employees waiting for mechanic to fix soldering irons.

4:17 p.m.: All workplaces occupied. Seven employees waiting for materials.

1. What do you think may have been wrong with Matt's planning and work schedules?

2. What are some of the conclusions you'd draw from the engineer's observations?

3. What will Matt have to do to make sure his department meets schedules?

enriching your viewpoint

To enlarge and improve your ability to make job assignments and plan work schedules, the following readings are suggested:

Bittel, Lester, *The Nine Master Keys of Management,* McGraw-Hill Book Company, New York, 1972, Chap. 5, "Act from a Plan"; also pp. 80–86 and 95–101.

Fiss, Barbara L., *Flexitime—A Guide,* Bureau of Policies and Standards, U.S. Civil Service Commission, May 15, 1974.

Katsanis, Thomas A., "Work Four Days, Off Two," *Modern Hospital,* July 1971.

Lindemann, A. J., Earl F. Lundgren, and H. K. von Kaas, *Encyclopedic Dictionary of Management and Manufacturing Terms,* 2d ed., Kendall/Hunt Publishing Company, Dubuque, Iowa, 1974, Sec. 18, "Production Planning and Control," pp. 123–130.

Rice, James W., "Production Planning and Control," in Lester R. Bittel (ed.), *The Encyclopedia of Professional Management,* McGraw-Hill Book Company, New York, 1979, pp. 966–975.

Richardson, Wallace J., *Cost Improvement, Work Sampling, and Short Interval Scheduling,* Reston Publishing Company, Reston, Va., 1976, Part IV, "Short Interval Scheduling," pp. 199–217.

Shue, Gene, "Overtime Efficiency—An Actual Test," *Industrial Engineering,* November 1970.

Smith, Martin R., *Short-Interval Scheduling,* McGraw-Hill Book Company, New York, 1968.

Wilson, Charles F., *How to Develop and Apply Work Plans: A Federal Supervisor's Guide,* Superintendent of Documents, Washington, 1974, Chap. 4, "Organizing and Staffing Your Plan," pp. 73–118.

Wixom, Theodore M., "Better Scheduling Helps Cut Direct Labor Expenses," *Industrial Engineering,* September 1971.

27

measuring and improving work methods

What is meant by work measurement?

The term is generally applied to any method for finding out how long it takes to do a job. Work measurement usually refers to the time it would take an individual to accomplish a specific task. However, when a worker is assisted by, or paced by, a machine, this may also be considered. Since human accomplishment is affected by how much physical effort and skill go into the job, work measurement usually takes those into account, too.

What are the main ways in which work is measured?

Making *time studies* of the actual job as it is performed (using some sort of stopwatch) is by far the most common way. Other methods range from rough-and-ready measures to ultrasophisticated techniques.

The crudest measures derive simply from looking at historical records that show how much an employee has produced in a day, week, or month.

The most elaborate approach uses tiny building blocks of time units based on *motion studies.* Experts add the time for every motion required on a job (lifting, pulling, straightening, and so forth) to find the total time needed. The measuring units are called *predetermined elemental time standards.* These may be known under a variety of proprietary names, such as MTM, Work Factor, and ZIP Standard Data.

Between time studies and predetermined standards are a number of other approaches. Most of them, however, are based on either (1) a direct measurement of time or (2) the knowledge of how much time it takes to make a particular motion (like grasping an object) or to perform some part of a well-known job (for example, when an electrician cuts $\frac{1}{8}$-inch diameter copper wire with hand clippers while connecting up a transformer). The knowledge of how much time is usually based in part on time or motion studies that have become *standards.* The standards are accumulated in a company's file or are available for purchase from consulting firms.

How is work measurement data applied?

Time data is widely used for a number of practical purposes. It enables managers and supervisors to:

1. Estimate accurately how long future jobs will take.
2. Establish reliable work schedules.
3. Provide employees with specific work standards in terms of either (*a*) time allowed to get a job done or (*b*) number of output units that must be produced in a certain time period.
4. Estimate the labor costs for products to be made or services to be performed.
5. Provide a basis for employee wages, especially those that include extra pay (wage incentives) for work that exceeds the time standard.

Must supervisors become experts in work measurement?

No. But supervisors should understand—and be able to explain to employees—several basic concepts: a fair day's work, standard time data, and leveling (sometimes called accomplishment rating or pace rating). These are the subjects of the greatest misunderstanding and number of complaints.

How is a fair day's work determined?

This is the basis of work measurement, and it is the most difficult to gain agreement on. The concept is that for a fair day's pay an employee ought to expect to give a fair day's work. So far so good. What is a fair day's work? By most definitions it is the amount of work an average (normal) person could do, working at an average (normal) pace, for eight hours without becoming unduly fatigued. The catch is, of course, what is meant by average or normal. To attain some kind of agreement on these terms, various sources (principally the Society for the Advancement of Management) provide films of common operations: walking, case handling, shoveling, clerical filing, machine operations, and others. These films are shown at speeds that represent agreed-on rates, say, 80, 90, 100, 110, or 120 percent of normal. Even untrained observers tend to agree quickly on the ratings, especially of the normal pace.

Why, then, are there problems with rating or leveling?

The problems arise when the concept is put into practice with an actual time study. At that point the time-study person must rate (or gauge) the operator's pace as the job is performed. The time-study analyst mentally makes a judgment of how the actual pace at that time compares with the analyst's feel for a normal pace.

While working, an employee may consciously, or otherwise, work as far below normal as 40 percent or as much above normal as 200 percent. The time-study person doesn't wait until the operator works exactly at 100 percent. It wouldn't be practical. So the operator's pace is rated, and the actual time measured by the clock is adjusted (or leveled) by the estimate of the operator's pace.

Take a man soldering wire ends to a television chassis. Mary, the time-study person, times John; he makes ten connections. The actual times for each connection are 0.13, 0.12, 0.15, 0.13, 0.12, 0.23, 0.12, 0.12, 0.13, and 0.11. Mary looks the times over and throws out the 0.23 reading as abnormal. Then she totals the remaining readings and divides by 9 to get the average time of 0.12 minutes. Now comes the critical phase of time study. Mary must apply her rating (or leveling) factor.

While Mary observed John making these connections, Mary mentally compared his pace with what she estimated was a normal pace for that kind of operation. Mary's estimate was that John was working at 110 percent of normal, or 10 percent faster than normally expected. Therefore, the time for the standard does not become the actual time observed but is increased to the rated time or, in this case, 0.12 minute × 110 percent = 0.13 minute. You can readily see that no matter how conscientiously or skillfully the rating is made, it is always a matter of opinion. Consequently, it can be a matter of debate. Many of the disputes with labor unions over time studies arise over the rating factor.

What assurance does an employee have that the standard calls for only a fair day's work?

Each time-study standard must take into account that it's nearly impossible for a worker to work at a fast pace all day. Fatigue causes most of us to slow down toward the middle of the morning and again toward the middle of the second half of the shift. So time-study standards allow time for relaxation. Otherwise it wouldn't be a fair standard, and it would be like asking for more than a fair day's work.

Factors to compensate for relaxation (and to allow for personal time in the washroom, and so forth) are usually built into the time standard. This *fatigue allowance* will vary from about 10 percent for light work to as much as 35 percent for heavy work, like cleaning molds in a hot and dusty foundry.

For the soldering job mentioned above, the fatigue allowance would be calculated in this manner:

$$0.13 \text{ minute} \times 10 \text{ percent allowance} = 0.013 \text{ minute}$$

$$\text{Standard time with allowance incorporated} = 0.13 + 0.013$$

$$= 0.143 \text{ minute}$$

Must a job be time-studied to set a standard?

Not if standard time data are used. Standard data are simply the recorded summaries of many time studies.

Take a machinist who turns down a spindle. Over the years this operation has been studied thousands and thousands of times. The standard times for each of the separate steps—or elements—in the operation are recorded in charts or tables. These charts can cover practically every possible variation. The tables show the standard times for several varieties of machines and chucks, for carbon and stainless steel, for short spindles and long, for heavy cuts and light, for wide tolerances and narrow.

The time-study persons need only analyze the elements in the job, the order in which they are performed, and the number of times they are repeated. Then they look up in their tables the standard data for each element and add them for the standard time for the specific job.

The use of standard data has proved to be a reliable and often economical way of setting rates. As logical as this may be, many employees ask: "How could they set a time for this job when they didn't study it?" Your informed answer will help to remove this issue. If the standard proves to be fair and practicable, that may be the most convincing reply.

What causes loose standards?

A standard is *loose* when an average employee putting forth normal effort is able consistently to undershoot the standard by a very large margin. Most fair standards, however, are set with the expectancy that good workers will be able to undershoot them by as much as 25 percent. Performance in excess of that should be investigated, for the standards may be loose.

Several factors determine the time allowed in the standard: methods and materials used on the job when studied, the way the job was set up, the way materials were supplied and taken away, the quality specifications, and the method of timekeeping. Changing any of these factors will loosen (or tighten, if the change causes the job to take longer) the standard.

You, as the supervisor, are responsible for observing when any of the original standard conditions are changed. If you slacken your standard of acceptance in order to rush a job through, you help loosen the standard. If you fail to observe and report a change in method or tool used, you help build slack in the standard.

Most supervisors are pretty alert to major changes in the way a job is done and quick to report them. But frequently standards become loose, not because of any one big change but as a result of the accumulation of many minor changes. This is all the more reason you should keep on your toes, watch for the first signs of a loosening rate, and then take action accordingly.

How much do you explain to workers about time standards?

Building confidence in the honesty of the system is where you should begin. More often than not, once you have shown employees that you and the time-study analyst in your department aren't trying to hide something, explanations will be easy and gripes held to a minimum.

Time-study methods can be explained in group sessions, or you can do it by taking your employees aside one at a time. If you begin with one of the older, more influential, and generally respected employees, he or she will be able to help spread the word to others.

Don't talk in generalities, abstractions, or big words. Get right down to cases. Use one of the jobs the employee has worked on as an example. Show how the job is broken down into elements with a studied time or standard-data time for each. Don't dodge the issue of rating. Show that rating is designed to protect the worker from a tight as well as a loose rate. Emphasize that the standard is kept fair by the inclusion of time for the operator to relax and attend to personal needs.

Let the employee examine the operation standard and the standard data tables. This will take much of the mystery out of the process—even if the details of the method are not completely understood. Make a point of showing how important job conditions, methods, and materials are to the standard. This way there will be more understanding when changes in any one of these conditions change the employee's standard time.

Impress on the worker your eagerness to see that credits are given for extra work or for delays—that your sole interest is to see that everyone makes the best use of time and that all employees get all that's coming to them.

All this explanation takes time, but not nearly as much of your time as unreasonable arguments and grievances over standards can take.

How do you handle complaints that the standard is wrong?

Time-study analysts do make mistakes, and they do not run the operating departments. That's your job. Along with it goes the responsibility to see that your employees get a fair shake.

When one of your employees questions a time-study rate, listen to the objection with an open mind. Perhaps the employee can tell you about some change in the conditions that does make the rate a wrong one. In any event, you'll want to get the facts as the employee sees them. On the other hand, don't assume the standard is wrong without looking carefully at the current job conditions. It may be that methods have been changed, material is off size, the machine is in poor shape, the employee has to hunt for supplies and tools or has to wait for jobs. Ask yourself, too, if you have shown the operator the correct way of doing the job.

Sometimes, of course, investigation shows simply that the complainer just isn't working hard enough to beat the standard.

What's the connection between time standards and wage incentives?

Where time standards are used to measure how much workers produce—and they are paid accordingly—the time studies are said to be part of a wage-incentive plan. Wage-incentive plans enable employees to increase their earnings over their normal hourly rate. Under such a system the company usually gets its share of employees' increased productivity two ways: (1) through the assurance the wage incentive gives of the employees' fully utilizing their time and effort on the job and (2) by getting maximum use of facilities and equipment when employees work at optimum effort.

Is there more than one wage-incentive plan?

There are at least 25 wage-incentive plans that have been dignified with a name. In the old days some plans were complicated, but the trend today is to keep them simple. Not only is the plan easier for the paymaster, but the wage-incentive system is a lot simpler from the employee's viewpoint.

Some of the confusion over wage incentives arises because of the way the money is connected to the time study. Piece rates mean exactly that—so much money per piece. If workers know that the piece rate on a mold is 30 cents, they know that if they make 100 molds in an 8-hour day, they will make $30. If their base rate is $3 per hour, they would make only $24 per 8-hour day if not on piece rate. If they make 100 molds, however, the additional $6 earnings is equivalent to a bonus, or incentive, of 25 percent over the base daily rate of $24.

It's more common today to state the standard in time—as so much time per piece. The worker figures earnings by comparing the actual time taken for the operation with the allowed or standard time.

The straight-line incentive system is very popular. It's called straight-line because for each 1 percent production over standard, the employees are paid 1 percent of their base rate as a bonus. For instance, if the standard time per mold is 6.0 minutes and they find themselves averaging 4.8 minutes per mold, they can easily calculate that their time saving will be 1.2 minutes. Consequently, if they can maintain their pace all day, their incentive bonus will be 1.2/6.0, or 20 percent.

How good are group incentive rates?

You'll hear a lot of pros and cons about group incentive rates. By pooling all incentive workers into a group, the supervisor can save time making assignments. This group method cuts down on inspection, timekeeping, and accounting.

To make the group plan work successfully, you must develop a lot of teamwork among its members. Otherwise, the efficiency of the group tends to be lower than the average efficiency of each employee working individually on incentives. That's because the more highly skilled workers tend to slow down if they think they are pulling more than their share in the department, and the person who likes to relax on the job finds a natural cover-up inside the group.

What is measured daywork?

Measured daywork really is time study without a wage incentive attached. Jobs are studied and effort is measured just as with an incentive system. But no earnings are directly based on the individual's or group's performance against these standards. Supervisors use the standards as an aid to supervision, since standards help them plan their work, make assignments, and find out where time is being lost.

Measured daywork is especially useful for indirect labor or clerical jobs like maintenance, material handling, housekeeping, engineering, filing, typing, and order picking.

What is work sampling?

Work sampling (also called *ratio-delay*) is another method of measuring work. By making random observations, you can find the ratio of delays, interruptions, or any other work element to the total process time. For instance, if you wanted to find out how much of the time a lift truck was actually out of operation, you'd visit the truck a predetermined number of times a day, say, ten. These visits would not be at regular intervals; they would be at random. If in ten days you made 100 observations, and during 23 of them the truck was idle, it would be statistically safe to conclude that the truck was idle 23 percent of the time. You could make the same sort of study on any number of items—so long as you make enough observations and the observations are made at random. If one were to make observations every hour on the hour, this would introduce a pattern that might bias the results.

How is a work sampling study conducted?

The observer records what each employee is doing at the instant the employee is observed. The record is made by checking a box under each of a set of previously determined categories. Different categories are used by different companies, but a fairly typical list might be:

Working.   This means actually performing work—running a machine, using a tool, and so forth.

Preparing to work.   Under this heading would come such things as observing a job to determine how to proceed, listening to instructions, asking questions relative to the job.

Travel.   This would include getting tools or supplies and walking or riding to the job in the case of, say, a maintenance worker who is sent out from a central location.

Delay.   This category is usually for delays for which the employee is not responsible—waiting for materials or waiting for some other worker to finish part of the job.

Idle.   This is time for which the worker is responsible—time spent talking (not about the job) or simply looking off into space.

Figure 27-1 illustrates a fairly detailed work sampling study of typical clerical operations.

Do employees object to work sampling?

Not usually, if it is properly explained to them beforehand. They should be told that the purpose is not to check up on individual employees but to determine what management can do to make it possible for them to work more steadily and effectively. Excessive travel, for example, may show the need for more convenient location of tools and supplies; waiting for other employees may indicate a need for better scheduling. Even if there is excessive idle time because employees are loafing on the job, the supervisor will realize that control must be tightened. Generally, however, sampling shows that the delays for which the employee is not responsible account for the greatest amount of wasted time.

FIGURE 27-1.

Work Sampling Study of Clerical Employees
Observation Sheet

Name of Typist	Random Observation Times								
	9:09	9:57	11:18	1:15	2:43	3:11	3:52	4:21	4:39
Chavez	7	8	1	1	3	5	6	3	1
Yost	2	1	6	4	1	3	7	6	2
Albers	7	4	5	1	8	1	1	3	8
Dowdy	7	8	7	4	1	1	2	1	8
Calabrese	4	1	2	5	7	5	1	4	1

Date: ___7/21___ Supervisor (Observer): ___F. Diehl___

Activity Category Code Numbers
1. Typing
2. Taking dictation
3. Transcribing from machine
4. Clerical activity at desk

5. Away from desk, but in office
6. Talking, telephoning
7. Personal
8. Not in office

Summary of 990 Observations

Category	Number of observations	Percentage of observations
1. Typing	487	49.2
2. Taking dictation	23	2.3
3. Transcribing from machine	86	8.7
4. Clerical activity at desk	71	7.2
5. Away from desk, but in office	36	3.6
6. Talking, telephoning	68	6.9
7. Personal	113	11.4
8. Not in office	106	10.7

What does methods improvement mean?

Methods improvement is any change in the way things are being done today that will show up in lower cost or better quality in the finished product or service tomorrow. The process of methods improvement is simply the organized use of common sense to find better ways of doing work. You need no stopwatch, no calculator, no motion-picture camera—only pencil, paper, good judgment, patience, and ingenuity.

More specifically, in methods improvement you put an operation, or a given way of doing a job, under close inspection and analysis. You give it this microscope treatment to eliminate every unnecessary step and to find the quickest and best method of performing each of the necessary steps.

For trained analysts, the basis of methods improvement is work measurement or work sampling data.

Is methods improvement known by any other name?

Methods improvement has many names, and it takes many forms. Sometimes it's called work simplification, time-and-motion study, operations analysis, methods engineering, systems engineering, waste reduction, or motion economy. Some people even believe that mechanization and automation are just advanced forms of methods improvement.

Methods improvement is usually effected by observing and recording each minute detail of a job, then analyzing the record for ways to do the job better. That's the kind of methods improvement we'll talk about in this chapter. There are many other approaches (like using motion pictures to observe and record, time studying, and so forth) that can be, and are, used effectively by methods engineers.

Where do methods improvements come from?

Any employee can have a good idea. When a company has a formal suggestion system, one of its main purposes is to provide a channel for handling employees' ideas. If your company does not have a suggestion system, you are the most likely one for an employee to bring suggestions to. Either way, a department whose employees initiate lots of ideas for work improvement makes a supervisor look good.

The best ideas for work improvement, however, are likely to come from first-line management. One authority has estimated that one work-improvement idea from a supervisor is worth ten from another employee. That's because the supervisor has a better overview of the job than a worker does. An astute supervisor can see the forest as well as the trees.

In many companies a methods department is staffed by methods engineers whose job is to simplify and improve work procedures. They help supervisors do a better job of lowering costs. They need your cooperation in spotting cost-cutting targets and in making the improved methods work after they are installed. You should form a habit of working hand in hand with the methods department. You can do a lot for them, and they can do much for you.

Can you give some examples?

Sure. Instances of methods improvement can be large or small, simple or involved. Take the job of drilling and tapping a $\frac{1}{4}$-inch hole. An operator drills first, then sets up and taps. Two operations are performed, but lots of effort is wasted between operations. Now the job is done with a single tool that has drilling threads on the lower part of the tool and tapping threads on the upper part of the shank. Both operations are done with a single setup.

Another example of methods improvement is in the garment industry. Formerly a cutter would cut only one piece of cloth at a time. Now the cutter stacks as many as a hundred layers of cloth together and cuts a hundred dresses at a time. This is done with powered shears; in the old days it was done with hand scissors.

Or take this example that involves switching to new materials. A plant crates small turbines. It used to take two persons an hour to fabricate $25 worth of lumber into a shipping case. Now one person does the job in an hour—using prefabricated, wirebound crates that cost only $10.

Just by cutting out a job that isn't necessary, precious time and money can be saved. One supervisor in a machine shop found by analyzing methods that dozens of machine parts were being finished to higher standards than the actual specifications called for. The supervisor cut out extra operations by seeing that workers produced mirror finishes only when specified.

Using a jig or a fixture to hold the work in place so that a packer can fold the shipping carton around it with both hands at once saved one company the equivalent of 12 weeks in labor time in a year.

Are methods improvements limited to manfacturing or production jobs?

By no means. They have been applied by expert and novice alike to such diverse fields as construction, supermarkets, and endless paperwork systems in offices. Lillian Gilbreth, a noted pioneer in work simplification, made great improvements in hos-

	Wrapping part	Drill hole	Typing letter
Operation ●	An operation represents the main steps in the process. Something is created, changed, or added to. Usually transportations, inspections, delays, and storages are more or less auxiliary elements. Operations involve activities such as forming, shaping, assembling, and disassembling.		
	Move material by truck	Persons moving between locations	Move material by carrying (messenger)
Transportation ➡	Transportation is the movement of the material or worker being studied from one position or location to another. When materials are stored beside or within two or three feet of a bench or machine on which the operation is to be performed, the movement used in obtaining the material preceding the operation and putting it down after operation is considered part of the operation.		
	Examine for quality and quantity	Review for accuracy	Checking for information
Inspection ■	Inspection occurs when an item or items are checked, verified, reviewed, or examined for quality or quantity and not changed.		
	Material waiting is "In" basket	Person waiting in line	Waiting for signature
Delay ◗	A delay occurs when conditions do not permit or require immediate performance of the next planned action.		
	Suspense copy in file	Material in warehouse	Filed for permanent record
Storage ▲	Storage occurs when something remains in one place, not being worked on in a regular process, awaiting further action at a later date, permanent storage or disposal.		

FIGURE 27-2. Flow-Process Chart Symbols With Examples of Shop and Office Work.

pital care by rearranging nurses' stations and by rescheduling food service, housekeeping, and patient care activities. Figure 27-2 illustrates how broadly methods improvement techniques can be applied.

How does a methods improvement project get started?

By plotting a job breakdown on a flow-process chart. A job breakdown (somewhat like that for training purposes) lists every

Summary

	Present		Proposed		Difference	
	No.	Time	No.	Time	No.	Time
○ Operations						
⇨ Transportations						
□ Inspections						
D Delays						
▽ Storages						
Distance Traveled		FT		FT		FT

Flow-Process Chart

Job _____

_____

☐ Worker or ☒ Material _____

Chart begins _____

Chart ends _____

Charted by _____ Date _____

Details of (Present / Proposed) Method	Operation Transport Inspection Delay Storage	Distance in Feet	Quantity	Time	Notes
1 _____	○⇨□D▽				
2 _____	○⇨□D▽				
3 _____	○⇨□D▽				
4 _____	○⇨□D▽				
5 _____	○⇨□D▽				
6 _____	○⇨□D▽				
7 _____	○⇨□D▽				
8 _____	○⇨□D▽				
9 _____	○⇨□D▽				
10 _____	○⇨□D▽				
11 _____	○⇨□D▽				
12 _____	○⇨□D▽				
13 _____	○⇨□D▽				
14 _____	○⇨□D▽				
15 _____	○⇨□D▽				
16 _____	○⇨□D▽				
17 _____	○⇨□D▽				
18 _____	○⇨□D▽				
19 _____	○⇨□D▽				
20 _____	○⇨□D▽				
21 _____	○⇨□D▽				
22 _____	○⇨□D▽				
23 _____	○⇨□D▽				
24 _____	○⇨□D▽				
25 _____	○⇨□D▽				
26 _____	○⇨□D▽				
27 _____	○⇨□D▽				
28 _____	○⇨□D▽				
29 _____	○⇨□D▽				
30 _____	○⇨□D▽				

FIGURE 27-3. Flow-Process Chart.

step that must be taken to make a product, carry out a process, prepare paperwork, or provide a service. The flow-process chart, a standardized way to record the job breakdown, is illustrated in Figure 27-3. The flow-process chart makes recording easy because it uses a kind of shorthand with only five symbols to remember. Here is what the symbols look like and what they mean.

○ An *operation* is anything that adds value to the product—that changes its physical or chemical characteristics, that assembles or disassembles, that prepares it for another operation, transportation, storage, or inspection. Anything you do not classify as a transportation, a delay, a storage, or an inspection is an operation.

⇨ A *transportation* is the work of moving an object from one place to another.

☐ An *inspection* is the work of checking an object for quality, size, weight, or any other of its specifications.

D A *delay* occurs when nothing happens to the object while it is not in storage. An object held in a tote box or bin awaiting the next operation is delayed.

▽ A *storage* occurs when an object is kept and protected against unauthorized removal—as in a warehouse.

For further explanation of these symbols and examples of how they can be used for product, process, and services charting, look at Figure 27-2.

How do you make a flow-process chart?

There are six steps in making a flow-process chart. Try following them on the sample chart, Figure 27-3.

1. **Choose the job to be studied.**   State clearly what the job is and what object (person, part or article, or paper form) you are going to follow on the chart. Stick to that job and the same subject all the way through. Don't change from a person to an object; every detail on the chart must be about the one subject. If you want to chart what happens to a person *and* the object being worked on, you'll need a separate chart for each—one that follows the person, another that follows the part (more about that later).

2. **Pick a starting point and an ending point.**   Choose short cycles at first, since they have fewer steps. But once you have decided how much ground you want to cover, write down every step of the job between these two points.

3. **Jot down a short description of each detail.**   Don't overlook any detail—no matter how simple or obvious it may appear. Write down each and every operation, transportation, delay, storage, and inspection.

4. **Put in the symbols.** In this example the supervisor has connected the appropriate symbols. Many companies furnish forms that have the five symbols printed in a row at each step. All the supervisor does is draw a line connecting the proper symbols from step to step.

5. **Enter the distance and the time.** Write the distance in feet for each transportation over 1 foot. Where the elapsed time seemed especially significant, make a note of it in the time column.

6. **Summarize the process flow.** Do this by counting the number of operations in the symbol column and writing the number in the summary block. Do the same for transportations, storages, delays, and inspections. Enter the total of all distance traveled and total time of the job in the summary block.

Will it help to make a sketch of how the job moves?

Yes. If the job involves transportation over a sizable distance, a flow diagram showing the line of movement helps make the job clearer (Figure 27-4).

In what phase of a job does the greatest room for improvement lie?

In the operations that actually do something to the product—shape it, change it, add to it in any way that makes it worth more. These operations are called the value-added operations because they add to the value of the product. Look at each job as if it were divided into three steps:

Makeready. This includes the effort and the time that go into setting up the equipment or the machine or placing the parts in the machine. A painter makes ready to paint a house by mixing the paint, raising the ladder, spreading the drop cloths, and so forth.

Do. This is the actual work that adds value to the product. A painter adds value to the house by putting a coat of paint on it. A worker adds value to a piece of $\frac{1}{8}$-inch iron rod by cutting it into 2-inch lengths for bolts. Value is added by heading it. And value is added again when threads are cut on the other end.

Put-away. This phase covers anything that's done after the "do" is finished. It included unloading, disposing, storage, transfer, cleanup. The painter puts away by taking down the lad-

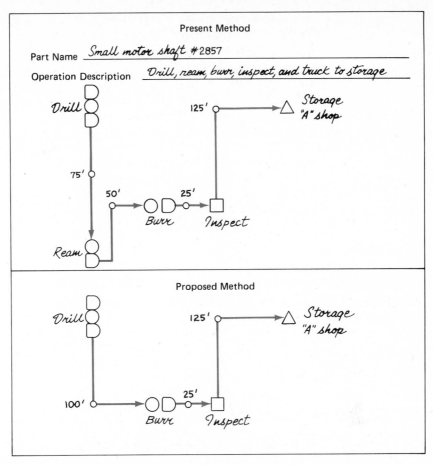

FIGURE 27-4. Flow Diagrams for Drilling, Reaming, and Burring a Small Motor Shaft.

der, removing the drop cloth, cleaning up any spots on the floor, washing the brushes, and storing the materials and equipment.

The reason you're advised to concentrate on a "do" operation is that if you eliminate it, you automatically eliminate the make-ready and the put-away associated with it.

How do you find places on the job where methods can be improved?

From study of the flow-process chart and the flow diagram. Challenge every step that has been charted. Ask yourself—and others—questions. (See next question in text.) Don't assume that the way things are being done today is the best way. Maybe it was a year ago, or even last week. But never conclude that there isn't a better way. New materials, new tools, new ideas always make a better way possible.

Look back at the flow-process chart in Figure 27-3. The supervisor who made it decided that it would be a good idea to combine the drilling (step 4) and the reaming (step 11) operations into a single, automatic operation using a new machine. The supervisor's new method eliminates the manual handling in steps 3 and 5. Then, the fact that the reaming at step 11 is now done along with the drilling at step 4 eliminates the need for steps 6, 7, 8, 9, 10, and 12, as well as 11. A look at the flow diagram (Figure 27-4) shows that these changes also reduce the transportation distance between drilling and burring operations from 125 feet (75 + 50) to 100 feet.

What kind of questions should you ask about the job being studied?

Ask challenging questions—questions that probe into every detail. You are probably familiar with Rudyard Kipling's famous poem:

> *I keep six honest serving men*
> *They taught me all I knew;*
> *Their names are What and Why and When*
> *And How and Where and Who.*

This often-quoted poem is your personal key to work simplification. Use it to remind yourself to ask:

- Why is the job done in the first place? Perhaps the job can be cut out altogether. Why is each of the details necessary? Give the third degree to each step. Is it really a must, or is it done "because we've always done it that way"?
- What is done? Have you recorded each detail so that you actually know? When operators pick up a part, for instance, they may not only be picking it up, they may be aligning it for insertion into the machine, or feeling the surface for burrs.
- Where is the detail done? Why is it done at that place? Where could it be done better, faster, more cheaply, more easily?
- When is it done? Why is it done then? When should it be done to do it better, faster, more cheaply, more easily?
- Who does it? Why does this person do it? Who might be better equipped, better trained, have more available time to do it more cheaply?
- How is it done? Why do we do it this way? How could the

method be improved by doing two or more operations at once, by mechanizing it, by using a fixture?

How do you develop new methods?

Uncovering delays and finding out what's wrong are valuable accomplishments, and their worth shouldn't be minimized. But this effort doesn't pay off until you've devised a better way to do the job. There are many approaches from which to choose:

Eliminate. First look for the chance of dropping out the detail or the entire operation. There's no point in wasting time improving methods if the job doesn't have to be done at all.

Combine. Doing two or more things at once saves time. Often it saves additional time by eliminating transportations, storages, and inspections that previously took place between operations.

Change sequence. Frequently you can do things more easily or cheaply by changing the order in which they are done. Ideally a part should be finished, for example, only after the shaping operations have been completed.

Simplify. After you've searched the first three approaches in this list, look for ways of doing the job in a simpler manner. Here's where you try to cut down on waste motions, replace hand operations with mechanical ones, provide fixtures for positioning, chutes for feeding. But remember, don't try to simplify until you've first tried to eliminate, combine, or change sequence.

In what ways does motion economy help?

Motion economy is the use of the human body to produce results with the least physical and mental effort. Figure 25-1 showed its value in designing workplaces. It's been given long study by methods engineers and physiologists. Here are some of the principles of motion economy that are generally agreed on as aids to getting a job done with the least labor:

Motions should be productive. Every motion a person makes should be concentrated on "do" operations, should bring the job closer to a finish. Hands, for instance, should not be wasted in holding the work; they should be released for more productive operations.

Motions should be simple. The fewer parts of the body used, the better. Use a finger and a thumb rather than the whole hand. Grasp an object by reaching with the forearm rather than with the whole arm. Motions should be along curved paths rather than straight lines, because most of the body members swing from a joint in a circular motion.

Motions should be rhythmic.   Arrange the work so that it's easy to work with smooth motions. It's easier, too, for hands to move in opposite directions and in similar motion paths.

Make workers comfortable.   The workbench, the tool, the chair should all be arranged so that the operator feels comfortable whether the work requires sitting or standing or walking.

Combine two or more tools.   Picking up and laying down tools takes time. It's quicker to reverse a tool with a working edge on either end than to pick up and lay down two separate tools.

Pre-position tools and materials.   Having things arranged so that they are already aligned before the operator picks them up speeds the job. If a part needs to be turned over or around, the job needs positioning.

Limit activity.   A person works comfortably within the swing of the arms forward and up and down. If the person has to reach or stretch beyond that normal work area, turn around, bend, or stoop, it takes time and is fatiguing.

Use gravity when possible.   Materials can be fed by gravity through bins and chutes. The part then comes out the bottom of the chute right at the worker's hand each time.

Where does value analysis fit into this picture?

To my way of thinking, value analysis (also called value engineering) is simply methods improvement focused on a product rather than on a process. However, Lawrence D. Miles, who conceived of value analysis while at the General Electric Company in 1947, defined it this way: "Value analysis is an arrangement of techniques which makes clear the functions the user wants; establishes the appropriate costs for each; then causes the required knowledge, creativity, initiative to be used to provide each function at that cost."

Miles's "functions" are of two classes: use and esteem. The use function provides the action that customers want from the product or service. An esteem function pleases them and causes them to buy it. Take an automobile. Use function: transportation. Esteem function: chromium trim.

The objective of value analysis is to keep the use and the esteem functions that customers want—but at a lower cost. Value people do not directly lower cost. They only provide criteria for decision makers (including supervisors) whose actions will lower cost. A value analysis study usually consists of five phases:

1. Gathering information to identify functions.
2. Creating ideas to serve functions at less cost.
3. Evaluating ideas as to practicality.
4. Investigating sources of supply and improvement.
5. Reporting findings to decision makers.

How good are employee suggestion plans for getting ideas from your employees?

It depends on the company, the way the plan is carried out, and the manner in which the supervisor supports the plan. Some companies have had phenomenal success with plans. Others have been unsuccessful. The National Association of Suggestion Systems reports that on the average you can expect 238 suggestions per year for every 1,000 eligible employees; of these suggestions, about 25 percent will be worth accepting.

To make your company's plan a success, get interested in it. If you adopt a negative attitude, employees will be cool toward the plan, too. Find out what part you play in the plan's administration, and recognize that the degree to which your employees participate will be a measure of how well you stimulate cooperation.

What's the connection between methods improvement and work simplification?

Work simplification is the brainchild of Allan H. "Mogey" Mogensen. He answers the question this way at his famous Lake Placid seminars:

> Work simplification **always** introduces the human element, is **always** designed for foreman (sic) and employee participation. This isn't true of many methods improvement programs. All too often the emphasis is placed upon engineering or top-side experting, and only lip service is given to supervisory and employee considerations. This was even more true in the old days. The engineer spoiled most of his opportunities by his "take-it-or-leave-it" attitude. Work simplification, on the other hand, builds into its program automatic methods for consultation with, and participation by supervisors and employees. That's the big difference. Without this participation, most methods improvement programs are only partially effective, if they don't fail completely.

supervisory word power

Work measurement. The determination, by systematic and (ideally) precise methods, of the time dimension of a particular task. Literally: how much work is there to be done? How long will it take a particular machine or a particular kind of person to do it properly?

Wage incentive. Payment of wages in such a way as to induce an employee to exceed some predetermined standard, usually for quantity of output but occasionally for reduction in spoilage or some other desirable result.

Daywork. Work in a plant or an office in which the hourly, daily, or weekly wage does not directly depend on the quantity of production or output, as it typically does when work is on a wage-incentive basis.

Work cycle. A pattern (or sequence) of motions or processes that is repeated with little or no variation each time an operation is performed. Also, for larger or longer sequences, the succession of operations or processes that is repeated with little or no variation each time a unit of production is completed.

Process time. The time required to complete a specified series of progressive actions or a specified operation's work cycle on a single unit of production; for example, the time, from start to finish, from the cutting of the bar stock to the final polishing of the threads, to make a steel bolt; or the time from mixing the flour and the water in a bowl to removing the baked loaf from the oven, to make a loaf of bread.

Other Important Terms in This Chapter

fair day's work
fatigue allowance
flow diagram
flow-process chart
motion economy
motion study
predetermined elemental time standards
standards
standard time data
time study
value analysis
work sampling
work simplification

reading comprehension

1. If the specifications for a polished metal product were raised to require a higher finish than previously, could the employee who works on that product expect the standard time to be increased or decreased? Why?

2. Compare a loose piece rate with a tight piece rate. Which is better for the company?

3. If industrial engineers didn't rely on rating an employee's pace, how would they arrive at the normal time to do a particular job? Why wouldn't this be a good idea?

4. What is the relationship between a wage incentive and a piece rate?

5. Why wouldn't it be wise for a supervisor to conduct a work sampling study by making observations at the same time every hour?

6. Compare methods improvement with work simplification.

7. One of the first decisions a methods analyst must make before breaking down a job is whether to focus on the person who does the job or on the object that is being worked on. Why is this important?

8. For what reasons is it just as important to challenge why a particular operation is performed as it is to try to improve how it is done?

9. What is a value-added operation? What is one in which no value is added?

10. Compare, for the sake of value analysis, the use function and the esteem function.

supervision in action

**THE CASE OF BILL SUDDS AND THE METHODS ENGINEER.
A case study in human relations involving improved work methods, with questions for you to answer.**

The Efferson Manufacturing Company is a first-rate old company that has built a quality line of office accessories for years—inkwells, staplers, dating machines, paper cutters, and others. Recently the company changed hands, and a new management came in to run the plant.

One of the first things the new manager did was to set up an industrial engineering department to study ways and means of improving manufacturing procedures and reducing costs. Ralph Abelson, the industrial engineering manager, was middle-aged, with an excellent record of accomplishment. He had been secured from his previous employer only by the offer of a sizable increase in salary.

Abelson spent the first month on his new job getting his feet on the ground and meeting the various plant supervisors. Most of the supervisors, who had expected the worst, found Abelson a pleasant surprise. In fact, it was remarked that he seemed to be doing more listening than telling. He certainly gave no evidence of wanting to shake up the plant from bottom to top. There was even some question in the supervisors' minds about when Abelson would begin to earn his keep. Abelson answered that question in February, when he began his methods improvement program.

The program began with Abelson's calling all the plant supervisors together. He carefully explained that the objective of the program was to enable the plant to reduce costs 10 percent so that products in their highly competitive market could be kept in the line. Abelson said that he expected the supervisors themselves to make the greatest contribution to the effort, since they knew more than anyone else about the plant's operations.

After the meeting, Bill Sudds, assembly supervisor, and Grace Keeting, shipping supervisor, talked the program over. It's a matter of record that Bill did most of the talking: "I see that the honeymoon is finally over. I wondered how long Abelson would play cat and mouse with us before he started to tap our brains for all we know. But he'll find it's a long, cold day in July before he gets anything out of me."

1. What do you think of Bill's reaction?
2. How successful do you think Abelson will be with his methods improvement program?
3. If you were Abelson, how would you have gone about selling your program to the supervisors?

enriching your viewpoint

To widen the scope of your understanding of work measurement, work sampling, and methods improvement, the following sources are recommended:

Fein, Mitchell, "Work Measurement and Wage Incentives," *Industrial Engineering Magazine,* September 1973, p. 49.

"Ideas Blow You to Tomorrow: Some Great Ideas Started With Just a Suggestion," *Industry Week,* February 22, 1971.

Johnson, Frank J., "Value Analysis," in Lester R. Bittel (ed.), *The Encyclopedia of Professional Management,* McGraw-Hill Book Company, New York, 1979, pp. 1178–1183.

Lindemann, A. J., Earl F. Lundgren, H. K. von Kaas, *Encyclopaedic Dictionary of Management and Manufacturing Terms,* Kendall/Hunt Publishing Company, Dubuque, Iowa, 1974.

Maynard, H. B. (ed.), *Industrial Engineering Handbook,* 2d ed., McGraw-Hill Book Company, New York, 1963, Sec. 3, "Work Measurement Techniques."

Miles, L. D., *The Techniques of Value Analysis and Value Engineering,* 2d ed., McGraw-Hill Book Company, New York, 1972.

Mogensen, Allan H., "Work Simplification and Improvement," in Lester R. Bittel (ed.), *The Encyclopedia of Professional Management,* McGraw-Hill Book Company, New York, 1979, pp. 1225–1233.

Niebel, B. W., *Motion and Time Study,* Richard D. Irwin, Inc., Homewood, Ill., 1967.

Richardson, Wallace J., *Cost Improvement, Work Sampling, and Short Interval Scheduling,* Reston Publishing Co., Inc., Reston, Va., 1976.

Shaw, Anne G., *The Purpose and Practice of Motion Study,* 2d ed., Columbine Press, Ltd., Manchester and London, 1960.

Work Performance Rating: A Motion Picture and An Industrial Training Aid, Vought Aeronautics, Dallas, 1972.

28

toward a higher quality of workmanship

How much does poor quality cost?

It costs industry billions of dollars each year. It is most obvious in the form of product liability suits (one million claims for $50 billion damages in 1976 alone) and manufacturers' recalls to repair defective goods. Billions of dollars are lost to poor quality, however, in other ways.

Corrective costs. This is money down the drain for any of the following: (1) damaged parts and materials that must be scrapped or, at best, reworked; (2) the time and effort of doing poor work over; (3) the cost of warranties that presume errors will be made that must be corrected later; and (4) the cost of handling customer complaints. Corrective quality is by far the most costly—from 2 to 10 percent of sales revenue.

Preventive costs. These are the costs of trying to prevent poor workmanship or defective goods in the first place. They include routine (1) inspection, (2) testing, and (3) quality-control procedures, including education and motivation programs. It is a rare organization where the costs of preventive quality exceed 3 percent of total sales revenue.

Are quality problems limited to manufacturing plants?

Far from it. Poor workmanship causes costly quality problems in just about every line of work, including clerical. For example, a close watch should be kept on any of the following that applies to your organization:

- **Accounting.** Billing errors, payroll errors, accounts payable deductions missed, percentage of late reports, incorrect computer inputs, and errors in special reports as audited.
- **Data processing.** Keypunch cards thrown out for error, deductions missed, computer downtime due to error, rerun time.
- **Engineering.** Change orders due to error, drafting errors found by checkers, late releases.
- **Hotel operation.** Guests taken to unmade or occupied room, reservations not honored, inaccurate or missed billing.
- **Marketing and sales.** Orders or prices written up incorrectly, errors in contract specifications, wrong copy or prices in advertisements and catalogs.
- **Maintenance.** Callbacks on repairs, wrong parts installed, downtime due to faulty maintenance.
- **Retailing.** Wrong product on shelves, incorrect pricing, merchandise damage in handling, storage, or shipping.

Philip B. Crosby, who conceived of Zero Defects, without which the United States would not have put men on the moon, states flatly: "There is no basic difference between manufacturing and service quality management except that one has tangibles as its product and the other does not. *Both require people to perform.*"

Who should have final responsibility for product quality—line supervisor or inspector?

Here's a question that gets plenty of batting around in many companies and has started many feuds between an otherwise successful supervisor and the inspection department. In the long run, responsibility must be fixed by your company's policy and its interpretation by your boss. But there's a long-standing rule of thumb that holds the best answer: Quality must be built into the product. No one can inspect it in.

Actually, few supervisors deny that they are responsible for product quality. The jurisdictional disputes arise over who's the best judge of quality—and who has the authority to stop production when quality falls below specifications. This is something you should try to have your boss make crystal clear for you. Otherwise, chaos will prevail.

Three plant operating executives I know were asked this same question. Here is the gist of each person's answer:

Supervisor's primary responsibility.   One chief engineer says:

> The quality of a product depends on the coordinated efforts of the people who design and the people who produce. The inspector acts as the last hurdle the product must leap on its way to the customer. Many supervisors still take refuge in the old saw that "our job is to make, it is the inspector's job to inspect." This type of thinking must be rooted out if an organization is to thrive and grow. It is the primary responsibility of the supervisor to turn out work of acceptable quality.

Supervisor's special duty.   A director of quality control says:

> The supervisor's responsibility for the quality of the department's products is not different from top management's responsibility for the profits of the company.
> The inspector's function is in many ways analogous to that of a treasurer. The inspector, like the treasurer, must compare present results against an agreed-to standard and, when the operation is not adhering to specifications, report these facts to the proper parties. This means that the inspector should forward this information to the department supervisor, who must make the decision of accepting or rejecting the questionable product.
> The key to quality of product is pride of workmanship, and quality is sharply reduced when the supervisor's duties are transferred to the inspection or quality control personnel.

Sometimes automatically controlled.   A factory superintendent says:

> In those industries where mechanization and automation have been gone into in a big way, the immediate responsibility for the quality of goods lies primarily with the manager of quality control and the designer of the machinery, because the quality safeguards are (or should be) built into the machine or process. For example, weaving machines or printing presses will stop auto-

matically if a thread is broken or if the paper is not properly lined up.

In other plants ... it is the responsibility of the departmental supervisors to train their operators so as to obtain the desired quality. Following this, the quality of the finished product becomes the responsibility of the supervisor, with the inspection department functioning primarily as the eyes of top management and the ultimate consumer.

What should you do if there is no inspection or quality-control department at your location?

If you make a product, the chances are that there will be an official inspection department somewhere in your organization —even if it doesn't carry on its activity in your department. If such is the case, you might first ask the central inspection department for advice in setting up your own quality checks. If you must go it alone, however, try this analysis of your quality problem:

* What is my inspection problem? What do I have to do to maintain quality?
* Shall I assign the inspection to someone as a part-time or a full-time job?
* Shall I do the inspecting myself? If so, how much time can I devote to it?
* Should I try to inspect all the work produced or only a sample of it? Or should I confine myself to the first piece on a new setup only?

Once you have considered these questions and decided on your approach, you can proceed to the next question.

How can you make your own checks of quality?

Keep in mind these ten points:

1. Set up some specific quality standards, such as dimensions and appearance. Keeping examples of acceptable and nonacceptable work on exhibit helps.
2. Put specifications in writing. See that your employees get a copy to guide them.
3. Allocate some of your own time for inspection. The total amount isn't so important as doing a certain amount each day.
4. Pick the spots where quality can best be made or lost. There is no point in spending your time checking operations where nothing much can go wrong.

5. Make inspection rounds from time to time. Change the order of your trips frequently.

6. Select at random 5 or 10 percent of the pieces produced (for example, letters typed) at a particular station. Inspect each one carefully.

7. Correct operating conditions immediately where your inspection shows material to be off grade or equipment to be faulty.

8. Consult with employees to determine the reason for poor workmanship or unacceptable products. Seek their cooperation in correcting conditions and improving quality.

9. Check the first piece on a new setup or a new assignment. Don't permit production until you are satisfied with the quality.

10. Post quality records, scrap percentages, and so forth, on the bulletin board to keep employees informed of how the department is doing qualitywise.

How can you get employees more interested in quality?

It's been popular to complain about the I-don't-care attitude of some employees. Your viewpoint should be that if employees don't care about quality, it's because you have failed to sell them on its importance.

To get a worker to become quality-conscious, start right from the first day by stressing quality as well as output. Emphasize that the two must go hand in hand in your department. Whenever you show an employee how to do a job—especially a new one—be specific as to what kind of work is acceptable and what kind will not meet specifications. Explain the reason behind product quality limitations, and try to give your employees the little tricks of the trade that help to make quality easy to attain.

Make no mistake: It takes a lot of understanding and coordination to make quality come out right. For example, in one case the difference was only a quarter of an inch. But when somebody dumped a supply of the shorter bolts next to the spot on the assembly line where the longer ones were needed to attach brake pedals, the result was the recall of 1,700 Chevrolets. An alert inspector caught this defect by spotting that there wasn't enough bolt protruding from the exit side of the nut. The inspector started the investigation that led to the recall. It happened on an assembly line where 2,000 employees put together 45 autos and trucks (five different models) every hour.

Why do employees make errors?

Generally speaking, there are six reasons why employees make mistakes—and most of them begin with management inadequacies rather than with employee shortcomings. Experience of companies who have improved their quality shows these potential causes of errors:

- Lack of training
- Poor communications
- Inadequate tools and equipment
- Insufficient planning
- Incomplete specifications and procedures
- Lack of attention

Poor communications, for example, can be overcome by taking the extra time to make sure each person fully understands the instructions. In written orders, don't leave loopholes that can lead to misinterpretation. One small company with a large staff of Spanish-speaking people had the workers repeat the orders that were given to them. It took a few minutes, but it actually saved time. Rejects and rework tumbled to a fraction of 1 percent.

Lack of attention, however, is completely different from the other potential causes of error and is perhaps the most serious. This is very personal and stems from employees' attitudes. You must reaffirm that management is interested in employees and will help them do their jobs to perfection. You, as a supervisor, must re-create the old-fashioned pride in one's craft. You must motivate employees so that they have a personal attachment to their jobs and will be proud of them.

It isn't all the employees' fault, of course. Quality experts, for example, observe that auto defects occur five major ways:

- A flaw in design that doesn't show up in testing
- A flaw in purchased or manufactured materials or parts
- A flaw in the manufacturing process itself
- A flaw in the tools and gauges provided
- A flaw introduced by sloppy or poorly informed workmanship

What can you do to help the employee understand that the customer is the real quality boss?

Try to provide employees with a customer's-eye view of your product. Workers who handle the same product every day tend to lose their objectivity. They begin to take minor defects for granted. To help them see the product as the customer does, get samples of customer complaints (about specific defects) and circulate them in your department. Explain how the customer uses your product—how it will be compared with a competitor's unit and how quality will affect its use. At an Ohio plant, supervisors and workers are selected to attend training sessions held for distributor salespeople. Employees hear at first hand the reasons for some of the things they do. "Our sales story really opened my eyes. I didn't realize what it takes to sell a pump," said one shop steward after attending the sales course. The net effect was a greater interest in high quality and lower costs.

At the plant of a manufacturer of small airplanes, where damage to aircraft bodies during production is a hazard, this approach is used to stimulate care among operators: "You wouldn't buy a $500 refrigerator with a patch on the door. Would you expect one of our customers to take a $250,000 plane with a 2-inch patch on it?"

Probably nothing is more dramatic in a painful and costly fashion than when a company issues a recall to the owners of its products so that a defect can be corrected. While the auto manufacturers get the full impact of the publicity (26 million autos were recalled in the first six years after the United States government cracked down on auto safety), many other firms in other industries have faced the same problem. For example, *The New York Times* cited on one day in the 1970s the following recalls:

- The electrical manufacturer who called back pacemaker heart machines with mechanical defects
- The major candy maker who recalled 4,000 fruitcakes with moth eggs in them
- The 20,000 tins of crab meat that went out with the wrong labels
- The thousands of cases of a soft drink that were ordered back because of contaminated lids
- The callback of the thousands of bottles of pharmaceuticals that went out with faulty caps

The granddaddy of all recalls occurred in October 1978, when Firestone Tire and Rubber Company announced its recall of 10 million steel-belted radial tires at a cost to the company of $230 million.

When things go wrong with quality or workmanship in your department, what steps should you take?

Supervisors at an Industrial Management Institute of the University of Wisconsin agreed on these 12 checkpoints for action:

1. Do you explain to each worker exactly what quality is expected on the job?
2. When work is rejected, do you make sure that the workers

concerned know what is wrong and exactly what is expected of them?

3. Have you a plan of close cooperation (for the purpose of improving quality) with the supervisor of the department from which your work comes and the supervisor of the department to which your work goes?

4. Do you get, or make, a list of all the defective work in your department each week or month so you can take definite steps to prevent similar defective work during the next period?

5. Do you set aside a definite amount of your own time for actual inspection of the work in your department?

6. Do you have a system for getting suggestions from your workers on how to improve quality?

7. Do you hold regular talks with each of your workers regarding the quality of the work that person is doing?

8. Are you making full and effective use of departmental bulletin boards for posting facts about quality and defective work and for exhibiting examples of good or bad work?

9. Do you keep your workers informed on the cost of defective work in your department?

10. Do you have any method for arousing pride of workmanship in your employees?

11. Have you systematically acquainted each worker with the relation between quality workmanship and job security?

12. Do your employees understand the value placed on quality performance when they are considered for raises or promotions?

If you can answer yes to most of these questions, you'll find that quality troubles will stay away from your door.

What is meant by statistical quality control?

Statistical quality control simply means that numbers—statistics—are used as a part of the overall approach for controlling quality. Statistics are tools and in no way relieve supervisor or employee from a concern with quality. Used properly, however, they can be of considerable aid.

In many industries, only the techniques of statistical quality control would make rigid specifications economically attainable. For example, J. C. Penney Co., Inc., orders millions of knitted garments each year. It uses various inspection and statistical methods to screen the thousands of samples submitted to the company for purchase. As a consequence, the company rejects 30 percent of the submissions, thus preventing subsequent disasters at the sales counters.

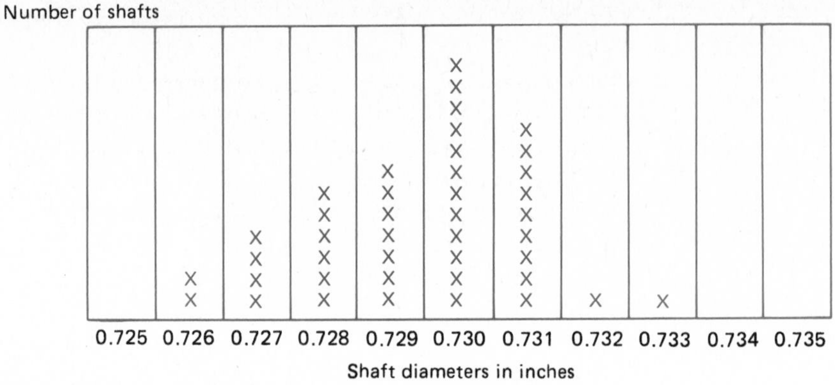

Number of shafts

| | 0.725 | 0.726 | 0.727 | 0.728 | 0.729 | 0.730 | 0.731 | 0.732 | 0.733 | 0.734 | 0.735 |

(tally marks)
- 0.726: X X
- 0.727: X X X X
- 0.728: X X X X X
- 0.729: X X X X X X
- 0.730: X X X X X X X X X
- 0.731: X X X X X X X
- 0.732: X
- 0.733: X

Shaft diameters in inches

FIGURE 28-1. Simple Frequency-Distribution Chart Used in Statistical Quality Control.

What are some of the tools of statistical quality control, and how do they affect the supervisor's job?

Greatly increased demands for precision parts have stepped up the need for better methods to measure and record the accuracy with which manufacturing people meet product specifications. Statistical methods speed this measuring process, and more and more companies use them in some form or other. Don't let any fear you may have of mathematics prevent your using statistical methods.

Three statistical quality-control tools are encountered most commonly:

1. **Frequency-distribution charts.** Hold on. It isn't as bad as it sounds. Probably you'll recognize it by its more popular name—a tally card. If you were asked to place an *X* in the appropriate space for every shaft diameter you gauged in a given lot, chances are that you'd come up with a tally that looks something like Figure 28-1.

In this case the nominal shaft diameter was 0.730 inch with a tolerance of ±0.002. This tally gives you a picture of just what and where the shaft variations are instead of merely recording whether a shaft is good or bad. This frequency-distribution chart (that's what it is in its simplest form) helps tell you the causes of the variation. The wide distribution in this case indicates tool wobble. A picture that showed parts bunched around a point below or above the nominal 0.730 inch (say, at 0.728) might mean that the setup must be adjusted.

2. **Quality-control chart.** This is an hour-by-hour, day-by-

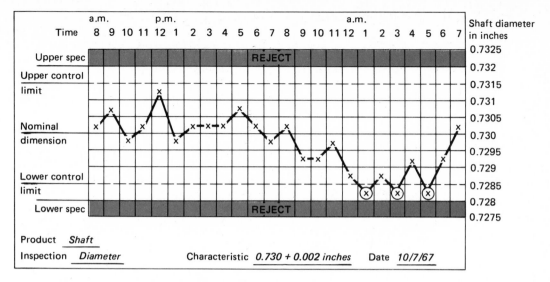

FIGURE 28-2. Quality-Control Chart.

day graphic comparison of actual product quality characteristics. On the chart are limits that reflect the person's or the machine's ability to produce, as shown by past experience. Statisticians make use of the knowledge of shop tolerances and analysis of previous frequency distribution tallies to establish these limits. Whenever the inspections plotted on the control chart show that the product is getting outside the predicted control limits, that's a signal for the supervisor or the operator to correct what is being done so that the product comes back into specification.

In Figure 28-2, the part being made is supposed to measure 0.730 inch. The tolerance specs are ±0.002, or from 0.728 to 0.732 inch. The quality-control statistician has predicted in advance from a frequency-distribution diagram that most production will vary within these control limits—the 0.7285 and 0.7315 lines. When quality stays within these limits, it is said to be on the highway. It is to be expected that a few products will fall outside the limits into the shoulder. But when the trend of measurements indicates that product quality is drifting progressively into the shoulder area, it's time to check the process. Any product that goes beyond the upper or lower specification limits (goes into the ditch) is rejected.

The value of the chart lies in its telling the supervisor and the operator whether they are within bounds or whether they are losing control of the process, before the process goes completely haywire.

3. Sampling tables.   The trend today has been away from 100 percent inspection, which is costly and often misleading. (In a 100 percent check of a load of oranges, does this mean that each orange has been inspected for color, ripeness, thickness of skin, appearance? Or does it mean that each orange was inspected for appearance only?) The first solution to less than 100 percent checking was spot-checking, but this proved unreliable. Today most sampling is done according to the size of the lot of goods produced and according to tables designed by statisticians for this purpose. These tables guide the quality-control manager in the determination of how large a sample to take and how often to take it.

Is there a connection between reliability and statistical quality control?

Yes, indirectly, and it often has a direct relationship to product liability claims. Reliability is defined as the probability of a product's performing a specific function, under given conditions, for a specified time, without failure. It must measure up specifically, therefore, to (1) what it's supposed to do (for example, for a bolt to hold 500 pounds of direct pull); (2) the circumstances under which it will be used (as at temperatures up to 450° F in an acid atmosphere); and (3) the length of time it should perform before it breaks or stops working (as for 25,000 fastenings or 39 months). Reliability can be determined either by direct test (using it until it fails) or by statistical computation (based on assumptions about the design and work characteristic of the product). Reliability is usually expressed as the (mean) time expected between failures—as, say, 1/0.002 or 500 hours. Because the assumptions made vary in the degree of confidence the estimator has in them, reliability figures are often qualified as having, say, 85 percent confidence (or being 85 percent sure to last as long as predicted but having a 15 percent risk of not lasting that long).

Reliability enters statistical quality-control considerations when you are deciding on the limits of variation, on how far from standard the product can be without being rejected. Obviously, the tighter the variable limits, the greater the reliability of the product. However, this does not mean that a perfect part will be reliable forever. It will be reliable only as long as it was designed to be under the specified operating conditions.

How important is nondestructive testing?

Increasingly so. The more valuable the product, the more important it is to test that product without destroying it. The farmer who candles eggs to be sure they are fresh is practicing nondestructive testing. Similarly, the company that X-rays a casting to see that it has no flaws is employing nondestructive testing. The principle of nondestructive testing is to make sure that your product is free of flaws without tearing it apart to find out.

The most common of all nondestructive tests is radiography, or, more simply, X rays. Also widely used are sound waves, temperature flow patterns, magnetic fields, liquid penetrating dyes that show flaws under ultraviolet light, and eddy currents induced by high-frequency alternating currents.

What is Zero Defects?

Zero Defects (ZD) is a quality-control program with a new wrinkle. It motivates. That is, it instills in each of us pride in our work. It puts quality on a personal basis. Zero Defects techniques stimulate us to care about accuracy and completeness, to pay attention to detail, to improve work habits. In this manner we work toward reducing our own errors to zero.

All other quality programs attempt control by rejecting work that doesn't measure up to minimum standards. Zero Defects reverses this philosophy. You aim for consistently high-quality products by eliminating all errors made by all the people designing, producing, selling, and servicing the item.

Zero Defects programs anticipated what lawyers have learned from product liability suits: Defective goods can arise from errors and poor workmanship anywhere along the line. Figure 28-3 illustrates this relationship.

What makes Zero Defects work so well?

Zero Defects gets results for a variety of reasons. The main ones, in my opinion, are as follows:

1. **A strict and specific management standard.** Management, including supervisory staff, does not use vague phrases to explain what it wants. It makes the quality standard very clear: Do it the right way from the start. As Philip Crosby says, "What standard would you set on how many babies nurses are allowed to drop?"

2. **Complete commitment by everyone.** Crosby denies that ZD is a motivational program, but ZD does work because every-

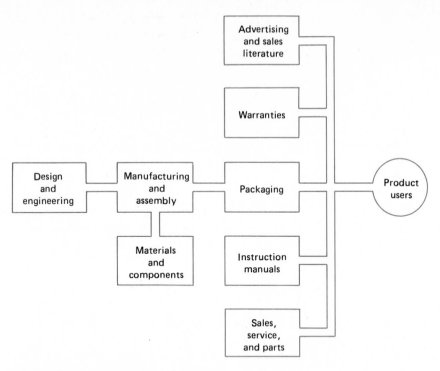

FIGURE 28-3. Where Product Liability Suits Arise. Adapted from "How to Control Product Liability Losses," *Journal of American Insurance,* Vol. 52, No. 2, p. 21, Summer 1976.

one gets deep into the act. From sweeper to clerk, everyone is encouraged to spot problems, detect errors, and prescribe ways and means for their removal. This commitment is best illustrated by the ZD pledge: "I freely pledge myself to make a constant, conscious effort to do my job right the first time, recognizing that my individual contribution is a vital part of the overall effort."

3. Removal of actions and conditions that cause errors. Philip Crosby claims that at ITT, where he's vice president for quality, 90 percent of all error causes can be acted on and fully removed by first-level supervision. In other words, top management must do its part to improve conditions, but supervisors and employees can handle most problems right in the department.

In what way is good housekeeping related to the quality of workmanship?

It is very hard to do good work in a sloppy shop. This applies to any kind of work, from assembling precision instruments to pouring white-hot iron in a foundry, from preparing purchase orders in a warehouse to sorting canceled checks in a bank. The insistence on neatness and cleanliness at the workplace also tells employees that the supervisor expects neatness and orderliness in their work.

Why are so many employees untidy in their work habits?

Neatness and cleanliness do not come naturally to most of us. Employees often feel that if they are working hard, the mess they create while doing so is justified. Supervisors, too, sometimes feel the same way. This is a mistake. Supervisors need to be sold on the value of good housekeeping before they can sell it to their employees, and then they must persuade employees that good housekeeping is a basic part of their jobs.

Won't employees resent having to do their own cleanup?

Some will. They will protest that housekeeping is menial work, that they are depriving the sweepers of their rightful jobs, or that they aren't paid to clean. Each of these objections must be met with the facts. Housekeeping need not be menial. Good care of the workplace has always been associated with craftsmanship. It is a foundation stone in apprentice training.

Improved personal housekeeping has deprived few custodial employees of a job. Usually it has enabled the custodial workers to become more effective and to show better results from their efforts.

As to housekeeping being part of the industrial worker's job, formal job descriptions usually include "care of the workplace."

Many workers have pack-rat tendencies, too. They accumulate an unbelievable collection of junk at their workplace if permitted. A certain amount of this should be left to the worker's own discretion—if it is kept neatly. But you should discourage collection of candy or food wrappers and old newspapers and magazines.

Poor housekeeping in the company is the result of poor work habits that have been tolerated by management—primarily the supervisor. The supervisor is the primary person in the drive to change these habits.

How can you sell a housekeeping program?

Housekeeping has many personal payoffs for those who practice it. When you are talking about better housekeeping to employ-

ees, don't present it in terms of just something the boss wants—
"We'll be hassled if it isn't improved." Instead, show workers how
good housekeeping improves the safety record and makes the
department a safer place for employees to work. Emphasize that
housekeeping actually makes production easier, quicker, and
more accurate and that clean and neat surroundings take much
of the drudgery out of work—and keep clothing cleaner, too.

Nothing is so convincing to employees as a demonstration of
what good housekeeping is—and what it can do for them. Many
people are puzzled when told to clean up. Each person has his
or her own standards of what "clean" is, and these standards
differ widely. So take a section of your department and see that it
is arranged and cleaned to a minimum of what you judge can be
maintained by your regular work force. Don't overlook anything
—from wiping out the inside of lamp fixtures to stacking boxes
squarely. Then gather your employees together so they can see
what you consider good housekeeping. Let them see if you've
missed anything, make suggestions, or protest standards they
think are unattainable. Then hold them to the accepted standard.

How can you make a
housekeeping inspection more effective?

Combine it with your safety inspections. Emphasize its relationship to quality efforts. To get more out of your inspections,
select different employees to make the inspection with you. Demonstrate your housekeeping standards to them, and let them
point out substandard conditions to you. Treat the inspection as
an educational exercise as well as a supervisory one. Employees
who participate will be better housekeepers—and they may help
you enforce housekeeping standards on less responsible employees.

What should you look for when making
a housekeeping and quality inspection?

Divide your observations into three areas.

1. Machines and equipment:
Unauthorized arrangements. Have machines, storage areas, or
operating areas been changed without approval in such a manner as to make housekeeping and quality workmanship more difficult?
Damaged or obsolete equipment. Are there unsightly, damaged,
defaced, or improperly guarded machines or other equipment?

Congestion with portable gear. Are air-operated or otherwise portable drills, guns, and tools or movable benches placed so as to hamper personal movement?

Leaks and drips. Are there leaks of air, water, oil, steam, coolant from pipes, tanks, or other containers?

2. Materials and storage:

Top-heavy piling. Are boxes or pallets stacked so as to tip easily or make proper materials selections difficult?

Cluttered aisles. Do employees leave boxes, tote pans, skids, or other work-in-process in the aisles so as to interfere with work or be hazardous?

Protruding obstacles. Do racks, bins, benches, or machines stick out into walkways or working areas in such a way that clothing might be caught?

Rube Goldbergs. Are there any makeshift arrangements of equipment when standard and safer setups are available?

3. Cleanliness and order:

Dirty floors and walls. Look under tables and benches, into corners and drawers, behind machinery.

Messy equipment. Are machines needlessly dirty? Are chips, scraps, wiping cloths, waste allowed to accumulate?

Unclean restrooms. Are fountains, washrooms, and locker and shower rooms spotless, regardless of their age? Are soap, paper, hot water, and towels available?

Rubbish and litter. Except where they are found in their proper containers, are cigarette butts, paper, bottles, or other rubbish accumulating?

Personal items. Is clothing kept in locker rooms or on assigned racks? Are lunch boxes, pocketbooks, toolboxes kept where they belong?

See also the safety checklist in Table 17-2 in Chapter 17.

Should employees be disciplined for poor-quality workmanship or substandard housekeeping efforts?

Yes, but only as a last resort and after you have set down unmistakably clear and attainable standards. Good workmanship is a job requirement. So is good housekeeping. But "good" means different things to different people.

Preferably, your standards for both quality and housekeeping should be written. They should be illustrated by examples, and they should be fully communicated to all employees.

Even so, the best approach to good quality and housekeeping is a positive one. Each employee should be encouraged to accept responsibility for them as a desirable way of working. Employees should know what the penalty for failure to meet standards is, of course, but the threatening approach should be avoided. (See Chapter 22, "How and When to Discipline.")

supervisory word power

Specification.   The definitions (preferably written) of expected performance of product (or service), usually stated in finite measurements of size, shape, finish, durability, and so forth.

Tolerance.   Essentially a statement of precision that establishes limits within which the product or the service must meet the specification; for example, a machined part specified to be 1 inch in diameter with a tolerance of ±0.005 inch.

Defect.   Any variation (in the product or service) from specifications that falls outside the prescribed tolerances and thus causes (1) the product to be rejected, discarded, or reworked or (2) a service to be interrupted, declined, or delayed.

Rework.   To remanufacture, adjust, modify, or otherwise repair a product or a service that has been rejected because of a defect.

Acceptable quality levels.   AQL is a more general form of specification that tells a supervisor the kind of tolerance (in terms of percentage of rejects, extent of rework, number of defects, number of customer complaints, frequency of stockouts, extent of delays in service) that will be judged as acceptable performance.

Other Important Terms in This Chapter

frequency-distribution chart	quality-control chart
housekeeping	reliability
inspection	sampling tables
nondestructive testing	statistical quality control
product liability	workmanship
product recall	Zero Defects

reading comprehension

1. Compare a line supervisor's responsibility for quality with that of an inspector.

2. The quality of the product is just as important—and just as variable—for nonmanufacturing workers like keypunch operators, supermarket checkout clerks, bricklayers, bank tellers, waitresses, and file clerks as it is in the factory. What kinds of errors or defects might be detected in each of these jobs?

3. In the absence of an inspection department, how should a supervisor proceed to assure the quality of the products the department produces?

4. How do automobile recalls reflect on manufacturing quality control?

5. How does statistical quality control differ from inspection?

6. In what way does statistical quality control depend on a reliability determination?

7. How good an idea is it for supervisors to conduct some of the inspections and tests themselves?

8. What makes the Zero Defects idea unique?

9. Compare the housekeeping typists might be expected to do at their workplace with that of custodial workers who come to the office each evening.

10. If you wished to have employees maintain a high standard of housekeeping in a particular area, how would you establish that standard?

supervision in action

THE CASE OF THE NO-FAULT QUALITY PROBLEM.   A case study in human relations involving quality control, with questions for you to answer.

Jane Borden, plant manager for Izod Precision Instruments Company, was puzzled. The plant had a sophisticated statistical quality-control program. Its suppliers of parts and materials were subjected to rigorous receiving inspections. Izod's employees were well paid, well trained, and appeared to be well motivated. Despite all this, however, the plant's defects record had slowly deteriorated. The number of units that did not pass final inspection had steadily risen. Worse still, Izod had received a number of complaints from aircraft companies that used the plant's products in their instrument panels. In fact, Izod was facing a lawsuit right now. A leading commercial airlines was suing Izod for $5 million, charging that a malfunction in one of this plant's instruments had been a contributing factor in a landing crash that had killed three passengers and injured seven others.

Jane called her key supervisors into her office to review the situation with them and to get their suggestions. After outlining the problem, several supervisors volunteered opinions.

"All I can say, Jane," said Will Smith, supervisor of the machine shop, "is that the problem isn't in my shop. We have complete control. Our stuff meets inspection 100 percent."

Marie Leonard, supervisor of the plating department, said, "I don't think the people in my department can be blamed. As you know, everything we get to plate has been okayed by the receiving inspectors. And everything we do is run through the automatic testing machine before it goes to the assembly operation."

Jack Jones quickly spoke up. "Well, it's not in assembly. We double- and triple-check everything before it goes to final test."

Jane thought for a moment and then said, "If the fault doesn't lie in the producing departments, it must have something to do with our inspection procedures."

Al Brown, the chief inspector, looked up. "Hey, wait a minute, gang. Our job in inspection is to tell it like it is. We can't inspect quality into the product. We check everything against product specs. Incoming material seems to be all right. Inspections at each major point in the process are coming out okay. But at final test, it falls apart. The problem must lie in the design and inspection specs."

Everyone at the meeting turned to the engineering manager, Charles Ruiz. "You are getting a runaround, Jane," Charles said. "Those specs have been proved out thousands of times. Every machine, fixture, tool, and inspection device is capable of turning out 99.9 percent acceptable product—if, and it is a big if—employees in each department follow them carefully. The in-process inspections can't catch everything that could go wrong with a part. It's after everything has been assembled and the completed instrument put on the test block that we're finding the problems. My guess is that each of you supervisors is really only working toward passing the 'set' inspections. You and your employees cut corners on everything else. That's not error-free production. That's simply going through the motions."

Every supervisor tried to speak at once.

"I'm the most quality-minded guy in the plant," said Will Smith.

"The plating operation is almost completely machine-controlled," said Marie Leonard.

"We put the stuff we get together right. We can't rework what's been done wrong elsewhere," said Jack Jones.

"Inspection and test just does its job. The rest of you will have to straighten this out," said Al Brown.

"It's a proved fact that the design and inspection specs are all right," said Charles Ruiz.

Jane Borden said nothing. She was now more puzzled than ever.

1. What do you think might be the real cause of the quality problem? Why?
2. Which supervisor or manager seems most at fault? Why? Which seems least at fault? Why?
3. What suggestions can you make to Jane to help her solve the quality problem at Izod?

enriching your viewpoint

To widen your view of quality control, workmanship, and good housekeeping, the following reading sources are suggested:

Crosby, Philip B., *Quality Is Free,* McGraw-Hill Book Company, New York, 1978.

Duncan, Acheson J., *Quality Control and Industrial Statistics,* 4th ed., Richard D. Irwin, Inc., Homewood, Ill., 1974.

Grant, E. L., and R. S. Leavenworth, *Statistical Quality Control,* 4th ed., McGraw-Hill Book Company, New York, 1972.

Gray, Irwin, with Albert L. Bases, Charles H. Martin, and Alexander Sternberg, *Product Liability: A Management Response,* American Management Associations, New York, 1975.

Groocock, J. M., *The Cost of Quality,* Pitman Publishing Corporation, New York, 1974.

A Guide to Zero Defects, Department of Defense, Quality and Reliability Assurance Handbook No. 4114.12H, Washington, November 1965.

Quality Improvement Through Defect Prevention, International Telephone and Telegraph Corporation, New York, 1967.

Thompson, James E., "Industrial Housekeeping," in Lindley R. Higgins (ed.), *Maintenance Engineering Handbook,* 3d ed., McGraw-Hill Book Company, 1977, Chap. 14-3.

Wise, David, "Housekeeping," in H. B. Maynard (ed), *Handbook of Modern Manufacturing,* McGraw-Hill Book Company, New York, 1970, Chap. 8–6.

SHOW 'EM YOUR MUSCLE!

29

improving productivity and cost control

If profit is the bottom line for top management, what is the bottom line for supervisors?

Cost control—or cost reduction. Supervisory effort contributes to profits, of course. What *you* do to conserve resources—people, materials, power, machinery—and to attain a higher output makes a big difference in how profitable a company will be. The decisions you make that have the most immediate effect are those involving costs and expenses. In fact, or principle, supervisors are given an expense budget to work against. It has two aspects: first, the command to spend no more than what is allotted; second, to hit a certain level of output in the department. As-

534

suming the second target is met, a supervisor's performance is judged by how well he or she keeps budgeted costs in line.

How does productivity relate to costs?

██████████████ It puts together the two factors a supervisor can control: outputs and inputs, results and resources. *Productivity* simply measures how efficient a person or an operation is by comparing (1) the value of the output result with (2) the cost of the input resource. It is usually expressed as a ratio (or rate). For example, productivity of a hand assembly department in a furniture factory might be stated as five chairs per labor hour. The number of chairs is the output; the labor expended is the input. If the furniture factory wished, it could convert both figures to dollars. If so, the value added to the chair by the assembly operation might be estimated at $3 each, or a total of $15. If an assembler is paid $5 per hour, then the productivity of the assembly operation would be $15 divided by $5, or 3:1.

It is common to compute productivity by making the comparison with labor costs only. It would be just as correct, however, to make the comparison with not only the cost of labor but also the cost of power, for example. In a factory that melts and casts an exotic metal like aluminum, the cost of electric power is far larger than the cost of labor. Thus, productivity could be calculated by comparing the value of a ton of the metal (say $500) with the cost of electricity (say $200 per ton) plus the cost of labor (say $50 per ton). The productivity measure would then be $500 divided by $200 plus $50, or 2:1.

Ratios can also be converted to percentages, and some companies state productivity that way. For instance, the 3:1 ratio is 300 percent and the 2:1 ratio is 200 percent.

Regardless of measurement technique, productivity tells how much a supervisor is getting from the available resources. It also tells how well costs are being controlled.

Value added? What does that mean?

██████████████ It is an economist's term for the value your operation adds to a product or service as it passes through your department. For example, a gear blank may be worth $2 when it enters the machining department. After having been bored and tooth-cut, it may be worth $3.50. The value added by machining would be $1.50. As the product passes from operation to operation, it adds value at each step. When computing productivity in dollars, it is important to know the dollar value that has been added. This figure is not nearly so easy to come by, however, as the dollar value of the input, such as labor or power costs.

For a single operation, value added is estimated by the accounting department. For a company's entire process, it can be calculated roughly by subtracting from the total cost of a finished product the purchase cost of its raw materials.

How can supervisors tell how good their departmental productivity is?

Few people can say for sure what is good or bad. But you can easily tell whether your productivity is improving or falling off. There are four basic possibilities:

- If output remains the same but costs go up, productivity is *falling*.
- If output remains the same but costs go down, productivity is *rising*.
- If output goes up, and costs remain the same, productivity is *rising*.
- If output goes down, and costs remain the same, productivity is *falling*.

If output and productivity both change, you will have to use this formula: Productivity equals output value divided by input costs.

Are productivity considerations limited to manufacturing operations?

No. The same principle applies everywhere. In many clerical and service operations, productivity measures are made exactly as in manufacturing. A typist's productivity, for example, would be the number of letters or lines typed per hour worked. A supermarket checkout counter clerk's output would be the number of items checked (or dollars taken in) per day. A bank teller's productivity would be the number of transactions handled per hour, day, week, or month.

The only limit to the application of productivity is the need to obtain a reliable measurement of output. It is difficult, for example, to measure the value of a nurse's output, although many hospitals talk about *X* number of patients tended by one nurse per shift as a measure of productivity.

Another factor to watch is the impact that quality demands make on productivity. If quality requirements are raised, output may drop accordingly. Or, if product specifications are loosened, output may rise solely because of this change and does not represent a real improvement in productivity.

Measurements aside, what factors contribute to productivity improvement?

There are two basic ingredients.

Technological factors. These include:

- Product or service design. Some things are easier to make or deliver than others.
- Plant and equipment. Up-to-date and well-maintained facilities and equipment make a big difference in productivity.
- Process layout and methods. Congestion and backtracking hinder productivity; order and unimpeded flow accelerate it.
- Condition of materials. Presorted and stacked parts speed machine loading. Carbonless forms with preprinted routing instructions improve typing efficiency.
- Extent of power used. Electricity, steam, compressed air, fuel—these all apply leverage to human effort.

Human factors. The obvious ones are ability, knowledge, and motivation. What is not so clear is the extent to which dozens of other people-oriented factors are important. Among those that deserve attention are individual education, experience, levels of aspiration, work schedules, training, organizational groupings, personnel policies, leadership, and—very important—pay practices.

What may not be so important as was once thought is the physical environment, but it cannot be ignored.

See Figure 29-1 for an indication of the relative input of human factors in operations with varying degrees of technology.

What role does employee job satisfaction play in improving productivity and controlling costs?

It is the most important factor not yet fully exploited. In high technology industries—such as petroleum refining—job satisfaction may be a smaller, though still vital, factor than technology. In most work, however, there is an increasing need to place major emphasis on the role of job satisfaction. In the long run, people control the work pace. They can be devilishly clever in thwarting machines.

Supervisors must try to match jobs with each person's own kind of job satisfaction. Productivity gets its strongest boost from

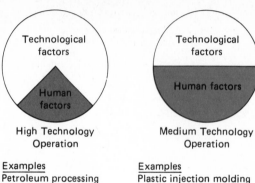

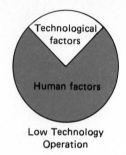

Examples	Examples	Examples
Petroleum processing	Plastic injection molding	Home construction
Word processing center	Credit card checking	Typing, filing, routine clerical
Auto assembly line	Semiautomatic spot welding	Hand, bench assembly

FIGURE 29-1. Relative Impact of Human and Technological Factors on Productivity.

the human side when supervisors support employees in their individual search for job satisfaction. The trick, of course, is to balance employees' needs for satisfaction with the organization's need for productivity and cost control.

Why so much flak about productivity?

On the national scene it is what enables one country to develop a better standard of living than another does. For years the United States was so far ahead of the pack, it had no worries. Since the 1960s, however, productivity growth in the United States has slowed to a walk, as shown in Figure 29-2. Other countries have suffered, too, but our relative drop in productivity has made a severe impact on the United States economy.

Most companies, understandably, do not take a global view of productivity changes. They are more worried about what is happening to their own operations. The demand placed on supervisors will always be for higher productivity in their departments, but it may be couched in different terms. The order is more likely to be stated as:

- Cut costs.
- Reduce expenses.
- Get more output from the same budget allowance.

How important is record keeping to cost control?

Unless you have accurate, available, and up-to-date records, controlling costs is next to impossible. When you say "control,"

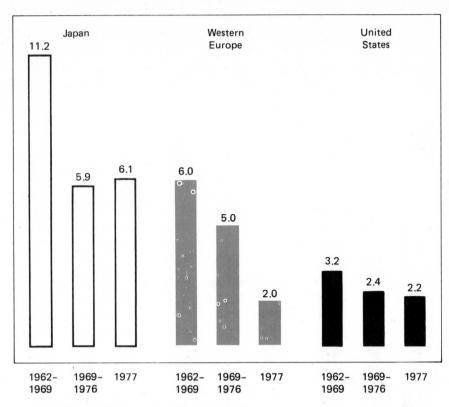

FIGURE 29-2. Comparative Growths in Productivity. From *Statistical Abstracts of the United States,* 1978.

it's the same as saying "keep within limits." If you don't know what the limits are or how well you're holding costs within those limits, how can you take any action?

How detailed should cost records be?

To make use of cost records, they should be in enough detail so that you can pick out where your department is out of line and where its performance is satisfactory. You wouldn't get much help, for instance, if all your boss told you was, "You've got to nip your operating costs. They went 10 percent over last month." You wouldn't know where to begin, and would probably have to work on hunches.

To determine which costs you ought to know about in detail, find out what costs you are held responsible for. Follow these from month to month. For instance, it's a safe bet that you are held responsible for the following:

Labor costs—direct and indirect.   Direct labor varies according to each company's definition, but it generally refers to labor charges for productive employees—those who operate machines, who work on assembly lines, or who fabricate or process materials. In service industries these are clerical people who process the forms and paperwork—as in banks and insurance companies. Indirect labor usually describes material-handling labor, shipping, and maintenance.

Maintenance and repair charges.   This is usually broken down into maintenance labor and maintenance materials—lubricants, replacement parts, and others.

Operating supplies.   Supervisors aren't usually held accountable for costs of raw materials. But they are responsible for miscellaneous supplies that don't go into the product, like wiping rags, safety clothing, sweeping compounds.

Power and utilities.   Especially in industries (like food plants or chemical or paper plants) where utilities are used in great volumes, supervisors would need to know about their department's use of water, steam, electricity, and fuel.

Waste or scrap.   Off-quality material is almost certain to be pinpointed as a "controllable" cost in your plant.

Many more items are often broken out for the supervisor's inspection, too, like overtime. An example of one company's cost report to a department supervisor is shown in Figure 29-3.

Won't costs vary according to how much work your department is doing?

Yes. Total costs, studied alone, may have no significance. Suppose labor charges in May were $20,000, then dropped to $15,000 in June. Did you cut costs 25 percent? You can't tell until you compare the throughput, or unit volume, for each month. If the throughput was 20,000 units in May and 12,000 in June, then labor costs actually went up.

You'll usually find your costs expressed as rates—so many dollars per unit, or per ton, or per gallon, or per dollar value of product. In the case described in the preceding paragraph, the rate of labor costs in May was $20,000 divided by 20,000 units, which is $1 per unit. In June it was $15,000 divided by 12,000 units, or $1.25 per unit. Cost per unit, then, went up 25 percent during the month.

SAMPLE

	Account No. Title	Current Month Rate	Current Month Amount	Year to Date Rate	Year to Date Amount	Total Allowed for Year Rate	Total Allowed for Year Amount
	60 DISTILLING CRUDES						
Rate Unit	RATE M GAL CRUDE DIST						
Equipment Hours	CRUDE STILL HOURS	138	2167	137	12478	145	20764
Manhours	MANHOURS WORKED	147	2303	186	16932	236	337
Throughput	GALS CRUDES DISTILLED		1570865		9092294		
Classes of Expense Reported in dollars & cents	LABOR PRODUCING GENL	169	285829	187	1699388		
	LABOR NON PRODUCING	11	17257	14	123651		
	EMPLOYEE BENEFITS	8	12640	14	131216		
	OVERTIME PREMIUM	12	19339	10	94255		
	M&R LABOR GENERAL	29	46045	65	594667		
	M&R MTL GENERAL	12	18930	31	285		
	M&R MTL CONTRACTED			38			
	FUEL PITCH			5			
	FUEL PETROLEUM OIL			44			
	FUEL GAS	183	285208				
	FUEL COAL						
	ELECTRICITY	28	43750				
	STEAM PRORATED DIRECT	231	363451				
	WATER INDUSTRIAL		676				
	SUPPLIES OPERATING	7	11				
	CONTRACTED EXPENSE						
	SOCIAL SECURITY TAXES	7					

FIGURE 29-3. **Sample Expense-Control Report for First-Line Supervisors.**

What should you do when your boss says to cut costs?

Some cynical supervisors just run for cover. "Here we go again" is their attitude. "We've been through this too many times to get excited now. This drive for cost cutting will blow over just like all the rest."

Other supervisors get in a sweat and run in six directions at once—lop off a worker here, an extra shift there. They do anything to cut the total department expense—temporarily, at least, even if it affects quality and morale.

Still other supervisors take their time. They don't act until they have gathered facts and figures. Then they plan a sensible, surefooted course of attack. They concentrate on the weak spots in the cost armor, get at the fat where it's easy to cut. Their efforts may be unspectacular and may even take a few weeks to show up. But when the record is scrutinized by top company management, their department is the one most likely to show lasting reductions in cost.

Which supervisor would you like to be? Which supervisor do you think has the most freedom to run the department? Which supervisor do you think enjoys the job most? And which supervisor do you think gets the raises and the promotions? Not old sour grapes! Not the fumbler! That's for sure.

How can you improve your cost and productivity record?

███████████ There are five good ways to chop away at costs. Each approach provides you with a different wedge for getting at the roots of each problem. If one technique won't work, try another—or a combination of two or three:

Reduce waste.   Where can you find waste in raw materials and operating supplies? How about people? Are you wasting their efforts? Are you getting the most from utilities, or are you wasting water, steam, electricity?

Save time.   Can you speed up or double up your equipment? Will time studies show you where time itself can be saved? Are you doing everything you can to get full cooperation from your employees?

Increase output.   You can cut cost rates—and improve productivity—by stepping up the throughput in your department. Sometimes there's a rhythm that goes with high production that's lost with lower production. Sometimes when you cut back, you need the part-time services of several different people, whereas if you increased output, these same people would be working 100 percent of the time. With the higher output base, cost rates would actually be lower.

Spend wisely.   Cutting costs rarely means that you stop spending. In fact, it's a popular and true expression that you have to spend money to make money. Often top management is more alerted to the need for spending to save during a cost-cutting campaign than at other times. So look for ways to spend money on mechanization or replacement of machines with slow feeds and speeds with newer ones.

Use space more intelligently.   Space—for storage, manufacturing, shipping—costs money. This cost goes on whether output is high or low. If you can figure out how to get more use of the same space, you cut costs. Double- or triple-stacking pallet loads, for instance, cuts storage charges for space by a half or two-thirds.

How good are one-shot cost-cutting campaigns?

If a cost-cutting drive is a shot in the arm administered to a never-ending concern for costs, then chances for the drive are pretty good. If you can recall the six-day bike race with its occasional sprint races, you'll have a pretty good parallel. The six-day riders raced continuously. But now and then they picked up their pace, and the leader had to sprint faster than the pack for a lap to hold the spot out in front.

The sour-grapes supervisor who looks at each drive as so much nonsense misses the point. New cost-reduction opportunities arise every day. New machines, new materials, new methods, new ideas, new people, and new products open more doors to cheaper production than you'll be able to walk through in a lifetime.

Where should you begin your cost-cutting efforts?

Pick the likeliest spots—those that your records show to be out of line with past performance. Be especially critical of operations that show a trend upward. Some costs will naturally be up one month, down the next. These may have little substance in them (although it's worth looking into them to see what causes the variation). Costs that creep steadily out of line might not appear spectacular, but in the long run they hurt most.

One supervisor, in checking cost accounts, noticed that charges for supplies had risen steadily for seven months—up $12.50 one month, up $9 another, up $17 the next, and so forth. Month by month the increases were nothing to get excited about. But in seven months this item had shown a net gain of $98.25 per month! Even if this expense were now to stay constant at the new level, in a year's time the additional expense would total $1,179! What was the cause? Seven months ago the purchasing department had changed the supplier of protective aprons all workers were required to wear because of the danger from acid splashes. The supervisor had heard the employees complaining about the inferior quality of the aprons but had shrugged it off as just another gripe. Actually, the new aprons were wearing out just a little bit faster than the more expensive kind—but this little bit more inched up until it meant $1,179 per year. How was the situation corrected? The supervisor got together with the purchasing agent and the supplier to find an apron that better suited the conditions in the shop—and as a result brought the operating supplies expenses back into line.

Can you overdo cost cutting?

Yes. It's wise for a supervisor to emphasize economies—even in small things like shutting down motors during lunchtime. But if you're penny-wise and dollar-foolish, employees will think the cost effort is a joke. For instance, don't set up a rule that an employee can't get a new pencil without turning in a 1-inch stub of the old, if at the same time you're spending $100 for new shirts for the bowling team.

Where do you get cost-cutting ideas?

Try these three good sources:

Yourself. Do this by building up a backlog of ideas year-round. Whenever you see something or read about something that might work in your department, jot it in a notebook or stick it in a folder. Call it your cost-cutting bank. Then, when your attention is drawn to costs for any reason, check your list to see what might work. (Check Chapter 27 for ways to improve methods and Chapter 32 for ways to solve problems.)

Your employees. The employees probably know more about the ins and outs of their jobs than you do. If you encourage them properly, they are likely to have ideas for cutting corners or cutting waste. Of course, one big way to stop employees from making suggestions is to explain right away why an idea is no good. If you must turn a suggestion down, before you do, examine it from every angle to see if some part of it has value.

Staff departments. If you can pinpoint the areas where cost reduction has the best chance of succeeding, staff specialists like industrial engineers and time-study and methods analysts frequently can be a big help in devising ways to achieve the reductions. That's their specialty, and they can call on a vast reservoir of examples of how similar reductions have been made in other companies and other departments.

Why are your money-saving ideas sometimes turned down by top management?

Because they don't pay off fast enough. Even though there's nothing much more exasperating to a supervisor than to come up with an idea that might save $250 a year, only to have it rejected by top management, there's often a good reason. If your plan to save $250 a year requires the company to spend $2,000 for new equipment, like a conveyor, that means it will take at least eight years for the idea to pay for itself. The cost of financing investments is so great that many companies adopt a policy that a new machine or piece of equipment must pay for itself in five years or less. Some companies insist on a payoff period of only one year.

What's overhead?
Isn't that where the money really goes?

Overhead, or burden, refers to the charges added to the cost of manufacturing the product. Overhead may include a variety of things right where you can see them yourself—like the cost of bookkeeping, mailing, shipping, depreciation of equipment, even maintenance and power if they are not directly apportioned to your unit production. These charges are usually called factory overhead. General overhead includes the cost of advertising, research, selling.

It's common for overhead to be expressed as a percentage of the cost of manufacturing. For instance, let's say it costs $1 to produce a tool in the shop. Factory overhead is 100 percent, and general overhead is 30 percent. Here's the way the percentages would be applied:

$$\$1.00 \times 100\% = \$1.00$$
$$\$1.00 + 1.00 = \$2.00 \text{ total factory cost}$$
$$\$2.00 \times 30\% = 0.60$$
$$\$2.00 + .60 = \$2.60 \text{ total cost}$$

The method of determining and applying overhead varies from company to company.

Now you can understand why supervisors who see the product turned out in their department at a cost of $1 often feel that the real money is being wasted elsewhere. If you'll look carefully, however, the whole picture hinges on how cheaply the product is turned out in the department. If the cost of $1 per tool were cut to 90 cents, the total cost would be $2.34 instead of $2.60. That means for a 10-cent reduction in the direct manufacturing cost, the total cost would be cut 26 cents.

What can you do to cut indirect labor costs?

First of all, let's settle on what indirect labor is. (Caution: Definitions vary in different companies.) According to accountants, it's all labor not directly applied to the product unit being manufactured. To supervisors it's any labor (including their own) that doesn't change the shape, size, or finish of the product. Indirect labor will ordinarily include work done by material handlers, inspectors, maintenance workers, supervisors, clerks, superintendents, even works managers.

One way to do something about indirect labor cost is to find out how it normally compares with direct labor charges in your department. Is it 1 to 4, 1 to 3, 1 to 1? If you can get a fix on this ratio or percentage, you can see whether it's going up or down. It's likely to go down when you add a new shift or up when you introduce a new piece of direct-labor-saving machinery.

One forging plant found that when it added a new machine, operators then had more time to clean their workplaces. As a result, they could eliminate the services of a janitor. Job redesign and methods improvements are good tools to show where indirect labor is being wasted. Take a good look at your paperwork, too. Maybe it's being overdone and could be reduced enough to drop a clerk.

Why do employees fear cost reduction?

Unless you can sell cost reduction to employees, they are likely to be indifferent at best, rebellious at worst. After all, to employees cost cutting may mean loss of work, overtime, their jobs. They feel that cost cutting threatens their security.

What are some chief criticisms employees have toward cost-cutting campaigns?

Employees often think that management itself throws away money by poor planning and downright misjudgment as to what's really important—and that applies to supervisors, too.

Here are some typical worker opinions:

"One employee saved the company about $2,000 one day and the next day almost got laid off for turning in 20 minutes overtime."

"We put in a new machine, then ripped it apart and sent it away. It probably cost the company $500 to do it. They waste lots of money by not planning the big things."

"They changed construction of this particular item four or five times, got just short of production, and then the whole thing was called off. What that cost I couldn't even guess!"

Sitting as you do on the management side of the fence, you can understand the reason behind many moves that look wasteful to employees. But the tip-off for you is that the employees frequently don't see the situation the way you do because no one has taken time to make it clear.

Your cue to selling cost reduction is to give employees the

facts and help them see that cost cutting (or profit improvement) helps them; it does not work to their disadvantage.

In the face of prevailing employee attitudes, how do you get the need for productivity improvement over to workers?

Remember, the biggest fear of both employees and unions is immediate loss of jobs. If the big picture means only that jobs will be shuffled, not entirely eliminated, emphasize this point. If there must be layoffs, handle the layoff procedure as well as you can. Show all employees who work for you that you'll do your best to protect their job rights (as well as you can in line with the improved methods). Take the lead in talking with employees about to be laid off to be sure they understand how to handle their insurance and hospitalization, how to apply for unemployment. Can you help them with suggestions about where to get another job? Be sure to tell them about their chances of being recalled to work.

What is the best way to get through employee resistance?

Try these five approaches:

1. Talk to employees about cost reduction in terms that are meaningful to them. Get their point of view, or they'll never be able to get yours. In face-to-face conversations, show them how the company's interest in profits is exactly the same as a worker's interest in higher wages and more security. Show that one can't be achieved without the other.

2. Get the cost picture down to earth. Don't talk in global terms of standard costs, of productivity ratios, or even about hard times. If company sales have fallen off, talk in terms of the reduction of specific parts being made in your department: "Where we made 250,000 the first quarter, our schedule calls for only half as much production this quarter." If rising material charges are a factor, pick up a product your employees make and tell them: "Last year, steel for this item cost 55 cents, now it costs 62 cents—a rise of 12 percent."

3. Set specific goals. Don't just say: "We've got to cut costs to the bone." Have a specific program in mind. "Our records show that machine costs have got to be lowered. We'll have to figure a way to use new tools or change our methods to do this." Or, "Scrap cost us $12,000 last month. This month let's get it down below $10,000."

4. Invite participation. Let employees know that you need their help and that help means more than just cooperation. You'd welcome their ideas on how to go about it.

5. Explain why and how. Reasons for a specific change should be spelled out. Employees need your help, too, in deciding how to accomplish the cost-cutting objectives you set.

How helpful are cost-reduction committees?

Many companies have achieved great results by using cost-reduction committees to spark a cost-reduction campaign. Committees provide lots of chances for participation and tap a big reservoir of people for ideas. The job of selling cost cutting can be difficult if you do it alone. If you know others are doing the same thing, it's a boost to your morale.

supervisory word power

Fixed costs.   Costs that tend to be constant, on an annual basis and which are not related to rate of production, services rendered, or amount of sales. For example: real estate rents and leases, taxes on company property, cost of money provided by bonds or preferred stocks, and—in many accounting circumstances—the cost of depreciation on machinery and other facilities.

Variable costs.   Costs that tend to vary (directly or indirectly) according to the volume of goods produced or services rendered or sales generated.

Direct costs.   Those (variable) costs that can be clearly identified with adding value directly to the goods produced or services rendered. For example: materials and labor.

Indirect costs.   Those (variable) costs that are essential to the production of goods or the rendering of services, but which do not clearly add value to them or do not do so in an easily measurable way. For example: material handling, inspection, maintenance, engineering and clerical support to manufacturing operations, advertising, and advisory staff services.

Standard costs.   The normal or expected cost of an operation, process, or product (usually including labor, material, and overhead charges), computed on the basis of past performance, estimates, or work measurement.

Productivity. The specific measure of productivity that compares the value of outputs from an operation with the cost of the resources used—expressed in time or dollars.

Other Important Terms in This Chapter

cost-reduction committee   output values
cost trend   overhead (burden)
input resources   value added
operating supplies

reading comprehension

1. What two factors determine the productivity of an operation? Why is high productivity better than low productivity?

2. What is the meaning of "value added"? Why is it important in a discussion of productivity?

3. A bank estimated that each transaction handled by a teller contributed 9 cents to the total value of the bank's services. The average teller receives $4.50 per hour and can handle 75 transactions per hour when fully occupied. What is the productivity of the average teller expressed as a ratio? As a percentage?

4. Distinguish between a unit cost and total costs.

5. How does saving time reduce costs?

6. How can a supervisor save money by increasing the department's output without raising the cost of running the department?

7. Why can cost-cutting campaigns often be so effective?

8. Dollars saved on the department floor can exert leverage in saving dollars of total cost. Why is this so?

9. If the ratio of indirect labor to direct labor in a furniture factory is 1 to 6, and there are 12 carpenters building furniture, how big is the indirect staff?

10. In setting up a cost-reduction target, would it be better to (*a*) urge employees to cut costs as hard as they can or (*b*) set realistic targets with specific numbers on them, like by $500, or by 42 percent, or by 125 rejects? Why?

supervision in action

THE CASE OF NED NORDEN'S COST OVERRUN. A case study in human relations involving cost control, with questions for you to answer.

Ned Norden had been a plating-room supervisor at the Glossy Trim Company for five years. Ned knew the plating operations from A to Z. When an employee ran into a problem, chances are that Ned would pitch right in. Working alongside, Ned would get the operator out of trouble in no time.

Ned was also known to top management in his company as a man who was willing to cooperate—especially in trying anything new. If the engineers developed a different kind of plating solution, they used to say, "If Ned can't make it work, nobody can."

Since the plating department had been looked on as a process-type operation, the company had never examined the department closely for costs. But when a new comptroller was hired, every operation—including plating—was put under a magnifying glass. The conclusion was that Ned had gotten sloppy about overtime, use of operating supplies, and waste of raw materials. Consequently, Ned was issued a budget for these items at the beginning of the next month.

At the end of the month Ned's boss called him into the office. "Ned," the boss said, "in checking over the figures for the plating department this past month, I find you're about 15 percent over budget. Will you see if you can't bring this back into line as soon as you can?"

The following day Ned called his work crew together. "People," he said, "we've got a real problem on our hands. We have an order from the front office to cut costs in our department 15 percent. It means there will be practically no overtime for a while. We'll have to watch how often we renew plating solutions. And I want you to keep your use of sweeping compound, wiping cloths, and aprons to a minimum." Without a dissenting voice, his gang vowed they'd pull together with Ned to make the necessary reductions.

At the end of the next month Ned was again called into his boss's office. "Ned, I hate to keep making an issue about this cost matter. I know that I rarely have to speak to you twice about any problem in the shop. But the fact remains that your department made no headway whatsoever against costs last month. I'm going to rely on you to make some progress by the end of next month."

Ned again went out to his work group. "Look," he said, "you're putting me in a bad light with the front office. We've got to get these costs under control. So I'm depending on you to give me cooperation."

At the end of that month Ned's department had cut costs approximately 3 percent. But by the end of the following month costs were back to where they were when Ned was first issued a budget. Ned wasn't surprised when he was called on the carpet again. When asked why he had been unsuccessful, his reply was, "I can't understand it. I expected my employees to give me a break. But now I don't know what to do except to get tough."

1. What do you think of Ned's approach to cost cutting?

2. What do you think of Ned's relationship with his employees? Why?

3. If you were Ned, what would you do to get costs back into line?

enriching your viewpoint

To expand your knowledge of productivity and cost control, the following sources are recommended:

Annual Report to the President and Congress 1977, National Center for Productivity and Quality of Working Life, Washington, 1977.

Bittel, Lester R., *Improving Supervisory Performance,* McGraw-Hill Book Company, New York, 1976, Chap. 10, "Output and Productivity," and Chap. 12, "Cost Control and Improvement."

Harrison, Jared F., *Improving Performance and Productivity,* Addison-Wesley Publishing Company, Inc., Reading, Mass., 1978.

Hershey, Gerald L., and Gene L. Houser, "Cutting Office Costs: Look Before You Leap." *Supervisory Management,* May 1975, pp. 29–33.

Higgins, Lindley R., and Ruth W. Stidger, *Cost Reduction From A to Z,* McGraw-Hill Book Company, New York, 1976.

"How to Promote Productivity," *Business Week,* July 24, 1976, pp. 146–151.

Katzell, Raymond A., and Daniel Yankelovich, *Work, Productivity, and Job Satisfaction,* The Psychological Corporation, New York, 1975.

Lane, Donald F., "Part 1—Organizing for Increasing Productivity," *Mechanical Engineering,* September 1978, pp. 25–34.

Lindemann, A. J., Earl F. Lundgren, and H. K. von Kaas, *Encyclopedic Dictionary of Management and Manufacturing Terms,* 2d ed., Kendall/Hunt Publishing Company, Dubuque, Iowa, 1974, Sec. 2, "Manufacturing Economics, Accounting, Budgeting, Costing, and Cost Control."

Richardson, Wallace J., *Cost Improvement, Work Sampling, and Short Interval Scheduling,* Reston Publishing Company, Inc., Reston, Va., 1976, Chap. 10, "Analysis of Inputs: Budgets and Costs," Chap. 11, "Analysis of Outputs: Products, Services, and Work Units," and Chap. 12, "Analysis of Input-Output Results."

Sutermeister, Robert A., *People and Productivity,* 3d ed., McGraw-Hill Book Company, New York, 1976.

30
CHAPTER the computer and management information systems

**What, really, is a management
information system? Why is it so important?**

At its root a management information system (MIS) is plain old
accounting, but with a broader base and an electronic twist. MIS
is important because it can provide an informed basis for all
management decisions. When the system is a good one, decisions are likely to be good. When the system is skimpy or overdone or misleading, decisions will suffer.

A modern management information system tries to keep track
of everything that may help to make a manager's decisions effective. In a manufacturing company, for example, MIS collects and

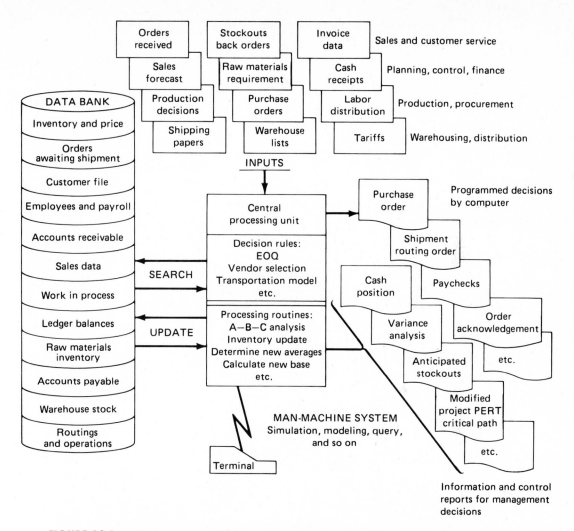

FIGURE 30-1. A Management Information System in a Manufacturing Company. Joel E. Ross, *Modern Management and Information Systems,* Reston Publishing Company, Inc., Reston, Va., 1976. Used by permission.

analyzes information about product development, production, marketing, and finance. In a service company like a commercial airlines, MIS may encompass other functions such as aircraft operation, maintenance, scheduling, and customer sales and ticketing. (See Figure 30-1 for an example of a comprehensive management information system for a manufacturing company.)

The ultimate objective of a MIS is to tie together all of a company's past and present data into a great big library with instant electronic recall. Managers at all levels draw from this library (called a data bank) any kind of information that aids short-range or long-term decisions. Few organizations reach this ideal. Most management information systems operate in functional pockets with separate systems for each important activity, for example, production and inventory control. These functional systems are only loosely tied into the overall company MIS, with little cross-referencing between them. The goal, however, is gradually to link all separate MISs into a fully integrated system.

In what way does the computer help MIS?

The computer makes a modern MIS possible. A management information system needs a device to collect, store, analyze, and transmit an immense array of data. The computer performs this function in the form of integrated electronic data processing, or EDP, and it does it at fantastic speeds.

How does the computer work?

Supervisors need not know its inner workings. It helps, however, to think of a computer as made up of four black boxes that are its *hardware.*

Memory or storage unit.   This operates by changing numbers coded in decimal form to binary form—known as the base-2 number system—so that each number (or *bit*) can be turned either on or off.

Arithmetic unit.   This device manipulates the bits—especially to add, subtract, or multiply them—at incredible speeds.

Control unit.   This handy device fetches instructions from the memory, decodes them, and then tells the other units of the computer what to do.

Input-output units.   These are what you chiefly see when you look at a computer. They connect the heart of the computer system to keypunch machines, card readers, tape and disk drives, and printers that spell out the typical computer report, or printout. Figure 30-2 shows how the various computer units are related.

What is the central processing unit?

This is the heart of the computer. Nicknamed the CPU, it includes the memory, arithmetic, and control units.

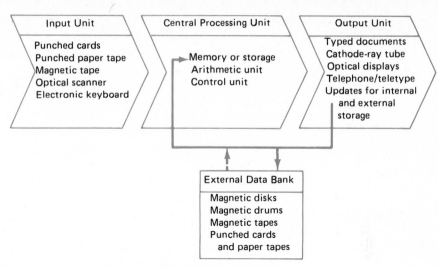

FIGURE 30-2. Elements of a Computer System.

How do operational information and data get into the computer?

This is done by programmers, highly skilled people who arrange data in such a way that it will flow through the computer to do what management wants. Programmers translate this data and its flow pattern into a computer language. COBOL and FORTRAN are two of the most common forms of this language. Programmers produce what is called a program. Programs are called the *software* of the computer.

Should a distinction be made between data and information?

It may seem like hairsplitting, but MIS designers insist there are good reasons to distinguish them.

Data are merely facts and figures that, until processed, bear little relation to decision making.

Information is data that has been processed for specific use by manager and supervisors in decision making related to planning, organizing, directing, and controlling.

Where does the computer input unit get the information it processes in the first place?

It may get it from you or your department. It certainly gets it from someone or someplace in your organization. Here are some typical computer input sources: a sales order, an invoice from a vendor, a record of the invoice when it is paid, a tally of the day's production output, the information on a quality-control chart. Whatever the input, it is usually copied by a keypunch operator who transfers the data to cards or tape by punching holes in them with a special machine. A card-reader machine then transfers the data from the card into the heart of the computer. Data may also be entered directly into the computer by a keyboard device—either an electric typewriter or a cathode-ray terminal (CRT).

What kinds of services do computers perform for MIS?

They can be classified under four main headings.

Recordkeeping. This is by far the most widely used service. It replaces or aids just about every imaginable kind of clerical activity that formerly was done by hand. Some experts say that 98 percent of all computer activity is recordkeeping. It can be done in batches, or it can be handled on-line as the transaction takes place. When a shipping clerk in a warehouse, for example, removes a case of goods from stock and keyboards this information at the same time into the computer, it is an on-line system.

Operations control. This connects the computer to a process, such as petroleum processing, or to numerically controlled machine tools. The computer's control unit gets feedback information (measurements) from the process or tool. The computer compares this information with the standard measurement in its memory. If there is a deviation, the computer then instructs the necessary valves or motors in the process equipment to do whatever is necessary for the process to proceed correctly.

Planning and simulation. This enables management to make forecasts and to try out a plan in advance. It does so by carrying out its procedures in a computer program modeled after its plan (a simulation).

Management control. This is, of course, the management information system. It works in very much the same way as operations control, except that management action—rather than a physical process—is being helped. The computer rarely takes the action; it simply signals management that something should be done. A computer printout that places an asterisk next to items that are running over budget is a typical output of this system. A supervisor observes the asterisk and does whatever he or she thinks necessary to correct the situation.

The computer end of MIS, then, is foolproof?

Yes—once the data gets inside the machine. Before data gets into the machine, however, there are innumerable chances for mistakes. Many errors in MIS occur at the very instant the original information is collected. This can take place anywhere along the line. The original sales order may have the wrong price on it, or the production figure written by the operator can be incorrect. Many errors are introduced, too, as the original data is prepared for input by keypunch and keyboard operators; and, of course, there is nothing to guarantee that the programmer has not made an error—or that the programmer was not misled by the manager who stipulated what the computer should do.

All these problems arise from human faults, not electronic ones. It is the reason close supervision is needed, together with an understanding of how the system works—especially outside the computer.

Where do supervisors fit into the MIS computer picture?

Supervisors become involved in computer operations in two basic ways:

1. You may simply be an end-user of computer output information. If so, make the most of this output. Understand what it means, what you are supposed to derive from it, and what kind of actions you are supposed to take based upon it. Is the computer printout you get a yard long, but only six items apply directly to you? Should you make a correction today? Or can you wait until the next report before you get moving?

2. You may be a *prime source* of inputs. If so, find out specifically what information your department is sending to the computer. Which records are selected for keyboarding? Exactly what form should they be in when they leave your department? Are the measures your employees are collecting exactly the same as those required for the computer? For example, are you tallying in inches when the computer needs metric figures? Or are you transmitting daily figures when the computer wants hourly data?

How can you get the most from your relationships with MIS designers and the EDP people?

▬▬▬▬▬▬▬ Four things will help:

1. **Ask for only as much data or information as you need.** It might be convenient to know what the reject rate is for every one of 578 parts in your department, for example, but this information would take far too many notches on a punched card. Instead, suggest that these parts can meaningfully be classified into only five types and that a reject rate according to these would be fine.

2. **Be ready to compromise when information overlaps occur.** Say that you want an inventory report with items listed by part numbers and the supervisor in the next department wants them according to order numbers. Suggest that a single report that lists items by both part and order number might be feasible and an inexpensive compromise.

3. **Let MIS and EDP people know about any excess information you get that you don't need or use.** Let them know also if you receive duplicate sets of the same reports. You may be able to help them reduce the number of items gathered and reports issued.

4. **Make your own data collections as accurate as possible.** Then relay this data to EDP as promptly as required and in the form specified.

Can supervisors design their own management information systems?

▬▬▬▬▬▬▬ Yes. Even if their parent organizations have a MIS, supervisors can and should develop their own concept of how information needed for decisions is gathered and routed to them. Part A of Figure 30-3 shows a basic management information system. Part B shows how a supervisor can adopt the same principle to explain departmental information needs, sources, and uses. *Primary data* is information that is collected and analyzed for the specific purpose of running a particular operation. *Secondary data* is any useful information published by trade associations, business magazines, the United States government, or any other outside source.

In part B of Figure 30-3 the supervisor set performance standards at 500 units per day, labor costs at $4,000 per week, and average weekly reject rate at 1.5 percent. The supervisor based the decisions for these standards on past records for the depart-

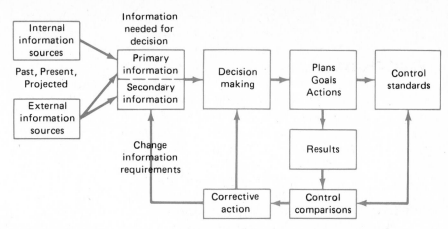

FIGURE 30-3 A. Basic Components of a Management Information System.

ment and what could be learned about industry standards for similar operations.

To make the MIS work, the supervisor requested the following: daily output figures from the shop clerk; weekly labor costs gathered from the time cards, processed by the payroll section, and recorded by the accounting department; and weekly defects rate from the quality-control department.

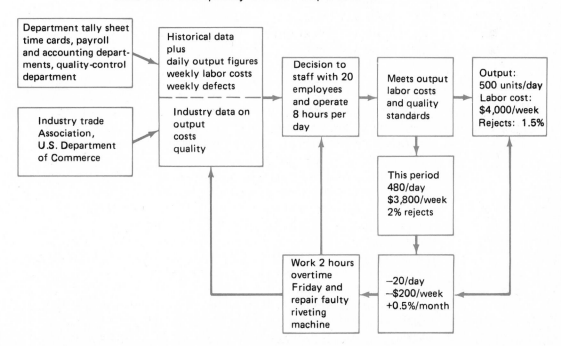

FIGURE 30-3. B. Assembly Supervisor's Departmental Information System.

For this week the supervisor's daily output has been only 480, or 20 below standard. Labor costs were $3,800, or $200 less than budgeted. The weekly reject rate was up to 2 percent, or 0.5 percent over standard. Based on these control comparisons, the supervisor decides to take corrective action. The entire staff will work overtime for two hours on Friday to raise output. The supervisor will also place a maintenance request to fix a faulty riveting machine, to which the higher reject rate is attributed.

How is employee job content affected by computers?

It is likely to be radically affected if the work is clerical. Skilled typists, for example, have to change their complete approach when servicing a computer-assisted word processing center. Where typists formerly entered data in selected places on a standard form, they may now type these entries into a minicomputer, which then types the entire form based on the entries provided by the typist. Check sorting, which is done by hand in many banks, will eventually be done by computer. The check sorters may still be needed, but their work will be directed toward gathering and presorting for computer reading. One check sorter will handle thousands instead of hundreds of checks per hour.

In many areas the traditional way of handling the job will simply disappear, if it hasn't already. Beginning in 1980, for instance, the Library of Congress will no longer prepare the familiar cards for library catalog files. Instead, the system will be shifted to keyboard operation. Most large libraries will follow suit, so that someone looking for a book will punch a keyboard and read the book's location from a cathode-ray tube.

Nothing, however, is likely to reduce the need for accuracy. Attempts to eliminate human error by computerization have generally been unsuccessful. Removal of one source of error, as when bank numbers are printed on checks with magnetic ink, simply highlights another source of error, such as placing checks upside down or backward in the optical scanner.

To what extent will computers replace people?

It is hard to say. During the first few decades of their use, computers created millions of new jobs. Unfortunately, some of these new jobs were created hundreds of miles away and in organizations different from those where jobs were eliminated. Some experts now believe the computer's impact on employment has topped out. It will neither create nor do away with jobs. Other experts foresee unimagined new uses that will again create millions of new jobs. Still other experts think that, if anything, the computer will now start to eat away at existing jobs. It is best to proceed on a case-by-case basis. Don't jump to conclusions about what computers will do to jobs in your organization. Wait until you gather all the facts.

How does the systematization of information handling, especially with computers, affect people at work?

It has its good aspects and its unfavorable ones. Even these draw conflicting responses. For example:

1. Systematization reduces job tensions and conflicts by making things more orderly. There will always be conflict among people, jobs, and operations. The computer should lessen their intensity, however, because the interfaces will be fixed and predictable. Once an information issue is resolved between the production and the maintenance supervisor, it should be less bothersome because it will arise in the same manner each time and can be anticipated.

2. Systematization creates job dissatisfaction because it requires individuals to fit their work into a rigidly prescribed format. Those employees who dislike close supervision and control will feel the same way about any system that makes similar demands. Supervisors must do a better job than in the past of placing people in work that best suits their concept of job satisfaction.

3. Systematization tends to make work monotonous because it reduces the opportunity to be creative. If the job is one that is fully dominated by the system, this will be true. People who prefer routine to initiative may like it, however. For many jobs the computer has just the opposite effect. It removes the routine and calls out for creative solutions to the problems it identifies.

4. Systematization depersonalizes work; people serve the machine more than the machine serves people. This is unfortunately true at lower levels of employment. At skilled and managerial levels, however, the system takes over much of the tiresome work and allows people to devote a greater portion of their efforts to work that matches their education, experience, and capabilities.

What can be done to make employees more adaptable to the MIS process, EDP, and computers in general?

Electronic data processing and other aspects of computer technology are with all of us to stay. Happily, employees coming out of high schools and colleges today are much more familiar with it than are those of previous generations. Nevertheless, there are several positive tacks that supervisors should take.

Try to reduce tension by allowing employees to bring their irritations into the open. Tempers are likely to flare highest when a new system is being debugged. Suppose Mike says, "Nothing matters anymore except getting the data to that electronic monster on time." Don't give Mike this reply: "That's too bad, If you can't keep up with it, maybe you better look for a job somewhere else." Instead, try saying something like this: "I agree that the computer now seems to be dominating our work in the department. Perhaps it won't be that way once we get used to it. After all, look how we adjust ourselves to the exact time for a TV show or a sports event. Let's stick with it and see if we can get the better of this situation."

Acknowledge that it's only normal to be fearful of what the computer may do to jobs and job security. Suppose that Selma says, "When they brought in the last computer, six people in the payroll section were transferred to the sales order department, and not one of them likes it over there. What's going to happen when these MIS analysts finish up with us next month?" Don't dismiss Selma's fear as something silly. Instead, agree that computers and EDP have made changes in the company. And, yes, some of these changes have been hard to accept. But assure Selma that you will do whatever you can do to make certain that higher management is aware of her present contributions. You will also look around to see where and how her talents can best be used if there is a change in her job.

Focus your attention on trying to make sure that people are assigned to the work they do best and like best. Abe, Edna, and Malcolm like routine work so that they can socialize to the maximum; assign them to repetitive work that is undemanding mentally. Ella, Dixie, and Vortek have strong creative qualities; assign them to work that requires initiative. All six persons may have to work in a computer-oriented world, but usually enough different kinds of work are available to satisfy individual preferences. People and job matches won't be perfect, of course. But when supervisors show they are willing to make the effort, this

act in itself helps to counteract anxieties about computers'
depersonalizing the work.

supervisory word power

Management information system.   A system made up of
data processing devices, programs, and people, which collects,
analyzes, exchanges, and delivers information to the organization in such a way as to help managers make the best possible
decisions.

Computer system.   A unique combination of self-modifying
(1) *equipment* (hardware) consisting of a central processing unit
that stores, manipulates, and controls data provided to it by input
devices and delivers information to users by means of output
devices; and (2) *programs* (software) couched in special lan-
guages that instruct the computer what to do and how to adapt
these instructions to the changing nature of new data (or feedback) it receives.

Information.   Data—past or present facts, observations, or
conclusions collected in numbers and words—that has been
selected, arranged, and analyzed (processed) to make it useful
for a specific human (managerial) activity.

Computer language.   A unique combination of symbols and
instructions that readily converts to the binary arithmetic form understood by the computer. COBOL and FORTRAN are basic lan-
guages for computer instructions.

Computer program.   A string of instructions written in computer language, which, when followed by the computer, carries
out a given operation—such as preparing a payroll, computing
merchandise prices, and maintaining perpetual inventory
records.

Other Important Terms in This Chapter

bit	hardware
central processing unit (CPU)	input-output devices
data	on-line
data bank	primary data
electronic data processing (EDP)	secondary data
feedback	simulation

reading comprehension

1. Why is it that a management information system can be said to be an extension of an old-fashioned accounting system?

2. List and describe the functions of the four basic parts of a computer's hardware.

3. Distinguish between data and information.

4. What is the purpose of the computer program? What is its nickname?

5. What might be some of the sources of computer input data for a fast-food chain? For an auto insurance company? For a manufacturer of baby food?

6. Suppose the supervisor of the woodworking department of a furniture factory was asked to reduce the number of specific items requested on the weekly departmental record report. Would it be better to cut out data on the number of defects found, the average number of employees on the payroll, or the number of orders backlogged for next week? Why?

7. List some examples of primary data and secondary data that might be used in a construction company, a department store, and a manufacturing plant.

8. Discuss the extent to which computers might change the jobs of a bank teller, a machine tool operator, and a parts clerk in an auto parts store.

9. Systematization of information handling may have three undesirable effects. What are they?

10. Besides the obvious value of providing better information on which to make decisions, what particular advantage may a smoothly operating information system offer to employees? Why?

supervision in action

THE CASE OF THE PEAK POULTRY SEASON.   A case study in human relations involving computers and management information systems, with questions for you to answer.

"You'll have to stick with it for at least another month. I know that keyboarding is not your cup of tea. But that is a vital spot that must be covered for now." Valerie Banks, head of the sales order department of Pappy's Poultry Packing Plant was talking to Don Wood, an employee of some five years. Pappy's is the largest chicken and turkey packer in the state. During the peak season, 120,000 birds per day go through the plant. They are dressed in various ways, frozen or packed in ice, and shipped off to dozens of supermarket warehouses in the Northeast.

During the fall and winter holiday season, the sales order department is a madhouse. Orders come in all day by telephone and teletype. Each customer presses for immediate delivery. But orders are far from standard. One customer may want a truckload made up of 1,000 whole turkeys in assorted weights, 500 cases of frozen parts, 200 cases of turkey loaf, and 300 cases of chicken breasts. Another may want a completely different make-up.

Clerks in the sales order department perform three kinds of work. First, there is a variety of low-skill jobs like typing forms, filing, and hand posting. Then there is the order entry keyboard operation that feeds input data to the computer. It requires a skilled employee who can work accurately at very high speeds. Finally, there is more complex work that involves liaison with the production and inventory control department. It has been the practice to hire college students temporarily to perform the liaison work during the peak season. They learn quickly and seem to have the flexibility and the initiative needed to handle the sensitive relationships involved.

"Every time the peak season rolls around, Val, you pull me off the production and inventory control job and sit me down at this keyboard," complained Don. "I've got seniority around here and I ought to get my pick of the jobs."

"When the work load is lower, I am glad to let you handle the liaison job," said Val. "But at peak periods I've found that part-time college students catch on quickly to the hand calculations needed to convert our orders to data for production control. Most of them already know how to work the punched-card machine, and speed is not an important factor on that job. Keyboarding the sales orders requires top-flight speed, and you are certainly the fastest person on that job we've ever had."

"I want to put the keyboard work behind me," said Don. "I've served my apprenticeship and should be allowed to work full-time on the liaison job with production control."

"Our department isn't large enough for that kind of permanent specialization," said Valerie. "We all have to work where the need is the greatest."

"If you would hire one or two of those college temporaries a couple of weeks before the work load began to peak, we could train them to be almost as good as I am on the keyboards," said Don.

"That wouldn't work," said Valerie. "The college kids catch on fast, I agree. But they get tired of the routine just as fast. And then they start to make errors. The mistakes we make inside the house between our department and production control can be patched up easily. The mistakes that affect our customers are nothing but trouble."

"Well, what about training Elda, the regular typist, to handle the keyboard work?" asked Don.

"Elda is simply too slow for that job. Besides, her accuracy isn't all that good," said Valerie.

"I don't care what you say," said Don. "It's not fair to marry me to the routine work when I have proved that I can use my know-how and skill on a job that is more challenging. If you can't see it my way, I'm going to complain to the general manager. I'm sure that a more interesting job can be found for me, probably in the production-control department."

This conversation took place early in the morning. Don found a chance to talk to the general manager right before lunch. By the next morning, Don had been transferred to the sales order liaison job in the production and inventory control department.

1. What do you think of Valerie's decision to place Don on the keyboarding job?

2. What alternatives might Valerie have tried? What are the strong points and drawbacks of each approach?

3. Assuming that Don had secured the transfer from the general manager, what would you do about it if you were Valerie?

enriching your viewpoint

Computers, MIS, and EDP are constantly changing and improving. Although it will be hard to keep abreast of developments, the following references should provide a sound basis for understanding changes as they occur.

"The ABC's of Surviving the Information Avalanche," a special 52-page advertising insert by the 3M Company in *Business Week,* April 24, 1978.

Bachtel, Charles L., "What to Do Before the Computer Comes," *Supervisory Management,* April 1974, pp. 2–9.

Burch, John G., Jr., and Felix R. Strater Jr., *Information Systems: Theory and Practice,* Hamilton Publishing Company, Santa Barbara, Calif., 1974.

Davis, G., *Management Information Systems,* McGraw-Hill Book Company, New York, 1974.

Norden, Peter V., and Jon A. Turner, "Computer Systems" in Lester R. Bittel (ed.), *The Encyclopedia of Professional Management,* McGraw-Hill Book Company, New York, 1979, pp. 188–197.

Ross, Joel E., *Modern Management and Information Systems,* Reston Publishing Company, Inc., Reston, Va., 1976.

helping yourself to succeed

6

PART

In the long run, all personal development is self-development. Supervisors who perform well in their work and who seek advancement do so mainly on their own initiative. For those who would assure their success, this part sets three key objectives:

- To analyze personal capabilities and shortcomings so as to construct a career plan with specific programs for developing knowledge and skills.
- To acquire an understanding of problem-solving and decision-making concepts and practices so as to be able to plan and manage more effectively.
- To anticipate the changes that lie ahead for supervision and management and prepare to deal with them as they occur.

31

CHAPTER **planning your career with self-development**

What can self-development mean to you?

Just about everything. Not only can it mean the difference between your holding a mediocre job and your holding a good one, but it can also mean the difference between your enjoying life and not enjoying it.

Self-improvement should mean continual growth for you—not physical, of course, but mental. It should mean constantly assessing yourself—as a supervisor and as a person. It calls for setting your personal standards a little higher each year because as you grow older, experience should tell you more and more about what is worthwhile and what is not.

True self-development calls for a certain amount of self-dissatisfaction. It's when you become too satisfied with yourself—

your performance as a supervisor or as an individual—that your growth stops and you lose your grip.

So be ambitious for yourself. Work holds high rewards for those who help themselves along. Mark it well: Over the long haul, your success will depend on your own efforts to improve.

How can you know how well you are doing on your job?

To map a plan for your self-improvement—the self-propelled road to a higher salary or a better job—the place to begin is with a no-excuses-permitted rating of yourself on your current job. To do so, answer the questions on the Self-Rating Job Quiz in Figure 31-1.

To evaluate your score, add the scores for each of the questions. A total of 70 is par. A score of 100 is tops. Anything below 50 means there's something seriously wrong with your performance.

If your score is between 50 and 70 points, your whole approach to your job needs an overhaul. If your score is in the 70s, better set up a plan now for improvement. If your score is 80 or above, don't take your future for granted. Look again at your low spots and decide to take definite action to bring them up within the next three months.

How are others likely to with potential for growth and improvement?

Your present employer will judge you most by what you accomplish on your job. If you have not yet mastered the art of meeting production schedules and quality standards and holding costs in line, you can probably forget about career growth. Assuming you can get these essential results, however, the other vital measures will be of your ability to plan, organize, direct, and control.

To make a candid assessment of this functional potential, try rating yourself against the characteristics listed in Figure 31-2 (Personal Effectiveness Inventory). Better still, ask a good friend or your boss to do the rating. The list consists of criteria that many authorities believe are needed for success in supervisory and management positions. The purpose of the assessment is not only to affirm your strong points but, especially, to identify areas that need further development.

On what is a career development program based?

It has four components.

FIGURE 31-1

Self-Rating Job Quiz

1. Outline employee responsibilities:
   Do you as a matter of policy see that all employees know what you expect from them in terms of output, quality, attendance, and safety?
   a. In specific terms and on a regular basis. ..... 10 points
   b. In specific terms but only when it applies to a new employee. ..... 7 points
   c. Vaguely and only when a discipline problem arises. ..... 3 points
   d. Can't remember when you last did this. ..... 0 points

   Score: _____

2. Relationship with your employees:
   Do you discuss with your workers your appraisal of their performance and other factors affecting your relationship with them?
   a. Regularly. ..... 20 points
   b. Not on a regular basis. ..... 12 points
   c. Only occasionally. ..... 8 points
   d. Hardly ever. ..... 0 points

   Score: _____

3. Working conditions:
   Have you tried hard to see that working arrangements for you and your employees are conducive to good work?
   a. By active, regular steps (inspection, etc.) to ensure for housekeeping, safety, and job enrichment. ..... 20 points
   b. By occasional but effective efforts to improve housekeeping, safety, and job enrichment. ..... 14 points
   c. Only when forced to do so by your superior. ..... 8 points
   d. Not in the last 12 months. ..... 0 points

   Score: _____

4. Contacts with other departments:
   Do you try (whether or not aided by the company) to become better acquainted with supervisors in other departments and to learn more about their duties?
   a. By taking advantage of every opportunity and trying to make more. ..... 10 points
   b. By attending company functions and following up all contacts. ..... 7 points
   c. By seldom attending company functions and failing to follow up contacts. ..... 4 points
   d. By never attending company functions and avoiding new contacts. ..... 0 points

   Score: _____

5. Further education and training:
   Have you personally made it a policy to improve your own basic education so that it will best benefit you and your company?
   a. By taking night or correspondence courses and following a program of self-education. ..... 10 points

FIGURE 31-1 (continued)

b. By conscientious efforts to train yourself when new problems arise on your job. — 8 points

c. By only rare attempts to improve your knowledge in the field of your work. — 4 points

d. In no way at all in the last 12 months. — 0 points

Score: _____

6. New assignments and ideas:

Have you searched for ways to contribute new ideas and to accept assignments beyond the limits of your current job?

a. By regularly submitting in writing carefully considered ideas, or looking for chances to carry out special assignments. — 10 points

b. By accepting additional assignments with enthusiasm and carrying them out with vigor. — 6 points

c. By occasionally suggesting ways informally for improving methods in your department. — 2 points

d. By doing just what your job demands and nothing else. — 0 points

Score: _____

7. Professional society activities:

Do you belong to, and participate in the affairs of, professional or technical societies like the National Management Association or the Industrial Management Clubs?

a. More than one and attend most meetings. — 5 points

b. At least one and attend most meetings. — 4 points

c. At least one but attend only occasionally. — 2 points

d. No outside activity of this nature. — 0 points

Score: _____

8. Keeping posted on new technology:

Do you make a point of keeping up with the latest developments that affect supervision and the technical side of your job by reading business magazines and technical journals?

a. Regularly on company time and occasionally on your time. — 5 points

b. Regularly on company time. — 4 points

c. Rarely. — 2 points

d. Never. — 0 points

Score: _____

9. Attitude toward company:

When not carrying out specific orders or under active supervision of your boss, how do you attempt to use your time?

a. Exactly as though you were running your own business. — 10 points

b. Follow policies and instructions to the letter but no more. — 7 points

c. Work effectively only under pressure for conformance. — 3 points

d. Look for loopholes to avoid work. — 0 points

Score: _____

Total: _____

FIGURE 31-2

Personal Effectiveness Inventory				
	Weak	**Adequate**	**Strong**	**Needs improvement**
1. Oral Communication: Effectiveness of expression in individual or group situations.	_____	_____	_____	_____
2. Written Communication: Ability to write clearly and correctly.	_____	_____	_____	_____
3. Leadership: Getting ideas accepted and guiding a group or an individual to do a task.	_____	_____	_____	_____
4. Interpersonal Insight: Perceiving and reacting to the needs of others, objectivity in perceiving impact of self on others.	_____	_____	_____	_____
5. Planning and Organizing: Ability to efficiently establish a course of action for self and others and get results.	_____	_____	_____	_____
6. Problem Solution: Identifying causes of problems, proposing solutions, and solving problems.	_____	_____	_____	_____
7. Stress Tolerance: Ability to perform under pressure and opposition.	_____	_____	_____	_____
8. Creativity: Ability to generate, recognize, and accept imaginative solutions and innovations.	_____	_____	_____	_____
9. Decisiveness: Ability to make sound decisions and take action.	_____	_____	_____	_____
10. Flexibility: Ability to adapt managerial approach to changing organizational needs and situations.	_____	_____	_____	_____
11. Reasoning: Ability to apply a sound reasoning and logical process to varying situations, problems, goals, and activities.	_____	_____	_____	_____

Adapted from *Guide for Preparing Individual Development Plans,* prepared by Richard F. Fraser and Chester C. Cotton for the Training and Career Development Branch of the U.S. Department of Agriculture's Argricultural Research Service at Hyattsville, Md., February 1977. By permission.

A candid self-assessment.   You will have started if you have completed the self-rating charts in Figure 31-1 and Figure 31-2.

Firm and realistic goals.   These should be based on what you want to accomplish in your career specifically and in your life generally. They will be limited, of course, by the weaknesses that stand out in your job quiz (Figure 31-1) and personal inventory (Figure 31-2).

A concrete program for development.   Every weakness points toward a corrective course of action. These actions should be spelled out in specific detail—a course to take, a book to read, a seminar to attend, an on-job practice to engage in. Action plans should also pin down the time to begin and complete each phase. A modest but concrete development program is far better than an ambitious but vague one.

Motivation and commitment.   Career growth has its pluses and minuses. Upward movement usually means greater status and a more affluent life-style. It also means very hard work, sacrifice of leisure time, removal from the easy friendship with people in the department, and an occasional unpleasant decision to make. That is the trade-off. To go ahead, supervisors have to value the benefits above the new obligations. Without personal drive and commitment to the goals you have chosen, a self-development program becomes an exercise in self-deception.

How can you plan for your self-improvement?

Self-improvement is paved with good intentions. To avoid misfires in your ambitions, don't attempt too much at once. Plan for continuing self-development. Check regularly to see what progress you've made. Try to put your plan into writing. The chart in Figure 31-3 suggests one way to do this.

It is easy to talk about self-motivation and commitment, but how does one develop it?

My guess is that you have a certain amount of it already or you wouldn't have come as far as you have. Nevertheless, the question has always bothered ambitious people. Here is one helpful way to think about this problem for yourself.

Try a force-field analysis.   This is done in five steps (see Figure 31-4).

   1. Pick a goal you wish to reach or an action you plan to take as part of your development program. This action should help

Supervisor: _Joe Smith_

	Weak Spots	Plan for Corrective Action	When to Do It	Action Com-plete
This Year's Plan	Telling employees where they stand	Prepare calendar with a different worker to be talked to each week	At once	√
	Poor department safety record	Hold monthly meetings with work group	Begin June	√
	Keeping up with job technology	Subscribe to _American Machinist_	At once	√
Next Year's Plan	No activities outside of work	Join International Management Council	Next year	
	Speaking in front of groups	Enroll in Dale Carnegie course in public speaking	Next winter	
Future	Cost estimating	Take correspondence course in accounting	Not sche-duled	

FIGURE 31-3. Self-Development Schedule.

you reach your goal by changing (improving) your present be-havior. This step is sometimes called the goal-action-change step. Your _goal_ may be to prepare effective reports for higher management to read. The _action_ may require your taking a night course at your community college in report writing. The _change_ will be improvement in your written communications.

2. Make a list of at least five important forces that are _driving_ you to make that change. For example, you want to get a promo-tion (key force is promotion); you hope to earn more money (key force is future income); your spouse would feel good about your improved status (key force is status); your boss is pressuring you for regular formal reports (key force is pressure); and you want the satisfaction of seeing your ideas influence higher manage-ment decisions (key force is influence).

3. Make a list of at least five important forces that are holding you back, or _restraining_ you, from making this change. For ex-ample, you can't find the time (key force is time); you hate taking night courses (key force is educational method); the course is only given on your bowling night (key force is interference with recreation); you are afraid that you won't do well (key force is fear of failure); and you don't like the idea that you will have to do homework (key force is homework).

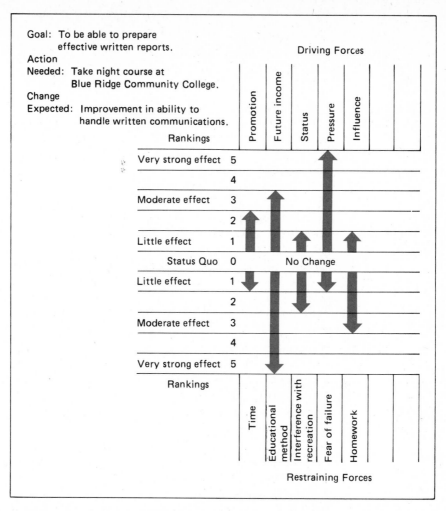

FIGURE 31-4. Example of a Force-Field Analysis. Adapted from George A. Ford and Gordon L. Lippitt, *Planning Your Future*, rev. ed., University Associates, La Jolla, Calif., 1976, p. 49. By permission.

4. Now rank each force, driving as well as restraining, according to how strong it is. Use a ranking scale of 1 to 5, ranging from 1 as "little effect" to 5 as "very strong effect." This singles out what is really important in motivating you and what is truly powerful in holding you back. It also helps to expose low-ranking forces for what they are—excuses.

5. Try to match opposing forces. A strong driving force like pressure may be all that is needed to motivate you to overcome a strong restraining force like educational method. Hope for a larger future income may overcome your dislike of homework.

The driving forces of promotion, status, and influence may not be so powerful as you thought they were when compared on the chart, but neither are the restraining forces of time, fear of failure, and interference with recreation.

How can you improve your education?

Face it, the person with the better education has an advantage over the person without it. But this doesn't mean you can't do anything about it. There's plenty you can do to improve your knowledge.

First, examine your own attitude toward further education. Is it strictly negative? If so, you'd better change in a hurry. Convince yourself that you, too, can learn new techniques and accept new ideas. If you want to learn, learning is made easier.

Next, pick out the soft spots in your educational armor. Is it reading and writing? Is it a weakness with figures? These can be improved quickly through correspondence and home-study courses or in an evening course at a local university. Adult education courses at your local high school also offer help in these areas.

If your weakness is in a technical line—say your company is processing chemicals or constructing complicated electronic equipment, or your job involves simple metallurgy—you can find courses at technical institutes and universities that will help you understand your processes better even if you don't become an expert.

Caution: You may not be able to take a course in physical chemistry, for instance, if you haven't had a previous course in basic chemistry. So your plan for improvement may often have to be a long-range one. Here's a suggestion. You may enroll in an advanced course just as a listener. You thus get a feel for the subject and its terminology, with only a little prior preparation.

In your programming, don't scatter your efforts indiscriminately. Pinpoint your educational efforts to strengthen your weak spots. Later on, if you like, you can add frills.

How can you take best advantage of your company's training and development program?

Show that you're interested. In most progressive companies today, the personnel manager or the training director is eager to help supervisors who want to help themselves. Don't be ashamed to ask for help, or think you'll be revealing a secret weakness. One of the necessary qualities of an executive is the ability for self-analysis and the determination to improve.

What is a management-development program?

Management development (it may also be called executive or supervisory development) is the term applied to the systematic inventory, appraisal, and training of management people. Programs vary according to an individual company's policies. Sometimes they include only top management people and often are not extended to the first-line supervisory level.

If there's a program in your company that applies to you, you'll probably hear about it from your boss. But don't expect your company to take care of your self-development program. It's really up to you.

Where can you go for outside help and guidance?

For educational guidance outside your company, try your local centers for adult education or vocational guidance, a nearby community college or university extension service. Or write either of the nationwide management clubs mentioned in Chapter 1. Another source to try is any nearby chapter of the American Society for Training and Development.

For information about specific correspondence or technical courses, write to:

American Society for Training and Development
P.O. Box 5307
Madison, Wisconsin 53705

American Society for Engineering Education
1 DuPont Circle, N.W.
Washington, D.C. 20036

National Home Study Council
1601 18th Street, N.W.
Washington, D.C. 20009

American Personnel and Guidance Association
1607 New Hampshire Avenue, N.W.
Washington, D.C. 20009

How can you draw favorable attention to yourself?

Just as you may take for granted employees who do what they are asked and mind their own business, so, too, will your company tend to consider you merely average unless you make a special effort to draw attention to yourself.

In the Army there is a saying, "Never volunteer". But plenty of people made their mark by taking this chance. In business, too, you must take chances—stick your neck out—if you're going to go far. So look for opportunities to prepare special reports, to serve on company committees, to volunteer opinions, and to point out problems.

While you may draw unfavorable comments from your associates if you're too much of an eager beaver or a "killer," the real danger lies in doing too little and in not making your accomplishments known. Too many supervisors hide their light under a bushel. If you've been making progress in running your department more efficiently, don't brag about it. But do draw attention subtly to this progress by preparing performance reports on a regular basis.

Your outside activities, such as membership in professional societies or civic and service organizations, should be reported to your boss and to your personnel office. Look for every opportunity to get favorable information about you and your accomplishments into writing and into your personnel file.

What will outside reading do for you?

Some people can learn a lot just by reading. Others find it difficult to get much from the printed page. But if you're one of the former, try to set up a planned reading program. Include in it at least one good newspaper (like *The New York Times* or *The Wall Street Journal*), one good news magazine (like *Time* or *Newsweek*), one good management magazine (like *Business Week* or *Administrative Management*), and one good technical magazine or journal that serves your field (like *American Machinist*). Don't just subscribe to them or have your name put on the routing list. Read them—and try to apply what you find in them. In addition, you ought to set up a library of business books for yourself. Selections from the references at the end of each chapter of this book make a good place to begin.

How important is your personal growth?

You spend only eight or ten hours a day at work. What you do as a person outside your job undoubtedly influences the way you conduct yourself at work. Consequently, it's important that as you grow older, you mature as an individual.

Upon reflection, it seems clear that one's advancement and ultimate sense of fulfillment depend on the extent to which personal achievements have brought one into a rewarding involvement with others. Many capable executives who lose interest after 35 or 40 do so because of the absence of emotional satisfaction. Yet it cannot be gained by psyching oneself up. It comes through deep and serious preparation for a meaningful relationship. Hard-headed Johnny Unitas, the great quarterback of the Baltimore Colts, observed at the close of his career, "As far as I'm concerned, it's a thinking man's game. Emotion may play a part, but it's 60 to 70 percent preparation—physical and mental preparation. Some players go along with the 'up' and 'down' business, but my theory is that these are the guys who burn themselves out."

Sound advice on this matter also comes from an unlikely source, artist Andy Warhol. This creative person, who first attracted attention through his paintings of Campbell's soup cans, was asked by an aspiring young artist what she should do to succeed. Warhol replied, "Work."

The supervisor's job, by definition, is packed with stress, isn't it? Won't pursuing an upward career make it even worse?

Not necessarily. But I agree that pressure and conflict are core elements in the supervisory environment. They can be managed and minimized, as much of this text demonstrates. In pursuing an upward career, however, it is more important than ever to find ways to take this pressure off whenever you can. For example, Dr. Friedman and Dr. Rosenman observe in their book *Type A Behavior and Your Heart* that supervisors (1) are under a chronic siege of time urgency and a constant involvement in multiple projects; (2) have the feeling that "only I can handle it"; and (3) have a tendency to hasten the pace of normal conversation as a result. As an antidote to these conditions, Friedman and Rosenman suggest these ten ways to cut down on stress:

- Plan some idleness every day—at work or at home.
- Listen to others without interruption.
- Read books or enjoy entertainment that doesn't demand concentration.
- Learn to savor food rather than to rush through every meal.
- Have a place for retreat at home, even if it's the garage or the basement.
- Avoid, if you can, irritating and overly competitive people.
- Plan leisurely, less-structured vacations.
- Concentrate on enriching yourself and broadening your life.
- Live by the calendar, not the stopwatch.
- Stay with one task at a time.

Easier said than done, of course, but these are pretty good guide-lines for keeping mentally and physically fit while handling your job and your career.

To what extent will career goals conflict with your other aspirations in life?

They can be compatible, but the higher one moves in a career, the more likely it is that other life values will suffer. This need not be, if you also build into the plans you make for your career a place for the other things you hold dear—family, friends, leisure, health, service, faith. You will be able to make such plans only if you have developed maturity, however. Maturity means the ability to stand outside yourself and make an honest judgment of your thoughts and behavior. It usually means—among other things —to exercise a great deal of self-control, to be able to hold your temper when others are losing theirs, to accept an oc-casional failure as well as success, and to evaluate the talents and the intent of others fairly, regardless of your personal views.

If you have developed such a maturity, you may want to try two exercises that will help you understand much more about what is important to you.

Try a life inventory. This requires that you go off alone for one hour and make up six separate lists about yourself.

- List 1. These are the things I do well.
- List 2. These are the things I do poorly.
- List 3. These are the things I would like to be able to learn or to improve: skills, activities, attitudes, and feelings.
- List 4. These are the things I would like to be able to stop: activities, habits, attitudes, and feelings.
- List 5. These are the things I would like to have in life that I don't have now.
- List 6. These are the things in life I value and would not like to lose.

Make each list as long as you like; each list ought to have at least five items, however. Don't worry about duplicates between lists. If you have compiled your lists thoughtfully and candidly, you ought to know more about yourself than before. Now, go back and look at your job quiz (Figure 31-1) and your personal inven-tory (Figure 31-2). Are there weak points on those lists that are explained by your life inventory? Are there items on your life in-ventory that would lead you to find new strengths on your job and in your personal assessment? Look at your goals and career plans. Do they conflict with your life inventory? In what way can your plans for self-development capitalize on what your life inventory shows?

Try keeping a 24-hour diary.   Do it for one business day and for one weekend day. Get a big note pad and write down (1) every single thing you do, (2) whom you do it with, and (3) how long you spend doing it. You will find that many things you do, especially at work, are repeated over and over. For example, talking with one employee about quality for three minutes may be repeated five or ten times with other employees. You may also discover gaps of time in which you do nothing. Don't worry about that, either. The purpose of the diary is to tell you exactly what two days in your life are really like. If you keep this diary carefully and candidly, you will find many surprises—and some valuable insights into your job, yourself, and your life. It, too, will help you plan a better self-development program and generate a greater drive to fulfill it.

enriching your viewpoint

To enlarge your comprehension of the fields that deal with, and support efforts toward, personal and career development, the following sources are recommended:

Bittel, Lester R., *Improving Supervisory Performance,* McGraw-Hill Book Company, New York, 1976, Chap. 14, "Planning for Performance Improvement."

Boyd, Bradford B., *Management-Minded Supervision,* 2d ed., McGraw-Hill Book Company, New York, 1976, Chap. 2, "Continual Self-Development."

Craig, Robert L. (ed.), *Training and Development Handbook,* 2d ed., McGraw-Hill Book Company, New York, 1976.

Ford, George A., and Gordon L. Lippitt, *Planning Your Future,* rev. ed., University Associates, La Jolla, Calif., 1976.

Fraser, Richard F., and Chester C. Cotton, *Guide for Preparing Individual Development Plans,* Training and Career Development Branch, U.S. Department of Agriculture, Hyattsville, Md., February 1977.

Kotter, John P., Victor A. Faux, and Charles C. McArthur, *Self-Assessment and Career Development,* Prentice-Hall, Inc., Englewood Cliffs, N.J., 1978.

McFarland, Dalton E., *Action Strategies for Management Achievement,* Amacom, New York, 1977.

Roach, John M. (ed.), *Career Planning: A How-to Chart for Your Future,* Amacom, New York, 1975.

Vance, Charles C., *Manager Today, Executive Tomorrow,* McGraw-Hill Book Company, New York, 1974.

32

CHAPTER

problem solving and decision making

What, specifically, is a problem?

A problem is a puzzle, a mystery, an unsettled matter, a situation requiring a solution, a plan or an issue involving uncertainty. Your work is full of them. Problems can be classified three ways:

Problems that have already happened. Examples are merchandise that spoiled, costs that got out of line, employees who quit, shipments that were missed. These may need immediate solutions to correct what has taken place.

Problems that lie ahead. Examples are how to finish the Ajax project on time, when to put on a second shift, where to place the

new press, whether or not to tell employees of an impending change in their work. These, too, require solutions now to set effective plans and procedures.

Problems that you want to forestall. These lurk in the future. You'd like to take preventive action now so that they never arise and thus never need solutions.

How can you recognize a problem or a potential problem?

A problem exists when there is a gap between what you expect to happen and what actually happens. Your budget, for example, calls for 2,200 insurance policies to be processed this week; the count at 5 p.m. on Friday shows that you completed only 1,975, a gap of 225 policies. Or you expected to hold the total number of employee absences in your department to 300 days this year; the total is 410, a gap of 110 days.

It is almost the same with potential problems. You know what you would like to have occur in the future: a project completed, a perfect safety record, fewer than ten customer complaints. These are your plans. But when you look ahead at your procedures and the potential for mishaps, you feel that your department will fall short of its targets—that there will be a gap.

How are problems solved?

By removing whatever it is that has caused, or will cause, a gap between the expected (or desired) condition and the actual condition. That's the main idea, at least. Suppose, for example, that your hoped-for safety record of zero accidents is spoiled by three accidents on the punch press machine. You will want to (1) find their cause (bypassing of the safety guard by the operators) and (2) remove it (by designing a foolproof guard).

Finding and removing the cause or causes, however, is usually difficult and requires considerable examination and thought. There will be more discussion about the problem-solving process later.

What is the connection between problem solving and decision making?

The two processes are closely related. A decision is always needed in the choice of the problem's solution. In many ways, problem solving *is* decision making. As you will see in a moment, any step along the way of planning, organizing, directing, controlling—and problem solving—that presents a choice of more than one course of action requires also that a decision be made. Take the safety record on the punch press again. A truly complete analysis of the problem might have suggested that the cause could be removed in three different ways: (1) use of an automatic feeding device that would remove the need for a guard, (2) institution of an educational and disciplinary program to instruct operators about the proper operation of the present guard, or (3) design of a foolproof guarding system. The supervisor, as decision maker, would have to choose among the three alternatives. The first might be judged too costly, the second not completely effective, and the third the best choice because it is relatively inexpensive and foolproof.

How can you recognize the need for a decision?

Whenever there is more than one way of doing things, a decision is needed. Any kind of choice, alternative, or option calls for a decision. You might ask, if this is so, why are so many decision opportunities overlooked? The answer is that managers and supervisors alike get preoccupied with the status quo. In effect they say, the way we are doing this is the only way. Such supervisors miss the point that there are always alternatives. There is always the choice to do something or not to do it, to speak or to remain silent, to correct or to let well enough alone. All too often a supervisor's decision is made by default. The supervisor does nothing. The tide of events carries the department until a crisis occurs. In reality, however, doing nothing represented a choice. It was a decision not to change, not to plan for improvement, not to anticipate a potential problem.

Must the approach to problem solving be systematic?

Yes. There are few exceptions to the rule that the best results come from a systematic approach. Here is a fundamental one.

Step 1. State the problem clearly and specifically. Stay away from a general statement, like "We have a problem with quality." Instead, narrow it down and put figures on it if you can, like "Between the first of the month and today, the number of rejects found at final inspection have totaled 32, compared with our standard of 15."

Step 2. Collect all information relevant to the problem.
Don't go too far afield, but do find data that may shed some light on process changes, materials used, equipment function, design specifications, employee performance and assignments. Much of the data will not tell you anything except where the source of the problem is not. If your information shows, for example, that there has been no change in the way materials have arrived or machinery has been used, good! You can look elsewhere.

Step 3. List as many possible causes for the problem as you can think of. Remember that a problem is a gap between expected and actual conditions. Something must have occurred to cause that gap. Most particularly, something must have been changed. Is the operator different from the old one? Was a power source less regular than before? Has there been a change, however slight, in the specifications?

Step 4. Select the cause or causes that seem most likely.
Do this by a process of elimination. To test a cause to see if it is a probable one, try seeing (or thinking through) what difference it would make if that factor were returned to its original state. For example, suppose a possible cause of rejects is that compressed air power is now only 75 psi instead of 90 psi. Try making the product with the pressure restored to 90 psi. If it makes no difference, then power irregularity is not a likely cause. Or perhaps you think that the new operator has misunderstood your instructions. Check this out with the operator. See if your instructions are, in fact, being followed exactly. If not, what happens when your instructions are followed? If the rejects stop, then this is a likely cause. If the rejects persist, this is not a likely cause.

Step 5. Suggest as many solutions for removing causes as you can. This is a good time for brainstorming. There is rarely only one way to solve a problem. If the cause of an employee's excessive absenteeism, for instance, is difficulty getting up in the morning, this cause might be removed in a number of ways. You might change the shift, insist that the employee buy an alarm clock, make a wake-up telephone call yourself, or show how failure to get to work is job-threatening. The point is to make your list of alternative solutions as long as possible.

Step 6. Evaluate the pros and cons of each proposed solution. Some solutions will be better than others. But what does better mean? Cheaper? Faster? Surer? More participative? More in line with company policy? To judge which solution is best, you'll have to have a set of criteria like the ones just listed. Evaluation requires you to make judgments based on facts. Consult the information gathered in Step 2. Also consult anyone who can offer specialized opinions about the criteria you have chosen.

Step 7. Choose the solution you think is best. Yes, this—like what you did in Step 6—is the decision phase of problem solving. In effect, you will have weighed all the chances of success against the risks of failure. The strengths of your solution should exceed its weaknesses.

Step 8. Spell out a plan of action to carry out your solution. Decisions require action and follow-up. Pin down exactly what will be done and how, who will do it, where, and when. How much money can be spent? What resources can be used? What is the deadline?

What approach is used for problems that involve the future rather than the past?

You must think forward rather than backward. What could change so as to cause a problem? An employee is retiring; you'd better have a trained replacement. The company has signed a contract with a new supplier; you'd better make sure the purchasing department relays the exact materials specifications to the vendor. Your plans call for ten new employees by the year's end; you'd better check with personnel to make sure these employees will, in fact, be available and fully trained when the new equipment is ready.

Potential problem analysis is essentially the same as basic, systematic problem solving. Its focus, however, is on step 4, listing possible causes. The fundamental difference is that you must transfer what your experience has told you about past causes to estimates of what may possibly recur in the future. You must, of course, also use your imagination to anticipate new sources of problems—causes that have not occurred previously but which might in the future.

How systematic must the decision-making process be?

Unlike problem solving, there are good reasons to believe that decision making need not always be systematic—or even logical. System helps up to a point. But when you are dealing with the future, hunches and intuition often pay off.

The systematic, or rational, approach to decision making takes place during steps 6 and 7 of problem solving: evaluating alternative solutions and selecting the best one based on the facts available. This approach can be made even more rational and more reliable by first setting goals that the decision must satisfy. For example, a problem-solving decision about cost cutting must be effective for at least six months and not involve employee separations. Or, if you are developing future plans, the decision may be required to fulfill the goal of assuring that production schedules are met without overtime.

This rational step of first setting a goal tends to make the quality of the decision better, even when they are ultimately made by hunch, because you know what your target is or what limitations will be placed on your choice or plans for implementation.

What is meant by mathematical decision making?

Mathematical decision making refers to the use of certain mathematical, statistical, or quantitative techniques to aid the decision maker. These are aids, very valuable ones in many instances, but they are only aids. The techniques do not make decisions. They arrange numerical information in such a way so that it can be analyzed mathematically, but the executive, manager, or supervisor must make the final decision, based on interpretation of the results.

Several popular mathematical techniques, discussed in the following questions, include payoff tables, decision trees, cost-benefit analysis, input-output analysis, and break-even analysis.

Payoff tables? What do they prove?

Payoff tables help you to make dollar comparisons between two or more different decision choices in a particular situation. Raw figures can be misleading. Payoff tables require that you also make a judgment about the chances that something will happen. Then these judgments (or estimates of probability) are applied to the raw figures. The result may be different from what you first thought it might be.

Take this example. Your department has been purchasing electronic assemblies from an outside contractor at $2,500 per unit. Your purchasing department wants to know whether you can make them cheaper in your own company. You are quite sure that you can, but a lot will depend on what kind of labor you employ. You have two choices:

• Alternative number 1 is to use unskilled labor at $5 per hour.

TABLE 32-1. **Cost per Unit at Three Different Levels of Productivity**

	Number of man-hours needed to build one unit in your company		
	200 hours	**100 hours**	**50 hours**
Alternative 1 Using unskilled labor at $5 per hour	$1,000	$ 500	$250
Alternative 2 Using highly skilled labor at $10 per hour	$2,000	$1,000	$500

Your guess is that their productivity (the number of hours needed to make one unit) will be fairly low.

• Alternative number 2 is to hire experienced, skilled artisans at $10 per hour. You feel quite sure they will have much higher productivity.

What is the decision? Which alternative will provide the greatest savings in the long run? First, set up a table that shows how much each assembly unit will cost at varying productivity levels for each choice. Obviously, the labor cost at each level is cheaper when you use the $5-per-hour labor. See Table 32-1.

The next step is to find out how much money will be saved by each choice at the various productivity levels. Again, Table 32-2 shows that at each productivity level the $5 unskilled labor will save the most money.

Here is the catch. Until now you have been using raw data. Your comparisons have assumed that $5-per-hour labor can actually build a unit in 100 hours or even in as few as 50 hours. Of course you have made similar assumptions for the $10-per-hour labor. But your experience tells you the chances that the skilled labor will reach the lower number of hours per unit is far greater than for the unskilled labor. So here is what you do now.

TABLE 32-2. **Savings per Unit at Various Productivity Levels (at Contract Cost per Unit of $2,500)**

	Number of worker-hours needed to build one unit in your company		
	200 hours	**100 hours**	**50 hours**
Alternative 1	$1,500	$2,000	$2,250
Alternative 2	$ 500	$1,500	$2,000

TABLE 32-3.
Weighted Savings According to Their Probability of Occurring

	At 200 hours per unit	At 150 hours per unit	At 50 hours per unit	Expected money value of each decision
Alternative 1				
Savings at each productivity rate	$1,500	$2,000	$2,250	
Probability of each productivity rate occurring	× .80	× .10	× .10	
Weighted savings at each productivity rate	$1,200 +	$ 200 +	$ 225 =	$1,625
Alternative 2				
Savings at each productivity rate	$ 500	$1,500	$2,000	
Probability of each productivity rate occurring	× .05	$ .20	× .75	
Weighted savings at each productivity rate	$ 25 +	$ 300 +	$1,500 =	$1,825

The next step is to weight the dollar savings you calculated above by making estimates of the probability of each alternative's reaching the various productivity rates.

Your guess is that for the $5-per-hour-labor, there is an 80 percent chance of hitting the 200-hour level, but only a 10 percent chance of assembling a unit in 100 hours, and only a 10 percent chance of lowering the labor input per unit to 50 hours. (Note that the total of your percentages is 100. Said another way: of 100 chances, the $5 labor will take 200 hours to make one unit 80 times, 100 hours 10 times, and 50 hours 10 times.) Your probability estimates for the $10-per-hour labor are much more favorable. You think there is a 75 percent chance of hitting the 50-hour level, only 20 percent chance of needing as much as 100 hours per unit, and very little chance (5 percent) their productivity will be so poor that it will take 200 hours. (Note again that the total of all probabilities is 100 percent or, decimally, 1.00.)

Now you weight the raw data by preparing a payoff table (Table 32-3). This is done by multiplying the savings at each productivity level by the probability estimate for each alternative. This gives you a weight savings figure at each productivity level. Now add the weighted savings at each level to find the expected money value (EMV) of each alternative. This payoff table tells you that a decision to employ skilled labor at $10 per hour (alternative 2) has a higher payoff expectation ($1,825) than if you were to use unskilled, $5-per-hour labor ($1,625, alternative 1).

The payoff table has helped you to plug your judgment about probable outcomes into the raw cost accounting data. You now have a more realistic knowledge of which choice may have the best dollar value—based on your judgment about risks. This is all you know. The great weakness of this method is that the weighted figures depend on how good your judgment is about the future. You may be entirely wrong. On the other hand, the great value in this method is that it forces you to make a firm judgment about what you think the risks will be. The payoff table won't make the decision for you, but it will force you to be more realistic about possible outcomes.

How can supervisors make use of a decision tree?

In much the same manner as they use the payoff tables. The decision tree is essentially a graphic portrait of how each alternative forks into various possibilities. It has the greater capability in that it portrays a series of cascading decisions. At each decision point, a payoff table may be constructed.

Suppose a supervisor is faced with a decision about how to treat Edgar, an employee whose attendance has been very poor. One alternative (A-1) is to enforce strict discipline by laying Edgar off for three days. A second alternative (A-2) is to provide constructive encouragement. A third alternative (A-3) is to try a little of both. Figure 32-1 shows how these alternatives work on a decision tree.

The supervisor can presume that there are only three ways Edgar can react. He may respond only to strict discipline, he may respond only to encouragement, or he may respond favorably to both. The probable changes in performance from each kind of response are diagramed, with a range of outcomes from very little improvement to great improvement. Thus, the improvement in Ed's performance differs according to each decision strategy and to each possibility of how Ed might respond to it.

To convert the decision tree to a payoff table, the supervisor must (1) assign probabilities to each of Edgar's possible responses and (2) assign a raw value to each of the possible outcomes—the changes in Edgar's performance. (See Figure 32-2.) The supervisor assigns a probability of .3 to a favorable response to discipline, .3 to encouragement, and .4 to a favorable response to both. (Note again that the total of the probabilities is 1.0.) The supervisor also assigns a raw value of 10 points for very

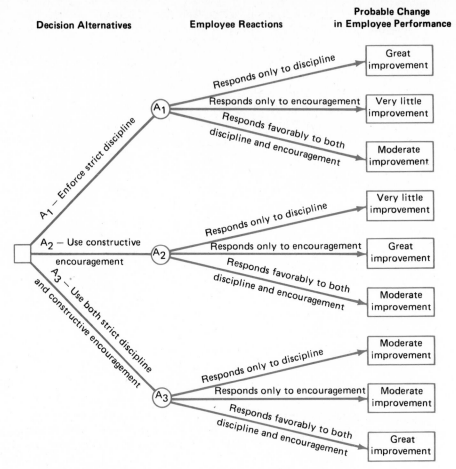

FIGURE 32-1. Basic Decision Tree: Discipline Versus Constructive Encouragement to Improve an Employee's Performance.

little improvement, 20 points for moderate improvement, and 30 points for great improvement. As with the payoff tables, the raw scores are weighted by multiplying each by its probability of occurrence. The weighted scores for each alternative are summed. This decision tree would predict that the best results would come from using alternative A-3, which has the highest weighted scores.

The decision tree has the same weakness as the payoff tables: It assumes that the estimates of probabilities are correct. They may not be.

The decision tree has the advantage of helping the supervisor to visualize what can happen.

Decision strategies	Probabilities of various responses (states of nature)	Probable outcome: change in performance	Raw value assigned to each outcome	Probability weighting	Weighted outcomes of decisions A, B, and C
A	(.3)	Great	30	X .3	9 ⎤
	(.3)	Very little	10	X .3	3 ⎬ 20
	(.4)	Moderate	20	X .4	8 ⎦
B Encouragement	(.3)	Very little	10	X .3	3 ⎤
	(.3)	Great	30	X .3	9 ⎬ 20
	(.4)	Moderate	20	X .4	8 ⎦
Discipline and encouragement C	(.3)	Moderate	20	X .3	6 ⎤
	(.3)	Moderate	20	X .3	6 ⎬ 24
	(.4)	Great	30	X .4	12 ⎦

FIGURE 32-2. Weighted Arithmetic Extension of Basic Decision Tree.

The tree in Figure 32-2 stopped after only one decision. It could have been carried on to a second set of alternatives. Suppose the supervisor chose alternative A-3. Ed, however, may in reality only respond to encouragement. His improvement will be only moderate. The supervisor can at that point on the tree set out two or more alternative actions. For example, the supervisor can (B-1) discontinue discipline but intensify encouragement, (B-2) discontinue both, or (B-3) try a Management-by-Objectives technique with Edgar.

The process would repeat in this way. The supervisor predicts Edgar's possible responses to each alternative and assigns probability percentages to them. Based on this estimate, the supervisor then predicts three different outcomes and assigns raw values to them. Finally, the supervisor multiplies the raw outcome scores by the probability weighting and chooses the best course of action, based on the resultant sums.

Decision trees can continue branching indefinitely.

What is meant by cost-benefit analysis?

It is not unlike the closing steps in problem solving and decision making. This is the phase when you examine the pros and cons of each proposed solution. Cost-benefit analysis has become a popular technique for evaluating proposals in the public sector. Take a proposal for a local government to offer a child-care service to its residents. Cost-benefit analysis adds all the costs of implementation and equates them with the value of the services to the community. Typically, the benefits of such nonprofit services are hard to quantify; that is, it is hard to place a dollar value on them. Accordingly, many cost-benefit analyses include quality judgments of benefits as well as dollar estimates.

Cost-benefit analysis is similar to *input-output* analysis, which tries to make sure that the cost and effort expended in carrying out a decision will at least be balanced by its outputs or results. In business, when outputs exceed inputs, the result is a profit. If there is an excess of benefits over costs in nonprofit organizations, the excess is called a surplus.

Some say that most decisions involve a trade-off. What is meant by that?

This is a way of saying that to attain your objective in one area, you must be prepared to give up something in another area. The department store maintenance supervisor who has only so much money to spend on new equipment may buy a powered floor sweeper and may have to forego the purchase of a powered platform to facilitate ceiling maintenance. Housekeeping will improve on the floors; meanwhile, it may get worse on the ceilings. This is a trade-off in which someone must decide which goal is more important at the moment.

Are decisions based on intuition as good as those based on logic?

If it works out as well, it won't make any difference as to how a decision was reached. Many decisions based on hunch have proved to be correct. They are harder to defend, however, when they go wrong. More important, any decision is likely to be better if its goals are clearly understood. The logical approach helps to strip away distractions and irrelevancies. Intuition often adds a valuable dimension by calling on some inner sense we don't clearly understand. Many authorities believe the best decisions come from the dual approach—a combination of logic and hunch.

In seeking facts to solve a problem or make a decision, what should be the cutoff point?

Stop looking when the trouble and the cost of obtaining the extra information exceeds its value. The rule is: the more critical and lasting the effect of a decision, the more you can afford to look for the last scrap of vital information. Don't spend two days hunting for background data on a purchasing decision, for example, if the item plays only an insignificant part in your process and will only be used once or twice. On the other hand, it might pay to defer a decision to hire a full-time employee until you have made a reference check.

Do guard against using the absence of information as an excuse for procrastination. Some decisions are especially hard to arrive at and unpleasant to carry out. When you are faced with these situations, there is a temptation to put off an answer (yes, answers are decisions—or should be) by asking for more information. Rarely is the questioner fooled by this tactic, and rarely does the additional information add much to the quality of the decision.

One final comment on this question: don't be too eager to rush into decisions—especially those involving people. Employees will often press hard for a quick answer. They catch you with your guard down. They may imply, for example, that unless you arrange for a transfer next week, something drastic will happen to them. If you feel that the urgency is forced, it makes good sense to wait a while. The situation may relax; the individual may find that the request for a transfer was only a passing inclination.

Do people approach decision situations differently?

Very much so. There are typically four kinds of decision makers.
- *Risk seekers* actively look for opportunities to make changes, to improve, to force action. Within limits these people make the best supervisors—especially in dynamic business enterprises where technology and the outside environment are very fluid.
- *Risk averters* tend to stand pat, to presume that what is working now should not be changed without very sound reasons. These people make good supervisors, too, especially in stable governmental organizations where it is important to have someone who can hold to a set and proved course.
- *Wishful thinkers* try to control the impossible or hope that good intentions will override harsh facts. These people don't make very good supervisors under any circumstances.
- *Biased thinkers* have limited vision. They often act from prejudice or misinformation. These people should not be supervisors.

Of course, all of us have a little of each kind of decision maker in us, depending on the situation. For this reason many experts advise that the best, and the most professional, approach to decision making is a contingency one. In effect, they say, use the technique and be the kind of person that best fits the problem at hand. Said another way, in times of great uncertainty, a standpat approach may be best. In times of great opportunity—when growth, for example, is taking place in your organization—you should look for chances to make changes.

What can be done to make your decisions more effective?

Besides starting with a specific goal in mind and laying a foundation of facts and systematic analysis, there are a couple of other kinds of insurance you can turn to.

Pick your spots.   First, avoid decision making, if you can, where risks are high. Second, try to make decisions only where the potential for payoff is great. You can identify the second kind of opportunity by using ABC analysis. The ABC concept is based on an established economic fact: A vital few problems or opportunities for action account for the greatest loss or greatest gain. Most problems and opportunities are basically of little consequence. Economists call this the 20/80 syndrome. It means that 20 percent of your problems will account for 80 percent of your losses or profits. Then, to turn the idea around, 80 percent of your problems will account for only 20 percent of your losses or profits. ABC analysis calls the vital few, "A" items; the inconsequential many, "C" items; and those that fall somewhere in between, "B" items. If you were to take an inventory of items in your stockroom, for example, it is a sure bet that only a relatively few items would account for most of its value. A great many items, however, such as paper clips and erasers, would account for only a small portion of the inventory's total worth. Astute purchasing managers concentrate on the vital few items, not the trivial many. You should apply the same principle to your problems and decisions selection.

Maintain your perspective.   Statistically, problems fall in what is called a normal distribution, and so do the results of most decisions. We say, "You win some and you lose some." That's really what a normal distribution tells us. If you make ten decisions, one or two will work out fine. One or two are likely to be "bombs." The rest will fall somewhere in between. Knowing this, you should keep the following guidelines in mind when you make decisions:

1. Don't reach too high. Don't set your objectives at the very top; allow some room for mistakes.

2. Don't overcommit or overextend your resources on one problem; you may need them later for an unanticipated problem.

3. Always prepare a fallback position, a way to alter plans and attain at least part of the objective.

How good are group decisions?

They have their good points and their bad points. Where a decision can be aided by shared views and mutual responsibilities—such as those affecting safety—committees have proved to be effective. Where action must focus for the benefit of a single area, group decisions may be weak and ineffective. The hidden objective of such group decisions often is, for its participants, to share the blame if anything goes wrong or to spread a scarce resource so that there are fewer complaints.

Generally speaking, decisions should be made by those charged with the responsibility to solve a particular problem. These decision makers may gain much, however, by seeking ideas and suggestions from others. But, in the main, they must make the final decisions themselves.

Just how good should you expect a decision to be?

The test of a good decision is: Did it meet the objectives set for it? Suppose, for example, the decision's goal was to prevent a recurrence of excessive turnover. At some point in the future, such as the end of the year, excessive turnover should have stopped. If so, the decision would be said to have satisfied its objectives.

How many of your decisions should be good ones? You probably make between 20 and 40 decisions a day. If more than 30 of them can be judged to be good, you've attained an excellent batting average.

enriching your viewpoint

Opinions about, and techniques for, problem solving and decision making vary. It will broaden your own perspective to consult the following references:

Bittel, Lester R., *The Nine Master Keys of Management,* McGraw-Hill Book Company, New York, 1972, Chap. 2, "Identify Vital Targets," and Chap. 3, "Prepare for the Probable."

Dale, Ernest, *Management: Theory and Practice,* 4th ed., McGraw-Hill Book Company, New York, 1978, Chap. 19, "The Theory and Practice of Decision-Making."

Flippo, Edwin B., and Gary M. Munsinger, *Management,* 4th ed., Allyn and Bacon, Inc., Boston, 1978, Chap. 6, "Decision-Making Models."

Fulmer, Robert M., *The New Management,* The Macmillan Company, New York, 1978, Chap. 4, "Effective Decision-Making."

Halter, Albert N., and Gerald W. Dean, *Decisions Under Uncertainty,* South-Western Publishing Company, Inc., Cincinnati, 1971.

Hicks, Herbert G., and C. Ray Gullett, *The Management of Organizations,* 3d ed., McGraw-Hill Book Company, New York, 1976, Chap. 15, "Quantitative Methods for Managerial Planning."

Magee, John F., "Decision Trees for Decision-Making," *Harvard Business Review,* Vol. 42, No. 4, July–August 1964, pp. 126–138.

Starr, Martin K., *Management: A Modern Approach,* Harcourt Brace Jovanovich, Inc., New York, 1971 Chap. 4, "The Decision Behaviors of Management," and Chap. 6, "Predecisions and the Value of Information."

Weisselberg, Robert C., and Joseph G. Cowley, *The Executive Strategist: An Armchair Guide to Scientific Decision-Making,* McGraw-Hill Book Company, New York, 1969.

33

CHAPTER

managing in a
changing environment

**What will give supervisors their biggest
challenge in the decade coming up?**

A changing environment—those outside influences over which
supervisors have little control—are already at work to make
the job of managing harder than ever before. Environmental factors impose themselves on the job situation from four different directions, as shown in Figure 33-1. They include:

• *Economic changes* like inflation, international competition,
and a flattening out in the growth of our standard of living.
• *Social changes* like later marriages, fewer children, more
women working, and a leisure-oriented life-style.
• *Resource depletion* as seen in the scarcity of energy reserves, pollution of air and water sources, and damage to the
ecological balance.

599

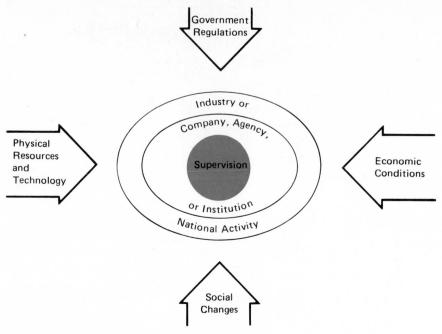

FIGURE 33-1. Impact of Changing World Environments.

- *Intensifying government regulation* of just about everything, including safety and health conditions; employment practices; product pricing and labeling; and credit, benefit, and pension plans.

What can supervisors be expected to do about economic changes?

Economic pressures at the supervisory level will call for sharper cost cutting and greater employee productivity. This is something supervisors can do something about. It won't be easy, though, since employees and unions will fight even harder to stretch their work and protect their jobs.

Shouldn't changes in the physical world of energy and technology be the responsibility of engineers and scientists rather than of supervisors?

Not completely. Conservation measures and resource protection are jobs that must be shared. It is hoped that the technicians will do a good job of making processes less destructive and energy more effective. But waste in any form has always been a prime responsibility at the front line of management. Supervisors will be expected to handle the nitty-gritty of conservation programs. You will be in charge of seeing that leaking pipes are fixed, lights are turned low, and pollutant spills are cleaned up before they reach the atmosphere. Supervisors will continue to be on the spot where the action really takes place. They provide a special value by serving as the early alert system for spotting potential savings or waste. Their observations and reports can enable engineering staffs to become more effective.

How will the new technology affect supervisors' jobs?

It is hard to say. Some developments, like computer control systems, should allow supervisors to spend more time analyzing results and making decisions. On the other hand, other technological advances, like the laser beam and the atomic sciences, can cause an unending series of process changes. These may prevent supervisors from establishing stability in departmental operations.

Where will social changes hit supervisors hardest?

In managing a work force with a different set of individual goals and standards. At all levels of employment, people have come to expect more from their work in terms of spiritual and financial enrichment. They also value their leisure almost as much as their independence. A growing number of people seek to work only periodically. Their need for material goods is relatively low, but they wish to make as much money as quickly and easily as possible. They can then have longer periods in which to pursue a life of their own choosing. For reasons like these, supervisors will increasingly be asked to involve themselves in the lives of their workers. A concern for each employee's individuality will be pressed by a society that expects not only equal opportunity in the workplace but also equal results.

This pressure will frequently come in the form of "jawboning"—by employees or union stewards, or both. Increasingly, United States citizens express their belief that employees should have a loud voice in what they do and how they do it. It is already more difficult to be selective in hiring. It will become even harder to apply simplistic reasons in trying to get rid of "obviously" incompetent employees. Accordingly, supervisors in the decade that is at hand will be expected to perform miracles. Social pressures, formal as well as informal, will force supervision to find ways to accommodate marginal employees despite higher management pressures for greater productivity. To do this, supervisors will have to learn just about everything there is to know about motivation, communications, and training.

As people press for special changes at work, which gets the bigger emphasis—formal or informal efforts?

Society puts effective pressure on both. It asks its governments —federal, state, and local—to pass laws that regulate the way businesses and other organizations can operate. This is formal, or legal, pressure. Society also exerts a great deal of informal, or psychological, pressure. Most people want to conform to group viewpoints. It makes sense also for organizations to go along with what the majority think about employment, conservation, safety, and security. To do otherwise is to invite subtle resistance. Customers don't buy products. Employees look elsewhere for work, or they lay back on the job. The net result is to make organizational goals especially hard to meet. This is true whether the organization is a giant firm, a government agency, or a departmental unit under the management of a first-line supervisor.

What areas will feel the greatest heat of government regulations?

Law tends to follow social changes. The social upheavals of the 1960s have been most evident in regulation of employment to protect the civil and the employment rights of minorities and women. There is little reason to expect this emphasis to change. It is already obvious to those in the ranks of supervision that implementation of equal employment opportunity laws ends up at their desks.

Following close behind as an irritant in the supervisory work load are the laws that protect the physical working environment. Few deny the contribution of the Occupational Safety and Health Act to the welfare of the United States worker. But there can be no denying, either, that OSHA places a major burden on supervisors. Preoccupation with safety and health often seems to work against employee productivity. As a consequence, supervisors must continue to find a way to integrate safe procedures with effective production methods.

Even the simple requirement of the Employee Retirement In-

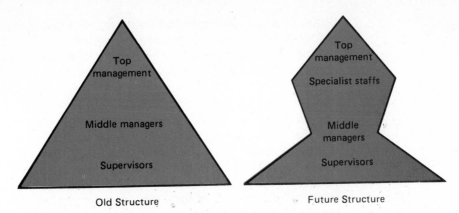

Old Structure   Future Structure

FIGURE 33-2. **Structural Changes in Future Organizations.** Adapted from R. Trewatha and M. Newport, *Management: Functions and Behavior,* Business Publications, Dallas, 1976, p. 507. By permission.

come Security Act (ERISA) puts the supervisor on the spot. The law regards supervisors as prime communicators in making the provisions of benefit and pension plans clear to their employees.

Government restrictions on product or service pricing, labeling, and safety also make an impact on supervisory activities. Pricing regulations tend to squeeze departmental operating costs. Labeling requirements call for more precise quality controls. Concerns for product liability demand better workmanship and stricter adherence to procedural specifications.

What will happen to the environment at the workplace?

Organizational structures and controls will probably place supervision in a fishbowl. There is evidence that the middle level of management is shrinking while the supervisory level is growing (see Figure 33-2). This seems to be a consequence of computerization of the coordinating function now performed by the in-between managers. It will tend to expose first-line managers to the scrutiny of those at the top. No longer will some supervisors be able to hide in the shade of their middle-level bosses.

Far more certain is the tightening of the organizational control system. It has long been clear to astute managers that they operate within a highly dependent system. This is a fancy way of saying that the supervisor in one unit can rarely do something without affecting the operations of another unit—often many other units. Until the advent of the computer, however, complete systematization of controls was a physical impossibility, and this placed a premium on those managers who could juggle—and balance—a great many things in their heads. Now we know that computers can tie together an incredible assortment of interdependent information. Not only can the computer do this, but it can also sort and present this data in a way that shows cause and effect between operations. This enables higher-level managers to spot out-of-line conditions quickly and to ask for supervisory corrections even faster. As before, supervisors will be expected to make the on-line decisions and to apply the hands-on controls. The big difference in the future will be that someone upstairs will be prodding for action and critically watching for results.

Specifically, where will the most far-reaching changes occur at the workplace?

A number of significant changes have already occurred, and their effect continues to grow. Among these are the following:

More women working at all kinds of jobs. Over half of all women between the ages of 18 and 55 were working or looking for work in 1978. Inevitably, women will move past a token presence in previously male-only positions. A far greater number of women will work as managers and supervisors.

Continuing assimilation of minorities. Gains in the employment of black and other disadvantaged peoples will be made in small steps, but the movement will be relentlessly forward. As with the employment of women, it will require positive attitudes and constructive action on the part of incumbent supervision.

Greater flexibility in working schedules. Flexitime schedules (see Chapter 26, page 473) are already commonplace in government and many office jobs. This trend will accelerate. Equally important will be the use of temporary and part-time help. These practices greatly enlarge the available labor pool and help to minimize dissatisfaction and turnover because of inflexible employment conditions.

More white-collar workers. Clerical employment continues to rise in spite of the changing nature of white-collar work. The new emphasis will be placed on technical specialization and professionalism, however, rather than on people imitating what office machines can do better.

Variety in compensation plans.   As the work force and work schedules move toward greater flexibility, the method of paying wages and salaries will move in the same direction. One example is a "cafeteria pay plan" offered by General Electric to some of its employees. It enables employees to opt for the most attractive combination of wages and fringe benefits. In effect, GE establishes the ceiling for the pay package, but employees may put together the combination each feels is most appropriate to his or her situation.

Greater emphasis on the quality of work life.   Work design programs (see Chapter 25) have made impressive, but isolated, advances in allowing employees to arrange work to suit their own inclinations. In the near future this approach is likely to become more widespread because such self-directed changes tend to improve motivation and productivity. Along with this trend will be a continuing emphasis on the career (or life) aspects of work rather than a narrow focus on work as a means of survival. Generally speaking, supervisors should welcome this trend since it enables supervisors to share part of their planning and control load with their employees.

As time passes, how will supervisory jobs be changed?

They should be changed for the better. They will not be easier, but they should be more clearly defined, far more challenging, and better paid. Supervisors will be expected to be (1) more accommodating to their work force and (2) far more participative in their approach to employees (which will require greater sensitivity and at least a partial belief in Theory Y).

On the other hand, supervisors will probably be under stronger pressures to conform to organizational structures and procedures. This may seem contradictory; it is not. What is happening and will continue to happen is that the rules of the organizational game will multiply, but their boundaries will become clearer. This combination will narrow the limits of supervisory discretion, but it will allow greater freedom within these limits.

Additionally, the supervisor's job will broaden in scope. It will require more, not less, responsibility; but it will also offer more variety. Obviously, supervisory performance requirements will be greater, and there will be a gradual upgrading of supervisory selection and training procedures. Almost certainly, supervisors will no longer be the forgotten people in the management field.

FIGURE 33-3

A Self-Check of Your Ethical Stance

Answer these questions as truthfully as you can; you will be the only judge of their ethical significance.

	Yes	No	Maybe

1. Would you ask a maintenance mechanic in your company to do a small repair job at work on your own kitchen appliance?

2. If offered a chance, at no cost to you, would you go on a fishing trip sponsored by the firm that supplies material for your department, if your boss has said it is okay?

3. If you had the opportunity to approve a promotion for a family member who was less qualified than other candidates, would you do so?

4. Would you take home for your personal use such office supplies as pencils, ink eradicators, or scratch pads?

5. If no one said you could not, would you use your employer's telephone to conduct a private, but noncompetitive, business of your own?

6. Would you use the company's telephone to make long-distance personal calls at the company's expense?

7. If given the opportunity, would you work on a private, personal, non-job-related project on company time?

8. If your boss asked you to pass on a small company gift to the local police officer who directs traffic at the company gate, would you do so?

9. If you found that part of the day's work in your department did not quite measure up to published specifications, would you try to slip it past inspection?

10. If you discovered a technicality that enabled you to dismiss a particularly troublesome employee, even though in this instance the employee was blameless, would you do it anyway?

**When it comes to standards
of management conduct and
managerial ethics, will supervisors be
lumped together with the good guys or the bad guys?**

Employees—and the public—make few distinctions between upper-level and lower-level managers. To most people, supervisors *are* the company, the institution, or the agency. You can be expected to be tarred with the same brush as your superiors. Consequently, the matter of managerial ethics is of vital importance to you.

Ethics is concerned with a person's doing right or wrong with respect to what the individual or, most important, his or her friends, associates, religion, and society at large think is right or wrong. This is a tall order, of course. There are often great differences of opinion about what is right or wrong. Almost always the line between acceptable and unacceptable behavior is faintly drawn. This is true in business in general and in organizational life in particular. You might try out your own ethical viewpoints against the list of questions in Figure 33-3. All these questions imply that a certain course of action is judged ethically correct by today's society. Unless you are a paragon of modern virtue, you will probably find areas in which you might tend to bend these ethical standards to fit the realities of your experience.

In earlier years supervisors and other managers could pretty much take these ethics or leave them alone. This is not so today. Society at large has come to expect managers to conform to society's standards of conduct. Supervisors are expected to respect to the letter the various laws and their regulatory specifications. They are expected to carry on in the *spirit* of the legislation as well. Even such a taken-for-granted goal as profit is under attack. Many people also feel that the bigness of organizations and the power that goes along with size are unethical.

Obviously, this heated concern for ethical practice among managers is a problem they must deal with individually and as a group. One approach has been for companies to prepare codes of ethics for managers and supervisors to follow. (See Figure 33-4.) Codes have the advantage of specifying a written set of standards to which each manager can look for guidance. They also provide a backdrop against which employees and customers can judge management decisions and actions. The weakness in organizational codes of ethics is that there is no assurance they will be followed or enforced. Codes also leave room for individual interpretation. Regardless of their drawbacks, however, such codes appear to be a step in the right direction.

FIGURE 33-4

Code of Ethics for Members of Institute of Certified Professional Managers

I will recognize that management is a call to service with responsibilities to my subordinates, associates and supervisors, employer, community, nation, and world.

I will be guided in all my activities by truth, accuracy, fair dealings, and good taste.

I will earn and carefully guard my reputation for good moral character and citizenship.

I will recognize that, as a leader, my own pattern of work and life will exert more influence on my subordinates than what I say or write.

I will give the same consideration to the rights and interests of others that I ask for myself.

I will maintain a broad and balanced outlook and will look for value in the ideas and opinions of others.

I will regard my role as a manager as an obligation to help subordinates and associates achieve personal and professional fulfillment.

I will keep informed on the latest developments in the techniques, equipment, and processes associated with the practice of management and the industry in which I am employed.

I will search for, recommend, and initiate methods to increase productivity and efficiency.

I will respect the professional competence of my colleagues in the ICPM and will work with them to support and promote the goals and programs of the institute.

I will support efforts to strengthen professional management through example, education, training, and a lifelong pursuit of excellence.

Another approach to a higher standard of ethical practice among managers has been a concern for professionalism. Many observers believe that licensing or certification of managers might raise professionalism by establishing ethical standards of conduct. One large voluntary organization, the Institute of Certified Professional Managers (ICPM), has already established a certification program. Its focus is on knowledge and experience, but it also features an ethical pledge (see Figure 33-4). The institute is supported by the National Management Association and the International Management Council. Its address is 2210 Arbor Boulevard, Dayton, Ohio 45439.

enriching your viewpoint

To gain a broader perception of the changing environment and its ethical aspects, the following readings are recommended:

Blumenthal, W. M., "Ethics, Morality, and the Modern Corporate Executive," *Dividend,* University of Michigan Graduate School, Spring 1976.

Carroll, Archie B. (ed.), *Managing Corporate Social Responsibility,* Little, Brown and Company, Boston, 1977.

Davis, Keith, "Can Business Afford to Ignore Social Responsibilities?" *California Management Review,* Vol. 2, No. 3, Spring 1960, pp. 70–76.

Drucker, Peter F., *An Introductory View of Management,* Harper's College Press, New York, 1977, Chap. 20, "The Limits of Social Responsibility."

Friedman, Milton, *Capitalism and Freedom,* The University of Chicago Press, Chicago, 1962, "Monopoly and the Social Responsibility of Business and Labor," pp. 119–136.

Johnson, Howard W., "Management Implications of Technology," in Lester R. Bittel (ed.), *The Encyclopedia of Professional Management,* McGraw-Hill Book Company, New York, 1979, pp. 1152–1156.

Kirkpatrick, Charles A., and Frederick A. Russ, *Business,* Science Research Associates, Inc., Chicago, 1974, Chap. 18, "Ethics, Business Law, and Taxation."

Miller, Roger Leroy, *Economics Today—The Macro View,* Canfield Press, San Francisco, 1974, "Sexism in the Labor Market," pp. 92–97.

action summary checklists

Effective supervision depends far more on action than on words. The thirty checklists that follow are designed to help you plan to put effective action into your supervisory job. Each checklist contains fifteen action points. Taken together, they summarize the key points presented in the first thirty chapters of the text. That way, they provide a quick and comprehensive review of the book's highlights. You can do much more with these checklists, however. By comparing each checkpoint with conditions on your own job, you can decide whether or not action is needed now. If your review assures you that a particular item is in good shape now or has already been taken care of, then check "NO" under the "Action Needed" heading. On the other hand, if you feel that conditions under that item need improvement, check "YES" for action needed. This means that you are not satisfied that conditions are up to standards described in the text and that you intend to do something positive to improve them. Don't stop there. Write down a date for when you expect to have that particular condition under control. When you have completed the corrective action, you can then check that item off your "Action Needed" list.

The Supervisory Management Job

1. Made a commitment to no longer work with your "hands on" the job and to embrace fully the management viewpoint.

2. Resolved to maintain good health, work hard, set a good example for your employees, and continue to learn.

3. Identified those individuals and groups to whom you now owe a responsibility: higher management (especially your boss), staff departments, fellow supervisors, and your employee work group.

4. Checked out the resources which enable you to carry out your job responsibilities: facilities, equipment, tools, power, utilities, materials, supplies, and information (dollar value of all this).

5. Gotten the "personnel jacket" particulars about your work force; personal data on each employee—age, length of service, work history, present job title and description, and pay rate.

6. Found out about current and upcoming production schedules and other output requirements and project deadlines.

7. Found out exactly what the quality requirements or specifications of your product or service are.

8. Pinned down the cost and expense limitations under which you will be expected to operate.

9. Accepted the fact that pressures upon you will be many and varied, with changing worker attitudes the most pressing of all.

10. Given thought to how well your present abilities measure up to the demands for technical, administrative, and human relations skills—and what you might do to improve them.

11. Prepared to balance your supervisory efforts between task-centered concerns and employee-centered ones.

12. Reviewed the managerial process so that you can anticipate problems and decisions requiring planning, organizing, staffing, directing, and controlling.

13. Accepted the fact that your supervisory role will often be ambiguous and will occasionally put you in the middle between higher management and your employees.

14. Guarded against pitfalls for new supervisors: poor relationships with others in the organization, failure to plan ahead, confusion about your managerial role, lack of initiative, discouragement, and the inability to successfully meet changing conditions.

15. Adopted an attitude of doing the best you can today with a plan for developing your knowledge and skills so that you can do even better tomorrow.

Action Summary Checklist 2

People at Work

1. Each task defined and analyzed; an estimate of physical and mental demands completed.
2. Thought given to the relative importance of financial and psychic rewards to each employee.
3. Departmental rules kept to the minimum needed for order and consistency.
4. Employees encouraged to provide feedback about job problems and to make suggestions about their work.
5. Emphasis placed upon organizational goals rather than your own.
6. Regular, open exchanges of conversation between you and your employees.
7. Older employees setting an example of job satisfaction for younger ones.
8. Allowance made for typical discontent of younger workers.
9. An effort made to see that work surroundings are as clean and pleasant as possible.
10. Variety and choice provided so as to minimize boredom in routine, monotonous, or repetitive jobs.
11. Opportunities provided for workers who wish to make their work more interesting and challenging.
12. An attitude toward work that sees it as a problem to be solved by the employee with the supervisor's help.
13. A periodic check to see that less than 20 percent of your work force is visibly unhappy with their jobs.
14. Flexibility in work assignments and the demands made upon each employee as a unique person.
15. Continuing effort on your part to be a member of the larger organizational management team.

Action Summary Checklist 3

Individual Motivation

1. Human problems approached from an informed point of view rather than assuming that common sense is all that is needed.
2. Alert to human interactions as well as to production problems.
3. Identification of differences in motivation, goals, and performance among your employees.
4. An assessment of each employee as to which levels of Maslow's hierarchy of needs are most important.
5. In trying to motivate employees, searching always for the unsatisfied need.
6. Provision of "satisfiers" at work for those employees who respond to positive motivation.
7. Open praise of employees who do a good job.
8. An opportunity for employees to provide their own self-discipline.
9. Challenging assignments for employees who want to achieve.
10. Wariness of your own overachieving to the extent that you become so task oriented that you minimize human relationships.
11. Friendship to those employees who value affiliation.
12. Resistance to your own power drives, while protecting employees from the power moves of their associates.
13. Maintainence of a general atmosphere of courtesy and comradeship in your department, in spite of occasional flareups.
14. Feedback to higher management of the absence of hygiene factors that may dissatisfy employees.
15. Restraint in jumping to conclusions about personalities; an attitude of "live and let live" with respect to personal preferences.

Action Summary Checklist 4

Work Group Behavior

1. Sensitivity to the dynamics of group relationships in your department.
2. Awareness of, but not prying into, informal groups in your department.
3. Willingness to share employees' loyalties with their work groups, formal and informal.
4. Integration of individual and group goals with company goals.
5. An opportunity for employees—collectively—to help in solving production and other work-related problems.
6. A sharing of relevant job information and know-how with employees, individually or in groups.
7. Action as a facilitator when work groups struggle to resolve intragroup squabbles.
8. Recognition that many individuals will look to you for protection from unreasonable group pressures so as to assure personal freedom of action.
9. Observation of changes in group behavior that may signal a radical shift in group attitudes, favorable or unfavorable, toward their work, the company, or to you.
10. The ability to describe the "personality" characteristics of your departmental work group and informal groups within it.
11. An assessment of your departmental work group as "weak" or "strong."
12. Development of a strong and cohesive departmental work group that is in general agreement with company objectives for it.
13. Assurance that your work group, while moving toward its departmental objectives also works in harmony with other company departments toward the greater objectives of the entire company.
14. A firm stand on goals, policies, procedures, and rules that are judged to be inflexible if work is to be coordinated in a safe and productive way.
15. Reliance upon performance as the best indicator of individual and group morale.

Action Summary Checklist 5

Conflict and Cooperation

	Action Needed Yes No	Date Completed

1. Main sources of conflict minimized: one way, downward communications; inconsistent directives and decisions; continual change in methods, relationships, and policies.

2. Prompt management of departmental conflicts as they surface.

3. A bargaining or compromising approach toward conflicts involving you and others.

4. A focus on issues and objectives rather than personalities.

5. Emphasis upon two-way communications and continued personal contacts, even when angry.

6. A sensitivity to the interests of others—associates as well as employees.

7. Recognition that demands for perfection are unattainable in most instances and threatening to most people.

8. A willingness to invite candid comments from employees about touchy departmental situations and to listen to them without recriminations.

9. Recognition that what is important is employee performance, not their attitudes; although poor attitudes may lead to poor performance.

10. Maintenance of your own state of good morale, seeking advice and guidance when it is low.

11. Encouraging employee cooperation by seeking to satisfy their needs for respect, challenge, and interesting or meaningful work.

12. Getting along with your associates by keeping your eyes on the common objectives of company productivity, quality, and cost control.

13. Cooperating with, rather than resisting, the advice and suggestions from staff personnel.

14. Seeking to maintain an attitude of "I'm OK, you're OK" when dealing with stress situations involving employees or associates.

15. Praising those employees who do cooperate in helping to meet departmental objectives.

Action Summary Checklist 6

The Arts of Leadership

	Action Needed		Date Completed
	Yes	No	

1. A concern for personal leadership as part of your total management responsibility.

2. Setting of good examples of personal commitment and a willingness to make sacrifices in order to help your team meet departmental objectives.

3. Maintenance of your health—physical and mental—so that you have the energy needed to handle the job actively.

4. Development of skill in applying all three kinds of traditional leadership approaches.

5. Proper focus on job objectives for yourself and each employee.

6. Balanced application of leadership techniques based upon each particular situation.

7. An attempt to match your leadership style to the followership inclinations of each employee.

8. A willingness to be autocratic or hardnosed when needed.

9. A concern for people equal to your concern for job results.

10. Regular self-study of human relations—formal as well as informal—so as to improve your leadership skills.

11. Demonstrated personal progress in the direction of point 9,9 on the Managerial Grid.

12. Determination through self analysis of your own assumptions about employees as either Theory X or Theory Y.

13. An ability to keep your head in the face of criticism, conflict, and routine job stress.

14. Consistency in the nature of your relationships with others for whose work you are accountable.

15. A conscious effort to treat employees equitably in similar situations; to neither play favorites nor to pick on those you don't particularly like.

Action Summary Checklist 7

Supervision and the Management Process

1. Each major problem or project approached with a plan.

2. A conscious effort made to regularly pursue the management process of planning, organizing, activating, and controlling.

3. Recognition given that the process must be repeated over and over, that it really never ends.

4. The conversion process for which you are responsible analyzed as to its function in transforming its resources into useful outputs.

5. The outputs or results required from your operations clearly defined: product or service—how many or how much, what quality, at what cost, when and where needed?

6. Work force resources carefully checked against conversion process and output needs.

7. Tools, machinery, and equipment resources carefully checked against conversion process and output needs.

8. Materials and supplies resources carefully checked against conversion process and output needs.

9. Money and capital resources carefully checked against conversion process and output needs.

10. Information and methods resources carefully checked against conversion process and output needs.

11. Markets resources (for sales and distribution supervisors) carefully checked against conversion process and output needs.

12. Use of and proficiency at handing the systematic approach to management.

13. Use of and proficiency at the human relations approach to management.

14. Use of and proficiency at the quantitative approach to management.

15. Adherence to Fayol's main principles of management regularly checked:

a. Division of work

b. Responsibility matched by authority

c. Discipline matched by loyalty

d. Unity of command

e. Unity of direction

f. Your interest second to organization's

g. Fair pay for employee contributions

h. Chain of command

i. Order

j. Equity

k. Initiative

Action Summary Checklist 8

Making Plans and Carrying Out Policy

1. Time set aside for planning: 5 minutes daily, 15 minutes weekly, 1 hour monthly.

2. Nothing new nor any changes attempted without prior planning.

3. Goals based upon a realistic look at departmental strengths and weaknesses and company-imposed restrictions.

4. Departmental goals arranged in order of priority.

5. Plans, procedures, regulations that fit into chosen goals.

6. Plans flexible enough to permit change when needed.

7. Control limits and control procedures established so as to enable you to monitor departmental progress toward goals.

8. Knowledge of your company's general policies, especially as they relate to personnel matters.

9. Up-to-date knowledge of procedures that affect operating practices.

10. Provision of feedback to your superiors about difficulties in policy implementation or the need for policy change.

11. Acceptance of company policies as your policy so far as employees are concerned.

12. Prudence in checking company policy implications before taking trend-setting action at the departmental level.

13. Willingness to explain and interpret policies, procedures, and regulations to employees in language they understand.

14. A commitment to goals that the company has set and to those you have set for your own operations.

15. Continuing alertness to the need to plan new goals and to establish up-to-date procedures.

Action Summary Checklist 9

Organizing an Effective Department

1. Your work force's organization focused upon departmental responsibilities and objectives.

2. Each employee knows what his or her job is and how it relates to others in the department.

3. An organization chart constructed for your department.

4. Your awareness of, but not conflict with, the informal organization in your department.

5. Identification of both line and staff responsibilities—in your department and with other company departments.

6. Knowledge of where and how your department fits into your company's overall organization structure.

7. Identification of your company's and department's organizational form—functional, divisional or product, geographical, customer, and/or project or task force.

8. An estimate of the degree of centralization and decentralization in your company and in your department. Satisfaction with the extent of your own span of control, neither too narrow nor too broad.

9. A clear understanding of your own responsibilities and their related authorities according to Figure 9-1 in the text.

10. Full development and utilization of your personal sources of authority.

11. Regular use of delegation within your department to relieve yourself of unnecessary work and to develop the skills and confidence of subordinates.

12. Willing acceptance of responsibilities delegated from above with an eye toward using them for your own development.

13. Knowledge of the chain of command in your company and general conformance to it.

14. Cooperation with and utilization of company staff departments.

15. Regular review of your department's organization structure to minimize communications problems, avoid having an employee answer to two people, assure clear designation of work duties, and retain flexibility for contingencies.

Action Summary Checklist 10

Staffing with Human Resources

	Action Needed		Date Completed
	Yes	No	

1. Alertness to symptoms of poor human resources staffing: high labor costs; excessive absenteeism, latenesses, and turnover; poor quality of work, and lowered output.

2. Periodic review to make certain that employees are placed on jobs that suit their capabilities best.

3. Periodic forecast of your department's work force needs, with care taken to neither understaff nor overstaff.

4. As an aid in carrying out your forecast, preparation of a work-force trial balance sheet that anticipates (a) payroll separations and (b) changes in scheduled departmental workloads (Figure 10-1).

5. Calculation or knowledge of your department's annual turnover rate.

6. Analysis of causes contributing to employee turnover.

7. Calculation or knowledge of your department's absenteeism rates.

8. Analysis of causes contributing to employee absences.

9. Improvement of your skill in assessing job seeker's potential from information provided on employment application form.

10. Periodic review to judge the applicability of performance tests as aids in selection of applicants for jobs in your department.

11. Periodic review of personal and performance requirements for each job under your supervision.

12. Preparation of job descriptions or specifications if required. (See also Chapter 26.)

13. Improvement in your employment interviewing skills: question asking, listening, appraisal.

14. Review of legal guides that must be followed in conducting employment interviews and in selecting and placing new employees. Checking with personnel department.

15. Insistence upon an employment reference check of an applicant before he or she is put on the payroll.

Action Summary Checklist 11

Activating the Work Force by Communications

	Action Needed	Date Completed
	Yes No	

1. A minimum of "noise" in your communication system; employees ready to listen, absence of conflicting instructions, employees and supervisors talking about the same thing.

2. Expertise in and reliance on many methods, rather than a single method of communications.

3. Your department's communications network plugged into the company management information system.

4. Choice of the kind of communication system—(web) open or (wheel) restricted—that best suits your operations.

5. Knowledge, but avoidance, of the grapevine as a method of supervisory communication. Rumors spiked as soon as they can be.

6. Emphasis upon the free flow of information up, down, and across your department.

7. Willingness to track down and retrieve job-related information for employees who request it.

8. Guarding against overcommunicating and talk on sensitive subjects.

9. Your boss kept regularly informed of accountable, controversial matters and the shop's attitudes toward policy.

10. Personal actions that back up your words.

11. Sensitivity to employee's feelings with a minimum self indulgence in personalities and prejudices.

12. Willingness to listen without taking offense, with an emphasis upon face-to-face communications.

13. Recognition that words mean different things to different people; dependence upon hard facts rather than vague generalities.

14. Development of your *person-to-person* communication skills: *spoken*—informal talks, planned appointments, telephone calls; *written*—interoffice memos, letters, and reports.

15. Development of your *group* communication skills: *spoken*—informal staff meetings, planned conferences, mass meetings; *written*—bulletin board notices, posters, displays, and visual aids.

Action Summary Checklist 12

Exercising Control of People and Processes

1. Departmental standards and controls related to departmental plans and goals.
2. Departmental controls established to cover employee performance, machine operations, materials usage, product or service quality, cost, and job assignments.
3. Control standards clearly written, numerically expressed where possible, and based either upon historical records or systematic analysis.
4. Standards set for employee's personal time to include attendance and tardiness, in-shop roaming, rest periods, and quitting time.
5. Standards set for quantity of production or output—for the department as a whole and for individual operations.
6. Standards set for quality of workmanship, product, and service—for department's output and for each operation.
7. Standards set for materials and supplies usage—yield, waste, storage, and inventory accumulation.
8. Standards set for all pertinent time factors, including job times, schedule fulfillment, and project completions.
9. Regular check to make sure that control measurements are accurate and relevant to the person or process being controlled.
10. Corrective action directed toward causes of variances rather than symptoms.
11. An understanding of intent of budgetary controls received and the degree to which you must conform to them.
12. A willingness to make the necessary cost/benefit decisions when setting, interpreting, or applying controls.
13. Application of the exception principle as much as is possible.
14. Sensitivity to the people problem in exercising controls. Emphasis on motivation rather than punishment.
15. Encouragement of employee's self control whenever feasible.

Action Summary Checklist 13

Giving Orders and Instructions

	Action Needed Yes No	Date Completed

1. A regular and candid assessment of whether your orders and instructions are getting through to employees and being carried out effectively.

2. Willingness to repeat an instruction so as to make sure that it is clearly understood.

3. An immediate search for feedback from an employee to assure that there has been no misunderstanding about required details.

4. Care in the choice of words so as to make instructions more clear, especially in terms of their quality, quantity, and time factors.

5. Use of the request approach as often as possible.

6. Avoidance of any semblance of a power struggle when issuing orders. Use of its situation as the basis for the order that is issued.

7. Commands reserved for emergencies or for situations where a high degree of immediate coordination is needed.

8. Selective use of the suggestion approach, reserving it for employees who have shown that they respond well to it.

9. Selective use of written orders and instructions, mainly to amend those already in writing or where the work is especially complex and varies from the normal in terms of sequence, timing, and quantities or quality required.

10. A curb on your anger and a concern for your tone of voice.

11. Regular demonstration of your willingness to share unpleasant working conditions with your employees.

12. Precision with group orders to make sure that all concerned know who is to do what.

13. Development of your skill as an active listener, using your responses to establish empathy and rapport.

14. A rein on any compulsion you may have to give too many orders or to give more details than the job or individual really needs.

15. Fairness in making assignments, with an objective of spreading the unpleasant as well as the attractive assignments equitably among willing and unwilling workers.

	Action Needed	Date Completed
	Yes No	

1. A grasp of the underlying purpose of job evaluation as it is carried on in your organization.

2. Focus on the worth of the job, not the person who performs it.

3. Evaluations that are independent of job titles, which may vary from department to department and from company to company.

4. Ability to describe a job accurately and objectively in terms of what is actually done, not what might be done.

5. Care in deciding exactly what a job's requirements are without basing this judgment on the type of person who has traditionally performed it.

6. An understanding of how your organization's job evaluation system values the various "compensable" factors such as education and experience.

7. Active cooperation with the specialists who handle the details of the job evaluation and compensation plan.

8. A clear-cut distinction during the evaluation procedure between the objective of properly classifying jobs and the assignment of wages to them.

9. Ability to make the necessary pay computations for employees on an hourly wage plan and knowledge of when time not worked is compensable in your organization.

10. Similarly, knowledge of when time not worked by salaried employees is or is not compensable in your organization.

11. Knowledge of the workings of the incentive pay system in your organization, if one exists.

12. Ability to communicate with employees about the organization's compensation plan and the impact of general wage increases upon that plan.

13. Knowledge of the workings of the profit sharing plan in your organization, if one exists.

14. Knowledge of the extent, application, and cost to the company of the various fringe (employee) benefits available to your employees.

15. Regular communication with your employees about the application, and the value to them, of the organization's benefits program.

Action Summary Checklist 15

Appraisal of Employee Performance

1. A focus on the major goal of improvement of the individual's performance so as to match the job's requirements.

2. Recognition of those factors which can be judged objectively and those which tend to be subjective.

3. A desire to base as many judgments as possible upon measurable, observable facts.

4. Maintenance of a file of critical incidents, or specific representative examples, of each employee's behavior so as to support the ratings you make.

5. Treatment of an individual's appraisal as confidential, with respect to his or her associates or peers.

6. A conscious effort to apply the same standards to all, so that your ratings are consistent from employee to employee.

7. Care in separating the discussion of an employee's rating from any talk or consideration of money.

8. Establishment of a positive, constructive atmosphere during the appraisal interview so that employees do not feel that they sit in the judgment of a person who believes himself or herself to be infallible.

9. Willingness to listen to an employee's rebuttal of your ratings and to change that rating if the argument is sound.

10. Avoidance of use of the appraisal interview to scold or punish.

11. Proper preparation for and conduct of the appraisal interview: privacy, enough time, emphasis on job standards, credit where it is due, mutual examination of the facts supported by examples of critical incidents, focus on the future, and sharing by you of responsibility for the individual's performance.

12. Your guard up against the halo effect, which discriminates for or against a person based upon a single incident or trait.

13. A continuing interest in and appraisal of the individual's performance, so that your judgment isn't a one-time thing.

14. Your active assistance to the employee in helping to shore up weaknesses or develop skills.

15. Thoughtful reexamination of conditions beyond an employee's control that may be contributing to his or her substandard performance: a poor skills-job match, inadequate training, work-group pressure, physical or emotional problems, supervision, problems in the process or procedures.

Action Summary Checklist 16

Training and Development of Employees

1. A continuing alert for symptoms of training needs—such as lowered output, off-standard quality, higher costs, accidents, or poor morale.

2. Care in orienting each new employee to your department, using the check list on page 264 of the text.

3. A systematic, rather than hit-or-miss approach to each and all training problems in your department.

4. Preparation of a simple job breakdown sheet with key points identified before beginning the training on a particular job.

5. Proper employee preparation and motivation provided before beginning the demonstration of a job.

6. Training demonstrations that emphasize both telling and showing.

7. Emphasis upon identification and demonstration of key points that make or break a job.

8. Breaking the training material into easily learned pieces, not attempting too much during any one session.

9. Arranging the training sequence so that the learner begins with the least difficult and progresses to the most difficult phases.

10. Allowing trainees to try out the job under your watchful eye before turning them loose on their own.

11. Regular feedback to the trainee regarding how well—or how incorrectly—the employee is learning the job.

12. Encouragement of questions throughout the entire training process.

13. Remaining available to trainees for help and guidance after they have been put on their own.

14. Training in your department based upon an analysis of skills needed (Figure 16-3) and a planned timetable for completion.

15. Your training approaches tailored to fit the needs and learning capabilities of each individual, drawing upon whatever resources you can muster (visual aids, operating manuals, etc.) and the advice and assistance of your company's training department, when one exists.

Action Summary Checklist 17

Employee Safety and Health and OSHA

<table>
<tr><th></th><th colspan="2">Action
Needed</th><th>Date
Completed</th></tr>
<tr><th></th><th>Yes</th><th>No</th><th></th></tr>
</table>

1. Knowledge of the safety standards that apply to your department.
2. Continuing search for potential safety hazards in your department.
3. Maintenance of conditions that affect general environmental controls and sanitation: ventilation, wastes, food consumption, washrooms.
4. Prompt reporting of occupational injuries and illnesses in your department so that they may be entered into the OSHA log.
5. Careful safety training for new employees and an ongoing program for all employees: especially for lifting, material handling, machinery, power transmission, falls, hand tools, and low-voltage hazards.
6. Knowledge of and protection of employees' rights under OSHA.
7. A continuing search for better accident prevention and safety procedures—the engineering of safety.
8. An ongoing program to educate and motivate employees to work safely.
9. Enforcement of safety rules and regulations, no matter how small—and without exception.
10. Insistence that employees wear the proper protective clothing in the established way.
11. The safety standards of performance in your department set by your own unfailing example.
12. Maintenance or knowledge of the safety records in your department, both frequency and severity, with an eye toward identifying recurring hazards, unsafe conditions, and people who have more accidents than others.
13. The making of key-point safety an integral part of employee training.
14. Prompt investigation of accidents and occupational illnesses, large and small, to identify and remove causes, not to fix blame.
15. Relentless surveillance of potential fire conditions in your department; knowledge of suitable extinguishers (by fire class), their location, their proper usage.

Action Needed
Yes No

Date Completed

The Supervisor's Role in Labor Relations

1. Full recognition that in the eyes of the law you represent your company in labor relations matters involving your employees.

2. Maintenance of a log or file of incidents that can contribute to contract negotiations when they next come up.

3. Diligence and precision in interpreting and applying contract matters during the life of the contract.

4. Care not to interfere or discriminate against union activity, as specified by the Wagner Act.

5. Protection of individual employee's rights to take up grievances directly with management, under provisions of the Taft-Hartley Law.

6. Clear identification of those employees who report to you as being either exempt or nonexempt under the Wages and Hours Law.

7. Firm observance of the proscriptions of the various Equal Employment Opportunity laws: equitable assignments, pay, and opportunities for promotion regardless of race, religion, sex, or national origin.

8. Support in action and spirit of your organization's affirmative action program.

9. Knowledge of and the ability to communicate clearly to your employees the basic aspects of your company's employee benefit programs under ERISA provisions.

10. Cordial, cooperative relationships with your department's shop steward, but not abdication of your rights or any form of co-management.

11. A neutral attitude toward unions and union membership, unless your company explicitly directs otherwise.

12. Knowledge of and adherence to the proscribed steps in your organization's grievance procedure.

13. A desire to resolve grievances in your department at your level, based upon knowledge of the facts and strict conformance to the labor contract and company precedents.

14. Willingness to check first with your personnel department or someone in higher authority more broadly informed than you before rendering decisions in labor matters that you suspect are sensitive.

15. Your grievance handling so thorough and fair that should an unresolved case go to arbitration, your case can be effectively presented.

Action Summary Checklist 19

Equal Opportunity for All

	Action Needed		Date Completed
	Yes	No	

1. Recognition and acceptance of a very broad definition of a minority: blacks, women, younger, disadvantaged, handicapped, older.

2. Knowledge of and respect for the basic legal protection against discrimination in all aspects of employment because of race, religion, age, and sex.

3. Determination to give black employees a fair chance to learn a job and to prove their ability to perform it satisfactorily.

4. Equal performance expectations from blacks and other minorities, once they have become an integral part of the work force.

5. Willingness to offer a little more patience and understanding to employees from disadvantaged backgrounds, especially those who have been part of the hard-core unemployed.

6. Care in using and interpreting test results for employment, placement, training, and promotion purposes.

7. Intensified—and perhaps longer than usual—training programs for disadvantaged minorities.

8. Avoidance of stereotyped thinking about why women work—and their interest in, and capability to perform, various types of work.

9. A desire to accommodate working wives and mothers (husbands, too) who have family responsibilities outside of work that occasionally interfere or distract from job routines.

10. Absolutely equal pay and treatment for women who perform the same work as men (and vice versa), with equal opportunities for training and development.

11. A determination to bridge the generation gap between you and younger employees by being supportive to their efforts, trying to make work more meaningful, and providing regular feedback.

12. Special encouragement and support for younger, disadvantaged workers who have a difficult time learning the discipline of routine work and attendance.

13. An alertness to obsolescence among workers over 50, with job assignments that make the most of their skill, good attendance, judgment, safe working habits, and loyalty while minimizing their slower pace, lessened physical strength, and often poorer eyesight.

14. Continued requirement of high standards of performance from older workers, with renewed opportunities for learning new skills.

15. An approach to selection, placement, training, advancement, and general treatment of each of your employees that is so fair and equitable that no charge of discrimination—even reverse discrimination—could reasonably be supported.

Action Summary Checklist 20

Counseling Problem People

1. Astuteness during the selection process in trying to avoid hiring potentially problem employees.

2. Awareness of and sensitivity to employees who display emotional problems, without overreacting to them.

3. Recognition that all of us, including you, have soft spots in our emotional armor and that this does not make us crazy.

4. Ability to distinguish between evidence of neurotic behavior (which may be tolerated) and psychotic behavior (which is bizarre and may become threatening to the individual himself or to others in the work place).

5. An attitude of wanting to help employees to adjust to their emotional problems—rather than to ridicule or punish them for these problems or to minimize their importance to the individual.

6. Recognition of the signs of poor emotional adjustment—sudden changes in behavior, preoccupation, irritability, increased accidents or absences, fatigue, too much drinking, or drug abuse.

7. Development of your skill as a listener, especially a nonevaluative one—a person who does not pass judgment on what he or she hears.

8. Conduct of your counseling sessions in a nonthreatening way, with emphasis upon nondirective interviewing rather than cross-examination.

9. Time set aside in your schedule to counsel employees who need attention.

10. Readiness to refer an emotionally disturbed employee to your company nurse, doctor, or psychologist for professional advice and treatment whenever your efforts are not fruitful.

11. A combination of firmness and empathy when counseling employees with problems of absenteeism, alcoholism, or drug abuse.

12. Separation of your approach to the willful absentees (vacationers, the directionless, moonlighters, and the aggressive) from the chronic and occasional absentees.

13. An alert for early warning signs of alcoholism among your employees: a sharp rise in absences, absences spread throughout the week, and part-day absences.

14. A willingness to confront the alcoholic employee with the choice of stopping drinking or losing his or her job.

15. Tolerance for the work-addicted individual, with your guard up to prevent this from happening to you.

Handling Complaints and Avoiding Grievances

1. Sensitivity to sources and symptoms of employee discontent: wages, nature of supervision, seniority, assignments, transfers, and promotions, discipline, safety and health, and general working conditions.

2. Respect for and attention to all grievances, real or imagined.

3. A desire to resolve the issue or grievance clearly, whether or not the solution is one that fully satisfies the employee.

4. Decisions based upon facts, thoroughly gathered and carefully examined.

5. An unwavering standard of fairness in judging the merit of complaints and grievances.

6. Candidness and the absence of trickery in discussing grievances with employees.

7. All discussions, with employee or union representatives, conducted in a businesslike manner and in a civil tone, with personalities set aside.

8. Decisions carefully explored beforehand, but made as quickly as possible.

9. Grievances with companywide implications discussed first with your superior or with the personnel department before decision is given.

10. Willingness to pass along and support rulings on grievances made by higher authorities as your own.

11. Decisions rendered in clear-cut terms with full explanation of your reasoning.

12. An opportunity for employees to save face when the ruling on a grievance goes against them.

13. Follow-up on decisions to make sure that promised corrective action actually takes place.

14. Strict adherence to your company's grievance procedure, if one has been established.

15. As much as possible, handling of grievances as confidential matters between you and the employees involved.

Action   **Date**
Needed   **Completed**

Yes No

How and When to Discipline

1. Discipline conceived of as an ongoing program to encourage desired performance and to discourage undersirable behavior.

2. Discipline used only for corrective purposes and never as a display of personal power or authority.

3. Establishment of rules that are reasonable and generally regarded by the work group as mutually beneficial to them and the company.

4. An understanding of the reasons why employees break rules: willfully by frustrated or disturbed employees and unthinkingly by untrained or misinformed workers or by employees distracted by personal problems.

5. Standards of performance and departmental rules enforced fairly, neither too leniently nor vindictively.

6. Discipline that stresses the positive rather than the negative, improvement rather than punishment.

7. An approach to meting out corrective discipline that is progressive, with penalties for successive infractions increasingly severe.

8. Advance warnings of possible disciplinary action communicated to employees through training sessions, bulletin boards, manuals, and face-to-face discussions.

9. Corrective discipline exercised without undue delay; the principle of immediacy.

10. Disciplinary action that is consistently applied in like situations and for similar failures to meet standards or to conform to established rules and regulations.

11. Discipline that is impartial and free from prejudice.

12. Knowledge of your company's policies, procedures, and regulations (and the influence of the labor contract if there is a trade union present) as they affect enforcement of performance standards and organizational discipline.

13. Determination to keep a cool head—and to be sure of facts and contributing influences—when administering negative discipline.

14. Care in making notations in your own records of oral or written warnings; maintenance of production, quality, safety, and absence records so that you can detect and correct off-standard performance before it gets out of control.

15. A double check of what it takes to make corrective discipline stick before taking action: clear-cut breach of a rule or standard, adequate warning, undeniable evidence, impartiality, credible back-up records, and appropriate penalties.

Action Summary Checklist 23

Supervising Office Employees and Clerical Work

	Action Needed		Date Completed
	Yes	No	

1. Ability to calculate the third profit generated by the savings you obtain in management of office and clerical employees.

2. Consideration in allowing office employees to socialize so long as it does not interfere with concentration or detract from total productivity.

3. A sensitivity to the work group's social standards with an aim toward helping newcomers to adjust and preventing the formation of rigid cliques or "in groups."

4. Conduct of business with your employees in a courteous and considerate manner.

5. Initiative in breaking the monotony of routine jobs by allowing variations in the routine or by job rotation.

6. A participative approach to individual or group work with freedom for employees who wish to develop their own methods to meet organizational goals.

7. Affirmative action on your part in helping employees to develop their skills and advance toward their own career goals.

8. A staffing plan for your department based on estimates of work loads compared with your company's standards of performance.

9. Continuing surveillance of individual and departmental accuracy and errors so as to maintain the desired level of service quality.

10. Some sort of forms control so as to keep the number of forms to the minimum required for efficient data processing.

11. Standards for files and records based upon long-term usefulness, minimum of duplication, ease of retrieval, and established retention requirements.

12. Periodic review of paperwork flow with the objective of simplifying procedures and records, as outlined on page 416, or by utilizing labor-savings machines, as outlined on page 419.

13. Reasonable, but firm, control over usage of the telephone for personal calls.

14. Long-range plans developed to anticipate and manage at the least cost the monthly and seasonal peaks and overloads typical of most office work.

15. An ongoing and effective safety program regularly communicated to your employees.

Action Needed

Date Completed

Supervising the Knowledge Worker

Yes No

1. Identification of those jobs under your supervision that are becoming increasingly knowledge and/or professionally oriented.
2. Flexibility in your approach to managing the knowledge worker, with a willingness to trade off organization demands for conformity for performance results.
3. Awareness that low performers as well as high ones, older knowledge workers as well as young, expect job freedom and challenging work and salary increments.
4. Care in proportioning your time so that high performers receive their share of attention and recognition.
5. Provision for varied, challenging assignments, with the majority of these requiring full use of the knowledge worker's talents.
6. Readiness to listen to new ideas and to evaluate them objectively; free and open communications encouraged across organizational lines.
7. Opportunities provided for knowledge workers to develop and display pride in the work they do.
8. Respect for the job demands voiced by knowledge workers, but caution and firmness in judging the appropriateness of requests and diplomatic firmness in denying those you feel are unjustified.
9. A broad—rather than legalistic—view of the definition of professionalism so as to encourage its practice by those who aspire to it.
10. Acceptance of the fact that those who work regularly with professionals—as so many health-care employees do, for example—are likely to consider their work professional too.
11. Use of supervisory methods and controls that reflect the stop-and-start nature (rather than assembly-line continuity) of many projects and assignments handled by knowledge workers.
12. Credit for the knowledge worker's achievements carefully identified with the individual, with assurance that higher management is aware of performance.
13. Paperwork requests held to the minimum that will yield adequate control information about progress of projects.
14. Performance standards established for output and quality of work; also, perceptive scheduling to reduce the possibility of featherbedding or excessive nonproductive time.
15. Recognition of the dual pressures that a knowledge worker feels—from functional manager and project manager—when working on interdisciplinary teams and task forces or in matrix organizations.

Action Summary Checklist 25

Job—and Work—Design and Enrichment

	Action Needed		Date Completed
	Yes	No	

1. Listing of jobs that would be improved by redesign, regardless of approach used.

2. Classification of jobs in your department according to whether they are hand paced, machine assisted, or machine controlled.

3. Knowledge of the process requirements in your department as they affect job design: product specification, process flow sequence, time constraints, and costs.

4. Review of jobs with the intention of improving (a) methods; (b) tools and equipment; and (c) workplace arrangements. (See also Chapter 27.)

5. Special thought given to workplace space allotted to each employee and its arrangement to best accommodate human movements. (See Figure 25-1.)

6. A focus on the structure of the work itself so as to make it as attractive and functional as possible for employees.

7. Sensitivity to organizational restrictions on job design as they affect the work of more than one employee or have an impact on other departments.

8. Jobs structured with the highest degree of motivation designed into them: as nearly as possible, a complete job that follows the product or process from start to finish—job enlargement.

9. As for 8, provision for an employee to have regular contact with the other employees, customers, or clients that use the product or service he or she produces.

10. As for 8, jobs that are enriched so that an employee is called upon to perform a variety of tasks and use a number of different skills.

11. As for 8, jobs that allow as much self-direction and self-regulation (autonomy) as possible.

12. As for 8, jobs that provide feedback directly from the work itself to the employee about whether the work has been done right or wrong.

13. As for 8, jobs that offer employees a chance for self-development and career growth.

14. Introduction of a strong element of goal-oriented supervision in your overall handling of the managerial process. (See Figure 25-2.)

15. Approval secured from your boss or personnel department before implementing job design changes.

Job Assignments and Work Schedules

1. Identification of assignments typically made in your department as either (a) repetitive routine, (b) variable routine, or (c) special projects.

2. Assignments that match employee skills and job classifications to the work to be performed.

3. At the least, use of a calendar or notebook to plan and record schedule commitments and job assignments.

4. Schedules that neither underutilize nor overload (over 95 to 100 percent capacity) your staff or equipment.

5. Special thought given to overtime and second-shift scheduling so as not to plan for the same productivity as for the day shift.

6. A willingness to accept flexitime schedule adjustments where company policy permits it, employees want it, and overall morale and effectiveness would be improved by it.

7. Knowledge of the extent to which your organization prepares a master plan and the way in which it is—or can be—translated into orders and schedules for your department.

8. Detailed, up-to-the-minute knowledge of what your employees and equipment can handle effectively in the way of output.

9. Care not to overcommit your staff or equipment or to make delivery promises that can't be met.

10. Verification ahead of time of the materials needed to complete a production run to be sure that they are on hand when the order is scheduled.

11. Preparation and use, when appropriate, of a Gantt-type production planning and/or progress control chart for work in your department.

12. An understanding of how PERT or CPM works so that you can make valid contributions in the form of task sequences and time estimates to the specialists who prepare the PERT plans.

13. For clerical work in particular, preparation and use of a work distribution chart as a basis for making job assignments.

14. Use of the short-interval scheduling principle in handing out variable, short-term job assignments.

15. Time spent once a month to plan ahead for schedules that must be met three months from now.

Action Summary Checklist 27

Measuring and Improving Work Methods

1. A knowledge of "how much time" it does and should take to perform the various tasks and work under your supervision, given the quality of workmanship expected.

2. A considered opinion of what constitutes a fair day's work for each job in your department.

3. Actual training, or self-directed practice, in judging the pace (compared with normal or 100 percent) at which your employees perform their work.

4. Knowledge of how time standards are made or derived, if your company used standards or has a work measurement program.

5. Continuing surveillance to keep time and output standards from becoming loose.

6. Regular communications with employees about the source or basis and suitability of their performance and time standards.

7. Knowledge of how time standards are translated into wage incentives, if your company has such a wage plan.

8. Periodic work-sampling check of your work force to observe the degree of travel, delay, or idleness that prevails.

9. Periodic review of tasks under your supervision to identify those that are least efficient so that they may be exposed to a methods-improvement analysis.

10. A methods-improvement analysis made of at least one departmental task every three months, including preparation of flow-process chart and flow diagram.

11. Routine thought given to improvement of each of the three task elements—"make ready," "do," and "put away"—of jobs performed in your department.

12. A challenging attitude toward existing procedures in terms of what is being done, where, when, why, and how.

13. Systematic application of (a) the *methods-improvement* checklist—eliminate, combine, change sequence, and simplify and (b) the *motion economy* checklist—productive, simple, and rhythmic motions; comfortable workplaces, combining of tools, pre-positioning of tools and materials, and use of gravity.

14. An alertness to value analysis applications, especially by substituting less expensive or easier-to-work-with materials and parts in the product being made.

15. General receptivity to employee suggestions and ideas for improving their work methods.

Action Summary Checklist 28

Toward a Higher Quality of Workmanship

1. Knowledge of what makes up both corrective and preventive quality costs in your company and especially in your department.

2. A watchful eye on service-related workmanship as well as product-related items.

3. Clear-cut understanding of your specific responsibility in maintaining quality in your department, including who has authority to shut down a line, stop a shipment, or order a job to be done over again.

4. Knowledge, or preparation, of specific quality standards for all the products made or work performed under your supervision.

5. Communication of these standards to each of your employees.

6. A continuing program to train employees in the proper methods for meeting their quality standards.

7. Close coordination, rather than combat, with the inspection and quality control people in order to anticipate and solve quality problems.

8. Regular, personal tours of your own to inspect product or work methods.

9. Action taken to correct conditions that interfere with good quality: repair of machines and tooling, upgrading of raw materials, providing proper workplace arrangements, adequate lighting, and sufficient storage space.

10. Knowledge of (or maintenance of your own) quality records for your department so that you know its trend compared with standards.

11. Continuing feedback to employees about quality performance in your department: face to face, on bulletin boards, in exhibits.

12. A plan, formal or informal, for encouraging employees to suggest ways to remove the causes of errors.

13. Emphasis upon the Zero Defects concept of "do it right the first time."

14. Insistence upon, and maintenance of, good housekeeping at each work place, with each employee apprised of his or her responsibility.

15. Periodic housekeeping inspections, made with the assistance of the employees involved and with an emphasis upon its relationship to quality workmanship.

Action Summary Checklist 29

Improving Productivity and Cost Control

1. Knowledge of which input resources and output values can be used to measure productivity in your department.

2. A record kept of the basic productivity trend for operations in your department.

3. Identification of the specific technological factors that can affect productivity for better or worse in your department.

4. Knowledge and surveillance of labor costs, both direct and indirect, in your department.

5. Knowledge and surveillance of controllable variable costs, especially operating supplies, in your department.

6. Knowledge and surveillance of energy (electricity, steam, water, heating, air conditioning) costs in your department.

7. Knowledge and surveillance of waste, scrap, reject, defect, or rework costs in your department.

8. A positive personal attitude toward cost control and reduction.

9. A periodic search to reduce waste in your operations—of any controllable raw materials, supplies, tools, forms, etc.

10. A periodic review of process time—of operations, machine cycles, order-to-shipment time elapse—with a view toward shortening it.

11. Maximum, efficient use of space for operations and storage.

12. Establishment of specific, attainable cost-reduction goals for factors your employees can control.

13. Encouragement of and receptivity toward employee ideas and suggestions for cost reduction.

14. An ongoing communications program to inform employees of the need for cost control by providing concrete examples and specific figures.

15. Knowledge of overall organizational cost goals, the priorities associated with them, and the way that cost and productivity efforts are measured in your company.

The Computer and Management Information Systems

1. Knowledge of the nature and extent of your company's management information system, including the main functions it serves.

2. Understanding of the way in which the overall MIS is served by computers, if any, including type, whether your company owns or purchases (shares) service.

3. Knowledge of which computer language is used by your overall MIS.

4. Specific knowledge of how your department feeds data to the MIS, and the exact form in which this data should be provided.

5. Constant surveillance of data collection in your department to assure its accuracy.

6. Specific knowledge of what information the overall, or functional, MIS furnishes you and of what actions you are supposed to take based upon this information.

7. Continual upgrading of your information-oriented performance so as to be a more effective decision maker as an end-user and a better source of input data.

8. Favorable personal relations with MIS and EDP people, asking only for the information you need, alerting them to information overloads and duplication.

9. A diagram drawn of the information system within your own department, using Figure 30-3 as a model.

10. Awareness of how information and computer systems in your company have changed, are changing, and will change the content of employees' jobs.

11. Regular communication with employees to demonstrate how the overall information system helps the department to function efficiently, and what they can do to assist it.

12. Care in making assignments that are computer directed or dependent, so that people who like routines and controls are closest to the computer system and those who like flexibility and show initiative are further removed.

13. Resolution of conflicts that stem from information or computer systems contacts—conflicts between your own employees and with those from interfacing departments.

14. Sensivity toward employees' fears about what computerization may do to their jobs and job security.

15. Continuing effort to counteract by your personal interest and attention any technological advances that employees feel are dehumanizing their work in your department.

index

Measurements, control, 198–199 (*see also* Work measurement)
Mechanical Engineering (magazine), 430
Media, communications, 190
Merit rating (*see* Appraisal, performance)
Methods (*see* Methods improvement, work)
Methods improvement, work, 498–510
  applications, 500–501
  defined, 498, 510
  examples of, 500
  flow diagram, 505
  flow-process chart, 501–504
  job breakdown, 501
  motion economy, 499, 507–508
  process time, 510
  questions, 506
  sources of, 505–506
  suggestion systems, 509
  techniques for, 507
  value analysis, 508–509
  work cycle, 510
  work simplification, 416, 457, 509
Michigan, University of, 476
Miles, Lawrence D., 508
Minimum Wage Law (*see* Fair Labor Standards Act)
Minorities, 317, 328–329, 352, 604 (*see also* Equal employment opportunity)
Mogensen, Allan H., 509
Monotony of clerical work, 28, 409
Moonlighting, 367
Morale, 71–72
  absenteeism (*see* Absenteeism)
  defined, 78
  of office employees, 406–408
  turnover (*see* Turnover, employee)
Motion economy, 499, 507–508
Motion study, 105, 452–453, 490, 499, 507–508 (*see also* Work measurement)
Motivation
  affiliation need, 42, 45
  attitude surveys, 70–71, 78
  and attitudes, 66–72, 78
  and behavior, 45
  career, 573–574, 580
  and compensation, 237–241
  and conflict, 61–66, 76, 78
  and cooperation, 73–78
  defined, 45
  disadvantaged workers, 332–334
  dissatisfaction, 40–41, 43

Motivation (*continued*)
  of groups, 49–58
  Herzberg, Frederick, 40–41
  and human relations, 34
  individual, 34–35
  from job design, 455–456
  of knowledge workers, 429–430
  and leadership, 82–95
  McClelland, David, 42
  Maslow's hierarchy of needs, 37–38, 40, 42
  morale, 71–72
  of office employees, 410
  participation, 53–54 (*see also* Participation)
  and personality, 37, 45
  power need, 42, 45
  and psychology, 35
  satisfaction, 39–41, 44 (*see also* Satisfaction)
  self-actualization, 39
  for training, 265, 276
  wage incentives, 239
  of younger employees, 345–346
Mouton, Jane S., 92, 93
Myers, M. Scott, 457, 458

N

National Association of Suggestion Systems, 509
National Electrical Manufacturers Association (NEMA), 235
National Fire Protection Association (NFPA), 283, 300–302
National Home Study Council, 577
National Industrial Conference Board (the Conference Board), 331, 333
National Labor Relations Act (NLRA), 311–312, 323
National Labor Relations Board (NLRB), 312, 315, 323
National Management Association, 17, 608
National Metal Trades Association (NMTA), 235
National Safety Council, 283, 287, 295
National Society of Professional Engineers, 440
Neurosis, employee, 358, 371
Noise, communications, 176
Nonexempt employees, 316
Nurses as professionals, 433, 439

O

Objectives, 113, 114, 125
  hierarchy of, 115
Occupational Hazards (magazine), 299
Occupational Safety and Health Administration (OSHA), 283–286, 318, 602
  employee rights and responsibilities, 286
  hazard classifications, 284
  National Consensus Standards, 283–284
  recordkeeping requirements, 285
  safety clothing, 296–298
  and sanitation, 284–285
  training requirements, 264, 286
Office employees, 604 (*see also* Clerical work)
  attitudes of, 407–408
  career orientation of, 410–411
  compared with blue-collar worker, 406–407
  defined, 422
  job evaluation, 235–236
  morale of, 406–408
  and pay, 408
  performance standards, 413–414
  safety, 419–420
  secretaries, 411
  turnover, 413–414
  unionization, 408
Office machines, 419
Office scheduling, 483–485
Office work
  quality control, 515
  work sampling, 498
Older worker(s) (*see* Employees, older)
On-line system, 556
Operation symbol, 503
Orderliness in workplace, 108
Orders, 212–223 (*see also* Communications)
  ambiguity in, 221, 222
  in anger, 218
  commands, 213–214, 223
  conflicting, 217, 222
  defined, 223
  directions, 223
  empathy, 221
  feedback, 222
  group, 219
  judgment in following, 216–217

Orders (*continued*)
  listening to, 219–220
    active, 220
    passive, 219
  meeting resistance to, 220
  missed, 214
  nonverbal, 214
  providing reasons for, 217
  refusals, 214–215
  repeating of, 213
  requests, 213, 223
  and tone of voice, 218
  unreasonable, 218
  wording, 221, 222
  written, 216
Organization, 130, 149
  accountability, 139–142, 149
  authority, 137–141, 149
  centralized, 136
  channels of communication, 143
  customer, 135
  decentralized, 136
  delegation, 142, 144–147, 149
  divisional, 134
  functional, 134
  geographic, 135
  informal, 131
  line-and-staff, 132–133, 149
  matrix, 136, 443
  product, 134
  project, 135–136
  resources, 131
  responsibility, 137–138, 140–141, 149
  span of control, 137
  staff departments, 132–133, 144
  Table of Organization (TO), 137
  task forces, 135–136, 442–443
Organization charts, 132–136
Organizational changes, 603
Organizational procedure, 114, 125
Organizing process, 129–150 (*see also* Organization)
  authority and responsibility, 137–141, 149
  chain of command, 143
  channels of communication, 143
  charts, 132–136
  delegation, 142, 144–147, 149
  example of, 148
  principles of, 147
Orientation training, 263–264
OSHA (*see* Occupational Safety and Health Administration)

Y

Z